Lessons from the Thorns
His Grace is Sufficient

The true story of how God's grace and mercy

transformed my shattered life

Sandra Maria Anderson

Website: Reach us at www.SandraMariaAnderson.com

Description: *Lessons from the Thorns* is the autobiography of a young girl's incredible journey Based on a true story, Lessons from the Thorns is the autobiography of a young girl's astonishing journey through the painful experiences (thorns) of life. It is a journey that chronicles the fight for mental health and wellness, freedom from abuse and addiction, and the search for her voice, the essence of the sacred soul. It is the story of a Savior—a Hero who paid the highest price to redeem her right to be free, and to be loved. *Lessons from the Thorns* is a journey that will guide the reader to the remedy for the formidable ailments that continue to plague society. From the words of great leaders, such as William Wilberforce, Malcolm X, and Martin Luther King, the solution remains the same. All people are created in the image of God. It is the love of God that retrains and changes the sinful heart. Nothing changes in the rage of violence nor in the silence of apathy. The nation continues to implode because of its defiant autonomy that has turned its back on the One in whom it is supposed to trust: The God of earth and heaven; the Creator of all things. The healing Love of God can do the impossible! You may find your secrets hiding here, and the courage to find your voice, take back your life and begin to heal through the power of the risen Savior, Jesus Christ.

Keywords: Autobiography, Addiction, Advocacy, Awareness, Childhood Sexual Abuse, Courage, Depression, Dissociation, Domestic Violence, Education, Excavation, Healing, HIV/AIDS, Mental health, Reconstitution, Reparation, Regeneration, Restorative Justice, Sex-Trafficking, Survivor, Transformation, **Transgenerational trauma.**

Disclaimer: This content is of a mature nature, including violence, and graphic sexual experiences and events. Reader discretion is strongly advised. I have tried to recreate each incident, including locales, and conversations from my memories of them. Some names and identifying details have been changed to protect the privacy of individuals. May the Holy Spirit guide you, heal you, and bless you as you continue this journey and your own, knowing, His grace is sufficient.

Scripture references: Holy Bible: King James Version (KJV; NKJV).

ISBN-10: 0692742522

ISBN-13/ 978-0692742525

DEDICATION

For my Sister, Joyce
A three-strand cord is not easily broken. –Ecclesiastes 4:12

For your sweet lullabies, tender kisses, and all the things you
taught me
Story after story, braid after braid, you helped me see
the amazing power of Christ living in me
With all my heart, I love you and thank you for the gift of who
you are

Your Sandy Patty

For my family and all families trying to make sense of the
painful thorns. You are not alone. God hears you, sees you,
and, in time, He will answer your prayer.

Dr. Alberto Mestre; for encouraging me to *"Tell My Story"* and
believing in my ability to rise above every circumstance.
My sincerest gratitude and love to you!

"Amazing Grace, how

sweet the sound,

That saved a wretch like me.

I once was lost but now I'm found,

was blind, but now I see.

T'was Grace that taught my heart to fear.

And Grace, my fears relieved.

How precious did that Grace appear

The hour I first believed.

Through many dangers, toils, and snares

I have already come;

'Tis Grace that brought me safe thus far

and Grace will lead me home."

~John Newton (1725-1807)

A reformed slave trader,

redeemed by the love and amazing grace of God.

Lessons from the Thorns:
The Moments in the Journey

Contents

Part lll: When sin is unmasked, the true nature of man stares back, utterly wretched, desperately in need of a Savior.

Part lV: Adolescence: A gateway of time where there is no time or rationale; there are only lessons where we are forced to pay attention or float through Neverland.

Contents

Part V: Life offers us choices. What we choose is everything.

Part Vl: The greatest lesson is learning to free ourselves from the slave masters of sin, pain, and fear.

Part Vll: Adulthood: The opportunity to change the course of time by choosing to break the cycle of secrets and generational dysfunction.

Contents

Part Vlll: The Awakening: The moment we finally let go, and fully realize that we have the power to decide and command our own life. There we find the most valuable gift of God: True love.

Epilogue

*The Symbol for lessons:

Prologue

The Call in the Rain

August 2005

It's 3 a.m. A thunderstorm awakens me, and a peculiar sound is coming from the falling rain. I hear a voice calling out, around me, outside of me, and from within. In the darkness, I turn away, squeezing my pillow tighter, trying to go back to sleep. But again, I hear it calling. Sitting up, I listen more carefully. I've heard the call before. I fear it.

"Sandra, you must go!" the voice commands. In an instant, I knew it was the voice of God. The sound is powerful, unmistakable. I have listened to it since the days of my youth, and the years I've wandered through the valley of the shadows of death. Walking over to my bedroom window, I stand, staring out at the falling rain. *Since escaping a lifetime of bondage, I only wanted peace.*

Again, the voice calls out to me, and I feel as powerless as I did when I was eight years old. I spent a lifetime asking unanswerable questions, wondering why God allowed the storms to come. I breathe in the soothing beat of raindrops as they splash and leap across my windowpane. I have tried to move on, forget the past ever happened, forget the nightmare of an unimaginable childhood and the ensuing fear that had paralyzed me for most of my life.

The past is over. I sigh, content to forget and stay in my comfortable place of apathy, satisfied with the quiet compromise that surrounds me inside its numbing embrace. I return to bed, stretching out in the beautiful darkness. Not very long ago, I was afraid of the dark, fearful of everything. Now, the darkness blankets warm around me, reminding me of the lessons I have learned in it, and through it. The fear is almost gone now — somewhere buried with the skeletons of the past…*as if nothing ever happened*. Outside, I hear the early morning rain picking up. The thunder rebounds in the distance. The wind shifts, moving from the outside to the inside. I feel His presence against my skin.

"You must go!"

He instructs again. I hear a guiding wind rustling through the trees near the outside of the window. It pitches higher. I stare back at the digital clock glowing in the dark. I breathe out again, hoping to escape this call coming from the wind. War is never easy. "The storm will soon pass," I whisper to myself. Sometimes when you are alone, your mind can play tricks on you. But I know that I am not alone and what is happening now is very real.

Suddenly, the air shifts in my room. The pulse of my heartbeat throbs inside my chest. The storm builds, traveling closer. "What's happening?" I whisper to myself in the darkness.

"Am I still sleeping or am I somehow awake?" There is no logic to why the curtains are not moving, yet I feel a strange wind encircling me. The wind beckons more pronounce, more powerful, and urgent. It calls out, "You must go!" My breath goes shallow, and suddenly the taste of bile erupts from my gut. I search around my room because I sense the invisible. I feel the intangible. I know God's presence. He is calling me out of my compromise and apathy. Between the raindrops, I am told:

"Do not be afraid. You must go and tell your story. Use the power that is deep within you, the same power that raised Christ from the grave. The Holy Spirit will lead and guide you. Go; tell all you know is true. Proclaim to all the nations how God makes all things new."

Thunder clashes in the distance. Then I hear a different voice, more solemn and frail. I clench my fist as horrible memories flash in front of me. Memories I have tried to forget, and secrets I swore I would take to the grave. Then, I hear another voice, and another, and soon, there are too many to tell. Some voices sound familiar; others are foreign; as if they are worlds away. Their voices sound like angry thunder, screaming across the sky. Voices imprisoned to a dark past, a monster's touch, and a broken trust. Some are dead, some are alive, but all the same, they cry out.

You can no longer remain silent; the small voice of a little girl calls from the darkness. Suddenly, I see images of endless gravestones with no names; only their terrible secrets remain. *No one must hear, no one must know, no one can see the shame hiding behind the pretense.* Pretending nothing has happened is all I know. After a lifetime of secrets and inner rage, ignoring the painful crimes against my life is normal. The secrets are like chains wrapped around me, not chains of iron but of piercing thorns. You dare not speak of it. You learn to breathe and be thankful that you survived another day.

"Can you hear them?" He asks me.

"Yes, Lord. I can." I exhale. Again, His voice echoes,

"You must go!"

Breathless, I ask, "What can I do? What difference can I possibly make? And where would I begin? How do I find the courage to forsake the pain and pride that demands the right to my solitude? After everything I've been through; I only want to live in peace, to be left alone." At first, He does not answer. For a moment, there is silence, but soon, all becomes louder than before. Like the distant tremors underfoot from an approaching dinosaur. I shudder. The ground beneath me quakes and trembles. Without warning, it gives way. Gasping, I fall back, trying to convince myself that I cannot be awake. I tell myself that *this must be a dream; only a dream.*

Comfortless chills grip my skin, propelling me through vast portals of time. Mysteriously, the storm intensifies, and soon, I am no longer in my bedroom, nor am I in the same dimension of time. Somewhere between life and death, I catch my breath, standing underneath a dimmed streetlight.

It is the fall of 1975. There, near the corner of a road, I see a green street sign. It reads 24th Street. A dense fog rises like a dark veil, hovering over the house. Against my will, I feel myself floating towards it. I reach out my hand into the foggy mist of a surreal existence. I begin to remember what I have tried for a lifetime to forget.

"I used to live here," I whisper to myself. "And it was in this house, I died," I remember. I can almost touch the sharp gray corbel stones jutting from the outer frame of the house. Suddenly, I feel consumed by immense emotions of desolation and fear. Scourges of exiling shame torment me all at once. It's all happening again. I cannot escape this horrible past, though I tried to let it go and forget it all.

"You must be here. My grace will cover you and keep you safe." Then there is silence. A mighty wind carries me to my backyard. A surge of memories greets me at the side gate. I feel the presence of the Holy Spirit standing next to me. My heartbeat begins to slow its frantic pace. This place is a field of dreams and the origin of nightmares.

Dazed, I wait. For what, I don't know. I listen as reminiscing winds stir up time, whirling around my feet, carrying me over the dewy grass. There, I see a tire swing, mango trees, and the sacred graves of my beloved pets. They all knew my secrets. Loyal to the end, they never told, and they filled the emptiness when I lost my soul that day. Gusts of rain and wind turn me to the back door of the house. I cringe, but I am powerless to resist the mysterious pull. It commands me onward. I hesitate, slowly turning the doorknob.

"Why must I come back here? I hate this place! Was it not enough? How much more must I endure of this terrible house? I don't want to be here!" He quietly guides me past the fear and sadness. I move forward. The feeling inside the house is the same: damp, cold, and emotionless. Weird sounds scurry through the walls like something is dying inside, trapped, unable to break free. It is something heinous; no one is supposed to know. I creep, slowly, inching from the kitchen to the hall. The corridor seems to go on forever, like the unforgettable memories it holds. Still, somewhere in my mind, I know this must happen. I must be here. I must confront the terror, the thorns, the fear, and the rage that has formed an emotional cage; no one can get through, nor can I break free. I must begin to heal. Being here begins the process. Though painful, this is a healing hurt. Like medicine on a festering wound; this is the cure.

I fall under a flood of tears. This house was never a home, but an apathetic lair where a monster roamed. In the bedroom, fear was birthed and became full-grown underneath the guile of lust. Dark secrets lurk through the rooms and halls. I feel them watching me, even now, restlessly crouching near my bedroom window. Secrets I swore I would never tell because fear is an evil taskmaster that uses blackmail, forcing you to carry the secrets to your grave.

"Do not be afraid." His voice wraps warmly around me. I breathe, trying to let go; but it is not that easy. Tears mix with rain. *Wake up, please let me wake up.* Outside the window, flashes of lightning cut through the darkened sky.

"This is not to harm you." His voice speaks in the storm: "Be still and see that I make all things new." In a blink, I am standing outside the house. I feel a strong wind blowing through me—like a tornado, it removes the roof, and soon, an unearthing begins. The rain penetrates deep inside the house with unyielding intent, uprooting articles of youth and innocence. In the whirlwind tossed back and forth, I see my comic books, my dolls, and a music box — where a ballerina dances to an unchained melody. I don't want to remember! Why can't I forget all of it? It was too much to feel again.

Lightning strikes in the distance. Between the flashes, I move through time once more. I close my eyes, and the scent of the ocean's air carries me across sleepy waves billowing against the seashore. Up ahead there is another street sign. It reads A1A. All at once, it happens, and I try to swallow. I taste the tears of a weeping child. Desperate, she runs away because it hurts too much to stay at home. I hear panting in my ear. It is not my own. The cruel sound mixes with the stench of sweat and sin from beasts that look and walk like men, but I could never tell the difference until the door locks behind me. I try to turn away from the memories. The fear, the rage, all take center stage, until the madness takes on grotesque shapes, trapping me inside my own mind.

"My God, why can't you just let me forget? Lord, you are the Prince of Peace. Please don't make me go! Please just let it be."

Just as quickly as I left the comfort of my room, I return. I exhale, relieved. I am safe, I breathe squeezing my pillow, but I could no longer escape the call in the rain. The wind continues to beat against the window, refusing to let up, refusing to allow me to stay in the comfortable place of apathy.

"Prepare to go back to the place of the thorns. Someone needs to know." His voice consumes me, tearing away the facade I have built up over the years. "But how do I speak of the unspeakable? Where can I find the courage to go back, and how do I summon the strength to tell the story of these sharp thorns?"

"The journey through the maze of a haunted generation is too heavy, too painful to relive again," I reply, feeling powerless in my own strength. Still, I hear the call.

"I am the Lord your God. I will go with you. I will never leave you. Be still and know the battle is mine, not yours. Go and tell of the mercy and grace that you have received. Not for yourself, but so others may hear, see, and believe." From the shores of the Atlantic to the peaks above the clouds; I remember His faithfulness—it is unfathomable, abundant, and endless.

"God, if you go with me, I will go. I will give myself away and tell the story."

For many years, I have hidden these secrets, buried them so deep inside, that even I could not reach them. But often, before we can move forward in life, we must first, go back. We must confront the past to heal, forgive, and move ahead toward a higher calling and purpose for being.

Freed from the trenches of my life's thorns, I had felt the duty of war too stressful. I wanted to rest, I needed peace, but the frontline of the battlefield is where I am supposed to be now; for such a time as this. And despite my frailties, I believe God will strengthen me to accomplish and complete His will for my life.

The Word of God affirms in 2 Corinthians 12:9, "His grace is sufficient. His strength is made perfect in our weakness." For this reason, I will not remain silent. I will tell the story.

It is the story of a little girl, helplessly lost. I sit alone, preparing to write about the incredible journey to find her, to love her, and to allow her to receive love—true love.

For many, time is a calculable concept of dates on a calendar that marks each era. But in my life, I have watched time sit still, offering an opportunity to set things right. The responsibility to do so belongs to each of us. As I write, a little girl writes with me, and with her, there is a warrior. They are free from the restraints of time. Therefore, in each chapter is the chemistry of three voices: the child, the warrior, and the writer; all are with me—the same; all are within me. I pray for guidance as I write about my journey; it is not for the faint of heart, but if you choose to start, I encourage you to continue; get to the mountain!

God's great love has brought me to an indefinite place where the only thing that is certain is His unfailing love and His amazing grace; I drown in it. All else is shrouded in the mysteries of life, death, and the dreams beyond. Behind the veil of our human existence, He is there, waiting to tell us who we are and whom we were created to be. He sent Jesus Christ: Immanuel (God with us) The Redeemer, His only begotten son to die for our sins and make us free, and to show us the wonders of what our hearts often fail to understand because the distractions of life blind us to His truth, mercy, and love.

The world needs to know there is a Balm in Gilead; a true Hero; a Savior who forgives sin, who heals diseases, who sets the captives free, and who came to make all things new. Today, more than ever before, I'm beginning to understand why my heart still aches and advocates with a burden for the hurting and the lost. It is because I can still hear their voices. Their cries are louder than ever.

Among the many voices is my own.

Eerie Ybor

"Everything you can imagine is real."
~Pablo Picasso

The house built on top of an old cemetery is the first house where I remember growing up. It was the beginning of awareness of my existence in the world. The third of five children, I arrived on a stormy morning on August 19th, 1967 at Tampa General Hospital. Perhaps the severe weather was a foretelling of events yet to come in my life. Still, the stories of my birth would wane beside the legend of the land on which our home rests. I was three years old when my eldest sister Joyce told my siblings and me the haunting history of the house and the town where we lived. I was too young to understand it all then, but the fear was real, unforgettable. My parents, Bertram and Lillie, moved to Tampa in 1962, buying the old house on the outskirts of Ybor City, a questionable area sensible people avoided after dark. And with all the disquieting rumors of Ybor's eerie past, it's no wonder why.

Some legends call Ybor one of the most haunted cities in the world, offering Ghost tours to those who have an affinity for fear. I never did, but fear would come to find me all the same. Tampa's tales of strange sightings, hidden tunnels, and haunted cantinas linger over the city like insistent dark smog. Ybor City takes its name from Vicente Martinez Ybor, a Spanish immigrant who in the 1880s became famous for his fine cigars and business savvy. The Cuban kingpin left a lasting mark on Tampa's economy and its people. As a child, riding in the backseat over Ybor brick streets, I was unaware of the mysteries that surrounded the historic district of the city, and I was utterly oblivious to the inner workings of a world that would challenge everything I grew to know.

Ybor is a moving kaleidoscope of shifting cultures and colors that fill the senses and stirs the spirit. In the early years, we grew up nearly colorblind in the town that mixes with a Spanish, Cuban, German, African, Jewish, and Italian effervescence; people were just people. The multicultural melting pot surrounded our home and our lives with an air of wonder and surprise. I remember hearing the strange stories of Ybor and the world around me. Whether embellished or true to form, in my mind, the tales were all very real.

There were stories of haunted tunnels, mob bosses, and drug

lords that ruled the streets of Ybor City in the 1920s. To this day, rumors tell of a hidden kingdom secretly intertwined with Ybor's refined restaurants, museums, and art galleries. Some would swear there is a dark underworld where ghosts and gangsters reign just below the surface of society. During the 1960s, that mystery would offer my family a glimpse into its secret world.

On the floorboards of our old home, I sit crisscross, staring out into an alien world. I always felt odd and out of place around others my age. So, it's no wonder why every opportunity, I would sit at the feet of grown folks. Minding my manners come easy for me. Awkward and shy, I'd play on the floor until my legs went numb. As my parents settled into their superstitious surroundings near Ybor City, they became hardworking entrepreneurs. Although the times were heavy with racial turbulence and inequality, God's favor followed them. After working tirelessly, they started their own business. "Live and Let Live" is the name of the barbershop and connecting grocery store they opened just off 15th Street, not too far from the creepy city of Ybor.

My mother manages the grocery store while my father runs the barbershop. My mom is a natural leader. Tough and assertive, she keeps the books and makes most of the decisions for the business and the family. And despite my father's unstable work habits, my mother manages to keep the business afloat. A workaholic by nature, my mom works multiple jobs to make ends meet. When she is not busy at the grocery store, she moonlights part-time at the Bay to Bay Nursing Home on Tampa's east coast. Before the sun awakes, she stirs to prepare for the day. Barely resting from her late-night shift, she is determined to get ahead. I remember feeling enchanted by her strength and independent charm.

She smiles and floats around as if she has found the secret to what Ponce de Leon was searching for when he set sail for the Florida coast in 1513. Work is her fountain of youth. She seems to thrive in the ability to provide and in the power of productivity. And if usefulness equates to youthfulness, she will live forever. Tirelessly, she runs the grocery store with a lively command and a permeating radiance that captures the hearts of her customers like bees to honey. My father, who is 20 years her senior, does not share nor does he care for her sparkling, confident personality. Quite the opposite, he is distant and closed. Inferiority seems to hold onto him like a faithful mistress. Most of the time, he appears to be far away, lost in thought. My small part of the world is quiet, and for now, the mystery of Ybor City is the only thing that kind of scares me.

My father preoccupies himself to the point of anonymity. Like the *Invisible man*, I find myself missing him even when he is in the same room as me. Known as Roadman by his closest friends, he never looks settled with himself. He appears to have two jobs, a part-time barber, and a full-time gambler. The Bolita gambling habit keeps him broke and bound to an illusion of hitting it big someday. And not too far away from the stash of numbers from the high stakes' illicit lottery game, is a bottle of Gin.

Liquor is like smooth talking spirits that keeps him numb to the sobering realities of the past and his present life. His silver flask is never too far away. He never really speaks of it, but there seems to be a weariness that hides behind his deep brown eyes. Whatever happened in his past must be unforgettable, because the pain remains alive in his lowly stride and downcast gaze. Whenever he catches me watching him, he quickly forces an easy smile.

In time, I would hear more stories of racial injustice. I see a heaviness weighing on my father like a thousand rusty chains. Unlike my mother who I often hear praying and talking to an invisible savior name, Jesus; my father remains silent—waiting on the world to change. He seems to lack the faith and optimism to believe beyond the hate and oppression; beyond what he could see. Despite the circumstance, I want him to believe things can get better. But sometimes, faith doesn't come easy.

The rising episodes of racial oppression in my parents and grandparent's era left me wondering, always thinking, why? As I grew the answers became more evident, but still, I could not make sense of it all. I suppose it's hard to make sense out of nonsense. Stories I heard from my youth, sitting at the feet of grown folk. Stories from slavery, *Roots*, and *Wildwood*; stories of tyranny—as if nothing ever happened. The beautiful yet cruel history of America tangled in my young mind. *In time, I would come to understand the reason why.*

There are lessons and stories in every family. Secrets that hide in the shadows of every life. Back during that time, the tales of Ybor City did not seem as scary as the guarded truth that was emerging. When I looked inside my father's sad eyes, I wanted to believe all the stories weren't true. I wanted him to dream, to be happy. But in the daunting days of my father's childhood, dreaming was a luxury many Colored folks could not afford. For an overwhelming majority, inhumane treatment left families in the depressive state of survival, lack, and hopelessness.

Before the equal protection laws, before the racial discrimination laws, and before the Civil Rights Movement of the 1960s, there was a promise of life, liberty, and the pursuit of happiness. And though I did not fully understand it all then, the world was preparing to teach me valuable lessons that would reach beyond the brick-ladened streets of Tampa and Ybor City; lessons of love, forgiveness, and humanity.

As a child, I watched my father sulk in anguish and apathy. What happened to his quest for life, liberty, and happiness? How did the times affect him, mold him, and cause him to look like the sky was always falling? It would be many years before I realized that laws could only attempt to enforce civil rights, but only God's law can change the sinful heart of men to understand human rights. This was one of the lessons from the thorns I was called to learn early. Life and time are masterful teachers. They both have a way of helping us make sense of the unthinkable realities we must face. Watching my father, I would learn the language of quiet sadness. A pang of sorrow you never speak of because, like breathing, it becomes a part of living, or more aptly stated, you perceive it to be normal.

My father wears the battle scars of a hard life. He was born on Independence Day, July 4, 1921, and witnessed a time in history some have only read about or watched on a TV screen. The irony of his birthdate would be as scornful as the events that followed. For many, true freedom is a snide paradox—a desert of mirages that confines you to its trickery. The dehumanizing stench of racial oppression and brutality carried far during his lifetime. Far beyond the distance of where my simple mind could reach.

The stories went on of how his parents were never married. Ancestors of slaves, marriage often culminated with a jump over a broom or sharing a room, waiting on the world to change. No silver spoon fed my father. No inheritance to pass on. His father died preaching in the pulpit, just after repenting of all the wrong he had done. No mothers love nurtured him. His young, teenage mother died days after he was born. I remember when I first heard the story of my dad's mother and his lost childhood.

Days after my father was born, before his eyes could recognize the one who gave him life, before his hands could hold onto the wisdom and wonder of all she would share, and before his lips could speak her name, she died. In the eyes of some family members, it was his fault, a bad omen.

The story goes on how in school, while other students wore a red rose, a token of love in honor of Mother's Day, his rose was a cold, breathless pale—the common color when ones' mother has passed away. During that time, superstition ruled the thoughts and actions of many; especially the uneducated and simpleminded. Belief has a way of giving delusions a heartbeat. Delusions that a child's birth can be a bad omen or that the color of a man's skin can make him more or less human; such is the lunacy of sin. I imagine apathy offered the mental escape my father needed to endure the tough times; that and a bottle of gin.

For a Black man in America, growing up with a dream was like trying to climb a mountain to capture the wind just to prove that you can, that you are worthy of love, life, and the pursuit of every other human right. These were hard lessons for me to understand, but the truth is often like that—strange and puzzling. Even so, as a little girl growing up near Ybor City, watching my father's misery, I can only see the greatest **man** on earth. My hero. My daddy.

Anger is essential when controlled. When we understand the true purpose of the emotion of anger, we can use it to make the world a better place for all people.

Dr. Myles Munroe spoke of a certain type of anger that connects us to the call of destiny. He said, "In life, purpose is defined by the thing that makes you angry. Martin Luther was angry; Mandela was angry; Mahatma Gandhi was angry; Mother Teresa was angry. If you are not angry, you do not have a ministry yet."

I didn't know it then, but destiny calls us years before we are in *the position* to answer. We will know when we are ready to answer 'the call.' It will be the moment when we can no longer stand by while injustice causes our fellow human beings to stumble and die. It is then we begin to understand why we came to earth.

Dancing on the Moon

"The ties that bind us are sometimes impossible to explain. They
connect us, even after it seems like the ties should be broken.
Some bonds defy distance, and time, and logic.
Because some ties are simply… meant to be." ~M.G.

Time turns, carrying me happily into 1973. I know
something special is going to happen today. My sister Joyce tells us
we are going to my parents' store, and she helps us get ready. I can
hardly wait. Work often keeps my parents away from home for far
too long. With five children and a gambling habit to feed, my
parents usually don't get home until late at night. I would try to
wait up for them to come home, just to hear the sound of their
voices in the house. But business is good near the peculiar town of
Ybor.

The responsibility of my siblings and I fall on my sister Joyce.
She is still a child herself, but she is maturing beyond her years. At
an early age, Joyce manages to take care of us, to help our parents
at the store, and to keep up with her studies at school. It all seemed
to come naturally to her. Always busy about the house and doting
on us, she rarely takes time for herself. "Get your jackets. It's cold
outside. Hold hands and stay together." She tells us. One by one,
like carefree ducklings, we follow her lead. Her presence is like a
sanctuary because she loves to sing praise songs and tell us Bible
stories. A few blocks from the store, the cold autumn air lifts my
thoughts away.

"Sandy Patty?" Joyce affectionately calls me. "Your laces are
untied. Please tie your laces before you fall." She watches us, with
an uncanny ability to catch every detail, from head to toe. At my
parent's store, a bell rings every time the door opens. I like the
sound, remembering a story I heard about an angel getting wings.

My mom greets us with a smile and a big kiss. "Hello babies
go get whatever you want," she says with a joyful tone. We dash
away. It happens every time. My mom lets us get bubble gum,
cookies, chips, soda pop, just about anything. Being here feels like
a child's paradise. Joyce watches my baby sister Linda, who is
fascinated with the menagerie of shapes and colors around her.
Michael, Leon, and I race up toward the candy aisle. This place
could very well be our favorite place in the whole store and
probably the entire world. Chico sticks, Sugar Daddies, Baby

Ruth's, and Tootsie Rolls. Michael's eyes glaze over. Once the sugar hits his system, he will be unstoppable. I head straight for my two favorite treats, Cracker Jacks, and Coca-Cola. I skip up the aisle, excited about the small prize hidden inside the box. Mama keeps the soda pop in an old deep freezer with a bottle top opener built into the upper left-hand corner. The freezer vibrates against the store window next to the front entrance. The frost on the outside of the deep freezer is thick enough to write your name on it.

Joyce says too much sugar is not good for us, but I like the bottle it comes in just as much as I like the cola taste. Mama told me I can get 5 cents for every bottle. So far, I have saved 3. I was thrilled. "Soon I will have 20 cents to put in my piggy bank. I am rich!" Shaking impatiently, I pushed down too hard on the opener. The soda bubbles fizzed out of the glass bottle like a volcano erupting, covering me with syrupy stains. I remember my mom's face. She smiles and laughs at me standing there, soda fizzing out of the bottle. My floral dress is a sticky brown mess, so I stare at the floor. Hearing my mom's laughter eased the tension I felt from the mess I made. It seems her laughter has a way of signaling all is right with the world.

I wish I had the power to make each moment last, so I do not have to leave. I try to be helpful, so that I can get to stay with her all day. Her kisses, her embrace—they are rare treasures. I cherish each one. A ray of sunshine drifts through the window. It touches near the ground where Joyce is standing with Linda. My brothers go off to the pool room near the back of the store. And with all the sugar coursing through their veins, it's just a matter of time before something gets broken or set on fire. Joyce meanders around the store, Linda is close to her with an insatiable desire to touch and taste everything she sees. I sit on the high wooden stool near the cash register, close enough to be near my mom, but far enough to stay out of the way. "Hello, sweetheart," Mom chirps cheerfully. She speaks to her customers as if they are all old friends. "How are you doing, dear? How's the family?" There is a glow around her, and her personality seems to be the heartbeat of the business.

I sit taller on the high seat near the cash register, watching my mother doing the same thing, time after time. Visit after visit, it slowly has begun to occur to me how strong my mother must be to work so hard. She gives herself away in her work, always going the extra mile to serve everyone. Once, I saw her take off a necklace she was wearing and give it to a customer who commented on how pretty it was. "Here, take it, it's yours," she said. I remember how the young woman's eyes smiled in disbelief as she looked at the necklace sitting in the palm of her hand. "We are all God's children," she'd often say. I've never seen her turn anyone away who was hungry, or in need of a listening ear. I stare out of the store's front window, thinking *I want to be just like my mom.*

"Daddy! Daddy…?" I shout, prancing toward the back of the store where my father is working in the barbershop. We can never be sure when we will get to come back to the store, so today I want to soak up all the attention I can. Approaching the door, I quiet myself and step back. Mama has made it abundantly clear to us that it is rude to interrupt when others are talking. I peek in and wait. He is busy with customers. Gray hair, dark hair, no hair—all sit in his barber chairs. Their voices boast so loud, I think they must be hard of hearing.

I watch him work, listening to the men rehashing the events of the day. His hands move as if they have a mind of their own. He seldom smiles or speaks. I watch as he bustles from chair to chair skillfully combing, cutting, and sweeping up hair. I wait until my legs go numb. I peek through the crack of the door of the shop, hoping he would notice me. The smell of aftershave and rubbing alcohol hangs heavy in the air among the baritone voices. A long, wide strap dangles near an array of scissors, combs, clippers, and a jar of weird green fluid. My father firmly holds the bottom of the strap. With an oddly shaped blade in hand, he moves with expert precision. Up and down, his wrist guides the blade against the broad leather strap. I think to myself; *I want to do that. I can cut hair too!*

Soon, my waiting is over. My dad senses my yearning for him and gives me a warm smile as our eyes meet. His big, light-brown eyes take my breath away, as only he can. "Sandra? Hey, baby." He stops his toiling and motions for me to come. The humming shears in his hand suddenly hush its drone. Quick flicks from a bristly brush send hair particles from his barber's apron spiraling through the air. All at once, his arms reach for me. I cannot contain my joy. It's not often I get to be with my Dad and being the middle child from his second set of children sometimes leaves me feeling lost, with no special place to fit inside his heart. The children from his first wife Victoria are all grown up. Now, with all of us, his second brood, he is usually too busy, too tired, or too preoccupied to notice how lonely the world can be without him.

At that moment, he lifts me up, and I feel like I can fly. My heart soars without a care in the world. I know I am getting a little too heavy for him to pick up, but he never shows it. He just smiles with pride, swaying me from side to side, as if I was light as a feather. The room transforms, and I am dancing on the moon. High up from the ground I can see my whole world. It exists in my father's eyes. During these rare sentimental times, my dad sees me; the real me, who would never need to pretend to be someone else because he has already made it clear who I am; I am loved, unconditionally. He sits in his barber chair and hoists me upon his lap, announcing proudly to his patrons, "This is my daughter, Sandra." I glow with delight, fluttering my feet nervously under his leg while I hide my face against his chest. The smell of his Old Spice is comforting. It must be his favorite because he always smells of it. He smells like Christmastime. His presence is my gift.

From that moment, I could no longer hear the exchange of words from the men sitting in the barber chairs. I listen to the beat of my father's heart. It matches the rhythm of my own. Our spirits bond ever deeper, composing our special song. We alone know the words. He dotes on me, pulling me close to his chest as he gently kisses my forehead. He whispers softly.

"Baby, Daddy got to finish his work." His eyes are full of love. "I'm sorry, baby; you go off and play now." He smiles at me, never showing his teeth.

"Yes sir, Daddy," I reply, leaning in to hear the melody again.

Every cell of my body drinks in the nourishment of my father's words. I give him a tight squeeze, close my eyes, and hold onto the moment with all my might. Knowing how busy he is, I want to make it last far into time. My feet reluctantly find the floor as he lowers me down, sending me off to play. His lap is my throne and there, I know I am a princess. Skipping away, I can't feel the floor. And before reaching the door, I run back to kiss his cheek. Bristles from his partly shaven beard tickle my skin. I love the scruffy feeling. An unspoken covenant passes between us; a promise of undying love, a promise to remember the moment always. Our hearts seal it.

I skip and twirl from the back of the barbershop to find Joyce helping Mama behind the register in the front of the store. Linda is sitting behind the counter. I listen for my brothers. The playful uproar coming from the poolroom tells me that despite their swashbuckling activities, we do not have to evacuate the store.

Thankfully, today, Leon and Michael cause no fires or explosions in the back room, unlike the times before when they would get into all sorts of mischief. Catching mice and lizards were second nature for my brothers and me, but one day, during summer vacation in Tallahassee with my grandparents, Leon lit a match under our grandparent's wooden house and almost burnt it down. Joyce caught him just in time before the fire got out of control. He said he was trying to toast bread. Boys! Go figure.

Joyce is always coming to our rescue, especially during the scary nights when the fights between my parents exploded with angry voices and pounding noises. For as far back as I can remember, Joyce was there gathering us together, looking into our worried eyes, and calming our fears. It was in those moments that I first learned about the practice of prayer. Joyce told us to never forget. It was as if she knew the heartache that awaited our family.

Besides, by all appearances, my parents seem to be no different from any other couple. The occasional arguments and the stewing silence are the norms in our family. Growing up, we learned to tread carefully through the suffocating atmosphere created by their heated clashes. In our hearts and minds, they were together. That's all that mattered. As children, fairy tales made us believe in magic. A mystical spell will overthrow both their stubborn wills and force them to love each other, for better or for worse.

I certainly believed in the childhood fantasies of a true love's kiss that would conquer all. Although battles of good against evil are written in every story, love always wins in the end. The spell breaks, the slipper fits, a gallant knight arrives just in time, and true love's kiss brings the dead back to life. That is the way life is supposed to work. Right? Enchanted by the magic and wonder of the implied messages, I believe; family is forever.

In this life, belief is essential—it is everything. What we grow to believe will often find its way to us in whatever form we've imagined, offering an escape from the present circumstances. However, the truth will never fail to exceed that which the human mind perceives to be real, although we may choose to deny it. Like gravity, there is a truth that is certain—fight against it with all your might, you will still fall because what goes up must come down, and what goes around comes back around.

Understanding absolute truth, no matter how it disagrees with our ideas and views, then becomes the principle thing. I was too young to understand the facts of historical trauma in my family; how it transfers and circles back like a boomerang; how it shapes our mindsets and emotions until we are unable to discern reality from conditioning; freedom from captivity. Most lessons will take a lifetime before we understand the truth of *being* human.

Whispers of a Savior

During the mid-1970s, memories of visiting my parents' store scatter across my mind like whimsical daydreams. Looking back, I find the more things change, the more they stay the same because true change must first happen within.

More often than not, in every relationship, the problem isn't the other person, but the underlying issue of perception. Like looking into a blurry mirror, perception makes you believe in its slanted reality, so you never ask or look for another option to find the truth. Blame is a distraction from the truth: it's all about you; no one else. For most, this is a painful lesson that involves the death of the ego —the one thing we are born protecting and defending; the main thing that keeps us from evolving into our true nature: the divine nature of love.

The occasional visits to my parent's store become less enchanted and more filled with stiff tension. Tonight, the store quiets down and so do my mom. Joyce prepares to gather us together to head home. She carries Linda, who is quietly sleeping, to the back room and waits for my mom to finish locking up and counting the money in the till. In the stillness, I notice a change. Maybe it was there all the time, but I am just too young to see or understand; something in her eyes—vacant, longing, like the sorrow of a sparrow that's kept clipped and caged. Her busyness hides it well.

Reality sets in as the last bell rung for the night. An unspoken sadness stirs in her eyes. I remember thinking that maybe she is just tired, maybe she misses being home as much as I miss her there, or perhaps it is because she and my dad had another fight. She tries to hide it, but I hear the late-night quarrels. Sometimes I feel guilty; like it's somehow my fault. I don't know why, but I do. I wished I could make it all better. But at least my mom and dad are together, and maybe one day, they will learn to love each other, and not argue so much. In the mind of a child, the answers are always that simple.

In the quiet moments, I hear my mom whisper,

"Jesus." She exhaustedly exhales and continues to say the name over and over again.

"Thank you, Jesus." Her eyes are open and focused. I wonder if she can actually see Him. My head lowers while my eyes search for Jesus. I want to see whom she sees, but I don't see anyone near her. Again, she whispers,

"Thank you, Jesus." I listen and sit quietly on the wooden stool by the store's front counter. Staring at my shoelaces as my feet dangle close to the floor, I began to ponder. Who is this Jesus my mom talks to and my sister sings to while she cleans the house? Who is the God of my grandmother, Rachel, and what of these miracles she believes? Mommy looks to the wind and whispers again, "Jesus."

After a while, my thoughts drift out to oblivion. Leaving my parents' store, lost in reverie, I lift away. When I find myself, I am on a magical quest, flying with the wind underneath me. In my left hand, I hold a golden wand—a magical scepter with which I wield against the evil forces of darkness. In my right hand, I carry enough food to feed everyone. My supply is endless. No one is hungry in my land, and no one is lonely. I wave my mighty scepter and golden sparkles of light fall, raining down glittery diamonds. Everyone it touches smiles. I am off to save the world. I use my magical powers to defeat a menacing, angry monster that stirs up malice and tries to destroy a village.

"Sydney" My mother's voice jolts me back to the store, away from my adventures. She has called me Sydney for as long as I can remember. I was never sure why, but it is the nickname she calls me.

"Sydney!" She calls again with slight agitation.

"Tie your shoe strings before you fall, sweetheart. When will you learn to keep your laces tied, child? Come down off that chair; it's time to go."

"Yes ma'am, Mama." I leap off the high chair like a mighty warrior, vowing to return to destroy the monsters. I look down at my shoelaces and sigh. They have a mind of their own. *I guess saving the world must wait until I can at least keep my laces tied.*

Time always answers the questions we are too afraid to ask. It will be only a matter of time before my mom and dad reach the breaking point. After closing, my father's anger ignites, apparently soaking in the toxic fumes of suspicion during the day. With his breath, heavy with gin, he heaves allegations of infidelity.

"Bert, when do I have time to be with someone else? We work in the same store all day, and we have one car to drive," my mom says defensively. Her voice shudders as though she is at her wits' end. But when you are under the influence of suspicion and gin, logic is overruled. He sees her friendliness as flirting; her carefree laughter most certainly means she is having an affair, and the tender way in which she warmly welcomes everyone is utterly intolerable.

Quite often, we do not realize that fear is a spirit—a real enemy. That which we fear the most, we surrender our energy to, and ultimately, our life.

Another long night ensues, another fight, another thorn begins to form inside me; it's becoming the norm. My dad appears to struggle with himself far more than with anybody else.

The mind can be a masterful deceiver, believing in its own deception. It can conjure a thousand lies and never question what's real and true. Strange how the facts can be so obvious, yet a lie allows us to think whatever we *want* and worship what we *feel*, no matter how absurd or contradictory it is to common sense. My father's addictions imprison him to the need to control the uncontrollable which often sends him into fits of rage like Dr. Jekyll and Mr. Hyde—a man one moment and a maniac the other. My siblings and I have been well trained to ignore my parents' civil war. The trouble is when you ignore the chaos long enough, it becomes normal.

The familial order to stay in a child's place is louder than the upheaval coming from their room. In silence, the thorns of fear and uncertainty began to form. So, I go to the only place that I can find comfort. I disappear inside myself. There, I journey far, far away. I learn to use my imagination, even more, to feel safe and calm. It is my hiding place, my sanctuary. Eyes open, I look out, into the wind. There, I search for Him and begin to pray:

"Dear Jesus, bless Mama and Daddy and my sisters and brothers. Bless everyone in the whole world. Now I lay me down to sleep. I pray the Lord my soul to keep. If I should die before I wake, I pray the Lord my soul to take. Amen."

During this same time, my parents' business begins to struggle. Times are hard for many families, especially the working poor. Under Nixon's presidency, the nation falls near economic ruin. What is more, the Watergate scandal would cause a flood of cynicism and doubt over the entire country. Then again, distrust was commonplace among people who spent generations disgraced and broken by the staunch injustice of racism and discrimination.

Justice waits while the blood of many cries out from across chasms of time. No reparations had come, no land—no real freedom. Communities imploded in anguish and disrepair. The country makes no amends for its horrendous crimes. In survival mode, many lost their lives.

The nation continues to steal that which it has promised to repay; reparations and land for centuries of slavery and its current shocking impact on the Black community; the extent of the economic and psychological damage would be innumerable. To this day, the aftermath can be seen and felt by the entire nation, and around the world.

Generation after generation, the stories are told. Veto after veto, the nation reneges on the liability of 40 acres and a mule that was made law after the war in the 1800s. America, the enslaving land of the free and home of the greed stays true to its deceitful history and its strategic tyranny. The wounds of bigotry will never heal entirely until the country finds a way to settle the debt it owes, fixes the damages, and get square with the house; a race of people referred to as; nigger, Negro, colored, black, and African American—different names, no identity. Until today, many human lives continue to be terrorized by the transferred trauma from hundreds of years of lynching, torture, branding, whipping, and illiteracy.

I was too young to understand how the social order and interplay would impact my life and my family. Nevertheless, hope would come amidst all the nonsense of a world plagued with thorns.

Joyce says God calls all people His children. "We are all the same—fearfully and wonderfully made," she'd say. However, I don't think everyone sees it that way. I guess it's hard to see with your eyes open. Such were the times. The political outrage over bribery and obstruction of justice presented an appalling contradiction. In the land of the free, twisted double standards remind you to stay in your place, granting only a false concept of *freedom*. Some people exist with a supreme sense of entitlement while the treatment of others is that of a slave. Unknowing, we adapt, assuming the same position of the past. These turbulent times would further test my parents' marriage. More hours at work, less sleep at home, and the arguments and fights linger. My stomach twists and turns with every fight as they ebb and flow in seething monologs of "I'm sick and tired of this!" *Please stop*! I scream inside, feeling nausea rising. I dare not tell them how their fighting scares me and splits my insides.

I learn to hold all the feelings in; the paralyzing fear, the uncertainty, the sadness. I feel it. Deep inside, like piercing thorns forming underneath my skin. There is an old saying—be careful little ears, little eyes, what you see, what you hear. The arguments directly affect our sense of self, safety, and the world around us. Strangely, the thought of them breaking up is scarier than the chaos of their fighting. Soon, the months would pass in dead silence. We never know where the landmines are. The next step could be the one to end it all. They become more like strangers to each other, and we feel the heavy tension that runs a divide between them. In the middle of the mess, my siblings and I hold tight.

Until we find the courage to confront our issues, things will often get worse. My dad's gambling spirals out of control, and he bets his entire paycheck in a dice game, again. So, with the quick toss of a hand, he loses it all, again. Financially defeated, a dark cloud rest over him. It is familiar darkness, one that he has known since his lonely childhood. Depression and apathy are obstacles he has yet to find the courage to overcome. He refuses to change, to let go of the past and resist his demons. Sometimes it's not that easy.

Today, Mom is angry because he skipped work. Instead of going to work, he goes to a poker house to try to win back some of the money he lost. In the middle of a hand, so the story goes, a player notices extra cards under his thigh. Just as a scuffle begins, police raided the place. Before the police could apprehend my father and before his bookie could catch up to him, he gets away. He hides in the one place he knew no one would search: the cemetery. My mother says the cemetery was a common hideout for my father and he was never afraid to go there to hide. No one there could hurt him or rat him out. I imagine hiding in the cemetery gives him a sense of peace—the kind of peace the living world couldn't offer.

Later that night we are awakened by frantic noises. We run to the top of the stairs in the house and see my mother. She is yelling. "Bert, how am I supposed to pay the bills when you keep gambling away all your money and stealing mine out of my purse? I am sick of this! You're just like your daddy—a liar and a cheat!" She scornfully confronts him. Firm anger replaces the look of sadness on my mother's face. The softness that once filled her eyes cement over, like a statue made of stone, sunken by the weight of her world. A world I could not fully understand at the time. My father fires back with a barrage of words that sound like gibberish. We get out of sight, closer to the shadows of the upstairs bathroom.

My dad staggers back and forth while he speaks. The house explodes in a blaze of angry words and threats.

Anger is like a bitter shadow that lurks in the corner of the house, keeping the laughter out. I remember praying for peace and love again between my parents. Before I fall asleep, I whisper, *"please stop fighting. Please stop!"*

Salvation Song

"Music is a moral law. It gives a soul to the universe, wings to the mind, flight to the imagination, a charm to sadness, and life to everything." ~*Plato*

Tonight, a tender hand touches my shoulder. "Come on, back to bed now," Joyce says. She senses the nerve-wracking effect my parents' arguments have on us. She quickly guides us back into the room and shuts the door. Joyce is wise beyond her years. Her eyes are patient and calm; her posture is poised and resilient. Seemingly untouched or immunized to the turmoil, she begins to sing softly in a gentle voice. It soothes me. She sees the frown lines on our faces. Perhaps she has gone through the same, though she never says.

As I rock back and forth, she rubs my back and runs her hands slowly over my cheek and kisses me. She continues to sing. One by one, she tucks us back into bed, humming the melody between the lyrics. Joyce kisses our foreheads, whispering, "Everything is all right, go back to sleep." She sings, and the chattering noises in my head fade quietly away. She sings, and her song moves the tension away from the air, transforming it into sweet harmony. It is as though she knows what's to come and somehow needs to seal our hearts to something greater than all the chaos around us. She sings peace over the uncertainty, until it suffocates the hate in the house, and fills me with hope beyond my knowing:

> *"Love makes the world go 'round.*
> *Love makes the world go 'round.*
> *It's a time for beginnings; love makes the world go 'round.*
> *When we're together, Love makes the world go 'round. It's*
> *a time for beginnings.*
> *Love makes the world go 'round."*

Joyce's lullaby calms us until Leon, Michael, and Linda fall fast asleep. My eyes begin to feel heavy, but I resist it to stay up with Joyce, to hear her gentle voice. I need to hold onto it before all the noises come back again, and the memory is gone. Her sweet lullaby becomes my salvation song—the tone, the vibration, the words, the melody; like a balm; it is healing.

This lullaby would continue to be my source of hope and strength for years to come.

Our Mom takes on yet another job to try to pull the family out of debt. A new business venture enables her to earn more in one night than she does in one week—tempting for a family struggling to make ends meet. My mother tells the story of a man named Caesar. While she is at work at the Bay-to-Bay Dry Cleaners on Columbus Drive, he walked through the door and made her an offer she could not refuse. Caesar is a suave, six feet five, Cuban mafia member with mustard-colored skin and an eye for colored women. He becomes love-sick with my mother, so the story goes.

Soon, Caesar becomes a regular customer and a mutual friend of both my parents. He runs the dog track and offers Mom a job running numbers on Saturday night. Mama gets many invites to the dog track, free of charge, courtesy of Caesar. He is crazy about her and makes no secret of his infatuation. She and Daddy visit the racetrack every week now, and the money rolls in faster than the greyhounds can chase the robotic rabbit around the track. Although the money comes easy, the risks are high.

The Bolita is an illegal and dangerous gambling operation: if caught, she could do time in jail; if the money comes up missing, so might she. She keeps the numbers in the freezer, hiding it with the frozen meat. Selling numbers for a mobster is risky business. But for now, Mom's charm and outgoing personality make it a profitable gamble. Looking back, the stories of my family seem almost impossible to fathom. However, the truth is like that. It forces you to survey the past, especially when the future looks impossible.

Tampa Bay became a hotbed for Bolita gambling in the 1960s. On the surface, the promise of getting rich quick is a tempting invitation, but what often lays hidden beneath most illicit fantasies are dark tentacles that stretch deep and wide. The game is serious business, and the gangsters who deal in its shadows would have no problem making welchers disappear.

During most of the 20th century, organized crime spawned disorder like a horde of locust on the streets of Tampa, giving it the name *Little Chicago*. The illegal numbers game became the focus of the mayhem. From Hialeah to New York City, it fed the fantasies of the working poor, and satisfied the greed of the most sinister racketeers. Tampa's notorious reputation grew in the 1940s and 50s as the infamous mobster named Santo Trafficante and the Trafficante crime family marked Tampa as their territory for the numbers racket.

Later, during the 1970s, organized crime families expanded its business to include prostitution and cocaine trafficking. Corruption spread like a fatal infection as many people went for broke and sold their souls for a piece of the action.

As a child, my simple mind could not wrap around the reality of crime and corruption. Many years would pass before I realized everyone has a soul, and every soul has a price.

In time, I notice how my dad's drinking began to affect his health. He becomes more elusive, more forgetful. He often complains of a headache, which is one of the symptoms of his worsening hypertension. Liquor only complicates the condition, but still, he never slows down. With red eyes and shaky hands, he backs out of the driveway. The last time he drove off with that *lost* look in his eyes, he did not come home for days. The old navy-blue Buick is the only means of transportation for the family. My mom was furious because she had to go to work with no way to get there. I don't remember her saying much on that day, only the quiet sadness that sat with us as we waited on the cracked-concrete step of the front porch.

She cries when she thinks no one is looking. I think my mom is trying to prove she is stronger than she is because often, when the burdens of life caves in on us, we are left with no other choice but to be braver and stronger than we are. She never talks about it. She sniffles and prays under her breath one word; only one name: "Jesus."

Footprints on the Stairs

"You must be careful how you walk and where you go, for there are those following you who will set their feet where yours are set." ~*Robert E Lee*

Something peculiar is in the house, but that too is becoming quite *normal*. Often, we are home alone, but Joyce is always there to care for us: cooking meals, combing, brushing, and plaiting our hair, checking behind our ears after bath time, singing lullabies at bedtime, teaching us to pray, and giving us a good spanking whenever we misbehave. Joyce is enchanting and the first person I remember ever praying over us at bedtime. Her hands are gentle and soft as the petals of a rose, yet strong enough to care for the five of us and keep up with the daily chores. It's getting harder to ignore the unusual happenings in the spooky house, but Joyce manages to keep things in order. She appears fearless.

Joyce is a natural-born teacher. She teaches through music, worship, and amazing Bible stories. Even the old house seems to listen when she begins her lessons. I hear weird clacks and brattles in the house. But the noises never appear to trouble Joyce. She just keeps right on teaching, singing, and praising as if she is caught up in her own world. After lessons, I sit on the steps watching Joyce sweep and dust while humming a cheerful melody, far away in thought and seemingly never weary from all her work. She prays and sings as if she is on a stage and her only audience is God himself. It seems her faith could move mountains, but it would take more than faith to endure the strange apparitions manifesting in our home lately.

Though we live in the eerie house, I suspiciously feel as if it doesn't belong to us but to someone from long, long ago who never wanted to leave, and never did. Upstairs is dark with a musty damp smell of decaying wood. A creepy shadow of fog lingers and stirs in the air. Confused and unsettled, the mist seems to search restlessly for a place to settle down and stay. Nighttime is especially scary. The house fills with hollowing noises so unnerving it chases the shadows out of hiding. Doors close and open like they are trying to talk. Glass breaks downstairs, and the sounds of cupboards slamming in the kitchen become more distressing as the night awakes. Tonight, Mom and Dad are away at work, and no one else is in the house.

"What is that," my brother Michael asks hesitantly.

"Everything is all right," Joyce says, reassuring us. She discerns what we cannot. Kneeling, she caresses each of us. Seeing the fear in our faces, she says, "Trust God; everything will be okay." The calmness of her voice and the confidence of her words comfort me. Hearing a faint rumble in the distance, she lifts her gaze toward the window. The floor creaks as she makes her way to the window and pulls back the nylon drape panel. The moonlight catches a sleepy moth as it flutters from the windowsill. It dances through dust particles rising from the old ruffled curtain. Joyce looks through the misty window. "A storm is coming," she warns us. Old folks say they can smell the rain coming from far off. Closing the curtain, she gathers us together to prepare for another stormy night.

Thunderstorms become welcomed guests in our home. Most nights, the roaring thunder drowns out the sounds of scurrying rats and other disturbing noises—at least long enough for sleep to find its way to us. I grow to love the resounding tide of the thunder and the lightning show glowing through the downstairs window. Joyce says God made the magnificent lightning show and the thunderous applause that follows. *My goodness,* I think to myself. *How powerful God must be.* I began to sense His presence, especially during the storms. The feeling is indescribably peaceful. Perhaps it's because the sight and sounds of the storms make me feel so helpless and small. Or maybe, it's because I was born during an early morning thunderstorm. Whatever the reason, the storms make God seem closer than ever.

We usually gather close during the storms. Most times Joyce sits in-between the middle of us and tells us Bible stories. The lightning and thunder present a dramatic backdrop that brings out an enchanted imagination inside of us.

"Come on. It's story time." Joyce announces. We snuggle up close to her. With a Bible in hand, Joyce says, "God is real, and He loves us so much. He is merciful and faithful, forever." Joyce tells us stories about Jesus and the miracles He performs. Blind eyes are open, the lame walk, and even the dead lives again. I am mesmerized. I want to hear more. I especially love the story she tells about Daniel in the Lion's Den and how God protected him from the wild lions. I imagine Daniel petting the hungry lions. In my mind, I can see their thick manes and sharp teeth. I can almost hear them purring as she speaks. *Wow, how mighty God must be,* I think to myself.

Cleverly, Joyce uses her stories to help us understand things that are not easily understood or explained. "God protects us from dangers seen and unseen," Joyce says with a protective gaze. "We must trust God in all things." Her manner is bold and confident. I hang on her every word. My hands clasped tightly together, waiting for the story's crescendo.

"Jesus speaks to the winds and the waves, and they obey His voice. When we have faith as small as a mustard seed, we too can speak to our situations with power and authority in Jesus's name."

A loud clatter of thunder captures our attention. My eyes wander skittishly upwards toward the ceiling. Suddenly, all the lights in the house go out. The shadows fuse with the darkness. This storm feels different tonight. We band closer together on top of the stairs. Sitting still and close, we listen. In the dark, sounds amplify as other senses come to life. The thunderstorm worsens as the night awakens, and I think about Mom and Dad at the store. They are working late again. I hope they are safe inside, out of the storm. Sharp thunderous blows cause the house to shake.

"The storm sounds angry," I think out loud. The lightning flashes through the downstairs curtains onto the stairs. My eyes rush downward to find the murky shapes on the carpet. They appear to move. With each flash of lightning, the forms in the carpet seem to come alive and take on weird shapes. Unlike the usual dingy spots left by an occasional fruit juice spill, these forms are strange and restless. Swirling patterns of Victorian, loops, and twists contort into the scariest shape of all: footprints.

Like a weird style of hide-and-seek, the footprints would vanish, only to return with the next bolt of lightning. "Did you see that?" Michael asks frantically. Our eyes search hesitantly for the owner of the footprints. I do not see anyone, only large disembodied footprints. Afraid of what the next flash might reveal on the stairs, I curl my knees in tightly to my chest, like a frightened turtle.

My eyes stretch wide as footprints climb higher and higher. My heart beats faster. What could it be and what does it want? Gasping, I hold tighter to Joyce. She is undaunted. Unflinching, she seems to study the moment, like a student of the supernatural; she looks out into the air and waits. The darkness yields no answers to my questions. The more I try to make sense of it; the noises, and rattling, the more I realize none of it makes any sense. I conclude some questions do not have answers. I learn to accept what is and let it be. The phantom footprints, the shattering glass, the unrelenting fear, and the distressing questions; I let go. I cannot understand it all, but it's okay. Joyce is here. That's enough for me.

Joyce begins to sing hymns of praise and worship again until the scary shadows fade. Her voice commands the atmosphere. Joyce says the evil spirits in the house did not like the sound of praise and worship music. For a moment, she stops singing. With her eyes closed and potency in her words, she speaks out into the air, "satan, the Lord rebukes you, in Jesus's name." She continues to pray as if she has authority over an unseen realm. With the fierceness of a warrior, she orders everything that is not of God to leave the house.

Bowing her head, she prays. We follow her lead, repeating the words, mirroring her posture. She prays, calling on the Holy Spirit to lead us, guide us, and keep us safe. One by one, she prays for our family. Joyce reminds us that songs of praise will subdue evil spirits, break the chains of fear, and create a haven of rest. "When times get hard, remember to praise God. Remember, God is always with you, even when you feel alone. His angels will guard and keep you. There is nothing too hard for God to do." She speaks in a matter-of-fact tone leaning towards us. As if she somehow knows the sorrows the dawn will bring.

Soon, the mysterious footprints vanish. The scuttling noises downstairs have long tired and faded out into the night. All fear is gone. Moreover, I discover the power of music and praise. Her heavenly voice chases away anything lurking about, whether real or imagined. It would be her faith, her songs, and her love that would significantly influence my character and carry me through the darkest times. Unimaginable storms were yet to come.

My sister's words and steadfast faith plants seeds in the fertile soil of my heart and the hearts of my sister and brothers. A secure foundation of trust and love grows deep beneath the surface of my life because of her loving care and tenacious faith. Joyce has no pulpit, no altar, and no system of religion or mystical phenomena. She shows us the grace of Jesus Christ through His words in Scripture, her Bible stories, and songs. That's it. There is only a relationship of the most intimate kind. Joyce said she learned it from Mom, and a person she calls the *Holy Spirit*.

Now, she teaches us the way of Immanuel—God with us.

I was too young to understand the concept of evil spirits. During this time, I often wondered how they got into the house in the first place. Like muddied footprints, can we bring them in from the places we have been and forgot to wipe our feet? The scary apparitions have never harmed any of us, as far as I can see, and truth be told, what I can see is far more frightening than what is invisible. Like wretched thieves, alcoholism and apathy steal my father's heart away, until my smile can no longer reach his heart. His absence is more frightening to me; more unnerving than the footprints on the stairs. He doesn't seem to know it, but a feeling of rejection, like a dark phantom, has taken the place of his arms. I wonder if he knows.

It often takes a lifetime to understand that we have the power to choose a different path; chart a new course; direct our footsteps towards wholeness and healing.

Reflecting on those haunting years, I realize the more I live, the more I find that we do not know who we are, for if we did, nothing around us would look the same. The way we see ourselves directly affects the way we live, parent, work, and love— indeed every aspect of life. My father, like most of us, view the world from a limited prism, a small, distorted speck that causes us to neglect the bigger picture, like focusing on a single star in a vast universe, when there is so much more out there; new worlds without end; more to explore and discover; beyond imagination.

When we look at ourselves for whom we were meant to be, we can never again live with the negative energies of fear, depression, doubt, anger, regret, and unforgiveness.

These toxic e-motions (energy in motion) distract us from furthering our evolution, blinding us from the inside out. When we begin to wake up and see the truth, we defuse these useless energies as they could no longer contend with the divine light from within.

Waiting for Miracles

Soon, my parents decide to move the family from Tampa after the business and their relationship further deteriorate. Likewise, the city itself undergoes a predictable downturn. Many areas in Tampa suffer the consequences of race riots, a decline in population growth, and an increase in organized crime. Bribery and extortion are a part of the problem as the corrosive effects of Tampa's underworld crawl to the surface during the 1970s. Corrupted political officials, along with the extremist group members of the Ku Klux Klan and the Black Panther Party find themselves under persistent investigation from the FBI for various crimes, which invariably led to the city's unstable infrastructure. Hush money has a way of snitching, especially when the feds are the ones asking the questions. The FBI in Tampa Division begins to track down the illegal gambling racketeers. No matter what side of a bet you were on before, the Bolita stakes rise after every arrest.

The Feds enforce new racketeering laws with harsh consequences; the risks are high; the penalty is prison. In 1972, agents took down the largest mafia figures of the time, including many of their co-conspirators. And though the new regulations primarily target the once-untouchable Mob bosses who ran the illegal lotteries in Tampa, my parent's ties with Caesar would implicate them as well. All bets are off. Rather than risk everything, my parents close the business and move the family to Fort Lauderdale for a fresh start.

They reopened "Live and Let Live" Barbershop on Sunrise Boulevard between 31st and 27th Avenue. My dad works hard to rebuild his clientele in the new city. He stays late cutting hair and keeps the shop going while Mom works at the 7 Eleven on 19th Street. Over the next couple of years, we move around more times than I can count. But I don't care; we're together. That's all that matters. We settle into an apartment behind Sunland Park Elementary School just off Sunrise Boulevard, a busy straightway of the city. Joyce tries to keep up with her studies while helping to care for us. Somehow, year after year, she manages to balance it all. School is challenging for me. After moving from place to place and school to school, it's hard to focus long enough to catch up.

I am usually somewhere lost between a history book and a daydream. My musings allow me to create a world of my own. In my daydream, anything is possible. *One day I will be rich, and*

Mommy will not have to work so much, I think to myself. One day I will possess the power to teach the world to stop all the fighting, let go of anger and bitterness, and see that we are all the same, just like the Bible stories I've heard. I will begin the lessons with my dad. I will teach him to smile more, not to be so angry all the time, and not to drink so much.

Subtly, I began noticing how my dad appears angrier when he gets home after a night of gambling and drinking. I hear him and my mom bickering back and forth. The air around the house feels different every time they fight and yell, like a war zone instead of a home. Behind closed doors, I swallow hard, waiting for miracles, praying for peace between my parents. The sad look I see in my dad's eyes makes me feel sorry for him. Maybe he realizes the booze does not work because when he sobers up the problems are still there. Whatever the reason for the drinking and all the fighting, it continues to rip our family apart.

In school, the teacher sees me daydreaming again, and threatens to call my parents—again. I try to concentrate, but it is hard to forget what I heard the night before. The screaming, the fights are impossible to ignore. My parents have a way of pretending as if nothing ever happened. Day after day, they go on with life as usual. I do a good job of acting as if I do not hear, do not see, and dare not speak of the fear and sadness I hide deep inside my heart and mind. Whether at home or in school, I am a student of life, learning the lessons of reading, writing, anger, and compromise, to which I have a front-row seat. Thankfully, at school, my teacher allows me to catch up on my schoolwork, but she warns me, again, "Stay focused Ms. Anderson." I try to do as she says, but it's getting harder with all the noise rambling around inside my head.

Since moving to Fort Lauderdale, John, my Dad's son from his first marriage, his girlfriend Lynn, and their two-year-old son, moves in with us. John is always telling jokes. His afro and swagger remind me of the singer James Brown. He keeps a black, wide-tooth hair pick with the handle in the shape of a fist in his hair. He likes to pick through his big curly hair, and then he pats it down with the palms of his hands, making it perfectly neat and round. At first, we breathe easy around his family. But things have a way of changing right before your eyes. When he drinks, he laughs loud and slaps his hand against his thigh after every punch line. Even if you miss the joke, you can't help but laugh at the way he amuses himself— then his temper changes when he would drink too much. He became more aggressive, less funny; more like our dad.

I begin to think alcohol makes people more of what they already are; freeing them from inhibitions, removing the masks people often hide behind. I remember thinking alcohol must be some sort of truth serum. After a few drinks, John would tell everybody's business, no matter how embarrassing or private. He'd say, "Laughter is the best medicine." But not everyone laughs, especially his girlfriend, Ms. Lynn. He takes dull-witted shots at her, making insensitive comments about her weight and other personal topics that no one with good manners should say. When he gets drunk, he becomes a different person. But he is not the only one with two-faces.

I'm not sure why, but John's girlfriend Lynn seems to hate us. Hate is a strong word, but I don't know of any other word to describe it. We become leery of her soon after they moved in with us. When she comes in the house, she looks through us as if we are invisible children. An intimidating contempt frames her round, puffy face, and I can feel a hardening chill crouching behind her stares. I pretend not to notice and swallow the sourness that wells up from the pit of my stomach. She doesn't know us, why would she not like us. I busy myself with play, assuring my growing fears that it's all in my mind. "Stop being so sensitive," I whisper to myself.

Saturday morning:

On the table in the living room, my stepbrother John is charming my brothers and sisters with a deck of cards. I stand next to the table, leaning on my elbows. "Hit me!" John yells out. My brother Leon, smiling as big as I have ever seen, slaps another card next to John. I smile at the way Leon's face lights up as he learns to play. He is a fun big brother.

"You bust, you bust!" Leon screeches loudly. "Let's play another hand." Leon explodes with new gusto.

"What are you playing?" I ask.

"I'm teaching your brother how to play 21," John announces as he gathers the cards together. He takes a big gulp from a can of Colt 45 malt liquor. High and low, he shuffles, moving with finesse, putting on a grand show for us. The cards ruffle, folding into each other so fast they make fluttering sounds, like the wings of a dragonfly.

He teaches us how to shuffle and lay the cards in the perfect angle on top of the table. John flips and deals the cards like a real magician. The cards fly across the table, landing smooth and exact. My brother Leon is awestruck. His eyes bulge with intrigue after every clever flip and shuffle. John puts an empty hand behind my ear. Suddenly, he brings his hand back in front of my face, holding a card with a funny looking clown on it. "Watch out for this joker, he is always up to no good," John laughs.

"How did you do that?" I ask.

"A real player never tells his secrets and never shows what's in his hands," John says, holding a grin that bears a striking resemblance to the clown on the card.

"Show me how to do that!" Leon begs.

"Me too, me too!" We all want to know how John did the card trick. He just smiles as he holds all the cards with a clear sense of satisfaction with himself.

"All right, all right, I'll show you a little something." John throws his head back and tips his can of beer upside down until it is empty. In a pounding thud, he crushes the empty beer can with one hand, flat against the table. I jump, shrinking back a little.

"See this here? The king is high, the ace is low — but that can change." He stops and let out a loud burp. The sour smell lingered long after the third can was empty. "Never lift your card off the table. Only bend the end of the card, like this here. You see?" John demonstrates using his thumb to lift the corner of the card. "Now, only you can see whatcha got. Never let nobody else know what's in yo' hand, you dig? You gotta know when to fold your hand and be quick." John shouts as if his tongue has swollen against his teeth. His words spray out over the cards and table. "But don't try to be slick, you hear. This is a real man's game." John looks square at Leon, whose fascination with the deck of cards would ultimately become a full-blown obsession.

"Show me what I taught you, boy," John slurs, sipping on his fourth beer, or that's where I stop counting — when I notice the change in his temper. I step to the side where a cold, unpleasant chill forces me back to my father's shop in Tampa and the house on the outskirts of Ybor. It's a familiar chill I have come to know well; it begins with a drink and end with the spirit of Dr. Jekyll and Mr. Hyde. I began to see my father in my stepbrother's glassy eyes. I can almost hear my father's voice in his heightened tone and slurred speech. It is garbled, like a man who is drowning his own soul, forfeiting his God-given destiny. John slams his hand on the table causing the cards to leap. "Come on now boy! It's your turn." He shouts. Leon cuts the deck and deals the next hand.

Another late night and I cannot fall asleep. Mom, Dad, and Joyce are not home yet. Work keeps my parents and Joyce away from home until late at night. And sometimes till early morning. I wish Joyce were here. Her lullabies help me sleep. Mom usually picks up Dad on the way home because she does not trust him to pick her up anymore. She is afraid he will detour to a gambling hall or worse, a bar. There, he drinks until he forgets himself and forgets to pick her up from work. John and Ms. Lynn watch us when my parents are away, but their fights keep them sparring in their room. What is it with the adult world? Why do people get together if they are going to fight all the time?

"I do everything around here." Ms. Lynn shouts. "And why I got to be looking after other people's nappy-headed children? They ain't none of mine!" she spits. John fires back at her. The noise rises behind the closed door. I cover my ears with my hands and try to find a daydream.

I learn to lay low and keep a safe distance away from the short fuses of the adults in the house. Tonight, I pretend to be asleep, until the house gets quiet enough for me to tiptoe out into the living room. I ease out of bed, limp to the couch, and wait for my parents to come home. I sway back and forth, trying to hush the noise in my head, long enough to hear the car pull up in the driveway. I make a mental list of things I don't want to forget. I need to tell my dad why I didn't take a bath; the big spider in the bathtub refused to leave. With six legs more than me, he could have the tub and the entire bathroom for that matter.

I need to tell my mom I hurt my foot today when I accidentally stepped on a nail that was stuck inside a plank of wood left outside in the grass. Although the pain stopped throbbing hours ago, I need to let her know what happened. Her love and attention have a way of making everything better. I know she will fuss at me for not wearing my shoes again, but it will be worth it because at least, she will be home. I wait, and wait, and wait until I fall asleep on the couch.

When my parents finally come home, it's the same argument: money, bills, drinking, gambling: different city, same fights. I think to myself that my family must have a lot of bills because they are always busy, and when they come home, they are always tired. I find myself daydreaming more often than usual to block the loneliness and uncertainty; especially when I feel out of place, which now, is most of the time.

Awakened in the night, I feel little bites on my arms and legs. John told me something earlier about not letting the bedbugs bite, but I thought he was joking. They wake me up in the middle of the night to a strange blackness. I try, but I cannot fall back to sleep. The night is long. And a new fear begins to settle in next to me. I am not sure what it is or why it chose me. I close my eyes and tunnel deep inside the reservoir of my mind. There, I secure the treasures of my sister's stories, strength, and songs. I see my mother's reassuring smile and the smell of my dad's Old Spice cologne. Before long, I remember a scripture from Psalms 23 —a seed planted in the soil of my heart during a thunderstorm at the old house in Tampa. "For the Lord is my shepherd, I shall not want. He leads me beside still waters. He restores my soul. Yea though I walk through the valley of the shadow of death, I will fear no evil, for God is with me." I whisper myself back to sleep.

Saturday morning

A new day unfolds in dual tones, vivid arrays of both hope and doubt. Lately, my parents have managed to get along with each other; I hope it lasts. It makes the house feel more like a home when they are not fussing at each other. Saturday morning and I am tired from the restless nights. I stay in bed a little longer than usual. Footsteps patter down the hallway toward the room. I know exactly who it is; it's John and Lynn's energetic son. He hits and spits, then runs up and down the hall until his diaper falls to the floor. Sometimes he likes to bite. I can never figure out why, but I guess he can't help himself.

We are not allowed to say anything to him when he makes a mess. Once he tried to bite Linda, but the moment I told Ms. Lynn, I got in trouble. She made it clear—we are not allowed to correct him about anything he does. I often wonder why he still wears diapers when he seems smart enough to kick, bite, and curse. I shake my head and hold my peace. I have learned to ignore his antics, wait for him to tire of himself, and run off to the other side of the house to play.

When I'm around Ms. Lynn, I feel like I can't do anything right. When she screams at me, I feel like a loser, believing I must have done something wrong to deserve her poor treatment. *I will do better*, I think to myself. After some time, her verbal assaults turn physical. She slaps me on the back of my head because of her son's toys scattered across the floor—where he was playing with them. I ask myself why: *what did I do?* Like the shattering glass inside the old house in Tampa, the answer does not come.

My baby sister Linda is almost five now. She plays with her See and Say pull toy while my brothers, Leon and Michael, are outside digging up worms or dueling to the death with razor sharp swords that resemble broken twigs from off the tree in the front yard. While on the bed, reading my picture book, I hear Ms. Lynn off to the side of the door. She speaks with short hawkish words. "Stupid! Fat ass!" She looks at me, giving no explanation before leaving down the hall towards the kitchen. I wonder to myself, *what did I do now*. A cold hush stays behind in our bedroom.

Peculiarly, when Joyce and my parents get home, Ms. Lynn acts as meek as a box jellyfish. I am afraid to tell Mom how Ms. Lynn treats us when she is not around. Mama always tells us to mind our manners. I will try harder to be good.

Moving to Fort Lauderdale was supposed to bring us closer together—a fresh start for our family. But the distance between my parents is farther now than ever. We live in the same house, but it might as well be different planets.

I miss Joyce; the weekend has come, and she is away again. Mama says she is visiting with family when she is not here. I'm not sure what that means. There are no explanations.

Culture has a way of teaching children far more than any classroom, and like breathing, we go along with the lessons it teaches, most times, without question. In a time where the cultural decree demand that children should be seen and not heard, my siblings and I wait quietly and obey the rules. The problem with laws in a culture that does not value children is that those children will grow up and become adults who do not value the culture.

Impossible Dreams

"It always seems impossible, until it's done."
~Nelson Mandela

I am afraid to go home from school today. Ms. Lynn made it clear that I was in trouble when I woke up. "Didn't I tell you to clean dis room?" she yelled. I was barely awake when her son left his toys all over the floor. Still, she blamed me for it. I don't answer back for fear I will get what I got the last time I opened my mouth to try to explain. I cleaned the room, but he messes it up again. My stomach ached all day in class—I could not concentrate on my schoolwork; my teacher sent me to the school nurse. I made up a story and said it was something that I ate. When I got home, Joyce was already there. God must have heard my prayer. I hoped she could stay with me, sit and read with me, and never leave my side. I missed her while she was away for the weekend. "After dinner, we will do something together," she says and begins to clean up around the apartment. Ms. Lynn is coiled up on the couch. A lump sit in my throat.

"When is Mom and Dad coming home?" I ask Joyce.

"Are you, all right? "Joyce asks touching my forehead. "You look a little sick." She leads me to the bedroom. We sit on the bed together.

"Yes, I'm all right," I reply, looking down at my hands. My fingers anxiously twirl the corners of a piece of tissue until it looks as alien as I feel. "I just was wondering when they were getting home."

She reaches up to move a barrette she put in my hair earlier. "There, that's better. They will be home soon. Why don't we start on your homework?" Joyce asks.

I explain that I was sick today at school and had to go to the nurse's office for most of the day. The school tried to contact Mom. "I don't have homework today." I feel sorry for not telling Joyce the truth of why I feel so ill.

For the first time in my life, I cannot express my fear to Joyce. I am afraid to tell her how Ms. Lynn has been treating me. I cannot form the words to explain what I do not understand. And what if it is my fault? Then I will be in double trouble. I keep quiet because Ms. Lynn reminds me of an angry storm. Not like the storms in Tampa; though thunderous, they were still kind. Ms. Lynn watches me while I talk to Joyce. She glares with cloak-and-dagger disdain as she hauls around the frame of a heavyweight prizefighter. I believe her cold, stare could freeze the sun. It evokes an indescribable feeling of doom, like looking into the eyes of the Greek monster Medusa from my library book. I look away, not wanting to test the fates.

I want to tell Joyce that when I am in school, I cannot focus anymore. As soon as one thought enters my mind, another comes, and then another. Before long, the wires are all tangled up and I cannot untie the knots. I shrink down on the desk, hoping the teacher will not call on me and will forget I was ever in the class. Before I can even try to master the new fraction worksheet Mrs. Watchcoat gave me over a week ago, I believe I have already failed. School is becoming harder and fear keeps me from trying any more. On the walk home, I threw away my math homework. With each new lesson in school, with every cruel word and argument at home, with all these escalating uncertainties, I begin to shut down, further inside a daydream. But I can't tell Joyce. I cannot tell anyone.

Later that night, we cuddle up together. Leon and Michael are on the right side of the bed, Linda is in the middle, and I am on the left. Joyce sleeps in the room across the hall. Sharing the room with my siblings is amusing, but when one gets in trouble, we all get in trouble. Joyce reminds us that we have school in the morning. "Settle down now," she says. It is past our bedtime, but we whisper, talking about what we want to be when we grow up. Leon says he intends to be an electrician and own his own shop. Michael is bent on running the world as an entrepreneur, while Linda looks at us with eyes as big and beautiful as a russet sunset, smiles excitedly and says, "I want to be Wonder Woman."

We cover our mouths, laughing giddily, trying to keep our voices down. "She's so cute," Leon says, looking adoringly at her.

"I want to be a police officer. I want to serve and protect everyone. I want to join the Army, and then, I will become a police officer." I say, just imagining how it would be.

"Girls are not allowed in the Army!" Michael protests with a spark of humor.

"Oh, yes they are! Anything boys can do girls can do better." I contest, waiting for him to sass me back. Michael pokes out his lip and smiles at me. His easygoing sense of humor is what I love most about him. He begins to make funny faces until we double over in laughter.

"Go to sleep in there!" Mom yells.

I imagine the night is a carousel of vibrant colors, decorated with images of our youthful imagination. In our minds, our dreams are real and attainable. They allow us to escape the confusion of our present reality and to cope with the chaos that is becoming a disquieting normalcy. The chaos has made us closer. A deep love grows between us, binding us together in a special way. We touch and hug each other as if it would be for the last time. As if at any moment, one of us could disappear. "I love you; I love you too." One by one, we close our eyes to rest, affirming our love for one another. Unguarded by pretense or rivalry, our affection flows freely. In the face of mounting adversity and instability in our home, our bond is fixed and sure. In the abstract portraits of our childhood hopes and dreams, there is a concrete reality. The reality of addictions and violent anger looms around the fringes of our impossible dreams. Still, we believe.

Spring seems to bring change and new life to our family. Somehow, my mom's work schedule is less demanding. The change enables her to spend more time with us. She arrives home before our bedtime, and sometimes we get to go to her job, just as we did in Tampa. The relief, the joy is indescribable. The change creates a new sense of safety in the house. And now, Ms. Lynn begins to stay in her room more than usual. Suspicion tells me my Mom knows about Ms. Lynn's deep hostility towards us.

Today she came home in the middle of the day. We walked home from school and noticed the pasty blue car in the driveway. Though her schedule has changed, I was surprised to see her home, this early. I smiled inside as I rushed to get to her, but my thoughts have a way of moving faster than my chubby legs can keep up. I stumble over the raised step leading to the front porch. Clumsy and awkward, I add another scar to my collection of scrapes and bruises. A tomboy at heart, I'm used to it.

Finding my feet, I grab my knapsack, brush off my knee, and try to catch up with my siblings. Without thinking, I pull the papers out of my backpack to show mama the drawing of flowers I made for her. "Mommy, I'm so happy you are home. I drew a picture for you." My arms reach out to hug her, but something is wrong. On high alert, she passes me. Confused, I lower my arms and follow her at a distance. She carries a troubled posture, with her purse and keys in one hand, the other on her hip. She stops and stands in the middle of the living room. The look on her face strongly advises me to keep my distance and keep my mouth shut until she is ready to speak. Inching back into the hallway, we hear the unspoken message. She scans the living room as if she was looking for something. I begin to think she forgot her wallet or maybe her work keys. A sudden outrage comes across her face. Her body tenses, and her right-hand forms a slow tight fist. Her eyes narrow until I can no longer see the pretty brown hue. Dumbfounded, we look at each other, searching for answers. I hear Mom talking under her breath. Nobody is in the living room except her. *Whom could she be talking to, and what has upset her?* I think to myself, looking for Joyce. She has not come home yet. She must take the bus from Rogers Middle School, which is usually an hour after we get back. I count the minutes. A thousand thoughts flooded my mind. I begin to ask myself if we did something wrong. The sleeping knot in my stomach wakes up. Did Mom and Dad have another fight? Did he blow his money gambling again? Did Mama find out about the way Ms. Lynn treats us?

My Mom turns and looks down the hallway. Suddenly, she asks us "Where is Lynn?" Again, we look at each other, unsure of what to say. I squeeze my fingers together, unsure of how to answer the simple question. Michael responds blankly, "Mama, we just got home, she might be in the room." Typically, Lynn is up late at night and hibernates in her room during the day. Lately, she has become more aloof and stays out of the way since Mom's schedule has changed.

Mom walks calmly to Ms. Lynn's bedroom door. My stomach twists with fear; I have heard enough fussing and fighting for a lifetime. My siblings and I huddle together peering out from our room. *What does Mama want to talk to Ms. Lynn about? Are we in trouble? Did someone tell Mommy about Ms. Lynn? Is that why she came home early?* My mind shifts from one thought to another.

Through the bedroom door, we hear Mom and Ms. Lynn talking. I cannot make out what they are saying, but I can hear her ask Ms. Lynn, "Do you understand?" with a harsh tone. When we hear the door close, we scamper quietly from our eavesdropping, back to the bed.

Understand what? I think to myself. The steady momentum of Mom's steps down the hall tells us she is leaving. When the front door closes, we make a beeline for the window. The engine revs and she backs out of the driveway. I remember wanting so badly to give her the picture I made for her at school. I know she would have liked the butterflies and flowers I drew around the border of it and the poem written especially for her. Maybe tomorrow she will find time to read it.

Year after year, I have watched my mom work hard both day and night. She tries her best to keep the bills paid and food on the table and to make everything better for the family. My mama has a way of making everything better, like one summer on my grandparent's farm when I got hurt. My parents sent us to Havana, Florida, a small town outside of Quincy, to spend time with Grandpa Eddie and Grandma Rachel. I was outside playing on the planks of wood Grandpa Eddie laid out on the grass near the house. He was preparing to build an indoor bathroom to replace the old outhouse that sat beyond the underground water well. Grandpa warned us not to play near the planks. But in my mind, playing on top of the planks was not the same as playing near them. The mind of a child can find a million excuses to get its own way.

Barefoot and boyish, I use the planks as a teeter-totter. Michael and Leon would take turns jumping on the other end; catapulting me higher and higher. I soar to the sound of the plank as it rebounds with every jump. That night, I feel so happy my grandpa is building a new bathroom onto the house. Glad my grandma would not have to go out into the night to use the old outhouse anymore, and happy I would not have to see the big hairy spider that creepily invaded your privacy as he watched from the corner of the rickety outdoor toilet. I was happy about everything. It's only as my feet start to swell that I remember what Joyce and Mama told me about keeping my shoes on when I go outside. In my eagerness to play, I had not listened. I was unaware that with each leap the soles of my feet are collecting pieces of splintered wood. Nor do I feel any pain; until the next day. My feet are swollen and tender to the point that I cannot walk. Mom and Dad came to take me to the hospital in Tallahassee. The soles of my feet are red, puffy, and full of tiny splinters.

"What were you thinking, child? How many times do I have to tell you to keep your shoes on your feet?" Mom was mad. I think when one of us gets hurt, somehow, she feels it too. Daddy's brown, deep-set eyes see into me. Although he does not say much, I know he understands how the urge to fly could get the best of you. With my mom and dad at my side, I lay still on the hospital bed. The doctor uses a shiny scalpel and a long set of tweezers to remove the splinters. The touch of my father's hand on my leg comforts me while the doctor removes each splinter. And even though she's upset, the warm concern in my mother's eyes covers me and makes it all better.

No mudslinging passes between them during the time in the

hospital. No harsh words pollute the air, no talk of splitting up and getting divorced. I feel as if I finally did something right. By some strange fluke, getting splinters in my feet offers a rare opportunity to bring my parents together; in peace. I rest my head on the pillow, happy. And for a little while, everything feels right again.

Strange how the mind works; how it frames a moment, shielding it inside a warm shell where it will stay, growing stronger, becoming a part of who we are. The pain of the splinters, the moments in the hospital, and the peace between my parents nestled deep inside me. Like the roots of a tree, moments like these grow wide and deep within the psyche. We will never know if we don't ask why, make the connections, and dig deeper until we find the root.

The thorn of martyrdom may have very well begun the day we tell ourselves; the pain is not so bad if it keeps the family together—if it keeps the peace and everyone is happy.

Never mind the splinters.

Angel in the Fire

As the years pass by, Joyce gets taller and prettier than ever. She makes it home from school and tells us to put on our shoes. "Where are we going?" Michael asks. "We are going to the park," she says. After finding one shoe in the closet and the other under the bed, I dash out the door. The park is adjacent to my elementary school, which is a short distance from the house. "Stay close," Joyce tells us. The soft rays of dwindling sunlight shine warm on my skin. Joyce shares a story on the way to the park.

We toddle closer to her, hanging on her every word. Through the years, her stories have become more real to me. She leads the way to the park, telling us the story of the three Hebrew boys who refuse to bow to a golden idol. In the ancient city of Babylon, the Hebrew slaves Shadrach, Meshach, and Abednego faced the rage of a madman, King Nebuchadnezzar. Goosebumps rise on my skin.

"What happened next?" I ask.

"Hush and let her finish telling the story," Leon says. Joyce says that the King heated the furnace seven times hotter because the Hebrew slaves refuse to bow to the golden idol. The way she tells the story makes me think she was somehow an eyewitness, exiled to the pagan streets.

Joyce ends her story, telling us that the slaves survived the fire because God saved them. "Not even their clothes smelled like smoke," she says, as we walk through the narrow opening of a short wooden gate that separates Sunland Park from the street. "Go play now. I will be right here, watching." Joyce says in her usual overprotective tone. Leon and Michael run off to roll down the small grassy hill in the middle of the park. The grass makes them itch, but they cannot seem to help themselves.

I hold onto Linda's hand and head for the swings. "Higher!" Linda says as I push her on the swings. Afraid she will fall off; I do not use all my strength. Instead, I tickle her every time she swings back toward me. Her laughter is like medicine. It reminds me to relax and let go. Letting go isn't that easy—especially when, at any moment, it could all fall apart. My thoughts have become more troubling. The noise around me grows distant; I am fading out. My daydreams call me away. I notice, with each new day, they do not allow me to stay present. When I begin to feel weird inside, they always come to rescue me.

Joyce walks up to the swings. "Sandy Patty, are you okay?"

"Yes," the answer comes out of habit.

"Come here," she motions, holding onto the chains of the other swing. "I will push you."

I sit but inside I hear Ms. Lynn's voice, jeering in my head. I blinked trying to ignore it. The phrase sticks and stones can break your bones, but words can never — well, that's a stinking lie; hurtful words can break your heart and spirit.

I do not want Joyce to push me, but she leans in and pulls back on the metal chains of the swing. Shifting from one side to the other, Joyce pushes us and sings: *"Somewhere over the rainbow, bluebirds fly. If bluebirds fly over rainbows, why then oh why can't I."*

We know the words and sing along. It is one of our bedtime songs. Joyce voice soon drowns out the noise that rushes in without warning. I imagine I am the bluebird in the song. In those moments, I feel free. Free from the confusion of a home where alcoholism and violence are paralyzing. Free to be a silly kid with crazy dreams and nothing to prove. Free from the thorns of fear that are secretly growing on the inside of me. Here with Joyce, I feel safe.

The dusk wakes up the sleeping bugs. I feel them before I see them. "Let's go; it's time for dinner," Joyce announces, waving her hands to get the boys' attention. Joyce gathers us together to walk home. Leon looks miserable as he scratches his neck, arms, and legs. "How many times have I got to tell you two about rolling in the grass? It makes you itch every time." Joyce shakes her head, looking pitifully at Leon and Michael, both sweaty and itchy from tussling in the grass. "When we get home, get right in the tub and take a bath." Joyce drills.

Holding Linda's hand, I mimic Joyce and shake my head at the patches of grass stains clinging to their clothes. Joyce combs her fingers through Michael's hair to rake out blades of grass and debris. He squirms and turns like he has ants in his pants. "Oooh, scratch my back please." He gives a silly look and tries to laugh it off. Michael is irresistibly funny and easy to love. Even when he is hurt or upset, he hides it with humor. He entertains us with his overdramatic antics on the way home.

It's getting dark. Joyce tells Leon to wait up and to stay with us on the walk back. Leon gives Joyce a don't-tell-me-what-to-do look and storms ahead. Leon is becoming more of a challenge for Joyce to handle. Similar to most boys his age, he becomes impulsive and unpredictable; short-tempered and aloof; he begins to mirror Daddy a little more each day.

"Where is Dad. He is never home?" Leon would often say with a bold tone. Leon used to wait up for Dad to get home, but not so much anymore. From the porch to the window, to the bed, and one day, the waiting slowly fades into acting out instead. In time, I watch anger replace the sadness. It hurts too much to wait for what never comes, so one day you just stop waiting, stop needing, stop feeling, and stop believing. Leon starts to break things and often misbehaves, sometimes to the point of hurting our feelings. I know he doesn't mean it, and though he never says, I think Leon misses Dad even more than I do.

Back home, I am not ready to go to sleep. I try to think of a thousand excuses for Joyce to stay close to me; just five more minutes, but I know she is tired because her shoulders slump a little. I believe it is from all the pushing on the swings. She kisses my cheek and says goodnight, and after she turns out the light, I ask her the question I wanted to know before we left the park.

"Joyce, who was the fourth man in the fire? When did he get there and why did He wait until it was almost too late to save the three Hebrew slaves?"

"It was Jesus. He was there all the time." Joyce replies, with a confident smile. Walking back to the side of the bed, she sits and pulls the blanket over my shoulders. "When we love God and seek Him with all our hearts, we will find Him." Her voice is soft, assuring. "We must have faith and trust His plan for our life. Even in the fiery trials, we must believe that God will show up, right on time." She sees the questions in my sleepy eyes before I can ask.

"But why would a good God allow the evil king to..."

"Shhh, Sandy Patty, go to sleep. In due time, the answers will come, and we will understand it all better then. Go to bed now. God is always there." She leans in and kisses me again.

When she leaves the room, I stare out in the dark, trying to understand the concept of a God who allows such heartache and pain. *Seven times hotter?* I think to myself. *Why didn't He stop it from happening in the first place?* Is life some cruel game? I cannot turn off the noises in my head, even after squeezing my eyes closed. The fear still comes—images of my parents fighting, Ms. Lynn's words: fat, ugly, stupid; they cut deep. I pull my blanket tight underneath my chin, and bury my face in my pillow, thinking, *Jesus was the fourth man in the fire. I hope He is here now.*

Mahalia's Song

"Put your mind on the gospel. And remember - there's one God for all." ~Mahalia Jackson

Months pass and time moves like the scattered clouds above. The sky looks sad today. The May rain is coming, but the world opens a delightful chance to spend time with my mom. The ride feels magical. On the way to my mom's job, memories lift me away. They are happy memories of Tampa's red brick roads, powerful thunderstorms, and my parents' store with the big candy cane pole in the front. Both joyful times and scary times follow me with each bump in the road. Being with my mom makes everything feel better. We have not visited her job since I can remember.

The chalky lines on the road shoot by like arrows from a bow. I make myself dizzy trying to count them all. Mom has a heavy foot and keeps one eye in the rear-view mirror and the other on the road. She drives fast as if she is always running late. But I like it; the wide-open road is freeing. The eight-track tape plays Mama's favorite songs from her most beloved singer, a woman named Mahalia Jackson. She plays the 8-track over and over again. We sway with the motion of the car and listen. Every word, every hymn, Mama knows and sings.

"How I got over, how I got over, my soul looks back and wonder how I got over..." my Mom's voice is childlike and beautiful, but the music is solemn and sad. I ask her why the woman sounds like she is crying in her song. She says it is because Mahalia and so many others have seen a lot of pain and suffering caused by injustice and racism.

"Where did racism come from?" I ask.

"It's always been, and it always gon' be till Jesus comes back; some people just evil!" Her tone is sour until you can feel it and taste it. The question seems to reopen an old wound that never healed. I quiet myself, resisting the urge to ask Mama if she knows when Jesus is coming back. The straight-ahead gaze on my mom's face tells me she is not only trying to concentrate on the road ahead, but also trying to make sense of the road behind her. Soon, she would tell of the grim details of a memory from her past, an unforgettable time when the nightmare of hate and slavery refused to allow you to wake up. For many children and families, waking up from the terror of racism came only after the final breath.

It was August 28, 1955. My mother was only 12 years old when Emmett Till, a 14-year-old young man from Chicago was kidnapped and murdered in Money, Mississippi. His body was found three days later in the Tallahatchie River, but a sense of real freedom and equality would not be found at all among the black community. The crime added more fear to the growing offenses among a people whose history of oppression refused to end — hung, raped, beaten, sold, and murdered dreams; families stolen from their own country, for no other reason but the sins of power and greed — the stories are copious.

I can't imagine how human beings could treat another human being with such cruelty. In my mind, the people who committed the crimes are not humans at all, but demons dressed up in human flesh. "The brutal crime went unpunished," Mommy says. "At least in this life it did." She mentions how the crime against Emmett Till had left a gaping wound in the Black community and in the minds of all those who did not share the sick societal belief. The possibility of such a crime happening again is all too real, and then she talks about the gruesome, open-casket funeral. I listen, holding my breath.

Her face assumes an unbearable expression. Pain and sadness twist across her beautiful cheekbones until all I can see is anger shadowed by deep disgust. Her words like smoldering embers glow and crackle in my mind. I look down at my hands, trying to move past the images her words conjure up, but they are too heavy, too unreal. I cannot imagine the heartache of Emmett Till's mother, looking down at her child — tortured and unrecognizable. Why does God allow such crimes? I look out the window, trying to find a happier place, a different memory. She drives ahead and prays. Repeatedly I hear her say, "Thank you, Jesus." She reaches for the volume on the radio and turns up the music. Appearing to pull herself away from the memory, she hums the words of Mahalia's song. No matter how hard I try, I cannot understand how she feels. So, I try to think of something else; the cars riding alongside us; the clouds above us like fields of cotton in the sky, but the music on the radio keeps bringing me back to Mahalia's song, the shocking image of a young boy, and questions of why.

Mama keeps a steady pace on the road. Mahalia's voice is powerful and deeply moving; I can hear why Mommy likes her music. She said Mahalia died three years ago, but her music makes me think she is still alive, just invisible now. Somehow, the words have a heartbeat. I hear it in Mahalia's song:

"I want to thank Him for how he brought me, and I want to thank Him for how He taught me, Oh thank my God for how He kept me. I'm gonna thank Him cause He never left me, want to thank Him for ole time religion, I wanna thank you for giving me a vision. One day I am going to join the heavenly choir. I'm gonna sing and never get tired…my soul looks back and wonders how I got over."

The rain pours and the car speeds on. I stare at my mom as she stares ahead, quiet. I wonder what she looked like when she was 12—imagining she was just as beautiful. I think of how the murder of Emmett Till must have affected her sense of safety as a young Black girl? And though I hide it from her, I know how insecurity feels. It is a dreaded feeling that you do not belong anywhere because nowhere is safe, not even inside your own mind. For me, the closest thing to heaven was when we were together in Tampa. No matter the fighting and the scary thunderstorms, we were all together, one big family.

Looking up at the stormy sky, I wonder if Emmett had a favorite hobby. What did he want to be when he grew up? What cartoons did he watch on Saturday mornings? Did he like to laugh and read as much as I do? I imagine what he looked like before the murder and the unimaginable description Mama told of his open-casket funeral. The whole black-white racism thing—it's all so confusing. Mama looks angry, especially when she rages about how black people must work harder to make ends meet because the opportunities are not the same; *why I think to myself. Why are they not the same?*

Though my mother is upset, she never taught us the language of racism and hate. She clears her throat. "No one comes right out and tells you; you just know it's true. It's just the way it is." she says, complaining about how low wages and the 'system' keeps people enslaved in an underhanded way. Gone are the white-only signs, but a system of greed and oppression remains. The need to work two and three jobs to survive has taken the place of the cotton fields of the South. The tension in the car is stifling when Mom goes on ranting at the air as if she is angry at the world. As if, life is unfair. We stay silent in the backseat. There are no answers to the many questions. There is only the rhythm of the road and ole' time religion on the radio, playing between the raindrops falling against the window like tears from heaven. I stare at the raindrops as they slide down the backseat window. I imagine the raindrops are the falling tears of Emmett Till and all those like him, reminding the world that they were once here; seen, but never truly heard.

The Artist

"If you could say it in words, there would be no reason to paint." ~ *Edward Hopper*

A big yellow sign flash ahead. It is the Shell gas station sign that sits just across the street from the 7-Eleven where my Mom works. Linda is asleep with her head resting on my shoulders. She is even pretty when she's sleeping. Michael drools with his mouth wide open and makes strange snorting sounds, while Leon peers out the window, silent and still. "Let's go," Mama says as she parks the car. I often think my mom is the manager of the store, maybe even the owner. Customers are waiting for her by the front register. Mama says we are staying with her all night at the 7-Eleven. Open-mouth, I am on top of the world. "Go get a treat and bring it to the register so I can ring it up." She says. The memories from her store in Tampa and my daddy's Old Spice cologne floats through my mind.

It does not take long for us to grab our favorite treats and bring it up to the front. Linda lifts on her toes and puts a Tootsie Roll and Pixy Stix on the counter. Mommy rings up each item and hands them back to us with a smile sweeter than anything ever put in a candy wrapper. When she smiles, I know everything will be all right again. The sadness in her eyes seemed to move away the moment she came to work. "Thank you, Mama." We say, and I ask permission to look at the magazines on the side rack near the front of the store. She nods and tends to the customers. Superhero comics and songbooks are my obsession. Michael and I look at the magazines together, losing ourselves in between the colorful pages and our imagination. We take turns talking about what we would do if we had superpowers. "Look at this, Sandra!" Michael says, pointing to a page in the comic book. We hit our knuckles together and say, "Wonder Twin powers, Activate!" We laugh, imagining ourselves to be comic book heroes.

The front bell rings, and an unusual-looking man walks in. He captures my attention right away. He wears a tattered beige overcoat with scruffy beige slacks. Slumped over with a slight hobble and covered in colorful speckles of splattered paint, he moves toward the front counter. "Hello Jim, how are you doing, my darling?" My mom gives a kingly greeting to a man who looks more like a pauper.

He seems to come to life with her friendly welcome. He grins and straightens his back. "Hi Lillie, I'm all right, just finishing a painting for you. You can come by the house soon and pick it up, or I can bring it by." His overcoat reminds me of the TV show detective, Peter Falk who plays *Columbo*. I like the curious way he scratches his head when he would ask questions to which he already knew the answers. He is funny that way.

Mom calls us all together to the front of the store. "Children, this is Mr. Jim. He lives just around the corner. He is a fine artist and my good friend." Jim smiles with a blush. He appears a humble man. His hand trembles a little as he reaches out to shake ours.

"Nice to meet you, Mr. Jim." I reach out my hand, mesmerized by the rainbow of dried paint splattered all over his clothes and shoes. His eyes are bloodshot as if he was up all night searching for something in the dark.

We smile politely. Mr. Jim walks away and shuffles to the back of the store. When he returns, he is carrying a bottle of red wine.

"Is that all you are getting today, my love?"

"Yes Lillie, that's all I need tonight." Mr. Jim digs into his pockets, pulling out pennies, nickels, a couple of quarters, and what looks to be a crinkled gum wrapper. Bumbling softly, he counts. Mama gives Jim an endearing glance, and then she takes money out of her purse and pays the bill.

"Put your change back in your pocket, sweetheart. I got it for you tonight."

He turns a new shade of red. "Thank you, Lillie." His voice cracks. He drops his change back into the pocket of his speckled coat. The comic book conceals my prying eyes and curiosity. I turn the pages pretending not to listen, but Mr. Jim holds my attention. There is something about him. He is more than what he appears to be — more than his disheveled hair, baggy eyes, and sun-burnt skin. I smile at him because if Mom believes he is a nice man, it must be true.

I place the comic book back on the rack and grab another one, the best one. My favorite one! Wonder Woman is beautiful with her bulletproof golden bracelets, flowing dark hair and red boots — she is the ultimate superheroine. No one else has a lasso of truth; I am crazy about her. Somewhere in my heart, I believe she is real, more than a figment of the imagination of animation in a comic book. I imagine flying in her invisible plane, living on Paradise

Island, battling evil forces with Superman, Batman, Flash, and the rest of the Justice League gang. Nothing scares Wonder Woman. She is strong and brave. "If only I could have this book," I whispered staring at the cover. My Mom already bought us candy, chips, and juice. To ask for more would be somewhat selfish. I sigh, holding the comic book for a few minutes longer before putting it back on the shelf. After a few more minutes of yearning for her, I pull myself away.

I miss Joyce tonight. She is away again visiting family. I keep wondering whom it is she is visiting. No one ever says. Again, I don't ask, but I can hardly wait for her to get back home. I want her to meet Mr. Jim. He is cute and makes our Mom laugh louder than usual. Mama allows us to go to Jim's house. He lives within walking distance, just around the corner from the store. Leon, Michael, Linda, and I walk with Jim to his home to help pass the time away. When we arrive at Jim's house, it was like visiting an art museum. You would never know from the outside looking in. His home is a colorful world where elaborate oil paintings fill the house from the walls to the floor. Canvases of every size display the beauty of his mind's eye; the odor of harsh solvents litters the air; brushes and tubes of paint in multiple colors and shapes are sprawled out everywhere, too many to count. I remember feeling awestruck at this simple man whose paintings captured the radiance of the night sky, the curve of windblown trees, and the rolling foam of the waves breaking upon the seashore.

A white, thick fabric covers the floor and some of the furniture. Jim shows us his paintings, telling us a little of the history behind the thoughts that brought the art to life. As I listen, I begin to see why Mom admires him so much. He places a small empty canvas on top of the white bulging fabric on the floor. "Take these brushes and paint whatever you want." Jim gives each of us brushes and one curved circular pallet of colorful paints to share.

We spread out on the floor and begin to paint the time away. Michael sticks his tongue out to the side whenever he is concentrating hard on something. I don't think he realizes how funny he looks when he does that, but I think it's an adorable habit. Leon uses every color on the pallet. His strokes are intense and broad. It's hard to tell if he is having fun or not. Linda draws circles and stars, and out of all the colors on the pallet, she chooses pink. She curls up on her side and hums a cheery tune, moving the brush with her melody. Wanting to see all his paintings, I walk over to the wall; there are so many colors. I don't know when we will have a chance to visit again, so I try to take it all in. Jim stands near me. I can smell the wine on his breath. He asks, "Do you like this one?"

"Yes Sir, Mr. Jim. I love it!" I reply without taking my eyes off the painting. "Mr. Jim, is this one dry?" My fingers touch the bluest ocean before he has the chance to answer.

"Yes, it's dry. I painted it two weeks ago. I use these oil and acrylic paints." He shows me the tubes. "So now, when the painting is dry, it still looks wet," he explains.

Jim shows me how he mixes the colors to make new colors, exciting and vibrant colors. He teaches me about pigments and adding texture to make the painting more interesting and alive. Linda comes and joins Jim and me near the wall. She shows me her picture. "I love it, Peanut," I say, holding her portrait of stars and circles. She smiles and holds onto my hand.

"Don't be afraid to make a mistake when you are painting," Jim says, showing me, a half-finished painting leaning against the wall on the floor. "Someday, I will fix this one, and finish what I started. When you mess up, just start over again. Don't throw it away; just start over." Jim looks at me. His eyes water and drift, maybe from the wine. But it appears he has traveled back in time to a distant memory.

Suddenly it feels like we are not talking about painting anymore. He wipes the side of his face with the sleeve of his paint-splattered overcoat and walks towards the bathroom. I watch him and wonder why he wears such a thick coat. It is not even winter time. *Is it to keep the paint from getting on his clothes?* I think to myself. *No, that can't be it.* Paint is already everywhere—his pants, his shoes, his shirt; there's probably paint in his underwear. *Why does he wear that disheveled overcoat?* Whatever his reasons, he wins my heart because he seems to be a kind, gentle, and patient man. With all the talk about racism in this world, there is no evidence of it in him. And he has a way of creating something beautiful out of nothing but empty canvases, paint, and brushes.

"Your mother will be worried. It's getting late. We had better head back," Mr. Jim says. Before leaving, I ask Jim why each of his paintings has his name on the bottom left-hand side. He explains that the signature indicates ownership for the artist. I read his name aloud: "Jim Crompton." I read it with a sense of pride, happy to have met him. Mom was right; Jim is a brilliant artist—I saw it for myself.

He walks us back to the store and opens the door with his arm stretched inside. "Ladies first," he says. Linda and I prance in, eager to tell Mama how kind Mr. Jim has been to us. "Hi Lillie, I brought your children back safe and sound."

"Thank you, my love. And you brought them back full of paint." Mom looks at the paintings and shakes her head at us. She is smiling, so I know it's okay. "I think you got more paint on yourselves than you got in those drawings. Give Mr. Jim a hug and tell him thank you for spending time with you." One by one, we thank him.

Jim looks at our Mom as if he would go to war for her. "No problem Lillie, anything for you." They talk for a few moments longer, and then he tells us goodnight. With a final wave of a hand, he walks out.

Mama finishes counting money and locks it up behind the counter. "Let's go, children, get in the car. It is time to head home." She looks tired, but she never says it.

"Yes, ma'am." We yawn, dragging our feet. The sugar rush from the Tootsie Rolls, Chic-O Sticks, and other treats has long since come to a crashing halt. Before I get to the door, I look at the Wonder Woman comic book, hoping one day I will get to take her home. We are too tired to fuss about who gets to ride in the front seat; we lean against the car, waiting for Mommy to turn on the store's alarm and lock the door. On the ride home, I think about Mr. Jim. I cannot wait to see Joyce and tell her about him and our exciting day. I know she would like him just as much as I do. He reminds me of the God she loves to talk to all the time. Just maybe not with the same shabby overcoat and paint-spattered shoes. But then again, like God, Jim is kind, and he paints in multiple colors. Each one of Jim's canvases is uniquely different. Mama says God made all people in His image. The colorblind way she treats Jim and all her customers make me believe what she says is true. We are all the same; all created by God, who paints with many colors to display His glory. Though my mom has seen tremendous racism and bigotry growing up, she seems to have a heart that cares for everyone—no matter the color of their skin. I admire that about her.

As we get closer to home, I scratch off some of the dried paint on the back of my hands. *Now is the time to ask*, I tell myself. If I don't ask her now, when we get home, it will be too late. She will make us go straight in the tub before I get a chance to ask her if I can do extra chores to earn money to buy the Wonder Woman comic book. I figure in two weeks I can save enough. Breathing out, I lower my head, afraid she will say no. For now, I let go of the comic book obsession and instead ask her about Mr. Jim.

"Mama, how long have you known Mr. Jim?"

"You ask so many questions child—does your mind ever stop thinking? Well, I have known him for as long as I have been working at the store, I believe. He buys his wine and dances around the store; he makes me laugh," she giggles, and then clears her throat. "But he is harmless enough and very respectable." She turns into the driveway. "We are home, children. Let's go." I shake Michael and Linda. Like zombies, they walk half-awake into the house. Leon is the first one inside. Before I step inside, I look up at the moon. It has followed us all the way home again. It makes me think of my daddy.

"Joyce, we are home!" I run towards her bedroom, eager to see her. Mom drops her keys on the counter and goes straight to her room. Dad is not home yet. After our bath, Joyce prays and tucks us in. She kisses us goodnight and begins to sing her lullaby.

> "Love makes the world go 'round,
> Love makes the world go 'round,
> It's a time for beginnings; love makes the world go 'round.
> When we're together, love makes the world go 'round. It's
> a time for beginnings; love makes the world go 'round."

Joyce has sung the melody more than a thousand times, but tonight, it is as if I have heard it for the first time because it takes on a new meaning. Today, something happened; I can't describe it. Spending the day with Mom and seeing Mr. Jim's paintings helps replace the memory of the sad story Mama told me about Emmett Till. I sense God's love more tonight because I feel a sense of peace, like the warm colors in Jim's oil paintings. I want to believe in this love that makes the world go 'round, the magical love my sister sings about at bedtime.

Lived experiences offer the most potent lessons. As humans, we once believed the earth was flat before we took the chance to sail beyond the horizon of our minds. Once we continue to evolve beyond the threshold of our limited thinking, we will discover that the living God created all human life; the Master Artist wraps the spirit of who we are in many shapes and shades for His Glory. Mr.

Jim and my mom supposedly come from two different worlds: one of white privilege, the other of black oppression. However, as I watched them together, I saw no trace of all the bigotry and hate that distracts humanity's progress. There were only a loving connection and a tender-hearted acceptance. We come into the earth as blank canvases, possessing the freedom of choice to create a masterpiece by how we choose to paint our life. Undoubtedly the outcome will be determined by whether we use the tool of our hearts or our eyes.

The Quiet before the Storm

"Those who do not forgive history are assigned to repeat it until compassion replaces judgment." ~*Alan Cohen*

In 1973, the war in our home seemed to come to a standstill, but the stark truth is my parents are too preoccupied with life to confront the years of strife in their marriage. I miss my dad. The house is quiet today, and he and John are working, waiting tables at Morrison's Cafeteria on Federal Highway. Between running the barbershop and being a waiter, I find out that my dad is a part of the Freemasons. Joyce said the Freemasons are a secret society that has passed down traditions of handshakes, passwords, and weird symbols known only to the lodge members. It's confusing to me because though it all sounds great, he doesn't seem any happier because of it. Joyce says that Daddy could build just about anything because of all he has learned through the years as a Freemason. "When we lived in Tampa," she mentions, "Dad spent much of his younger years working on different construction jobs," I remember listening to her, feeling special just thinking that I am the daughter of a great builder, a stonemason, a skilled bricklayer, but deep inside, I would much rather have him around to spend time with us. My heart longs for the sound of his voice, his words, his attention, and his love.

The days' pass and my skin cry out for the affirmation of his touch. I try to recall his smile and the sound of his laughter between the long spells of his absence. I wonder if he still loves us. A hundred times a day, I ask myself the question. I wait for him to take me dancing on the moon again the way he did in his barbershop in Tampa. I will wait forever if I must. Until then, I must compete with his jobs and habits. When he is not working, he is too tired or too busy trying to settle his relentless debts. Debts owed to bookies and his brutish wardens, Mr. Gin and Jack Daniels. I don't think he knows how lonely it gets waiting for him. He doesn't seem to realize that he is the only man I love, the only dad I have. How will I ever learn what true love is if he does not slow down long enough to teach me?

Time passes, and I fear that while we are growing up, he is missing it. Leon's behavior is becoming more distressing. He begins to defy Joyce a little more every day. When she tells him to do anything, he gets angry and throws things. We all miss dad in our own way. All too often, parents have no clue how important their presence, time, and interaction are to growing hearts and minds. My soul waits to hear his words, trying to remember the last time he said, "I love you." So much is going wrong inside my head; I can't explain it, and I'm afraid that one day I will get lost inside myself.

Someone knocks at the door.

"Is Roadman home?" A man outside is calling out. He pauses, and then pounds at the door; his voice is scratchy and deep. We do not look outside. We've been taught never to open the door when we are home alone. We lay low, pretending the house is empty. Mom and Joyce will be back soon. We wait for the voice to leave. When he finally goes away, Leon, Michael, Linda, and I play made-up games in the room. Our imagination runs wild. Our room transforms into a jungle where we swing on moss-covered vines like Tarzan and Jane. Then, we pretend to be crime fighters; Michael plays Superman and Linda is Super Girl. The four corners of the room widen and become the city of Metropolis; Leon plays Lex Luthor, pretending to rule the world. I tumble onto the bed, laughing at Michael's silly face. He has a way of always making me laugh — like no one else can. He ties a sheet around his neck. It is his magical cape. He swears he can fly as he jumps from the bed into a pile of dirty clothes on the floor. Linda wants to jump too. She climbs up on top of the bed. Ready to jump, she stretches out her arms fearlessly. "No! Peanut, wait!" I say, afraid she will miss the pile of clothes.

We take turns catching her. She smiles, bursting into giggles. "Do it again! Do it again!" She pleads. "Sanwa!" she calls out, reaching, laughing, still unable to pronounce my name. We spin her around and around until she is dizzy. Before we lower her to the floor, she laughs, "Do it again, again, again!" Our childish sense of fun and play is delightful, but it would not last. Without warning, something goes wrong. Like the flip of a switch, Leon's temper fly's off the handle. He frowns and yells out, "I quit, I don't want to play this stupid game anymore." Leon throws a fit, kicking toys and clothes across the room. Leon withdraws in cold isolation, and we are unsure of what triggered his outburst. "Where is Daddy?" He yells across the room.

As time passes, I begin to realize my brother is growing up faster than our parents or anyone around could understand. He needs more than what their time can give a growing young man trying to find his purpose in a world of uncertainty. There is no one around to catch him as he shifts through puberty and the complex impulses of adolescence. No arms stretch toward him as he jumps from one stage of development to manhood. Children seem an afterthought in a world where survival commands the schedule. The effects would last a lifetime.

Leon's outburst was scary. Just a moment ago, our brother was standing right there: happy, playful, loving. I saw a rage in him I don't think I have seen before, but the signs were there for a while now; like bricks scattered strangely out of place, built day after day, by a little boy who once waited for his dad to come home. Sometimes, waiting on miracles can take a long, long time.

"What's wrong?" Michael asks. "Why don't you want to play anymore?" Leon does not answer. Cold and quiet, he stands in the middle of the floor with his hands down to his sides. Michael, Linda, and I sit on the bed and wait for the foul spirit to pass.

In moments like this, Joyce taught us how to pray and believe. We get on our knees by the edge of the bed and pray the Lord's Prayer. Leon joins us, and we all pray aloud, "...*Thy kingdom come, thy will be done, on earth as it is in heaven. Give us this day our daily bread and forgive us our debts as we forgive our debtors and lead us not into temptation but deliver us from evil; for Thine is the kingdom, the power, and the glory forever.*" We wait to hear Leon say Amen. He doesn't. Instead, he continues to pray. "God forgive me for all my sins. Forgive me, Lord. I'm sorry — in Jesus' name, Amen."

We huddle close near the window, knowing in our hearts there is a love between us that will never fail. Linda lays her head on my lap. I hold her and stroke her hair to ease her off to sleep. Michael's remedy is comedy. No matter what is going on, he finds the silver lining of laughter in every storm cloud. Tonight, he laughs alone. Leon's despondency shows in his face. I remember how the pain of rejection started early, passing on a wave of quiet anger, like an inheritance of bricks to build another wall of isolation. Our father can teach only the lessons that he has learned himself. Parents cannot give what they have never received.

In the formative years of our lives, these moments are critical. The number of times we jump and fall, waiting on the arms of a love that cannot catch us, depends on our ability to hurt long enough to stop jumping, and finally, just stand up. These are painful lessons that we cannot learn on our own. We hold tight to one another.

No Matter What!

Words are powerful, holding within them the forces of life and death according to Proverbs 18:21. They have the power to build up, to renew, and to defy the odds, even after all hopes seems lost. I remember them well—three words spoken in a moment in time would become the foundation on which faith in God would prevail in the midst of terrible thorns; yet to come.

Michael leaps up and runs to the window after Mom and Joyce pull up in the driveway. A huge smile lights up his face. "Mama is home!" he yells, running to the front door. The noise surprises Linda awake. She smiles instantly. Leon has been in the bathroom for quite some time now. Michael knocks on the bathroom door, "Leon, Mama is home."

She comes in the front door and calls out to us. "Get the rest of the bags out of the car." She is carrying two bags. I spy my favorite breakfast cereal, Captain Crunch, sitting on the top. We help Joyce put the groceries away, while Mom goes into her room and closes the door. Leon follows behind her.

"Mom is tired," Joyce explains. "Let her rest." Leon does not listen. He knocks. "Leon, I told you, Mom is tired, she just finished working and grocery shopping for the house. She is tired. Let her rest!" Joyce stresses again.

"I just want to tell her something," Leon explains.

Mama hears Joyce and Leon in the hall. "Yes, Leon, what do you need, sweetheart?" Her voice sounds like a sleepy sparrow.

"Ma, my tooth is hurting bad," Leon moans. We look on from the hallway when she calls Leon to the room. She is in bed. I notice her nude colored pantyhose has a rip at the toe that runs down to her heel. She looks uncomfortable, and I want to go in and straighten the lopsided pillow under her head. I stay to the side.

"Open your mouth and let me see," she says. Leon leans over her, opening his mouth wide. "That looks bad! What have I told you about eating so many sweets? Now look at that tooth; it looks awful!" She tells Joyce to get the Orajel out of the medicine cabinet. She shakes her head, making noises as if she has a toothache. She puts the ointment in Leon's mouth and tells him not to spit it out. He makes a face that tells us the ointment must taste as awful as his tooth looks. "You got to stop eating so much junk, you hear?"

"Yes ma'am, Mama," Leon replies with his head to the side and his mouth slightly open. "Thank you, Mama." Leon seems to smile with the pure satisfaction of time and attention. A moment later, her mouth falls open. Her eyes close. She is sound asleep.

Joyce closes her room door softly and begins to prepare supper for us. I ask Joyce if I can help her cook. She laughs, reminding me of the time in Tampa when Linda and I climbed up on a chair next to the stove to cook a pot of grits, some eggs, and a can of Spam; a bad idea I blamed on boredom and curiosity. I remember thinking how difficult it was to open the meat container. Joyce said she caught us just in time. I was almost four-years-old, and Linda was two. "We were living in Tampa; it was around two o'clock in the morning. I found you and Linda in the kitchen with a pot on the stove. Linda was still in diapers at the time. I took you both down just before the pot started to boil. There were eggshells, melted butter, and salt everywhere," Joyce laughs and smiles at me. I vaguely recall making such a mess, but I distinctly remember wanting to cook because I want to be a hard worker—like Mom and Joyce. I lean against her side, smiling, laughing at myself: *The need to feel useful gets the best of me.*

Joyce teaches me to measure the ingredients and clean up after each step. "Don't wait to clean up after you finish cooking. Clean up as you go. That way, the kitchen will stay in order while you cook, and you will have less to do when you finish," she says, wiping off the top of the stove. She makes cooking fun. Together we make mashed potatoes, meatloaf, green beans, and cornbread. Before dinner is ready, the kitchen is spotless. I do my best to follow Joyce's instructions. Linda helps set the table, and we sit down to eat. Joyce says grace: "Precious Lord, thank you for the food—" As Joyce prays, my mind wanders. I want to ask Joyce where she goes when she does not come home. On the lonely weekends when she is not here, I want to know—where does she go? I don't ask. Instead, I ask her about the mystery of how she could wake up without a fire alarm when Linda and I were cooking in the middle of the night.

"How did you know we were out of bed? What told you that we were in the kitchen?" Joyce said that the Holy Spirit woke her up and told her to go to the kitchen. She explained that when you pray and walk close to God every day, He guides you in all your ways.

"God woke you up?" Linda asks with a bewildered glance.

"Yes Linda," Joyce replies. "God speaks to His children."

Leon and Michael begin to ask questions about the Bible, God, and the devil. Joyce tells us stories about good and evil. Some stories I know about; others, I'm too afraid and do not want to know. We talk for what seems like hours at the table. Joyce tells us we must trust God always, no matter what. It is her recurring sermon. I do not know what the voice of the Holy Spirit sounds like, but I know her voice. It is consistently caring and hopeful, but today something is different in her tone. She seems unsure, almost vulnerable. I have never seen Joyce look frail or helpless; however, tonight, the look in her eyes is unsettling.

Life seems to have a way of testing you, pushing you, and taking you to a place that is beyond your control. I wonder if the Holy Spirit told her something was about to happen—something unspeakable; something her lullabies could not soothe away so easily.

I turned my head when I heard the key click and the doorknob turn. Ms. Lynn and her son walk in with my stepbrother John behind them. Excited, I ask if Dad is with them. Leon and Michael run to the door before Ms. Lynn or John can answer. Ms. Lynn walks past us as if we were dark shadows beneath her feet. She does not look in our direction, nor does she speak a word to us. John tells us dad left work before he did, and he is not sure where he is.

"You know Roadman," John says of Daddy. "He is always on the road somewhere." John sways to his room, leaving behind the sour smell of beer, which tells us one of two things will happen tonight. He will either fall asleep or start a fight with Ms. Lynn. If they fight, Mom will wake up, and all hell will break loose because, in her words, "She ain't having it." Mom's temper is short, especially when she is tired.

Joyce tells us to take a bath and get ready for bed. She reminds Leon to brush his teeth so she can reapply the Orajel to his cavity. Linda and I grab our dolls and get in the bathtub. We love when Joyce puts dish detergent in the water, making millions of lemony bubbles. As I wash my doll's hair, I think of what Joyce told us at the table. I teach it to my Barbie doll.

"Trust in God, no matter what," I say. Her blue eyes stare back at me, fixed into place along with her pretty plastic smile. My mind trails away, thinking about my dad. "God, please watch over Daddy, and please keep him safe."

My doll stares back covered in bubbles. I don't hear God. I wonder what He sounds like because He is quiet again, and I don't know if He is even listening. Joyce tells us to say our prayers. I pray because she tells me, but deep down, I don't think God hears me in a world full of people all praying at the same time. Our bedtime comes, and dad did not make it home yet.   After the lullaby, I pray silently: "God bless my mom and dad, my sisters and brothers. God help me be good, so Ms. Lynn will not hate me. God bless all the sick and hungry people in the world. Amen."

I try to hold tight to the words Joyce taught us. "No matter what," she'd say, "Trust in God," but by the Mid-1970s, the fighting between my parents begins again, and in-between the bouts, there is an awful gnawing inside, like the grinding sound of maggots feeding underneath the decaying foundation of our family. Helpless, we listen and wonder when the ground will finally give way—when all the fights and threats, and anger will explode, leaving nothing behind but rubble and memories. We hold tight to each other; praying, hoping for peace between our parents.

When the house gets quiet again, the details of their fights replay. His suspicions and anger, her disapproval of his gambling and drinking all night—back and forth in their tug of war, my insides twist and turn. The intensity is shocking. The language, no child should ever hear. Terrible things breed in wounds left festering in the darkness of apathy and bitterness. Nevertheless…no matter what, I will believe what the Bible stories tell me; "with God, all things are possible." There is still hope for my family. There is always a chance for peace. No matter what, I will believe.

The way parents treat each other will either harm or bless their children. The damage comes from the volatile clashes and the passive-aggressive silence; children cannot separate themselves from it any more than they can remove their DNA; all are one. The blessing is in the art of communication; where conflict is resolved with dignity and peace, and above all else, with love and respect.

In the Clouds

The heart of every child is unique, yet all similarly longs for love, time, and attention. When these fundamental needs go unmet, a deep sense of rejection can settle inside the empty space; that's where the thorns grow, and the place of emotional wilting begins.

My teacher, Ms. Watchcoat congratulates me on my test grade. It made my day at school. Somehow, I could ignore the noises that echo from home and focus on my spelling test long enough to complete it. I prayed for God to fix things between my parents. If they would learn how to talk and listen instead of screaming, maybe then everything will be okay. Joyce once read us a passage from Proverb 10:12 that says "hatred stirs up strife, but Love covers a multitude of sin." *What happened to love and forgiveness? I ask myself. Don't we all make mistakes? If love covers a multitude of sin, why can't they just love each other and cover each other, instead of cursing at each other?*

After school, I could not wait to show Mom my test grade. Joyce will be so proud of me because I took her advice. I wrote each word ten times and repeated the spelling aloud, again and again, until I memorized them all. It worked, just like she said it would. I got an A! I float on air walking home from school. Nothing can bring me down. From a distance, we notice our parents' car parked crookedly in the driveway. Michael gives me a peculiar look; it is only a little after three. Did she get off early? Maybe she came to surprise us and take us to work with her again. We race to the door.

John and Ms. Lynn are in the kitchen. John asks us, "How was school today?" Ms. Lynn is next to him, cutting her eyes at us as if they were sharp daggers, before turning away.

"I got an A on my spelling test!" I say, digging through my papers to show him my grade.

"That's good," he says and walks away toward the room.

"Is Mom home? The car is outside and… I?" The door closes before I can finish asking the question. *I guess he did not hear me.* The TV is on in the living room, but no one is watching it. The music on the television captures my attention. A beautiful woman with long raven-colored hair is singing. She is tall, slim, and she looks very refined and exotically beautiful. As she sings, her body sways from side to side. A short man with a thick mustache sings next to her. At first glance, they are an odd-looking couple, but they look happy together. I like their song: *"I got you, Babe."* I hum along as I put my school bag away.

Eager to show Mom my grade, I rush to her room. A sense of pride swells inside me like a helium balloon as I stare at the red circle my teacher made around the capital A on my paper. I feel unsure but happy to see the car outside when I raised my hand to knock on my parents' bedroom door.

"Who is it?" My dad asks with a harsh tone. *Is Daddy home?* I wonder to myself, disbelieving that I heard his voice on the other side of the door. For the first time since I can remember, he is home early; God must have listened to my prayers.

"Daddy, it's me!" I run in and throw my arms around him, falling into his arms. Old Spice and perspiration hang onto his polyester shirt. I squeeze him tighter. "Daddy you're home! I miss you. How was your day? Are you okay?" I cannot contain my joy. All at once, a familiar melody play. The song of our heartbeat shifts me back in time. A time before the thief of addiction and rage stole his smile and heart away from me. I lay on his chest, and with every heartbeat, I can hear it. I dance on the moon again. I would have held on a little longer if I only knew how soon the song was going to end.

Sullen and quiet, my Dad slumps on the edge of the bed. Deep lines plunge down the sides of his mouth. Michael and Linda walked in. He remains unresponsive, staring out into the air. He does not look at us. I lean back, touching his shoulder. "Daddy, are you okay?" I ask. He does not answer at first. He stares off as if he is not here, but somewhere locked far away — inside the cell of his own private Alcatraz. Respectfully, we do not interrupt the silent desperation that detains him. Content to be in his presence, we wait for the blessing of his words, his voice, and his attention.

With a curious look, Linda breaks the silence. "Did you eat something daddy. Are you hungry?"

"No baby," he says with a short breath. "Daddy is just tired." He huffs. Puffy pouches sit beneath his lower lashes while red lines stretch out like lightning across the white of his eyes. I wonder the last time he slept. I try to think of something to say; something funny to make him smile, or something witty to make him proud. But I keep my mouth shut and resist the urge to show him my spelling test. Even with the bright red marker around my grade, he is too far away to see it. Michael stands close to me and wraps his arms around my waist. I rest my head on Michael's shoulders, wondering why our dad looks as if life has cheated him out of an all or nothing bet. We are unaware of how serious it is. We're oblivious to how much our lives are about to change.

He clears his throat. "Get in the car; we gonna go for a ride." he gasps, barely forming the words. Our faces light up. Did we hear what we thought we just heard?

"I got front seat!" Michael shouts. He runs out the door making his usual silly face. We hustle behind him, laughing, racing to the car, excited at the chance to spend time with our dad. We wait inside the car until it feels like an arid desert. I begin to think that he changed his mind, but we have no intention of getting out of the car. In my heart, I believe love has no expiration date. I will wait for him forever if need be. Sweat trickles down the side of our face as we sit and wait. When he finally shuffles out with the car keys in his hands, we breathe and settle into a special joy. Since moving from Tampa, this is the first time I can remember that he came home early to take us for a ride. I only wished he looked as happy as I felt.

Our clothes are sticking to our clammy skin. The wind blows in through the window and chills me to the bone, but it feels good at the same time. Daddy is quiet. He slumps behind the wheel of the car and drives. Emotionless, he steers quietly away. It doesn't matter where we were going. Just being with him is enough for me. It's a rare and magical treat. He drives, and we fly. He is my hero, but I wonder if he knows. I stare at his hands on the steering wheel as he peers blankly ahead. Random tremors, like hiccups, cause his fingers to twitch. I pretend not to notice and pray silently. *God save my daddy. I do not know what is wrong with my father's hands or his heart, but he does not look well. Please, please, God, make my daddy happy. Amen.* I stare up at the clouds.

The window seat feeds my imagination. Clouds in the shape of dinosaurs, bunny rabbits, and mermaids drift magically in the sky. "If you look hard enough, you will see it too," I tell Michael as we ride. "Do you see that one: an old man with a beard? Look over there. It's a ship sailing by." We go on and on, entertaining each other with our heads in the clouds. We are completely unaware of how terrible things had gotten between our parents, and that bad had gone to worse.

Dad is quiet, almost too quiet. We wait for him to say something, anything. After he parks the car, he finally speaks. "I will be right back," he says, hobbling out of the car without another word. With a few off-balance steps, he disappears through the back door. We sit in the parking lot of the Melody Bar on Sistrunk

Boulevard. Over an hour passes, and I wonder about the people who are walking in the same door. My stomach growls, and my mind race with questions. *Who are they? Do they serve food in there?* I hope he is getting us something to eat. We sit and wait, watching every time the barroom door opens, hoping it's him coming out.

"I'm hungry," Leon grumbles.

"Me too," Linda repeats. Almost six o'clock in the evening, the late-day wind carries the delicious smell of soul food from a nearby restaurant. The aroma of collard greens, barbecue chicken, and cornbread whips in the air, making my stomach growl even louder.

Sleepiness quiets our cravings. We wait in the car nearly two hours with no sign of our dad coming out. My mind runs away with me, wondering if he is all right. I forget where I left my spelling test paper; I am always misplacing things. "Michael, do you remember where I put my spelling test? I want to show Mama when we get home."

"Michael...Michael?" He does not answer. I turn around to see his mouth wide open; he has fallen asleep—beads of sweat run across his forehead. Linda has nodded off to sleep as well. Leon is awake, with his arms folded and his chin caved inside his chest. *Where did I put my spelling test paper?* The thought pesters me until our dad finally comes out of the bar.

He gets in and leans forward with an awkward posture as he drives. His eyes are glazed, and he looks just as sad now as he did when he first walked into the bar. But the deep crease that rippled his forehead is gone, and his hands are different. They are steady and no longer tremble. I want to ask him questions about the barroom. *What did he do? Did he see any of his friends? Can we go in with him next time he goes? Do they serve food in there?* To ask any of these questions would be out of line and disrespectful. Such are the times. We stay in a child's place; seen and not heard. We follow his lead and keep quiet. However, the quiet is about to become deafening. Today will be the last day of my family as I know it. The day my world stop turning.

If parents realized the devastating impact divorce has on their children, divorce courts would be empty, and homes would fill with more patience, kindness, acceptance, humility, and understanding.

Casualties of War

"War is what happens when language fails." ~*Margaret Atwood*

Uncertainty exists in every life, every home; mainly a home where contention and hostility live and breed for days, months, and years. Our world is about to change forever. Seeds of anger and bitterness sprout up like tall weeds; thick and overgrown. We could not know what would be around the next turn of a key when we returned home from the bar. We would soon learn as we stepped out of the car that life, as we knew it, was over.

Our Dad goes straight into combat mode as he steps through the door. With an urgent pace, Joyce meets us at the door and hurries us to the bedroom. She puts one hand on the doorknob, eases the bedroom door closed with the other, and huddles us together and tells us to pray the Lord's Prayer. We do not ask questions. We do as she says.

My stomach churns with uncertainty and fear. *What is happening!* Soon the answers become more evident. Suddenly, we hear screaming, and a physical fight erupts. In the corner of the room, we cringe, praying that it would soon end, and everything would be all right again. But between my mom and dad, everything would not be all right. The build-up of unresolved disputes would come to a nightmarish end. My blood curdles as they scuffle—I hear my mama scream. I beg God to stop it. Hitting, pushing—the dresser tilts. I try to swallow. The sound of perfume bottles falling, hateful grunts, a solid punch, and something hits the wall. The terrible sound crashes inside me. My mind plays shocking scenes. I pray harder, folding my hands tighter until they go numb. But God does not intervene. I question everything I know. What is love, anyway? Does God even hear me? Is He listening? Can He hear my prayers over the sounds of the chaos? I cannot swallow for fear of hearing something worse. I know Daddy hides a gun under the seat of the car, and Mama has one of her own inside her purse. We gather closer, unblinking, just breathing.

Like a shield, Joyce's arms wrap around us, cocooning us in the corner of the room. "Everything will be all right. Just pray. Remember what I told you. No matter what, you—must—trust—God." Joyce explains. I try to hold onto her words and remember what she tells us, but the scuffle is earsplitting. In those moments, I cannot remember anything. Leon and Michael sit down on the floor near Joyce's feet. Linda hides her face in my chest. With every thud, she jerks and looks toward the door, squeezing me tighter. Profanity like acid pollutes the air. The words are damaging and cruel, like fireballs thrown against the walls of a house made of dry wood. Our world is set ablaze.

Hopeless, we wait for the madness to end. We wait for peace, but it will not come. The damage is beyond repair. We had not known how bad my father's drinking and gambling had spiraled out of control. Nor did we know what had happened earlier in the day—the story of how my dad went to my mom's job, threatening her with a gun after he found out another man was visiting her at work. My parents' marriage could endure no more. No more threats, no more fights. The battle between my parents came to a bitter end when my mama says, "Enough!" She packed her belongings, declaring, "Either he will kill me, or I will kill him!"

Powerless to stop her, he yells back, "You ain't taking my kids!" His voice is full of resentment. The verbal crossfire between them burns and stings until my nerves twitch all on their own. She opens our bedroom door and grabs Joyce out of the room. Both flee out of the house. Panicked, I can't take in any air. *What is happening? Where is Mama going, why is she taking Joyce away, and why is she leaving without us?* My heart waits for the answers. Unnerved, we run to our bedroom window that overlooks the front driveway. She turns towards us before getting in the car.

"I will be back to get Y'all," she gasps. Her eyes are watery, her voice hollow, defeated. I groan at the sight of my mother and Joyce putting clothes and bags in the car without us.

"Mama," Michael presses his face against the glass. I open my mouth, but nothing comes out. Helpless, I scream inside my head, *don't go!*

Seen but not heard, I am too afraid to say the words—afraid to move, afraid to think. *Wait! There is still hope. She hasn't left yet,* I say to myself, praying from the window. *Mama wait!* I remember now. I remember what Joyce said. No matter what, I must pray and believe that God will make a way. He will put it all back together again. I believe! There is still a chance for my Dad to say he is sorry, for Mom to slow down—for them to kiss, makeup, and begin again. *I believe. I believe! Please, God! Make everything okay! Please stop my parents from tearing our family apart.*

My heart stops when the sound of the car's engine starts. Joyce sits in the backseat, motionless. We stare out of the window in disbelief.

Later, we will come to understand why Joyce went, and Mom left us behind. All those times Joyce had gone away for the weekend without us, she was with a man named Willie. Joyce was visiting *her* father's house. Willie is her biological father. Terrible things happen behind closed doors—that's where we learn to keep secrets. Years would pass before the truth came out about her weekend visits and the *secret* abuse she endured at the hands of trusted *friends*.

On that last day, Joyce could not stay, and when Mom backs out of the driveway, it feels like the world crumbled beneath our feet.

Leon, Michael, Linda, and I freeze to the bedroom floor. She speeds away, and as the dust settles, we cannot move. We stay in the same place—motionless, shell-shocked mannequins staring out the window. Our static faces display the ashes and rubble of a domestic war we had never signed up for, never agreed to, and never had a say in the matter.

In the aftermath, all is quiet and still. Dad does not say a word. He returns to his room and closes the door. No one talks or explains what is going on in the war zone of our home. It's like nothing had ever happened. We refuse to walk away from the bedroom window. We stand there, waiting for a miracle. *Maybe she will change her mind and come right back, or maybe this is all just a bad dream.* The only movement in the room is silent tears falling. We are the casualties of war. Tonight, we do not talk. We do not dream. We gather on the floor, holding each other, weeping, waiting for the storm to end. We wait for the world to turn again.

Every day after school, we sit by the window, still watching, still waiting. The window becomes the portal of our time machine. Time stopped the day Mom and Joyce went away. Staring out of the window, I travel back in time to the days at my parent's store in Tampa. I can almost hear the fierce thunderstorms of Ybor between the chords of my sister's sweet lullabies. Leon is hopeful. Even when he cries, he believes everything will be all right. He talks about when Mama returns and how happy we are all going to be. We sit, huddled together on the floor, listening to his heartfelt sermons.

"Yes! She is coming back; she said she would," Michael says with firm confidence. We force a smile, staring at each other, nodding our heads in agreement. When Mama says it, we know it is true. She will be back. We wipe our tears and wait.

The Lineup

"Young alienation, disappointment and heartache are all a
part of the first real growing up that we do."
~*Judd Nelson*

Time rewinds and plays on slow repeat, preparing to freeze
us into place altogether. It's a sin what happens to children behind
closed doors. Even worse is the secret pain little hearts hide, afraid
to tell a soul, and so, we don't say a word, and soon, the thorns grow
deeper. Until one day you wake up far away from yourself because
being you is no longer safe. That day was coming. The day the
sound of silence leaves you because the noise refuses to stop; the
day when you learn to fly away — vanishing into thin air — the day
of detachment where a magical tunnel opens, helping you to
escape.

You know when you are not wanted. It is an unspoken
spiteful feeling that lingers in the air, like the smell of fish left out
too long. The rotten smell overwhelms the senses, making you sick
to your stomach. Since Mom and Joyce left the house, I have become
more of a jumpy hermit. Most times, our Dad is away from home,
leaving us in the care of Ms. Lynn. She makes it no secret; she hates
us. I do not know why. With Mama and Joyce away, it is open
season, and we are easy prey. Ms. Lynn appears enraged at the
mere sight of us. School is a refuge, but at night, Dad and John are
at work, leaving us alone with Ms. Lynn. The days pass slowly. In
the morning, the lash of a cord bites us awake. She uses it like a
skilled cattle driver. "Get yawl asses up for school. Dis room better
be cleaned befo' you leave, and you bet' not be late," Ms. Lynn
orders snidely. Her tone is how I would imagine the bite of a
scorpion would feel; it matches the lashes. Half awake, we move
mechanically, skidding across the room.

Clothes on, room cleaned, we get to school on time. I try to
avoid my teacher's careful attention. I do not want her to see me. It
is not a good day. I walk into the class and sit quietly behind my
desk, wanting to disappear. When my teacher sees me, she greets
me with a hug. Her long brunette hair is soft and smells freshly
washed. "Good morning, Ms. Anderson."

"Good morning, Mrs. Watchcoat," I reply, standing up,
never looking her in the eye. She puts her hands on my shoulders

and stands arm's length away.

"What happened to your head?" she asks. I think of something to say fast, but nothing comes out of my mouth. She sits down while I remain standing. "Ms. Anderson?" she looks squarely at me.

"Yes ma'am, Mrs. Watchcoat."

"Did you hit your head on something again?" she asks suspiciously.

"Oh, yes ma'am. I'm so clumsy," I say, looking away, putting my hand over the silver-dollar-sized bump on my forehead. "I was daydreaming again. I ran into the wall." I smile dizzily to escape her suspicion. I feel guilty about lying to her. She is so sweet to me, but I know that I will be in trouble if ever she learns the truth. I never tell. She starts the class, and thankfully, she does not call on me. I kick up rocks on the way home from school. Almost there, I turn around, looking over my shoulder; feeling like someone is watching me.

After school, I try hard not to step on the landmines that trigger Ms. Lynn's temper. You never see them coming—the explosive strikes of a cord or a fist upside the head. We obey without question. Despite our submission, she makes us regret we are alive. At night, we wait by the window, staring up at the moonlight, hopeful with every car that passes. Sleep comes in spells because we can never tell when Ms. Lynn will come in, and the nightmare begins. Leon starts grinding his teeth in his sleep; Linda cries and often hides in the closet. I sit with her, rocking her side-to-side, humming the melody of our stolen lullaby. It's too painful to sing the words.

Dad comes home after dark most often, never seeing our faces, and never noticing the legion of welts and scabs embroidered on our skin. He never sees, and never asks. Leon detaches. He buckles under Ms. Lynn's brutal mistreatment and our Dad's failure to intervene. A hollow marionette with hidden strings, his personality seems to break and fade. Anger becomes his puppet master. He begins to break things again and throw the broken pieces across the room. He later cries because of the damage. Michael hides his hurt in humor that is becoming somewhat bizarre. During our darkest nights, he tells jokes, acting like everything is fine. He often laughs to himself, ignoring it all. With each passing day, the thought of seeing Mama and Joyce keeps us anxiously hopeful.

After finishing my chores, I look for Linda. I hear faint whimpers coming from the closet. I find Linda hiding between loads of dirty laundry in the corner of our bedroom closet.

"I want Mommy," she cries. Her beautiful bright eyes eclipse with sadness.

"It's okay, Peanut; Mama is coming to get us soon. She said so. She is coming. I promise," I whisper, holding her tight to me.

"But I want her now!" Linda moans inconsolably. I feel helpless, unable to comfort her. Leaning against the dark closet wall, we cry together. I close my eyes and watch little specks of light dance between each breath.

The imagination is a gift from God: a magical place where you can hide, and no one can find you. Since Mom and Joyce left, my imagination has become more vivid, more powerful, and I learn to vanish safely away into the obscurity of my daydreams. There, I learn to cope with the overwhelming feelings of fear and distress. Mom said she would be back. Days pass, I daydream of the moment she would arrive. I hear her car's muffler dragging against the rocky pavement on the street. Hurrying to the bedroom window, I watch her pull into the driveway. My heart leaps out of my chest from the delight of hearing her call us to come out. The sound of her voice fills me with joy. I listen to her calling us. *"Leon, Michael, Linda, Sandra, come out, come out, I'm here."* I hear her clearly, and my smile is as bright as the sun.

Suddenly, I feel a stinging on my face. The pain in my jaw knocks me to my knees, bringing me back to earth. "You hear me calling yo' dumb ass," Ms. Lynn shouts. "Get yo' fat ass to the table." Lost in my daydream, I did not hear her calling. I touch my face, stunned. Blinking, I do not cry. It takes a minute to realize where I am. Blindsided, I feel a flush of tears fall like water. In shock, I feel no emotion at first. A tinge of blood trickles down from my lip. I taste it before I feel it.

At that moment, I feel like an orphan. I look around the room for my doll Mama got me for my birthday. She is nowhere around. I need to touch her, to hold her, to feel the sympathy she will give me. Then I begin to remember. After Mom had left, our toys were put into a big black garbage bag. I haven't seen my doll since. Finding my feet, I stand up and ease guardedly to the table. My face stings, but the pain inside is worse. Everything I love someone takes from me. Silently I scream, *Mommy! God, let her hear me.* My thoughts race, and though I try to think straight, I cannot. Pieces of me are all over the place; still scattered across the floor.

Leon, Michael, Linda and I sit solemnly at the kitchen table. Vacant and afraid, we look down at our plates at sweet peas, rice, and off-colored mystery meat. I am not hungry. My stomach tells me something worse is about to happen. I try to go far away in my mind to prepare. My head slopes forward—the left side of my face throbs. Blood collects in my mouth, but I cannot get up from the table to go and spit it out. I swallow it along with the sweet peas. I do not chew because chewing hurts. Nauseated, I feel the eruption coming from deep inside my belly; peas and blood mix with anxiety.

I peek at Leon. He notices my eyes watering. He can tell I cannot hold it; I cannot keep my food down. I run to the bathroom, vomit, and slowly walk back. Ms. Lynn nostrils flare as I return to my seat. She wears a grim smirk, completely in control of her insanity. She scoffs across the table, informing us of what we did wrong today and the way in which she plans for us to pay. Leon's leg shakes, making the side of the table vibrate. Michael bites his bottom lip, but the rest of him remains motionless. Linda begins to cry. Her face distorts with fear. Powerless, we shudder. We know what is coming: The Lineup.

We've been here before—positioned in a straight line, usually from the oldest to the youngest; we are not to move. The thrashes will be worse if we do. We obey without question. Why she hates us so much remains a mystery to me. I think to myself, *did something happen to her to cause her to be so unhappy, so miserable, and so cruel? Did something happen when she was a little girl? What did we do?* I cannot remember, I don't understand. I rummage through my cluttered memory for answers. Sometimes, if you can find reason, it makes the punishment easier to endure. Gasping, I come up empty.

One by one, we shake, forming the lineup. "Don't you move!" she calmly warns. It's hard to stand still when everything in you is screaming for help.

She sits wide-legged on a chair facing the hallway and sturdies herself. A chorus of sobs fills the air before she ever wields the first lash. Leon is first. She lashes him, targeting his back and legs. He recoils and twists. She never moves off the chair. To make her move toward you would call for dire consequence. I cannot think of what could be worse. We do not test her. We crawl to her as she commands. Leon prays aloud with every whip to his back. The anguish of his gasps makes us hurt before it is our turn.

I weep for him. Incapable of saving him, I could feel my heartbeat fading. "Jesus help me, God forgive me," repeatedly he prays. God does not intervene. Pain collides with an undercurrent of rage; still, Leon begins to pray even louder. His words seem to fuel her anger. Inflamed, she swings. The cord whips through the air like lightning from an angry storm. "I'm sorry! I'm sorry!" he moans. She does not stop.

Where is Daddy? I scream silently inside my mind. No defense, nowhere to run, no place to hide. We cry and recite all the scriptures that we know. Joyce hid the treasure of God's words inside of our hearts a long time ago, and now, like breathing, it comes out. While we were still in diapers, she told us of the stories of faith and courage in times of uncertainty and fear. During the thunderstorms in Tampa, we remember the songs and scriptures. Joyce told us to remember and never forget.

I fold my hands together under my chin, waiting for my turn. Tears roll over my knuckles. Linda rocks side to side, never taking her eyes off Leon. "The Lord is my shepherd; I shall not want...." Leon stutters to finish the passage. I cry for him, more than for myself.

"I got to go pee," Michael squirms; a reaction he has at every Lineup. He holds a brave expression on his face. The closer it gets to his turn, the stronger the urge to use the bathroom.

Unable to restrain himself, he breaks the line without permission. Ms. Lynn takes the transgression out on Leon. She stands up and beats him harder. Breaking Lineup is not allowed. Leon falls to the floor.

"Leon!" I scream.

"Shut up. Shut up I said!" she spits. I motion toward Leon, reaching out, somehow trying to catch his fall. He goes quiet.

"Leon," I exhale, falling next to him. I close my eyes, trying to wake up. At this moment, I welcome her whip. Anything to take away the heartache of seeing my brother crumpled on the floor. I hold onto him. So, for a second in time, everything is all right again. I feel his skin, his warmth. We are connected. I hurry to vanish far away in my mind.

" Get yo' fat ass back in line!" Ms. Lynn rails. With a cold glare, she utters profanities. She beats me off him. I scamper across the floor, rubbing the welts swelling on my arms, legs, and neck. The stinging pain takes my breath away. I get back in line. "Don't try me!" Ms. Lynn warns.

Michael is next. Linda slumps her shoulders and presses her

face into my stomach. "I'm sorry, Sanwa," Linda sniffles and sobs, not understanding why we must endure The Lineup. There are no answers.

I hold onto Linda in the hallway while we wait our turn. I want to protect her, to stop it, but I cannot. I suppress the pain, way down deep inside. I hear Michael cries just before I begin to fly away. Flicks of light, like fireflies, scurry through the darkness in my mind. I lift off and take flight.

All goes blank, and a low humming noise drowns out the commotion. The hallway becomes a secret tunnel through which I turn and spiral through the passageway. Dissociation becomes an unintentional rescue. Unlike my imagination, where I am free to daydream, detachment carries me away on its own. There, I dangle in a strange place. I straddle two worlds, unsure how far away I am from either. Divinely, it is my saving grace. It releases me after The Lineup ends. By that time, I'm welted and disheveled. Unclear of time, I wait for the answers to come — there are no answers. Linda is clutching my arm. Ms. Lynn tires before beating her. I am relieved and thankful that Linda was spared from The Lineup today.

We learn that the Lineup ends after Ms. Lynn has thoroughly exhausted her anger, and the fire of the dragon inside her is somehow satisfied. "If I hear a sound, I will beat yawl asses again." Ms. Lynn walks calmly to her room and shuts the door — like nothing ever happened.

We make our way to the room and lay together on the bed. Muzzled sighs, bloodshot eyes — our noses are sore from wiping and sniffling. Together, we languish. Trapped inside this house, inside this skin, marked up like sick graffiti.

"Mama, please come soon," I whisper, trying to find a comfortable side to rest, but the welts swell, making it feel like lying in a bed of thorns. Suddenly, Leon looks at us. "Where is Daddy!?" he gulps under his breath. His voice is irate and strict. A profound sense of sadness and anger cuts through his tone. He stares at us as if he demands an answer. After a while, the questions become more agonizing than the lashings. There are no answers to our many questions of why. No one comes; no one hears our cries. We stop asking and accept what is. Linda and Michael fall asleep. Leon turns his face to the wall.

My stomach growls, but I miss Joyce and my Mom more than anything. I close my eyes, trying to find the melody of Joyce's lullaby to settle the storm; it is hard to hear. The gross profanity in my head and the grumbling noises coming from my empty belly are all too loud. The whole "sticks and stones" mantra is a flat out lie! *Swearwords are hurtful.* I relive it all again: the cruelty, the heartache, the cries, and the fireflies that come out of nowhere. My last thoughts before falling asleep are of green peas. I can still taste them in my mouth. To this day, I hate them.

Parental neglect is rampant in our culture. The need to survive, to work, and to provide leaves the door wide open for demons and monsters of every kind. Despondent, exhausted, and distracted, parents and caregivers seem to forget that children need so much more than food, clothes, shelter, and gadgets; they need to be seen, to be heard, and to be loved.

Hurt people will often act out the same degree of hurt on others, and sometimes it only gets worse until we take the time to heal and deal with our own inner madness. Today, families are out of order because when the sadness is not seen, when no one talks, and everybody screams, the entire family, community, and nation implodes and before anyone knows, everything explodes
until we all

fall

down.

Yellow Eldorado

Listen to that sixth sense that tells you that you are not alone—even when no one else is around. God is there. Intuition is there for a reason; to teach us, to guide us, beyond what we think we know. Insight is a gift from God; we must learn to trust and develop it; only then we can see with new eyes. Eyes of faith that looks beyond what we see and understand.

Days pass. I cover up. Long sleeves, long pants, and I head out to school. I cannot wait to see Mrs. Watchcoat. She is kind and makes me feel special. Her smile warms me. But I can't let her know, and I don't want her to see. Before leaving the house, I make every effort to look *normal*. My head is throbbing, and I have an open cut on the back of my thigh, but I walk to school, ignoring the pain. Sometimes I think I deserved it. What other reason could it be? Why would someone be so mean, so cruel? Why! *"Seen and not heard. What happens in your house stays in your house."* These sayings create a culture of secrets I dare not tell for fear of something worse happening. You learn early in life to take the pain and dig a deep hole to hide it in a place no one will ever find it. I learn to hide it well.

I must hurry to school. I am running late because Ms. Lynn had told me I had to stay behind and clean up the room. My siblings walked to school without me. When they leave me behind, it feels almost as bad as the reason why. The room was already clean, but Ms. Lynn had another excuse for making me stay back.

"Clean up dis room. I done told yo' fat ass befo!" Ms. Lynn screamed at me before school. I do what she says without question. After I start cleaning up the room again, she orders me to sit on the floor between her legs; my back turned towards her. I am afraid, but I sit. She grabs my hair. Unaware of what she is about to do next, I prepare myself, bracing for the angry licks she often gave me. Her big fleshy thighs pen me in while she pulled my hair. With a fist, she hits me, yanking my head from side to side. "The next time I tell yo' fat ass to clean dis room, you betta have it done before I come in here."

"I'm sorry, I'm sorry!" I groan and squeal. Nobody hears. Nobody comes. The louder I cry, the harder she pulls, so I force myself into quiet submission. She wraps her fingers around the strands of my hair, snatches up, and then, all at once I hear a snip. I feel a release and watch my hair fall to the floor. She cuts my hair and tells me to get my black ass to school. Off balance, I try to stand up. Vertigo causes everything to move around me. The room spins so fast that I fear I'd fall and get into more trouble. Determined not to fall, I move through the spinning motion of everything around me. I stumbled out of the house and walked to school alone—as if nothing ever happened.

I think of my teacher all the way to school. Her classroom is my sanctuary. I hurry, walking with my head down. The pain in my head causes my eyes to hurt and blur in the bright sunlight. As I approach the corner, I notice a yellow car, fancy with clean white-trimmed tires. It is following me. I cross the street. The car stops on the curb. There, our eyes meet on the dusty rock-covered road, just a few feet from Sunland Park Elementary. I stop and squint, recognizing the driver over the glare of the sun. At first, I think my eyes are playing tricks on me. I thought I saw her many times before, but it was not her—only my imagination, my longing. She motions for me to come. Only as I moved closer to the car door did I finally allow my heart to believe.

"Mommy!" I cry out. My eyes fill with tears of both joy and sorrow. Awakening from the Nightmare, I begin to feel again. And suddenly, I feel everything at once: pain, fear, shock, elation. My body goes limp from the weight of emotions. She looks inside of me. She seems to see the nightmare I cannot describe. Her eyes are ablaze with anger. She looks as if she will explode. Her words are short as she breathes deep, speaking through her teeth:

"I'm coming today, baby. Do not say anything. Be ready."

"Yes, Mama." I squeeze my hands tight as if to hold onto her few words, like a secret treasure. As quickly as she came, I watch her leave, burning down the road. She furiously speeds away leaving a cloud of smoke. I hurry to my classroom, still hearing my mom's voice—fearing the vengeance in her face; my stomach twists. My mind races and I cannot convince my thoughts to sit still. I know of my mother's passion and her fury. I have seen and heard them both. When mixed, the result is volcanic. I run towards the door of my school. Another tardy is all I need, but it doesn't matter now.

Mama is coming. I know I will have to leave my school today. I wait for the sound of the bell. The sound of liberation: Mom is coming. The happy thought overrides the pulsating pain in my head. After Mrs. Watchcoat completes her lessons for the day, I quietly collect my worksheets, drawings, pencils, and crayons out of my desk. I hope Mrs. Watchcoat does not ask me any questions. I cannot tell her goodbye or why I'm leaving school. Mama said not to say anything. Tightlipped, I act as if this is just another day. I am getting better at pretending. If my teacher asks, I must make up another lie.

Joyce taught us to tell the truth. She showed us the Ten Commandments in the Holy Bible and told us to do our best to follow God's law. I have lied to my teacher before about my head having an encounter with a deranged bedroom door, and no doubt, I will lie again; and perhaps I will have to lie a million times more because I'm not sure who or what to trust anymore. *Seen and not heard*, I obey the orders that scare me more than the words of the prophets who warned of hell's fire. In my life, fear is a place called hell. And hell is a place called home. The voices there are louder, more frightening.

The school bell rings, signaling the end of the day. I ignore my nervous gut and push my chair under the desk. Mrs. Watchcoat stands in her usual place inside the threshold of the classroom door. I walk towards the opening, watching her smile and wave.

"Good job, students. See you tomorrow. Study for Friday's vocabulary test, and do not forget to have a good breakfast in the morning," she says. I walk toward her, and the floor feels lopsided.

"See you in the morning, Ms. Anderson," she says. I reach my arms up for a hug. She bends down, wrapping her arms around me—It feels so good. She could never know what her gentle touch means to me. Her patience and kindness salve my hidden wounds. I squeeze her tight and forget to let go. She gives me a squeeze, lifts my chin, and tells me I am a smart girl. Her kind words feed my starving soul. I fall into her again and rest my head on her shoulder. I hold onto her, trying to stay long enough to believe the words she spoke to me—long enough to dream of a better tomorrow, long enough for my heart to let go and say goodbye.

"Good-bye Mrs. Watchcoat." I smile and walk away. After that day, I would never see her again.

I think it has been several weeks since Mom and Joyce left, but it has felt like a year. After school, I say nothing. I cannot breathe a word to anyone. I look around and down each corner of the street. I breathe heavy, wiping the sweat away from my eyes, searching for the fancy yellow car. The noise in my head magnifies with every step towards the house. Riotous noises that I cannot turn off. Mixed emotions, like a demolition derby, crash into each other. In my muddled state, I slip and almost fall. My loose shoestrings break my speedy stride. I have no time to stop and tie them. I must get home.

"What's wrong? I don't want to rush home. Why are you walking so fast?" Michael asks. I try to calm my nervousness.

"I have to go to the bathroom really bad," I tell him, trying to pretend as if nothing ever happened as if I did not see Mama today, as if I have fallen under the delusion of a fantastic dream. I look toward the house. There is still time to get ready. The fancy yellow car is not in the driveway. We walk into the house and immediately begin to perform our daily tasks. Ms. Lynn is in her room. I pray she is asleep and stays asleep until after Mama comes and we are gone. Her son is playing up and down the hallway with a toy truck. Linda is trying to whisper something to me, but I cannot focus long enough to hear what she is saying. Panic and hope overwhelm me.

Someone is outside. *It must be Mama,* I think to myself. I dart to the window. The neighbor next door is standing outside talking to someone. It is not her. She told me to be ready and not to say anything. I still have time. *But how do I get ready? What must I do?* And if I knew what to do, how can I do it without saying something. I want to tell Leon, Michael, and Linda that I spoke with Mom today and that she said she is coming. I wait without saying a word. Mommy's voice is louder than all the questions and clamor inside my head.

Leon and Michael are busy in the living room and kitchen. I start to clean up after Ms. Lynn's son. He must have eaten something that did not agree with him. He makes a mess that leaks out of his diaper. The smell turns my already sensitive stomach inside out; I quickly bathe him and change his diaper. An hour passes, and Mom is not here yet. I whisper under my breath, "she is coming. I know she is coming." I miss Joyce so much it hurts, and I hope she does not get too upset when she sees our hair. Joyce had always told us how pretty we looked after she braided our hair. Now, my hair is a cut, tangled, nappy mess, but I hope she still thinks that I am pretty. I notice that Linda has been in the bathroom for a while now. When I go in to check on her, she is slumping and groggy. She quietly weeps.

"Peanut, are you okay?" I ask. She sits on the commode. I touch her forehead and neck. She is hot and clammy. "Peanut, what's wrong!"

Her mouth moves, but I cannot hear what she is trying to

say.

"What is hurting, Peanut? Say something! Are you hurt?" Kneeling down, I lean into her. Stroking her hair, I lift her chin. Sad lines fall down the corners of her mouth. She frowns, huffing in short, choppy breaths. Faint snuffles ascend and then release all at once. "Peanut!" Panic rips through me. She wheezes and starts crying. She looks as if she is trying to stand up in the ocean, but her feet cannot find the seafloor.

"Sanwa, I don't feel good. My stomach hurts; I hurt all over. I want Mommy." She exhales and then cries again. Beads of sweat roll down her forehead. Her feet dangle listlessly over the commode.

"I'm sorry, Peanut. Mama is coming. She is coming," I whisper, cutting my eyes to the bathroom door. "I saw her today! Everything will be all right." I yell for Leon and Michael.

They rush to the bathroom. "Peanut is sick. She is hot. What do we do?" I say, sinking back against the bathroom wall. An awful sense of guilt rips my heart. I could not hear when Linda was trying to get my attention earlier. After school, she wanted to tell me something was wrong.

"I 'm right here, and everything is going to be all right," I say the words, but I am falling apart. Linda is getting hotter. Leon looks through the medicine cabinet. Suddenly, a dark shadow stands in the doorway of the bathroom. We freeze in place; the noise roused Ms. Lynn. She glares at us as if she has a bad taste in her mouth that she desperately wants to spit out.

Leon squares his chest and stares back into Ms. Lynn's face. "My sister is not feeling good," Leon says with a defensive attitude.

Ms. Lynn pauses, looking coldly at us. "She ain't none of my damn child." She rolls her eyes and walks away toward the kitchen.

Leon rakes through antacids and old prescription bottles. "She can't take this stuff." He slams the cabinet door shut. His face falls. No remedy — we do not know what to do.

I run water over a cloth, ring it out, and place it on top of Linda's forehead. I remember. Joyce did it before when we lived in Tampa. Linda cries louder, holding her stomach.

"It's okay, Peanut," Leon says tenderly.

"Did you eat something bad?" Michael asks. Linda doesn't answer. She moans louder. Michael lays his hand on Linda's head, and begins to whisper over her, "Lord, please touch my sister..." In desperation, the seeds Joyce planted inside our hearts begin to surface. Together, we bow our heads and pray.

Mama's Retribution

Call me absent-minded, but the moment I had most anticipated would sneak up on me. We could not tell when it happened. We only knew that one moment we are praying for Linda, and the next, we would be praying for Ms. Lynn. Mama was in the house. As we came out of the bathroom, hell was breaking loose in the living room. Now, more like an uncivil courtroom, our home explodes with scenes too mortifying for me to ever forget. My mom is the judge, the jury, and the executioner—all to Ms. Lynn's regret. Ms. Lynn quails, halfway off the couch. Mama scowls at her with a harsh tone.

"I told you not to bother my children, didn't I...?" she shouts, hitting Ms. Lynn repeatedly, charging her with the crime of mistreatment.

"Who told Mama?" Puzzled, we whisper among ourselves. We would soon learn that the adult world has secrets too. The wall has ears and the night has eyes. When Mom had left the house, she also left a spy watching us, listening from somewhere on the outside. Naively, we had never known, until now. Mom strikes Ms. Lynn in the face, and then she seems to wait for her to fight back and counterpunch. It never comes. Ms. Lynn appears to be no match against Mama's vengeance. With a riotous glare, Mama turns and looks at us; a huge vein swells in her neck and runs up the side of her head.

"Take her stuff and throw it out in the front yard!" She roars. I hear her, but my feet feel like they are stuck in hardened cement. I cannot move. My nerves shake like they are no longer a part of my body.

Leon and Michael dash away and start throwing Ms. Lynn's belongings on the porch and sidewalk. I hold onto Linda, still crying, feverish, and scared.

Mama, still screaming at Ms. Lynn, instructs us again. "Throw it all out the door! All of it!" I hear her. I am trying to move. My brain received the signal to move, but my body detaches. I stand in a state of shock. Driven by rage and fierce retribution, Mom doesn't stop. A part of me feels sorry for Ms. Lynn. Under my breath, I pray. I try to close my eyes, but I cannot blink. I pray it would all end. *God, make it all stop.* I pray for peace. But it will not come today, not for Ms. Lynn, not for my Mom, my Dad, nor my siblings and me. Nobody wins here. There can be no winners in this madness. Mama growls and argues our defense,

"I told you not to mess with my children, didn't I? Uh-uh, didn't I?" A blow follows every word. And Mama is long-winded.

Ms. Lynn shrieks and grunts beneath Mama's anger. Her arms whirl, trying to deflect the strikes. Violently, Mama punches her in the face and head. Repeatedly she jabs, landing solid hits. At once, Mama pulls back. I think it is over, but it is not. Never taking her eyes off Ms. Lynn, she reaches into her purse and pulls out a straight edge blade. I have seen it before at my dad's barbershop in Tampa. Fear unties my hands long enough to allow me to cover my mouth. She swings the blade across Ms. Lynn's hair like a sickle through a wheat field, slitting off the top of her hair. Ms. Lynn's hair falls over the couch and floor.

Mom tells us to go stand outside on the porch.

"Don't move until I tell you," she says. We gather outside—we do not move. Ms. Lynn's belongings litter the porch and sidewalk while her most prized possession will soon join the eviction.

Neighbors stare and chatter from next door and across the yard. In the chaos, I feel a presence—sweet and gentle. Suddenly, I spot her. Joyce is in the back seat of the fancy yellow car, waiting on the curb near the driveway. The engine is running. A strange man sits in the driver's seat. Before I can think, Mama comes out of the house carrying Ms. Lynn's TV. She lifts it up, high into the air and throws it down onto the sidewalk. The television crashes into smithereens on the hard concrete. The noise grabs more attention, and before long, we hear sirens. Someone has called the police.

"Get in the car!" Mama says, moving with the speed of a bank robber. We sprint behind her, jumping in the backseat of the fancy yellow car. The car skids away from the curb. Mama vents and cuts her eyes in the side-view mirror. The car moves fast and smooth as the strange man drives. He makes short, unclear remarks. He and my Mom talk back and forth about the violent incident. *There is too much noise in the world.* The car cuts the corner sharply, swerving in and out of traffic before slowing down off a back street.

Joyce coddles us in the backseat. We are quiet; no one cries; no one moves. Only slight tremors push through to the surface of my hands and legs. I think of Daddy. *Where is he? Does he love us? When will I see him again? Will he miss us? Dad, where are you?* My heart calls out with a thousand questions. In the canyon of my mind, I hear only the echo of my own voice. I'm not sure what else

I expected to hear. Wishing I could silence all my senses, I lean into Joyce.

She gently pats my leg, and whispers, "It's okay, it's okay." My leg stops shaking, but my mind will not be still.   I twirl the corner of my shirt around my finger. Tighter, I twirl until I can feel the blood stop circulating. The sharp, tingling sensation somehow soothes me because, at least, this is a pain that I can control. I twist tighter.

We move further and further away from what has felt like a nightmare. There are no words, no answers. Words are lost somewhere in the wreckage behind us. Somewhere underneath the piles of broken promises and shattered dreams of my family, the answers await. Somewhere wedge tightly in-between this seen-and-not-heard generation, are the reasons for all the hate, the anger, and the madness. It is hard to breathe, hard to move when the stress of anxiety and blame sits on your chest accusing you of everything. It talks to me, and I believe what it says. *This mess is all my fault.*

Children internalize almost everything!

Unable to fully understand the conflict within my parent's marriage, I twirl my shirt tighter, wanting to hold my doll. She got left behind. Tighter, I twist until my finger hurts from the pressure. *I am sorry I forgot you, Dolly.* In my head, I feel sorry for everything; in my heart, I want my dad to make everything all right. Why can't he just say he is sorry? Why can't my parents make it right again? If we could just pull over, turn around, and go back for a minute or two, I know we can work everything out.

In arithmetic, my teacher said, "You must work *through* the problem to find the answer." I believe if we can go back and sift through the rubble, maybe then, we could find what went wrong and fix it. But we don't pull over; we do not go back — the whitewall tires on this fancy yellow car move on. I close my eyes, trying not to let the tears fall. *Daddy,* I whisper inside myself, *we are leaving; where is the melody of our heartbeat and our dance on the moon?* More questions surround me. Where are we going? Who is this strange man? My stomach sours with more grief and unanswered questions. I twirl my shirt tighter. Quick flashes of color and sounds move at random. And even though no one is talking, I can still hear screaming — too much noise in the world. Straight ahead, we ride, in the backseat of this fancy yellow car. No one speaks of these tattered emotions. No one acknowledges the fear and uncertainty. Like stowaways, they hunker down and hide in the insecure places of young hearts and minds. No one can see them, but they are real, sitting right here next to me, staring out into an uncertain world, near the window seat.

Since that last day at our home, I felt sorry for Ms. Lynn. Sorry for whoever hurt her so badly, that she could not understand her own madness, or how to express love and kindness. I would never see her again. Years later, I will hear of John's alcoholism and his early passing. I miss his card tricks and the sound of his laughter.

When healthy singleness is our primary focus and foundation, a healthier family unit can begin. In today's ego-driven culture, broken homes appear to be more common than catching a cold, but the aftermath is perhaps the single most cause of societal dysfunction in the home, community, and the world. Divorce does not only sever the sacred union of the two adults, but it also distorts the identity of the children, leaving them vulnerable to abuse, revictimization, and emotional scattering. The world never looks the same again, and deep within their young hearts and souls, the grief and loss of what was, turn inward, where, oh so silently, the thorns of isolation, self-blame, and shame begin to grow.

Stop, think, and listen. Ask children how they feel, take the time to gently explain, and patiently answer their questions; all of them. Both parents must help them understand it is not their fault. Only then can children regain a sense of balance and emotional wellness to alleviate the lingering fear and anxiety of what they may not be able to fully convey. Bless their future with words and actions that assure them that they are safe and loved; no matter what.

Dixie Court Projects

"Hope is being able to see that there is light despite all of the
darkness." ~*Desmond Tutu*

The clouds are formless. They drift above, looming in the
sky, like dark puffy masses of nothing. Inside this fancy yellow car,
we whisk away to someplace new with a strange man. His skin is
the color of butter pecan ice cream, but it is hard to see his face. As
he drives, I peek at the back of his head. His hair coils with tight
ringlets, dark and sleek. He focuses sternly ahead and never looks
in the backseat. His hands are strong and steady on the wheel,
steering us away. *Who is he?* The question nudges me in my sides. I
tell myself to hush, quiet down.

A cigarette dangles loosely between his thumb and
forefinger. He takes a drag, pulling hard and deep before releasing
a cloud of strong-smelling smoke. It rises, winding through the air.
Michael is fast asleep when the car stops. Linda's head is resting on
Joyce's lap. Leon scans the parking lot before eyeing the stranger in
the front seat. Smoke dances from the silver ashtray. The smell
stings my eyes and burns my nose. I do not let it show. Like staring
or asking questions, that would be impolite. I pretend the smoke
doesn't bother me.

As the strange man steps out of the car, the world seems to
stand at attention. His broad shoulders canopy over a physique I
have only seen in books on Greek mythology in my school library.
He is tall and strapping with a polished appearance. Horizontal
lines run across his forehead, militant and strict. Head high, back
straight: he stands and waits. We do not move until Mom tells us
to. Her face has softened a little.

"Let's go. We are home, children," she says with a heavy sigh
of relief. The sound of her voice is calming. It helps me push away
the puzzle in my mind I have been trying to put together. There are
too many missing pieces to make sense of anything. A green
dumpster sits to the right of a modest sign that reads Dixie Court
Projects.

As we walk into our new home, I turn around briefly. I look
out at the sky. Somehow, I try to collect all I have left behind: my
dad, my books, my doll. There was no time to pack properly. I
cannot let go so easily; they are all a part of me. In this unstable
world, you have no choice but to let go.

"Watch your step, Sandy Patty," Joyce says. The step on the porch is high. She takes my hand and leads me inside. Mama stands, waiting by a long floral blue sofa. It is pretty, and there is no place to sit. New toys and gifts take up all the room. She bought new clothes, a tiny red ball with ten shiny jackstones, a hula-hoop, and dolls for Linda and me. Leon and Michael have a new bike, a big wheel, and water pistols. Wide-eyed, we stare at each other and then back at Mama and Joyce. Sleepwalkers, we float above the ground. It must be a dream. Everything is here, everything brand new — all for us!

Mom's cheeks lift joyfully at our shocked expressions. Seeing our faces, she seems to glow with the kind of happiness only a mother knows. She looks weary, but happy at the same time. It feels like Christmas. My heart tries to leap for joy, but my mind tells me to wait. I can't trust the moment. In disbelief, I want to hold up my hands and try to protect my face. It feels too dreamlike, too wonderful. I remember what happened the last time I felt this way. Staring up from the floor, my own daydream betrayed me. I hold my breath, steadying myself for the strike; the worst hit is the one you don't see. If I see it coming, it will not hurt as much. On guard, I prepare, waiting to make sure the joy I feel is real.

"Thank you, Mama!" Leon says. His voice nearly sounds like a child again. A sense of calm and safety thaws his face — his eyes light up the entire room. My heart warms. I miss that look. Watching him, I smile too, and I try to breathe out the terrible images that creep around the corner of my mind. Michael jumps on his bike; with no time to waste, he beams down the sidewalk. Mama rests on a green recliner near the TV. Linda snuggles with her new doll on the sofa; her legs stretch out in front of her. Joyce gives her juice and coddles her close. I sit on the floor, toss my jacks, and throw the small red rubber ball in the air. I try to pick up more than one jack at a time. I can't. Still, I am determined. Once the twitching in my left- hand settles down, I know I will be able to pick up more. Until then, I will keep trying.

Mommy has a sparkle I have never seen before. She leans forward with her elbows on her thighs, watching us play. Through the screen porch, I hear Michael riding back and forth on the sidewalk. More delightful than the toys are the joy of feeling safe. Having Mama here with us makes the world feel right again. Her presence is like a sun shower at the end of an awful drought. The excitement of it all takes our minds off the strange man inside the house. He is in the back room. He has not said anything to us, and we do not ask about him. We know better. We mind our manners, play with our toys, and try to forget about the memories of the lineup.

Mom pushes herself off the chair after sitting for only a few moments. She takes a pot from beneath the kitchen counter and begins to cook. She starts dinner and tells Joyce to finish because she must get back to work.

"Yes ma'am," Joyce replies respectfully. Driven beyond her obvious exhaustion, she prepares herself for the night shift.

"Where did I put the keys?" she asks. The strange man's voice riddles back from the bedroom. I hear a sharp click. He locks the door. I toss up my ball and pick up another jack, blocking out the unanswered questions. Mom gives Joyce instructions for the night. She takes her purse and heads out the door. I am surprised that mom is going back to work. As if nothing happened, she pulls it together and keeps going. The screen door slams shut as the strange man walks out behind her. The strong smell of his Winston cigarettes lingers long after he is gone. The odor is nauseating.

I put my ball and jackstones to the side and grab my new doll. "Why does Mama have to go? Why does she work all the time?" I ask Joyce, pouting because I wanted her to stay home with us, at least for a little while longer—just until the tremors stop, and the uncertainty goes away.

Patiently, Joyce explains, "She has always worked hard, for as far back as I can remember. She works hard to keep the bills paid." I sit back, holding my doll, listening, but unable to understand fully.

Time moves on, but I am finding it hard to keep up. My mind thinks too much—about everything. I worry about my dad, and hope he knows how much I love him, miss him, and that I need him now more than ever. Something's wrong. I feel it inside. I cannot explain it, but it feels like when you are running and running so fast, scared, nearly out of breath, but when you look down at your feet, you realize you never left the place you were standing.

That's exactly what it feels like.

The Trench

Grief is a natural human response to loss and heartache, but it needs to be seen, heard, and felt if it is going to heal. For when grief is unresolved, it creates a vast crater within, burying us alive from the inside until the day we awaken with nowhere else to go, but up. Awakening, for me, would take a lifetime.

I thought the war was over, but I can still hear it inside my head. I sit on the floor and try to hide inside an invisible shell, hoping no one can see me. Joyce is cooking. She puts a ladle to the side and glances my way. Somehow, she sees me and the disruptive emotions that make me feel out of place.

Lingering questions scatter about the floor around my feet as I play with my metal jackstone set. I try to pick up more jacks, but the clamors and images will not go away. They surround me, chanting the war cry of my parents. I wonder if anyone else can hear the ruckus. It's easier just to sit and stare away from everything.

Joyce is calling me—I see her, but it's hard to hear over the noise or respond on cue. She calls me again, "Sandy Patty, your blouse is wrinkled. Stop twirling your finger inside your clothes." I look down at my hand. My finger is tucked tightly inside my blouse. It happens automatically, without thinking. Joyce begins to call me Ball-e-Bee because of the habit of twisting and balling my shirt or anything in my hand. The habit helps me deal with an inner ache that I cannot explain. The memories run deep and wide, like an endless circle of a massive trench.

"Sandy Patty," Joyce calls me again. "Come here." She pulls me up on her lap and gives me a tight squeeze. Then she does what she has always done. She kisses my forehead and pulls me in even closer, rocking me side to side. I drop my head, believing I am too fat to sit on her lap. "I am right here, and I love you," Joyce says, looking at me as though she can see through me. I lean into the sensation, the feeling of her arms, the comfort of her words; I find a safe harbor in her presence—a place where the vexing voices are not allowed to stay. Still, I often feel ugly and stupid. Maybe Ms. Lynn was right. Inwardly, I blame myself for everything that has gone wrong. I'm not sure why, but I do. She holds me tighter. I tilt my shoulders away and lower my head to my chest, but she does not let me go. Joyce begins to sing silly songs and teach me the words. She tickles me all over until I can hardly breathe. Like a magic potion, the laughter unties the knots and set me free to try and just be a child again. Like medicine, she uses love and laughter to heal the hurt inside.

Days turn into months and before I know it, another year goes by. One by one, Joyce tries to give us the time and attention we need to heal from the past turmoil and our parent's divorce.

Mom comes home late at night from work with the strange man. Joyce does not say much about him. I ignore the terrible smell of his cigarettes. The strong scent stays behind, clinging to the curtains and furniture. I think of my dad. Since moving to Dixie Court projects, I have not seen him. Not even once. Mom continues to work hard year after year. I begin to think that when I grow up, I must work just as hard to make her proud of me. Then, maybe, she will take the time to sit a while and get to know who I am becoming. Until then, a part of me refuses to grow up because my parents are not here. The very ones who gave me life are not here to share it with me.

I attend North Fork Elementary School, and soon, fall behind. Daydreaming makes it nearly impossible to keep up with the rest of the class. I find myself shuffling around the hall of the school, feeling like I do not belong. After school today, mom surprises us. She comes home early with McDonald's Happy Meals. Heaven comes down to earth in the moments she spends at home, although it is short-lived. She tells us she must get back to work. I waited for her to notice Linda's and my new hairdos. Joyce spent hours washing and braiding our hair. The colorful bows and barrettes match our dresses—Joyce is fussy about that. Mom tells Joyce to lock the door behind her. She does not notice. After a while, I stop expecting her to. The smell of her perfume lingers in the air.

"Sandy Patty, please stop balling up your dress, and stop sucking your tongue," Joyce says. I look down at my hands and then back at her. Again, I hadn't noticed. It seems I lag in time, back to another state of mind whenever my mom is near.

After schoolwork, Joyce begins to clean the house. I think cleanliness is an obsession for her. Her eyes look tired like she has not been sleeping well. Still, her voice fills the small apartment with the melody of a lively song. She sweeps the floor and sings. With each new day, Joyce seems to become more beautiful, more kind, more patient, and more of everything I want to be when I grow up.

"No matter what, you must trust," Joyce reassures us,

teaching us that faith is an invisible thing—something intangible. Her faith seems to be the only thing that never changes and the very source of her beauty. She has a lesson to teach, even when she is cooking and doing chores. "Everything will be all right," she says with steadfast confidence.

"Can I help you in the kitchen?" I ask, wanting to be with her every moment I can. I am not sure when I became so clingy. For that matter, I am not sure when I became so afraid of being alone, afraid of the dark, and afraid of the noise.

"Thank you, Sandy Patty. Of course, you can help. You can put the napkins on the table for dinner." I work hard to make sure the napkins are just right. Straight with no wrinkles, the corners must all face the same direction, I tell myself. I stand next to Joyce to see what I can do next. "It's time for dinner, wash up. "Joyce says. In his room, Leon fidgets and grumbles at a project. It consumes much of his time. He creates a lamp out of an old Budweiser beer can. His hands fumble with wires that sprout out the top of the tab. After a few moments, he connects them to a light bulb and waits. Impressed with Leon's creativity, Joyce applauds his design. I am amazed that he even thought to make a lamp in the first place. In an ingenious way, he recycles the beer can to make something useful of it. I think it's really neat.

"It does not work!" Leon grumbles. Deep wrinkles swell on his forehead as his fingers wrestle with the wires until he finally connects the bulb.

"Leon, you did a good job. You made a lamp. It looks good!" Joyce says with a smile.

"Yes, but it does not work!" Leon spits the words through his teeth. His jaw clenches. A mist of angry tension hovers around him.

"It's okay, Leon, you will make it work. Keep at it, and you will get it to work." Joyce encourages Leon and calls us over to the table to eat. Before we can bless the food, Leon throws French fries across the kitchen table and knocks over his chair. His temper goes from zero to a hundred in a split second. We jump up and step back, away from the table. Joyce moves in. She stretches out one arm to guard us, and the other towards Leon. He unhinges. "Leon, calm down!" Joyce tells him. "I know you are hurting, but you can't hurt others because of it."

"I don't care!" Leon screams. His aggression seems to appear out of nowhere, but it has been building for years. It was in his eyes before we moved that last time—before the divorce, before the

Lineup, before the disappointment of waiting for a father that does not come home, before he jumped and waited for arms to catch his fall; the signs were all there. Standing around the kitchen table, we watch him lose it. He shadowboxes, moving his arms defensively against the air. He looks as if he is carrying a load of bricks on his back. Joyce reaches out to him. Her face mirrors the sadness in his eyes. She tries to soothe him, but the wounds of rejection are unreasonable. He seems to stand outside of himself, looking in, unsure.

After a few more angry huffs, he stomps into the bedroom.

"I want Mama." When the angry spell finally breaks, he cries. Michael, Linda, and I wait by the doorway. "I'm sorry, Joyce." His words fall sad and desperate. "I didn't mean it. I am sorry, sis." Anger and shame sweep beneath his apology. He withdraws to a place it seems no one else is permitted to go. Mom and Dad are our world. The loss of connectivity, the breakdown of our family, seems to leave Leon in a perpetual state of grief and anger. Leon drops his head in his hands. Joyce is silent at first. She seems to know she cannot solve a problem that she did not cause, but she helps him cope with his manic emotions.

"Leon, I understand how you feel," Joyce says rubbing his back. Her eyes offer the respect and validation he craves. "I have been there too; there is nothing we can do except pray and trust in God. I know you want Mama and I know you miss Daddy. I understand, but they are not here; I am here. We must trust God. I love you, and I am right here with you." She puts her arms around him as he breaks and cries. Tears fill our eyes as we watch from the hallway. Sniffling, I wipe my nose and try to be strong like Joyce. It's not working. I want to make it better, to fix it; I cry because I cannot fix it. So, I look at his lamp. Abandoned on top of the dresser, it lays on its side; wires sprawl out at random. He must have tried to connect it at least a hundred times. Perhaps it is what triggered the outburst—an old beer can, some wires, and a light bulb. It is hard to find your way in the dark, especially when you are trying to find your place in the world. That's what it feels like since before mom and dad split up—just kind of dark and uncertain. Joyce listens and flows at our pace to help us cope, in our own way, and at our own time. Like a sweet nightingale, she sings us to sleep.

Time is a peculiar thing. It seems to move in circles, and like a boomerang, it comes back to the place where we tossed it away, offering the chance to begin again if we are ready to learn the lesson that it wants to teach. Being teachable is the key to new beginnings. But all too often, unresolved pain and grief will keep us defensive and stuck, unable to redeem the precious gift of time, and live in the present; the here and now. May God help us to be teachable and seek to heal our families from grief and trauma. Every day, this will be a conscious and purposeful process.

The Bully Slayer

"If there are no heroes to save you, then you be the hero."
~*Denpa Kyoshi*

A gentle breeze blows by the porch as we sit with Joyce, watching the winter turn to spring. A butterfly flutters by the ivy-covered pillar that separates our home from the neighbors. I wonder if Mary will come by and visit as well. She lives in the apartment behind us with her mother and older brother. A few days ago, Joyce took us over by Mary's mother's apartment and let us play on the grass. Mary reminds me of warm apple pie because she is cute and sweet. About a foot taller than me, Mary likes to play all the same games that I do. She taught Linda and me new clapping songs last week. "Miss Mary Mac" and "The Slide" are fun, but the best one is "Rockin' Robin." It is something about the words and the rhythm that makes me feel like I can fly:

"He rocks in the treetops all day long
Hoppin' and a-boppin' and singing his song
All the little birdies on Jaybird Street
Love to hear the robin go tweet. Rockin Robin…"

Mary can clap faster than anyone else I know. Her hands move like a hummingbird when we play. I can't keep up. *One day, I will be able to play the game without missing a beat*, I think to myself.

After riding up and down the sidewalk, Michael parks his bike on the side of the porch and sits with us a while. I look at him and shake my head. That boy cannot sit still for more than five minutes, six minutes' tops. The day is more peaceful than it is quiet. It fills with the usual noises of the world: the chatter of passersby, the occasional barking dog, and the sound of stillness inside. I breathe them all in. Content to simply be together, we relax and enjoy the gift of a new day.

"How are you doing, Ms. Jimmie Lee?" Joyce asks our next-door neighbor as she steps one foot out of her screen porch door.

"Just fine Baby. Y'all all right?"

"Yes, ma'am. Thank you." Joyce answers politely. Ms. Jimmie Lee is the neighborhood watch person. If something is happening in the neighborhood, no matter the time, she seems to know. She gives the playback of the day, adding how the lives of the characters from her TV stories *As the World Turns* collide with the ones here in the Dixie Court Projects. I roll my ball and jacks in my hands, staring out from the porch.

"How's ya' mama?" Ms. Jimmie Lee asks, stepping the other foot onto the porch.

"She is fine…Ms. Jimmie Lee." Joyce says, slowing her speech to a sudden halt. We hold in a chuckle at the sight of Ms. Jimmie Lee's slip hanging halfway off her hips. Michael looks away bashfully. At first, Leon seems entranced at the sight, but then turns away, and drops his head. I smile at him, thinking about how he finally got his lamp to work. Joyce told him not to give up. He listened—he did it. It works perfectly now.

As we sit in the garden of each other's company, I notice how the sky moves with a vibrant shade of blue. The distant sound of the ice cream truck captures Linda's attention, along with the other children in the neighborhood. The tune "It's a Small World After All" blares magnetically from the streets.

"Joyce, may we please get some ice cream?" I ask.

"Yes. Hurry; go stop him before he drives away." Joyce says, looking over the clearing where the sidewalk meets the road. She runs inside. "I will be right there," she says. Joyce rarely ever says no.

"Ice cream, Ice cream!" We yell rushing toward the ice cream truck. I wait for Joyce near the side of the road. The day feels magical as I swing Linda's hand in mine. Linda gets a rainbow pop with bubble gum at the bottom; Michael and I get éclairs—they are our favorite ice-cream. I like chocolate, and he loves strawberry. Leon cannot decide. He stares at the pictures on the side of the truck with his hand on his chin.

We move to the melody, waiting for him to make up his mind. After a few minutes, he finally decides to get an ice cream sandwich. Before we get back on the porch, Michael is holding his ice cream stick.

"What happened to your ice cream?" I ask, still licking mine.

"I ate it," he replies with a silly grin. He plops the stick in his mouth and chews on it. I shake my head at him. Up ahead in the distance, I notice Dennis coming up the sidewalk near our porch. We are invisible to him now. He makes no eye contact. When he sees Joyce, he walks on the grass to the other side to avoid her. He swiftly moves on across the courtyard. Dennis the Menace we called him. A portly teen, he walked around as if he owned the neighborhood. He bullied us after school like it was a part-time job. He even shoved Michael to the ground and dared him to get up. But that all changed the day I came home from school crying.

It happened nearly a year ago. Joyce had noticed my face the moment I walked through the door. "What's the matter, Sandra?" Joyce uses my proper name with a firm tone when she notices something wrong. Sniffling, I had told her that Dennis touched my butt and pushed me down. I dropped my papers and ran home. "Where is he?" she had said. Her light skin turned an unusual shade of red. Joyce ramped her feet into her flip-flops and took off like a fireball out the door.

"Show me who he is!" Joyce simmered on the edge of the sidewalk. I have never seen her that upset. Like a fire crackling in a fireplace; contained, but just as hot. Standing outside, I pointed down the sidewalk where Dennis stood casting his haughty shadow over a group of boys.

"Is that him?" she asked.

"Yes. That is him, right over there with the red-striped shirt."

Joyce bolted down the sidewalk towards him; Leon, Michael, Linda and I followed a stride behind. At first, I feel queasy; confrontations bring back too many bad memories, but then, after that moment, I stood there — unafraid.

Fearlessly, Joyce ran right up to his face. In weight, he was twice her size. She stopped close enough for him to feel her breath on his broad, bullish snout. Eye to eye, she warned him. "You better not ever touch my sister again!" She moved toward him with every word; her head cocked to the side. Poised, she seems to have waited for him to give her a reason to open fire. Chest to chest, she readied her fists. My siblings and I stood next to her; astounded by her lack of fear.

A crowd quickly formed. Dennis made his move. He inched back and took a swing. Joyce weaved to the side. With her shoulder down, and head up high, she invited the next punch. He hooked the air. Joyce countered with a hard right to his face, followed by an underhanded left below his waist. As he buckled under, she pushed him over.

"Now you know what it feels like to get pushed around," she said with one breath, and with the next, she hit him again. The force of the blow lifted his shirt. His flabby belly shook over his belt. The fight incited the crowd that steadily grew. Dennis' gang scoffed, but they all knew to stay back.

Joyce continued to jab with a driving stagger. *She fights like a guy*, I thought to myself. The circle of onlookers rippled out, spreading wider as Joyce drove into him. She struck left and right until he broke away and backed off. The crowd heckled and shouted about how Dennis got beat up by a girl. His jaw swelled like a puffer fish. Unflinching, Joyce held her position. Calm, but still flammable, she did not blink, nor did she say another word to him. The message was clear. Dennis retreated; his wounded ego hurled threats from a distance. Joyce flared and started to sprint after him, but he high-tailed it and ran farther away. Though the fight was over, a fire still burned inside her. Her chest moved up and down, like a flame refusing to burn out.

In that instance, I saw the reflection of our Mom. The same fury and unquenchable energy flowed through her. "Let's go." Joyce had said with her arms stretched out behind us. She squinted down the path towards the direction Dennis vanished. *This is my sister,* I thought to myself. *The bully-slayer is my sister!* The same girl who sings lullabies in the night hides a fire inside, and I had never known before. We strutted proudly back to the porch, a foot taller than when we left. A new sense of confidence and self-worth redefined my view of the world and my place in it because she fought for it. She took back our sense of safety, handed it to us, and dared anyone in the neighborhood to try and take it again. Dennis never bothered us from that time on, nor did anyone else in the area.

Today, as I watch Dennis walk across the grass, I imagine, he will never forget the lesson my sister taught that day. The lesson of the Bully Slayer: "Keep your hands to yourself. "

God made human beings to need relationships, attachment, and security. When we feel safe and protected, the connection grows, bonding us to a sacred love, unbreakable and timeless.

In our world, beyond words, life, and time, Joyce is that sacred love. Her selflessness and enduring life lessons of love and faith would remain steadfastly in place throughout our life.

May I Have this Dance?

"Everything in the universe has rhythm. Everything dances." ~ Maya Angelou

The weekend comes, and we sit together on the floor to watch a movie. The creature feature show is coming on tonight. After watching *The Blob* last night, I conclude I'd much rather watch Popeye the Sailor or the Three Stooges. The sight of people and animals being eaten alive by a flesh-eating alien mass of goo has me completely paranoid. I like to laugh—I have seen more than enough scary stuff in my life. Joyce puts a thick blanket on the floor for us to sit and watch the show. I pull the blanket up to my chin when the show begins. The voice of Vincent Price is spine-chilling. I snuggle closer to Joyce.

"Sandy Patty, you okay?" Not wanting to ruin it for everyone, I don't answer. After a few moments, she gets up unexpectedly and puts her hands out towards us. "Who wants to dance?" she asks. I look at her as if I am missing something. "May I have this dance?" Joyce asks again, holding her palms open.

"Yes! I want to dance!" Linda springs to her feet and takes Joyce by the hands. The blanket falls into my lap. Looking up at Joyce, I forget to be afraid of anything. She begins to teach us how to dance the waltz.

"Follow my lead," Joyce instructs. "Head high, shoulders down, hand in hand we step one, two, and three, one two and three..." She spins Linda around.

"My turn," Michael says, looking like he needs to take a nap since eating dinner. Joyce turns to him and pairs us together, Leon with Linda, Michael with me. She moves the blanket off the floor and turns off the TV.

"Boys always take the lead; girls put one arm around his shoulder and your hand in his hand." Linda and I are excited to learn the waltz. Leon and Michael stand square-footed in the middle of the living room. Michael is full of energy, but Leon looks as if he just got off a bus and stepped into a foreign country; we have never danced the waltz before.

The living room turns into a ballroom. Our imagination creates the lighting effects and the elegant ball gowns that flow with every spin. Michael starts acting goofier than usual, making up his own moves, which are embarrassingly less than graceful. I change partners. I walk up to Joyce, and she takes my hand.

"Do you want to lead, or would you like me to lead?" she asks.

"I want you to lead," I reply, smiling — partly because I feel shy, but mostly because she asks me the question. In this seen and not heard culture, no one asks, everyone tells you what to do. The question, in some way, makes me feel special; I have a voice, an opinion. She bows then rise, puts her hand around my waist, and cups her hand in mine.

"Follow my feet, and I will lead. One, two, three, and one, two, three." I look down. "Don't forget to keep your chin up. Don't look down," Joyce says, before spinning me around again. Then, she brings me in and dips me back. For the first time in a long time, I don't feel clumsy.

One by one, Joyce turns us, dips us, and brings us back up again. She begins to sing as we sway and spin:

> "I know you
> I walked with you once upon a dream
> I know you
> The gleam in your eyes is so familiar a gleam
> Yet I know it's true
> That visions are seldom all they seem
> But if I know you, I know what you'll do.
> You love me at once
> The way you did once, upon a dream."

She says the song is from a Disney movie she loves called *Sleeping Beauty*. Joyce sings the tune, we change partners, and the dancing starts all over again.

"How did you learn to dance the waltz?" I ask.

"Watching the Lawrence Welk show on TV." We float on air. Dizzy, we spin. She blesses us with the gift of movement and dance, and everything feels new. The dance movement begins to feel like therapy. A melodious baptism begins in my spirit. Open-mouthed and carefree, Linda takes another turn. Joyce takes her and dips her close to the ground. Linda free-falls backward, throwing her arms over her head. She laughs contagiously. There is no room for sadness here. Joyce makes it clear we are loved, and in our tiny corner of the universe, our lives fill with the magic and wonder of a waltz; until, we begin to dream again.

Living Dolls

September 24, 1974

Mom and the strange man get married today. His name is Robert. He is a military man, a merchant seaman in the Navy; the captain of his ship. He does not smile or laugh or play. It must be against some government policy. And I don't think he likes kids very much. He hardly talks to us when he is home on furlough. But one thing I know for sure: he likes guns. He seems to have guns of every shape and size. Joyce says he keeps most of them under the bed. Long ones, short ones, and some in-between. Guns scare me, and so does the way he stares my way, out of the corner of his eye. But at least Mom looks more at ease. In the passing moments when Mama is home, she looks happier, less stressed. Joyce says mom is finally going to take some time off work. I smile when she tells me the news. Robert will be on active duty in Spain and Mom will fly out on Saturday. I must get a kiss before she leaves. Spain is so far away.

I play with my jackstones on the floor. I can pick up five now without dropping the ball. With practice, I am getting better. Joyce gets her tin of barrettes and bows.

"Linda, it's time to get your hair braided." Joyce fluffs pillows on the floor. Linda sits between Joyce's knees, watching *Captain Kangaroo* and *Mr. Rogers' Neighborhood*. I get excited because my favorite cartoon is coming on soon; the *Underdog* show. *Underdog* makes me want to be a superhero. Sitting on the floor near Joyce's feet, I hum the theme song and sing the chorus: "There's no need to fear, Underdog is here!" The show makes me believe that anyone, no matter how small or clumsy, can do remarkable things.

Joyce puts bows on the ends of Linda's hair while Simon Bar Sinister is putting phony phone booths around the city to try and trick Underdog. Simon is a power-crazed schemer who tries everything to destroy Shoeshine Boy—the innocent, law-abiding puppy whose secret identity was an indestructible hero.

"Come on, Sandy Patty," Joyce calls. "It's your turn. Time to get your hair braided." I look at Linda. Her head lays limp against Joyce's inner thigh. Joyce picks her up and stretches her out on the couch. Pink and white bows lay across her forehead. She is sound asleep. I hop on top of the pillow, smelling the blue bergamot pomade Joyce uses to oil our hair. It smells of soft perfume.

I rest my head on Joyce's thigh and try to stay awake long

enough to see the end of the Underdog adventure. It seems every adventure involves a phone booth. There must be something with phone booths and sudden superpowers: you go in normal and come out with superhuman strength. The show captivates my imagination. Sweet Polly Purebred, Shoeshine Boy's sweetheart, uses her damsel in distress voice to call Underdog. He hears her pleas and comes to her rescue. I keep watching, and braid after braid, Joyce styles my hair. Her hands are gentle, and it gets harder to keep my eyes open. By the end of the adventure, Underdog saves the day again. I laugh when he crashes into a tall building. He is so clumsy, but that's one of the things I love about him. Joyce finishes my hair, and I ask her if we can have a puppy. I want to name it Underdog.

"When you are responsible enough to take care of a puppy, we will ask Mom, okay?"

I smile. "Okay."

It's getting dark outside. Joyce walks to the screen porch and tells Leon and Michael to come inside the house. Linda is still fast asleep. Leon runs his bath. Michael plays the dual roles of Chief and Indians in his room. Joyce sits on the green recliner in front of the television. She tells me it is almost time for the *Hee Haw* show. Only she and I watch the show together. It is our special time to sing out loud and act our silliest. *Hee Haw* made me fall in love with country music. The silly sketches made us laugh until tears filled our eyes. Joyce taught me the words. Now, I know them by heart. We sing at the top of our lungs every time the skit comes on:

> *"Where, oh where are you tonight.*
> *Why did you leave me here all alone?*
> *I searched the world over and I thought I found true love.*
> *You met another and PFFT! You were gone!"*

We spit raspberries at the end of the chorus. Our eyes hold fast to each other as we topple over in laughter. The green recliner becomes a garden where seeds of laughter, joy, music, and acceptance grow deep roots. Giddy and free, we blow into our hands, pretending they were old moonshine jugs. We sing all the *Hee Haw* songs until the show is over. It is our bonding ritual. The love we share is unbreakable.

While Mom boards a plane for Madrid, Spain to spend time with Robert, Joyce changes the living room around again, putting the couch next to the front window. It makes the place look new each time she rearranges the furniture. Chores, homework, dinner, and now instead of watching TV, Joyce reads to us and prepares to tell us another story.

We climb on the couch together and listen. Joyce talks to us about the days before we were born, when Mom and Dad worked in Tampa. She speaks of it as though it was yesterday. She talks about days gone by, telling us that in the sixties, many children stayed home alone while their parents earned a living. Children had to fend for themselves. The times were tough, and the children had to be strong.

"I had a doll to keep me company, and sometimes when it was too quiet in the house, I watched TV," Joyce said she had to grow up fast, from an early age.

She skipped a grade in school because she studied hard and long in the lonely hours. Joyce tells us about Grandma Rachel, Sunday school in Tampa, and my favorite story of all, the story of God.

"With God, all things are possible. If you believe, you will see miracles. The greatest miracles aren't always found inside church buildings but inside your heart." Joyce explains and helps us understand the context of her words by telling stories, incredible stories of a supernatural world. I see the pictures in my mind. Though I do not understand it all, I want to believe. Her voice is like a song; it rises and falls as she speaks. She tells us how she would sit in Sunday school with her Bible on her lap and study the scriptures. In my mind, I can see her wearing the prettiest polka-dot dress.

Joyce opens the Bible and begins to tell us about a madman. A story in the book of Exodus:

"It looked impossible for the children of Israel. Caught between the ocean and pharaohs army; there was nowhere else to run." Joyce sits on the edge of the sofa, moving her arms like water. I can almost feel the gust from the sea as she tells us the story of Moses and Pharaoh.

"What happened next?" I ask. Our faces are full of anticipation.

"The breath of God parts the sea. Moses told Pharaoh to let God's people go, but he did not listen."

Joyce takes us to other worlds with her stories; other dimensions where there are no impossibilities. She makes us believe there is so much more to life than what we have seen. I imagine Joyce had to create a world of her own when she was younger; a safe place not built with wood or stone, but with walls of faith, prayer, and songs that she now shares with us. It is an amazing gift; more valuable than the toys we received when we first moved to Dixie Court. Joyce teaches us to build our life, in the same way, using the elements of faith and love. I trust her safe, peaceful world. Over the years, it has been our refuge and saving grace.

A gentle light shines in Joyce's eyes as she shifts the conversation. She begins to talk about Leon. She dotes on him with her words as she recalls the year of his birth.

"I can still remember the day you were born," she says to him. He listens and pushes out a chuckle as she goes on and on about when he was younger.

Joyce tells us of the day Leon came home from the hospital. Her soft manner is more like a surrogate mother: changing diapers, helping with meals, cleaning up spills. The responsibilities are heavy. She tells us about our other siblings we never knew, infants who lived for only a day or two before passing away. Born prematurely, they never left the hospital.

"Then Michael was born," she says. Michael smiles when Joyce mentions how happy Mom was that Leon had a playmate. Joyce looks up with her hands clasped together and smiles.

"I prayed for a sister, and during a thunderstorm in Tampa, you came." Joyce's eyes fall on me, covering me with a sense of purpose. Then she looks at Linda and continues down memory lane.

"A year and a half later, Mama had you, Peanut. Then I had two sisters and two brothers to love and take care of." Like living dolls, we have replaced the ones from her short childhood—a childhood shrouded in secrets she had yet to share. Joyce strokes Linda's hair and turns her eyes upward.

As we sit and listen, I notice how tired Joyce looks. She tries hard to keep it all together, but with Mom so far away, the load is heavier. Through each new day and circumstance, she carries on. But something is peculiar in her face. Joyce has a look about her; I had seen that same weariness in Mom's eyes when we lived in Tampa. Something is hiding behind her glance, like a secret you cannot tell.

"Joyce, are you feeling all right?" I ask. She does not answer. "Joyce...?" I whisper, rubbing her knee. Then she looks at me with a distant smile.

"Are you okay sis?" Leon asks, sitting up straighter.

"I'm okay; I was thinking about Mom and Dad when we lived in Tampa before we moved here. So much has happened, but I don't want you to worry about all that." Joyce leans back on the couch. She seems to lock away something she could not say, something she felt we were too young to know. That's just her way: to protect us, to shield us, just as she did during the thunderstorms in Tampa. Linda cradles her doll and sits quietly listening. My finger begins to twirl inside of my shirt.

"Joyce, would you sing us a song?" I ask, knowing that the melody will make any sad memories fall back to sleep.

"Sure, Sandy Patty." She looks up and sings:

> *"Climb every mountain, search high and low,*
> *Follow every byway, every path you know.*
> *Climb every mountain ford every stream*
> *Follow every rainbow, till you find your dream.*
> *A dream that will need, all the love you can give,*
> *Every day of your life for as long as you live*
> *Climb every mountain,*
> *Ford every stream,*
> *Follow every rainbow, till you find your dream."*

Joyce's high soprano voice is beautiful. As she sings, a steady resolve resonates between each note. I feel it down deep, capturing my soul. In every line and space, there are traces of her faith that leads us to her truth. A truth that exists beyond the words of her songs and what our human eyes can see. A belief in a God that works mysteriously; I believe it. A truth that we would need to survive the unimaginable course set for our lives. There was a dark storm forming in the distance. It is headed straight for us.

After she sings, Joyce says God has a purpose for everything we go through in life.

"I like that song, Joyce," I say, surrendering to the freedom of trusting in an all-powerful God. Inwardly, I remain unsure. Blind to the deeper meaning of faith, I see only her love for us. I hear only the beautiful melodies.

"That song is from *The Sound of Music*." She tells us before busying herself around the house.

"We can watch it together when it comes on again," she says. I smile, thinking that you can search for a dream, climb a mountain, and follow a rainbow. I can't imagine where you would begin to do such amazing things. It all sounds like a great adventure.

Through the years, Joyce stories and songs decorate our lives with the wonder and mystery of faith in Christ. We listen, we grow, we believe. We are her living dolls. She dresses us up in spiritual clothing, like the armor of a soldier where faith is a shield, prayer a sharp sword, and the Word of God, an impenetrable breastplate that no fiery dart can penetrate. She girds a great truth inside us. At the time, we could not know or understand that her faith, stories, and songs were all an arsenal of weapons; preparing us for a fateful journey, yet to come. A journey that would test everything we were taught to know and believe.

My heart smiles when I remember the angelic spirit God sent before us; to welcome us, to care for us, and to teach us of the greatest love of all. The hardest lessons were yet to come; nevertheless, God's grace is sufficient to heal the brokenhearted. His promise is that He will never leave us nor forsake. He said it beforehand because He knew in this life, we will often feel forsaken. To this day, I must remind myself, encourage myself to never forget: "The just must live by faith" (Romans 1:17).

Bacon Grease

"I cannot think of any need in childhood as strong as the need for a father's protection." ~*Sigmund Freud*

We've heard nothing from our father; maybe he will come by tomorrow. I think it's only been a few days, but the world feels a little lonelier since Mom went away to Spain. I hope she is all right. I have no idea how Joyce does it all by herself. She keeps it all together and tells us that Mom is due to arrive home by next weekend. Maybe we will get to go to the movie theater with her when her plane lands. She said we could go when she gets back.

The worse scars are the ones we can't see.

Joyce looks more tired today; she reminds me of Mom—strong and confident, yet worn-down. Like my favorite cartoon, Underdog, I imagine she must have some magical phone booth she visits when no one is looking. Still, I can tell something is troubling her. *I will surprise her with breakfast*, I think to myself. That will make it better. No matter what is making her look so sad, a delicious meal usually helps. Joyce is always cooking and cleaning. This will be my way of taking care of her for once: breakfast in bed. She will be so surprised when I wake her up with eggs, bacon, toast, and a glass of orange juice. Excited, I get up early and prepare.

I hurry; if she gets up before breakfast is ready, it will spoil the surprise. I tiptoe to the kitchen. As I peer through the olive-green curtain, I see no sign of the dawn breaking. I have time. The surprise must be just right. I reach under the counter and take out the frying pan, and quietly open the cabinets and drawers. After turning on the front burner and putting the pan on top, I take a pack of bacon out of the refrigerator. One eye on the stove and the other in the hallway, I tell myself to hurry. I can't help but smile, imagining how happy she will be that I made her a special breakfast. The bacon begins to sizzle noisily in the frying pan. I hope she does not hear it. I am seven years old, but I feel like a big girl. Through the years, watching Mama and Joyce cook has made me want to cook every day. I will make her proud. Thrilled, I hum a quiet tune, looking for the salt and pepper to season the eggs. As I open the cabinet, I see the containers.

After cracking the eggs, I push a chair to the base of the stove. I put one knee on the counter and my other foot on the chair.

I grab the salt and place it on the side of the counter, and then I get the pepper. As I come down off the chair, the edge of my left-hand hits the handle of the frying pan. The hot bacon grease spills over the top of my hand. Only then, right at that moment, did I understand why Mom and Joyce turn the handle of the pan inward, away from the front of the stove. The hot bacon grease sears my skin. I scream, falling over the chair and onto the floor. "Mommy!"

The pain is unreal, and I believe I'll never be able to write or use my left hand again. Joyce runs into the kitchen and lifts me off the floor. She is saying something to me, but I cannot hear her. I do not feel her arms around me as she lays me on the couch. She kneels next to me, looking at my hand, and then runs to the kitchen. She returns with ice and a cool, wet cloth. When Joyce puts the ice on my hand, my screams turn into frantic wails. "Mommy!" That's all I can remember saying.

Joyce hold me, rocking back and forth. "I'm sorry, Sandra. Mom is still in Spain. She won't be home for another week." My right-hand squeezes tighter around my left wrist. She pats my right hand gently. "It's okay. It's okay," she whispers. "I am here." She strokes my head and lets me cry until the ice begins to numb the pain. Hours pass and Joyce stays close to me, putting a white cream on the burnt areas. It cools the burn, but it doesn't stop the heckling. Voices in my head wake up, accusing me of being stupid and clumsy. They jeer and say *You big, fat, clumsy loser; you can never do anything right.* I bury my face in the pillow on the couch. I ruined the surprise.

When I finally gather the courage to look at my hand, I see that the skin looks raw—reddish brown blisters speckle across white flesh. The bacon grease burned off the top brown layer of my skin. Blinking, I look up at Joyce.

"You will be all right. Everything will be okay. You must learn to use your right hand until your left hand heals." She never blames me for making a mess of the kitchen or forbids me to cook again.

"I wanted to surprise you with breakfast," I sob pitifully. "Sorry, I ruined it. I ruined your surprise."

"You tried to do something good. That's what matters. Now, you will get better; your hand and your cooking will get better. Give yourself time to grow." The last thing I remember is Joyce humming a slow melody. I lean into her and fall asleep.

Mom gets home on schedule from Spain. She looks happy

until she sees my hand. Joyce tells her what happened.

"What were you thinking, child?" She asks with a painful look on her face. I look up at her not knowing what to say, how to respond. I smile, happy she is home safe. She drops next to me, examines my hand, and shakes her head. She searches in her drawer and pulls out a white glove. She tells Joyce she did well by putting the cream on the grease burn.

She tells me I must wear the white glove on my hand until it heals completely. "The glove will keep the wound from becoming infected when you go back to school."

"Yes, ma'am," I reply, but I don't want to wear the white glove outside of the house. I feel awkward enough when I go to school. Now, I am sure to get picked on by the other students. I can already hear the jokes from my classmates: A white glove on a chubby black girl who uses the wrong hand to write with, and who is prone to tripping over her own two feet. I dread going back to school.

When I return to school the next week, I find that Joyce was right; it wasn't so bad. I must learn to use my right hand now, but my handwriting looks like scribble-scrabble. Balled up papers are scattered atop my desk. If I cannot understand what I wrote, how in the world will my teacher understand it? Thankfully, the teacher gives me extra time to catch up with my classwork, but it is hard to think and focus. Worse than the burn on my hand is the ache of missing my dad. I have not seen him since we moved to Dixie Court. I raise my hand for permission to go to the restroom. I only pretend I need to go; just to be alone.

In the bathroom, I slide the latch on the stall and wait until no one else is there. When it is completely quiet, I say a silent prayer. "God bless my daddy and keep him safe. In Jesus' name, amen." I whisper the words out, like sending a secret telegram. I tell myself that God will deliver the message for me, and Dad will come to see us soon. I have learned to whisper prayers from listening to my Mom when she is driving in the car and Joyce when she is working around the house. On the way back to class, I count the spots on the floor. I don't know why. I guess it takes my mind off other things.

As I take my seat, I remember what Joyce told me. *All things are possible if you believe.* I settle into the belief that I will see my dad soon. I hurry to copy the words on the blackboard before class is over, but my right hand is uncooperative. A tune plays in my head from days of being home after the bacon grease accident. While healing, I watched *The Mary Tyler Moore Show*. Mary is smart, funny and very pretty. Sitting at my desk, I hum the tune. The song is catchy and reminds me of Joyce; a girl *"who turns the world on with a smile and takes a nothing day, and suddenly makes it all seem worthwhile."* At the end of the show, Mary spins around and throws her hat way up into the air. Like worries in the wind, the hat lifts away. Lost in a daydream, I ball up another piece of paper.

I am somewhere out there with Mary, turning around in a circle on a crowded Minnesota intersection, tossing all my worries away.

Wheat and Tares

My mom comes home early today with Robert. He is on furlough for a few days, and our home smells like him again. During his stay, he does not say much. There must be some classified military rule for consorting with children. As he walks by, the authoritarian click under his shiny black heels makes words unnecessary. We take heed and stay in our place. The tip of his cigarette glows between his fingers while a trail of smoke follows him to the room. The walls vibrate when he shuts the door, and I exhale, wondering how old he is. *Mom could pass for his daughter,* I think to myself. Maybe it is the saltwater or the sea air, or perhaps, it's the smoking that causes his skin to look so scaly and cracked. Mama seems happier now, and when she is happy, our world seems happier too.

Oddly, Joyce is not home yet. We sit on the floor and watch *Fat Albert and the Cosby Kids.* Where is Joyce, my mind wonders? I get up and look out of the front window. Mom and Robert are in the room. I hear their slurs through the thin drywall. I wait for the answers to nudging questions that tell me something's wrong. When Joyce finally gets home, she looks as if she has a tummy ache, and her face is sad and drawn. She doesn't say what happened. She knocks at Mom's bedroom door, walks inside, and closes it. After a few moments, Joyce comes out of the room, goes back outside, and stops to talk to a young man. It is Mary's brother. I remember waiting for her to get back inside the house, worried about the agitated look on her face. When Joyce comes back inside, she sits on the couch and wraps her arms around herself, as if she is protecting a precious gift.

"Joyce, are you okay?" I ask. She rocks back and forth as if caught in an invisible storm. I move closer to her. Quiet, I wait for her to speak. I pick at my nails and glance her way every so often just in case she is ready to say something to me. I was not ready for the news; none of us were.

She takes my hand and only stares at first. She wraps her arms around me, still silent, almost shaking. When she finally speaks, her words are short. "I love you, Sandra." She has said those words to me at least a million times, but right at this moment, the three words seem to take on a different meaning. Like the way she braids my hair; she entwines each word tightly together. I try to understand the seriousness of her tone, her touch, but I cannot. My stomach begins to hurt, afraid—I twirl my shirt and wait for answers. Is someone hurting her? Did something happen while she was in school? Joyce means the world to us, and now, the fear has returned.

"I love you, too," I tell her, waiting to hear the reason that would explain the worried look on her face. That day, she walked away without another word.

Life has a way of sneaking up on you. All this time, I never realized it. All while Joyce is teaching us, caring for us, and growing us up, she is becoming a woman herself. It happens in the next few weeks. Joyce takes on a new role. Mom and Robert drive her to the Broward County Court House and sign the consent for her to marry. At the age of 16, Joyce marries, and several months later, she becomes a mother. When Joyce moves away from Dixie Court to begin a new life, she leaves seeds behind; seeds of stories, songs, discipline, and faith deep in the soil of our young hearts. For years, she covered them with warmth and love to be sure they take root.

Some time ago, I remembered hearing the parable of the tares and the wheat: good seed struggling to grow in the same garden with harsh, relentless weeds. During that time, I was too young to grasp God's concept of gardening; the idea that something or *someone* could appear to be good, caring, even "righteous" yet the whole time, be wicked.

Our world is about to shift again.

The storms are coming, preparing to water every seed.

This was a hard lesson to understand.

Jeremiah 17:9 says, "The heart is deceitful above all things and beyond cure—who can understand it?" We can spend a lifetime trying to understand why terrible things happen, or we can let go, surrender, and trust. God's sovereign will and permissive will is not easily understood. He alone controls time and has the answers to all of the questions of why. The answers come, only when the harvest is ripe. And so, there are some things we must experience before we can fully understand the meaning and the reasons why.

Monster on 24ᵗʰ Street

There are forbidden places no one should go, things no one should touch; boundaries set before the dawn of time—no one should cross. When we cross these lines, the sacredness of life gets lost or worst, redefined. For God, has said, "Thou shalt not," and when we forsake His laws, terrible things can happen; unspeakable things.

1975

Our world moves like an earthquake. The devastating aftershocks come subtly and will last for years to come. Joyce moves to Sunny Reach Acres, off 18th Avenue and Broward Boulevard. An apartment complex not two miles from us—but it's not close enough to keep the monsters away. Since moving from Dixie Court, I lost count of all the places we lived. Now, a house on 24ᵗʰ Street in Lauderdale Manor is where we call home. Gray sharp marble stones jut out from the surface of the front of the house. In the backyard, two tall mango trees begin to bear fruit among its leaves. The trees serve multiple purposes: some good, some not so good. The good thing is we get to eat the delicious fruit, but when we misbehave, Mom tells us to go pick a switch off the tree. The stinging switch accomplishes what her words sometimes fail to do. My mom does not believe in sparing the rod. The thin tree branch makes us listen, and it trains us to be respectful and considerate of one another when we get beside ourselves. Like most children, we can be hardheaded, especially during times of change and uncertainty.

Growing up on 24th Street started out like a daydream: a blurry detachment from the world where you learn to adapt to the uncertainties of life. My mind learns to escape from reality to the pleasant places of my choosing. Most of the time that place for me is sitting up high on a branch of our mango tree watching my feet dangle in the air. The trees are fun to climb, especially for a tomboy like me. Michael and I swing upside down and play for hours at a time. Those times are magical, carefree, and I feel like I am one with everything. There is something about the leaves, the branches, and the above ground hideaway that intoxicates me. Inside the thick foliage, nothing can reach you; nothing but the wind.

I pick a few mangos for Joyce and put them in a bag underneath the kitchen sink. She had said she would be over to visit soon. I can't wait to see her. I miss her so much.

The clock ticks and our Mom ride each minute. Between working at the dry cleaners, the 7-Eleven, and the Honeywell Security Company, I wonder when she will be home. For a while, she worked at the Post Office, but soon quit. Only so much can fit into a 24-hour day. She looks so tired coming in, changing from one set of clothes into another. Her dark blue security uniform makes her look like a savvy police officer. She rushes in and unlocks her bedroom door.

"Sweetie, come tidy up the room for me, and put this in your piggy bank." Mom hands me a one-dollar bill and four quarters.

"Thank you, Mommy!" I glide to my room and squeeze the dollar through the slit in the back of my tall, poodle piggy bank. I smile, counting each quarter as it clanks to the bottom.

Mom goes into her bathroom and changes her clothes. "Sydney, do you see my pantyhose on the bed?" she calls out.

"Yes ma'am, right here." I hand them to her, thinking how itchy they look. I hurry to finish cleaning before she is late for the night shift. Helping her makes me feel great, useful. The responsibility delights me because I know it is one less thing my mom must worry about. I empty the wastebasket and make up her bed. "Mama, which shoes do you want to wear?" I asked, straightening up her shoes underneath the king-sized bed.

She yells out from her bathroom, "I have my work shoes already. Just make up the bed and put the clothes on hangers."

"Yes, ma'am, I already made the bed." Even without any allowance, I love helping. I dream of becoming rich, so she does not have to work so hard anymore.

Uniformed fastened, perfume sprayed, and she is out the door. "Keep the front door locked. Keep out of the front yard. Play in the backyard, you hear?"

"Yes, ma'am," we reply before she hurries away. By now, I am somewhat used to her working all the time. I have no choice but to accept the fact that the adult world runs on a merciless clock. All the same, I long for her time, the treasure of her presence. The scent of her White Shoulders perfume stays behind. I breathe it in, again and again, holding onto any part of her I can.

"Bye, Mama," I whisper, watching my breath fog on the living room window. I walk back to my room and count all the money in my poodle piggy bank. *One day, I will have enough money saved to buy my mom 1,000 bottles of her favorite perfume*, I think to myself; *one day*.

Every neighborhood has it's good and bad. During the 1970s, it was not good. "Hoodlum Palm," some people call our neighborhood, including my sister, Joyce. She didn't approve of the area at all. With Mom at work, and Joyce busy with her family, we must learn to fend for ourselves. But it doesn't seem all bad. We have each other, and from time to time, a strange, yet peaceful, Caucasian man with short brown hair and a gentle glow comes by the house and tells us about faith in God. He leaves tracks with Bible verses and offers to take us to Bible study. Sometimes we'd go, enjoying the time spent where the familiar stories of love and grace connected us to others we didn't know. I am not sure when it happened, but one day, he stopped coming.

The walk to and from school is long. On hot days, it feels even longer. We often stop by Mrs. Freedman's house to buy treats to take on the walk. She sells freeze cups in every flavor: cherry, grape, orange, and more. We stuff Big Blows, Chick-O-Sticks, and other candy in our backpacks; my allowance money is enough to get each of us a treat before school. We hurry so we are not late for the bell. My new teacher, Mrs. Smith, is strict, but I like her. She does not allow students to chew gum or eat candy. And if she catches us talking or passing notes during class, she will make us read it out loud and share it with everyone—good thing I keep to myself. I already feel awkward just being me, let alone being forced to read a private message in front of the entire class.

Overall, Mrs. Smith is nice and always takes the time to answer my questions. She never makes me feel slow or stupid because I can't learn as fast as the other students. The hardest part of school is catching up with assignments after moving around from house to house. Though it puts me behind in my schoolwork, daydreaming is my escape from it all: all the uncertainty and all the noise in my head. Behind my desk, I can drift away to my own private, peaceful island.

After school, we rush home. Oriole Elementary School is nearly a mile and a half from home. Sometimes the walk is scary. To walk back home too slow is to ask for trouble. We make haste before the neighborhood troublemakers find their way to our street. Ernest is the ringleader of the pack and lives on the next block over. He is thin and lanky, with an arrogant swag that pushes people around before he ever lays a hand on them.

Once, he and a couple of his underlings followed us home. He wore the same mean mug smirk on his face until we got into the house and locked the door. He and his posse have a reputation for bullying younger kids and breaking into homes, even in the middle of the day. When they walk away, we move from the corner of the curtain and head for the room.

Later in the day, I stay in the house and read, while Leon, Michael, and Linda go out and play. The kids who live on our street are friendly. Colin and Chester's family live just across the yard and often keep up a ruckus with Leon and Michael. They go back and forth with whose daddy is bigger and tougher. Linda has made friends with the family who lives near the end of the block. One of them goes to my school. Her name is Pamela. She is sweet and carries a softness inside her eyes that reminds me of a warm breeze on a cool starry night. I feel comfortable around Pamela, and I try to be social, like my sister Linda, but I much rather stay home to read and cuddle with my new pet, Midnight.

She is a stray cat that followed me home. Somehow, she found me and now, I am not so lonely. I named her Midnight not because her coat is black, but because her moods are as mysterious as the night sky. She is more humanlike than a pet. She looks at me as if she sees, hears, and understands the world in ways I cannot. She reminds me of important things humans sometimes forget. Midnight seems content in the poetry of her own soul. I believe animals must have souls because they are so godlike. She purrs and teaches me her language while I rub behind her ears.

Lately, the house has become spooky. Not like the house in Tampa, where thunderstorms visited in the night and shadows like spirits seem to move among the floating mist in the air. Something here is more real, more ominous than the translucent shadows that hid between the flash of lightning. I try to brush off the suspicions and lay on the bed with Midnight. We watch *The Wizard of Oz*, but watching the movie is not the same without Joyce. She was always here. Nostalgia carries me back in time to her lullabies:

> *"Someday I'll wish upon a star*
> *And wake up where the clouds are far behind me*
> *Where troubles melt like lemon drops*
> *Way up on the chimney tops*
> *That's where you'll find me."*

Midnight likes my singing. I stroke her until we both fall asleep.

Spring of 1975
Mom surprises us today. She takes us to the movies and then

to the mall. We wait in the car while she shops. The sky is bluer when she is with us. Content to be together, we sit in the backseat of the car, and before long, my brothers begin to tease each other. As usual, Michael starts it. Michael is the master of telling knock-knock jokes, yo'-mama jokes, and fat jokes. It is all in fun, but I don't tell him that it hurts my feelings. Ms. Lynn's voice echoes in my head after the punch line. I guess I don't have much of a sense of humor. When Mom returns from shopping, she has new Easter clothes for all of us, and Easter baskets for Linda and me. The baskets are huge and filled with chocolate and toys. I have a pink bunny rabbit with my favorite malts and candy inside. Linda's rabbit has a flower bonnet.

Mama tells us Christ's resurrection is the reason she loves to celebrate the holiday. Later that night, she takes me to get a perm, Linda gets a lovely hairdo, and Leon and Michael get brush-cuts at the barbershop. The next day, we take professional Easter pictures at Mizell Studios. I feel so dressed up. I cherish the time with my Mom. After the holiday, things go back to normal, and my siblings and I spend the days goofing off and trying to stay out of trouble. I place a white towel on my head, pretending it is locks of golden blonde hair. I was not sure why I like doing that, but somehow it made me feel more acceptable and pretty.

Somewhere in my mind, I am not pretty because my hair is not long and blonde. As a black girl, I just know I am *different*— different from my dolls and everything *deemed* beautiful. Hidden like poison in the air of the culture, are the insidious messages that you and everyone else in society naturally adjust to, without question. It is as normal as breathing. Such are the times.

Science is my favorite subject in school. The school's library books feed my curiosity like nothing else. Books on history, animals, space exploration, and nature fascinate me the most. I check out as many books I can on the subjects. From the Bermuda Triangle to Saturn's rings, my collection of books fills the long and often lonely hours at home. Yesterday, I read a book about the moon. It sits so still and quiet in outer space, yet it has a powerful gravitational pull.

My teacher, Mrs. Smith tells the class that on July 20, 1969, Neil Armstrong made history when he landed on the moon. I was only two years old then, but now when I think of the moon, I think of my daddy. It holds a memory that belongs to only him and me. And like the moon, he sits quiet and still, somewhere out there. A force stronger than the pull of gravity tugs at my heart; I miss him dearly. And I often look out my bedroom window and imagine him driving by to see us, to take us to the park and maybe to get an ice cream cone. Waves of joy wash over me when I see his face. I am all aglow, imagining his blue-brimmed hat tilted to the side. I stare out my window, waiting on a fantasy until my legs go numb. Still, I wait.

My mom and Robert seem to be blissful, but I am not sure what they have in common. He's not the fatherly type and appears to have lived a long life before meeting my mom. The way he looks at me when he is home on furlough makes me happy when he is away. I am not sure how the military works because Robert comes and goes with no set schedule as far as I can tell. We never really know when he will show up on furlough.

A few months ago, he made enemies in the neighborhood by pulling his gun on a gang member. Though the details were left out, Mom had told him not to mess with the hoodlums around the area. She warned of the trouble it would bring to the house, explaining he wouldn't be around when the thugs came back looking for him. He did not listen. Soon, break-ins become a part of our life. First, it is a broken window, then a jimmied lock that broke the back-door knob, and later it became more brazen. The gang begins to steal things out of the house: a radio, a TV, a vase. We never knew what would happen next. We simply pray: *if I die before I wake, I pray the Lord, my soul to take.*

Although the fear and uncertainty never cease and becomes quite normal for us, it is getting harder to hold on to the stories and songs we learned through the years. Terrible things can happen when no one is watching.

One day, I overheard my mom talking to someone on the phone. She said Robert's merchant ship carries him to many faraway places. Foreign lands, with strange food, different languages, and independent rules you make up as you go. Once, we all traveled to Cape Canaveral in Cocoa Beach, to visit Robert as his ship docked at the port. The ship was massive. Once inside, a new world introduced itself to us. Inside of his ship is gray. The walls and ship deck were all gray. I looked for color; not sure why, but there was none. From the ladder, we climbed down on, to the ceiling, and the floor: all gray. I caught Mom as she smiled, watching us look out through the porthole; I smile too. Robert wore a blank face; I figure it is another military regulation; another unspoken rule.

I could smell the sea air through the small round window.

The smell of the ocean filled the tight quarters of the lower deck. I loved the smell of the sea, and overall, the tour was exciting. Robert stayed, we traveled home—but I had so many questions I wanted to ask. Questions about the way he stares at me.

I keep the suspicions to myself, imagining instead all the places he has been. *It must be exciting to visit different worlds,* I think to myself. I had wanted to ask about the ship and the way it works. How can a small rudder turn the massive ship—in any direction? I had wanted to know about his voyages and about mermaids. Are mermaids real or make-believe? If anyone knows, surely a First-Class Merchant Seaman would. The mermaids I have seen in my library books are beautiful exotic sirens. I wonder if Robert has ever encountered one while sailing on the high seas.

I remember flipping through the pages of my book, *Mermaids, Myths, and Monsters.* It is one of the books I find hard to put down. The stories are mesmerizing. The tales of strange sea monsters lurking beneath the depths of the ocean are fantastic mysteries—some of which I believe are true. Surely Robert would know. I want to ask him if the stories are real or the illusions of weary sailors. However, Robert's strict disposition does not permit such childish questions. I never ask.

My life would forever change on the day Robert came home in mid-1975. Like most cataclysms, he arrives unannounced. Unpredictable and cold as the seas he sails, no one can ever tell what's lurking beneath the surface. But I was about to find out.

Some days, Mom takes us with her to work at the store, but she can barely work trying to keep an eye on us anymore. Other days, we are home alone, or worse, home with Robert.

I have saved almost $20.00 in the white poodle piggy bank Mom bought me. She always tells me to save some of what I earn. I save up enough to buy the comic book of my dreams. Finally, it is in my hands. The Justice League, with Wonder Woman and Super Friends—the world's greatest crime fighters in history! I am on top of the world; I dream out loud and wide-awake—I am ecstatic. After reading the comic book for the fifteenth time, my mind is set! I know what I want to be when I grow up: an officer of the law, and a crime fighter. I will join the Army, and just as soon as I complete about ten years of service, I will join the police force. It's settled. I cannot wait to tell Mom about my plans. I cannot think of anything else that would make me happier than rescuing and serving others. In my mind, it was like joining the Justice League.

The pictures of Wonder Woman's beauty and courage inspire me beyond my clumsiness and lack of confidence. She is an ordinary girl with a special identity and purpose. She fights for justice, love, and peace; I am crazy about her. The comic book is my treasure. Flipping through the pages, I think of how proud Mama is going to be. I read until I fall asleep. Visions of being a police officer follow me there. I dream I can fly in an invisible plane. Up, up, and away I go.

When I awake, the pages of my comic book crinkle against my face. I yawn, and suddenly, as I turn to stretch, I stare into serpentine eyes hissing over my bed. It is Robert. I blink to convince myself that I am awake. After smelling the pungent scent of cigarettes from his breath, I am sure.

"Come into the bedroom." He says sternly. Leon, Michael, and Linda are all outside. Mom is at work.

"Yes, sir," I answer to the air. He has already walked away. I stop at the door, quietly wondering what he wants. I wait while he stares into the beige, framed mirror attached to the dresser in their room.

"Your mother wants you to clean the room," he says, never taking his eyes off his reflection.

"Yes, sir."

At first, I don't think anything strange. My mom has asked me to straighten up her room before, a least a hundred times or more. The last time, she gave me two dollars to put in my piggy bank. My mom said I did a good job. Now that Robert is home on furlough, perhaps she wants him to rest. I fold the clothes that are laying over the side chair and pair Mama's shoes together. She has a lot of shoes. I like the strappy shoes that make her look taller than usual. The smell of her delicate perfume lingers in every corner of the room, but the toxic smell of Robert's cigarettes makes me want to choke. It's strange how two completely different scents can exist in the same place.

I work hard and hope Mom will notice how clean her room looks when she gets home. When I finish cleaning their bathroom, I tell Robert that I am all done. As I turn to leave the room, he tells me to close the door, but to stay inside. I shut the door, confused; I make the mistake of asking him a question: "Why?"

He tells me to come and sit on the bed. I sit. He looks down at me and asks me a question I do not know how to answer. "What did you say?" He demands. His posture and tone shift the atmosphere around me, like an earthquake that causes everything to tremble. He stands close, angled within reach. Afraid to speak, I begin to stutter. My mouth moves against the advice of a small voice inside my head that was trying to warn me to keep quiet.

"I was just asking why I needed to stay—" Before I could finish my words, a leathery palm whacks my right temple. The impact of the blow sends me to the floor. The world blurs and spins. One hit was all it took. I am petrified, unsure which direction is up or down, my legs go weak, and I scream silently, *Mommy, he hit me. He hit me!* I hear a sudden click on the bedroom door, and a buzzing noise hums inside my ear. I think he is still standing over me, but everything looks blurry. I keep my head down to avoid the next strike.

He seems to wait until the blood comes back to my head. I feel him there, looking at me, like a swatted insect, my nerves shudder and twitch.

"Get on the bed," he orders. Flailing, I reach for the covers and pull myself up from the floor. In shock, I do not cry. Fear is all I feel. It is paralyzing. I am too afraid to move. Braced for the next hit, I can hardly breathe. He moves in closer.

"I'm going to ask you again. What did you say?" My hands shake near my face—the room is still spinning. It will not stop. Caught in a dark spiraling cloud, I want to disappear. But there is no way out. His silk shirt brushes against my skin. I will not answer. If I do, he will hit me again. My mouth will not open. He backs away and reaches underneath the pillow. He slithers to the front of the bed and places a black revolver on the dresser. I do not move.

He lays the gun on its side next to bottles of perfume and Mama's hairbrush. My elbows pin to the front of my rib cage. My knees knock together, as silent tears roll down my face—the barrel of the gun points directly at me. In my mind, his gun is an evil Cyclops. Robert places a magazine on the bed. The title in thick bold letters reads *Hustler*. It has pictures I have never seen before. Pictures of naked men and women tangled together in knots of arms, legs, and body parts; pictures I know I am not supposed to see. He turns the page and shows me an image of a naked woman with a German Shepherd behind her. I recoil. Acid boils in my stomach as he closes the book, ordering me into positions. I cry, trying to escape in my mind. I can't. My mind would not allow me to miss any parts of this horrible incident. It is all too real.

His eyes move back and forth, trailing an intimidating path from his gun to me. He tells me what he wants me to do and explains how he wants me to do it; never taking his eyes off his weapon.

"Yes… sir," I stutter, moaning deeply, sniffling with the terror of a living nightmare. I don't understand what he wants from me or why, but I know it is wrong. I rock back and forth, still trying to disappear. I pray for my mom to come or Joyce to show up. *Hurry, hurry*, I say inside, praying while time begins to freeze me in place. *Daddy, please come get me*, I scream inside my head. *Daddy, please hurry. Please! I'm sorry for all I have done. Please! I am so sorry for everything?*

Nobody comes. No one stops it.

My flesh crawls as he touches me in places I have never been touched before. Sensitive places awaiting the day I grow up, mature, and marry. Private places that belong only to me: he steals it all away. I can't move, I can't speak, I can't think. *What is happening?* I scream inside, but there is only the lamenting echo of a wilting voice within.

On the bed, tears of disgrace and shame fall inside the folds of the sheets. I feel something breaking, ripping inside of me. My world shifts with every disgusting touch and stroke. All innocence dies underneath the stench of lust, sweat, and the bitter smell of Winston cigarettes. The assault violates the sacred parts of all I am—my body, soul, and spirit. I feel it. Sick with mayhem, I will never be the same. Mentally, I scatter in every direction of time. I disconnect from myself, imagining these are the moments when angels cry because they know of the insanity that waits in the silence of such a crime.

In the haze of madness, I begin to detach further from myself, escaping the reality of what's happening. While my body lies underneath a monster, I feel my spirit fading, drifting away, like a sad ghost through my mother's bedroom wall. I blink through tears, disoriented, as my world turns upside down. *Why is this happening to me?* More tears fall, and I could feel my soul hovering just above my face. I see her. She whispers, "I must go tell my Father what has happened, I must go to be with Him." And then, in a blink, she was gone. I remember the moment she left me there. I felt alone, like a hollow shell; empty. Numb.

My next thoughts are about my dad. I need to let him know how I died. I need to tell him that I had waited for him, just as I promised. I waited to hear our melody again and to dance to our song on the moon. I need to tell him that I am sorry for not fighting back, for letting it happen. I never learned how to fight, and now I fear no one will ever love me. Not even he can love me; not anymore.

Robert finishes his nefarious trade: his lust for my sanity. He looks at the gun again, and warns, "I will kill you and your mother if you say anything." He unlocks the door, opens it, and evil-eyes me on my way out. I glimpse at a repulsive spectacle as I pass the bedroom mirror; it is my reflection. I turn away in disgust. I went into the room a little girl — I walk out a sideshow freak. I lower my head and heed Robert's warning. Not for me, because in my mind, he already killed me, and now, the whole world looks unsafe and ugly. But for the sake of my mother, I will not breathe a word. I love her, and if telling her what happened today causes her heartache, I will bury it here with me, deep below the surface of a graveyard of isolation and shame. Robert shuts the door, and I stand alone — incapable of moving forward. Frozen in time, there is no moving on.

I remember standing there, in the hallway, like a corridor that goes on forever, leading to nowhere. Seen, not heard; a hollow shell with a stolen voice, I blink with nothing behind my eyes. Outside of myself, I listen to the quivering voice of a child, carrying a dying plea. "*Daddy, where are you? I needed you today, but you never came. I died today. I need to see you before I vanish away, forever.*"

Stripped of every dignity, I try to take another step down the hallway, but the world is spinning. Everything spirals downwards. The ground opens, and I fall. A voice calls me; I hear it but can't respond. Michael is leaning down near me, but his voice sounds like he is talking in the tin can with a string on it; the one we use to play the telephone game on.

"Why are you on the floor?" He asks, leaving his mouth open. I do not answer right away. There are no answers.

Unaware I had fainted, I keep quiet. I don't know how long I was on the floor when Michael found me. The last thing I remember seeing was small flicks of light floating in my eyes, and then there was a dark trench. Michael helps me up to my feet and walks me to the living room couch.

"Are you, all right?" Michael asks, holding onto my elbow and hand.

"I am just dizzy, Michael. I just got dizzy, that's all. I think I got my period today." I reply, eyes down, too ashamed to look up at him. Damaged and dirty, I don't want him to see my stains. I pivot myself away from him. The cruelest thieves have come into my life. Nothing can undo it. I will bathe myself over and over again, but it will not change what has happened. Because of this, my life, my body, and my mind will become a free-for-all. A misfit with no boundaries, no lines; in my undeveloped mind, the sick acts will demand that I assume the position; without question. A day and a month are both the same; time doesn't matter anymore.

The concept of right and wrong stumbles out, naked in front of me. It mutates and deforms into an imprint of obscurity—sick and twisted. Nothing is clear anymore. Rescue is impossible because no one can ever know. I curse the day I was born and swear I will never trust anyone. *I am soulless; don't look at me; don't touch me. Leave me alone!* These words are my anthem. I will be eight years old on my next birthday, but I will never age again because dead things don't grow.

A sick sensuality awakens, and now my thoughts feel as filthy as my flesh. My dolls do not look the same. No longer do I desire to brush and comb their hair, because all that I can see are their breasts and body parts that remind me of Robert's pornography. I begin to draw pictures of body parts, and I don't want to play anymore, dream anymore, or live anymore. A quiet rage begins to replace my desire to dream. The world is not safe; no place is safe—not even in my imagination. Perverse images rush in from out of nowhere, violent and naked. Unwanted but still, they come. These are the imprints of a monster's touch.

My cherished comics once made me believe that good would always triumph over evil. But it doesn't matter now; life is but a dream. Alone in my room, I hear voices, hissing near me: *"Tell anyone and I will kill you and your mama. You are a big girl now. You gonna learn to like it. You belong to me."*

Robert soon leaves and goes back overseas, but I can still hear his threats. They squeeze until I can no longer feel my own heartbeat. A toxic shame keeps me hostage to its secret. With no antidote and no hero, death is slow, and the shame drives me to a dark place. I pile up the things that once made me dream: my Wonder Woman comic, poetry, and the drawings I made at school. I throw them all away. One by one, they fall to the bottom of the grimy trash can in the backyard.

Robert's physical and sexual abuse would continue for years. Voiceless, I learn to keep secrets, to look like I am alive when inside I'm a dead girl; floating through time.

Children are sexually abused at rates beyond accurate calculations because many cases go unreported and are undetectable by the national statistics and bureaus. All over the world, children languish in silence; seen but never heard—never telling a soul. Over 90% know their abuser. What does that say to us?

Until mankind understands the nature of sin within every human heart, society will continue to spiral downward into the deep trenches of depravity where nothing is sacred; this rebellion is the very sin of witchcraft (1Samuel 15:23). We must understand this truth!

We are in desperate need of a Savior.

Grandma Prayers

Winter 1978

Three months ago, I turned 11 years old, but age is nothing but a number. Clocks and calendars are only for those who care to keep up with time. I don't. When you are trying to make sense of life, time has a way of stopping until someone comes along to help you make sense of the nonsense. Stuck in place, I go through the motions with a peculiar look on my face, as if nothing ever happened.

Life continues to shift. The storms rage on.

"We have to go!" My mother says. The family prepares to travel to Havana. "Cancer...terminal...it won't be long." I hear the words, and I remember my mother's face as she held the receiver. She looks lonelier than I have ever seen her look before. The phone call came in from Ms. Maggie, a neighbor of my grandmother Rachel. My mother is heartbroken at the news.

The endless road moves my mind in every direction of time, and I add a new word to the list of things I hate: sweet peas, furloughs, and cancer. Robert comes home and drives the eight-hour distance from Fort Lauderdale to Tallahassee General Hospital. I watch my mother hold a solemn stare over the winding road. I turn and look out the window, thinking about my grandmother.

Memories of Havana rush over me. My grandmother's arms around me, her hands calloused and leathery from laboring in the fields, yet I long for the feel of them because they are *her* hands. She would always say that we belong to each other. I'd always smile hearing her words. The sounds of crackling wood and snorting sow hogs send me back to the dirt streets of the small town of Havana.

Nothing has changed since my siblings, and I last visited. The same oak tree slouches in the front of my grandparents' home. The same scorch of land sits beneath it where, after hunting in the woods all night, my uncle and cousins would build a fire, burn the skin off the kill, and prepare it for the smokehouse. I never wanted to see what animal they brought back from the long nights of hunting. My heart would break if I did. I was too young to understand the importance of it all. Instead, I would run away alone through the tall fields of green to see my grandfather's huge sow hogs that sat in the large pen off in the distance of the farm.

One hundred pounds of muddy pink skin jiggled when they would see me coming. "I missed you too," I'd say, feeding them tall blades of grass through the wired fence, listening to their short grunts and snorts. "Here is some for you too. You must share." That was a lifetime ago. Everything has changed.

At the hospital, the smell of bedpans and bleach ambles by us down the halls of the hospital, while the sounds of beeping machines crisscross between the voices of nurses and family members who have gathered in the room. I wonder if there is still hope for my grandmother. As I walk to the bedside, I see a woman sleeping on her back with a peaceful look on her face. She looks nothing like my grandmother. My mother is standing near the bed, holding the sleeping woman's hands, sobbing quietly. A flash of memory catches my attention as a ray of sunshine streams into the room. My mind daydreams at will. My eyes follow it outside, to a happier time. It was nearly two years ago when we spent the summer here in Havana. The kettle whistled, and my grandmother made coffee. She kissed my face and told me how much she loves me. She loved everyone she knew.

One night during that time, Grandma told us to quiet down and go to sleep, but Michael would not stop cracking jokes. We bundled together on the queen-sized bed, so there was no escaping his clowning. Leon made it worse when he put his hand under his armpits and squeezed. Gassy noises blurted out from underneath the sheets. Grandma had warned us repeatedly to quiet down and go to sleep, but it was all too funny. When she pulled back the sheet, she had our full attention. Grandma gave us a good switching, reminding us to mind our manners and be respectful of everyone in the house. The next morning, she'd sit me on her lap and let me sip her coffee. In a house filled with voices, she had a way of looking at you and listening to you as though there was no one else around.

But those days are gone, and now, everything has changed. The concept of "respecting everyone in the house," is gone, and I wonder in my world of secrets and thorns, if respect for all, ever existed, especially between children and the adults who are sick and twisted. The beeping machine brings me back. The family gathers here and there, in and out of the hospital room, waiting. Strange how life works; we wait to hear the first cries of life, time pulls the dates in between the dash a little closer together, and then, we wait to say goodbye.

My mother cries in bouts of prayers and whispers of "Jesus." Some days are better than others for her. Old folk say the dead wait for their loved ones to cross over. To greet them and welcome them home on the other side.

It is Wednesday, November 22, 1978. The curtains are open with a dazzling stream of light spraying in. The sleeping woman suddenly wakes up. Her beautiful eyes, like a russet sky near sunset, looks out over the room. I recognize those eyes. They are the peaceful eyes of my grandmother. She speaks for the first time since falling into a coma, three months ago.

"Open the curtains so you can see! It is beautiful! Look, look, the streets are gold, everything is beautiful!" I recognize her voice. The same voice has whispered prayers over me while I sat watching her cook on her old potbelly stove. "The bridegroom is coming! Pull back the curtain. Open up the window so you can see!" she says. Then, just as quickly as she had awakened, her voice faded away. She fell back to sleep. Before the sunset, my grandmother flew away. She was 57 years old when she died.

In the peaceful summers spent with our grandparents, jumping on wooden planks, feeding blades of grass to snorting hogs, and running through fields of green, I never knew my grandmother lived with secrets—voiceless skeletons quietly tucked away behind closed doors. In time, I would learn about the dangers of secondhand smoke. My grandfather smoked Camel cigarettes for most of his life. Although she never smoked, my grandmother would pay the price for inhaling the fumes. Many years later, I will find out the secrets my grandmother never told. A terrible truth of fear and abuse hides in the shadows of my family's history. For over four decades, my grandmother was the victim of domestic violence at the hands of my grandfather.

My grandmother's priority was always her family. Her children were her focus, her everything. I've never heard her complain, not even once. I never knew of her hidden pain, nor do I remember hearing her cry; perhaps because the generation before hers believed it to be a man's right to beat his wife. In a male dominant society, being both black and a woman is a slap on both sides of the face. I imagine she was simply thankful for the blessings of children and a place to call home. Such were the times in my grandmother's world, where until 1923, many women of every race and culture had no voice, and the absence of equal rights and respect left them no choice but to assume the position for the sake of marriage, family, or religion. I could not imagine my grandmother's misery; she never spoke out; I never heard anyone say a word. Not one word—as if nothing ever happened.

I hear whispers of Jesus: the mighty savior of the world, and in the same praised-filled atmosphere, these secrets float around like toxic fumes. I live in the shadows of my family secrets and instinctively assume the position. I learn to stay in a child's place, though my childhood is long gone, stolen away. I learn to go along to get along with the order of things, knowing deep inside something is very wrong. *What is law?* I question. I learn to hear but don't hear, see but don't see, feel but don't feel. Until I can no longer tell the difference between what is real and what is fantasy. In my isolation and fear, I question faith. What does it all mean? The lullabies that linger beside the insanity? I question morality. I question God. They say that Jesus is coming again. In my secret despair, I wonder, *where is He?*

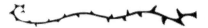

The worst thing you can do with pain is to do nothing. Sooner or later, it will surface, rising to the top, demanding the time and compassionate energy denied for its resolution and healing. To continue ignoring it, acting as if nothing ever happened, signs the consent for the next generation to endure the same dysfunction. I know this all too well.

We must confront our issues with a teachable spirit; this is the only way to renew our minds, transform our lives, and heal the brokenness. Healing is a personal journey and sacred responsibility.

My Secret Place

"We need to find God, and he cannot be found in noise and restlessness. God is the friend of silence. See how nature - trees, flowers, grass- grows in silence; see the stars, the moon, and the sun, how they move in silence... We need silence to be able to touch souls." ~*Mother Teresa*

August 1979

My stomach hurts today. I don't want to go to school. My attendance is pointless. When I go, I cannot focus, cannot see, nor can I concentrate on what my teacher expects from me. I hate this place. The blackboard is just a blur. I need glasses because spots float around in my eyes like tiny specks of light. They come and go without notice. It is worse when I hold my head up straight. I've stopped trying and just stare down. Mrs. Robinson stands at the front of the class talking about a math test. It doesn't matter. Nothing adds up in this sick society.

I take up space and wait for what's left of me to decay. Secrets have a way of killing you from the inside out, and the smell begins to give me away. I have not bathed in days because I no longer care about my appearance, nor what others may think. The way I see it, the worst I look and smell, the more people will leave me the hell alone. The teacher sends me to the office, again. I couldn't care less. I'm getting used to it all now—the stares, the whispers, the bullying, and jokes. I hear and don't here. I feel, and I don't feel. It's whatever.

In September, Hurricane David forms off the Atlantic coast. The Category 5 hurricane damaged the roof of Lauderdale Lakes Middle School. That year, students must attend Boyd Anderson High until reconstruction is complete. It is a tough time for me, mainly because today, I get detention to the principal's office. There are too many questions to which I had no answers. The principal asks me about my hygiene and overall disheveled appearance. Unsure of what to say, I chew gum and keep quiet. He asks me again. I blow a bubble, pop it, and cut my eyes to the wall, wishing this man would leave me alone and mind his own damn business. The principal stands and takes a wide, flat paddle from behind his shiny mahogany desk.

A picture of a happy family sits on top next to a penholder

and a notepad. *Being in this office must be what hell feels like*, I think to myself, having an attitude about almost everything. This man does not know me, nor does he care, and his voice is irritating.

"What's going on with you Ms. Anderson?" He asks again and warns me of the consequence of being disrespectful and disobedient. I do not answer; I know of this adult game and its unfair rules—the rules are: there are no rules. *"Disrespectful,"* he says with his flat tone and paddle? If eyes could kill, I'd be charged with murder. His threats and paddle cannot intimidate me. Unresponsive, I do not care about his punitive remarks. Dead things can't bleed. This man is wasting his breath trying to talk to me with his shiny desk and know-it-all tone.

"Whatever," I whisper out of the side of my mouth.

"Excuse me, Ms. Anderson?" He asks rhetorically—he heard what I said the first time. Inside I am raging. I have a terrible secret to keep. I hear the constant hiss of a dark creature, scarier than his paddle, more controlling than his blind authority. The fear surrounds me and steals my voice. Inside I am screaming, but no one can hear me. No one cares. No one stopped it: the fights, the divorce, and the rapes. *Get out of my face*; I want to scream at this entitled, pompous jerk. I sit calmly, holding my peace. Unable to speak, even if I wanted to, I could not form the words to say, *there is a monster living on my street, inside my house.* How do I explain the unspeakable things that happen behind closed doors? How exactly would this principal like me to enlighten him of colorful images of pornography Robert force me to see when his demons prepare to exploit me like a two-bit whore? Just how do I answer his questions like a respectable child? The child inside me has died, and all that's left behind is an outcast, seething with an intense desire to set this shiny mahogany desk on fire.

I wrap my arms across my chest, thinking *I cannot stand this man*! The principal snarls at my "insolent attitude." His ears turn red, no doubt clogged with the noise of his own importance. He, like the rest of this stinking culture, does not take the time to look deeper, to probe and see what is hiding underneath the rage and aggression. Straightaway, his ego inflates. He says a bunch of words to which only he is listening. I am already gone. I slouch over and tilt my head to the side.

"I should have never come to school today," I mumble to myself. A mistake I will not make again. Next time, I will skip school and go to my secret place.

Pale-faced, the principal orders me to lean over his desk. He paddles my backside twice. The sting of the paddle against my skin is a welcomed reprieve from the anguish inside my heart. Leaning against his desk, I clench my teeth and refuse to cry in front of him. Instead, I imagine watching his desk burn until it smolders.

My anger builds as he wields his paddle. A quiet fury crouches deep inside of me; it simmers next to the fear. All the same, I breathe out a sigh of momentary relief. It feels strange, but the burning sting from the paddle soothes the deep emotional pain. The world shifts again and prepares to toss me wherever the wind blows.

I don't remember when it happens, but slowly, I begin to be afraid of everything and nothing, all at the same time—the signals in my mind cross, mixing like the smells of perfume and Winston cigarettes. For me, the world is unsafe, like driving a hundred miles per hour through thick smog. I never know what's ahead of me, but I know when it hits, it will be the end of it all. I prepare to quit school—the one place I had loved, but no longer belonged.

Michael Tascarelli sits in a desk in front of mine, talking to his friends. We are from two different worlds. For most of the school year, I have silently watched his light brown wavy hair, listened to him laugh with the other students, and dreamed that one day I would marry someone like him. He seems so happy all the time, and that made me happy as well. I want to say goodbye and tell him that I won't be back. *But that would be a waste of time.* He doesn't know I'm alive. He never looks at me, even when I have said hi—he smiles and walks right past me as if I were invisible. A girl like me never stood a chance with a boy like him.

Sitting back in my desk, I plan my exit strategy. School is no place for misfits like me. I walk out of class, down the hall, heading towards the side exit door. As I pass the library, a song stops me. The music is coming from the chorus room. I turn my head, and for a moment, the music holds my attention. I know the song; it is a song I love from the brother and sister group called The Carpenters. Since fifth grade, I've listened to their music.

Through the small window of the chorus door, I peer in. The chorus of students sings "Bless the Beast and the Children." Fog forms on the glass of the window as I whisper the words:

> *"Bless the beast and the children;*
> *For in this world,*

They have no voice,
They have no choice.
Light their way when the darkness surrounds them,
Give them love, let it shine all around them..."

Standing outside the door, I imagine what it would feel like to be a part of their world: a world of polished uniforms, rosy cheeks, and the confidence of knowing where you belong. The teacher plays the piano, smiling proudly, as she directs the next verse. Not wanting anyone to notice me, I pull away from the window and step back inside my own silent, secretive world. Music no longer plays here. There will be no first kiss, no homecoming parties, no prom dates. Not for me. In the emotional dungeon of secrets and abuse, the ability to learn, to function, and to see a future move beyond my reach. This is my reality. No cap and gown, no graduation with family gathered around to celebrate the milestones of life. Education is pointless in the dark trench of my mind. I step away, back inside the fate that has replaced the distant dream of a lullaby — the song my sister used to sing to me back in Dixie Court Projects. It was a melody about climbing a mountain and following a dream. But dreams are impossible illusions, and I don't want to care anymore — I tell myself not to care because caring hurts. Not giving a damn about anything is a safer option.

I make a path through the grass on the west side of the campus yard. I walk to my secret hideaway: a wooded area located off 26th and Martin Luther King Avenue, a few blocks from the main road. It is an extraordinary place. There, I created my own world among the trees and the shallow pond that sits in the midst of a sleepy glade. It is a safe, quiet world. No one, except for my friend Pamela, has ever been here with me.

She came one day after school when a group of students was making fun of my clothes, the smell, and calling me all sorts of names. Bullying was nothing new for me. Especially from black girls who began to make fun of the way I spoke and acted, saying I didn't talk or act "black." In my mind, it was ridiculous because I always thought I spoke and acted like I was human; just a person. However, deep inside I knew as a misfit, I would not be accepted in any group or click. So, frankly, I couldn't care less. In my world of thorns, it seems people haven't a clue of another person's truth, so it's just easier to make assumptions, bully, and judge according to what *we* see with the imperfect vision of our two small eyes, rather than looking deeper. Looking back on that time, I realize people are people—clay containers like gardens of soil, filled with seeds of love, hate, or apathy; what sprouts up is most likely what was planted.

Whatever we say, or do; however, we act or react is often based on the facts of environment, culture, and experiences: nothing more, nothing less.

I know Pamela felt sad that day. Her eyes said it. That day when we were in the cafeteria, she stood up for me.

"Why are you hanging around that weird girl?" one of the girls had asked Pamela.

"She is not weird! Leave her alone. She is my friend," Pamela fired back, letting me know she would be loyal to the end. Still, I lost my appetite and walked away. It wasn't long before the bullies caught up with me on the walk home from school, but I knew from that day on, the bond Pamela and I shared would never be broken. It was during that time I invited her to my secret hideaway. I had felt so happy that she came. The grasshoppers and dragonflies seemed to come alive as we stepped through the woodland; they are always so welcoming. This nature is so serene, and here, I feel accepted.

"Wow, San. I didn't know this place was here," Pamela said with a look of amazement. From the street, no one could tell what's hidden inside, just behind the brush of trees.

"I am not sure if anyone knows. No one is ever here when I come, except for the birds and little critters," I replied, hoping she would stay awhile with me. She did.

"How did you find this place?" Pamela asked. Her eyes stretched wide with every step.

"I was walking home from school one day, and something pulled me in." It was something I couldn't explain. "No one knows I am here. I have always loved nature." I whispered. Pamela listened as I rambled on. I told her how I come and sit just to find peace. The tall trees, the birds, the scurrying ladybugs: they all fill up my senses and set me free to just be me—without judgment.

Pamela looked at me as if seeing me for the first time. She holds a sweet compassion inside her eyes, looking at me with empathy as if she knows the secrets I hide behind a cagey smile. I never tell, and she never pries, though I notice reflections of regret when she turns to look away. A gentle wind blew, sweeping through the leaves around us.

"How long have you been coming here, San?" Pamela had asked, sweeping back her long, beautiful hair from her face. I breathed, watching her eyes take in the overlay of the marshland. Muddied rocks gurgled half-sunken in the wet sandy clay near the pond's shoreline. Wild vines climbed in every direction on the trunk of moss-covered trees. They had found a way past the sharp prickly shrubs sticking out near the bottom.

I breathed out, searching for a way to answer her question. Looking away, I shrugged my shoulders. "I can't remember," I responded cautiously, looking over the pond. It is an honest answer, though not entirely true. I withheld the vile facts of the matter.

The fact is I did not want to remember. The details are too disgusting to reveal. I couldn't tell her that I started coming here after every assault. I threw a rock as hard as I could into the muddy pond. Pamela placed her hand on my shoulder.

"It's okay, San. Whatever it is, God is with you." Her eyes began to tear up before she looked away.

The cool breeze rustled across the surface of the pond, thick with white clayish sludge that moved undecidedly. Moss-covered rocks decorated the edge of the lake. The air was getting colder, but still, Pamela stayed. We sat against a smooth boulder near the water's edge and listened to the tranquil sounds around us. Birds flew over, chirping as they nestled in the treetops. The sky moved the clouds back like a curtain. The dusk summoned a symphony of critters waiting to perform their evening overtures. The ground filled with the sounds of crickets and beetles stirring about excitedly. Nightfall brought them out of hiding, and like every living creature, they seemed to wait to be seen, to be heard, and to be loved. Busy ants teem up and down the Swamp Rose-tree that sits behind us. They were so small but seemed to move with intense purpose, as if they have a schedule to keep.

"Um..., it's getting late, San. I have to get home." Pamela said, her face drawn with sadness as though she did not want to leave. She knew I was not ready to go, and I knew she could not stay. I walked her to the edge of the glade, and we hugged each other goodbye.

The bond of true friendship will remain with us long after we part ways. In the moments we shared in the hideaway, I discovered another part of Pamela's beautiful heart. She stood up for me against the bullies at school; she knew my secret hideaway and did not tell anyone. She has never judged me for the outcast I have always believed I was. I will always love her for that. In time, school becomes an afterthought. Before long, I will drop out of

Lauderdale Lakes Middle School, and come every day to my secret garden.

I have a few months before the monster comes back home on furlough. I make plans to run away from home before his ship docks in Port Canaveral.

I overheard my Mom talking to Freddie, a friend she met. I think his fondness for her is more than friendship. Freddie is a funny man with a sweet spirit, but he had an awful problem with drinking until he loses himself. We call him Uncle Freddie. He comes over when Robert is away. When he is drunk, he makes crazy faces until he vomits. He swears he sees things no one else can see. Once, during a drunken episode, he refused to put on his shoes because he claimed he saw tiny people inside of them. He said he was afraid to squash the small village of people living in his shoes. Another time he was driving and suddenly ran out of his car. He grabbed onto a telephone pole and refused to let go. He said he saw my mother on the top of it and did not want her to fall off. He openly admits he is an alcoholic, but I am not sure if he is doing anything to help change the problem. He cries a lot, only to get drunk again. I have never seen a grown man cry, except in the *Hee Haw* show Joyce and I used to watch.

I feel sad for him. I try to understand alcohol addiction, but I cannot. All I know is that it's the same wretched thief that stole my dad's heart away from me. Joyce taught us never to use the word *hate*. She said it is not a nice word. But I have no other options. No other words can describe what I feel. I hate it. How potent alcohol must be to make sensible men worship at its feet, and then tie them into a knot so tangled it becomes impossible to break free.

Freddie drives over to our house to check on us sometimes when my mother is at work. He brings food and seems very nice. One day he comes, and we beg him to drive us to Joyce's house. Unfortunately, he agrees.

"Sure, I'll take you to see your sister," he slurs with a glassy cross-eyed look. My heart lifts at the thought of seeing Joyce. We have not seen her in a while now—she will be surprised. Leon is not home. *He is going to miss the trip over,* I think to myself.

Linda smiles big and puts her shoes on. Michael is already out the door. Excited, we ignore the wobbly way Freddie gets into the car.

"Climb on the top. Let's go see your sister!" Freddie says, and then he takes a drink from a beer can. *We get to ride on top of the roof of the car!* We look at each other and Michael, Linda, and I climb hastily on the upper part of Freddie's sky-blue Oldsmobile. Pure insanity, there is no covering for us, except for the prayers stored up over the years. We fly down the road from 24th Street to Broward Boulevard and 18th Avenue. Past red lights and stops signs, Freddie floors it. We hang on to nothing. There is nothing to hold on to when you are riding on top of a roof. Our naiveté fails to inform us of the imminent danger ahead. Freddie turns into Sunny Reach Acres and slams on the breaks. The joyride is over.

After the sudden stop, we soar through the air like dice tossed in a game of craps. Michael somersaults against the pavement; It snatches the skin off his shoulder and arm. I roll off and hit the sidewalk; my big toe bursts open and bleeds. I stagger up, fueled by adrenaline and fear because I do not see Linda from the side where I fell off. Frantic, I limp around to the other side of the car. Linda is lying on the ground, curled up into a ball. She has flown off and landed between the road and sidewalk. Quiet moans escape from her closed lips.

"Peanut, are you okay?" I ask, afraid of the answer.

"I can't move my arm," she murmurs. "It hurts." Freddie sits spaced out behind the wheel. He has not moved yet. Michael and I pick up Linda and take her to Joyce's apartment. We tried to hide the bruises from the incident. Pretend like nothing ever happened — it was the norm. The pain will never heal in the darkness of secrets. Furthermore, we wanted to protect Freddie. We knew he would be in trouble if mom found out. And we should have known better than to get on the roof of a car. What we didn't realize was the extent of the damage of our joyride. During the next few days, Mother notices the kink in Linda's arm. It gives the secret away. She calls Linda in her room. Michael and I follow.

"Why are you holding your arm like that?" She asks Linda. Her brown eyes look up. She stays quiet, then hesitates and answers with a shrug.

"Umm," Linda pauses and looks at Michael and me. When Mother touches her arm, Linda winces in pain.

"What happened?" she demands. Afraid of her reaction, we are all silent. Mom looks at Michael. "Michael! What happened to your sister?" Michael tells her everything.

Furious, she calls Freddie on the phone, screaming about how stupid it was for him to drive us on top of his car. "They could have died! "she yells. After a trip to the emergency room, we find out Linda's arm is broken in two places. She must wear a cast for months to allow the broken bones to heal. It's peculiar, how we learn to adapt and cope with pain without ever saying a word. I cannot imagine Linda's pain. We are all secret keepers. What goes on inside, stays inside; until *"we all fall down."*

Freddie is remorseful and says he will try to stop drinking. Easier said than done—the attempt is as feeble as his driving. I can smell the booze on his breath within ten feet of the doorway when he comes over to the house. It is another rough day; one of the painful lessons I am yet learning. It appears men have a lustful way about them. Even the ones you least expect. Though Freddie is not the monster Robert is, he possesses a lewd craving all the same. Lust seems to be a demon that possesses the loins of empty men. Gluttonous, it feeds on a need that can never be satisfied—like the craving for sin. That day, Freddie crosses another line. The gentle, kindhearted man who seems to care for us, confirmed my belief that all men are just alike: lust-riddled, sin-sick, scalawags.

While my mother is at work, Freddie comes and sits next to me. Suddenly, he reaches between my legs. With eyes, as empty as a dark pit, he begs to touch me. I recoil, pulling my elbows and knees together. He stops when I start to cry. He slurs an apology, stating that he was drunk and sorry. In my mind, his heart has always outweighed his alcoholism, but now trust is broken between us. I come to realize a horrible truth. This world is not safe for children—not at all. Drunk or not, I question what would make a man desire a child and justify the horrible act in his twisted mind. I doubt my own sanity; my understanding of how the world is supposed to be. Seen and not heard, I keep quiet and fall deeper inside myself and a trench of secrets. These are painful truths, hard lessons to wrap my mind around.

Many years later, time would also reveal the painful truth of sexual abuse with other members of my family. Like a generational root, sin is inescapable and has no boundaries. So, it seems we all have a secret place where we go; a hideaway where no one else knows. There, we can breathe and suppress all the shame, the pain, and the questions of which we can't seem to find the answers.

We must confront and address our family secrets to heal!

Fireflies

In the darkest places, guiding lights will appear. Be it the lights from the heavenly constellations, or the lights from within the infinite imagination; the source of these mysteries is the same. It often takes a lifetime to understand that there are things that we will never fully understand on this stormy planet. Faith is the light that guides us through the darkest misery and leads us home.

Midnight does not like water. I must postpone my plans for running away to the beach, and instead, save up enough money so she can go with me to someplace dry. Perhaps we will go back to Tampa or maybe even New York City. Years ago, watching Frank Sinatra and the Rat Pack on television made me want to go to the city that never sleeps. I think Midnight will love New York too. On my bed, I pour out the money in my white poodle piggy bank. Midnight and I have five dollars and change. I am not sure when Robert is coming home on furlough, so I prepare in advance. I flip through the pages of an overdue library book and read it to Midnight. It's called *Where the Wild Things Are*. I imagine going to the island on the pages and never coming back.

I keep a picture of Joyce with me. The portrait captures her big smile perfectly — it gives me hope, but at the same time, it hurts. I miss her. She is busy being a wife and mother, but she came by to check in on us the other day. The sun had shined brighter that day. Those are the best days. On the days when she picks us up and takes us to her house; I never want to leave. Spending time with her makes me believe beyond my fear and the insanity of what was happening in my life. Joyce likes exercising and teaches me all she knows. Jogging, step aerobics, walking: we work out for hours together. I love it, mostly because I love being with her. I never want the time to end, and I pretend to be okay when she drives away.

"I love you guys. See you soon!" she says before driving off. We all stand outside and wave until her old, brown Ford fades out of view. Staring down the empty road, I think of how much I miss her lullabies, her stories, and her songs. I will not tell her how sad I am because I do not want her to worry. She has enough to manage now. I dare not say what has happened since she moved away. I don't want her to go mad. I keep it all in, pretending I am just fine. Only my precious pets know my secrets.

I have a brown hamster now. I am not sure if it is a boy or a girl. I name it Cindy. That was the name of my girlfriend when I attended Oriole Elementary. She and I were close. We would hold hands in school and play together at recess. We seem to share the same spirit and clumsiness. The black girls called me a cracker lover. I am not sure why, or what it means. At that time, I had never heard the term before, but I tried not to let it bother me. I loved Cindy, and I thought she felt the same way about me. It's funny how quickly things can change. The friendship we had during our time in school would come to a sudden end the day I asked if I could walk her home. When we got to the door, Cindy told me she wanted me to say hi to her mother. Her mother took one look at me and told Cindy she could never play with me again. I waited for her to say goodbye. She never did.

Her mother had yanked her through the door. Before she closed it, she said the word "~~nigger~~," looking at me. I just stood there, stunned. *Am I missing something?* I thought to myself, standing in the middle of the sidewalk. Cindy peered out from the corner of the window and looked at me as if I was a stranger. Her face distorted as if she had bitten a poisonous apple and now, sees me through her mother's slanted eyes. I turned and walked home, thinking about all the times Cindy and I had played together, ate lunch together, and walked the halls of the school. Call me naïve or slow, but I remember wondering what went wrong. Though it was a long time ago, I will never forget the look in her mother's eyes. It was a long walk home.

Seeing how people treat each other makes me love my pets even more. My pets become my best friends. They do not switch out on you. I see no judgment in their eyes, only a complete and honest acceptance, just the need to give love and receive it in return. I think my hamster is colorblind, but I am not sure.

A stray dog gave birth to puppies in the bushes in front of our house, and now, I have three pets. She had been thin and full of mange when she gave birth to six puppies, two of which die the first day. When her other puppies got a little older, she died. The surviving puppies wander away, except one, which I secretly keep. I have not decided a name for him yet. He is beautiful with a cocoa brown coat. I don't have permission, so I sneak him food and milk outside and sometimes hide him inside the house. Midnight is not too fond of my hamster or my new puppy. Her tail snaps at the air when I coddle my other pets.

Still, she manages to relax on the edge of the bed and wait for me to watch TV with her. Animals must have a unique purpose on earth. They are so affectionate and kind. When God created them, He must have known that humans would need to understand unconditional love.

I also believe my pets have incredible senses and can hear my heart, even feel my sadness, and share it with me, making it easier to bear. I would be so lonely without them here with me because whatever faith is, it is getting harder to believe. Harder to trust in anything. Harder to fall asleep because I am scared Robert might sneak up on me. I try to recall the stories of faith and hope I have heard about all my life. I want to believe that somehow, I will find my way through this sickening maze of noise and fear racing in circles in my head. The trouble is I do not know how to believe anymore. I thought I could be strong, courageous, like my mother and Joyce. But the fact of the matter is I was wrong. Everything is wrong. I never learned how to fight. Somehow, I missed that lesson. Somewhere between the dream of joining the military and the nightmare of a shameful secret, I never learned much of anything. I cannot tell my mother about a pain that I cannot begin to explain. I cried out for my dad—I waited and waited. He has never come.

As I sit in my room, cuddling up with Midnight, she presses her nose underneath my chin and rubs her face on my neck. Her green eyes glow like emeralds against her black fur. She purrs contently and nestles on my lap. We sit quietly and watch TV together. My mother bought me the new TV for Christmas last year. She buys us nice things, especially for Christmas. Of all the holidays, my mother loves Christmas best, but my greatest wish cannot fit underneath a Christmas tree—and if it is the birth of Jesus Christ, I wonder does He see what I see and if He cares what is happening on this sick planet?

Elvis Presley is dancing on TV and Midnight sits and stares. She seems star-struck at the sight of him. She watches the screen, ears straight up, swishing her tail to the beat of "Hound Dog." For the first time, I realize that much like the rest of the world, Midnight is also a fan of Elvis. I stroke her from the top of her head to her tail.

"I like him too, Midnight, but no one dances like Fred Astaire. He moves like magic." I talk to Midnight as if she can speak back to me. I tell her everything, and she listens. We understand each other's language. "I love you Midnight," I whisper in her ear. I doze off.

Moments later, I feel like I am dreaming—an awful dream. Michael runs in my room. Sweat pours down his face. "Come quick, Leon's been hit!" Michael shouts. His face warps in fear. I leap off the bed, praying, feeling like the world is moving in slow motion.

"What happened?" I scream at Michael. He is moving fast in front of me. He does not answer. I try to swallow, but I cannot close my mouth. "Michael, what happened?" He rushes onto the street. I am still screaming to the back of his head, "What happened to Leon?" Flicks of light float in front of my eyes, as a thousand images of what could have happened crowd inside my mind. Michael stops in the middle of the road. He looks back at me. The terror in his eyes tells me to hurry.

One block away from the house, a crowd has gathered around a brown station wagon at the cross-section of 24th Street and 23rd Terrace. The air turns metallic when I realize that Leon is in the middle of all the commotion. I move, feeling the hot asphalt underneath my bare feet. Afraid of what I will see, I pray. *God please, please let everything be all right.* Trying to catch my breath, I press through the crowd of people surrounding the accident scene. I nearly faint at the sight of my brother's body halfway underneath the front wheel of the station wagon. A solid punch to my heart, I fold over, holding my stomach.

"Leon!" I scream. Neighbors hurry to get him from underneath the car. Road rash covers large parts of his face and body. My voice trembles in disbelief. "Leon! Leon, I am here."

Car doors slam and more people gather around. I hear bystanders giving mumbled accounts of the accident. "He was going too fast," one man says. But no answers come that could change this. Nothing can rewind the present course of events.

Leon stares out holding his upper thigh. Blood pours out of his knee and leg. His nails dig into his skin just above the wound.

"Stay calm. Don't let him fall asleep. Help is on the way!" The station wagon is locked in a dead axle to the left. Buried underneath is Leon's moped.

"Jesus! Oh, my God!" the voices mutter on the crowded street. I want to touch him and hold him, but I cannot. Any touch might cause him more pain.

At the sight of his distress, my arms shake uncontrollably. My hands reach out frantically, grabbing the air. Lightheaded, I feel a floating sensation.

"Leon! I am here." Gravel imbeds in the palms of my hands, as I scuttle against the road, inching closer to him. "Leon, hold on! God is here. He is here with you. Hold on! Please, God!" I plead, staring at his blood, begging God to help us. Each minute feels like an eternity, and with each heartbeat, more of him spill out on the ground.

Voices from witnesses and onlookers crunch above us. Their shadows seem to block the air and the sun. Sirens blare in the distance. The sounds mesh into a low drone, and they funnel out over the top of the crowd. Leon is not talking, but his mouth is open. He wheezes faintly.

"Leon, I am here," I whisper close to his ear, hoping he can hear me over the chaos.

"Sis!" He grimaces in pain.

"Leon, I love you. I am right here. Everything is going to be all right." I look for a place to touch him, to feel him, to let him know he is not alone. Parts of Leon's skin lag through his torn, blood-soaked clothing. Grayish pieces of gravel set inside the ripped pleats of raw flesh from where he'd been dragged underneath the car. The smell of gas and tire rubber chars the air. A shiver thrums out from his throat. "Pray for me, sis."

Suddenly, he begins to hyperventilate.

The sound of a deep voice commands the growing crowd. "Get back. Give him air!"

Michael's eyes lock with mine. He stands over us and begins to pray aloud. Leon grimaces in pain, clenching his jaw. His head rears back, and he stares out. Michael looks down the road.

"What is taking the ambulance so long to get here?" someone in the crowd yells out. I hear the sirens, but I do not see the ambulance. Leon's leg twists in the wrong direction. Torn flesh exposes a pearl-white colored object—it is his bone.

Helpless tears fall under my chin, and then, I see a tunnel. Right in front of me, a corridor opens in midair, like a portal to another dimension, a different world. It beckons me: *hurry, hurry away*. The specks of light appear in my vision from out of nowhere—they jump around like fireflies. I blink my eyes, but they are still there. Like a magical colony, the fireflies seem to move through the tunnel and turn back towards me. I stare down the tunnel, tilting my head. I have seen it all before, at least three times, last I counted. The tunnel has appeared during The Lineup, during my parents' bitter fights, and during the dreadful hours that followed Robert's furlough. His ship docks, he calls me in the room, and before I can feel his sickening touch, the tunnel opens.

The fireflies come to lead me away to a quiet place. I see it now, but this time, I need to stay present—Leon needs me. As I try to fight away the dizziness, the world slows its rotation; a high-pitched sound rings up against the base of my ears; the noise grabs my attention, and then, The ambulance rushes away. Thickened hues of red and black remind me of what the fireflies were trying to help me escape. A round blotch of blood splatters the ground, like a cracked scarlet mirror. Soundless feet shuffle around me. Soon, everything begins to speed up again. I remember. The squeaky wheels of the ambulance gurney and Leon's gut-wrenching moans as the paramedics lifted him off the ground. The clamor sounds of witnesses and neighbors talking at the same time are too much. Too much noise; too much chaos; I detach.

A few weeks later, the rain came, washing away the blood-soaked gravel. Leon survives the horrific car accident. He needed over 70 stitches in his leg, and after the surgeries, he must learn to walk again. I am thankful for God's grace and mercy. The strain of the accident takes a toll on my mother. The following days, she seems more tired than usual when she gets home from work, lifting her head just high enough to put the key in the door, or when she looks up to pray. I think to myself that being a mother is not easy, especially when society demands you to work sun up to sun down to make ends meet. A regretful sadness rests in her eyes. She never wanted Leon riding on the moped in the first place. She works harder to catch up with time lost from work due to the frequent trips to the emergency room and follow-up doctors' visits. First Linda's arm, now it's Leon, what's next? I don't want to cause further stress for my mother. I pretend to be fine, lying about school, acting as if I am not losing my mind—it's all becoming quite normal.

Leon's gait has become more like our dads since the moped accident. He limps around, and his moods border two extremes, between quiet and angry. When he is quiet, I see a reflection of Daddy in his eyes. When he is angry, I see a desperation that drives him until he becomes undone. I know he misses dad, though he hardly says it anymore. Twisting the corners of my shirt, I stare out of my window until the pain in my finger takes my mind off everything else. I don't know what I am waiting for, but I feel restless and afraid. Afraid of loud noises, a knock on the door, a ship docking for furlough bringing the sea monster to shore, and more than anything, I fear getting stuck in that place inside myself and never finding the way out.

Bedroom Window

The baffling and complex conditions of "mental illness" has an origin; a starting place where it slowly sprouts like weeds, silent yet hostile. No one sees or hears when it breaks from the ground. The spirit of fear is the birthing place of many mental and emotional woes. As triune beings, the body, mind, and spirit can take but so much before the breaking begins — when all that is sacred splits, allowing the advocate of insanity to come to the rescue. In my life, I've found that the mind knows where to go, where to escape in the attempt to survive the madness. It is more prevalent than anyone can imagine, and quite often, it comes as a saving grace.

There is whispering. *You had better go now while you still have a chance. Hurry, hurry up; he is coming.* Then, the voices grow louder. I play possum until the house gets quiet. In the still of the night, I get ready to take flight and run away from home. Slowly, I turn the handle, rolling out the eastside window in my bedroom. The fear of Robert coming home is more dreadful than the unknown shadows of the outside world. I slip out of the window with a small black duffle bag. The bag holds only two items — all I need: a picture of my sister Joyce and a prescription bottle full of pills.

I stole the pills from my mother's medicine cabinet. I have never stolen anything before, but after the last time Robert made me come into the room, I could no longer stand the disgusting reflection staring back at me in the bathroom mirror. While the water ran, I quietly hid the bottle in my pocket and walked out.

I hate him for the things he does to me. I hate myself for not being strong enough to fight back. In my mind, I believe the bottle of pills will be strong enough to stop the noises in my head, and lethal enough to keep Robert far away from me. By the time his ship docks, I will have beaten him at his own game, taking my own life, and dare him to touch me in my grave. Finally, I will be free from the secrets and shame, and there, I will have some sense of peace.

I sneak down the street, feeling a shadowy presence following me. In the corner of my eye, I see it. I whip my head, looking back. I must hurry to my secret hideaway. My mind races a thousand feet ahead of me. *Hurry, before anyone sees you, finds you and drags you back. He is coming.* I quickly dip out of sight off 24th Court and 28th Terrace. The rain is coming. I stumble over slippery stones that pave the side road of the street. *Get up, hurry, I am almost there.*

"Where are you going?" a voice calls out in the darkness. But anxiety tightens the muscles around my throat. I hold my breath and wait to see if the voice is real or a figment of my mounting fear.

"Hey." A slim, silhouette steps out into the moonlight. I see his gentle face. It is Cleveland Mack, a neighborhood boy we call Junior. He has always been nice to us ever since my family moved to the area. He has a polite, coy way about him. I am not sure how old he is, though he looks to be around seventeen. I never asked.

"Where are you going so late?" he asks. My stomach churns; *I can still get away,* I think to myself.

"Hey, where are you going?" He questions again. I keep moving.

"Hi, Junior," I whisper, holding my head down, trying to get out of sight.

"Is everything alright? You should not be walking out here alone. Whose house are you heading to this time of night?" I keep moving without a word. *Hurry, feet, hurry.* My mind races onward.

He follows close. There are no headlights on the road— almost there. I cut across the grass and cross over 26th Street. I see my secret hideaway, finally. I drop my shoulders and breathe. *I made it. I will sneak inside, take all the pills, and never come out.* I stand outside of the meadow and wait for Junior to leave. *No one can know where I am.*

Be cool, I tell myself, hoping he will be gone soon.

"What are you doing out here? What's in your bag?" Cleveland asks.

"Nothing!"

"Then where are you going?"

"Nowhere!" I say impatiently. I have a schedule to keep, and he is holding me up. I wish he would just leave. "What's in your bag?" he asks, reaching out his hands. He takes it and opens it.

"Give it back!" I demand; I'm sick and tired of people taking things from me.

"I will give it back when you tell me why you are out here. And what are you planning to do with these?" He holds up the bottle of pills and looks at me. I sit down on the sidewalk, shadowed by trees and the night sky. Putting my head between my knees, I turn away.

The night air causes chill bumps to rise on my skin. An evening wind blows dead leaves across the empty side street. In the distance, sheets of rain move toward us.

"I just don't want to live anymore," I cry, never looking up.

"Don't say that! Nothing can be that bad," Cleveland says, touching my shoulder. "I can't let you kill yourself." He puts the pills in his pocket, reaches down, and helps me off the ground. He looks at me, incapable of understanding. We are from two different worlds. He has his family, drums, and music; I have mounting fear, shame, and disgusting secrets. He, like so many others, have no clue of this reality and the madness that closes in on you.

"You don't understand," I mumble, wiping tears away. Unable to escape the vexing hiss of Roberts's threats, I go silent.

"What is it, what don't I understand?" Junior asks again, moving closer to me.

"Nothing, it does not matter." I look up at the moonlight and imagine my dad is there, waiting for me. I lift away in my mind. I want to fly away to the moon. The closer I get, the bigger I smile. I shoot past the moon and fall back. He is there to catch me. I am in his arms, dancing on the moon to our special song. The melody is the same one that played in his barbershop, the rhythm of his heartbeat and mine.

"Hey? Are you okay?" Junior asks. I hear him, and I don't hear him. I am too far away to answer.

The raindrops mix with my tears. I blink, feeling them roll down my face. A chill reaches inside my bones, shaking me back to earth, back to the dark road, back to reality. The moon is so far away.

"Sandra? Hey, let's get out of the rain. Come to my parents' house. Don't worry; you can stay the night. My parents won't mind."

Cleveland's home sits in the corner on 30th Avenue, a few blocks away from our house. Michael, Leon, and I visited there a couple of times to hear Cleveland and his brothers play the drums on their open-air patio. Inside the house feels warm. Pictures of his family decorate every wall and on top of the wooden coffee table in the living room. I think, *how blessed he is to have his family*. They have a set of drums sitting off to the side, along with other musical instruments. "Let me get you a sandwich and a dry shirt," Cleveland says. He shows me the bathroom. His family is asleep.

A few moments later, he rushes back in. "Here is a sandwich and iced tea." Cleveland hands me the plate. I sit on the bed, while he grabs a blanket and gets comfortable on the floor. We sit up and talk a while. I don't eat. No appetite, but I want to be polite, so I nibble a bit and listen. He goes on and on about his family and his plans. I listen to his dreams, smiling, believing he will do wonderful things with his life one day. Cleveland appears to be a loner, just like me, but he has a quiet confidence that sees the world through hopeful eyes. He reminds me of a sweet Sunday hymn that you love to sing because you know all the words. He continues to talk, but my mind wanders away from his carefree glance. Like a broken timer in my head, my mind floats at will, without me knowing when, and without my consent. It comes back only when it knows the coast is clear and I am safe.

I resist the urge to twirl the edge of the shirt around my finger as I thought about asking him why he was out so late tonight; how he happened to show up on my path to Neverland. I don't ask. Instead, I flow with his calm energy and try to ignore the voices in my head.

"Here, let me get this for you." He stands and pulls back the sheets and blanket on his bed. "You can sleep here tonight. I will sleep on the floor. In the morning, you can start over. It will be a new day." He takes an extra pillow, bundles up underneath the blanket on the floor, and says goodnight without another word. Sleep does not come as easy for me. I take the picture of Joyce out of my bag and put it on my chest. Imagining she is here, I listen to her lullaby, and soon,

drift away.

The next morning, I wake up and prepare to go back home. I stroll slowly, uncertain of my fate, thinking about Cleveland all the way. I never met a guy like him. When he looked at me, I could see no signs of lust or disapproval. He was kind and sensitive. My assumptions about all men must be wrong. And perhaps maybe he's right. Today is a new day. Still, I dread going home.

My stomach twists as I turn onto 24th Street. No car is in the driveway, so I sneak in through the back door; the lock has been broken for a while now. Midnight is waiting for me. She greets me, rubbing her fur across my legs. I pick her up, go inside my room, and wait for the backlash. To run away from home is to ask for two things to happen: a whipping and a label, for trying to be what the grown folk call "grown." My mother punishes me for running away and tells me to stay in my room. No problem there; I am always in my room anyway. I feel guilty for causing her more heartache. She looks hurt, confused, and just plain tired. Unable to tell her why I ran away, I do not say a word, telling myself *the secret must go to my grave.*

The isolation is comforting. I disappear inside my mind; my

own inner world where no one else is allowed. A world no one else understands. With my chin against the windowpane, I look out at Michael and Linda playing in the front yard with Colin, Crystal, and Marshal. I look further down the street for Leon. I don't see him and haven't for a while. My thoughts drift back to Tampa. The smell of my daddy's Old Spice cologne and my mother's smile that had let me know everything would be all right. Now Tampa's scary thunderstorms seem but a gentle rain compared to this trench of thorns that life has led me in.

Midnight gets my attention. She lays her body against my legs. Her green eyes look caringly at me as if she understands what the rest of the world can't, or at least that's what I tell myself. I smile at her, caressing her soft fur, thinking of my mother. The whipping has seemed to hurt her more than it bothered me. The welts from the switches will heal, but the pain in my mother's face is perplexing and static. Her beautiful brown eyes dilated, wide and weary. It is as if she knows she cannot reach me anymore. When she asked why I ran away, I said nothing because I feel nothing, except fear. My mother was so angry.

One of the first set of rules you learn in this culture is to answer when an adult is speaking to you. The first hit came to my face. Sworn to secrecy, I cannot explain, no matter the pain it causes. I must protect my mother. Robert told me he would hurt her. I believe him. I won't say a word. I love her too much, and I know what he is capable of. Some time ago, my siblings and I saw him hitting her during an argument in their room. That day I wanted to kill him with my bare hands. He stood over my mother, yelling at her, slapping her face. With every strike, I clenched the inside of my jaw until I tasted blood. I wished him dead.

What gives anyone the right to treat another person that way! I screamed inside. If only my mother could read my mind and see inside my heart. This seen-and-not-heard culture is blinding. She is too exhausted from working two jobs, too weary of being a mother raising children alone in a culture that is changing beyond the oppressive restraints of her own past.

It is a past where children are not permitted to speak freely about their feelings and fears without coming off as weak and disrespectful. My mother's generation was forced to go along to get along—mentally conditioned to nurture the twisted lies that a man is different because of the color of his skin. Black people seem to lose the value of who they are and pass the distorted perception to the next generation—to the degree that their blood, sweat, and tears are less valuable compared to the rest of humanity. It seems the entire world becomes brainwashed into believing its bigotry. Such were the times. For children like me, seen and not heard, we too must go along to get along.

While my mother tries to keep up with the changing culture, rage sets a fire inside of me. I did not know it then, but my pen would become the torch that would begin the inferno. Children living in this seen-and-not-heard society will soon give birth to a menacing offspring. Rebellion will be its name. A generation seen and not heard produces a forest of thorns; thorns growing from the inside out, springing up, angry and wild, and that same generation will set the forest on fire, sit back, and watch it burn. Trusting no one, cursing the sky, they will shoot without aiming because the entire world has lied to them with its twisted contradictions. Something is very wrong when the messages are mixed and unclear. No one tells you, so you are forced to find out as you go.

The fallout from the time I ran away shifts into second gear when Robert gets home on furlough. There is a disgusting aroma in the air—a mixture of Roberts's cigarette smoke, his cologne, and his lies. He sits smug-faced in the living room and tells me to stand there and not move. My mother's expressions go from troubled to angry and then back again. I stand in front of them with my hands down by my side. Robert looks at my mother. He talks about how grown and "fast-tailed" I've become since he left overseas; as if I am not standing there. My blood boils. I can't stand the sight of him. My mother drops her head as if she is searching for answers. I want to tell her the truth about the scaly snake she calls her husband and the way he touches me when she is away at work. I remain quiet, listening to the convenient cover-up he uses to hide the truth of who he really is—a sea snake, a monster. I rage.

He seems to believe his own lies. They continue to question me, and I can see the flick of Robert's split tongue; it sneaks out even with his mouth closed. I cut my eyes away.

"What is wrong with you?" My mother screams, desperately trying to understand why her once-happy middle child has become detached to the point of running away from home. Concern, anger, and sadness mix inside her brown eyes. I keep quiet. Robert's warning still hisses in my ear. *How do I answer my mother without hurting her heart?* In silence, I stand condemned. If I speak out, I will cause more trouble than if I just stay silent—either way, I am guilty. Guilty of being alive in a culture that kills you and then asks you why you died; I remain silent. Robert interrogates me about why I ran away from the house. More rage boils in my gut. A damn pretentious question if I have ever heard one—he should already know the answer; the seawater must have given him a severe case of amnesia. Motionless, I say nothing. Perhaps somewhere in his perverted mind, he believes it is his right to rape, to hit, and take whatever he likes. I want to scream; *I left because I knew you would be coming home soon. I knew you would touch me again. I ran away so I could finish dying in peace.* But I keep quiet. To say anything would be to head into dangerous territory; my mother must never know.

She yells, "Don't you hear your daddy talking to you?"

The question incites me beyond rage. I could explode. My flesh crawls, and then, the words fly, instinctively, like vomit.

"He is not my daddy!" Robert strikes me hard in the face. I take it, steadying myself for the next blow. He has already killed my spirit, my sense of safety, and my view of sexuality, but I'd be damned to hell if I ever call this sea creature my dad. *My daddy would never touch me the way he has!* Robert hits me again, knocking me to the floor. The room spins, and I hear voices, chattering up from the ground. They sound like ghosts, whispering in my head. *Stay down, keep quiet, and do only as you are told. Don't make it harder on yourself; you must go along to get along. Do not think; do not ask questions, just die quietly. This is the way it is. This is your fate; the way it has been for generations.*

From inside the trench of my mind, I hear voices, feeling like I've gone completely crazy. Unsure how to respond or what to believe anymore, I swallow the acid that explodes in my stomach. It burns as it moves in both directions. A concoction of fear, hate, and rage mixes inside as I waited for my mother to stand up for me, to tell him that he cannot treat me that way. She didn't. Such are the times of this *seen and not heard* culture. I tell myself she is afraid of him—fear has a way of making you watch from the inside out and never say a word.

When I get up off the floor, a chill runs over me. My world shifts and the trench deepen. In my room, I repress every emotion, thinking of my dad. In my mind, I drift through the catacombs of apathy; a graveyard for the living where you barely move and breathe because it hurts too much to think, to dream, to feel. I know my father is there, somewhere. I will search until I find him. When the house becomes still and quiet, I journal the rage; it is my weapon, my only way out. In time, I find that writing is a defense; a secure hiding place where I build impassable walls of paper and ink, and there, only there, can I set myself free.

Monster

This poem was written years after I ran away from home.

I must run away. Far and fast, I will go away beyond his monstrous grasp. I will run. Lost and alone, there is no home sweet home for me. Not anymore. There is only fear, shame, and the pursuing pain of a monster my mother did not see. But, how could she? How could anyone even tell? What features can unveil a handsome visitor from hell? Self-absorbed and vain, I imagine that is how he came, with perverted passions left wild and untamed. Set free to roam with just enough cologne to cover up the stench of fire and brimstone. It's a Monster!

See him dressed up all tall and fine, driving a yellow Eldorado from 1969, and saying a whole lot of sweet nothings to soothe my mama's stress and ease her worried mind. He is her Superman, her hero; who would ever know her way out of the ghetto would arrive in full military fatigues. Who would ever believe he is not who he appears to be! He smiles a beguiling smile, looking at her but all the while, lustfully inspecting her child. Watch him! A slithering snake, he lays low and waits for the perfect time to strike. Fangs emerge as he hisses the words, "tell anyone and I will end your life!" The fear is paralyzing, and so no one ever hears of the wickedness these monsters commit. Could it be only me, or is there a lamenting symphony of boys and girls silenced by a serpent's hiss? A secret so haunting, it screams; the venom, so toxic it murders your dreams. The terror is so constricting it enslaves, and the shame is so degrading, victims dig their own graves.

Heed this warning.
Be careful with your little girls and boys, when they lose their childlike ways and forsake their precious toys, and the light in their eyes disappears. Careful when their fairy tales turn into a living hell. The clock ticks loudly pass the hour of twelve, and you never even notice when the last petal fell. Listen well—listen well; be careful! Some monsters are difficult to detect, creeping in with secret cravings you could never imagine or suspect. I once believed a merchant marine with training and skill would surely know wrong from right. But now I know better. Monsters only care about satisfying their sick appetites. They take what only God can give and believes it to be their right. Lost in the abyss of a twisted mental pit, they are captives of their own perversion; Hitler's shoes would be a perfect fit.

Rage, only rage; I am a slave to it. An outcast damaged and rejected. Touched and now, I'm it. No one to trust, because no one stopped it. So, I just give up. I belong only to the wind, and where it blows, I will go; hiding the rage deep inside, so no one will ever know precisely how or when I died. The Bible says you gotta watch and pray, but behind closed doors, no one is watching, no one is listening for what little lips are too afraid to say. When children go quiet, slow down, stop to see them, to hear them. Look at their faces, search their eyes. Ask them tenderly questions of why. Parents, please stop being so busy, quit your bickering, and spend more time listening.

There may be a monster lurking by.

Many years would pass before I settled into these thoughts, but when we are arrested in development, we tend to straddle dimensions of time. This poem was written in three voices: the voice of a child; the one who ran away because no one saw the tears or heard the cries. The voice of a soldier shouts in between the rhymes; the one that died inside the battlefield of my mind before ever having the chance to solemnly swear the oath of "defense against enemies, foreign and domestic…So help me God." There are enemies, not made of flesh and blood, yet they are more horrendous than these could ever be. The voice of the writer carries a lesson from the thorns in this poem, this warning: Please take heed; Protect the children! They are the future.

Prize Jewel

The world is filled with "odd" people; you know those people who seem a little quirky or strange; even insane. Never judge them, because you never know when, why, how or what happened. Judgment only brings more judgment. One of the most valuable lessons from the thorns is: be graceful with others; for the kindness you give will return to you — one hundred times more.

As the sun begins to set, Michael and I walk back home from the Oakland Park Flea Market. He bought a book on spells and curses while I became obsessed with a new series of comics I came upon in the graphics section. The Nightmare comics are a hair-raising assortment of strange tales that have attached themselves to me. Stories of zombies and gory pictures of the living dead; I emptied my piggy bank to buy the newest volume; the books are an escape from the grand illusion of life. Another day passes, and I wake up to disappear inside the graves of the tormented souls that lurch through the pages. Their shadowy world accepts me, and among the rotting flesh of the undead, I don't feel as ugly and alone. Hidden behind an awkward smile, so no one sees, and in-between the pages of my magazine, no one ever knows I am gone.

I miss my Midnight. The mango trees in the backyard shade her grave and those of my other beloved pets; I trusted them with my secrets. Midnight, my hamster Cindy, and the puppy that I never got a chance to name — he never made it past six weeks old. Animals have a divine nature. They are so unlike humans; they love unconditionally. It is getting lonelier without them, but maybe it is best that I do not have any more pets. Robert has said that I love animals too much, insisting that I should not have pets if I cannot learn to treat them like the animals they are. His accusation confuses me. What could he possibly know about the love of human or animal?

Midnight loved me as much as I loved her; she died on a chilly morning when Robert started the car; it had been early, just before the break of dawn. Robert told us to get in the car. I am still not sure how she got out of the house or when she made her way up into the warmth of the engine block of the car. From the backseat, I heard a sudden snap when the key turned inside the ignition. I could have never imagined it was the sound that killed my Midnight. Leon, Michael, Linda and I looked on from the backseat as Robert lifted the hood and pulled her out from the fan belt of the car. He slung her mangled body to the side of the house and slammed the hood shut. He has more regard for the butt of his cigarette than he did for my Midnight; he never looked back at her. My eyes saw it, but my heart refused to believe. Stuck in a dream, I looked in the opposite direction. *Soon, I will wake up.* I tried to convince myself that the sudden snapping sound was not real; the black object lying lifeless in the dirt was not real. *The tears running down my face are not real. This is just a dream. Midnight is in the house, somewhere, waiting for me. But it is impossible to cry in your sleep; isn't it?*

Robert restarted the car and waited. He placed a cigarette in the corner of his mouth; nose to the sky, he struck a match and leaned back against the seat. He had one arm across the armrest, the other, on top of the door panel. The smoke burned my watery eyes, letting me know this was no dream. As the cigarette sags between Roberts' lips, his words were cruel and just as caustic as the smoke that carried them.

"You loved that damn cat too much. You caused its death. I told you before! You don't need to have any pets. Always carrying it, and petting it, you loved it too much; it is your fault it is dead. Get out and go bury it." Robert ordered. He stared dead ahead. Smoke sputtered from his nostrils and mouth with every breath.

Leon, Michael, and Linda got out of the car to help me bury Midnight in the backyard. Like gravediggers, we creep through the dewy grass. We had found a place to lay her to rest, near the base of the mango tree. Leon limped to the tool shed to get a shovel. We gathered close with no words as he dug a hole. Michael placed Midnight inside the shallow grave. Guilt-ridden, I cried. Robert said it was my fault, and maybe he was right. She belonged to me. I should have made sure she was in the house. I should have checked twice before I got in the car. *My fault, it is all my fault.* Around the site of Midnight's grave, the spirit of guilt floated in front of me, whispering, "You killed her." I could hear it. I heard it before; accusing me of my parents' divorce, Ms. Lynn's anger, and Robert's mistreatment. Now, the same voices judge me, blaming me for the horrible incident, cementing the belief that every grief, past, present, and future, would be my fault.

I whisper to her, "I'm sorry Midnight. I am so sorry I let you down."

The morning wind blew through the mango trees as Michael rubbed my back.

"It's all right, Sandra." He tried to comfort me, but he cried too — we all did. Forming a circle and holding hands, we bowed our heads while Leon prayed over Midnight's grave. She was more than just an animal to me. I would swear she had a soul because she shared it with me after mine was gone and expressed a love and sensitivity many humans do not have. Some people will never know how to love so unselfishly.

In the empty days that go by, I let go of trying to understand a man who says an animal is just an animal, yet his actions are as debased as a hyena or a slithering grass snake. I think of the story I once read about Cain and Abel. The first murder in history did not involve animals, but humans: blood brothers, one became consumed with jealousy and hatred of the other. How then can anyone say the life of my Midnight does not deserve the depth of a love that adores and values its life, its purpose for being alive? And how can someone love something too much? The contradictions puzzle me.

The stories of faith Joyce taught us clashes with my reality; everything is wrong. I hate it here. Like a kite flailing in a violent wind, I wrestle with manic emotions. The pain in my stomach is getting worse. My mom gives me antacids, but nothing helps the ache of losing Midnight. *We had plans. We were supposed to run away to New York together, but she left without me.*

The death of Midnight drives me deeper into an emotional trench where I feel completely lost. Not like in a daydream, not like anywhere really. My thoughts evaporate, like the morning dew when the sun rises. They drift away to nowhere. I lose the concept of time, unsure when I leave myself or when I return. The present is too painful, and the future too impossible. The nothingness is a blessed reprieve. It disconnects me from everything.

The neighbors begin to talk. On the way from Ms. Freeman's storehouse, Michael stays close to me when our neighbors across the street stop to ask questions. "What happened to your forehead?" Mrs. Williams asks about the knot that sits above my left eye. She gives me a sidelong look when I tell her I fell off my bike. The same stare my teachers used to give me. No big deal; all is normal.

The nosy neighbor continues to probe, and I turn quickly towards Michael. There is an old saying: "What goes on inside this house, stays in this house." I hear her chatting with another neighbor as we walk away. "I haven't seen her riding a bike," she asserts. At that moment, I have a fervent desire to lose the manners

Joyce and my mother taught me. Instead, I drop my head to the ground and walk to the backyard with Michael. I try to avoid contact with people. They are too nosy. My stomach boils because I do not like people up in my face, asking questions which I cannot explain and if I could, it would not matter anyway. I would just be another topic of their gossip. Inside, I scream, *mind your own damn business.*

Amid the scattered clouds above, I walk to meet Linda after she gets out of school today. Through the years, we have become closer; still, there are some things I hide from her. Secret things no one must know. I do not tell her about school. I can't take the chance of her slipping up and telling Mom. And I do not tell her my plans for running away again. I reckon she will find out soon enough. The day she wakes up, and I'm gone, then she will know. Time has a way of telling all our secrets. Though we live in the same house, Linda and I exist in two different worlds. She is in the fifth grade this year at Oriole Elementary. Beautiful and confident, she gets prettier as the days' pass. Her school is almost out, and I wait for her near the wooded area off 31st Avenue, near the Oakland Park Flea Market.

A narrow sidewalk separates the wooded enclave from the streets. We meet near the shallow edge of the opening. I wonder if there is a hidden pond inside this glade, like the one at my secret hiding place.

"Peanut let's go inside and see what's in there," I suggest, looking curiously into the thicket.

"Yea, let's go," Linda agrees. She is usually up for any adventure within reason. We go into the woods, past the thick brush, stepping over fallen branches. The land looks untouched, unvisited. Vines crisscross in every direction. Dried twigs snap under our feet. The noise from the traffic falls quiet as we make our way further inside the woodland. The area is dense with thirsty-looking trees. Their branches spread like scrawny fingers, begging for water. The stalks are splintered and flaky. Flecks of light from the treetops move about the dead leaves that blanket the ground. I look for birds, a squirrel, and any signs of life. Nothing stirs, nothing creeps; not even in the spiders' web. There is only stillness here; I absorb it.

We stoop, crouching under bowed foliage, moving closer to the middle ground. In the distance, there is a clearing. It dips off into a dry ravine where a few aging trees lean into traces of light.

Linda stops suddenly, seeing something on the ground ahead. A strange object rests quietly among the dirt and leaves. A sense of uneasiness creeps alongside us. We stay close together and cautiously step toward the spectacle. Looking down, we see it is the skull of an animal resting alone among the falling leaves. I can only think about its life. *What was it? Did it have a family? What caused it to die?* I think about my Midnight and reach for it. Linda becomes terrified. Panic-stricken, she reaches her own conclusions about the skull.

"Something must have killed it," Linda says with alarm. Her wide eyes scan over the glade hastily. She looks forward and back and forward again.

"Something must be in here!" she gulps.

Linda does not stick around to ask questions. She shrieks so loudly that the sound could almost wake the dead. Gripped with fear, she runs, kicking up dried leaves, creating a new way out of the glade. Unafraid, I watch her run. I catch up with her on the outside of the woods, but not before picking up the skull. I will give it a new resting place. I find an old shoestring and route it through the eye sockets of the skull, making a necklace, wearing it; never once believing it was morbid or strange.

After that time, Linda remarked of how I wore the skull like it was a prized jewel. While she had appeared freaked out by it, I felt relaxed, because I could relate to it. And besides, it took the attention off my forehead.

Dis-ease begins in our mind; the storehouse of thoughts—deep within the subconscious; the seat of the human soul. Childhood abuse and neglect create distorted beliefs, where reality hides behind rage and silent tears like tainted glass, blurred and obscure. Our perception of reality is then made clear by our actions, and every action or inaction is caused by how we think. We must guard the way we think, and challenge our reality based on God's truth, not merely on our limited thoughts and feelings that trauma often skews; for we may be dead wrong. "Whatever we think, *that's* what we will become" ~Proverbs 23:7.

Loveless Love Songs

Science has yet to understand the magnitude of music. It can inspire, heal, incite, comfort, and unite humanity beyond the distractions of race, class, and culture. Music is undeniably powerful as it moves, weaving its magic inside of us with vibration, rhythm, and energy. Like a grand hypnotist, music reaches deep inside the mind, creating streams of limitless ideas before capturing the soul to an intended goal; there is a message in the flow of every beat. Be mindful of that message; for it can serve as a deadly poison or as the greatest therapy.

Mid-day afternoon, my mother is home earlier than usual. She goes into her room and keeps the door partly open. That's peculiar, because she usually walks in, closes the door, and goes straight to sleep. Robert is overseas, and I pray he stays away and never comes back, imagining him shipwrecked on an island of hungry cannibals off the West Atlantic coast, preferably adrift inside the Bermuda Triangle. Somewhere I read there is no chance of coming back from that place. As I step into the hallway, I hear my mom singing. The song is beautiful, but her voice sounds sad. The lyrics are that of a love song that surprisingly has no lover. It is a loveless love song. From the room door, she looks tired, a little more than usual. The song flows and circles back slow, like sleepy waves upon the seashore.

> *"You're nobody till somebody loves you.*
> *You're nobody till somebody cares.*
> *You're nobody till somebody loves you.*
> *So, find yourself, somebody, to love."*

I drop my head, looking away from her. I cannot understand the extreme demands society places on her life. Still, she seems to demand much more from herself. Sick or well, she goes to work, driven by some force that keeps her going despite the circumstances. Day in and day out, year after year, I've seen her toil. The strain on her face tells me the load is heavy.

"Mama?" I tap on the door. With a starry smile, she motions for me to sit next to her on the bed. She keeps singing. I sit on the bed, staring at her. In my eyes, she is the most beautiful woman in the world. She smells like the sweet gardenia flowers that bloom on the tree near the front yard. The soft fragrance envelops the entire room. I put my hands on my lap and breathe in the treasure of her presence. Grateful that she is home, I hold onto the moments. Her presence is a priceless gift. She pauses and whispers, "Thank you, Jesus." I have heard her whisper those words all my life. I fidget with my shirt, restless from so many questions without answers. *What is love? What is the true meaning of the word? And why is she always thanking Jesus, when she looks so tired and downcast?* I don't trust this culture with the answer. In my wounded mind, any answers it supplies will be a barefaced lie. I have seen its hypocrisy and disgusting contradictions. I slump my shoulders on the bed and wait for my mother to tell me the grand mystery of this confusing life.

I wait to feel safe again, to feel alive again, where my heart beats without fear and pretense. But my mother is tired. She sings herself to sleep. I sit on the edge of the bed, remembering when the world was a quieter place where I dreamt of becoming a police officer and joining the military. Now, something is telling me that I will not live to see the age of twenty. The sharp pains in my chest are getting worse, but like everything else that hurts, I learn to ignore it.

"Mama? Mama, do you want me to take your shoes off, so you can rest better?"

Her eyes push open. "No baby, I got to go back to work. I'm just resting my eyes."

"Mama, are you hungry? Do you need anything from the kitchen?" I ask, wanting to do anything to help her rest.

"No thank you, baby, I'm fine." She replies, never looking at me. Fatigue creases the outer corners of her eyes. *She works too hard,* I think to myself, glancing at her hands and arms. An assortment of scars has my attention. I've never noticed them before.

Burn marks scar her hands and underneath the sides of her arms, all the way up to her elbows. My mother never told me she suffered from burns, and I wonder how she got hurt. The charred parts look painful still. I touch my hand, rubbing my fingers across the scar from the bacon grease burn, remembering the indescribable pain. I can only imagine how painful my mother's scars have been.

"Mama, what happened to your arms?" Asking the question makes me feel uneasy, but curiosity has always gotten the best of me. My mother stretches out her arms, touching the scars.

"I got burned at work. It is a part of the job." She says in a loyal manner.

"Does it still hurt?" I ask.

"I am used to it now; it doesn't bother me anymore. Child,

you gotta be tough in this world. I ignore the pain and just keep going." She shoots the words out, switching her posture, fully awake. Her temperament becomes firm and defensive. I pull my scarred left hand underneath my shirt, twirling the corner of it around my finger.

My mother sits up on the bed and tells me of a time in history. She talked about when she was growing up, she had to work hard and basically fend for herself. A child of the 1940s, she was not born in a hospital, but at home, on my grandparents' farm in Havana. A midwife, hot water, and tattered rags welcomed the second of seven children for my grandparents.

"The Holy Bible serves as the certificate of birth and death for Negroes," she says. My mother speaks about her siblings and their humble beginnings in Havana, Florida. No electricity, no indoor plumbing, a wash bin serves as a bathtub. "In those days, nothing was wasted; not food, not water, not nothing. Our clothes were passed down to the next youngest, and we respected our elders. We were grateful for what we had." My mothers' tone turns serious.

"One of my first jobs was at the Three-Way Cleaners and Laundry in Tampa." She explains how, as a young teenage mother, she worked hard to earn a living. "It is not easy for Black people in a racist world. I don't get tired because you do not have the choice of getting tired." Her voice scorches the air, and her eyes betray her words of not "getting tired." She looks exhausted.

"I thank God I had a praying mama." She pauses for a moment and then continues. "We never would have made it through the tough times without my mother's prayers. Ever since I was a little girl, I heard my mama pray and sing. Working the fields picking beans, cleaning the house, cooking our meals, washing our clothes on an old scrub board, she would sing like an angel. All she knew was work, church, and her children. She would walk to church, even when her feet were too swollen to fit inside her shoes." My mother speaks about my grandma Rachel as if she was a saint. "God has been too good for me to complain about anything. My mother didn't complain, and neither will I," she breathes.

My mind travels through her stories, her journey, from there to here. I begin to feel selfish for running away, guilty of causing her more pain. She has been through more than I can imagine. Self-condemning voices scream inside my head. They tell me to keep quiet, suck it up, and stop causing trouble. *Just pretend you are fine.* My mother has been through enough heartache. Other voices ask me why I was even born. *Where do I fit into her life? What is my worth? What is my price?* Compared to her harsh history, and that of my grandmother, I feel weak, like a soldier unfit for battle. How could I think I could make it in the Armed Forces, let alone the police academy? I try to sort through the array of conflicting emotions and the voices in my head—it is too impossible. Time after time, I try to bury the pain, but it reappears, like sharp thorns breaking through the surface of my skin.

I tell myself, no matter what, my mother must never know my secrets. It would be devastating for her to find out. The trench deepens where I must not only hide the truth from my mother, I must also find a way to hide it from myself. My mom seems to deny herself the permission to feel her own hurts, to cry her own tears, and to find comfort and empathy of being human. Sometime, long ago, the right to be human must have been denied. *How do you give the understanding and support that you never received? How do you find empathy for another when your heart still bleeds?* And because no one stopped the bleeding, misery becomes normalcy.

The questions and inconsistent rules are confusing. The stories, the songs, the whispers of Jesus—what is it all about? Why would a great God send His Only Son to sacrifice His life on a cross for people who never need to cry, never get tired, and never feel weak? What is the point of it all? Life seems to be a complex game of time and secrets, a futile game of perfection, where you hide from self-expression, weakness, and any sign of being human.

On my mother's bed, I sit still and quiet. The chasms between the cultures are too wide to cross. No one talks of emotions in this seen-and-not-heard culture. Any signs of emotions— sadness, fear, anger, contempt, and disgust are unacceptable in my family, so you learn to "get over it" or bury it deep inside. Zero validation, the penalty for having emotions labels you with an accusation of "trying to get attention," which is utterly unacceptable. Such are the times.

Developing a self-protective nature became normal; believing I must fend for myself, learn how to work hard, sing a sad song, and never speak of sorrow or pain—all became "normal." I must learn how to play the game, to be acceptable, to be okay, to smile when inside I want to scream and stop the world from turning long enough to get off the ride. Like breathing, hiding inside myself became normal, but truth be told, I had folded a long time ago. So, like my dad, I sat pokerfaced, waiting for the world to change, among the tombs of a childhood that was long gone. Still, I waited. I waited for the noises to stop long enough for me to hear a love song; a song of truth—a song where the lyrics will not betray the melody.

Stolen Generations

"Racism is a much more clandestine, much more hidden kind of phenomenon, but at the same time, it's perhaps far more terrible than it's ever been." ~*Angela Davis*

Some storms are unpredictable, inescapable. Like destiny, you cannot control them. You must ride them out, to learn what only they can know. There are lessons only the storms can teach. The body snatchers have come with badges and guns. They call themselves: "the police." I look around and see a world full of thieves, men without conscience—cold-hearted beasts with no sense of justice or respect for their fellow human being. I remember the rage I felt that day; I remember it well.

A fierce wind travels up 24th Street. The cyclone catches Leon in its grip, but he would not be the only one. Even before the 1970s, the mass incarceration of young black men for nonviolent offenses forced families apart. Four centuries later and the same system of tyranny and control circles back. Some may call it jail or prison, but truth be told, its covertly, another stolen generation. Once again, history repeats and the thorns grow deeper.

Michael, Linda, and I stare out the bedroom window. Red and blue lights flash through the curtains.

"What is happening?" I ask Michael. Michael's leg shakes as he bites his lower lip. Linda's eyes appear motionless and confused. My chest hurts at the sight of my brother in handcuffs. Leon is up against the police car in our driveway. His eyes stretched wide like he is trying to find his way through the dark. We stay in the room, quietly pacing from the window to the door and back again. The voice of my mother and the police mingles with gibberish coming from the police radio. A fractured look topples over Leon's defeated posture. I wanted to scream. *Why are the police arresting our brother?*

I sit on the bed, pushing myself up against the corner of the wall, disappearing inside a memory—a magical, happy memory. Leon, Michael, Linda and I were together. "Pick a card, any card." Leon's tone pulled us into the game. He loved to play the same one. "The hands are quicker than the eye," he'd eagerly proclaim. We sat together in our room. Leon has always been excited and high-strung, especially when he performs with his deck of cards. He has gotten better through the years. "Come on now! Watch closely because the hand is quicker than the eye," he said again and showed us three cards: one red, two black. "Find the red card. Watch carefully, because the hand is quicker than the eye." He wowed us with one trick after the next, smiling the entire time.

The flashing police lights bring me back to the present. A look of betrayal outlines Leon's face. We watch helplessly from the bedroom window as the police place Leon in the back seat of the patrol car. I want to reach him, to touch him, and whisper in his ear that everything will be all right. But I have heard the stories of police brutality, and I am afraid for my brother. I scream inside, *Leave him alone! He is my Brother! Take your hands off him!* I continue the inner tirade until the red and blue flashing lights fade away down the street. My left index finger is numb. The blood cannot get through the twisted knot of my shirt. What will they do to him? Where will he sleep? What will he eat? Will he be safe? Where will he live? In jail, prison, slavery: different names, same destination. Michael, Linda, and I stare out in silence.

The conduct of the police reminds me of the principal who paddled me. In his office, I had been just another black girl with an attitude. His punishment was swift, no compassion, only action, and reaction, crime and punishment. He had a job to do—that's it. He did his job. The police reacted with the same blind authority. *Who did they serve and protect,* I think to myself; *What did my brother do to deserve the way the police handled him in the front yard? It was as if he is guilty before any trial ever starts. No judge, no jury, they have already decided the verdict by their abusive treatment.*

My grasp on reality slips further away. I am not sure if I ever had a grip on it. What is real? *How can a society handle people so cruelly and then expect them to submit? What happened to dignity?* The oxymoron is maddening. I remember how my insides quaked with feelings of injustice for my brother. *What is justice, what is liberty?*

Michael and Linda sit next to me on the bed.

"What did he do wrong?" Linda asks. Michael opens the door and steps out into the hall. When he comes back in, he tells us the story. "Mama said he stole something, a TV, I think," Michael answers, but appears uncertain of his words. He drops his chin in his hand. The blank expression on his face begs the question of what is true. Linda draws her knees to her chest and drops her head. I say nothing. What words could possibly make sense of the stolen generations? Despite the accusations against Leon, I do not believe any of it. And if the allegations are true, my heart defends him all the same. Right or wrong, there is a deeper truth. I feel it, somehow, I know it. The truth echoes in between the hidden places; unseen places that tell me Leon is hurting, trying to find his way in a world that double deals, and hides its hands. I know of his heartache from years of jumping, falling, and waiting for a father to catch him in his arms, and teach him about a life that is as complex as the stars in the universe. I rage against the law, and the bandits we call "the police" that stole him out of his own house. With my own eyes, I witness their brutality; inhumane treatment that contradicts the law they are supposed to uphold. Innocent until proven guilty is a sick joke.

I remember growing angrier, believing there is more hypocrisy than humanity in the social order of things. *How can the law accuse him of stealing when the same law is a grievous thief, who enslaved and raped countless people throughout the world's history?* I have read the inhumane stories—from Harriet Tubman to Martin Luther King. In my mind, every pain magnifies, and the issues are not merely black and white. Shadowed hints of truth lay hidden in the gray areas of life, where only the conscience can decide what is wrong or right. But what if the conscience is distorted? Who then makes the rules? Who gets to choose what is right and what is wrong? The law, the police, a merchant marine, an angry grandfather; who gets to decide? More rage! I implode, trying to make sense of nonsense, but the growing frustration muddies every attempt.

Later, I will discover the charges against my brother were hearsay, claims of stealing a TV that was never proven and never found. No evidence, yet he will spend time in prison. He is a teenager: a child! The Pledge of Allegiance, we recited every morning in school loses its gleam. "One nation, under God, indivisible, with liberty and justice for all." What travesty! *Where is the justice for my brother and others like him?*

There was once a time when all I believed in was my sister's stories of faith, her sweet lullabies, and the whispers of Jesus between my mother's sighs. The world made sense with a simple message of love and new beginnings, but rage has replaced hope and piercing thorns surround me in this complex society of unsolvable riddles. *How do you believe when everything is wrong? Now, my brother is gone, and I want to set the world on fire!*

Baseball Bat

"You must face your monsters to defeat them."
~Wienna Jane Hamilton

Just a few days after the police takes Leon, Joyce drives over to the house. She wants answers and is not leaving without them. Big knots in my stomach dissolve sending acid like lava up my throat as she questions me.

"What is going on?" Joyce asks, confronting me about my recent behavior. She refuses to leave without knowing why I am not in school, wearing a skull of a dead animal and becoming a complete mess. Someone must have told her. *Gossipers make me sick to my stomach,* I think to myself. Arms folded, head down, I don't answer.

Robert is home on furlough. This time, he stays home longer than usual. Joyce takes me outside to speak with me alone. We sit in her car on the curb, near the mailbox. Afraid he will come out, I keep an eye on the front door. Trembling hands, vacant eyes; Joyce sees it and questions me past the lies I hide behind. I tell her I am fine, but she is not buying it. The look in her eyes tells me she knows the answers to the questions.

"Why did you run away before?" Joyce asks. I keep quiet.

"What is going on? You are running away, Leon is in jail, and no one is telling me anything." Her hands strangle the top of the steering wheel. She exhales and asks again. "Sandra, tell me what's the matter; talk to me," she pleads, but it is hard to hear her voice over the hiss of Robert's threats in my head.

While she talks, I quietly plan the next run. Leon is gone, and I know my departure is not too far behind.

Joyce sits sideways. She leans close to me in the front seat, waiting for an answer. When I try to talk, nothing comes out. *If she knows my secrets, she may not love me anymore;* that's what my mind says. The thought of her not loving me is too much to bear. I must continue to hide and pretend to be the same little girl she once taught to dance, to sing, and to dream. But now, my only wish is for everyone to leave me alone.

Not knowing what to believe anymore, I Look out the passenger side window, questioning everything I once believed. *What is real? What is truth? And if faith, love, and hope exist, then, where is it?* Faith did not stop Robert from hurting me, hope did not prevent the police from taking my brother, and the elusive concept of love sat idly by and watched it all happen.

Joyce leans in closer, determined to get answers. The air outside is still as if it is listening, like an informer, ready to squeal just as soon as I open my mouth. I do not trust it.

Joyce takes a deep breath and turns away. I glimpse the side of her face—flushed red, her temple pulses. It tells me she may already know the answers to her questions. Joyce touches my hand.

"Sandra, I've known you all your life. I changed your diapers and cared for you. I love you. Tell me what's wrong? I am here." With her next to me, I begin to feel safe enough to talk, to open my heart and dig through the remains of a lost childhood and speak the words I swore I never would.

Joyce strokes my hand as I begin to tell her everything. I do not look at her reaction at first, afraid of what I might see. I tell her about what Robert has been doing to me while Mom is at work. I tell her everything. Quitting school, the constant fear, the isolation, the shame, and the rage I can't explain. Joyce listens calmly, drawing me closer to weep on her shoulder. She brushes my messy hair with her fingers. "I'm sorry I wasn't here to stop it," Joyce says, wiping away tears from my face.

"He told me he would hurt Mama and me if I said anything. I was too afraid to tell you. I'm sorry."

I run my shirtsleeve across my runny nose. "How long has he been hurting you?" Joyce asks me. Her nostrils flare.

"It started when we moved here, to 24th Street. Don't tell Mama," I plead. An anxious shiver runs over me at the thought of my mother finding out. The strain is unbearable. What a mess I've made of things. I want to disappear.

Joyce prays, and my thoughts scatter. I want to live with her, but she already has so many responsibilities. Now, she is stressed out about Leon and me; how much more can she take? I feel guilty for telling her, getting her involved in this mess. I stare out, through the front window of the car, wanting to fly away. Maybe my grandmother and Midnight will be waiting for me. When rage and hopelessness blend, you just want it all to end.

The sun sinks low behind us, and the air turns cooler than before. Joyce tells me a story. I have heard her stories all my life, but she tells me again as if it was for the first time. "God gave His only begotten Son, because of his great love for all humanity," she says, stretching out her legs in the car. I listen to the story of the Cross of Christ: a crown of thorns, His resurrection, His suffering, His mercy, and His love. She tells me He will never leave me, nor forsake me. I rub my puffy eyes, trying to listen, but the chatter in my head never stops.

"God will fight your battles," she says with confidence, pulling her head back before peering at the front door of the house. "Though you may feel you are alone, God will always be with you. Do you understand this, Sandra?" I nod, wanting to believe anything she tells me. A glance towards the front door and everything is still, almost too quiet. A part of me worries about Robert finding out I told Joyce. The other part of me, too angry to care, waits to run away.

Joyce does not leave. She stays with me, and we talk until the clouds move across the moon. I look down the street. A stray cat jumps from behind a garbage can near Pam's mother's house and quickly scurries out of view. I think of my Midnight. I stare up into the heavens where only a few stars are shining. By early dawn, the old brown Ford transforms into a sanctuary, and for the first time in a long time, I feel a sense of safety. Leaning back, I rest. I do not fall asleep, but I find something that sleep has not offered me in a long time: peace and rest. We both stay wide awake, and before we knew it, the night transformed into a new day.

The sun cradles us in soft sparkling rays, climbing from the eastern horizon.

"Do you believe it's morning already?" Joyce says, stretching her arms out. She peers curiously out the window, toward the front door, and then back to the clock on the dash of the car.

"No," I answer. "Where did the time go?" I say, grateful that Joyce stayed with me. The grass in the front yard glistens with the morning dew. Chirping birds announce the dawning of a new day. Joyce watches the time, but she does not rush away home. Instead, she seems to wait, calculating the minutes. For what, I do not know. I would think she would be tired and ready to go home after talking in the car all night. But an intense energy flows from her calm exterior. We stretch out and continue to talk past the constraints of time. Joyce tender heart shines through her eyes. A divine presence seems to have found a home inside her. I have seen it my whole life. I begin to notice how Joyce kept one eye on the front door and the other set on the button that opens her trunk. Her tone is soft as the petals of a rose, but something is stirring inside.

She turns casually, looking in every direction, rolling her shoulders and stretching her neck. Her eyes narrow, and then, in a blink, it happens. The front door opens. It is Robert. I try to swallow, but my breath is gone. I freeze. Hearing the trunk pop open, I turn towards Joyce, but she is already gone. Out of the car, into the trunk, she grabs a baseball bat. Just then, flicks of light jump around in front of my eyes. The fireflies appear out of nowhere.

Joyce rushes to the front door towards Robert. Dizzy, I step out of the car, cringing near the back taillight. Afraid Robert will find out I told Joyce; I feel the acid rising. What have I done? I've seen his guns; a militia of Cyclops loaded and ready to carry out his pass threats.

"Please God protect my sister," I whisper as I watch Joyce snap. He towers over her five-feet-five-inch frame. Joyce moves quick and fearless, right up to his face—she does not flinch. A crazy calmness sets up her swing. Elbows high, she rears back.

"I'm gonna crack your skull for what you did to my sister!" She wails and swings. He catches it midflight. I gasp; afraid he is going to hurt her. But Joyce is not intimidated. She rotates like a tornado. Tightening her grip, she spins, swinging again and again.

They tussle, jerking, scuffling until he brushes her back with a hard shove. She rebounds with fierce momentum, switching the direction of her aim. Sideways, she draws back. High in the air, the bat chops, barreling down. Robert raises his forearm to block. Intent on the conquest of a cracked skull or a broken bat, Joyce will not stop. My mother appears in the doorway. With shock and exhaustion in her expression, she says "What is this?" They argue, but I can't hear over the noise in my head. Then, the air is still; only huffs and cutting glances fill the silence. Neither Robert nor Joyce explains the truth. Robert sends my mother back inside.

"Get off my property!" Robert orders from the doorway. Fist clenched, Joyce will not back down.

"Who do you think you are? You can't run me off! This is my mother's property! This is my family!" Joyce firmly shouts. Her face glows red; there is a secret between her and Robert of which I was not aware. Later I will find out he tried to molest her when she was a young teenager, but she is a born fighter—he never tried her again. It would be sometime after that I would begin to understand the fury in her eyes. Old rage puts up a fervent fight; it is a rage she keeps locked inside from a history of sexual abuse that started before the age of 5. A world of thorns is not safe for children.

Outside the house that day, before she leaves, Joyce looks sternly at Robert. "You will pay!" she declares before walking away. Her words plant a fateful seed. Joyce places her bat in the trunk, and as she walks towards me, sweat trickles from her face and neck.

"Sandra." Her voice shakes. "I'm not gonna let nobody hurt you. You tell me if he touches you again and I will kill him dead!" Her jaw clenches. She tells me to always trust in God, no matter what. "I will be back soon. I love you," she says. But I already know, by the time she returns, I will be gone.

"Okay. I love you too."

Joyce leaves. I prepare to run.

Looking back on that time, I'd imagine the first swing of Joyce baseball bat brought it all back to his memory; his perversion and the sick secrets that comes with it; he was mindful of the fact that Joyce did not care about his scare tactics — the confrontation made it clear. The baseball bat confirmed the point that she could snap at any moment and crack his skull. And given the new rules of engagement, I wonder how well slept that night. But it did not matter; I wouldn't be around to find out. I knew there would be consequences.

Beat m*e or kill me, either way, I am out.* I am leaving to find my dad, and no one will stop me. I will find him, and at that moment, I will dream again. In his arms, I will listen to our melody play, the music of his heartbeat with mine. Just like old times in Tampa. I wanted to say goodbye, but I don't think my family will miss me too much; I cause too much trouble.

Michael is with Mr. Walker, a kind neighbor who lives at the end of the street. He treats Michael like a son. He has a tree-cutting business and teaches Michael the trade. Linda is over at Pamela's house again, which is a couple of houses away from Mr. Walker's. I will miss them, but I must run without telling them I love them, without knowing when I will see them again. I pull the black duffle bag out of the closet and begin to pack. Robert has taken my mother to work; the house is empty. I hurry and pack only what I need.

"I wish you were here to go with me. I miss you so much," I talk to Midnight as if she is still here. Talking to her calms my nerves. I take two items: a picture of Joyce and my *Top Song Hits* magazine. Reading song lyrics helps to quiet the chatter in my head. And the picture of Joyce reminds me that I am supposed to have faith, no matter what. I don't take any clothes; clothes and shoes are of no use to me. I can't care less about fashion and girly things. Misfit is not in fashion, nor do I feel the need to be. Thinking of the things Robert has done to me makes me hate being a girl.

In my mind, nothing really matters anyway. Something tells me I will not be around long enough to concern myself with material things. Black top and blue jeans, I prepare to run, holding onto the picture of Joyce. She is standing in a hallway wearing a shirt with pink and green floral prints, a short skirt, and black shades. She looked happier in the picture. Voices in my head tell me to hurry as I place the picture inside the duffle bag.

I try to decide where I am going or if it even matters at all. *What if I get caught running away? What if I cannot find my dad?* Adrenaline surges through every part of me. Either way, I must run. I have caused enough trouble for everyone. Running is my defense, but I must do it right this time: *no messing up, no getting caught, no coming back. Ever!*

More often than not, children run away from home because they no longer feel safe to stay. As the stars in heaven shine above, children escape to the street unaware of the predators that await; risking it all to be seen, to be heard, and to be loved.

Lost Melodies

"Change will not come if we wait for some other person or some other time. We are the ones we've been waiting for. We are the change that we seek." ~*President Barack Obama*

Northwest Seventh Avenue, Fort Lauderdale

I don't look back. Everything in me says fight or flight. I run. Hurrying off the main roads, cutting across back alleyways, I stay out of sight. Almost instinctively, my heart leads me to find my dad. I'm nearly twelve years old, but I feel aged and tattered. Still, I know my dad will still love me, just the way I am; that's what my heart wants to believe. The world opens wider when you are on the run. I won't turn back, hurrying straight ahead, remembering the bar off Sistrunk Boulevard. Some time ago, I heard my father might be working there.

The wind blows and whistles around me until I reach the northwest corner of Sistrunk Boulevard. Fear makes me feel like someone is watching.

I dart inside the Melody Bar, breathing out, hoping he is here. My stomach feels like someone punched the air out of it. Hungry, tired, and scared, I tremble unsure of the next step to make. "Please God, let me find my dad," I whisper, searching desperately through a haze of cigarette smoke and particles that float aimlessly through the stuffy air of the bar. Across the room of scattered chairs and faces, I see him.

"Daddy!" I shout. In that instant, I feel weak, but it doesn't matter because I know he will catch me. Tears of joy begin to flow at the sight of his face; it has been years. My clumsy feet cannot carry me fast enough; I run to him. Nothing else matters now; he will make everything okay.

"Dad!" I wave my hands, moving toward him.

Daddy! It's me!" I beam like a child again, standing in front of him, almost breathless. He wears a burgundy shirt, and his hair is thin and gray. He stands behind the bar. Customers lounge around the smoky saloon, but in my mind, it is only my dad and me. The light inside the bar is dim. "Dad!" I move closer, pushing myself against the edge of an old sandstone countertop standing between us. "I miss you! It's me!" Row after rows of bottles sits behind him on a shelf, sparking a happy memory of a song we would sing on the long road trips to Havana in the summer: "*You* take one down, pass it around, 99 bottles of Beer on the wall. 98 bottles of...” The chorus speeds by, and I feel a new fear. Something is wrong. My father does not seem to hear me or see me like I am a ghost.

“Daddy!” I tilt my head, leaning closer to him. “I came to see you, and I wanted to...” I hush myself, staring at his hands. They are still trembling, just as they had years before, but worse. A tired look of surrender bends his shoulders over, like a storm-damaged tree. Years have passed since I last saw him. His face bristles, unshaven and frayed, he wipes the counter with slow circular motions. I try to clear my throat, but something is stuck inside, making it hard to swallow. He glances up, looking out over my head. Hands still moving, making circles over the counter. It appears he has had a stroke.

“Daddy, I came to see you. I miss you. I...I wanted to see you and... tell you...” In midsentence, I stop talking. He stares blankly through me. That same empty stare, looking out at everything and seeing nothing. I try to pull myself together. The light is too dim, that's all. That's what my heart tells me. Any minute now and he will recognize me and speak my name.

“It's me...It's me, Sandra.” The words fall heavy from my quivering lips, and I suddenly realize my appearance is not that of the little girl he once knew.

No colorful barrettes or ribbons adorn my hair; many things have changed since he last saw me. The soul of his little girl has gone missing, somewhere out there. The freakish-looking spectacle standing in front of him is all that is left. Dropping my head, I turn my face to rake back the dry, tangled mats of hair with my fingers. I become awkwardly aware of the bra straps digging into my chubby shoulders from my double D cup size chest. No wonder he does not notice me—even I don't recognize me. I'm a mess.

I breathe out, suddenly thinking of school. I remember crying to my mother about the girls in my classroom who would bully me and make fun of my weight and breasts, calling me names like “Dolly Parton” and “Titty City.” I hate my body for more reasons than one and have wished I could become invisible to the cruel jeers; standing in front of my father right now; that wish must have come true.

The wrinkled jeans, oversized t-shirt, and dirty sneakers hide more than mismatched socks underneath. Somehow, I feel I have interrupted his life; I stand quietly to the side. My eyes water and my left index finger tugs at the edge of my shirt: twirling, waiting, twirling. My dad is still unresponsive. Swollen sacks of skin sit underneath his eyes. He limps from one end of the bar to the other, cleaning, making circles, stopping only to sip from a shot glass on the side of the counter. The sound of a loud crack from the back room causes my shoulders to jerk. I catch my breath, wincing in the direction of a small poolroom. The break shot of men playing pool streaks through the smoky air of the bar. I remember hearing that sound in my parents' store when we lived in Tampa. Striped and solid colored pool balls ramble out over the green baize covering. Watching his hands, I move towards the edge of the counter.

"Daddy?" I walk behind the bar, crossing the boundary of the counter that separates me from his arms. I wrap my arms around his waist and lay my head on his chest, and exhale. The worst that could happen is that he will push me away. *But I have nowhere else to go — nothing else to lose.*

"Daddy, it's me. Sandra."

Zero gravity, I feel his skin against mine, and I lift away to the moon. The need to breathe in again fades into the background of his heartbeat. I hear the melody of our song, and suddenly, I could feel the traces of the little girl I used to be. "Dad, I miss you." I squeeze him tighter, refusing to let go. The strong smell of gin blends in with the faint smell of Old Spice cologne reminding me of Christmastime.

A carousel of memories spin around me, and I begin to remember when it all fell apart: the years of coming home late at night, the gambling debts, and nerve-racking fights. The bottles of gin that sat up high on the throne of our home and all the angry words parents never think their children hear and know — words like stones; sharp and painful. He blinks at me as if he is trying to wake up from a deep sleep. And then, for the first time in years, I hear him say my name.

"Sandra?" He steps back and looks at me. The tattered rag dangles near his off-balanced hips. "Baby, how did you get here?" He slurs, staring at me as if I was someone else.

"I walked all the way. I needed to see you. Daddy, I miss you. How are you?" He hobbles to a small round, two-chair table that sits between the counter and the poolroom. I follow closely, remembering how I've dreamt of this day for so long; I have imagined every detail: Our eyes would meet. I would fall into his arms. He would see my broken heart and painful thorns and make it all go away. *Surely, he will tell me I can stay with him,* I think to myself. I can cook and clean and take care of him, and never see another monster again.

On the side of the room, a short-skirted woman with heavy makeup and glittery high heels sit alone. She crosses her legs, an elbow resting on the back of one hand while the other plays with a cigarette. She lifts her chin and strikes a pose. She is pretty and looks to be waiting for someone.

"Daddy?" I whisper, tilting toward him, needing to tell him why I came, wanting him to say to me that I can stay and never leave his side. A sudden burst of laughter pours loud behind me from a chunky, round-faced man tending the bar. A couple is standing at the counter.

"I got it, Roadman," the round-faced man says, wearing a white apron tied around a beer gut. My dad never looks his way. He nods slightly.

Blades of light wedge in as more customers enter the bar. I push my dirty sneakers under the chair and cross at the ankle, waiting for my dad to say something. Anything! Nervous, I want to twirl my shirt. I resist the urge because I have so much to say. He folds his hand slowly across his lap, sitting sideways, leaning slightly into the table. He is still quiet, but the circles have stopped.

So much has happened, and I need him to know. I want to tell him how I cried when the police took Leon away, and that I am afraid of everything. I want to tell him that I have sores hiding on my arms and thighs, places where I have tried to scratch the skin off, but the reek of Robert's touch still crawls inside, refusing to die. Now I am caught somewhere between six years old, and seventy-five and I don't know what to do. I need to tell him that I can't dream of joining the army and the police force anymore. The only dreams I have left are those of falling and dying—it feels real, not like a dream at all. The noise in my head will not stop. I need help.

But I stay quiet because nothing has changed. Somehow, I feel my telling him will only push him farther away, deeper inside his own inner pain. After all these years, his eyes tell me he is still unavailable, unreachable.

"Daddy, are you, all right?" I look at him, the frayed edges of the bar rag trembles with his hand. A moment later, he speaks.

"How…how you doing, baby? How's your mama?" He asks with a soft slur. The stroke must have affected more than his gait— froth forms in the corner of his mouth. Before I can answer, I notice his eyes drifting away to the corner of the bar. With a saddened heart, I watch, biting my lip, unable to tell him what I desperately need to say. In those moments, I find a treasure and a tragedy. The treasure is seeing my dad again after all this time; my heart still intertwines with the first man I have ever loved, and always will. The tragedy is seeing him again—after all this time, the thief of alcoholism and apathy still blinds him, until he cannot see how my heart bleeds.

I pray to vanish away into the air, disappear from this chair, so I don't have to get up and walk away. "Daddy, I love you, I have to go now," I say, looking at the side of his face. Quiet and still, only his hands move with steady quivers. He does not seem to hear me. "Daddy?" I whisper, tears falling against my will. "I love you."

Holding on to the fading melody, I turn my face and push the tears away. I stand to go. The chair scrapes against the tile floor, and my father looks up at the sound. "I love you, Dad, I have to go now. It's getting late." His glassy eyes widen until I can see my reflection and that of our lost melody. He clears his throat.

"Bah, baby, how you been doing? How's your mama?" The words tremble out. I look down, twirl my shirt, and swallow every pain; it does not matter anymore. His trembling hands cannot bear my heavy burdens. For the first time in my life, I will lie to my father, hoping to soothe the tremors in his hands somehow.

"I'm all right, Daddy. Mama is okay too." I turn away and walk out of the barroom.

Joyce taught us that one of the greatest gifts God has given us is the gift of imagination. The idea of using my imagination was easier to do in the warmth of her lullabies or between the pages of my favorite book. I never imagined when I was sitting in between my sister's knees in Dixie Court, getting my hair braided, watching my *Underdog* cartoons, that tonight I would be crossing over railroad tracks, running farther away from home.

A cold chill blow in the air as I hurry out of sight. I waited in vain for my father to call my name as I left out of the smoky bar. He did not call. I even slowed my restless pace just in case he decided he had more to say. He didn't.

The farther I walk away, the smaller the bar becomes. I remember how, from a distance, the bar started to resemble a small booth like the phone booths in my *Underdog* cartoons. I peered over my shoulder to see if there was the slightest possibility that he would leave out of the bar and come after me; fly through the air, defy his alcoholism and apathy, and save me from myself and the mounting fear. He never came.

During that time, I didn't understand the depth of my father's pain, but I knew he loved me. I felt it the day he lifted me up in his barbershop in Tampa. Safe in his arms, we flew to the moon together and danced to the melody of our heartbeat. The look in his eyes, the smile on his face told me that I was his princess and that it would always be that way—no matter what.

Profound loneliness settles inside when you realize no one is coming for you; no one cares enough, or maybe, there is a reason why; an unknown purpose for all the pain; a lesson that only the thorns can explain.

The evening was falling as I crossed the street. Memories can be tormenting, especially the good ones; I tell myself that was a long time ago; those days are gone. Memories are all that's left. There is no going back home. I run, heading to nowhere, believing my father has a secret identity. He is really a superhero, but he is just stuck right now, brainwashed, like Underdog inside a bar; a phony phone booth set up by another face of Simon Bar Sinister.

I was too young to understand it all then. The pieces didn't fit. It would be years before I made the connection of how art imitates life and how life seems to move in circles. Some lessons are more painful than others—this thorn would pierce every part of me.

I walk past the train tracks feeling like I am living and breathing outside myself—detached and restless. I go through the motions, still feeling sorry for my father. He cannot hear my cries for help while he's stuck inside his own personal hell. Head down, walking toward the eastern sky, I journey on, making my way to, Neverland.

Bathroom at the Biltmore

Oceanside — Fort Lauderdale, Florida

The evening wind blows cold. I wrap my arms around myself, trying to rub away the tiny chill bumps rising from beneath my skin. The duffle bag shifts against my shoulder as I walk swiftly, unsure where the fear is leading me next. The right shoelace of my sneaker flops about carelessly; tying it would be a waste of time; I don't bother. Darting behind houses and buildings, I try to keep out of sight.

With eyes wide open, I recapture a warm memory sitting between my sister's knees while she braided my hair. The biggest concern in my life was missing my favorite cartoons and staying awake long enough to see my mother's face after she returned home from her second job. Now, unsure when I will see my mom again; I sigh heavy, keeping my head down as if it will somehow make me invisible.

I look up only at the intersections; hungry and thirsty, my stomach growls, but I keep moving; walking toward the Beach. The streets are livelier than what I had imagined before I snuck out of my bedroom window. Cars speed by; sketchy faces appear in the corners of my eyes. Anxiety makes my stomach turn. It tells me to avoid eye contact with anyone and stay off the main roads. Joyce taught us to pray to God when we are afraid. But prayer doesn't come easily. The darkening sky sits over me, whispering; *Hurry out of sight!*

The beach strip is alive with music and beauty. A majestic night sky stretches above lofty luxurious hotels, while just a few feet away, I notice a few homeless people scattered here and there in the frigid wind. A man sleeps on a bench. It appears the sum of his possession's piles inside the plastic bag he clutches to his side. I remember looking at him, wishing there was something I could do to make it better. Unsure of what "it" was; perplexed of how the world could be so rich and yet so poor all at the same time; I keep moving, turning towards the mouthwatering smells that linger through the wind from the surrounding restaurants on A1A.

On the Fort Lauderdale beach, I hang among the shadows near the sand and gaze across the street at the pizzerias and cafes. The delicious aromas cause my stomach to ache more, but I ignore what I cannot change. Walking through the grainy sand, watching the waves roll into the shore, brings in a memory of the last time I was here. It was one summer morning; my mother dropped us off to play for the day. After leaving the International Swimming Hall of Fame, we ran, leaving footprints in the sand, and watched as the waves would slurp in and roll away.

Everything looks different tonight; the wooden pavilion we use to play on is gone; the shoreline is closer to the sidewalk, and the ocean looks darker now that I am alone. The tide foams, swishing—it rolls in and out, making its own music. In the sea, I hear a song, a lullaby. Perhaps I hear it because I am scared, and the lullaby was always so comforting. Whatever the reason, I hear it, wrapping itself around me;

> *"Love makes the world go 'round. Love makes the world go 'round; it's a time for beginnings; love makes the world go 'round. When we're together, love makes the world go round…"*

The melody plays in the waves, and tears begin to blend with the spray from the sea. The salty air tosses up bits of sand in every direction. Nearby, a couple is holding hands, strolling along the beach. I stare at them until their bodies merged into one along the shoreline. I miss my family. But I dare not return. The sound of Robert's voice howls through the wind, "I will kill you if you tell anyone." The fear of his threats is louder than the growl in my stomach and scarier than the shadows that creep near the dimly lit areas on the beach. I shake it off, rubbing my hands together, looking out over the vast ocean.

Tall palm trees line the sidewalk down the strip. I sit on the side of a small concrete building, watching rats scurry out from beneath the door of the structure; the hairy colony crawls through the tall grass near the sidewalk, into the garbage cans. Graffiti marks the entrance to the underground passageway that leads from the beach into Hugh Taylor Birch State Park. The parks tunnel links across Sunrise Boulevard and A1A. I remember going inside once, years ago, before the world became cold and turned upside down.

I look for a sign from God to tell me what to do and where to go. Seeing the stars, I wonder if God can see me. I move up the beach, passing strangers who look just as lost. Still, I pull my gaze away, keeping my head down; Ms. Lynn taught me that. I remember the lessons well. I try to stay close to the water's edge where it is easier to breathe. Less light shines near the shore. My legs are tired from the long walk to the beach, and I hadn't planned on it being so cold. A fluorescent seashell takes the attention off my rumbling stomach and the voices telling me how stupid I was for not packing a jacket in my duffle bag. I collect a few odd-shaped shells and put them inside. Then, a bright sign from across the street catches my eye. Red neon lights on a two-story resort spell out the words: The Biltmore Hotel.

The need to close my eyes for just a moment is consuming. Mindlessly, I walk near rows of apartments off A1A and spot a stairwell with a solid wall that covers the base. A quick look to the right and left, no one is around. I sit on the cold concrete, unable to lie down because a group of ants already occupy the space. They march up and down the cement stair wall and back on the ground next to me. I wonder; *do they ever get tired?* I do not think I ever remember seeing a sleepy ant. I scoot closer to the middle of the floor under the stairwell and try to rest.

After some time, I hear footsteps approach, and my heart jumps—I must have dozed off. Swallowing hard, afraid of getting caught, I inch closer to the inner wall, waiting for whomever it is to move on. *You're nobody till somebody loves you.* The irony of my mother's song is heavy, and I think about this word called love. The night winds reach underneath the stairwell, chilling my bones. I remember wanting to disappear, wanting God to come get me and take me far, far away from here. But He doesn't come. When I think the coast is clear, I get moving, sneaking away from underneath the stairwell.

"Alhambra." I sound out the word as I turn the corner, thinking it is a strange name for a street. I keep moving, wandering onto Las Olas Boulevard and then back toward the strip where a group of sandal-wearing beachcombers is standing near a pub called the Elbo Room on the corner of the block. They chuckle in a happy-go-lucky kind of way. *Life is but a dream,* I think to myself crossing over to the other side of the street and walking back towards the seashore.

I watch as people walk in and out of a hotel. How blessed they must feel to be warm, fed, and at peace. Tonight, it is too cold to disappear inside the shelter of my imagination. Relentless and unkind, it reminds me who I am; I am no one, invisible, a runaway. I ran away because I have a secret, disgusting and unchangeable. The monster told me not to tell. I believe his threats, and a part of me shamefully feels it's my fault. The reality is that there is a real scourge of shame that presses its incriminating forefinger against the base of my skull, accusing me of letting it happen. Ignore it all I want; it will not leave me alone. I have no voice and no defense against it. Robert had said I would learn to like it, and with his perverted hands, he'd touch me again and again until something inside my body would betray me and succumb to his demands. But he was wrong. The only thing I've learned to like was a thousand ways I imagined he'd die.

I don't know why, but I walk toward the back of the parking lot, near the Biltmore Hotel. *Head down, eyes low; act normal,* I tell myself as I cross back over A1A for the second time. The clamoring noise of traffic and pedestrians fade as I dodge in between the parked cars, looking for a quiet space to hide and sleep. Hotel guests pass by, and to my relief; they do not seem to notice me. I watch the ground, then dart my eyes delicately to the side, pretending I have a purpose for being there. Life has taught me to be a master pretender. I am good at hiding, keeping secrets, being seen and not heard. I'm here, and I'm nowhere. I catch my breath near an outdoor poolside bathroom at the back of the Biltmore Hotel.

I sit still and quiet inside the bathroom stall, waiting for the slightest hint of sound outside the door. The bathroom is small with two toilets that sit about two feet away from the entrance. There is no lock on the door. I listen with hushed breaths. Fear twist the nerves in my stomach with thoughts of being caught on the private property of the hotel. *The police will come. I will be charged with trespassing, or worse; I will be forced to go home.* I stay in the bathroom stall, sitting inside on the commode, half-asleep and half-awake. The duffle bag hangs at my side. I take out the picture of Joyce, staring at her as I lay my head against the stall. I breathe out and let the tears roll across the bridge of my nose, onto the floor. Closing my eyes, I let go of the need to know, to ask questions, to pray, to think, to feel. This is where the heartbeat of life and the hand of time settles me. I am here, in the bathroom of the Biltmore Hotel.

Over my Head

A peculiar thing happens to those who are touched, mistreated, and abused. A deceptive grooming process takes place, casting its spell on you. Instead of going forward, time rewinds making you believe that it is on your side when the truth is, time is running out.

Time will never heal trauma any more than acting like nothing ever happened could. Healing is a purposeful journey of resolving the pain and grief through varying degrees of understanding and acceptance — a lifelong journey that requires humility and patience.

My thoughts are cloudy the morning I walked out of the Biltmore Hotel. I cannot say I was sad or angry. I was merely there; stuck between a fantasy world where nothing matters, and the reality of being eleven-years-old, alone, and homeless.

Sore neck, stiff back, I hunch over at the bathroom door, listening, breathing quietly. No one came in last night, but I hesitate to go out into the dawn. Thinking the early morning risers may catch me leaving, I ease the door open to see if anyone is standing outside. While the chilly morning air rushes in, I run out towards the back lot, trying to hurry before anyone can see me. I head for the water — always the water. It's hard to explain, but the water draws me unlike anything else. The sun yawns and fiery colors awake, glowing in beautiful hues of red, yellow, and orange, setting the horizon ablaze. The sea sparkles with the reflection of the sky. I breathe it in, thinking of nothing apart from its beauty.

A seagull flies above me on a crisp breeze. The lifeguard tower is empty, and no one sits under the blue beach umbrella that mushrooms from the sand. Staring out over the waves, I think of how the ocean is so immense and mysterious. Sand sticks to my skin and I notice my clothes are a little looser. I have not eaten; the thought passes by me without a care. Insensible to the need for anything other than to exist in the moment, I brush the sand off my hands and walk into the ocean. The waves do not scare me at first.

The warm seawater feels inviting. Still groggy, I close my eyes for a moment and just breathe. The vast ocean makes everything else in the world looks small, irrelevant; I walk out deeper. My eyes sting from the salty air and lack of rest. But the stinging doesn't matter; I step out deeper. Captivated by the glorious creation around me — the sky, the sun, the ocean — I disconnect.

The water comes up past my chest. I go out deeper until my feet can no longer feel the bottom. By the time I realize it, the current sweeps me away. I look for shore, but it is too late. The water is over my head. I know how to swim, but I never learned to swim in a rip current. I begin to drown. A powerful flow pulls me under, and farther out, away from the shore. Fight or flight, I panic. I flail at the waves, nothing under my feet, nothing in my reach except for more of what's drowning me. Caught in the undertow, I surrender to whatever it wants.

Life and death, they feel the same as the sea pulls me out. I realize that the stories I've heard and read are right; my life flashes before my eyes, every memory, sound, and smell; I see it all — every scene. I thrash up. In the colorless waves, I experience it all in a flash, gulping, heaving forward and backward. It is as if life is but a dream. As I sink, a part of me is frantic, but for only a second. With no other choice, I let go. And a strange peace breathes itself into me; *this must be death; it feels peaceful.*

Sunbeams move above me like fireflies on the surface of the water. Ears clogged, I hear only a quiet swooshing between extended intervals of a heartbeat; swoosh, beat, swoosh. Suddenly, an orange tube resembling a small, oblong-shaped rocket lifts me up, under my chin. It totes me back towards the shore. I flounder on the sand with my head still spinning, looking up at the obscure frame of a man. My eyes and throat burn, and water trickle in my eardrum. When I regain focus, I hear him. He has brownish blonde hair and sun-kissed skin. He wraps a large sienna-colored towel around me and tells me to cough up the water.

"Are you okay?" he asks, looking at me with wide-eyed concern. He watches me breathe and tells me he is a lifeguard. "Do you need to go to the hospital?" I look down at the sand.

"No, sir. I don't need a hospital. I know how to swim, but the tide was taking me away." I explain, pretending my nose doesn't sting, and my lungs don't hurt. The seawater whooshes in my ears and stomach, causing a tunneling sound, like trapped air flowing from a pearly conch shell, echoing around me. I push an easy smile, pretending I belong somewhere and to someone. "Thank you, sir, I will be all right." I rub my nose, rake back my hair, try to act normal, and avoid probing questions. "I'm glad I came to work early today. Be careful out here. There are dangerous riptides that you won't be able to see until it is too late," he warns, looking out at the ocean. The lifeguard doesn't know that I'm used to dying and getting back up as if everything is fine as if nothing ever happened. It has become routine; the straddling of life and death feels the same. "Yes, sir and thank you again." I gather myself to my feet, wanting to leave before he asks any more questions. "You can keep the towel if you like," he says. I nod, thank him again, grab my duffle bag out the sand, and make my way up the beach.

While a part of me is grateful for the lifeguard saving my life, a part of me had reconciled with destiny, prepared to accept the ocean's gift of eternal solitude and safety. Seen and not heard, you learn not to ask certain questions, but for a moment, I wanted to ask God, why? *Why was I born, why so much pain in the world, why tie the hands of fate, and why not let me die?* God is quiet today. I leave the questions in the wind and keep moving. I make my way up the strip, passing rows of stores and restaurants. The towel cloaks over my shoulder, making me feel less exposed. That's good. My clothes are heavy and cold. With sand and water squishing in my shoes, I keep my blurry eyes toward the ground, walking aimlessly, to where I haven't a clue. I merely do what runaways do—I try to outrun it all: the rage, the anxiety, and the shame. The trouble is; it's not coming from the outside world; it is all coming from inside of me. There's no escaping; life is but a dream.

Missing

Every day in the United States and around the world, children go missing; there are many reasons. Please don't judge them; ask why. And then, just listen.

In 1974, Congress passed the Runaway and Homeless Youth Act to address the growing problem of youth living on the street. Subsequently, the Juvenile Justice and Delinquency Prevention Act added to the goal its "core protections" to curtail the epidemic of homeless children; seen and heard as delinquents rather than victims of trauma from violence and assault. Today, we must ask how much has changed. The decrease in family and societal values foreshadows an increase in the population of Neverland.

A quick glance over my shoulder, and the lifeguard tower and the blue beach umbrella begins to fade in the distance. In the corner of my eye, I see her; a girl who looks like me: young, black, and lost. She walks the strip.

"Hi, what's your name?" she asks with a carefree stare. Caught by surprise, it takes a moment to realize she is talking to me. Cookie is her name. She wears her hair in a small afro. Her skin is like black velvet, and right away, I notice her spunky attitude.

"BJ, my name is BJ," I answer guardedly, turning away towards the ocean.

"I know my way around the strip, stick with me, BJ. It's not so bad out here once you learn how to use what you got. You gotta be smart, and watch who you trust," she says. We walk towards Las Olas Boulevard. She tells me she is fifteen, but she walks with the grace and sway of a woman twice her age—each step begs for more attention than the last. She leads me to the Burger King that sits close to a crowded bar called Summer's on the Beach. We stood on the strip, near the oceanside Bar, listening to a crowd of men hoot and scream, "Take it off, take it off!' Shoulder to shoulder, the men lifted their bottles of beer high into the air, shrieking like wild hyenas.

"What are they screaming at?" I ask Cookie, unable to see through the crowd.

"Let's go around the back." Cookie says. At the back of the building, the bar stands open with a small stage in the middle.

There, a blond woman with long legs stands in high heels, a stringed bikini, and a t-shirt. She shimmies her shoulder as buckets of water pour over her breasts. The crowd explodes with jeers and whistles. Arms folded, I watch the women, one at a time, come onto the stage. Water pours, men scream, and soon the t-shirts come off. Unashamed, the women seem to enjoy the lustful outbursts. Cookie leans against the sidewall like she owns the block. She looks like she has seen this contest at least a hundred times. My mouth is still open.

The judge, a burly-looking man wearing a checkered shirt, holds a beer bottle in one hand and a microphone in the other. His bushy mustache looks like a fat dead caterpillar. With a proud smile, he announces the winner. The rowdy crowd chants as she steps forward. I remember thinking how beautiful she looked. I wonder who she is, where she came from, and why she allows them to treat her that way. Her golden hair wisps over sleek shoulders, her wet skin glistening. Though I know it's rude to stare, it is hard to turn away. Her body looks like a poem; only God could create with the pen of his finger, but their hoots and gawks seem to mock every verse. I look at her and wonder what she had won. More barks, more booze—the attention must outweigh any inkling of disgrace from a crowd of oafs that reduced her worth to the size of her breasts and the contour of her face.

Cookie is waiting near the edge of the street. "Let's go, BJ. We can get something to eat at Burger King." She says it is open late and the manager often gives food to the runaways and the homeless people who loiter after hours.

"I can work. I will work for my food," I say, telling her how I learned to earn money by helping my mother clean up and doing chores around the house. "No one has to give me anything. Besides, I would hate feeling like I owe somebody for something I can work to get."

Cookie gives me a jived look and sways inside the fast food restaurant. Beach sand tracks in behind flip-flops and bare feet of people filing in line to order. Napkins and trash sprawl over the tables and floors. I don't ask; I see the mess and get moving, picking up crinkled hamburger wrappers and half-emptied plastic cups. I grab a handful of napkins and wipe off the tables. Cookie stands off to the side with a puzzled look on her face. Burger King is a two-story eatery. I climb the stairs to the second floor and clean the trash off the top of the tables and the floors. A comfortable energy flow through me. While cleaning, I have no time to entertain the scattered memories. The self-assigned task relaxes me, and surprisingly, I have not thought about my own hunger.

" What you doing that for?" Cookie asks, her head tilting as if she is trying to figure me out. I walk past her and place the trash in the garbage can.

"Cleaning." I look at her, turn away, and keep moving.

"You don't have to do that. I told you, the manager gives away food at the end of the night," Cookie says with a slight attitude.

"I told you, I don't need anybody to give me nothing. I can work." I keep moving.

"And what if he doesn't give you anything after all your work?" she asks, pointing her forehead towards me. I shrug my shoulders.

"Then at least the store will look nice and neat before I leave. I will come back every day and clean the tables and floors until the manager notices me. Maybe I can even get a real job!" I smile at the thought of feeling useful and working hard like my mother. The towel capes around my neck. I walk downstairs and sit at an empty table. Cookie tells me she has someone she needs to see and walks near the rear exit. A thin, white man with dark hair and eyes the size of silver dollars stands, holding the door open. Cookie walks out with him.

I wait, sitting at a corner table, watching customers come in and out. I drift off until the sound of hunger pangs pushes me awake. As the sun fades, I stare down at my dirty sneakers. The pavement has eaten off parts of my shoelaces. The smell of burger and fries has upset my stomach, but I don't dare ask for food. Daydreams usually keep me busy, and when my mind is occupied, I don't feel as hungry. Cookie hasn't made it back. But then again, she never told me she would. I figure she must be busy doing whatever she does.

I make my way out of Burger King, wrap the towel around my shoulders, and take the back street towards the bathroom at The Biltmore. Tired, I just want to rest, eating will have to wait for another day. On the way, I find a piece of wood, a two-by-four plank, and tuck it underneath my arm. The towel hides it well. The dark of night becomes my ally; beneath the stars, I am just another traveler, well-hidden from my past. Walking between cars in the back of the parking lot of The Biltmore, I scan the sides and front of the entryway with one glance. The poolside lounging chairs are empty. No one is in the pool, but near the edge, a rectangular-shaped inflatable raft floats on the water. I take it and sneak into the bathroom, placing the two-by-four between the bathroom door and stall, creating my own lock and sense of security. I breathe out, wanting to rest, too tired to cry or worry about anything else. I stare at the piece of wood up against the door; it makes me feel safe. Before anyone could come in, I would have time to get up and leave out. The sound of silence outside tells me it's okay to drop my guard and try to sleep. Weary from the day, I listen to the silence more than the condemning voices that plague me, accusing me of breaking my mother's heart, causing more stress to the family, and being born. I lie on top of the raft I took from the pool, wrap myself in the towel, and draw my knees close to my chest. The temperature is colder near the ground, but the raft is soft, and the towel lessens the shudders. During the night, I often wake up, trying to catch my breath. I listen for noises on the outside, but all is quiet out there. The vexing sounds are coming from inside my mind. I try to sleep, but when I close my eyes, I feel like I'm drowning, falling, farther away inside a trench. After some time, it will all begin to feel normal: the falling, the drowning, the detachment. I hide inside myself and get lost in a place where there is no earthly location. A place no one can find me. Not seen, not heard... just missing. Neverland.

Wolves Behind the Wheel

"The world is a dangerous place to live; not because of the people who are evil, but because of the people who don't do anything about it." ~Albert Einstein

The morning air wakes up the aches in my back and side from where the plastic raft went flat during the night. But having a sore back is not a part of my plans. Life has taught me well; I ignore every twinge and make my way towards Burger King with one agenda today: get a job. I will clean up the tables and floors at Burger King again, gain the attention of the manager, and get a job. In my mind, it is that simple. The obsession to work overrides everything in the world around me. The fact that I have not taken a bath, brushed my teeth, combed my hair, or eaten in days is irrelevant. In survival mode, all fundamental human needs move away from my conscious thinking. I have a heartbeat; that's good enough; I want to work.

I walk with my duffle bag across my shoulder, ratty sneakers, dirty jeans, and the same black sleeveless shirt. I keep moving. Moving makes me feel better. When I sit still, the memories catch up to me and then swarm around me like giant wasps. Cleaning the tables at Burger King had offered me a sense of control. The feeling is empowering; even without pay or food, it makes me feel useful, with a sense of purpose I cannot explain. Three blocks away, I watch for Cookie. I do not see her; only a few kids loiter by the back door of a pizza shop. I can usually tell the runaways when I see them; an unspoken kinship connects the scattered faces of youths that flock to the ocean; perhaps it is the only thing bigger than the reasons we run away.

Two blocks from Burger King, the sunshine falls around me, thawing out the stiffness. *I must do a good job,* I say to myself, praying to be able to work, to eat, and to find somewhere to belong. I'm almost there. One block away from Burger King, a silver car pulls up close to me. In the warmth of the sunlight, I don't see who's driving. The tint on the windows deflects the light. I keep walking. In my detached excitement of cleaning tables and floors, I didn't notice how deliberately the tires slowed.

I will prove to the manager that I am a hard worker. I stop to tuck my shoestrings underneath the tongue of my shoe. Rising too quickly, I feel lightheaded and dizzy; I keep moving. The driver's window rolls down, catching my attention. I think nothing strange about the question.

"Excuse me, do you know where there's a good place to eat around here?" he asks in a mild tone — his kind face and brown skin shrouds with meekness. I thought nothing of telling him that Burger King was one block away. "Hop in. Is that where you're going? I'll give you a lift." His polite smile seems sincere and friendly; sheep-like. I thought nothing of getting in the backseat of the car. After all, Burger King is only one block away. I thought nothing of it; I thought nothing...

There are terrible realities that live next door to our disconnected perception of our human existence. In the blink of an eye, a thousand questions rush in. What is human; what is beast; what is reason; what is insanity? Time stands still, almost purposefully, because it is about to reveal its wisdom. It is about to tell you its truth, and it needs you to pay close attention to the lessons it is about to teach you.

I remember playing with my sister, Linda; "Paddy cake, Paddy cake, baker's man, bake me a cake as fast as you can, roll it, pat it, and mark it with a "B" and put it in the oven for you and me. Let's play again Sanwa," Linda would say, her hands pressing forward. Her smile shines from between the spaces of her outstretched fingers. Linda and I would often play Paddy cake clapping games, never tiring of each other's company. No matter the uncertainty around us, we knew the love we had for each other would never end. *I hope she remembers that I love her,* I say to myself, once I realized that I might never see her again.

"Sir, you are passing Burger King, it's back there," I say timidly, feeling the blood drain from my body as if I was sitting upside down. My palm pressed against the window. He does not answer. The sound of the car doors locking strikes thunder inside me. As it speeds past Burger King, I go weak. In the backseat of the car, I twist forward, nothing in my stomach but boiling acid mixing with fear. My throat burns, trying to swallow the eruptions.

"Don't worry; we just going for ice cream first." The driver says, with a soft, sheep-like grin.

What is human?

I almost believe him, as I once thought mermaids were real; something is beneath the surface, something toxic, like an invisible poison that suffocates you before you ever know it's there. The tint on the windows hid the face of another man reclined in the front seat. A hairy man; more hair than face, and a voice that snarls; unlike the driver, his intentions are crystal clear.

"Keep still, and you won't get hurt." His mouth moves, but I cannot see it. Hairy dark bristles and yellow eyes carry the threat towards the backseat. My thoughts scatter, remembering Robert's warning; the cruel echo is the same. More acid, more fear. I could not eat now, even if I had food offered to me. Afraid to move, to think, to cry—I know the position; I assume it. Seen and not heard, I freeze, dropping my head, drowning in the thoughts of what will happen. I yearn for the ocean, the waves, and the undertow. I pray underneath my breath. *God, please take me away now, if you are real; please take me to heaven, before it's too late. Hurry God; please hurry.*

What is beast?

The engine revs on the highway, 95-South. The car takes the left lane. I squeeze my eyes tight, waiting on God to speak. Just as He spoke before the planets were formed—the sun, the moon, the stars. God has the power to speak me away as if I have never been on the earth at all. Joyce said God is real, but right now, God is quiet. The sound of the road drags beneath me; it is the only sound I hear. The drive is long; I imagine at the end, there will be a cliff, sudden and endless. A rancid smell pushes from my quivering lips. Nauseated, I squeeze my hands together against my belly, folding inside myself, wishing my breath away. But wishing doesn't work.

The last things I remember about the drive were the signs that said Miami, the stain of my palm print on the window, and the sense of evil poisoning the air around me. I once believed wolves only hunted at night; I was dead wrong; it is a sunny day. The car finally stops in front of a one-story apartment complex. The wolves flank to the right and left. They walk alongside me; one snarls, and the other continues to grin, sheep-like. I move, unable to feel my feet on the ground. The sidewalk is narrow, and it feels like a one-way trip. Knots swell up inside; the knots are all I can feel. A little girl is skipping across the grass, moving outside of me. Bows swing on the ends of her hair. She tells me to be quiet and not to move. She vanishes just as quickly as she came.

What is reason?

Behind closed doors, the nature of the beasts comes out. The driver with the sheep-like grin is still smirking as his fist retracts. I remember the blow before hitting the floor, flat on my back, hard against the bedroom carpet. I also remember thinking; *he didn't have to hit me; why did he hit me. I know the position – without force. Please don't hit me again.* I shudder inside. On top of me, his breath vibrates in my left ear. I cry out, but it does not matter, no one hears. His eyes look soulless. I turn away, sensing the little girl nearby, watching. I listen to a small voice echoing from a tunnel. She is the same little girl I saw before. "Quiet now. Be still; quiet yourself and pray," she whispers, sitting in the corner with her knees drawn up to her chest. She turns her eyes away from me. Tears roll into the fibers of a stained carpet. I open my mouth wider to breathe, to pray, but my ribs feel crushed under the weight. God has abandoned me, but still, I pray aloud, "Our Father in heaven hallowed be thy name, thy kingdom come thy will be done on earth as it is in heaven..."

The prayer comes out of my mouth without effort or thought. The words had been planted in my heart years ago, alongside lullabies and whispers of Jesus. I tell myself that I must say the words before I die; they are the only words I can remember. I believe today would be the day of my physical death, and my soul and body will be one again. *So, if I am to die here, in this wolves' den, then I will choose the eulogy.* Again, and again, I say the Lord's Prayer. I pass out with the prayer on my lips.

When I awake, the hairy, yellow-eyed wolf has taken the place of the other one. Something moves across the room, closer to me, near the closet, but it is hard to see with the sweat of wolves in my eyes. Through blurred vision, I can see a little girl with a red ball and ten metal jackstones cupped in her hands. She sits crisscrossed on the stained carpet.

"Be still. Lay quiet." I hear her. She speaks softly, raising her finger to her lips. "Watch me; I want to show you how many jackstones I can pick up now." She throws the ball into the air; the colorful barrettes dangle at the bottom of her braided hair, while she hums calmly and throws out the jackstones. They flutter out, lifting away, into what looks like shiny fireflies.

I blink through the tears, needing to touch her. But she vanishes away again.

What is insanity?

It is strange. I hurt all over and yet; I feel nothing at the same time. I could've sworn they were flesh-and-blood men. How naïve of me to think there was only a monster on 24th Street. Frozen and quiet, I wait to fly away, but there will be no such mercy. I hear the men talking. Their voices speak outside the tunnel. They order me to clean myself up because I was going to meet someone. I don't remember the walk back to the car, only the shame that shoves me in the backseat. Tires roll again; a smeared handprint reflects off the window, and I stare out, angry at God. I waited for Him to come, to spare me from this cruelty and disgrace. I sit motionlessly. My mind searches for any sense of reason, but it only finds the numbness of insanity.

The wolves drive me back to the Fort Lauderdale Beach. The car stops at a building that connects four apartments near Seville Street and Birch Road. The sun is setting. I stare out at it, figuring it would be the last time I see it; but I felt okay with that. The two men take me from the backseat to the front door of a small studio apartment. A pale, gangly man opens the door; his eyes sit back inside the sockets in his head. The two black wolves take me to a corner of the room. "Sit!" The man with the sheep-like grin orders me. The white wolf looks me over. He looks like he is in his late forties to early fifties. I imagine his grungy mustache is full of spiders, weaving each word he speaks, waiting to crawl all over me. He takes a wallet out of his back pocket and hands the black wolves' cash.

"You won't have no trouble out of this one; she's young." The yellow-eyed wolf says. Staring away, I see everything and nothing, all at the same time. I squeeze my duffle bag tightly across my chest. The door closes, and the black wolves prowl out into the darkness, no doubt to hunt again. The white wolf locks the door and takes his turn. But this time, I'm already gone. No need to stay; I know what happens next. I hurry away, escaping inside a dark corner of the wall of the tunnel, watching the dance of the fireflies.

The years have taught me how to keep quiet. I have learned to disappear inside the mercy of another dimension. It is a place where the pain is not allowed to go, nor any other human emotion. My mind disconnects, far away to a place that is quiet and safe. It is a gift; from where or who I am not entirely sure. When the white wolf finishes, he casually asks if I am hungry. I do not answer. Dead things do not need food; still, the question confuses me. The idea that someone can rape you yet be concerned if you are hungry is baffling. The evil of the first two wolves left nothing to question. Their cruelty had no hint of kindness or concern.

"You can have some pizza when you want it, but you can't leave, or my boys will be waiting to bring you back," he explains in a calm, gentle voice. I stare at the floor, waiting for it to open, and swallow what's left of me. When my mind is fully aware, agony engulfs me beyond the physical pain of the rapes. I drown in a murky swamp, still straddling two worlds.

Round tablets layout on the table next to powdery lines; it is my first time hearing the word Quaalude. White powder cut in parallel lines reflects on a small rectangular mirror; it is my first time hearing the word cocaine. He turns on the TV and tells me to watch; he leaves pizza on a side table and tells me to eat. I do nothing without instruction, except breathe; all else is suppressed — pushed way down deep until I forget where it is.

Clocks and calendars do not exist in this world. They are useless here. In the outer limits of this gravity, time has no relevance. Day and night are the same. Nothing makes sense because there was once a time you could have sworn you were a human being. I don't remember when it all got easier, but in the following days, it did.

Later, I will find out his name. While the shower runs, I glance briefly at a letter sitting face up on the top drawer. The first name is easy: Edward. My lips silently attempt to pronounce the last name on the letter, "Eke-el-burg." I wonder if that is his name, a name his parents gave him when he was just a baby boy before he became a wolf; another monster.

The shower stops, and it all begins again. But no amount of soap and water can wash away the sin of this. After each rape, he huffs around, pulling at his nose, sniffling as if he has a cold, peering out the corners of the window like there is a bounty on his head. Fear keeps me in my place, believing his two guard dogs are not too far away. I do as I am told, without question. Robert taught me the position years ago — mechanically, I assume it. Unlike Robert and the wolves behind the wheel, Edward never hits me; I guess he knew he didn't need to. A part of him appears to be human — the part that lets me watch TV and asks if I am hungry — the part that looks away, soberly, as if he knows God is watching.

After a while, it all collides. I learn to let go and wait for time to begin again or stop altogether. My mind adapts and unlocks hidden treasures I never knew I had. I find passageways to help me escape farther away from this reality. I soon learn to play tricks on Edward, fooling him to where he thinks I am here. I smile inside because he does not know that I have gotten away. The little girl with the pretty barrettes is waiting for me by the window. She waves her hands, motioning for me to come. By the time he climbs on top of me, I'm gone. The fireflies arise, and together, she and I climb through our secret tunnel. It is dark up ahead, but step-by-step the fireflies light the way.

The little girl and I embrace and giggle with our foreheads touching. I notice she is wearing a pretty purple dress. "You look beautiful. I've missed you," I tell her. She blushes a downward smile and hurries me on. "Let's go!" She says, skipping ahead. Edward has no clue he is alone on the twin-size bed. We look back at him. His hips gyrate ridiculously, grunting like a clammy pig, he is unaware I have already slipped away from underneath him, far away from his reach. We laugh at him and hurry away, further inside our Neverland.

"Come on. Let's go!" She says with a carefree smile. Our fingers interlace, and we follow the fireflies. The glittery sparkles of light lead us to a peaceful place. A spacious green field, adorned with upright monuments of stone and bronze markers, stretching far as our eyes can see. Each slab holds a universal truth; a comforting epitaph; it declares the weary will find rest and the evil of this world will one day come to an end. We walk through the tombs and sit with our legs crisscrossed on an unmarked grave. Grateful she came to get me; I breathe and pull at blades of grass bordering the crypt. The years between the dashes mark the time of life and death on each grave. I can clearly see it, but I question its accuracy. Birth and death have nothing to do with life, in my eyes. Given a birth, I do not remember, marked with an existence I want to forget—what then is life except for time marked with strife—a mystical dream. A gentle hush sits on the grass like dew. I look over at the little girl. She sits close to me, carefree and content.

The delicate chiffon dress flares out across her knees, exposing a scar where Michael accidentally hit her leg with a broomstick when we lived in Dixie Court. I ask her if it still hurts. She shakes her head, no, shifting the red ball and shiny jackstones from one hand to the other. "He didn't mean to do it. He was swinging the broom, and I got too close," she explains with a lighthearted tone, never looking up from her jacks. A burn mark speckles between her knuckles and fingers on her left hand. We sit together, looking over countless gravestones.

"How many jackstones can you pick up now?" I ask. She looks at me, colorful barrettes swing on her braids. "I can only pick up seven, but I am practicing every day. Soon, I will get all ten." She says with confidence. She lays her head on my shoulders. I close my eyes when I smell the bergamot in her hair. I think of my sister, Joyce.

I miss her lullabies.

"You know the words of the song. No need to miss something that you already have," she says to me. She bounces her ball on the slab of the grave, picking up another jack. In the moments, I feel no anger or sadness — only the reality of the lessons from the thorns.

"I like it here," I tell her. The cemetery is such a serene place. There are no tears, pain, or memories, only dates of births and deaths. I begin to understand why my father would choose to run away here when he would hide from the bookies in Tampa. Here, nothing else matters.

No cruel touches can find you. I feel safe and free. A blue jay flies on the evening breeze, and lands to perch on a nearby branch. The field is immense, with no gate or fence to keep anyone out.

Since the dawn of time, the thorns have sprung up, sharp and fierce; what have we learned from them? I remember how my mind, under profound stress, shifted, allowing me to see what we should have learned by now: the lesson from beyond the veil of this flesh and bone existence. In this place, we will see with different eyes. All are welcome here, and here, no one is obsessed with sex or the color of your skin, your class, your culture, or ethnicity. Only the living waste their time with such foolish, pointless distractions. Even the mindless earthworms know better; they feast indiscriminately on rotting flesh. Only the living lives in vain. The dead have no memory of such trivial things. And I would imagine that now they understand it all never mattered in the first place. A reflection of vanity echoes from each gravesite: Here lies humanity; cold mounds of ash and dust finally freed from their idols of lust, greed, and bigotry.

I exhale, feeling a shift in the air.

The little girl looks behind her shoulders and then back at me. "He is finished now. You have to go. It's getting late." She stands gracefully fixing the creases in her dress. She whispers in my ear. "Remember, no matter what, we must trust God." She takes a few steps and hoists up on a raised white-washed tomb that sits above ground. She crosses her legs at the ankles and motions for me to come. Tears well up in my eyes; I don't want to leave. The living world is too cruel, too painful. I will forfeit my sanity for the serenity of this burial ground. "You must go," she says with a look of peace about her. Her scarred left-hand reaches down towards me. I stumble up.

It is harder to breathe; I feel the weight of his body. No matter how many times it happens, it still hurts. I beg her not to go, but she vanishes away.

"You my good girl." Edward snorts, lifting his bony chest off me.

His sweat stinks, and traces of the white powder stick like dried mucus around his raw nose. I listen to the water running in the shower, trying to remember and forget at the same time. All I feel are the thorns, piercing in and out, turning, spiraling like razor wire on a prison fence. To move in any direction only causes more pain—so I don't move at all. It's easier that way. I stare down at my feet, dangling near the floor.

Time passes, waits, or stand still; I can't be sure.

When Edward leaves, I watch TV. He goes out, he comes in, and he goes out again. I stay in my place—seen and not heard. Days later, I sit crisscrossed on the floor eating pizza and watching rats run across the TV screen. A sad little boy has a pet rat named Ben. Skinless tails scurry in tactical hordes, attacking the people who insist on bullying the boy. The movie ends with hundreds of dead rats, but Ben survives. The film is sad, but the ending made me happy. The boy and his rat can begin again. The credits run, and I listen to Michael Jackson sing the song about Ben. I imagine the boy and his pet rat stayed together forever. The burning acid in my stomach has settled a little, but I do not think I will survive very much longer. Something tells me I will be dead before the age of twenty. Surely my family thinks I am already dead, and they would be right; I wonder if they care. Either way, it does not matter. Nothing really matters; I doubt it ever did. Life and death feel the same—only a dream.

I grab my duffle bag from out the corner to look at the picture of Joyce. It is all I have left; it is all that matters. The only thing I have in the world that connects me to the lullabies and a fairy tale life I once knew in Tampa. The beautiful portrait of my sister wearing shades, a white shirt, and the loveliest smile. I hold the picture to my heart, telling her about my day and the rat movie. I imagine she can hear me. Like playing the telephone game, invisible wires connect our hearts together, and tonight, I begin to listen; a voice inside pushes aside the shame, making room in my cluttered mind. I listen.

"The water! Listen to the water." The voice is coming from the smiling portrait in my hand. Edward is in the shower, again — some things are not easy to wash away. He stays in the bathroom for quite some time, and as the water runs, I hold the picture close to my face. The TV is on, but I am not paying attention to it anymore. A sense of urgency runs through me. "Listen to the water." I turn around and back again. My heart beats faster.

"Get up," the voice says louder. I hear it, trying to swallow, afraid to move. Instinctively, I do it. "Walk to the door." Afraid, but I walk.

"Unlock the door." The water is running. *The water!*

"Slide the chain away." I slide it.

"No one will come after you. Go…now!" I run out the door, into the night. I don't' look back. I run. I do not think. Dizzy with the rush of adrenaline, my feet move without telling my brain the plan. There is no plan. I run. At the corner of Las Olas Boulevard, I stop running, unable to take another step. The weight of the world is heavy; I look for the fireflies to lead me where to go. They do not come. I stand on the sidewalk, stiff, numb. Feeling as if my body is not my own. The night air blows through me, as a police cruiser pulls up to the curb. The red and blue rotating lights are blinding. I don't move, or think, or feel. I am just there; breathing.

"What's your name?" the officer asks. I do not answer. "Where are you going?" I turn my head away, saying nothing. At this point, the sight of any man disgusts me and turns my stomach inside out.

Without another word, he puts me against the car. My chest presses against the cold rear frame. He pats me up and down, checking my pockets as if he is expecting to find something other than my black skin and the baggy clothes that hang from it. Cold cufflinks pinch tightly around my wrists. He puts me in the backseat. I keep to the script of my life of being seen and not heard; assuming the position, I do not resist. The police officer reports a detailed description of me on his radio. I don't understand the muttering reply from the dispatch, and I don't care. I will not talk to this pig or any other filthy swine that walks with two legs. In my wounded mind, all men are alike; uniform or not. Looking at him, I have one thought: dirty, disgusting scalawag.

In the back of the police car, I cut my eyes at him, acting tough, but the truth is I am afraid of everything and everyone. I remain silent, but I inwardly vow never to go back home. He can take me to jail for all I care. I have seen enough to know this world is out of control; from the cops who are supposed to protect and serve, to adults who order children to obey their perverted rules. *Mind your manners;* they say, all while they have none. It is all a bunch of crap. Be seen and not heard, the inconsistencies are absurd, and I want to set the world on fire, lean back and watch it burn.

Riding in the back of the police car, I stare off, traveling toward another destination of which I have no voice, no rights, and no control. I assume the position.

Suddenly, I realize I've made a terrible mistake. Something was missing. I look down at my shoulder and panic. Turning to the other shoulder, I know it is not here. Hands behind my back, I lurch to the window, looking out, down, back toward the sidewalk. I feel crazy, shifting my body, searching the seat, the floor; it is not here! *Where's my bag*? I ask myself. "No! No, wait! Where is it? Please! Turn around!" The police tell me to calm down. Somewhere behind me on a patch of trampled grass, the sidewalk, or at the door of Edward's apartment, I lost the portrait of my sister. My only possession in the world is gone. There was no way of retrieving it; no going back. I remember; just like before my parents' divorce — there was no going back to fix it all. We need to go back! I squeeze my eyes together unable to control the manic emotions. I fall, headfirst, down the backseat, thinking of how much I hate this world, I hate this cop, and I hate myself for leaving my bag with my sister's picture. I rage until the numbness comes to my rescue.

In the moments of detachment, the concept of time is lost. I don't remember the length of time I was missing, and some events remain repressed to this very day.

Life is but a dream.

Upon this revolving planet, there lies the harsh reality of our humanity: sin has no limits, no boundaries, no rules. Robert's pornography; Edward and his wolves, sex trafficking and on and on, these are all a part of the grand scheme of the thorns — the consequence of sin and the stubborn defiance of mankind.

Did we not understand the words of the Creator who in

Exodus 20 said, "Thou shalt not have other gods and no graven images? Do not take the Lord's name in vain, remember the sabbath day, honor thy father and thy mother, thou shalt not kill, thou shalt not commit adultery, thou shalt not steal, thou shalt not bear false witness, and thou shalt not covet. Although given these clear instructions, humankind acts as if nothing ever happened, as if God, the Creator of all things, never spoke these directives, and so when we see the results of our own doing and destruction, we ask, "Why; what happened?" The lessons we fail to learn, we will be forced to repeat.

With the current crisis in families around the world, this message cannot be overstated.

"Politicians want you to speak up about them when it comes time to vote, yet they never speak up about protecting children from abuse." ~*Unknown*

Oakland Park, Florida

An unprecedented number of sex crimes go unreported. Trafficking is one of the many plagues of a sin-sick civilization. Shame often blames the victim. Many victims believe the lie. The rapist will usually get away with committing one of the most heinous of crimes. And on and on it goes; the blatant disregard for life and the sacredness of the human soul. If God's eyes are on the sparrow, I pray He is watching us on this planet of thorns.

1980

The cuffs stay on at the station. I must look dangerous or crazy or something in between the two. Sitting in a chair with my hands behind my back, I ignore every question. I do not remember how long I stayed at the police station, but I will sit in that chair for hours staring at a desk and a cop who appears disconnected and uncaring. The damn desk has more personality than this cop. Having a badge and a gun must give him some sense of power as if he is no longer flesh and blood but an armed deity. He questions me like he already knows the answers and has already reached a conclusion as to why I was on the corner of the sidewalk. I do not speak, leaving him to write his report based on the "facts" of his egotistical gut belief. He cuts his eyes up at me from his paperwork. His brow presses down with indifference. There, we find something in common: he couldn't care less; neither could I. *Freakin traffic light cop.* I cut my eyes away to the floor.

A stocky officer walks in and steps behind the desk. They both begin to talk about me as if they know me, and as though I am not sitting there in front of them listening. In the middle of the conversation, words like *delinquent, prostitution,* and *runaway* leak out. Straight attitude, I can spit fire if I open my mouth. I squint in their direction, having a few words to add to their report: *stupid, pig, moron.* I roll my eyes to the corner of the room, keeping the rage just below the surface.

The cops are still talking when I doze off with my hands cuffed behind my back. The metal digs into my wrist, cutting the circulation just enough to take the edge off the inner turmoil. I lift my head to look around the station before staring at the ground again. *Men are an evil species,* I ponder with my eyes closed, as the images rush in and out. Pompous, greedy, lustful scalawags, I rant silently. Self-absorbed cavemen who believe they are above rebuke and free to sin and do whatever they damn well please without conscience or remorse. Underneath the blue uniforms, the sheep-like grins, and the military discipline, they are all the same; sin-sick beast. More rage! The cop places me in a holding cell for the rest of the time I spent there.

Car tires roll.

The door slams on the car of a blank-faced social worker. The sound wakes me up in front of Lippmann Youth Shelter, a crisis center that offers temporary shelter for abused and troubled kids in Fort Lauderdale, Florida. The shelter resembles a compound with clusters of connecting room-like apartments facing out towards the front office. The sidewalk forks in three directions, and the social worker heads up the middle. She has barely looked at me from the moment I met her at the Juvenile Detention Center. I had stayed at the correctional facility for juvenile offenders after the cops were done "questioning me." Freakin Jerks! The place was ridiculous and added insult to injury. When the cops found out I was a runaway, they sent me to a juvenile center on Broward Boulevard. When the Juvenile Center found out I was only 12 years old, they called the social worker to get me. After hours of questioning, with arms folded across my chest, I had only one thing to say. "I am not going back home!" She drives me here to the shelter.

We walk into what appears to be the intake office. A row of chairs faces a single desk to the left of the office. I sit and wait. For what, I do not know. No one explains anything. They tell you what to do; they say sit, so I sit. They say wait; I wait. But I got plans of my own.

For now, I play it cool, as if to follow the disconnected rules of these human traffic lights. Other kids are waiting, slouched back in gray folding chairs. The air is stiff, and only pens move in the rigid atmosphere from strict-faced caseworkers taking notes. My arms stay folded across my chest as I glance at the faces of the kids around me. Without ever exchanging a word, the universal pain of rejection, abuse, and neglect connects us, each with a story, a prelude of how it all went wrong.

I sit by the window, a place where I can look away and feel free. I imagine I am a bird, a tree, a cloud — anything else but me.

After some time, the intake worker calls my name. Soon, another woman walks up to me. She introduces herself.

"Hello, my name is Ms. Helen Kennedy," I remember her eyes were soft, angelic. She sits down to speak with me, but it is hard to listen when I'm already gone—when the pain builds and transforms into a monster of its own. Rage, fire, more rage, I can see the flames. I can smell the ashes inside of me, smoldering with fury. My cloudy eyes stare at her, sensing kindness inside, and for a moment, she reminded me of my grandmother. The shelter takes children ages twelve to seventeen, she tells me. I am now twelve-years-old. I get in. But getting in does not matter because I have already mapped four ways out.

After the "talk" with Helen, I go back to the chair and wait again, for someone to tell me what's next—as if they know, but the truth is, they don't have a clue. Angry and sick of rules, I've just about had it. And if I have to sit in front of another desk, I swear I will snap. I no longer need to talk or ask questions. The time for questions has passed. Questions do not matter in a society that speaks out of both sides of its mouth. I trust no one with the answers. I mark time, waiting for the right moment to disappear into the night.

A girl with sunlight hair sits next to me. I try not to stare at the purplish bruise on her arm or the way her eyes aimlessly float away. We look at each other and share a passing exchange. Almost instantly, I feel close to her. This is where life has brought us, internally bleeding, waiting for everything to make sense in the world again. I secretly scorn the adults around me. *Just who do they think they are? Telling us what to do, when to do it, and how they want it done. I have no respect for authority. Everyone can get out of my face,* I scream silently, wearing an emotionless expression the whole time. These people have no idea of the pain we lock inside the cages of our minds. By now, I have convinced myself that no one sees, no one hears, and no one cares. So, everything is whatever!

The shelter's rules and routines are direct and straightforward: attend group meetings, no fighting, no sexual contact, clean up your space, blah, blah, blah and more freakin' blah. I've already mapped another exit. It's only a matter of time, and I will be "so out of here," I whisper out so I can hear myself say the words. I sit quietly, wondering what the hell is wrong with these people. What exactly is a group supposed to do when the rage inside colors the world a bloody red mess and the maddening noises sounds like an Uzi firing off in your head. I relive the past;

thinking of how no one stopped the attacks, the violent assaults. And now they expect me to attend a group and talk to people whom I believe do not have a clue of what it feels like to be me, to feel so dead inside that nothing else matters.

No fighting, they say! Really? What the hell? What kind of freakin' rule is that? I have been fighting all my life without ever throwing a punch—more rage. And if anger could start a fire, this place would be a blazing heap of desks, case folders, and files. I could almost smile just thinking about how high the flames would leap.

There will be no time for me to participate in any of the lists of outlawed activities. I'm out! Judgmental eyes have already judged me a troublemaker, a delinquent, a prostitute, a runaway— a stupid black girl with an attitude. I got nothing but tears and rage as payment for whatever they claim I did. A staff member blabs away about something or other, but I am not listening. My mind gets busy planning the details of my escape. I stare at the floor, completely distrusting in a world where up is down and down is up. I lean forward, feeling a sharp pain in the bottom of my stomach. There is no language to express what can only be described as splintered thorns piercing inside. I keep quiet about it.

Another night, another group; we sit in a circle. Sick and tired of circles, I play the role and stick to the script of being seen not heard. Buying time, watching a clock with no hands, I lean on my elbow and stare ahead. Nearly fourteen of us are together in one room during group sessions. I do not remember who leads the group, what they say, or what it means; because I do not care! Many of the kids cannot sit in their chair without shifting, jerking, or picking at scabs. Others seem more like me: quiet, detached, hiding everything inside so no one sees the extent of the damage. Stuck in what feels like an endless monsoon, the future blurs into nonexistence. *I doubt I will make it to the age of twenty,* I tell myself again. So why even try. No need to dream about a future that will never come.

My brain feels broken, and I hope no one calls on me to say anything. I vacillate between trying to remember and trying to forget. It is best to try to forget, or better yet, act as if nothing ever happened. I don't know how long we have sat in the group, but my stomach aches most of the time. No one asked you how you feel. No surprise there.

After the group is over, the kids huddle together in what appears to be a multipurpose room. When the adults are gone, the masks come off. I pick up bits and pieces of stories, versions of abuse and neglect, kids trying to find the missing pieces of a world they never asked to come to. I listen, and our pain connects us in a way nothing else has. The beatings and addictions, middle and high school dropouts, suicide attempts, and on and on the stories go. Fathers, who got drunk, got angry, went crazy. Mothers, who got restless, got high, went missing; children who had it all and gave it all away in exchange for their idea of love and safety. Others had nothing to begin with, so they had nothing to lose. Everyone has a story, but without a heart connection, we will take it to the grave.

A boy who looks fifteen or sixteen years old pulls out a cigarette and blows smoke rings into the air. I wonder how he learned to do that because he seems too young to smoke. It is a stupid thought on my part. In this perverted society, being too young for anything is unheard of; you are forced to assume the position, disgusting positions, regardless of your age. For so many, childhood is a cave—you go in and never come out.

"Hi, my name is Randy," he says, smiling. Dirty blonde hair shags like a mop across his face. I shift in the opposite direction. He changes his accent, tilting his head towards me. "Gidday mate. Ow ya goin this fine day?" he says, sounding like an Australian nerd. He acts as if he is at summer camp or on vacation. Like he does not have a care in the world. I shake my head and look down at my raggedy fingernails.

"See, got you to smile a little," he says, exposing a chipped front tooth. I had not noticed I had smiled, but I had seen the usual silliness that reminded me of my brother, Michael. A memory rolls over me like a gentle wave of how Michael would make us laugh. Years ago, back in Tampa, he had put on a green dress and a wig. He strutted around the house, swaying his hips, imitating May West. "Why don't you come up and see me sometime, big boy." His voice sweet and girly: one hand on his skinny hip and the other puffed up the curls on the old bouffant wig. He always put on a show. Joyce turned red with laughter until tears rolled out the corners of her eyes. I smile to myself thinking about him. Acid churns up, and that was the end of that memory.

"What's your name?" Randy asks me.

"BJ," I say, peeling off the edges of my fingernail. I don't look up for more than a quick glance. He tells me he has been at the shelter for a while, and that it is not so bad after you get used to it. *I heard that somewhere before.* I think to myself. *It is among the top five lies that kids create for themselves to survive reality. A lie that forces you to adjust because anger is not allowed. So, you learn to adapt and exchange the pain for folly.*

"I will keep you company if you like," he offers. I shrug my shoulders, with no intentions of staying around long enough to see much more of this place.

"Okay," I reply, watching the clock.

At twelve-years-old, I do not know much of anything about the Department of Children and Families. But what I can tell this far is they remove children from danger. They provide shelter, food, and safety, but something is missing—something beyond the basic needs. There is no connectivity. A housed body, a lost soul, I am already gone; too far gone to care about their social work, treatment plans, and freaking therapy. Rage is blinding. Lost somewhere between a lullaby and a gravestone, I do what I do best; I prepare to run.

After dinner and lights out, I wait for sleep to fall over the children in my room. I'm tired, but anxiety keeps me wide awake. The night was still, and crickets begin to sing outside. That was my sign. I run. Out the window, through the back way, where the streetlights could not snitch on me. I run. I do not bother to look back. I have learned the secret of getting control from every prison and stronghold in my life. I run.

I take no caution, no thought of anything else but getting to my sister's house. *Joyce will want me.* I cross over Oakland Park Boulevard, staring straight ahead, moving toward Broward Boulevard and 18th Avenue. I see nothing else, nothing but her face, her smile. I must hurry. *I'm running out of time.* My head feels dizzy, swimming with everything and nothing.

I don't remember when I reached 18th Avenue, but seeing the old gas station, I knew I was close. A cop drives past me and instantly my thoughts rage with contempt. *If the police want to pick me up, so be it,* I tell myself, keeping my stride. If a social worker takes me back to the shelter, I won't make a fuss. I will go. And just as soon as I hear the cricket's wings, I will run again. The night air blows cold, and the cop doesn't stop. I keep moving. I notice a lake near a narrow bridge. The moonlight bounces on the water, and I pause. Swept away by the stillness of the lake, I suddenly feel calmer. A field of grass connects the bridge to the entrance of Sunny Reach Acres apartment. When I reach the stairs and look up at Joyce's second-floor apartment, I become doubtful.

One foot on the stairs, I step up, but then, I back away.

It is late, and Joyce and her family are probably asleep. Afraid of what she will say, I do not go up the stairs. Cold wind chills me to the bone as I wait on the sidewalk, questioning where I belong. Part of me needs to see her, while another part of me wants to stay away. No one stirs outside. It feels about two in the morning, but I can't be sure. Among the cars parked in front of the complex, Joyce's brown Ford sits in the middle. The back door is unlocked. I open it, sneak inside, and lay down across the back seat. Restless, my mind will not stop moving, running anxiously, as if it is not mine to control.

What if Joyce is mad with me, what if she thinks I am ugly, and no longer worthy of her love? What if she can tell where I've been? Will she still love me when she smells the stench of the wolves reeking from underneath my skin — these are my thoughts, my fears. In the backseat of her car, I curl myself into a tight ball to get warm. A feeling of dread blankets over me, reminding me of what I am: a misfit, an outcast of society. A harsh reality seeps inside the doorframe of the car and sits behind the driver's seat. It tells me not to cry anymore; crying is useless. It tells me to accept life as it is and to toughen up. Moonlight shines faintly through the backseat window. I shiver, close my eyes, and decide the voices must be right. I don't bother to pray, thinking about if faith is even real. The backseat is real; the cold is real; the monsters are real, and the hurt is real. Should I ignore it all and pretend like nothing ever happened?

This is where life brings me. "Where is the God of the lullabies?" I whisper to the wind, and with the next breath, I fall asleep.

During those angry sessions, I was utterly unreachable; unable to learn — to see beyond the thorns and the rage that grows from the sense of hopelessness. There is an inescapable truth I could not run from: life tends to move in circles. Resist all we wish, the iron grip of the subconscious will not let go until we stop running from the problem and learn the skills to rise above it.

Until I became free from the fear within my mind, nothing was going to change on the outside. We become teachable when we let go of anger. The challenge was to increase awareness of all that was hidden beneath the pretense.

Dance of the Manatees

The water in the lake ripples over the backs of mammals swimming up to the surface and back underneath the water. I stand next to the gate that separates the complex apartments from the brackish river water of a long lagoon that curves underneath a bridge. Numb, I lean against the gate, watching the manatees move slowly through the water. My thoughts float out with the widening ripples. It is my first time seeing a manatee, my first time staying at my sister Joyce's home, and my first time seeing the terrifying signs of something very wrong in Joyce's life.

When Joyce and her husband find me sleeping in the backseat of the car the next morning after the run, I am afraid they would try to send me back home. I awake looking up at their shocked faces, unsure of what I see. In disbelief, their eyes stare down at me and then at each other. Joyce feeds me and welcomes me into her home. The cops never come; neither does the blank-faced social worker. And after a couple of days, I stop jumping when I hear the telephone ring or when someone knocks on the door. I am happy to see Joyce again, but something inside of me knows not to tell her what had happened on the beach. It's too much to tell, to remember, to relive. I keep the secret of the wolves locked away. Besides, Joyce is already going through her own family issues. Many times, I feel she is mad at me for coming. *Did things between us change from the days she would sing lullabies until all the noise faded away?* The picture begins to become clearer as the days go by.

The stress on Joyce's face is disheartening. More than I could understand at the time, she had been breaking under the pressure of taking care of everyone except herself. Worse is seeing the bruises on her arms and legs—her light skin shows what she doesn't tell. On the way to the bathroom, I catch the tense sight of white pieces of plaster on the carpet in her room. Looking up from the dusty pile of drywall, I turn away. A fist size hole in the wall reveals a familiar portrait of the fights and arguments my mother and father used to have from Tampa to Fort Lauderdale. The memory burns my stomach, but the thought of Joyce being abused cuts even deeper.

I try to ignore the holes in the walls and broken furniture. Most times, I stay in the bathroom, holding my stomach, rocking back and forth. *Is this what life is all about? Was this just the nature of things? Or am I missing something?* The tension in the air circled me, moving closer. It was too much—thinking of my parents' marriage, and now, my sister. The fights, the arguments, the violence, and the silent depression: it's all back again. I keep quiet and try to simply do as I am told—it's easier that way. Joyce looks exhausted. She covers her bruises and seems to bury her sorrow somewhere deep. I exhale thinking of how she took a baseball bat and fought for me; what was happening now that she couldn't fight for herself? I felt helpless. One day, as I am about to walk to the lake to see the manatees, Joyce faints on the sidewalk. I run to her, kneeling by her side, thinking she must have had a heat stroke or forgot to eat again. It's happening more often now.

When she comes to, she seems more concerned about me than the fact that she has just collapsed on the hot cement. Her eyes are cloudy-looking as if she is lost in a storm. I cannot understand what is happening to her, and I begin to regret that I came to her home. I believe I have added more stress to her life. Joyce has given so much of herself to our family through the years. Her love and loyalty drive her beyond fatigue. She forgets about herself, trying to take care of everyone else, and I pray to see her smile again. I wash dishes and help around the house, hoping to make her life easier, but often, I think I just get in the way. I walk to the lake and stare out over the water, waiting for the manatees to swim up to the surface. Through the years, I have learned how to wait— not moving, just breathing, waiting for the world to change.

The water calls to me; it always has. Be it the ocean or a sleepy lake; there is something about the water that soothes the aching inside. A fish leaps, catching a ray of sun before plopping out of sight. And as the ripples spread wide, I think about life, death, and God. The thoughts consume me.

Birth of Codependency

Near the lake is where I meet Bruce. He is a neighborhood teen who lives across the street with his family. He speaks to me. I glance away. Then I remember hearing the words that broke past my hard pretense.

"God loves you, and I love you too." I stopped and stared at him like he was out of his mind, but still, his words seem to water the dry places inside.

"You don't even know me," I answer with a bit of an attitude and zero social skills.

"But God knows you," he replies. His skin is as rich as the

night sky, covering a thin frame that carried a Bible and an empathetic smile.

He talks, I stare. I talk, he listens. Time passes, and we become more acquainted. I remember being impressed with his knowledge of God, the Bible, and the world. He likes fishing and church. I love the lake, the trees, and watching the manatees dance in the waves.

The church is an abstract concept in my mind. I have always believed the church was a place inside of you; a place you created with a whisper to a savior you cannot see. In Tampa, Joyce would turn the platform at the top of the stairs into a sanctuary. Bible stories, singing, and praying; she taught us that we are the church because God lives in our heart. I miss the Bible stories, and the way hearing them made me feel invincible. Just thinking of a little boy who brought a giant to his knees made me believe that miracles are real. Joyce said it. I believe it. Especially now, because I got giants too.

I long to find truth amid all the noise and chaos. I want to hear the stories again to block out the blatant contradictions life keeps showing me. Like a huge spider web, the confusion of life traps me until I can no longer move, and no longer feel what is real from what is fantasy.

Bruce teaches me about his idea of church, its rules, and membership. He often walks with me to the lake and stays with me, watching me look out over the waves. In time, my defenses begin to fall. And though I have an inner hatred of the male species, Bruce seems different. Gentle, kind, and charismatic, Bruce regularly speaks about his church and his beliefs. I like to hear the stories, and I like the attention he offers me. Better yet, he doesn't seem to mind my awkwardness. I feel like I can almost breathe normally around him. At first, I make every attempt to hide everything about my life: the rapes, the shame, the self-loathing. But I still feel he can see it, smell it, and it will be a matter of time before the secrets come out.

Soon I will realize that I am not the only one with secrets. We all have a side of ourselves we hide from public view. And given the right circumstance, the other face of who we are will awake and rear its ugly head. On my thirteenth birthday, Bruce buys me a green diary. The first gift I had received in a long time. I treasure it. I write my deepest secrets, but soon I became afraid someone will find it, read it, and uncover the disgusting monologues. Nearly a month later, I destroy it, ripping out each page. I tear them into tiny bite-size pieces before tossing them all away; feeding them to a smelly dumpster that sits near the edge of Sunny Reach Acres.

Shortly after, Bruce and I kiss. The first kiss is in a tree I climb when we walk together one night to Stranahan High, down 18th Avenue—the same school where Joyce graduated in 1977. Tree-climbing is second nature for me. It arouses pleasant memories from 24th Street of my siblings and me hanging upside down in the mango trees laughing, imagining we are superheroes. *Wonder Twin powers activate*; I think of Michael, wishing he were here to fist bump with me, so I can turn into whatever I want to be. *I'd take the form of anything with wings, so that I could fly away.* The memory feels like a lifetime ago.

I climb higher up the tree. The higher I go, the better I feel. Bruce climbs up after me. He stops halfway from the top. I am surprised when he climbs that far. The treetop is quiet, and I keep climbing until I reach the tallest branch. I perch like a dove, staring out over the schoolyard. We stay up late talking about life as the world presents it to us. Family is a huge sore spot for both of us. Acid swished in my stomach as I open up to him about parts of my life.

The conversation flows, and I realize Bruce and I have a few things in common. Fathers that had little to no reference for fathering, and how much we had missed them when they were not around. We both have mothers who work hard on thankless jobs and often come home too exhausted to understand and engage the generation of children growing up way too fast, and parenting in the shadows of a past plagued by bigotry and oppression in a post-civil rights America was not easy. These realities are the upshots of a nation that pretends nothing ever happened.

We both have brothers who went to jail at a young age. The ache of their absence throbs between us as we share the stories of their arrests. Strange how much we have in common, how the passive heartache connects and binds.

"I can write your brother sometimes if you have the address. I like to write, and it may make him feel better to know someone is thinking about him." I tell Bruce. We speak in simple language about a complex world we are unable to navigate. We look for something to connect to, and here in the treetops, we find each other. Broken and left alone to fight our own demons and the demons of our fathers, we sit listening to the breeze rustle through the leaves. A bond begins to build between the long gaps of silence that fill up the spaces where logic refuses to explain any other options. Passive and absentminded, I learn to flow out with life's current, accepting whatever position it commands — no questions asked.

Sometime later, at Bruce cousin's home, when no one was around, Bruce gets on top of me. Our first time together sexually is mixed with secret shame and the detached emotions of allowing myself to experience the touch of what I inwardly despise. I hate sex, but like an animal branded with a hot iron, the act becomes a part of the acceptance of an initiation of validation. Groomed to assume the position, I naturally go along. Sex tells me I have value and a sense of purpose. At times, it made me feel special, even loved. Sex whispers my usefulness. And if I give myself away, it promises me a sense of control in a world where I have none.

Later I will find out the truth about the whole concept of control; it is an illusion, a liar, and a double-dealing con artist. While sex offered me a sense of worth, it demanded my will, hindering my ability to find my worth in the only place it could be found — inside my soul; a soul I felt I'd lost a long time ago.

Worse yet is the double standard of sex outside a healthy marriage relationship. It offers neither control nor value. It detracts it, morphing into an abusive cycle of dominance, void of true love and value, where you become a means to an end, something used, owned, and exploited. But for me, it is just another thorn among the many, and as the relationship shifts into a new phase of abuse, I assume the position.

The first hit came soon after the first sexual encounter. I was no longer a girlfriend but a piece of property, a slave; that's how it felt. Sex is no longer a choice, but a demand. In my broken brain, I think having sex will earn me love, respect, and acceptance. I am very wrong. It does the exact opposite, making me a slave in a controlling mind game.

A shove, a slap, a fist, a kick: I am sure I did something to deserve it. I guess there must be something wrong with me. Why else would this keep happening? So, I figure I need to change whatever I had been doing to make him angry. I try, but at thirteen, everything in my life is already wrong. I take it. Whatever happens to me, I let it happen. I never fight back. A misfit, unworthy, devalued, frozen in place, this was my lot, my destiny, my fate.

I take it all. Years ago, I had learned that the best way to deal with problems is to ignore it. Disregard the crimes and wait for the next ripple to carry me out; out of reach, out of my mind. Anywhere it chooses to take me I will go willingly. Sexually active, emotionally disabled, I conclude this was my life, although the seeds of a lullaby did not agree. Something buried deep inside among the thorns, rages against it all. I tell myself to be tough, be strong, but I frankly don't know how.

Fight, flight, or freeze—I only know how to run. On the outside, I pretend to be okay, a normal human being, and a part of the acceptable society. But inside, I am a dry thorn bush with skin on, and when the stress rises, I have but one option, I must get away from it all.

Watching the dance of the manatees, I prepare to run again.

No Way Home

1981, spring ends, and like the rhythm of the season, the ripples in the lake circles wide and back again. I stare out, mouthing the words to a song I heard years ago by Barbara Streisand; it is a love song that moves me to wonder if such a love exists. Love that is "soft as an easy chair, fresh as the morning air, ageless, and evergreen." I stay for long periods of time, fixated; staring out over the water. It's calming.

My sister's old Ford broke down a few weeks ago. She parks it on the far-right side of the apartment complex. It is in the perfect place for me. The backseat becomes my hideaway — away from the anxiety, away from Bruce, away from my sister's arguments with her husband, away from the echoing of the wolves, away from everything. In the backseat of the rusting Ford, I can close my eyes for a little while and hope time moves on without me.

Joyce begins to work even harder. She reminds me of our mother. I see glimpses of the past, and the fear comes back again. The domestic brawls increase. Until one day, Joyce says she has had enough of the fighting. She packed her things and heads up Broward Boulevard towards Interstate 95: On foot. I follow her as she walks up the bridge, lugging two heavy sacks.

Helpless, I feel unsure of what to say to make it all better; desperate, I search for something. I pray under my breath, trying to keep up with her hurried pace. She keeps walking on the thin path of the road that separates the cars from the grass. Once she makes it up a distance, she puts one bag on the ground and lifts her thumb to hitchhike northbound. Standing close to her, I plead, hoping to make it better, to fix it.

"Joyce, don't go, please!" I cry, not understanding the weight of life she carries. I can feel the rush of air from the cars whizzing up the highway.

"I can't go back, Sandra. I am going to kill him, or he is going to kill me. I can't go back." Her voice roars over the loud sound of the traffic. Her eyes are full of rage and pain. Deja vu, the past has returned, staring me in the face on this highway. History repeats itself — refusing to die.

I remember the same words my mother had said before leaving my father before all the monsters came.

"But Joyce, what about the children, your home, please Joyce. Don't go?" Unsure of how to change her mind, I drop my head.

"What home, Sandra? Do you think those children don't see the holes in the walls, the fights between their dad and me? Do you think that does not affect them? I do not want to subject my children to that. There is no peace in that house. There is no home! I want better for my children and this ain't it." Angry tears collect in her eyes, but she won't let them fall.

She doesn't seem to notice how close we are to the speeding cars. The pain is tangible, forceful, like walking 1,000 miles with bare feet on sharp pieces of broken glass; you're going to bleed, no matter which direction you go in.

"Joyce, please!" I cry, begging her to try again, pray, and believe that the God she has taught me about all my life will somehow make a way, make it all better, make all things new.

"Please, Joyce, please, you must trust God! Remember what you taught us. Please, don't go!" I break down.

Suddenly, she drops her shoulders and takes a breath.

"Don't cry, Sandy Patty. I don't want to see you cry." She wipes the tears that fall from my eyes. I am not sure what makes her change her mind, but she does. Love has a way of making you bear the unbearable. A brush of wind whirls close by us from the speeding cars. Joyce stands motionless, holding onto the heavy load of clothes and knickknacks in her bags.

As I stand there waiting for her to make the next move, I feel helpless to change the sadness in her eyes. My mind finds its only refuge. I disconnect to a place in time when life was carefree. I see the green painted apartments of the Dixie Court Projects, where we had laughed and sung silly songs until we burst with joy. Blissful memories of watching the *Hee Haw* show, dancing the waltz, and listening to lullabies at bedtime. It all swirls around me until there is no road, no cars, no packed clothes, no tears, and no broken glass. We turn to walk back to the house together. Our pace is slow. Home feels so far away — like the lost feeling you get when there is no way home.

Days go by, and Joyce is busier now than before. I spend my time in scattered places: at the lake with the manatees, Bruce mother's house, or in the backseat of Joyce's old broken Ford. When you are an outcast, it seems only the wind welcomes you. I busy myself and make plans to go away; somewhere I cannot cause pain or feel the constant dread. Perhaps no such place like that exists on this side of heaven.

On the top of Joyce's kitchen table, I notice a beautiful sketch of a woman's face and a few sketches of characters from her Archie Comic books. Joyce tells me she likes drawing when she gets a quiet moment. The moments are few. She says drawing helps her relax. I remember thinking, *after all this time, I did not know that she liked to draw.* But then, there are so many things I didn't know. I think of school. Though I desire to learn, to read, and to explore life beyond the secrets, school is out of the question. It's impossible to dream when you believe tomorrow will never come. In my mind, there is no tomorrow to dream about; even the next breath is questionable.

A lifetime ago, on top of the stairs in the city of Tampa, my brothers and sisters were all together. My parents had worked hard to manage life. The scary thunderstorms outside did not matter. We were all together.

Now, the storm rages on the inside, and it's getting worse. I blame myself for causing Joyce more worry and frustration. When she looks confused and overwhelmed, I tell myself it is my fault. I should have never come to her home. I feel as if my life is one great big mistake. Lately, I am feeling dizzier than usual, with severe stomachaches and nausea. The sick feeling is normal for me, but something is different this time. Something else is happening.

I have not seen my period in two months. Usually, I don't bother to keep up with that time of the month. Schedules are useless in my world. I only react to what is happening now. And right now, between the uncertainty and depression jutting like thorns from inside, life was growing, preparing to shift me away, towards a new direction.

In June 1981, I found out I am pregnant. Anxiety mixes with a love beyond any I have ever known. At thirteen, I prepare for my next run, but this time, I will not be alone. I feel her growing inside me. I know my baby will be a girl. The wind whispered it to me; yet, I'm so frightened by my circumstance and remorseful questions: *how can I have a baby with all these thorns, these shameful stains? How do I hold her and keep her safe when I can't even find my way?*

God, please help me.

In the Wind

"It is the Holy Spirit's job to convict, God's job to judge, and my job to love." — *Billy Graham*

Roadman's daughter, I make plans to chase the wind, hoping it will lift me up and carry me to a safe, quiet place. I don't remember where I was when I tell Joyce that I am pregnant. She is the second person I've told; Bruce was the first. Joyce wastes no time walking across the street to Bruce's mother's house to confront him. She pounds on the door. Bruce opens it.

"What are your intentions with my sister?" Joyce asks pointedly. I do not remember the answer. My focus stays on Joyce and the vein pulsing from her neck to her forehead. "Do you know how old she is?" She doesn't wait for an answer. "She is only a child. She just turned thirteen years old two months ago." She breathes; her face is red, and her bottom lip still moves after she finishes talking. I don't remember the rest of the conversation. I only remember thinking I don't like confrontations. I disconnect.

Later that day, Joyce goes to work. I go to the lake. Staring over the water, I watch the manatees dance as I plan my next run. In constant motion, anxiety keeps me skittish, looking about as if there is some evil bounty hunter after me. Anticipating the next sneak attack in my life, I convince myself the next one will take me out. But it will need to chase me down. A moving target is harder to hit. The clock is ticking, and the pistol in my head prepares to pull back the trigger.

After some time, my mother gets the news that I am at Joyce's house and that I'm pregnant. I do not remember all the series of events that take place with my mother during this time. My life is a wreck, and I do not know how to report the fact that my boyfriend is beating me. The same boy who has said he loves me and want to be a good father to our baby. It is the way life and love goes. Such is all I have seen. And I've never heard different. The world continues to spiral. Here a little, there a little; I see only glimpses. When my mother comes to the house to talk to Joyce about my craziness, I hide in the room. Knowing her temper, I avoid any contact.

Linda comes too. She finds me squatting near the closet in Joyce's room. I am happy to see her, but all the same, I want to keep my distance. I don't want her to know what had happened on the beach. As she sits down beside me, I shift, smiling to keep up the facade of being the same sister she once knew. But that girl is long gone—somewhere in the wind. I know my mother is hurt and disappointed, but I have no language, no words to explain to her what happened to me years ago while she was at work. Silence is golden. I wait until the coast is clear to slip out of Joyce's home. Sometime later, my mother comes by and finds me underneath the stairwell; I hide there to get away from everything, but the hiding place proved to be a crappy one; she finds me.

With hands on her hips, she looks at me with a deep ache in her eyes. I don't remember what she was shouting about because I shut down the instant I saw her standing there. I want to vanish inside of the concrete wall, but there was nowhere to go.

I will never forget the pain in her eyes—crammed with sorrow and anger; she looks as if she will explode. My heart sinks knowing the heartache I have caused her. She does not force me to go home. She must know I would only run away again. When she leaves, I know I must run farther away. That day, I walked to the lake hoping to see the manatees before I go. They do not surface today, but Bruce does. I tell him I was leaving. I don't remember the excuse I give him, just that I needed to go. I had wanted to trust Bruce, especially now that I was pregnant, but my fragile mind cannot make the jumbled pieces fit. *How can love be love if it hits you with one hand and strokes you with the other? What is true love? Does Bruce care about me? At thirteen years old, does it even matter? Does anything matter at all?*

I'm only sure of one thing: I want to be left alone. I wanted the noise in my head to stop and longed for the peace and quiet of solitude. Solitude is safe; it never slaps you in your face or holds you prisoner in a room when you want to leave, as Bruce has done on several occasions. The solitude respects my wishes, and if I need to scream out, it reacts just the same. There is kindness in solitude. Unlike the many moods of Bruce, the solitude allows me to be angry. Bruce makes it clear the first time I got upset, that it will be to my regret, so I learn just to let it go. All the rights of being a human being are forbidden. Such is the transfer in this culture. Such are the times.

My comfort comes from knowing Joyce will have more peace without me making her life more complicated than it should be. I leave her house with only the clothes on my back. That day, I learned that sometimes those we trust the most would often let us down, not intentionally, but because the thing we most need; the essence of all we seek cannot be found outside of ourselves. The truth of who we are, our value and identity, must first be understood, within. This lesson would take years to understand fully.

"God, please take care of my sister," I whisper, cutting through the dirt path on the side of the lake. The impulse is the same: walk eastward. The pull is unexplainable. I move towards the ocean again. From the moment I walk away, I feel peace. I walk on guard, always cautious of the predators waiting. The familiar winds of the Fort Lauderdale beach strip carry me under the same stairwell of an apartment complex. Another night I sleep inside an enclosed lifeguard tower. It is warm, and the scattering noises don't bother me too much anymore. I've gotten used to them. When I am too tired to keep out of sight, I nod off near the ocean and listen to the sounds of the sea.

Like the waves in the ocean, I move in and out of time, drifting back and forth from the present to the past. I am learning to let go and accept the things I cannot change, or maybe I am learning what it feels like to finally lose my mind altogether. Whatever the case, living in the wind is peaceful because the wind does not scare me anymore; only people frighten me.

On the run and pregnant, I try to remember to eat. Life is uncertain, especially when there is no safe place to sleep. The dawn was overcast as I walk back to my mother's house looking for Linda and Michael. Exhausted, my feet swell from the long walk, but the driveway is empty; that's a good sign. I sneak through the back door. Nothing has changed—the lock is still broken.

The fear still lives here; it hisses pass the broken hinges of the doorframe. *I will kill you if you tell anyone.* Other voices say, *your time is almost up; You will be dead before you turn twenty.* I keep moving. A moving target is harder to hit. I know my mother's schedule; she is working, always working. I am not sure if Robert is home on furlough or out of the country. With no car in the driveway, I take my chances.

When I walk through the kitchen, I find Michael and Linda in the living room. "Sandra!" Linda says with a big smile.

"Hi, Peanut. Hi, Michael, I miss you." I smile, acting in complete control. To my relief, no one else is home. Michael heats a Banquet Chicken TV dinner for me. We sit and talk, laughing as if life is but a dream. I pretend to be okay when Michael and Linda ask me how I am doing. But the truth is I am not well. *What have I done? How could I have allowed myself to get pregnant with nothing to offer my baby?* No home, no education, no stability, and no future. The emotions torment me.

I eat again and laugh at Michael's endless jokes. I take another bite of food, wondering, *who will raise my baby after I die?* I force a smile and take a sip of the sugary red Kool-Aid Linda has made. I watch Linda staring at me as if she knows it will be a long time before we would see each other again. She can't pretend as well as I can. I turn away, swallowing another bite of chicken and mashed potatoes.

"Don't go, Sandra! I will hide you here in the house." Linda says. Michael echoes her plea for me to stay and takes my empty plate to the kitchen.

"Don't worry about me, guys." I continue to play the game, pretending to be strong, even fearless—anything to protect the secrets. Sitting in the living room, I suppress every vulnerable emotion, shifting back to BJ. BJ reminds me that I must be tough. So, I won't let them see me cry. Not here, not now, and not in front of anyone. No one can be trusted because no one stopped it; all the madness and the pain. What's more, is nothing can turn back time. Nothing can change what has happened.

The pseudo-personality of BJ gives me a safe place to hide from myself and pretend that nothing matters. BJ couldn't care less about the conflicting crap smelling up this seen-and-not-heard society.

While time slips away from us, laughter turns to an unspoken hush of uncertainty. Linda's soft brown eyes shift away as if searching for something to say to make me change my mind. "Don't go," she pleads, wrapping her arms around me. When she lets go, she hurries to the couch and angles it caddy-corner to the wall. "See, you can hide in the back, behind the couch. No one will find you here." She reassures me with a sympathetic glance.

"This should work too," Michael says, moving the tall artificial tree plant next to the arm of the chair to conceal the makeshift hideout. My mother has had the same plant for as many years as I can remember.

I want to stay and be close to my sister and brother, but the feel of the house still makes me sick to my stomach. For the sake of love, I decided to stay for as long as my nerves can hold out. Linda smiles, and for a brief time, I lay low behind the couch. The set-up works for a little while, but my mother soon finds out I was there, and so does Bruce.

He comes by the house and stands outside in the driveway, waiting for me to come out. In the cluttered world of my mind, I do not bother to keep up with the details of the next few days. The mounting stress tells me when it is time to run. And now, time is up. Before I could say goodbye to Michael and Linda, the yelling started. My mother screams about me getting pregnant and for thinking that I'm, as she puts it, "grown." I don't remember all of what she said, only that it hurt. After that, BJ takes over, and I am fine again because it reminds me not to give a damn about anything. Bruce and Robert talk outside near the driveway. I only catch the tail end of the unexpected encounter.

Over a year ago, I had told Bruce about my stepfather. I never imagined he would confront Robert, face to face. And after the experience with Bruce's controlling and angry nature, it was like the pot accusing the kettle of boiling.

"I'm gonna watch you die for what you did to her!' Bruce tells Robert as if he could see the future. After that day, Michael walks me down to Mr. Walker's house on the corner of 24th Street. I am ready to disappear again, but Michael is worried and doesn't want me to be alone on the streets. He is certain Mr. Walker will offer me safe shelter. When we get there, Mr. Walker welcomed me in, but I do not want to stay too long at his home. It is too close to my home and the monster living in it. Though Michael is well acquainted with Mr. Walker, I do not want to live with any man. I view men all the same: as evil opportunists, who will surely find a way to exploit or abuse the vulnerable and the weak-minded if given the right day and time. After a few days, Mr. Walker agrees to drive me to Tampa to stay with my mother's sister, Aunt Murline. During the drive up, Mr. Walker sings gospel hymns and makes music by clapping two spoons together. He says he is a born-again Christian. Songs of praise fill the lawn truck along with the sound of his lawn mowers and tree cutting equipment that shift every time we hit a pothole or make a sharp turn. The open road is freeing. The farther away we move from Fort Lauderdale, the more the anxiety subsides.

The sky is alive with vibrant hues of blue, and the clouds move over with no sign of rain. When we stop for gasoline and bathroom breaks, Mr. Walker takes a moment to show me how to play spoons to his favorite song, "It's in My Heart."

"See, take it like this and tap it against your leg," He says, holding the two spoons between his thumb and index finger. I have never heard the song before, nor have I ever seen someone create such a pleasant melody with silverware. I practice with the spoons while Mr. Walker teaches me the lyrics on the nearly five-hour trip to Tampa. The words of the song wash over me, calming the impulsive twitches that hiccup without notice. The melodious sound of the clanking spoons pushes aside the noise in my head long enough for me to enjoy the moments. By the time we reach the Hillsborough County line, I can recite the entire song,

> *"It's in my heart, this melody of love divine.*
> *It's in my heart that I am yours and you are mine.*
> *It's in my heart; I can't help but sing and shine,*
> *It's in my heart; it's in my whole heart."*
> *Though some may **sing** to pass the weary night along*
> *Though some may sing to entertain a worldly throng*
> *I sing because I worship God in song*
> *It's in my heart; it's in my heart.*
> *You ask me why I know His blood can **cleanse** alone;*
> *You ask me how I know He sits upon the throne*
> *And why I know He chose me as His own*
> *It's in my heart; it's in my heart.*
> *You ask me how I find the time to read and **pray**;*
> *You ask me how I smile when things are far from gay;*
> *You ask me how I sing His praises come what may;*
> *It's in my heart; It's in my whole heart."*

Singing the song with Mr. Walker, I begin to recall the three words Joyce told us years ago. Simple words she said we should never forget. "No matter what, trust in God, no matter what." As I listen to the words of the song, I begin to hear the connection. I must remember to trust God with my whole heart, but I am not sure I know how to trust anyone or anything. How do I hold onto blind faith? Terrible things have already happened. How do I believe in a God who allows the storms to keep raging in my life? He stands by and allows it to happen. I have many questions with no answers.

In Tampa, the town looks the same as it did before my family moved. Windows of dilapidated buildings, barely steady enough to hold in the heat, stare out like cold glazed eyes. The open-air coin laundry mat sits on the same corner, just across the street from the liquor store, and an old juke joint. The timeworn roads bring back fond memories of lunch in the park with my cousins. We'd spend some summers there, hanging out at the community center just outside of Ybor City. Mr. Walker stops at my aunt's house on 22nd

Street. The song is still playing in my head when we arrive. I breathe, looking over the front porch.

"Thank you, Mr. Walker. I will continue to practice playing the spoons," I say as I get out of the truck. But before I could leave, Mr. Walker takes my hands and says a short prayer, asking God to watch over my baby and me.

"Let me know if you need anything," he says before backing his truck away.

My aunt Murline is standing on the porch. She reminds me of a Nubian queen with her high cheekbones and her tall, elegant frame. She is extraordinarily beautiful. I reach up to hug her, feeling grateful she allowed me to come. And though she welcomes me warmly, I knew within a couple of weeks; I would leave.

Once again, the noise comes back, whispering just behind my left ear, *you do not belong here. Outcast, misfit, you'll only cause trouble.* In my mind, I could not do anything right. Like my father, I long for the road, the wind; it is where I feel content and free. In less than two months, I will be on my way back to Fort Lauderdale. There is something about the beach there. It calls to me, and I long to feel the spray of the waves. Something about the ocean makes me feel alive. It listens, giving and receiving at the same time.

During the short stay with my aunt, she keeps to herself, mostly isolated in her room, seldom talking in complete sentences. Aunt Murline used to be joyful and friendly, but something has happened since the last time I saw her. Empty Budweiser cans sprawl out in the backyard of her home. Near the back door, the pile reaches above the level of the doorknob. I thought my aunt was recycling the aluminum cans for extra cash. I later will find out she had suffered from depression and began to drink heavily. She had changed, or perhaps I just never knew her truth.

One night, she took me out. I can still hear the music playing in the bar. She had dressed me up in a wig and large floral dress. We walked to the bar a few blocks away from the house. She told me to tell the bartender that I am eighteen. I told her I do not drink. I have just turned fourteen, and I am pregnant. She said it's ladies' night at the bar and I did not have to drink.

"Just tell the bartender you are eighteen and don't worry about nothing else," she assured me. The wig itched, and the high heels cramped my tomboy ankles. *I cannot walk in heels!* I think to myself. I wouldn't dare say it aloud, but I had known it wasn't a good idea. *The bartender is going to see right through me, this oversized dress, and the fifties style wig that kept sliding down to the left side of my face.* The walk to the bar was excruciating. I don't know what hurt more, my toes or my conscience. *How am I going to lie to the bartender?* I would much rather stay quiet, sit to the side, and let my aunt do whatever she came to do. I was not going to fool anybody. Even I knew that.

When we walked into the bar, it was nearly empty, except for a few people lounging along the corner tables. This was my second time inside of a bar. A different city, but the same numbing haze hung in the air like an obscure hypnotist waiting to take your worries away. The bartender threw her eyes on me before I ever made it to the counter. Her head tilts.

"How old are you, child?" she asked — one side of her jaw slightly bigger than the other. Her tone reminded me of my elementary school teacher from Sunland Park. She had known the answer before she asked.

"Fourteen, ma'am," I reply, forgetting to breathe in again.

My aunt gave me clear instructions on the way to the bar; simple orders of what to say and how I am supposed to say it.

The bartender grumped with a southern drawl, "You too young to be in a bar, child." Chewing tobacco slurped in her jaw like thick brown syrup. Pointing her finger towards the exit, she had told us to leave. The walk back to the house was long. My aunt did not fuss at me for telling the truth, but the whole way back, she was quiet. The sound of my heels flopping against the sidewalk was the only sound in the world for those moments. With her arms folded, and her head low, my aunt walks with a nowhere-else-to-go kind of pace. Though she never mentioned it, I felt as if I let her down.

"I can't even lie right," I whispered, scratching underneath the itchy wig. I had just wanted her to be happy. On the way back to her house, the only thing that felt worse than disappointing my aunt was my aching feet.

For most of my pregnancy, I stay on the run. Driven by strong emotions, I have learned to become a chameleon, blending with each new place, but only for a moment. My stay will be short. I trust no one to love me enough, past the stains, past the torment of an inner world that drives me to run away. I will beat the agony of rejection at its own game. I will run.

In a matter of years, alcoholism would claim my aunt's life. Cirrhosis of the liver was an awful price to pay. I was too young to understand it then, but there was a reason for my aunt's sadness.

Years earlier, so the story goes, she had a secret lover who shot and killed her husband. He came home early from his work as a truck driver; it was after midnight. He drew his gun a few seconds slower than her lover. My aunt was never the same since. In 1986, she lost her battle with depression and addiction. She was only 40 years old.

When I left my aunt's home in Tampa, I stayed with Mr. Walker for a few days, sneaking back and forth to see Michael and Linda. But soon, Bruce finds me. And again, I play the game of house with no house, having sex while hating sex, living but wanting to fly away. I feel as if I am prey for Bruce. And now that I am pregnant with his child, there is no getting away. A part of me wants to believe he loved me, but I can't get beyond his need to hit and control me like I am a pet or cheap lakefront property. For a while, I ignore what I cannot change. Paying no attention to the fact that I have no direction, no plan, and no purpose of my own, I go where instinct takes me. Nearly seven months pregnant, I see life, not in days, months, or years, but restless breaths.

"Where are you going now?" Michael asks with a worried look. His deep-set eyes and jawline twinge, reminding me of our father.

"I'm all right. Do not worry about me. I just want to tell you I love you guys before I go." We kiss, and I turn to walk away. Linda starts to cry. She stares at me, and then at my belly.

"Don't cry, Peanut. Everything is all right. Don't worry." I hug Linda, pretending to believe my words, but really; I hate to see her cry.

Anxiety builds, telling me to make my move before anyone comes home, or before Bruce shows up again. I tell Linda everything will be all right. Just like Joyce used to say to us. I wipe her eyes and tell her God is in control. Saying the words are more out of habit than belief. The words drift out, from years of hearing my mother whisper the name of Jesus and listening to her play the song "God's Got It All in Control" by Shirley Caesar. But I question what I believe. Too many questions with no answers.

"Linda, there is something I need to teach you before I leave," I explain. I teach her about her cycle. I want her to know what to expect and how to manage the monthly cramps. I do not want her to be afraid like I was when I first got my period. Such topics are not explained. The language of the culture withholds the issues that are perceived to be taboo. Issues like sexuality, addiction, and human emotions. In blissful ignorance, you walk blind until you fall in and find the pitfalls of life, or until they find you.

Linda and I hug and kiss again before I leave 24th Street. I know Linda would be all right because she spends a lot of time at Pam's mother's house. The bond Linda has with the family is special, and I know she will not be alone while our mother was working. And either way, she will be safe from any attempts from Robert. Joyce's baseball bat has made sure of that. He never touches her. I vow never to come back to the house on 24th Street.

I hurry my pace, eager to sit near the waves and feel the spray from the sea washing over me. Behind me, I hear footsteps swiftly approaching. He refuses to let me go by myself. "Everything is gonna be all right, Sandra. God is with us. You are carrying a child, and I will not let you be alone on the street. We will trust God together," Michael says, rubbing his hand gently across my back. Tomorrow is not promised, the next meal or where we will lay our heads tonight is uncertain; all we have is each other. Michael has always been sure of himself even before we left Tampa. Despite the fears of our troubled childhood, he appears unscathed. His stubborn demeanor helps me breathe easier. I'm glad he is with me tonight.

The night breeze blows hard from the ocean. Michael and I make our way up the busy strip. We blend in with a sea of faces moving in both directions. The prattle of voices mingles with the sounds of punk rock and the various smells rising from the bakeries and fast food restaurants. I tell Michael about the bathroom at The Biltmore Hotel, and that no one comes in during the late hours of the night.

Michael hears me but does not seem to listen. He scans the strip, looking up and down each side road and building. I am not sure what he is looking for, but I know he is about to make something happen. That is his nature. The people who know him best call him Mr. Swap Shop because he always has a hustle. With his trusty beeper and his bag of tricks, Michael could charm his way inside the Pentagon.

I am not sure how many days' pass before we met Ron: a young man who looked to be around seventeen and had the same wandering look about him. Sitting against a wooden blockade, we notice the young man watching us. Possibly a runaway, he comes and sits on the same weather-beaten barrier that separated the beach from the road. I watch him watching us. With Michael by my side, I felt more confident and prepared to meet crazy with crazy. Whatever happens, I ready myself.

Sand covers his feet up to his knees. "Hi, I'm Ron," he says politely.

"Hello, my name is Michael, and this is my sister, Sandra," Michael says with a businesslike flare. I follow with a swift hello.

He and Michael continue to talk. I quietly zone in and out, staring at his tanned skin, wavy blonde hair, and ocean blue eyes that lets you see right through him.

"Come on, Sandra," Michael says, motioning me to follow him and Ron. I do not think twice about where we are going. I trust Michael. Crossing A1A towards the backstreets, we climb stairs up to a small group of studio apartments. Ron leads us to an apartment he says he shares with some friends.

"If you need a place to crash, you guys can hang out here," Ron said introducing us to his male roommates. We sit on a black couch. Michael is trusting and cordial. Guarded, I follow Michael's lead. Ron's roommates are four same-sex, mixed race couples. They arc kind to us. But Ron seems too nice. *Why would he invite strangers in his place? Why does he want to help us?* I question his motives, waiting for the ugly truth to slip in through the back door. But it doesn't. There are no double crosses or hidden agendas. Ron and his friends offer us a place to rest. Nothing more, nothing less.

Ron and I talk about why he ran away from home. The story went from his dad, to drugs, to rejection. He spoke in circles as the conversation went on, avoiding direct answers to the questions about his family. I do not press for any. Sometimes there are no logical answers. Life is what it is. A dream, a grand illusion where we don't remember our birth and the appointment for our death is set by the same mysteries of time. In this life, there are no easy answers. Perhaps that is why we run away to the ocean. The vast sea helps us forget all the questions that have no logical answers. The sound of the waves drowns out all the nonsense and condemning voices that tell us that we are not good enough, and never will be.

"You don't look like you should be out in the cold," Ron says, looking at my belly and then up at me. "You can crash here until you and your brother figure something out." We thank him, and Michael and I stay on the sofa. And though I am still somewhat suspicious, the doubts begin to fade.

No one hurts us. No one asked anything from us. These are complete strangers, but they show us compassion. *There is a lot I do not know about life, about love, about anything,* I think to myself. With Michael by my side, I drift off to sleep. When I awake, I capture a glimpse of sexuality that is unknown to me. Men embrace on two queen size beds in an exchange that seems to give everything to the other without force and control. The intimate display causes me pause, but never alarm. I remember hearing about the vileness of homosexuality in a church I had visited years ago; stories that warn of the wickedness of Sodom and Gomorrah, and of how fire and brimstones rained down from heaven because of the sinfulness of greed, arrogance, and the heartless disregard of the poor and needy. The topic was taboo when we were growing up. But in my broken world, some beasts walk on two legs, fed only by their insatiable lust. Sitting here tonight, I question what is normal. In my mind, I don't trust anyone with the answers. In a world filled with blatant contradictions, I haven't a clue. All I know is that tonight, I feel safe among men who cared enough to take us in out of the cold.

For a short time, Michael and I stay together on the beach. Our bond grows closer than ever. Michael gets us a studio room just above Ron's apartment—Michael makes things happen. I am not sure how he does it, but he does. We have no furniture, but at least we have our own space to sleep, and we have each other. I tell Michael I want to work at the Burger King down the beach strip. I know I could be an excellent employee if given a chance. The plan is to clean up the tables and floors, impress the manager, and get a job. The strategy sounds good in my head just as it did the first time until I got there and saw Dirk, the manager.

Short and brawny, he has a commanding presence. Dirk shouts orders from the side counter. "If you got time to lean, you got time to clean," he says to the workers behind the counter. I liked him immediately. His army-cut brown hair stands as straight as he does. I notice a few of the crew members look like teenagers. *I am sure to have a shot,* I think to myself, looking around the store to see what needs cleaning. But the tables and floors are already spotless. I sit at a table by the window, facing the ocean, thinking of a plan B.

After a few moments, I feel a presence behind me. It is a young woman. She is wearing a Burger King uniform and has a long-handled dustpan and broom in her hands.

"Hi. Don't I know you?" she asks. On high alert, I do not answer. I do not want anyone to know me. To know me suggests you know I am a runaway. The risk of juvenile or worse, being sent back home becomes a threat. I look down, and then off to the side.

"Hi, um. Miss, are they hiring here? I want to get a job. I can clean the tables and chairs," I say, darting my eyes over the restaurant. "My name is MaryAnn. What's your name?"

"BJ ma'am. And I can clean the bathrooms too if you need someone to do it." I hold my breath, afraid she will ask a question that eventually will require the truth.

She gives me a relax kind of look, smiling at the same time. "I will talk to the manager for you. How old are you?" she asks. I panic, feeling like I have already blown it with the look on my face. I try to think of something to say without telling her a lie.

"How old do you have to be to work here?" I ask worried that answering a question with a question would sound disrespectful and prove I am trying to hide something.

"14, I think, part-time only. I will ask to be sure."

After some time, Ms. MaryAnn comes back. "Sorry, he is not hiring now," she said.

"Thank you for asking." I take in the ocean view from the window seat. My thoughts trail off over the waves.

"Looks like you need this. Don't worry. I got it for you." Ms. MaryAnn places a tray on the table with a Whopper with cheese, fries, and a soft drink.

"Thank you, ma'am," I respond shyly, feeling uncomfortable because I did not work for it. She smiles and returns to the kitchen area. I save half my food for Michael. In the coming days, Ms. MaryAnn and I become closer. I can always get a meal and a smile from her. Whenever I come to the store, I pick up trash and clean the tables and floors by hand. It becomes a habit. Cleaning makes me feel useful in a way I cannot explain. *What once was dirty, I have the power to clean. I can wipe up every stain and spill until it looks like it never happened.*

Michael and I often stay inside the restaurant after closing. When the tables and floor are clean, I sit on the stair steps that lead up to the second floor, watching the crew work behind the counter. Dirk glances at Michael and me from time to time but never seemed to mind us hanging around. We weren't the only ones. After hours, he gives food to the homeless and the growing number of runaways who loiter around the area. Night after night, it is all the same: so many kids out near the beach with nowhere else to go. Probably, there is a monster living on their street, and perhaps like me, they come to the sea to listen to the waves and the winds, hoping it will reveal its mysteries, so the world will somehow make sense again.

I question God, wondering if He can see us from wherever He is; life is but a dream. Years later, in 1985, the Covenant House will open in the area on 733 Breakers Avenue. The crisis center provides emergency shelter, food, and counseling to the growing number of runaways seeking refuge near the beach. Like so many runaways during that time, Michael and I were a few years too early. Left on our own, we were among the nation of runaways with no place to call *home*.

We are the children of the wind and sea.

The Book at the Bus Stop

"God moves in a mysterious way, His wonders to perform. He plants his footsteps in the sea, and rides upon the storm."
-William Cowper

Time winds up, and Michael and I say goodbye near the Biltmore Hotel. When it all falls apart, I tell Michael to go back home. No place to run, nowhere to hide, we are out of options.

Just the other day, everything had changed. I am not sure how, but my mother had found out where Michael and I have been staying. And so does Bruce. *How did they find us?* When Bruce comes over, the conversation centers on my unborn child and his plans for us to have a life together. Not long after the *chat*, he is on top of me. Such has been every encounter since the first time. I've always felt as though I don't belong to myself, and the requirement to have sex when he wants is a given. Each position speaks of my usefulness, my place, my price. There is never an argument because he is always right. No opinion, no rights, no voice; I instinctively obey. Empty hearts with lost souls will always yield control to the takers.

Still, there is another part of me that waits, watching the clock. Running farther away from him is the only plan I honestly have in mind. I feel like I have been running all my life, and now, I'm good at it. My memory is intact, and I don't trust the Dr. Jekyll/Mr. Hyde ways of Bruce. He tells me things will be different. My heart tells me to run. It doesn't have to say it twice. Bruce soon leaves, and the paradise Michael and I have created will not last.

When my mom shows up at the studio apartment, I climb inside the bathtub. The studio design is one way in and one way out. There is no furniture to hide behind and nowhere else to go. The dread of seeing my mother is overwhelming. The shame of my life, and the disappointment I feel I caused her, makes me shake uncontrollably. My mother comes into the bathroom. Face to face, we stand worlds apart. She is angry and despondent. I am seen and not heard. As she screams at me, I remain silent, never saying a word. The same hopeless look bellows in her eyes, like a deep cut that will not stop bleeding. She uses the same angry words, like a coarse sponge desperately trying to wipe up the spill between us. Two separate cultures, no connection, no understanding. It will take a lifetime before the blood dries. My mother rants on again about how I think I am "grown." Secrets hide in the palms of my clench fist as I shrink against the shower wall.

In anguish, I fall deeper inside a dismal trench: a seen-and-not-heard abyss where no matter what I say, I will not be heard; no matter what I do; the real me will not be seen. So, the best thing to do is *nothing*. As she stands in front of me, she dares not ask me why I keep running away, or why I prefer to stay on the street. Asking such questions of children has been as foreign as a black man living in an all-white town. It just didn't happen when she was growing up, and it scarcely happens now. Children don't question, and parents use the tools they were given to raise the next generation: hard work, anger, and oppression, while faith seems to be the cushion in between the three. The time in which my mother grew up seems to prevent her from seeing me as a separate human being, rather than an extension of her past, her oppression, and the racist plight she had to fight to demand respect for her life.

I want to scream out, "Mama, this is me! I am not your past! I love you! I am sorry!" Up against the bathroom wall, I remain silent.

There seem to be two kinds of people in the world: the slave master and the slave. No middle ground appears to exist between the two extremes. My mother is emotionally unreachable. In the bathroom, unresolved anger floats around her, like ghosts desperately trying to right the wrongs of her time before they can finally cross over. Heartache melts away any sign of empathy from her face. After the surge of cutting words, she frowns deeply, and I pray to disappear. *Oh, how I wish to be anyone but me, anywhere but here.*

The way I see it, the word *grown* doesn't fit me at all. What is it to be "grown?" Whatever it is, I did not choose it—it chose me. This isolation chose me. The shame, the distress, the anxiety, it all chose me. I don't want it, but it refuses to let me go. I keep my mouth closed, inching closer to the corner of the tub. She knows I will not go back home and does not try to force me. I only wish I could tell her why. Some secrets are stronger than fear. By the time she walks away, my nerves could take no more. When she leaves the studio apartment, I break down, weeping. Mostly because she thinks I am someone who I am not. She hasn't a clue about who I am. Such is a culture where children are raped and beaten, seen and not heard, snatched from their own childhoods, and still expected to behave like good boys and girls. The very notion is absurd. But no one ever knows because we don't say a word. For nearly ten minutes, Michael stands over me, rubbing my back as I vomited in the toilet. Only one thought came to mind: it's time to run again.

Michael and I leave the studio, determined to keep moving around so no one can find us. We stay for a short time at Ms. MaryAnn's home, and then, back to the beach. This time, we try to keep out of sight. But it is not easy. No matter where we go, we stick out like nighttime above solid snow in the dead of winter. A pregnant girl and a young boy wandering around the beach is usually no big deal. Unless that boy and that girl happen to be black, and the area, in 1981, happens to be densely populated, mostly by people who are white.

The misty rain makes the air feel colder than before. The horseshoe-shaped structure of The Biltmore Hotel keeps the brunt of the wind away from the pool area. Once again, I find a refuge here. The same poolside that I used to sneak by to sleep inside becomes our hideaway. But this time, I do not hide in the bathroom. Out in the open, we rest on the lounging chairs near the pool as if we were paying customers. Tired and hungry, we are out of options. I watch Michael sleeping soundly. His shoulders still tremble even after I wrap a towel around him.

Guilt overtakes me, seeing Michael out here like this; I can bear no more; I love him too much, and I know our mother will let him come back home. At that moment, I decide it's time to do something.

"Michael, Michael," I whisper. "Michael, wake up. It's time for you to go home." His eyes wander around as if he is trying to remember where he is.

"Okay, let's go," he says, rubbing his eyes.

"I'm not going. You are. I can never go back there again."

Michael yawns with a confused look on his face. "I will be okay. I have a plan. But you have to go home." He stares back at me. He looks unsure as if he is thinking whether he wants to debate or not. Perhaps he knows it would be a losing battle. From our childhood, he has always seemed to listen, letting me have my way. Years ago, Joyce had told us stories of how inseparable we were, even as toddlers. She was right. Michael and I have always shared a special bond. Tonight, I know the love we share will always be there, no matter what. I touch his shoulder.

"Trust me, Michael; I got a plan. I've been here before, remember, I told you. But I need you to go home now. I will be fine." His eyes glaze with sadness as he stares back at me. Only the sound of the wind moves around us.

I smile and nod, wanting him to get moving. He drops his head and says a quiet prayer. We embrace and kiss each other goodbye. Michael is fifteen. It will be the last night I see him for almost a year, the last time I stay at the poolside of the Biltmore Hotel, and the last time I tell him a straight-faced lie. I have no plan, no known options, nowhere else to go. Desperate, I would say anything to get him to go back home where I know he will have food and a warm place to rest.

Alone, I feel everything. An unexpected pressure comes across my lower back. The intense pressure reminds me of the mess I have made of my life. For a moment, I think back to Tampa when I spilled soda pop all over my clothes. I had made such a mess, but my Mom just smiled and laughed. The world was a different place back then; there is a harsh awareness that I cannot escape nor fix — no one can. On my own, I think, *what kind of mother can I possibly be? I have nothing to offer my baby, nothing but secret thorns and this unpredictable wind that blows me to and fro towards Neverland?*

On the shifting sand of the beach, I walk. My footprints vanish with each oncoming wave. As if they were never there at all; only a dream. The sound of the sea no longer comforts me. I can only think about my unborn child. Something inside me shifts, and I am too tired to pretend anymore. Alone again, I am free to be myself. I sit on the sand, disconnecting from the pretense. BJ moves on, somewhere in the wind, until I can feel every emotion. I let go, allowing the tears to fall. In this incomprehensible reality of my life, tears are the only outlet to help me grasp any sense of sanity. I imagine that is why God created us with the ability to weep and shed tears. He must have known about the nonsense that would go on down here on this stormy planet.

The chill in the air signals the hours before dawn. After a while, I learn to tell time by the shift in the wind and the hue of the sky. Sitting near the shore, I touch my belly. "You deserve so much more. I'm so sorry, my baby," I whisper.

The reality is what it is: fourteen, pregnant, unwed, uneducated, homeless, and full of thorns; I let go of what I cannot change. There is no need to pretend anymore. I take off my shoes and let the waves wash over my swollen feet. I don't remember the last time I had something to eat but all the same, the last thing I feel is hunger. Though my stomach grumbles, I hear it and don't hear it. *Life is but a dream;* I think to myself looking out over the rolling waves in the sea. After some time, I get up and walk alongside the ocean's shore. Restless, I keep moving. Near the open sea, nothing hinders the wind. Like a free spirit, it blows through the waves, kissing up particles of sand and seawater in every direction.

Nothing covers me except the blue flower-printed shirt on my back and a lint-filled pair of pants. The cold wind blows; I feel it and don't feel it. The reflection of the moonlight fades over the ocean, and I think about my dad. And then, I think about my black duffle bag I lost somewhere a long time ago. I haven't even thought about it until I look for something to hold a pretty seashell I've picked up. With nothing to put it in, I leave the seashell on the shore where it belongs. Somewhere, a long time ago, like the empty seashells, I lost the part of me that felt alive, that dared to dream, and that believed all things were possible. Since that first day I went in the room with Robert, I left out empty. The emptiness remains. I feel soulless. *Who could love someone like me?* Hope is as obscure as the concept of love. And in my muddled mind, the unrelenting voices tell me my value, my worth, my price. When I try to add it all up, it totals less than zero.

Tonight, I have one question for God. *Why was I ever born?* I sit on the sands of the shore, too tired to walk anymore, waiting for His answer. *Why has the God of my grandmother allowed my life to continue this way?*

"God, if not for my sake, please help my baby," I whisper, looking up at the cloudless sky. The heavens are quiet. Only the wind blows around me. A sharp pain pushes around my lower back again, and I feel the flutter of life inside. I miss my family, thinking of Joyce till it hurts. I pray for Leon, hoping he is okay. I think about Michael, Linda, and the games we would play in the backyard underneath the mango trees. I miss my mother's laughter and my father's Old Spice cologne that always smelled of Christmas.

Sitting by the shore, I tell myself those days are gone forever. I question what is family, what is faith? It feels like some made-up fantasy—figments of the imagination, like Santa Claus and the Easter Bunny. The thoughts roll out with the waves until a sound in the wind captures my attention. It calls to me. I turn my eyes towards the distant horizon. The sky wraps itself around the sea like ancient lovers, falling into each other. I breathe out, believing I am crazy and just hearing things out of desperation. Then the voice surrounds me until all I can do is listen. It is all consuming, as it silences every question and every sneer from within.

"Get up," it whispers to me. Instinctively, I move, standing to my feet. "You must walk," it instructs. Almost like breathing, I move, walking in the direction it leads. I have no control of the navigation.

The wind picks up, and the voice guides me towards a bus stop, near Sunrise Boulevard and A1A. There is a bus bench near the edge of the road. I stop, sit, and rest without thinking, just breathing. And then, I noticed a book next to me. It is a New Testament Bible with a beige cover. *Someone must have left it behind before getting on the bus,* I reckon. I sit back on the bench too tired to think or read; still, my fingers move, opening the book.

And without searching, my eyes immediately focus on the words of Mathew 6:31: "Think not of tomorrow, what you shall eat or drink or what you shall be clothed with, for your heavenly Father knows what you need before you ask." The air around me turns strangely still as if heaven was listening, waiting for me to speak.

Leaning back against the bus bench, I question God once more. "Lord, if you know my needs before I ask, why so much pain? Why am I here, no home, cold, hungry, and afraid?" I close my eyes, puffy and sore from bouts of crying, salty air, and lack of sleep.

At this very moment, I experience what I can only believe to be the supernatural. It is something beyond reason, life or death, color or class, flesh, and bone. Beyond this earthly realm of emotion, want, and need. It is a sound, like a vibration of motions that consumes every part of me. The voice left nothing to doubt, nothing to ask for. The God of my grandmother, my mother, and my sister revealed Himself in a way that I cannot fully explain. And human language fails to describe the details of the events of what happens in the next few moments.

As I become aware of the scripture, and confront God with His Words, the wind shifts, moving inside me, around me. The simple acknowledgment and acceptance of the scripture, as it relates to my homelessness and despair, set in motion an unseen realm beyond anything I can imagine.

Infused with energy, I feel a pulling. An invisible guide immediately compels me to get up and walk towards the west. As I start walking away from the beach, I do not know where I'm going, only that an unexplainable energy is leading me. Shepherded by an overwhelming force, I look back at the bus bench where I was just sitting as if I will find a reasonable explanation for what is happening. There is none. Soon, I approach the corner of Andrews Avenue and Oakland Park Boulevard. Peculiar, my feet are swollen inside tattered sneakers, yet the three-hour walk has felt like 10 minutes because mysteriously, a part of me feels like I was being carried.

"Rest here," the voice tells me. I sit down to rest on a yellow patio table that sits outside of a McDonald's restaurant.

Early morning, but still dark outside, peace surrounds me. For the first time during my homelessness, I give no thought to sleeping outside in the open—the strong presence, almost tangible near me, watching, protecting me. At this very moment, I am not alone. I put my head down on the table and close my eyes. The wind blows, but I can't feel it. I have not eaten in days, but at this moment, I'm content; satisfied. I hear the voice again saying, "I am here. I have always been with you." I fall asleep.

Early Morning: McDonald's – 265 West Oakland Park Boulevard

"Hi, would you like to come in and get breakfast?" Her name is Ms. J. Peck; it's on her name badge. She is a young fair-skinned woman who looks to be in her mid-twenties. She is wearing a McDonald's uniform. Right away, she reminds me of my sister Joyce. That morning, when she touched my shoulder, I had been in a deep sleep, and I almost forgot where I was.

"Don't be afraid," she says, smiling with her eyes more than her mouth. She invites me inside to get something to eat. The McDonald's is just opening for the morning shift. I sit in the corner by the window. She goes behind the counter and starts working the register. After a few minutes, she brings a tray to my table. On top of the tray are two cartons of milk, a breakfast sandwich, a card, a five-dollar bill, and a couple of quarters.

She tells me to sit and eat while she begins her shift. After a few moments, she came back and sat down next to me. She told me she knew me, and God was with me. In shock, I stare at her.

"Call the number on the card. Don't worry; you can trust them; they are nice people." I am speechless and in awe. How does she know me? She must have read my thoughts because, in the next moment, she answered the unspoken question. "Your family lives on 24th Street. I live on the next street over," she says. "Everything will be all right. Use the change to call the number, and a van will come to get you. Don't be afraid," she says, looking at my tray. "Would you like more to eat?"

"No, thank you," I say, wanting more, but too stunned to digest what I've already eaten. She hugs me and goes back to work, but not before telling me to trust God. "Thank you," I reply.

I slowly regain my bearings to leave. I am thankful for her kindness, the food, and the money, but the thought of a strange van picking me up made me question: who, where, what, and why. *Who are these* nice *people? Where are they going to take me? What are they going to do to me once I am there? And why would anyone care about a misfit like me?* Hesitant, I walk down Oakland Park, waiting, pondering the questions until nightfall.

Denny's – 3151 N.W. 9ᵗʰ Avenue

I walk to the Denny's on the corner of Powerline Road and Oakland Park, just about a half-mile down the road. I sit in a quiet booth trying to explain to myself what happened at the McDonald's.

The card in one hand, money in the other, and the book tucked under my left armpit, I shake my head, trying to wake up from this trance-like dream where God has spoken to me, and a beautiful lady I have never seen before has fed me and told me to trust in God. It is all too unreal, and for hours I struggle with what to do next. *This card doesn't even have a name on it. What if it's a set-up to take me back home? Who are these people anyway,* I ask staring at the card, flipping it over again, as if the answers to my many questions will magically appear on the opposite side. In my world, you must earn trust, and I have a terrible habit of trusting things that hurt me; mistakes I am trying to correct. My baby moves and a peaceful feeling come over me. The same presence I felt on the beach, I feel now.

A woman humming on a high stool near the front counter catches my attention. She sits alone. Her hair is thin with traces of gray and brown flowing off gaunt shoulders. Deep wrinkles run across her sunburnt skin. She stares off, singing as if she has lost someone she loves:

> *"Lay your head upon my pillow*
> *Hold your warm and tender body close to mine*
> *Hear the whisper of the raindrops*
> *Blowing soft against the window*
> *And make believe you love me one more time, for the good times."*

She sings the song as though she is heartbroken. I've heard the sad melody somewhere before. Business is slow at the Denny's, and I try not to stare at her, but I can't help it. I wonder why she is sitting all alone and if she has a family somewhere, waiting up for her to get home. For a while, I forget about my own sadness, to make room to hear another loveless love song about an elusive lover — a deceptive fairy tale with no happy ending. I turn away, towards the fogged window. I wrap my arms around myself, staring at my vague reflection through the thick glass. The parking lot is half-empty. I stare, wondering, *what is the true meaning of life and love. After some time of looking out the blurred window, my thoughts trail away into stillness.*

Simon House

"In every community, there is work to be done. In every nation, there are wounds to heal. In every heart, there is the power to do it." ~*Marianne Williamson*

Winter, 1981

A phone booth sits on the far end of the parking lot, across from Denny's; in the same shopping plaza. At first sight of it, I think about the *Underdog* cartoons I used to watch as a child. As I get closer to it, I think about my father. I wonder if he misses me as much as I miss him. The quarters drop inside the coin slot, and I hesitantly put the receiver to my ear. I dial the mysterious number on the card with no name. A phone number written by a sweet woman who says she knows me, and that I must trust in God — a God with no face, who works in mysterious ways, and is as predictable as the powerful winds.

A caring voice answer and asks for my location.

"Are you safe? Someone will be there to pick you up. Stay where you are." The concerned voice of a woman asks if I needed her to stay on the phone until the driver came. I told her no, mainly because I wasn't sure what else to say.

In less than 20 minutes, a van comes, picks me up, and takes me to a place called Simon House where I receive a bed, clothes, food, and a new Bible that had both the Old and New Testaments. Ms. Susan, a staff member of the center, stands near the bedroom door, asking me if I was okay and needed anything else.

"No, thank you. I'm all right."

"The clothes in the closet are all new, donated from different organizations, but you will need maternity clothes. Tomorrow, we can go to the store to get clothes and shoes that will fit you. After you get some rest, I will show you around the center. Snacks are in the kitchen if you want more to eat, and our women's groups meet in the morning and evening. Let me know if you need anything at all." She gives me a look as if she knows what it feels like to be me.

"Thank you, ma'am," I reply, barely moving my mouth, unable to express the emotions, the shock, and the uneasiness; I fear waking up to realize the joy I feel is only a dream.

She closes the door as she leaves out of the bedroom. I stare outside myself. I wait for the hit, wait to awake and realize I was fantasizing again. Facing the closet, I stare at clothes lining the entire space with an array of shoes underneath. A twin bed sits at an angle on the other side of the room. It is empty. I am alone, but not really. I begin to realize there is a world beyond the one in which I was born—another realm, unseen but just as real. The realm my grandmother, mother, and sister spoke about. The next moments in the room are indescribable as the same presence reveals itself to me, just as it did on the beach. I am awestruck. Safe inside my new room, the chill bumps have gone. It is warm here. The twin bed is soft, and my unborn baby and I eat from the hands of complete strangers; again. My new Bible has a brown matte covering. On my lap, I trace my finger across the embossed words: The Holy Bible.

I touch it like a priceless heirloom, remembering the incredible stories that were told to me throughout the years: Sunday school stories of how Jesus came to set the sinner free and the miracles that caused many to believe that Jesus was the Son of the living God. I lift my head, feeling the air change in the quiet room. And then, with my thumbs on top of the pages, I open my new Bible, and in that instant, I learn a valuable lesson about faith.

Without ever looking for a page, the same scripture shows itself to me again in Mathew 6:31: "Think not of tomorrow what you shall eat or drink or what you shall be clothed with, your heavenly Father knows your needs before you ask." My mouth falls open. How has this happened twice? Without me ever trying to find the scripture, it reveals itself—as if the Words have life. In awe, I hear a distinct voice, all-consuming yet merciful. I do not fully understand what is happening or why it is happening now. All I know is I heard His voice, clearly saying, "All you have asked, you have. I promise that I will never leave you, nor forsake you. I will be with you always."

The voice spoke clearly to me, without question, I knew it was the Lord. The God I have heard about all my life: The God of Abraham, Isaac, and Jacob. It was The Holy God of my grandmother's tears, my mother's whispers, and my sister's lullabies. He heard me. Cold and hungry, on the beach underneath the scattered stars, *I cried out and He heard me.* I breathe out. Somehow, the book at the bus stop was there, at that very moment in time, so I could learn His words and experience the power of His promises—for myself. Less than twenty-four hours after finding the book at the bus stop, I have received food, clothes, and shelter. A community of support surrounds me from the moment I arrive at the Simon House. I have given no effort in the search for the scripture in either instance. All I know is that I had been lost and alone, and now I am warm. I am safe. I am found.

Journaling has become a habit since arriving at the Simon House. It lifts the heaviness that sneaks up on me when I least expect. Writing helps calm my panicky emotions. A pen is like a lightning rod between my fingers. I cannot write fast enough to keep up with the torrent of thoughts that need to escape at any given moment. Inside my Bible, I use the white space that runs down along the right side of the page to journal and cast away every care out of my mind; I feel a little lighter every time. The last time I wrote down my feelings was inside the green diary I got for my thirteenth birthday. The Bible is different; I trust it with my secrets, the rage, and the shame. I write it all down and now, I can almost breathe again.

The Simon House has group counseling. Preferring to be with the children, I do not go at first. A member of the staff monitors us on the outside play area. I feel more comfortable around the children; I trust them. Watching them run and skip makes me smile. I throw a ball and clap my hands when a little boy catches it. "Great job, sweetheart!" I say. Back and forth, the ball goes, from one child to the other. Again, we clap together, smiling, carefree. One little girl drops the ball—I run, pick it up, and put it in her hands.

"Great job, baby, you got it! You caught it!" We clap our hands until she smiles and throws it back again. On and on it goes. The monotony is wonderful—nothing to think about except for a rainbow-colored ball and the joy of sharing it. The moments offer me a vicarious gift. We play together until the group is over. A trace of childhood is borrowed and returned. I feel grateful. But my stay at the Simon House is short.

The lesson is becoming abundantly clear; you should never unpack your heart in a place where you cannot stay. I learned these lessons the hard way and I hate them the most. For the winds, might come at any time to send you off to another place.

The need to leave the Simon House came unexpectedly. A hard lesson I was not ready to learn, but I had no other choice.

Ms. Susan taps on my door. "Sandra, a caseworker is here to see you." My heart seizes.

"Yes ma'am, Ms. Susan." My voice cracks. A familiar dread comes over me. *Who could it be, and why?* Ms. Susan tells me to gather my things. I must leave today. A caseworker from the Department of Children and Families is here to pick me up. I gather the nerve to ask Ms. Susan why.

"Why can't I stay here?" I feel a mix of tears and resentment welling up all at once.

"You will be better cared for where they are sending you. You are very young and far into your pregnancy. We want what's best for you, and this shelter cannot provide the care you need." Susan touches my hands.

"I don't want to leave. There are other kids here. Why can't I stay? I do my chores and mind my manners. Why can't I live here like the others?" I cry the words, knowing Ms. Susan is right. But right or wrong, I am tired of moving from place to place. I feel safe, welcomed, and I desperately wanted to stay. She mirrors my sadness and tells me everything will be all right. I wonder how she could be so sure.

"Yes, there are other children here, but they are the children of women who are fleeing abusive situations. When you came, we did not know you were just a child yourself. You are in a vulnerable position right now. Your needs require special attention. We care about you and want you to get the help you and your baby needs."

She moves closer to me, holding my twitchy hands. "Don't worry; they will take good care of you and your baby." Her hands are tender and caring. "Will you try to understand what I am saying to you?" She leans down and tries to look in my eyes.

I refuse to look up. Tired of being moved around, sick of being afraid, fed up with not being in control of my own life—I let the tears roll down as they please. Emotionally drained, I do not bother to ask questions anymore. No more protest, I lift my head. "Yes ma'am," I whisper. Wiping my runny nose, I begin to gather my things and thank Ms. Susan for all she has done for me.

She tells me to come and say goodbye to the rest of the staff and families. I have come to love them since arriving at the shelter, but I do not want to see anyone. I was not ready to say goodbye. But isn't that just like life. It sneaks up on me, forcing me to let go of what I think I have. I should have learned that lesson with my cat Midnight.

Out of gratitude and respect for all they have done for me, I dry my tears and pull it together. We hug and say our final farewell. The children squeeze my neck and grin as if they will see me again tomorrow. I try to hold back the tears, learn to pretend again, and go along to get along. All life skills I have learned well. To feel and not feel, to bleed inside from the anxiety that eats a hole in my stomach until I feel as though I will pass out. For whatever reason, God gives me the gift of this place and then takes it away. Tires roll; I hear the road beneath me; it is a familiar sound. *What's next*, I think to myself, but I haven't a clue where I am going. *Away, away; off to Neverland.*

Life is but a dream.

I was too young to understand the legalities of a women's crisis shelter, and why at fourteen, I could not stay.

The real name of the shelter was undisclosed for the protection of the women and children living there. Later, I will learn that Women in Distress is a twenty-four-hour crisis shelter in Broward County that helps victims of domestic violence and their children escape abusive partners. The shelter was a haven for my unborn baby and me. It gave me both peace from the storms of life and a sense of purpose for the future.

You will know when you have a calling on your life; the signs will be there—circumstance that will demand you to live by faith and not by sight. When you believe, no matter what, you will see miracles beyond imagination.

Just keep holding on to God's unchanging hands. Even when we feel lost and alone, God knows who you are, and where you are right now. You are not alone.

St. Vincent's Girls' Home

Miami, Florida — 1981

"You will be fine," The DCFS caseworker tells me. I presume the words are caseworker protocol; something they say to kids in transition. I don't remember her name. It does not matter anyway. Words are just words. Like empty cups in a cabinet: useful, but full of nothing. *How does she know I will be fine?* She might as well tell me the truth; no matter how harsh; the truth is better than not knowing. *Where is she taking me?* I wonder. She does not say. Maybe she does not know herself. Maybe she thinks it does not matter to kids like me to know what's next. But it does. I never wanted to leave the shelter, and not knowing where I am going next only causes more anxiety. The women's shelter has been the one place I felt safe and accepted for who I am. There, we speak the same unspoken language. We learned the language of chaos — when nothing makes sense, and we must learn to straddle two dimensions of time, between the past and the present. The women at the Simon House understood me without me ever needing to explain.

Head down, Bible to my chest, I close my eyes, listening to the tires roll. The sound of the road calls to the hidden parts of me; the parts that belong to my Dad, Roadman.

The DCFS worker is quiet on the ride to my next Neverland. It seems when you want answers, the world gets quiet, and when you want the noise in your head to stop, the world gets chaotic. In the crazy cycle, I disconnect. Wherever the car stops, that's where I will be. On the highway, southbound, I glance up from the backseat, remembering the days when the moon would follow me all the way home. *Home* is such an elusive word. Just when I think I've found it, the picture is gone, like clouds shifting in the sky. A home turns into a sailing ship, and before you can imagine it, a sea monster swims by.

The backseat is such a voiceless, powerless position. The stress of the sudden change triggers me back to the haunting memories like bloodsuckers feasting on the happy times I want to remember. They leave behind everything I want to forget.

Smoke slithers, dancing up from a dirty ashtray, his voice still commands: *Open your legs, open your mouth; do as I say, don't make a sound.* Miles away from 24th Street, the uncertainty triggers it all.

With no choice in the matter, I swallow what I cannot spit

out. I want to ask the caseworker to let down the window so I can breathe. But I don't. I have learned to live my life barely breathing. Nothing changes that now. Quiet and composed, I hold it all in as the car moves on.

"I'm all right," I say to myself. I wipe away tears that fall past my pretense, wishing the world would leave me alone. I am just fine! Opening my Bible, I take my pen and write a question to the only one who I believe has the answer. "Where to now God?"

Multi-colored flowers border the outside of a girl's home. The smell of spaghetti swirls in the air as we pass two cobblestone pillars on both sides of the walkway. In the middle of the grounds is a huge courtyard of lush green grass. The lawn reminded me of Dixie Court Projects, where Joyce taught Linda and me how to turn cartwheels in the meadow.

The caseworker walks me inside, and I sit in front of yet another desk. The first impulse is to knock it over, but I remain still and quiet. A woman with short dark hair stares down thick-framed glasses. I stare back, narrowing my eyes with a defiant attitude because I'm sick and tired of caseworkers, backseats, and desks.

After a few inaudible words between the two, the caseworker walks out. The woman behind the desk introduces herself as the residential supervisor of St. Vincent's Catholic Services. She looks up from paperwork, pen in hand, and tells me she wants to talk about my options after I settle into the new surroundings. *Options?* I think to myself. *What options could she possibly be referring to?* A member of the staff takes me to a single floor dorm-like room. She is a courteous woman with a gentle smile. I don't remember her name. I will call her Marcia. Upon first impression, she has a pleasant personality, though her words are few. Dragging my swollen feet, I notice Marcia slowing her steps to match mine. The pressure in my lower back has become increasingly worse since the swift move to St. Vincent's. Two beds, one bathroom. "This will be your room," she says, and then she gives me the choice of the twin beds. I chose the bed closest to the window. I put my Bible on my pillow and my bag of belongings on the side of the bed. She waits patiently for me.

"Where are we?" I ask.

"Miami, Florida," Marcia replies, taking me on a short tour of the grounds. The social worker had never told me where she was taking me.

"Miami?" I echo under my breath. I've had just about

enough of these disconnected social workers. The social worker might as well have been a taxi cab driver — but at least taxicabs have the decency to let you in on your destination. Miami, of all places. I drop my head and breathe.

The kitchen looks like it can feed a small army.

" I hope you like spaghetti. We are having it for dinner tonight," Marcia tells me, and then we go into a multipurpose room where girls are playing table tennis, watching television, and reading magazines and books. I notice there are rooms adjacent to the north wall in the multipurpose area. They remind me of classrooms without chalkboards.

A memory visits me of a time when I once sat in school, drawing hearts around a big circle, daydreaming of doing something great with my life: becoming a cop, joining the military, and changing the world with the love of a lullaby.

Faith is hard to hold onto when every time I believe things can get better, something changes and causes me to question everything I thought I once knew. With no control over my life, my thoughts scatter like ashes in a whirlwind. *Of all the places to take me, she brings me to Miami?* I try to get past the irony. My thoughts drift. I hear Marcia calling me, but she sounds far away.

"Sandra?" Marcia asks, touching my shoulder.

"Ma'am?" I ask, needing a moment to remember where I was.

"Are you okay?" she asks again.

"Yes, ma'am. I'm fine."

"Do you need to sit down?"

"No, ma'am. Thank you."

"You can participate in any activity you like. The books you were just staring at are for you and the other girls here. You can read at your leisure." Marcia goes on to tell me about the residential program services, rules, and expectations of the girls. At first impression, St. Vincent's is a different place with the same rules as the others. Chores in the morning, breakfast, and group counseling; however, the program's construction is unique in that it connects the lives of hurting girls from different ethnicities and languages — all underage, all pregnant, and all in need of a miracle.

We relate to each other in ways the adults cannot. Most adults have no idea of our reality. I believed they are blind to the fact of what it feels like to be in our shoes, in our skin, and behind the closed door of a place we once called home. I ask Marcia about school. Her answer is surprising. She says St. Vincent's provides tutoring and classes. She also mentions St. Vincent's is a temporary placement facility that houses girls only while pregnant. Social workers and residential counselors work to help the girls with every aspect of their lives from medical expenses, counseling, parenting classes, foster care, and adoption. Since I'm close to my third trimester, my stay will be short. *I'm getting use to short stays.*

The Department of Children and Family Services coordinate services with the St. Vincent's program, and I have no idea what is next in my life. And even if I did, I have no voice, no say in the matter. Uncertainty lingers around me like shapeless faces in the dark, whispering words about me that I cannot understand. Before I have the chance to settle in at St. Vincent's group home, I prepare for the wind to blow again. And so, I don't unpack. Lately, I discover that the more I move my body, the better I can cope with the rising stress. Exercise calms my nerves, so I practice the aerobic moves Joyce taught me when I was younger. The squats and stretches help to relax the muscles in my lower back. It also helps to calm the relentless anxiety that keeps me on the edge of a cliff where I look down at the outstretched arms of death. Lately, especially at night, I feel the fear growing, wearing a thick black cloak and a haughty smirk. He waits to catch my fall. *Before twenty*, it taunts.

Reading and writing keep my mind occupied during the passing weeks at St. Vincent's. Writing poetry makes me think about love, and I find myself thinking a lot about Bruce and the promises he has made to me. I imagine what true love should feel like. Shouldn't true love accept you the way you are; thorns and all? Or does it supposed to hurt you and manipulate you into doing what you don't want to do? Perhaps true love doesn't exist, especially not for misfits. Still, in the solitude of my room, I dream of a brave prince who falls in love with a humble maiden. Against all the odds, they live happily ever after.

The last time I saw Bruce, he seemed to be sincere. Maybe he has changed, I think to myself. But I am not sure that I can forget so easily. I love him, as far as I can understand the meaning of what love is, but when he is angry, he becomes someone I don't want to know. I move past the thought and stay true to my word to write to his brother in prison. Don becomes my first pen pal. So, between watching the Tonight Show with Johnny Carson and Ed McMahon, I write letters telling Don about my time here at St. Vincent's. I try to encourage him with scripture verses and poems. He writes back, and I notice his penmanship is unlike any writing I have ever seen. His handwriting sways stylishly across the pages of his lengthy letters. We continue to write one another during my stay in Miami.

I share a room with Gabriella, a fifteen-year-old Spanish girl who speaks very little English. She is shy and nearly seven months pregnant. We become friends, teaching each other words in our languages while sharing the hard language of a broken home, an abusive relationship, and the fear of motherhood. Gabriella tells me the story of a boyfriend she once trusted. Her brown eyes gloss over with tears, and though her English breaks into a Spanglish kind of dialect; I understand her. Sadness is a universal language; tears are all the same color.

"He hit me, but I love him. I got embarazada. I got pregnant. Mi novio es con otra chica. My boyfriend is with another girl," she explains.

"I'm sorry," is all I know to say. I remember feeling angry, upset at the fact that she is crying. Meanwhile, he is somewhere with another girl.

I read to her, hoping she will understand all the words. I read slowly, "John 14:1 says 'let not your heart be troubled. Believe in God and believe in me.' Bruce had taught me the scripture when we first met, before the sex and the hitting started.

I share the scripture with Gabriella, hoping we both can learn to trust in something bigger than all our worries. The double standards in this world are confusing, but I believe there is a God who hears. He heard my cry on the beach that night at the bus stop. Now, I want to believe for Gabriella. We sit together, alone in the room, two young girls brought together by some unknown destiny. She sniffles, wiping her tears away, while I twirl my shirt, thinking of something to say that would make her happy, if only for a little while.

"My sister taught me how to braid. Would you like me to put a braid in your hair?" I ask her, trying to find a new memory for the both of us.

"Si, yes," she answers. After dinner, we pass the time quizzing each other with English and Spanish vocabulary words, stopping only to feel each other's belly when our babies kick and turn.

"Put your hand here! She is moving!' I say, slightly exposing my stomach. Gabriella touches my belly and smiles in amazement every time she feels my baby moving underneath my skin.

"Sandra, tocar aqui; touch here!" Gabriella says. Her face is radiant.

"Wow! What are you doing in there, playing basketball or

something?" I say, talking to her belly. We both laugh and learn to adapt to life at St. Vincent's. Gabriella makes the time enjoyable. But in the quiet hours, when all the chores are complete, when we have exhausted our energies with doctor's appointments, birthing videos, and group sessions, the calendar reminds us that we may never see each other again. Our due dates draw closer. And once we give birth, we will not return to St. Vincent's.

Today fills with physical exams, assessments, nurses, and doctors until I cannot keep up with it all. "Have you ever experienced insomnia? Are you nauseous? Have you experienced heartburn or any other gastrointestinal problems? Do you have shortness of breath?" A barrage of questions comes at me, but they are all easy to answer because, for most of my life, I have lived with all the symptoms. They are the symptoms of life. Whether they have anything to do with my pregnancy is beyond me.

Between questions, I watch my shoestrings dangle back and forth underneath the examining table. I float into a peaceful trance and hear the faint echo of my mother's voice: "Sydney, tie your shoestring." The smell of alcohol pulls my attention in the direction of a small counter in the corner of the room. Cotton balls, bandages, and wide popsicle-looking sticks lean to the corner of a jar next to a sink. *I miss my dad.*

"Breathe deep. Again. Stick out your tongue. Open your mouth. Say ah." The doctor gives me a complete oral, breast, and pelvic examination. I hide my disgust of his hands touching me, floating away until it's over.

There's no expression on his face, just a slight look of concern is all I can perceive. *Is my baby okay?* I want to ask him. *What happens when I give birth? What happens after? Will it be like my father's mother who I never had the chance to meet? Will I be like her after I have my baby? Will I fall into an endless sleep and never get to see her?* The doctor leaves in a matter of minutes. I keep my questions to myself. A few days later, I receive a message to go to the front office.

My second time visiting the residential supervisor is the last time. She asks me about the future, my plans, and my goals. I cannot answer. I am a fourteen-year-old pregnant runaway. *How can I foresee a future when my past continues to haunt me?* I am afraid, always afraid and unclear of what the future holds. Now, the anxiety is worse because I have an innocent baby with whom I must share this uncertainty.

The residential supervisor sits back in her desk. A pen flips between her fingers. "I want to tell you about your options." Her pursed lips look as though they would vanish if she were to smile. She doesn't. "We specialize in the maternity care of young girls. And we want you to make the best decision for yourself and your unborn child. You are very young, and considering the complications, we believe it would be in your best interest if you were to put your child up for adoption."

She sits back in her chair, pen tapping the desk, waiting for my response. I slant my eyes coldly at her, waiting for the blood to return to my heart after what she has just asked me. *Did this woman just ask me to put my baby up for adoption?* I don't remember taking another breath. My answer is short, and somewhat rude, possibly out of ignorance or plain selfishness. Either way, I say it so she can understand me clearly the first time because I will not repeat it again.

"I'm keeping my baby!" I jab the words across her desk, push back the chair, stand up and walk out.

Storming across the grass of the courtyard, I mumble angrily towards my room. *Why would she ask me that question — to what complications and in whose best interest is she referring?* Manic emotions flare inside of me. Set on reactive, I rage. *Just who does she think she is for even suggesting such a thing?* My baby is all I have in the world. She might as well tell me to give away my heartbeat. I storm inside my room, slamming the door behind me. Shifting on my bed, I twirl the corner of my bed sheet around my finger, thinking of a few things I should have told her before I left her office. The circulation in my finger stops. My mother had taught me never to use profanity, but I swear, if that woman says another word to me, I will tell her off in both English and Spanish.

After I calm down, the anger turns to shame. The nail on my finger is turning dark. After years of twirling the blood out of it, the nail bed is slowly dying. Anger feels like a deadly sin. The guilt that followed feels like the punishment. The residential supervisor is doing her job — like the cops, the caseworkers, the principal, and the rest of the world. Everyone is just doing their job. Staring down at me from their elevated positions, like traffic signals turning green, yellow, and red. The world is full of dutiful people, functioning without feeling, just doing their damn jobs. No one sees the lonely tears, the scars, and the fear locked deep inside. No one bothers to ask the question "why." But, the craziness of it all is that if someone were to ask me why I'd almost assuredly tell a lie. Pretense is a self-imposed prison; I cannot get out, and no one can get in. *Stay away, keep out, leave me alone.* No one stopped it. I was supposed to be safe in my own home, but it seems no place is safe. Not even inside my own mind.

I ask God to forgive me for being angry. I cannot fully understand the severity of my condition, both mentally and physically. My anger shoots without aiming, and I must admit even I cannot understand the intensity of it. It's better not to get mad at all. I cannot see the supervisors' position, nor can I imagine giving up my baby for adoption, even if it is, as she puts it, "in the best interest of my unborn child." All the same, my mind is made up. I am keeping my baby. I have already given her a name. She is my Casita; my little house. I will give her my middle name, Maria. She will be mine, and I will be hers; all I have in a world that has stolen everything else away from me. Nothing can change the fact that we belong to each other. No one can steal that away.

And though I know I am young, I will learn whatever I must to care for her and teach her about God's love. The love of a lullaby, the kind of love that makes the world go 'round. Something inside my heart tells me she will love me too, no matter what. Even when I fail and fall on my face, my little girl will teach me to be better; I just know it.

For many days after my visit with the residential supervisor, I struggle with my decision. *What kind of mother will I be? How can I give my baby what she needs? Where will we live? How can I manage to stay in one place when the memories of my past keep chasing me, smothering me, and trying to kill me in my sleep? Will I live long enough to see her grow up? God help me make the right decision for my baby. Perhaps I am too young to parent a child, too unstable to be a good mother. Maybe the residential supervisor was right.* The stress and anxiety of the decision send me back to see the nurse more times than I can remember.

On Saturday morning, I stay in bed. My feet are swollen, and the back pain is getting worse, probably because I stood on my feet for hours in the multipurpose area, where I braided a couple of the girls' hair last night. Gabriella has left the room early this morning, most likely to meet with the other girls, eat breakfast, and watch TV. I stay in the room. Here I can be myself. When I am alone, it is easier to breathe. I journal, pray, and sing to Casita. I know she hears me and hope she will see past the mess that I made of my life and love me anyway. I rub my big tummy and sing:

> *"You and me against the world*
> *Sometimes it feels like you and me against the world*
> *And for all the times we have cried*

I always felt God was on our side
You and me against the world..."

I listen to Helen Reddy, singing the song over and over again. Casita floats quietly inside of me as if she is listening. At least that's what I tell myself, so I do not feel so alone.

I'm worried, more today than usual. I count the days when she will arrive, trying to prepare myself, trying to keep from falling apart at the thought of being a mommy; an impossible belief that I can have someone who will love me unconditionally. The doctor has given me a due date. By the end of January, she will be born. In nearly a month and a half, she will be here. My mind races in different directions. Excitement collides with worry. Gabriella comes into the room and asks me if I want to watch TV with the others.

"No, thank you, Gabby. I'm okay, just resting." I force a smile. She stands over my bed for a moment and tells me she will be back later. When she walks out, I flip through the pages of my Bible and journal four words: God, I am afraid.

I must have fallen asleep because I do not remember Marcia walking into my room. I open my eyes, and she is standing near my bed, smiling a sweet smile.

"Sandra, you have a visitor. She is waiting for you in the office."

"Yes, ma'am." I sit up, forcing my plump feet inside my shoes. *Who can it be?* I squint in the bright sunlight, heading towards the office. Dizzy from the unexpected news, I waddle across the grass of the courtyard. As the door opens, I try to catch my breath. I see her face, I scream.

"Joyce! You are here!" I cry, overwhelmed with emotion.

"Hi, Sandy Patty, I missed you. How are you?" she asks, looking at me as if I was the only person in the world. My mouth opens with so much to say, but nothing comes out. I held onto her for what seems like twenty minutes before letting go. *How did she find me;* the question comes and goes amidst the excitement of seeing her.

"Joyce, you came!" My words hang in the air until the doubt clears, and my mind registers that she is here in front of me.

"Of course, I came. I had to come check on my little sister," she says with a big smile.

Joyce spends the entire day with me, walking the grounds and talking about her children and her work as a nanny. We take

Polaroid pictures by the lake and laughed at how *big* I have gotten since the last time she saw me. I have gained over 15 pounds since arriving here.

"How are you, Sandra?" Joyce tone changes. "Are you scared?" She touches my hand.

"Yes," I reply with my head down, embarrassed to admit it aloud, believing fear is a sign of weakness.

"I know you must be scared. Having a baby is a scary experience. I am praying for you. Trust God, Sandra. No matter what, you must trust Him. He will never leave you nor forsake you. He is with you always." Joyce tells me about a time when she was younger.

We sit near the lake, by a flower garden on the outer edge of St. Vincent's. "In Tampa, Mom and Dad would fight all the time. Dad would come home drunk and would fight Mom because he was so angry with himself. He would take his money and gamble it all away. When he got home, he'd take it out on mom. Mom would pray and tell me that God would make a way for her to get out. In my room, during every fight, I'd hold onto my dolls and cry. I prayed and believed that God hears our prayers. He hears us. We must believe that He hears." Joyce words of encouragement wrap around me like a warm blanket.

We walk back from the lake as if we owned time. St. Vincent seems brighter with Joyce here with me. She is impressed at how I have learned to braid. She meets Gabriella and a few of the other girls as she enters in the lounging area.

"This is my sister, Joyce," I say proudly. "See Joyce, I practice braiding just like you taught me; three strands, folding in, over, and around the other." I show her Gabriella and another girl's hair I braided earlier.

"Keep it up, Sandy Patty. You are doing a good job," she says. My head rises a little higher. I smile. Joyce sits with us in the multipurpose area, watching me smile at her.

"Will you braid my hair next?" one of the girls asks.

"I will tonight, after my sister leaves," I reply. I can never say no, even when I am tired or in pain. I simply ignore it and keep moving.

The group counselor lets Joyce stay an hour past visiting hours. I am grateful. When her car backs away, I try to keep a smile, but it is hard to see her go. "I will see you soon, Sandy Patty. I will be back in mid-January. Take care. I love you."

"I love you too, Joyce." I wave. Long after she drives away, I am in the same place, staring down the road. *She really came. This is what true love feels like*, I breathe.

For the first time, today, I feel the winter's air.

Mercy Hospital

3663 South Miami Ave, Miami, Florida

January 1982

Sewing class today has been fun, and I complete the final stitches on Casita's gowns. Two tiny pink and white robes to wrap her in when she is born; I cannot wait to see her wear them. I am thankful to the staff members who have provided the fabric for us to sew. Some of the girls make baby booties with tassels. Others knit blankets. In the group classes, the counselors talk to us about the risks and possible outcomes of giving birth. I try not to think about the part when she said some women must have what's called a cesarean section. But the thought of surgery is not easy to ignore. Since coming to St. Vincent's, I have learned a lot, but Gabriella and I know it is almost time to say goodbye. For the last two days, my stomach tightens and releases, stronger and stronger the contractions become. Marcia tells me I will not be returning to St. Vincent's after I leave the hospital with my baby, and so, I prepare to say my goodbyes now.

January 23rd, 1982

I wake up around 6 a.m. with a pain, unlike anything they have explained to me in the group sessions or on the videos. I collapse on the tile floor of the bathroom; I am convinced that this will be the day. The day I give birth and the day that I die. *I hope I see my baby's face before God takes me.* The thought is consuming.

"Sandra! Mama!" Gabriella gasps and hurries to get Marcia.

"How far apart are your contractions?" Marcia asks.

"I'm not sure, but I don't want to go to the hospital right now. I will be okay for a while." My bags were packed, but my heart is not. I will miss Gabriella, the girls, the staff, the spaghetti, and the quiet lake. I'm not ready to never come back. I need more time to prepare before I say goodbye.

Marcia tells me to let her know when the next contraction comes. I don't say a word for fifteen or twenty minutes, pretending to be in control. "When the contractions are closer, we must get to the hospital," she says. I nod through the pain and pressure. Marcia stays with me, and we sit outside the opening of the multipurpose area. I have heard walking would help with the labor process. Up and down the sidewalk, I keep moving, buying time.

"Gabriella, let me braid your hair before I leave," I say, wanting to do one last thing for her. Hoping she will remember the times we shared. She sits in a chair on the sidewalk, and I begin to braid. Three sections of hair, I take my time, until I can no longer bear the pressure. The other girls sit around outside, watching the time, counting down five minutes between contractions. It's time to go. The girls and I hug and say goodbye.

"Remember to practice the English I taught you, Gabby."

"Yes, remember your Spanish, I pray for you and your baby."

"Okay, si, que tengas un buen dia. Have a good day." The sentence is the only Spanish I can remember between the hard contractions. Marcia puts my bags in the car and rushes me to Mercy Hospital. It is 2 o'clock in the morning on January 24th.

"Take care of yourself. I wish you and your baby all the best." Marcia tells me goodbye and leaves me in the care of the nursing staff. It was the last time I saw her.

The hospital ward is cold. I lay on a gurney and the nurse checks to see how far I have dilated. *Only five centimeters, with five to go before Casita is here;* I think to myself as the nurse walks away. I wait alone in a room that is freezing. The sheet on the bed is pure white and thin. Hours pass, and I shiver between the contractions. They are becoming closer, stronger, and more painful. The nurse finally comes back in and checks for dilation; it hurts worse when she does that.

"I need you to start pushing," she says. My limbs move uncontrollably, and I am afraid of pushing, afraid something will go wrong. The wheels of the gurney roll, heading into the delivery room.

"When you feel the next contraction, I need you to push again." The doctor presses against the top of my belly. A hard pressure replaces the contractions. The forceful spasms are intense.

"One more push," the doctor says. My heart beats loudly inside my ears as an overwhelming pressure tightens and then squeezes around my lower back and abdomen. Outside of my control, everything in me bears down. Automatically, like the beating of the heart, my body does all the work.

At 7:52 a.m. on January 24th, 1982, like a blossom born from a dry thorn bush, I see her, and the world no longer look the same. The sight of her drives out the memory of labor. I smile.

"Thank you, Jesus," I whisper. My sweet little house, I will never be alone again. Casita is beautiful. 6 pounds and 4 ounces, 17 inches long—the doctor says she is a healthy little girl. Gratitude is all I feel. After spending months on the run, haunted by shadows, impaled with thorns, God has blessed my daughter to be well. She is so small, yet she will be strong enough to do what I believe is impossible.

My mother comes to the hospital, and there is calm. For the first time since I ran away, the stressful lines that dug into her face softens. We sit together in my hospital room, gazing in silent wonder at the gift of this little life. No angry words pass this time. There is only acceptance of what is and hope for what is to come.

"She is beautiful, Sydney." My mother says with a feathery voice. Her presence, here with me now, means everything. Sometime that night, after everyone has gone home, I breastfeed Casita—I felt so inadequate. As she lay in my arms, I whisper, "Thank you, Jesus." My mother and I have embraced for the first time in what feel like a lifetime. *Who would have known that such little hands could build a bridge where two cultures could sit in peace and find a reason to begin to mend the years of brokenness?* The nurse comes in and takes Casita back to the nursery. I am exhausted yet elated. Grabbing my Bible out of my bag, I fluff up my pillow and begin to write. The journal entry is short tonight. Just three words: *I am thankful.*

Surviving hardship requires letting go. Learning these lessons happens when the mind is free to expand and see beyond the borders of this human existence. Matthew 18:3 says, "unless we become like a child, we will not see the kingdom of heaven." For if God controls all things, why then do we allow conditions to puppet our reactions? One day happy, the next, sad, and on and on we go, controlled by the yo-yo reactions of life's circumstance. Letting go helps us to see patterns more than people; understand energy over emotions, and to nurture the inner world of the spirit over the outer of the flesh. There is a knowing within each of us; an embodied, indescribable consciousness, created in the image of God, which is not affected by circumstance nor the mental and emotional pain which imprisons the ego; the self. A child grows, first inside and then out of the womb, without thought of trying and without fear. Years would pass before I learned the lesson of rebirth and the freedom that comes from fully trusting, letting go of the need to know, to feel, to think, to control, and learn to just be still.

DCF: Department of Cracked Foundations

The Department of Children and Family Services transports my daughter and me from Mercy Hospital to a foster home in Fort Lauderdale. The foster family is bilingual, so I get to practice the words Gabriella taught me while at St. Vincent's. But change is not easy. Casita and I sleep in a cot near the back of what looks like a small glassed-in porch. I try to fit in, but nothing I do changes who *I* tell myself I am—*an outcast, a misfit.* It would be years before I understood the triggers that cause stressful emotions to rise, dragging me back in time, hindering me from going forward in life.

Ms. Polly's home is the second foster home, but it will not be the last. A misshapen mindset forces me to believe that everyone sees me the way I see myself: damaged and unworthy of love. I try to follow the rules and do what I'm told. Casita and I move along the currents of a social service system that appears to take more time behind desks, buried inside mounds of caseloads and files rather than building connections and families. The uncertainty from day to day causes my insomnia to worsen. Maddening sounds still arise from time to time, sneaking up like an ambush. Change and uncertainty trigger noises in my head, like the sounds of constant clawing and scuffling. Sleep comes only in spells.

Something is wrong, but I have no way to know or communicate exactly what it is. I do what I have always done; I ignore it. All that matters now is my baby. The problem with that outlook is if a mother is not a healthy, functioning individual, how can her child grow to be one?

"Sandra...? Sandra?" Ms. Polly knocks on the bathroom door.

"Yes, ma'am."

"You have been in there for a while. Is everything alright?"

"Yes, ma'am." I clear my throat. "Casita is asleep. I changed her diaper and fed her before she went to sleep," I tell her, never opening the door.

"I am talking about you. Are you okay in there?" she asks again. Annoyed, I open the door. Knocking sounds bothers me.

"Yes, ma'am. I am fine. I was just thinking about stuff," I say. But the truth is when the anxiety comes, I need to find a place to be alone, a quiet place to shut out all the noise in the world and tell myself I am not crazy. The bathroom is the only place where I can handle the fear and uncertainty. It is relentless, but no one must know. Everything is okay.

Ms. Polly reminds me of a smart businesswoman; she wears a short-cropped afro and a vestal disposition; her words are few. I learn to read the implicit language that dawdles in the restricted airspace of her home. And it goes without saying that you have a place in the house, but not in the heart. No tenderness, intimate talks, or hugs—nevertheless, she manages her position as a diplomatic foster parent with an air of concern.

She tells me about a condition called postpartum depression and talks to me about the symptoms she believes I may be displaying. She explains that some women give birth and experience the 'baby blues' where the emotions of excitement, fear, and worry can clutter up their mind, causing extreme sadness. *Postpartum depression?* I think to myself. I listen, but I want to tell her about an incredible story. A story that started before I ever gave birth, before I ever got pregnant, when all the monsters came; when I found out the world was not a safe place.

I want to tell her about the voices that follow me around, and the stains that I cannot wash away. No matter how hard I try, the damage feels irreparable. I hold my peace, staring off into space. *How do you separate one condition from another?* If I have postpartum depression, it must have hitched on unaware with the locomotive of lunacies in my life. Like a hobo on the back of a moving train, the condition joins a cargo full of thorns that all look the same to me. I once believed my child would change my world, but since being in foster care, the fear only increases. Ms. Polly means well. She does her job, providing my child and me with the basic needs of housing, food, and clothes. But there is no connectivity. I plummet deeper inside an emotional trench.

I pray to have the courage that will change my daughter's world. The problem is I do not know how. Looking at her, lying still and quiet in her bed makes me want to try. Ms. Polly goes into the kitchen. I go back and forth between the bathroom and the bedroom. I need just a few more minutes to try to pray the anxiety away, but prayer does not seem to be working.

"God?" I whisper. "Am I doing this right?" Unsure of the rules of prayer and life, I feel hopeless. But something inside me tells me that God hears, even when He does not stop the storms from coming. I know His voice. I try to remember His words. I think of Gabriella and the other girls at St. Vincent's. I miss them so much and hope their babies will all be okay.

Days pass and Ms. Polly changes our room from the back area to the one nearest the front driveway. I am happy to be near the window; it is freeing; solid walls are suffocating. Near the window, I can look out at the trees and clouds and imagine what lies beyond the sky—beyond what my eyes can see.

A car pulls up, and to my surprise, it is my mother. The moment I see her I feel nine again. She brings clothes, pampers, and baby wipes for Casita. I sit quietly next to the window, watching her hold her granddaughter. I cannot explain the delight of having her here. She smiles and talks to Casita with a sweet voice.

"Make sure you burp her to get all the gas out of her stomach," she says, patting Casita on her back after giving her a warm bottle. The bottle was a second choice after I had tried breastfeeding. During my stay in the first foster home, I wasn't producing enough breast milk, and after two months, I had felt she needed more than what I had to offer. The doctor said that stress could cause the problem, but I felt the lack of milk proved my deficiency as a mother. It was depressing for me, but I have learned to accept the things I cannot change.

"Yes, ma'am. I will remember to burp her."

Casita's father comes over often to visit me in the foster home and bring Casita gifts from his family. He beams looking at her, holding her like a proud father. One night, Bruce and I sit on the couch for hours, listening to Gladys Knight and the Pips singing "Neither One of Us." Casita sleeps, and the record plays again and again on Ms. Polly's old record player. Our words are few. I wonder how different life would have been if I had the strength to fight against the rip current that is about to take me out into the deep. But I have never been a fighter. I sit next to Bruce, listening to another sad melody about a love that could never be:

> *"There can be no way*
> *This can have a happy ending*
> *So, we both go on, hurting and pretending*
> *And convincing ourselves to give it just one more try*
> *Because neither one of us wants to be the first to say*
> *goodbye."*

With no tools or manuals on relationships, and no points of reference on how to navigate effectively as parents, we prepared for life with what we knew and what we had: a baby girl, broken hearts, unresolved grief, and faith cushioning in between the three.

As I look back on that time in my life, I realized one of the most important lessons is to "forgive on credit." This requires us to take nothing personally, understanding that we all have a story; we are all human. In the 17th chapter of Luke, Jesus was speaking to His followers about the importance of forgiveness and the "70 x 7" decree. "Offenses will come;" those things that cause people to stumble and fail will happen in this life. I had a lot to learn, and many years would pass before the concept of forgiveness and accountability were reconciled.

Cruel Lessons

In DCFS's custody, I flow with the current of social workers and case managers, never staying in one place too long; such is my existence. The Department of Children and Family Services I now refer to as the Department for Cracked Foundations—because children like me keep falling through the cracks; *it's all so absurd*, I think to myself. I look at them, wondering why they are here. *Come, stop, go*, says the traffic lights with their blank faces. They look at me but never see me; only another case number, another file.

Mrs. Williams becomes my next foster mother. One morning, during breakfast, her husband tells me that putting ice in your cereal makes it taste better. I try it and found that he was right. When the milk is colder, the cereal seems to stay crunchier. In every interaction, Mr. Williams is a kind man and makes me feel welcomed. That year, two other girls are placed in the foster family with me. Shortly after being at her home, Mrs. Williams teaches me another cruel lesson about this stormy life: not every smile is a sign of acceptance; not even from someone who you least expect. You would think I would've learned by now not to trust, and that you must earn it. In short, I had to learn the hard way. During my stay, Mrs. Williams falls in love with my baby. She decides she wants to keep Casita as her own and attempts to take my daughter away from me. I never see it coming; it appears the world is full of takers.

Mid-1982, the Department of Children and Family Services returns me to Lippmann Shelter until the "great and powerful" state of Florida decides differently. My daughter stays at Mrs. Williams' house. A social worker tells me the split is only temporary until the state can find "suitable placement" for both Casita and I. Days turn into weeks. In a confusing haze of social workers and court hearings, mumbling their legalistic jargon, my nerves unravel. A part of me, unable to cope, disconnects from the madness. I drift through time, like a ship without a sail, unable to bear the separation. Bruce tells me not to worry. He attends the reunification hearing, holding my hand, swearing to put an end to my foster mother's obsession. I am grateful he is with me. During this time, I remember the complications the residential counselor at St. Vincent had warned me about. I had not understood it then, but now, her message is becoming crystal clear. I feel like I am fighting against the world, blindfolded and with both hands tied behind my back.

Apparently, when placed in state custody, the firm arm of the government stakes its claim over you and everything you possess. Similar to slavery, you go along to get along. You have no say. Seen and not heard, you stay in your place. Under the supposed care of the Department of Children and Family Services, I get lost in the translation with little to no rights to decide my own life or that of my child.

The authorities make it no secret: I am a slave to its surrogate authority. The government agencies make decisions for my life as if they are a great deity that somehow knows what's best for my baby and me. But the truth is, like the great and powerful Wizard of Oz, many are just flesh and bone stage magicians giving the illusion of restoring safety and order in the broken lives of children and families. Many of the social workers I have met are disconnected and arrogant know-it-alls, working behind the curtain of the law with their social services degrees; clueless of the reality of the scars and secrets that are hiding behind adolescent eyes. I swear, for one of them to smile or show empathy violates some state code. Like the numbers racket in Tampa, broken people seem to be the new lottery of a system where hitting the number on a caseload appears to matter more than healing the heart and soul of a human being. I remember the many interactions with caseworkers, void of the pure compassion that separates the human component of the work from the stoic traffic signals that hover above the streets, just doing its job.

Several weeks later, the courts' rules in my favor; we're reunited; my little house, Casita. Bruce has played an important role in helping me win the reunification battle. He has worked it out where Casita and I could move in with his aunt, and at the age of 15, I reach legal emancipation. The government has no more say in my life. I remember feeling utterly indebted to Bruce for fighting for our daughter, and for being by my side during the lonely times without her.

But despite the state's emancipation, I am far from being free. In the weeks that follow, I come to respect and admire Bruce, though the fear of him keeps me on guard. He is everything that I am not. He is confident, loves to cook, and he helps provide for my daughter and me during our stay at his aunt's home. Bruce's steadfast support has caused me to trust and love him despite his past abuse. Even with his controlling temper, he has a caring side as well.

Weeks later, on a Monday morning, I sit at Parkway Middle School, determined to get my education. Since having Casita, school is all I think about; I want to try to be a good role model for her, but I cannot teach her what I do not know. I hunger and thirst to learn, to read, to study, and to become something other than me. Someone she can be proud to call Mommy. I sit in the back row, dropping my eyes away from the swift unfriendly stares. The students watch me, avoiding me as if I come from another planet. I keep my head down, doodling circles on my paper. The blackboard is a blur, and my hands will not stop shaking from the persistent surges of anxiety. I keep waiting for the past to go away, to forget it all. But it still haunts me.

Sitting behind my desk, I scribble more circles across the lined paper—circles sprawl out wider and darker. The teacher keeps his distance, and from the position of his desk, I appear to be working from the textbook he had handed out at the beginning of class. The only lesson I complete today is in circle drawing. Circles resemble the trench of my life: dark and confusing. I feel claustrophobic, like being stuck in a place with no walls, windows, or way out. It's worse when I am under stress. The desk closes in on me, and it is getting harder to breathe. In the corner of my eye, something is moving, crawling.

Just above me, it vibrates like spider's legs moving to the sound of Edward's rhythmic huffs.

"You my good girl," the voice stalks and crawls towards me. I flinch at the air, and then catch myself, pretending to scratch the back of my neck, hoping nobody saw me, and think I'm crazy.

When you think it's over, thankful you made it out alive; think again. The past is never over until we face it, and if we don't deal with it, if we pretend like nothing ever happened, it will continue to deal with us as if it had never ended.

"Get a grip. There is no spider. Keep your hands down. Act normal," I whisper, calming the anxiety that causes my stomach to boil. My mind tells me to escape because it believes the assaults of the past are still happening right now, in real time, in this classroom. Nagging voices whisper that everyone is in on it and that I must leave now. I know it is not true, but my body, which has always felt as though it doesn't belong to me, refuses to believe. I raise my hand.

"Yes, Miss Anderson?" the teacher asks.

"May I please be excused to the restroom?" He writes me a hall pass. I feel awkward in public, and restless shadows surround me as I walk out of the classroom. I crumble up the hall pass in the folds of a tight fist, thinking of how much I hate desks, and though it's nothing personal against the teacher, I can't stand looking at his mustache; it arouses feelings of disgust.

I hurry to the bathroom; there, I can breathe, and take off the mask of pretense. Once the stall door closes, I don't want to come out. Unsure of what it is that I am afraid of, I stay in the bathroom until I convince myself the coast is clear, and the ghosts are all gone; at least for now. Splashing cold water on my face, I tell myself that something is wrong. Nearly forty minutes have passed since I've been in the restroom. And as much as I wanted to attend school and get an education, learning is almost impossible in such a suffocating place; I don't fit. *How can I fit in with students my own age when I feel lost, somewhere between a child and an alien life form from Mars?* I look at the hazy outline of a girl staring back at me in the mirror. Despite my efforts to try, I cannot see myself. The reflection looking back at me is wretched, soulless, an obscure mist; I learn to avoid mirrors. The struggle for acceptance in a society where I just don't fit in is too much for me to endure. Walking out of the bathroom; I don't bother going back to class for my books and folders. A few blocks away from home, I walk, head down, watching my shoestring flopping in every direction; some things never change.

There are cruel lessons I have learned in this world, lessons of deceitful smiles and yellow-eyed wolves. Lessons of love songs empty of love. Lessons of life where you learn to pretend that there is meaning and truth behind the lies of your pretense, so you fool yourself; *only yourself.*

On the way to the house, I kick rocks thinking; *School is useless.* But I wanted to learn more than anything. I bite the corners of my lip, believing life has already given me a grade. I get an F for stupidity: I should have known better than to get into a car with strangers, especially after Robert had taught me the true nature of sin and the men who practice it. I receive another F for believing that Bruce could love a misfit like me. And yet again, there is an F for foolishly thinking that I could attend school with my peers and succeed. Too much has happened, too many thorns, too much noise drowning out the lessons on the chalkboard. I tried to believe that, no matter what, everything would be okay; just like my sister used to say. But I doubt even the teacher will make a fuss about my absence. I belong nowhere. That's how I feel every day; like an alien who woke up on the wrong planet and is forced to stay; forced to pretend that I fit in, but the reality is nothing makes sense. *Who was I fooling really?* The bitter lessons of this world have already taught me its harsh truth. I've learned it well, so I do not feel like a complete failure. I give myself an A+ in the art of pretending. I have learned to smile like I always do, to laugh and nod, right on cue, and agree with everyone and everything, even if it makes my heart bleed from the need to scream: *Leave me alone!* Honestly, that's all I want; just to be left alone.

I make excuses. I'm good at it now. But I might as well stay home where I do not have to cover up the shame of being beat anymore. Since childhood, I've made excuses for every injustice, every scar, every tear. Bruce's aunt says she has heard the fighting in the room, but she does nothing to stop it. No one intervenes; not even God. Casita is just a baby, but I believe she sees and knows; I feel ashamed. Just yesterday, it went from bad to worse. Colin, a friend from the old neighborhood, had come over to visit me. Michael or Linda must have told him where I moved. I was surprised he came by, mainly because I have not seen anyone from 24th Street since running away.

"How have you been? Everyone was wondering where you had gone again," he said. I had evaded the question, asking him how his family is doing. After we had talked for nearly a half hour about his brother Chester, his mom and dad, Colin wished us well and said goodbye. I remember feeling so happy that a friend had taken the time to stop by to see my baby and me. My joy is short-lived. Bruce beats me for having the unexpected guest. No explanation, no warning, just a clear message: No visitors. I take it, climbing up from the floor just as I have done many times before. The quiet submission comes as natural as breathing. The years have taught me well.

Defiance is not allowed; anger is out of the question. I know the position and assume it. Seen and not heard, I understand the rules. They have always been the same. But secretly, I feel anger building, rage forming clusters of new thorns inside me. Terrible things happen behind closed doors. That's where the thorns grow. Behind closed doors where no one else can see, so no one else will know. I take life one day at a time, reckoning the bad must come with the good. I tell myself to be better, *a better mother, a better girlfriend, a better lover.* But nothing I do seems to be good enough. All my life, I have seen the face of this anger and hostility. Since childhood, it has haunted me. A rage that hits and controls with an angry fist. My grandmother had died in the secrets of its resentful shadow. My mother has battled its bitterness until she could endure no more. My dear sister, who sung lullabies over me, has followed the fateful course of holes in the walls, broken furniture, and fickle promises to love and cherish "until death do you part."

Now I sit in a waist-high trench, trying to make sense of it all. Days, weeks, and months pass — nothing changes. Around and around this fateful trench I go. Sliding back down the wall, my hands covering my head. Like a good pet, I obey, wondering when I became the enemy.

Late one evening, his aunt tells me again, "I heard you two fighting in the room. Sometimes a woman has to do whatever it takes for the sake of the family." *Whatever it takes,* I think to myself. *What exactly does that mean?* I do not respond. I had no answers. Years ago, Joyce told me no matter what, I should trust God. But this can't be right. *What does trusting God look like when I am on the losing end of this twisted game.*

When all is calm again, Bruce pretends as if nothing happened. He prepares a meal, laughing with his friends that visit him; the rules are different when you are the one making them. At his whim, he comes and goes with his friends — women, and men he grew up with; I don't say a word; mostly because I have nothing to say. I watch from the corner on the couch, trying to figure a way out of this trench. I miss my mother and my sisters and brothers. I long for my father and wonder where he is now, and if somehow, he is somewhere, still making circles too.

Time moves on, and I sing to my little Casita, the same songs that I heard as a child:

> "*Somewhere over the rainbow*
> *Bluebirds fly.*
> *If bluebirds fly over rainbows*
> *Why then oh why can't I?*"

Imagination sets us free; it is a gift from God. As a child, I'd envision all kinds of magical things happening in the world. There were no limits to my powers to grow, to evolve, to become whatever I wanted to be. But then, as the outer world changed around me, the inner world of impossibilities fell asleep. We can wait for something or someone to rescue us from our trenches, or, we can wake up to who we are; wonderfully created beings, with the power to change the world.

Burger King

Casita and I move in with my mother to a house off 8th Street, between Broward and Davie Boulevard. The look in my daughter's eyes after every fight was too much to bear, and I've had it with being beat by someone who says he *loves* me.

Domestic violence has a sick element to its duplicitous nature: no one can love him or herself and hurt another; therefore, self-hatred drives every brutal act.

Like always, Bruce finds us, claiming he has changed and wants to be in his daughter's life. He seems to still know the way back inside my fragile heart. Perhaps if it weren't so broken before I met him, getting in wouldn't have been so easy. The same as always, my heart skates on thin ice—easy to forgive. I should've thought twice about all the other times he has claimed to have changed.

Robert no longer sails the seven seas. He has retired from the Marines since becoming seriously ill. He runs high fevers and often vomits. The constant doctor's visits and late hours at work have slowed my mother's hurried pace. Through a half-cracked door, I watch her lean over his sunken body as he coughs, gasping for the next breath. She lifts herself from the edge of the bed and wipes dribbles of vomit from the sides of his mouth. I feel sorry for him. Later, my mother will tell us that it is cancer. The years of smoking cigarettes have caught up with him. When I'm home, I offer to help my mother with his care. When it comes to Robert, I have only one emotion: sympathy.

I apply for the job I had wanted for as long as I could remember. Dirk hires me, and I begin working at Burger King on the strip of Fort Lauderdale beach. It feels like a dream come true, and I love the job. Working makes me feel useful; in control. The team on the evening shift is fun and teaches me how to run the register, work the broiler, and make perfect sandwiches and fries. In the busyness of serving customers, I find a haven. In the steady structure of the job, I find rest. Work is like a drug that helps block out the constant barrage of unstable emotions.

"If you have time to lean, you have time to clean!" Dirk tells the crew. He has no clue how much his words are like therapy. I smile every time he says it because the busyness gives me no time to think of the past because his voice out commands the others. I stay in the present moment cleaning, never "leaning." I volunteer to work overtime whenever a crewmember is running late or calls in. I may understand one of the reasons why my mother works so hard; In a strange way, it is freeing.

One of my coworkers, Alexandra, gives me rides home when it is too late to catch the bus from the beach area. She goes by the nickname Alex. She likes photography and asks if she could take pictures of me.

"Anytime you're ready, Alex," I tell her. She is an older woman, maybe in her early twenties. Heavy set with creamy dark skin. Easy to love, she is always helpful and offers to take my shift on the days I need to take Casita for her checkups. One night after work, we go to the beach so she can try out her new camera. I think she wants to go to college for photography. She seems to come alive behind the camera lens. On the shore, the weather is just right; the ocean is calm, and the wind blows warm over me. For the first time in a long time, I feel free just to let go. I spin around on the sand like I am seven years old again, while Alex takes pictures of me in the surf and on the shore. Later that same week, she took me out to see *The Rocky Horror Picture Show*.

The night is alive. Inside the theater, another world unveils itself. A world where I feel accepted among others who appear to be just like me: misfits. The stage fills with all sorts of characters. Some dressed in drag; others hardly dressed in anything at all. Laughter and smiles fill the audience and on top of the stage, just in front of the playhouse screen.

"Did you enjoy the show?" she asks.

"Yes! Thanks, Alex."

"What did you like best?" she moves closer with the question.

"Well, I love music, and I like to laugh. The show was funny, but mostly, I like being with you. I feel safe around you. You make me feel safe. That's what I liked best," I tell her, folding my hands on my lap. She drops her head with a smile and moves her hand shyly across her forehead. Alexandra is a sweet friend who I soon come to love. The air around her is calming and carefree. I want that. She listens to me and makes me laugh when the anxiety rises unexpectedly.

Soon, I begin to have strange feelings for her, deep butterfly feelings that force me to question my sexuality; a part of my life in which I never had a voice. *Is it a sin to feel this way? And if it is, why then do these unnatural affections feel so natural, and most of all, so safe?* When I am around Alexandra, I don't have to pretend to be something that I am not. She seems to like me for who I am: thorns and all. My wounded sexuality started early in my life, but I dare not tell a soul of where I've been. When you have lived your life in the wind, there are not many family traditions to embrace. There is nothing to anchor you beyond your volatile emotions and brokenness. I do what I know how to do best—stay silent and suppress the forbidden emotions. I wait for the wind to tell me where I belong and who I belong to. My feelings are not merely lustful for Alexandria, but they are forbidden longings all the same. And still, my eyes naturally follow the silhouette from her smile to her thighs. I will never tell her all my heart needed to say.

At work, I listen to Janet Jackson on the radio, excited about her concert, especially after seeing her on the TV show *Good Times*. I clean the broiler and prepare to sweep the floors. The store has been busy today, and Dirk needs closers. As usual, I offer to stay late. When our shift is over, Alexandra drives me home. In my mother's driveway, we sit in her car, both of us hiding our emotions behind short words and nervous tension.

"Thanks for taking me home again, Alex," I tell her.

"Sure, Sandra, it's not a problem. I want to ask you something," she said. The tone of her statement shifts the air inside her car.

"Okay, what is it?" I unbuckle my seatbelt, clutching the bag of leftover burgers and fries I have saved for Michael and Linda. I wait for her to ask her question, but she doesn't speak. After a few seconds, she leans over and kisses my lips. Soft and gentle, her kiss feels safe and sensual. I am breathless and wait for the oxygen to return to my head. It is the first kiss that has ever felt this way. It feels strange and extraordinary, all at the same time. Not because she is a female, but because I have never thought anyone would want to kiss someone like me. I don't remember stepping out of the car; perhaps because the blood in my heart forgot to move toward my feet. As her car pulls out of the driveway, I stood by the front door for several minutes; smitten by her kiss.

I would soon leave the beach franchise. Alex and I never spoke much after that time. Afraid, I never let anyone too close to me, and perhaps she already knew.

Suicide Watch

"No one commits suicide because they want to die...
They just want to stop the pain."
~ *Tiffanie DeBartolo*

Early summer — 1983

My first driving lesson ends with the fender of Bruce's car stuck in the wire fence near the rear of Westwood Heights Elementary School. I am fifteen and Bruce teaches me to drive. In the back parking lot of the school that sits to the left side of my mother's home, my right foot gets stuck on the accelerator. The next thing I know, the fender of the gray Cordova is in the fence.

The driving lesson comes along with many other experiences that year. In June, I had started working another job at Wendy's on Davie Boulevard. The extra job keeps me busy and helps me to save money, and the restaurant is walking distance from the house. One day, Bruce shows up at my job to drive me home. He starts the same fight as before; nothing had changed. In the middle of a back road, he throws me out of the car while it is moving. I remember sitting on the pavement asking myself, *is this really happening all over again?*

Bruce accuses me of doing what I would soon come to find out he was doing; the typical move of most cheaters. His plan is a sick validation for his ego, which seems to inflate after every angry episode. The more he gets away with it, the haughtier he becomes. Often, I remain in shock, while he appears calm and relaxed, without a hint of remorse. The old adage must be true: it takes one to know one; to which I am a clueless fool. I couldn't mistreat an animal. I try hard to be acceptable, and to prove to him that I am innocent of his blindsided accusations that come without a moment's notice. It doesn't work; I assume the position, always terrified of him. I work hard at not making him upset. Blaming myself is all I have ever done. I defend Bruce to my mother and family when they ask me about the abuse. Violence was the norm; I've seen it all my life. When he is not angry, my heart pity's Bruce, believing that someone had hurt him too, maybe a long time ago. Perhaps his father or someone he trusted. Pain demands to be felt; the way we express it says more about us than our words let on. Maybe that is where the anger comes from. We all have secrets — two sides to who we are; the one we hide, and the one that hides itself from us.

When Joyce ask, I refuse to tell her of his mistreatment; she would lose it, and for a while now, she has enough of her own struggles to deal with; she has not come by since I moved back to Fort Lauderdale. I take the good parts of Bruce along with the bad, determined to cope by keeping myself busy. Unfortunately, being busy does not resolve the issues that require the courage and skill to confront them.

While I am at work, my mother and Linda help care for Casita. Other times, she spends the day with Bruce's family. Work for me means more than just earning a paycheck. I lose myself in serving customers, cleaning the tables, and taking lunch orders through the drive-through window of Wendy's.

"Have a nice day. Hope to see you back soon," I say, smiling at every customer. Often, while I'm at work, I think about going back to school to get my education. School calls to the inner parts of me. *I will try harder this time,* I say to myself. Casita is growing fast, and I want to set a good example. I miss her when I am at work. *Our walks by the water and the adoring way she smiles when she sees me coming. I want to give her so much more, but with the stress of life building, how can I?* Achieving my high school diploma seems out of reach, but when I see my Casita, I tell myself that I must try.

Today, Linda and I sit in the kitchen talking about two of our favorite singers, Janet Jackson, and Barry Manilow. Linda begins to sing a beautiful rendition of "When October Goes" by Barry. I sit opposite her at the table, listening to her lovely voice. With all that we share, we are worlds apart. Linda has grown into a beautiful socialite. Witty and fun to be with, she has friends who adore her as much as I do.

Since moving in with my mother, I have made only one friend in the neighborhood. Kay is her name. She lives at the end of the street with her family. I visit her home once or twice, never staying too long. Just long enough to say hello. Both Kay and I are awkwardly shy and slightly overweight. We talk about slimming up together, but time never allows us to put our plans into action.

In late summer, Linda introduces me to Sophia, one of her friends from school. I remember thinking how pretty she was when I first met her. She sits at the kitchen table with Linda, and as they begin to talk, I move towards the back den where Michael is sitting. Uncomfortable in my own skin, I prefer excusing myself immediately after any introduction. Casita follows me, and we begin to watch TV with Michael. I give him a big squeeze around his neck, and we snuggle up close on the sofa.

Soon, I hear Bruce come in the house. He sits down at the kitchen table with Linda and Sophia. The words between Bruce and I are few when he comes over. And when my mother is not home, sex seems the main reason for the visit. Words only get in the way. Sex has been an act void of intimacy, caring, and genuine love. I don't fully understand it; this thing called love. But what I will grow to understand is that love will never hit you, slap you, dominate, and manipulate you, but I routinely gave myself to it, believing somewhere in my empty soul, this was the closest thing to love, as I understood it. I never had the mind or the ability to say, "You can't hit me. You can't mistreat me. I will not allow it." You take it and lose yourself in the mind game until it becomes 'normal.'

Passively, I take life as it comes, unaware of the tidal wave that is about to cave in on me. I don't know when it got this bad, but it is about to get much worse.

Bruce begins to come over more frequently. One day, I go into the house, and him, Linda, and Sophia are talking in the living room. I don't think anything of it. I am tired and want to spend time with Casita before taking a nap. I walk into my room to read to Casita, imagining all the places we will go. She loves when I read to her. I think about the stories Joyce used to read to us. They were wonderful and made me feel like I was a part of a magical world. Now, I share books and stories with my princess.

I put Casita on my lap and begin to read. "I do not like green eggs and ham. I do not like them Sam-I-Am." She listens with her head resting on my chest as I read the Dr. Seuss storybook, *Green Eggs and Ham*. "Would you like them here or there? I would not like them here or there. I would not like them anywhere." I breathe, secretly wishing I had the power to say what I do not like and do not want in my life. Looking at my little house, I play pretend. I make a sour face as if I have just taken a bite of the green eggs and ham right off the page. Casita mimics me and then she smiles with a giggle. I smile back at her.

She is my world; my wonderful little girl. Her little arms hug me, cuddling tightly around my neck as if I have no thorns at all. Brown stardust eyes look at me as if she sees something special.

"I love you this much, Pooh-Bear," I say with my arms stretched out wide in front of her. She falls into my chest. I swing her around until we are both dizzy. She giggles happily, looking at me as if I was someone worthy of the gift of her love, worthy of the word: Mother.

One week later

Flashing lights move in and out of the darkness.

"Swallow, I need you to swallow." A voice, a face, it is a woman. My eyes are heavy. I cannot keep them open. "Keep her awake. What is your name? Can you tell me your name?" I feel my mouth hanging open. I cannot close it. "What is your name? Tell me your name?" The same voice, like an annoying mosquito, will not leave me alone. Noisy beeps, sirens, and screeching voices echo up against the walls of a hollow tunnel. I am trying to tell her my name so she will stop asking. I feel my mouth moving, but nothing comes out.

I waited for God to come. I tried to find the fireflies, but they never came. The bed is shaking side to side like a storm cloud is carrying me away. "What is your name? Do you know what day it is?" I do not remember my name. I have no name. The words spin around inside my head, but nothing comes out of my mouth. There is no time. Time has run out, and nothing matters anymore. There is nothing else for me to believe in—there's only blackness. Stinging tubes run through my nose, down my throat, and into my stomach. In and out of darkness, I see the extraction of colors mixed with mucus-looking fluid moving slowly upward. I gag from the plastic tubes and the smell of charcoal. Tiny red and yellow pills pump from my stomach going somewhere. I cannot see where. *Why hasn't God come to get me yet?* I think to myself.

Medics swarm around me, and then blur out, like looking into a tarnished mirror. I look around the inside of the ambulance and begin to remember: A love letter. I found it with the details of a relationship between Bruce and Sophia. I don't know how long it has been going on. And I do not care. In a confrontation, I tell Bruce it is over between us. *Love does not hit you and love will not cheat!* The sordid details in the letter give me the courage to end the relationship or better said the tyranny. The repercussions come while I am holding Casita. I pay a harsh penalty for speaking my mind, for being angry, and for wanting to break up with him. Bruce punches me in my face and snatches my daughter out of my arms. I scream for her, but he says if I do not want him, I do not want his child.

"She is my baby. Give her back!" I reach for her; he rears back his fist and knocks me to the floor again. I stay down. I do not want Casita in the middle of this. She is looking, she sees; I cannot bear her eyes staring at me; powerless. I remember my parent's fights. I feel helpless. Children should not witness such chaos; this should not be!

I turn away to hide the shame and disgrace from Casita. I am dazed, wondering how this can be happening: my baby, my little house, my home. He puts her in his car and drives away. In the ambulance, I try to focus my eyes on something that is not moving, but everything is moving, shifting. The sky had fallen. Now, I remember, and I was mad as hell to still be on this planet.

He has taken away my baby because I broke up with him. It all rushes back. I vomit again. No one had been home to hear me scream for my baby. I waited for the fireflies to come and take the pain away. They never came. I could take no more. *No more thieves, not one more thing will be stolen from me. I am done!*

I had cried out to God as I walked to the medicine cabinet. "You let him take my baby out of my arms. You did nothing! You just let it happen. Why do I pray and believe in you? All my life, you have allowed everything to happen. All my life you watched. You watched me get raped and beaten, and now this! Why God! Why!" I scream at the top of my lungs. My throat burns from screaming out into the air. There was no answer. Heaven was quiet while I prepared to end my life. I emptied a bottle of pills in my hand and swallowed them all.

"Forgive me, God." I cried as I hurried into the second bathroom… swallowed more pills. As the tears ran down my face, I searched inside my drawer and found the Dextrin pills I have been taking to lose weight. One by one, I pushed them out of the aluminum package and crammed them down my throat.

I swallowed every capsule. I searched the kitchen and bedrooms for more. I needed to make sure I had enough drugs for a one-way ticket off this thieving planet. I had always heard that suicide takes you straight to hell, but after having my daughter taken from me, beat out of my arms, I could take no more! God forgive me, but I'm willing to take my chances with the uncertainty of an afterlife rather than the surety of these painful thorns. "No more!" I scream. *No more.*

"God, please watch over my baby and my family. Please take me away. Forgive me." I prayed, kneeling on the floor near the door where I last held my Casita.

And then, the darkness came. No tunnel, no fireflies, no little girl with colorful bows in her hair. There was nothing; only a thick darkness.

In the ambulance, the heartache comes back. I remember

everything that I want to forget. I had waited for God to rescue me, take me away; the wait was in vain. The noises, the tubes—awful nausea spins the room; if I wanted to die before, I beg for it even more right now.

Suicide had seemed the only way out of the trench. To have my baby taken was the final assault—I could take no more; no more oppression, and abuse, no more cover-ups. Some strange force has demanded my life since childhood; I figured I would help it out, give it what it came for years ago.

Before my discharge from the hospital, a nurse asks if I still want to kill myself. Hesitant, I bypass the question. She waits for an answer. Chest burning, I give her one.

"I wanted my daughter. She was taken from me. Now I want to be left alone!" Bits of food particles mixed with medicine and stomach acid lurches to the roof of my mouth.

Do you still want to die, what kind of question is that, I think to myself? I turn my head, facing the bed rail on the other side of the room. The nurse on suicide watch turns and walks out. *Why would I tell her anything? She does not know me and has no idea what it feels like to be me.* Rage heats like fire, burning my stomach. Anger has a way of shooting without aiming. *I have already died what feels like a hundred times;* I wanted to tell the nurse. I want the world to leave me alone. *Just leave me the hell alone!*

When I return home, my mother is angry and asks me how I could do something so stupid. She says I would have "died if no one called 911." I keep quiet, listening to the rage in my head. The hurt in her eyes is intense, incomprehensible. Still nauseous, I stand near her bed, woozy and sick to my stomach. Staring over her headboard, it's clear that my actions have hurt her, yet again. The reality of the pain I caused sits heavily on her face. She looks down tiredly at her hands; her tone softens, drawing back as if she has reached the dead end of a long road with me. Medical bills spread across the dresser. The ambulance and hospital charges are costly. With no insurance that covers suicide attempts, the burden of payment cripples an already tight budget. *I am probably worth more dead,* I think to myself. *If only she knew the truth of my life, and the heartache that I hide. I have no words to begin to explain.*

Alone in my room, I blame myself for my mother's heartache; all of it; *she has dealt with so much and now I have made everything worse.* I can't do anything right. I can't even die right. The tunnel has gone; it's no longer escape there. So I spiral through an emotional black hole, distancing myself from everything and everyone. "You are such a loser. I hate you," I say aloud to myself. The dark shadow of depression finds me and wraps itself around my heart until I might as well have died. I feel nothing. Nothing matters. I must not allow myself to feel anything; that way, I can never be hurt again. That's the answer—*to feel nothing.* I disown my anger and heartbreak; this is my protection from the world—*whatever happens; it does not matter,* I tell myself. Apathy grips me. I move through life disconnected, nearly unconscious. I vanish into a familiar trench filled with thorns that creep along the sidewalls like wild spiky vines. Fed up with life, mocked by death, I settle into a ghostlike existence. Breathing out, I let go of my will; the need to know, to feel, to think, to control, and just be; breathing in the moment of what is and nothing else.

Rage and hopelessness are a fatal blend and is often the mixture that creates the perfect storm of implosion. The terrible thing about suicide is that amid the desperation of the circumstance, the pain can feel like an unrelenting torment, causing us to believe the sorrow will never end. The fact of the matter is trouble won't last always; we must see beyond the present painful situation, so we don't forfeit the future. What I didn't know at the time was that life was teaching me a valuable lesson; although painful, it was the beginning of the teaching in the law of nonresistance; a divine law that wars against the ego that demands vengeance. Only the law of love conquers evil.

In the book of Matthew 5:39, the principle of nonresistance is taught when the Lord said, "But I say unto you, that you resist not evil, but whosoever strikes you on the right cheek, turn to him the other also." Christ taught the lesson of loving those who persecute us, returning grace, not evil, for every assault. The process was just beginning; after what seemed a lifetime of running, fear, and rage, I was right where God wanted me to be; in the dying place; a place where you stop, breathe, and let go of all resistance and negativity, to just love. Letting go is an ongoing journey—a lifelong process of dying to the self.

God will take care of the rest.

The Choice to Love

The days melt together as the clock rewinds. The last time I saw my daughter we were singing together; she was teaching me how to feel again. Time moves slow, watching me mope around like a snail with a broken shell; lost and exposed. I can no longer tolerate strong smells, especially spices. The discharge nurse told me it would take some time before my sense of taste and smell becomes normal again. I'm not sure I know what *normal* means, in any sense of the word.

At work, I spend a lot of time in the bathroom, hiding, praying, scared — of what, I am not sure. My manager at Wendy's notices the lengthy bathroom breaks and asks me if everything was okay. "Yes, I'm fine. My stomach was hurting a little that's all. It must have been something I ate. I'm fine. Be out in a minute." It takes nearly a half an hour for me to talk myself out.

After work, I walk home past St. Thomas Aquinas High School. The students wear the finest plaid-blue uniforms I have ever seen. *Oh, what it would be like to attend that school, to be one of the students with a blue and white uniform, carrying books instead of thorns.* I pray, looking up at the open sky above me.

"God, I want to learn. I want to go to school; I want my baby, and to be a good mother; to be normal and not scared all the time." Snowy-colored stones border the outer edge of the school's property. I walk, kicking a rock halfway home. Looking down, I follow the tumbling stone; I empty my mind, kicking it again. There is only the stone — nothing else. My mother comes home between jobs to check on Robert. He has become sicker. She says the emphysema is getting worse. The lung cancer has spread to his stomach, and the prognosis is poor. She walks with a sad, heavy pace.

"Mama, can I help with anything," I ask.

"Just listen out for Robert in case he needs anything. I must get back to work," she breathes.

"Yes, ma'am."

Robert's shoulder bones stick out from under his flannel pajamas. Cancer has ravished his once tall, soldierly frame. He no longer looks like the same person who sailed across the seas and shattered the soul of the child in me. And staring at him today, I do not see him as the same person who hurt me. Now, he is barely there. The fear is gone; only sympathy rests in its place.

"Robert, do you need anything. Are you thirsty? Can I get you something to eat?" I ask him. But he has no appetite—neither for food nor anything else. His only request is for ice. I bring him a cup of ice and return to my room, unable to stop myself from feeling regret and sadness at the sight of his skin shriveled against his bones, as if he is a phantom, waiting to vanish into thin air.

I'm sorrowful for the man he has been, and for his worsening condition. Moments later, Robert lumbers to my room door. He is wearing a robe over his pajamas with blue slippers, and car keys in his hands.

"Get in the car. I am taking you to get your daughter," he says, never looking at me, nearly out of breath. He coughs after every few words. For the first time since I had run away, I sit next to him in the front seat of the car, unafraid. Visibly weak, his body convulses with a hacking cough. The ashtray is empty. He does not smoke anymore, but the same stifling air moves around him. He drives me to Bruce's mother house. "Go get your daughter," he gasps, clearing his throat. He keeps the driver's side window down and stares out with sunken, stone eyes at the front door.

My feet move as if I am walking through tall murky swamp grass. I am afraid of Bruce, and I do not know what is coming, what to expect. I knock. Bruce opens the door. He and Robert exchange no words, only a hard glance. Bruce must have understood the nonverbal message. No words, no confrontation: I walk back to the car with my daughter in my arms. Robert does not speak on the drive home. The only sounds are the tires against the road and Robert's constant coughs. I remember thinking; *Robert must have called him or something. I am not sure what happened.*

I am grateful to him for taking me to get my daughter. We return to the house, and Robert hobbles to his room. He closes the door behind him, but the wheezing sounds escape loudly from underneath the door frame. Deep shudders and hacks remind me of the sounds of a car engine that sputters but cannot start because there is something stuck inside. The constant gasps and coughs grind away at the air until all I could do is close my eyes, waiting for the sound of silence.

Casita lays her head on my chest. I feel unworthy, unfit to be her mother. Unable to fight for her, unable to fight for myself, she watched me cowering, too weak to fight back. I hear Robert's rattling coughs again. It's louder than the noise in my head. I rock Casita side to side, listening, wishing I could make him better, but it appears to be too late. The wheezing grows louder as if the air around him is backing away. In the years that have gone by, at the moment when I am faced with the choice to love or hate, I feel only compassion.

There is no room for hate. Hate requires an exhaustive will and tormenting strain. The weight of hate is too heavy for me to carry, too stressful to hold onto; the thorns are enough. I choose to serve and love him in his sickness, despite the years of his sexual abuse and mistreatment. The morning Midnight died in the fan belt of his car, Robert had said I love too much, too hard. I had never understood the accusation, but perhaps, after all this time, he was right. Among the sharp thorns are seedlings of a lullaby; the melody of a love that makes the world go round and makes all things new. Now, the roots grow deeper.

Months feel like days, and my mother moves to a house on 32nd Court, a quiet neighborhood off State Road 7, closer to her job. The house is enormous with an empty room in the far back; the room has no carpet, and a sliding glass door separates it from the kitchen and dining room area. She allows me to make the room a workout and dance area, under one condition: I had to keep the music down. The warning comes because sometimes when the noise in my head won't stop, the loud music drowns it out. A few hours a day, I lift weights, dance around with an air guitar, and practice ballet moves I have learned from a fitness book I bought at Publix. When my mom was shopping for groceries, I headed straight to the book and magazine aisle; a habit that has never changed. Reading fills up the part of me that longs to get back in school.

One of the magazines I buy is Joe Weider's *Muscle and Fitness*. The articles make me want to be more, do more, and dream again. I read the articles, learn new exercises, and follow the recipes. Some workout moves I remember from working out with Joyce. Exercise is healing for me—it allows me to change and channel the anxiety into energy. The time I had spent working out with Joyce had been like therapy, where I can sweat out all the toxic emotions and silent frustrations.

All my life, I've watched the transfer of violence in my family, grooming me, demanding that I assume the same position. Still, the choice to love outweighs it all; it offers an indescribable release and sense of freedom, unlike anything I have ever felt before.

Breadcrumbs on the Lake

Michael exercises with me when he is not busy practicing karate or working with Mr. Walker's lawn service. Bruce Lee has become his obsession. He made a pair of Nunchaku's, of which he mistakenly hits himself with more than anyone else. I keep my distance until he gets better with his practice; since getting hit with a broomstick he was practicing with years ago when we lived in Dixie Court, I know better. Life slows down a little in the quaint neighborhood. Linda makes new friends and spends her time between our home and theirs. Soon, Bruce comes over and apologizes, again—just as he has done many times before. He swears he has changed and speaks of marriage.

"Everything will be different," he promises. I imagine my father made the same promises to my mother many years ago. The promises to love, honor, and cherish somehow changed to anger, fighting, apathy, before finally getting divorced. For that reason, I never want to get married.

Love seems a ridiculous war where you fight against the wrong enemy. A battlefield of no survivors and no apparent reason what all the fighting was for in the first place. Indifferent, I go along to get along with Bruce, waiting for something to change. I am not exactly sure what I am waiting for—maybe a sign from heaven or the courage to make my own decisions and take back my life. Or perhaps I'm waiting for acceptance, for true love. Whatever it is, Bruce finds me right where he wants me. Incapable of saying no.

He knows of my wounded soul, the insecurities, and the tender part of me that is no match against such cunning schemes. He denies the rumors floating around about the other girls—three to be exact; one comes up to my new job at Burger King on Oakland Park, turning the suspicions into a hard-cold fact. I know he cannot truly love me. I know it because I have not learned to love myself.

In quiet apathy, I allow him to take sexual and emotional ownership of my life again, with no responsibility for my heart, my mind, and my future. At the onset of our relationship, the signs had been there, but defenseless eyes will almost always miss the clues and red flags. Stained by a past that haunts me, blinded by the little attention he offers, I consent to his wishes. I skin my knees on the carpet trying to please him. The way to his heart is to become a slave, on my back, assuming the position. In time, I discover the sobering truth about sex: it is not love. Nor can it ever be.

Possessive and controlling, he grooms me with a different kind of fear. The worst kind, one that speaks of love in one ear yet justifies abuse and lies in the other. I watch outside myself, allowing it to happen. Sex and submission take a twisted shape, masquerading as something it could never be. Love can never be violent, and abuse can never be love. Regardless of how it shifts, one moment you laugh and the next moment you cry, disrespect is still a lie, a nasty lie that tramples your spirit, and expects you to spread your legs and take it. I oblige, uncomplaining; I know the position expected of abusive men. I learn to die again and again, until I become merely a body to be used, a cheap possession.

The problem is that for so long, there have been so many parts of me scattered and broken. From identity to education, I do not know who I am or where my life is going. I wish my father were here to help me with that part. When I was little, he had a way of making me feel like a princess, and now, with zero self-esteem, I feel inferior and unworthy of more than what life has offered me. Maybe this is just the way life goes. Your boyfriend beats you, so what's new? You take it, just like everyone else. The first time we had sex, it was as if I signed a dastardly contract, some back-door deal that demands you to meet his needs at all cost. That was three years ago. Now I am fifteen, the mother of his daughter, and the contract still binds.

Soon, Casita and I join Bruce's church, Refreshing Springs Church of God in Christ. It feels good to be a part of a group of people who accept my daughter and me. The church encourages me to grow in my faith. Although I am antisocial, it feels nice to belong. The smiles seem genuine, and I begin to feel connected to a family of believers. One evening after I return home from an outing with some of the church members, Bruce comes over and rings my mother's doorbell.

When I open the door, he slaps me across my face. A flash of Ms. Lynn and The Lineup immediately resurfaces, and the taste of sweet peas and blood brings the memory from the past to the very cold present. I flinch from the sting of his hand; he was so calm that I never saw it coming. The hand grenade is the punishment for going to the beach with members of the church who had asked me if I wanted to go. Bruce says I should have declined the offer and that it better not happen again. His two-sided nature strikes me on both sides of my face. I take it without a word. Straitjacketed, I blame myself for his anger. The broken part of me believes his reaction must be out of love. *Why else would he give so much energy and attention to me? Or maybe, I am just crazy.* Whatever the facts, I do what I have always done when under the gun of cruelty: I go numb. I repress my anger and settle into the refuge of apathy.

Every time I tell myself that it won't happen again, it always does, and now, it's getting worse—the apologies are few. What is the point of saying you are sorry if you keep doing the same thing? I once read when things start out one way; it usually stays the same until you decide to change it. But the last time I tried to break off the relationship, my daughter was taken. I take the easy road. Flight or fight, I am just tired. I want to be with my daughter; Bruce is a part of that. I believe there is no other choice.

Tonight, Linda has made a casserole. She has become a fantastic cook, always in the kitchen, creating something new and delicious. Casita licks her lips and fork after cleaning her plate. She is usually a finicky eater, so I am happy to see her finish all her food. Casita and I share the room closest to the bathroom. By now, I would think the dark could no longer scare me, but it still does. The bathroom light stays on all night. It is late, but I stay up to tune into the radio program called *Night Sounds*.

Casita and I listen to Bill Pearce almost every night. His radio show plays the most peaceful music, and in between the songs, I listen to the sound of his gentle voice; it is so soothing. Casita snuggles up close to me, and I sing the songs to her that come on the radio until she falls asleep. Tonight, I wait for one of my favorite songs by Amy Grant. When it plays, I feel a peace that surpasses the uncertainties. I pray that when Casita grows up, she will remember the words, just in case I am not here to sing them to her:

> *"El Shaddai, El Shaddai,*
> *El-Elyon na Adoni,*
> *Age to age you're still the same,*
> *By the power of the name.*
> *El Shaddai, El Shaddai,*
> *Erkamka na Adoni,*
> *We will praise and lift you high,*
> *El Shaddai.*
> *Through your love and through the ram,*
> *You saved the son of Abraham;*
> *Through the power of your hand,*

you turned the sea into dry land.
To the outcast on her knees,
You are the God who really sees,
And by your might,
You set your children free."

In the coming weeks, news of Robert's condition worsens, and my mother continues to work around the clock. Sun-up until sun-down — she is often too tired to eat when she gets home. Linda and I listen out for Robert's calls. In the final weeks, he calls out for ice. It is his only request.

"Ice! bring me ice!" Linda and I take shifts carrying him large cups of ice. Every day, the same. We take ice into the bedroom, which resembles more of a hospital room, where multiple lines hang from a double-headed pole that attaches to an intravenous machine. Sealed bags with medical supplies and tubing sit on the dresser next to perfume and cologne bottles; an emesis basin sits on his bedside table, exposing a puddle of green phlegm tinged with dark red blood. A portable urinal sits on the floor near the edge of the bed; I empty it and return it to where he can reach it.

The room reeks with an uncomfortable eeriness. Clear fluid drips slowly from the bags hanging on the metal hooks into a tube-shaped chamber. The tubing hangs like jellyfish tentacles, attaching to ports in his arm. I lower my eyes to the floor as I remember a conversation my mother had on the phone.

"The doctors have done all they could. Winston cigarettes caused the cancer, and the last tests showed it has spread to every part of his body. The palliative treatments are the last resorts. It is only a matter of time." He receives medications intravenously to combat the aggressive form of cancer and to manage his pain. He is due to have surgery to remove the growths that have spread to his stomach.

The last week of Robert's homecare revealed the gravity of his condition — it was not merely physical. His calls for ice continue day and night, until the week he was admitted to the hospital. During that time, Linda and I do not know what to do. Although a cup of ice sits at his bedside table, he continues to call out for more of what he already has. "Ice! I need ice. Bring me ice!" We sit still, listening, unsure of what else to do.

The lake is a peaceful escape for me. Casita and I take walks to the lake that sits in the middle of the neighborhood over on the next street. The farther away we walk, the freer I feel. Casita skips up the sidewalk, and my heart soars just watching her. She is beautiful and carefree, like a butterfly dancing on the breeze.

Linda joins us and takes pictures of Casita running pass the lawn sprinklers. It is a sunny afternoon. Linda stays with us for a few minutes and then leaves to visit her friend who lives nearby. Casita carries a plastic bag with a few slices of bread. She makes it a point to remind me to get bread before we leave the house so we can feed the ducks that waddle by when we sit near the water's edge. She beams, throwing breadcrumbs on the lake.

"Look, Mommy," she says, pointing at a flock of birds landing on the pond.

"I see them, baby. They are hungry today." Casita sits on my lap, and our legs dangle back and forth over the water. The lake is calming, and as the birds feed, the water ripples, carrying my thoughts out and away.

The sun feels warm on my skin, and I breathe in the tranquility of being near the water. Nothing else in the world matters except to be right here, right now with my little girl, my little house…this is true love. Casita turns and smiles at me.

"Baby, I love you this much," I tell her, stretching out my arms.

"I love you this much too, mommy," she says, stretching out her arms as wide as she can, copying me like she always does; it is our sweet routine.

"I love you always." I press my face into hers and give her a squeeze. Casita giggles, staring back over the water, in her own little magical world; a delightful world she happily shares with me. My child is my everything. I want to protect her and preserve moments like these, so she will always remember that she is my princess, the best part of me.

But it will not be. Destiny prepares another onslaught. The trench of violence widens, making way for an inconceivable course of events that I could not foresee or prevent. Lost in a trench of piercing thorns, breaking free would be nearly impossible.

God's training is never easy. But He promises that if we must face it, by His grace, we can bear it. He orders our steps according to His will for our life. The Lord invites us to learn of Him. In Matthew 11:30, the words comfort us, letting us know that, despite the circumstance, His yoke is easy, and His burden is light. Sometimes He orders us into green pastures, and other times, He sends us to the frontlines.

Chasing Smoke

The human mind was created to reason, the human spirit, to worship, and the human heart, to bond within a symbiotic union—the giving and receiving of love and acceptance; we are triune beings. When the soul can't find a safe refuge in which to trust and belong, there will be a deep void where anything can come along and sweep you off your feet. It is the element of bonding that will either nurture or neglect us throughout life, forcing us into captivity with no strength of our own to stand. It's all a matter of who or what we bond to that determines the condition.

February 17, 1984

There is something worse than death. I feel it as it skulked into Roberts's hospital room. My mother looks at me, unable to speak as she moves to the side of the hospital bed where Casita, Bruce, and I are standing. She senses it too. The hairs on my arms and the back of my neck stand up. Something is in the room, moving intently through the air as if it has an appointment to keep. Casita is two years old; she holds tightly to my leg, looking up at me, uneasy and agitated.

Earlier today, my mother had called me to the hospital to be with her; I came immediately. Bruce drove with me; his presence will be the fulfillment of a prophecy spoken years earlier on 24th Street. Robert has been in a semi-comatose state up until today. His eyes open, and the look on his face is terrifying.

He pants rapidly, eyes widening as if he sees something we can only feel. But the entity is as real as the past events that went on behind closed doors. It was at this very moment that I begin to understand the scripture I had read about the wages of unrepented sin. My mother draws her hands to her face. "Go get the doctor!" she tells Bruce. As he darts out, she closes her eyes and prays. The heaviness travels across the floor and seems to lie on top of the bed. Robert's eyes are bulging, and he looks as though he is no longer living, though he is still moving and breathing. I had heard the stories about cigarettes and the damage it does; damage that causes tremendous suffering before the final gasp for breath. I remember wondering why anyone would ever smoke knowing the outcome; still, something else was happening to him; something worse than the natural process of dying. Green fluid, like thick lava, secretes from his ears and mouth. He convulses, and my mother backs away, near the window.

"Where is that doctor? What is taking the doctor so long to get in here?" she says. Incidentally, the doctor does not come in the room—only a priest. The minister speaks with my mother, says a prayer, and walks out.

My mom and I walk to the left side of the bed. When my mother picks up the phone, Robert takes his last breath. The green fluid stops running from his mouth, but his eyes are still open. I stand close to my mom, comforting her. Suddenly, the air is still, and it feels as if the same presence that walked in moves away from the bed and walked out; it was tangible.

We thought it was all over, but after a few moments of calm, Roberts's eyes move, looking to the left side of the bed where my mother and I are standing.

"He must have done something very wrong," my mother says, staring back at him then quickly away. I put my arms around my mother as she calls Boyd Funeral Home to make the funeral arrangements. Loyal to the secrets, I will continue to hold onto the memories of 24ᵗʰ Street and the wolves that came in between. Even after his death, there is no freedom. The thorns are a part of me. The whispers still come from a childhood that is long gone. *"Get on the bed. You are going to learn to like it. Say anything, and I will kill you!"* To this day, I only feel sadness for him. Someone must have hurt him terribly when he was a little boy; that's my logic, my way of making sense of sin. How else could he be capable of such cruelty as he grew and became a man with the understanding of right and wrong?

January 5, 1985

I climb the stairs of my new apartment. Bruce, Casita, and I are moving into our first home together. The neighborhood is scary; the kind of place where you want to be in your house with your doors locked before the sun goes down. The two-story complex sits right across the street from the Sunset Memorial Cemetery. Tiredly, I move up and down the staircase carrying mirrors, boxes, and furniture. I am sixteen years old and almost eight months pregnant. It is my first apartment since leaving my mother's house.

Exhausted from the move, I'm glad when I finally get to lie down and rest. It is nearly 1 a.m. The moment I stop moving, the hard labor starts. The pain is odd; unlike the labor of my first child, there is a wrenching sensation I cannot describe. Bruce rushes me to Broward General Medical Center. Dr. Clarke, the emergency room doctor, checks my cervix. I am not dilating, but the pain has become more excruciating, and then suddenly, there is no pain or movement.

The nursing staff rushes me into surgery with no time to explain the details of what's about to happen. "What's wrong? Why do I need surgery? Is my baby okay?" I try to speak, but the questions come out in fading sobs.

"The umbilical cord is wrapped around your baby. You must have surgery!" All at once, the condemning voices come. *How could I have been so foolish to move furniture and lift heavy boxes? I should have known better. What was I thinking? God, please save my baby! Please let me hold my baby before I die!* Unable to manage the stress, my body responds as it always has under threat; replaying the fear of what happened to my father's mother.

The nurse wipes a cold, brown liquid over the lower part of my belly. I'm awake! I see it. I smell it. The nurse straps my arms down, while a cloudy mist seeps through the side holes of the contraption covering my mouth and nose, sharp flashes of silver flicker in front of a face covered by a surgical mask. I'm still awake. I see the scalpel and suddenly remember the fight with my mom and Ms. Lynn, as if it is all happening in real time.

Darkness.

When I awake, I am in recovery. I have no memory of why I am in the hospital.

"It's a boy," Bruce says. A nurse walks past the bed, pulling the pastel curtain closed. He is premature but doing well. He is five pounds and seven ounces.

"The doctor got him out in time," the nurse says. I am grateful, but it's hard to let go of the guilt of moving furniture while so far along in my pregnancy. I meet him for the first time, and I cannot believe the amazing gift God has given me. He is the most handsome baby I have ever seen. A strong spirit, he is my BJ. I name him Bobby, and as his little fingers wrap around mine, I feel his strength. Holding him, I feel his courageous spirit.

Moments later, the weight of it all falls heavy as feelings of inadequacy hammer me: *What can I give my children when there is so much I still don't know? When the secrets of my life linger around me like haunting shadows? God help me; I can't do this alone.*

That evening, my mother visits me in the hospital with gifts of a new white robe with matching slippers. The proud look on her face makes me smile. The nurse tells me to press a pillow over my belly when I laugh or need to cough. She says the pillow will help relieve the pressure from the abdominal spasms and help with healing. The horizontal cut would heal long before the deep wounds left unresolved in my life.

Roughly one month later, Bruce goes out of town to be at the side of his lover while she gives birth to a second son. I have suspected him of cheating, but my suspicions mean no more than my objections to the physical and emotional abuse. No voice, no rights, not even in my own eyes; I assume the position.

The world learns how to treat you by how you allow it to treat you. Emotionally brainwashed, I enable the cheating, the hitting — whatever Bruce says, goes. A playground for his use, I see myself as an ignorant black girl, a misfit, the ideal type that will permit the abuse. He comes and goes as he pleases. Quiet submission, I say nothing. A long time ago, I had forfeited my right to be angry with anyone about anything, and now, cruelty has no limit, no boundaries. I assume the same position demanded of me my whole life; I know it well. Seen and not heard, I learn to smile like a tired rodeo clown at the end of every fight.

In the silence of the night, when my children are asleep, and the crickets' wings catch the wind, I stare up into the sky. That's when I let the tears fall. During those times, I feel like a lost child because I inwardly long for my sister's arms, her stories, and lullabies — as if I have not aged at all. I close my eyes and see my mother's face. I wish I could tell her what is happening to me, and pray that maybe someday; she will see me and hear me for who I am. That day, I will tell her my innermost secrets. Moonlight glimmers against the bed sheet hanging in the window, and I wonder where my father is tonight, and if he thinks of me as much as I think of him. Isolated in a world of thorns, I wait for the world to change.

Casita is three years old. She is as beautiful as the day she was born. Her arms stretch out wide with a curious look on her face. "Mommy, I love you this much!" Dimples in her cheeks, she holds the position until I copy her and pick her up, like always.

"I love you too, baby." I swing her around in a circle until she laughs as if nothing else matters in her world. BJ breastfeeds for the first two months until I need to pump milk before my shift starts again at Burger King. *If I study hard,* I tell myself, *I will be able to take the GED exam and earn my high school diploma.* As the months go by, school is all I can think about. I want to make my children proud of their mama; getting an education will be a good start. I have worked and saved up enough money to buy my first car. Bruce is away again; I don't know where. I don't ask, and sometimes I could care less. The isolation grows, and I do not have many friends, but I remember one. My children and I ride over to Kay's house.

Kay is an old friend that I have not seen since my mother moved from the neighborhood. I want to surprise her.

We stop by unannounced, hoping she is home and that my unexpected visit is not an imposition.

"Hello, is Kay at home? I just wanted to stop by and see how she is doing. I hope she doesn't mind me stopping by. I don't have her number." I say to a lady walking towards my car. At first glance, I do not recognize her.

"Hey BJ, it's me. Kay!" She is standing right in front of me, but my eyes never saw Kay, the girl I once knew. She has lost a lot of weight, and as she leans into the window of the car, I notice something else has changed.

"I miss you, Kay. How have you been?" I ask, noticing the profuse sweat rolling down her face and how her cheekbones pointed out like she just arrived from a third world country.

"I'm good." She says with an excited smile, moving like she needs to use the bathroom. We talk for a few minutes, and she invites us inside her home. Kay is a mother now as well. She has two young children, and they all live with her mother and siblings. *How blessed she is to be with her family,* I think to myself. Kay moves back and forth from the living room to her bathroom. We wait patiently on the couch, smelling a peculiar odor coming from her room.

"How about we take the children to the beach for a picnic sometime? I can get burgers and fries, a blanket, and a toy bucket with a shovel for them to make sand castles," I suggest. But Kay is not interested in going to the beach.

I do not think it is strange at first, especially since the bathroom is sort of a hideaway for me. It is the look on her face when she finally comes out that last time that makes me question. *What is happening to her? What happened to the person I use to know or thought I knew?* Sweat rolls into dilated eyes that are stretched twice the size from before she went in; a look of desperation sweeps across her face when she asks if she can borrow money. I say what I always say when asked for anything.

"Yes, sure no problem."

"Can you take me down the street to get something?" She asks, moving in place as if bugs were crawling on her skin.

"Sure. Are you ready?" I jump at the chance to be a hero, perhaps because I need one so badly.

We pull up to an apartment complex, that was less than ten minutes away. I hand Kay twenty dollars from my glove box. She tells me to wait in the car. When she gets back, she tells me to hit the gas, and the look on her face mixes with elation and paranoia.

"This place is hot," She says, looking out the side view mirror. I have no idea what she means. Later, I will find out she was referring to the cops that were casing the area. The drive back reveals why her mood has changed so radically. She opens a small piece of foil on her lap, and suddenly, it is as if no one else is in the car—no one else except her and the crystal object she holds onto like a talisman. I've never seen the drug before, and at first glance, I think whoever sold it to her cheated her out of the money. *Why would she pay so much for such a small stone object?* I would soon find out.

People are like vessels; I once heard in a Bible story. Clay pots made from the dust of the earth. The sad thing about empty vessels is that when it is left empty, anything can come along to fill it.

When we get back to her home, she takes me in the bathroom, places the small white rock crystal on a small, clear-stemmed, pipe bottle, and lights the end of the stem with the flick of a lighter. When she inhales, the tension surrounding her vanishes in a cloud of smoke. The hard-branching lines that crease her face from the side of her eyes to her hairline are gone. "Take a hit," she says.

I did, and at first, I felt nothing. I had never smoked anything before and had never seen the small rock drug. Except for Edward's evils and the pills I took during my suicide attempt, I didn't have a clue about any drug, especially the drug called Crack Cocaine. Unsure of what I am supposed to feel after taking the first hit, I stare at her, then down and then back up, waiting for something magical to happen. But I only gag and cough on the smoke.

"Don't pull so hard. Drop your shoulders, and don't swallow the smoke. You never smoked anything before?" Kay asks before taking another hit.

"No. Not that I can remember."

After coughing the smoke out of my throat, I ask her the same question again. Walls suffocate me. I want to get out and go anywhere where the air feels free, and I can watch the quiet waves.

"Do you want to take the children to the beach? We can get KFC if you want. The weather is nice, and I have a blanket in the car." Again, I wait for a response. Kay tiptoes to the window and peers nervously out over the driveway; she does not answer at first. So, I ask a third time. She paces, nodding her head, looking at the floor as if she has lost something. I'm not sure if she ever heard the questions.

Kay and I never make it to the beach, and it was naive of me to think we ever would. After being isolated from my family and the few friends I thought I have, I desperately want someone to talk to, to connect with; someone who can help me make sense of all the craziness. After the visit, the children and I head back to the apartment. During the ride home, I cannot stop thinking about Kay. *How different she is now.* The girl I had thought I once knew is gone.

Unknowingly, I have walked into a slave camp where the slave master rises, pretending to be a genie in a bottle with the power to grant wishes and command all your worries away.

The present woes will almost pale in comparison to what was about to come. The world opens its arms wider to show me a whole new realm of crazy: the dominion of addiction. In the coming months, Kay's house becomes a place for me to run, away from the anger and isolation that has been building inside, mainly after every fight at home. She welcomes me with open arms and a readied crack pipe. Riding on the passenger's side, she shows me the way. I supply the cash, but when the money is gone, so too is the *welcome*. At least for a little while, I feel safe from Bruce's reach. He cannot find me here.

I sit at Kay's home, leaning against the bathroom wall, waiting for the tranquilizer that will take all the hurt and fear away. It is an effortless process, but with catastrophic consequences. In the haze of smoke, I couldn't see it coming. Kay loads the pipe and flicks the lighter. I pull hard, swallowing, choking.

"Hold your breath and let it come out slow." Kay demonstrates. In time, I discover another tunnel to which I can escape it all. Dark and void of light, no fireflies flutter up—there is only dancing smoke from the genie's bottle. Crack cocaine takes me beyond the hidden passageway of the fireflies, beyond any realm I have ever experienced. As the fire of the lighter rubs the pipe, I've already made my three wishes: no more pain, no more fear, and the final request is the same one as always: to fly away. I take a hit, close my eyes, and wait to disappear.

In the grip of addiction, there is no past, no present; time does not exist; a week feels like a day enraptured by the bliss of cocaine. Basic human needs are an afterthought; there is nothing else. No need to eat, to sleep, to take a bath; no need for love or lies; crack cocaine becomes the perfect alibi — the escape from all the nonsense. The drug reminds me that it alone matters. It demands everything, and after all the thieves I faced, I have nothing else to lose. I bow to its ability to make me feel free, unchained, and flawless.

As a runaway, I was used to living day to day with no thought of food, clothes, or having a place to sleep. In survival mode, the next breath is the only commodity I can afford. But then again, in my broken life, there is one difference between my days as a runaway and the drug that now makes me its slave: crack cocaine has a high price. It grants you three wishes with one caveat, one warning; it demands everything: your family, your hopes, your dreams, your life!

Even in my sleep, I'm chasing smoke, flying through mind-numbing clouds, dreaming of getting high. The addiction didn't take hold at first. Like a secret lover, it waits for me to be ready, to be beaten enough, broken enough that I will run into its arms. After every slap and punch, I run to it, knowing it will be waiting to rescue me. All it takes is the kiss of fire to awaken my lover. My hands tremble as I flick the lighter, inhale, and watch as the rock melt inside the glass pipe. Instantly, the unbearable memories melt away with it, as if nothing ever happened.

The bonding begins as I exhale. The smoke wraps around me and holds me tenderly until the shivers in my hands stopped. After the first hit, the constant noises in my head go silent and the shame of my past, the wolves, the stench of it all, can no longer torment me. It was blissful. Only minutes later, there is an intense craving for more. It doesn't take long before I felt emptier, more desperate, and more broken than ever. Like an unfaithful lover, crack cocaine also has two sides: it promises to take you higher than you've ever been, and then, it turns you into a different kind of slave; a slave of circumstance where pain and self-pity feed the genie of addiction.

Freedom from addiction has a high price, far beyond what I could ever afford; far beyond the ransom the genie demands as payment for the bondage of what would become a savage stronghold on my life. Naturally, I assume the position; the same pathetic powerlessness; chasing smoke inside a widening trench until I could no longer tell the difference between what was real and what was complete insanity.

Fly Away

"Insanity - a perfectly rational adjustment to an insane world." ~R. D. Laing

A generational saga unfolds, and I stay the fateful course; no resistance, no struggle; the vortex is too strong. As my addiction worsens, the cycle of neglect circles back, catching my children in the whirlwind of a familiar pattern—a history that never dies. Full speed ahead toward self-destruction, my mind races against a clock with hands moving in the wrong direction. Everything spins, like Dorothy's house in *The Wizard of Oz*.

In the throes of alcohol and drug abuse, I do not hear the cries of my children, nor attend to the hunger in their eyes from the lack of care and my emotional absence. Powerless, I'm incapable of giving them the stability they need. Parents cannot provide what they do not possess. During the bouts of sobriety, I've tried to hide the addictions from my children, but children hear and see even when we hide behind closed doors.

I do what I do best. I run. Bruce's mother and sister's care for my children during my many relapses, loving them back to life after the many times I fail to be the mother they need. Days, weeks at a time, I disappear into the night, chasing smoke, fed up with life. I exist in and out of sobriety, straddling two worlds: one of smoke and make-believe, the other a harsh reality of being a sixteen-year-old alcoholic and crack-addicted misfit. Between lucid moments of sobriety, I see the questions in my children's eyes. But I have no answers to give them, no words to describe how my manic emotions drive me to self-destruct from the inside out.

After days, weeks in the streets, Bruce tracks me down and brings me back. I go where I always go when I get to the house: the bathroom. There, the threatening voices pull me in and then push me away. Like bullies on the playground, they surround me, telling me, "You will not live to see twenty; you will never belong here; you will never belong anywhere." The voices are familiar; I have heard them all my life. But now, addiction makes the delusions worse. The images are sharper, more alive than ever. I jump and flinch at the air. Shadows peel off the wall, crawling, jumping at me. Images, grossly deformed, carousel around me, vanishing only to reappear; they feel real. Addicts know when it's getting worse but feel powerless to stop it. During one of the many breakdowns, I hit myself, swatting at my arms and legs, trying to kill what I cannot see.

Everything in me craves the high, *just one more hit from the crack pipe will make it all go away*, I tell myself. My tolerance for the drug transforms into a total physical and psychological dependency. Sun-up to sundown I think only of it—to disappear in the smoke of crack cocaine and to drown in the abyss of the liquid spirits of alcohol. The toxic balance of both drugs was necessary to grant my wish of feeling nothing. Like magic, it works.

One night, after using heavily, I began to feel a tightening in my chest and felt that if I took one more hit, I would die. Still, I loaded the pipe, flick the lighter, and inhaled with all my might. These are the realities of addiction; sick with a twisted form of vengeance; we wait for the end to come with no intention of quitting until the odds are even.

From relapse to sobriety, addicts exist without direction or purpose. More than a decade ago, I sat in the car with my siblings watching my father walk into the Melody Bar. Now, history prepares to repeat itself in the month of December 11, 1986.

I am driving down 31st Avenue with my children in the backseat. Heart racing, I pull over and run inside the bathroom of the Shell gas station. My children are waiting for me inside the car.

Once inside the small restroom, I cannot come out, I can't swallow, or breathe. The manic anxiety overpowers me; I need a hit. Matches burn my trembling fingers, and I drop the rock on the grubby floor littered with cigarette buds, crumpled paper, and dirty shoeprints. An old beer can with holes poked in the top serves as my crack pipe. It stays in my bag for moments like this—the times when I can no longer cope with life. Ashes from a half-smoked cigarette lying on the ground were all I needed to cover the holes in the aluminum can—the rock genie nests on top of the ashes. In the smoke-filled bathroom, I cannot see the fear, the distress, and the uncertainty in my children's eyes as they had ridden in the back seat before we arrived here, nor while they wait for me to come out. There is only smoke.

There was no coming out; at least not on my own. Paralyzed in a mysterious world I have no power to break free from, I cower in the corner of the stall, remembering all the times I have prayed and cried, believing maybe one day, my life would matter. Time passes; I am not sure how much. The police came to take me out of the bathroom after I ignored the demands of the station attendant. My children go with family members; I go to jail after the substance the cops test for turns blue; the color that signifies the presence of cocaine. They could've saved time if they had listened when I told them exactly what it was in the first place. My second time in the backseat of a police car felt no different than the first. Now a captive to addiction, not much has changed. *Life is but a dream.* Bruce bonds me out the next day. But the truth is I wanted to stay locked up; away from him; away from everything. As a minor in the eyes of the law, I get out of jail with no "serious" legal charges filed this time.

After my release, Bruce drives me to the apartment. He has his own idea of the law. His rules, and his way. Nothing has changed there either. I pretend to listen to his ranting; pretend to care about his threats and remarks about disgracing the family. I remember thinking, *what the hell! What family? We are nothing more than property in the grand illusion of a family.* Whatever he says or does from here on out is of no consequence. It's whatever! *What could anyone possibly do to me that has not already happened?* Now, there is one agenda, one destination, one plan: get to the bathroom. Get high. Stay high. Repeat.

Crack cocaine becomes the great equalizer. More than just a high, it counterbalances the fierce assaults against my life. It evens the odds, releasing inhibitions, allowing me to escape and disappear into the pungent air: nothing matters, only the next high, the next fix. My children, my jobs, my responsibilities—all get lost in the smoke of crack addiction. After another hit, like magic, I forget it all; assuming the position of a thousand nightmares from a childhood where some strange entity has declared war against my life. How do you know where to begin or how to try to take control of what you felt you never had power over in the first place?

Weeks pass in and out of consciousness since my arrest. My mind scatters, even further away from any sense of sanity. No bathing; no appetite—the smell of food nauseates me. I stay in the bathroom, like a dugout in a war zone. The battle is all in my mind.

There is a knock on the bathroom door—my heartbeat races with paranoia. A voice inside my head tells me to swallow, but I can't. Saliva accumulates in my mouth, and my mind races against itself. *Swallow! Swallow, turn, fold your hands, unfold your hands, swallow, before anyone comes in, you must swallow. If you do not swallow, you will die.* Lumps of spit and mucus pile in my throat. Suddenly, I hear faint whispers and hissing saying, *you are nothing. Dirty crack whore, you will never be anything.* I listen to the knocking. Afraid to open the door, I freeze. This is the insanity of crack addiction.

"I will be right there," I stumble, trying to stop my hands from shaking long enough for me to grip the handle. As I turn on the faucet and spit in the sink, I notice thick black mucus, like soot from a chimney, coming out of my mouth. It holds onto the side of the sink, refusing to go down the drain. "I will...I will be out in a minute." *Hurry, hurry, get away, get away,* the voices warn me. *You must run. Get out now, before it's too late. Before twenty!*

Since my childhood, death has seemed to toy with me, and in my sick mind, it is only a matter of time before the ax comes down and I can finally be rid of its torment. In a state of constant fear, like a death row inmate, I wait for the inevitable. After a few minutes, I drag myself out of my bathroom and slowly open the door. Wide eyes, I stare at her.

It is Casita. She is waiting on the other side, patiently sitting, bows still in her hair from the last time I braided it. She is four years old now. She steps towards me with something in her hands. I blink, and a memory flashes across my mind to a place and time when we were close, inseparable.

She is skipping through water sprinklers with a quarter loaf of Dandee bread in her hand. The bag swings as she hops and skips joyfully to the lake, excited to feed the birds and ducks.

The uncontrollable tremors bring me back to the present. We do not take walks anymore; we do not sit together beside the peaceful lake to feed the ducks and watch the birds fly. The lullabies are gone. Everything is gone, lost inside a smoke-filled trench of thorns.

"Mommy," she says, moving closer. Her brown eyes hold no memory of her mama's arrest and abandonment. I tilt my head to the side and look away. "Mommy, I want to show you something I made for you." She smiles at me and hands me a drawing. Flowers and hearts surround the words: *Mother, I love you with all my heart.* She must have used every color in her crayon box.

"I...I love it. It's beautiful baby." The words stumble out from dry, cracked lips. The kitchen light shines near my bedroom door. I turn my sunken face away before she sees the dark circles and puffy bags underneath my eyes from the many sleepless nights.

Casita stands with her arms by her sides, staring up at me, as if she sees no wrong. Leaning against the wall, I place an unsteady hand over my mouth to cover the stench of my breath from days without eating or brushing my teeth. The constant flare-ups from my empty gut cause me to back away from her.

"I made it just for you!" She stretches her arms out wide to her sides and says, "Mommy, I love you this much." Somehow, she still remembers how I use to stretch out my arms, hold her close, and tell her how much I love her. Incredibly, her little heart remembers the person I use to be. She looks at me as if she sees someone else; someone who is not entirely hopeless, someone worthy of her colorful portrait of hearts and flowers. She wraps her little arms around me and holds on tight—like a blossoming flower on a thorn bush, refusing to let go.

In our wretchedness, it is difficult to see what God is doing and why. In pain, all we can see is the pain. Depression takes on many forms with one primary effect that causes us to neglect the divine within and to wallow in self-pity. In Romans 7:14-25, the Apostle Paul explains, "For we know that the law is spiritual, but I am of the flesh, sold under sin. For I do not understand my own actions. For I do not do what I want, but I do the very thing I hate. Now if I do what I do not want, I agree with the law, that it is good. So now it is no longer I who do it, but sin that dwells within me. For I know that nothing good dwells in me, that is, in my flesh. For I have the desire to do what is right, but not the ability to carry it out. For I do not do the good I want, but the evil I do not want is what I keep on doing. Now if I do what I do not want, it is no longer I who do it, but sin that dwells within me.

So, I find it to be a law that when I want to do right, evil lies close at hand. For I delight in the law of God, in my inner being, but I see in my members another law waging war against the law of my mind and making me captive to the law of sin that dwells in my members. Wretched man that I am! Who will deliver me from this body of death? Thanks be to God through Jesus Christ our Lord!

So then, I myself serve the law of God with my mind, but with my flesh I serve the law of sin."

Paul clearly understood his wretchedness and the inner war with sin. The problem with addiction and every malady known to man then becomes the same one that caused the fall from the beginning. There lies the law of perseverance through faith, understanding the importance of God's love and grace that covers a multitude of sin (1 Peter 4:8).

History's Encore

April 20th, 1986

At the altar in a long pink dress, I stand pigeon-toed big underneath it, pregnant with my third child. My mother bought a hat with a veil for the occasion. My father is not here to walk me down the aisle, but all the same, he gives me away. History prepares its encore: it all begins again—the transfer is becoming complete. The church fills with family and friends, faces I can barely see. My eyesight is weakening and so has the enamel on my teeth from my past drug use. During the past year, I fight to stay clean and sober; again, it will be short-lived. The call of addiction is powerful. There is no outrunning the genie.

"Repeat after me." The pastor performs wedding vows. Sacred vows to love, honor, and obey. At eighteen-years-old, I stand there, at the altar, pretending everything is fine, play-acting in a skit where I smile for the cameras while wilting inside. Ever more a master of disguise, I repeat the vows verse by verse, line by line, moving through time but never growing up. Blood still runs through my veins, but inside, nothing feels alive: that's why now, I invite the pain—it allows me to feel something. I stand there, a body in a wedding gown going through the motions, living a life that feels as though it is not mine. I am here, and I am not here. My body, my mind, and the children I have carried and birthed into the world—a slave has a right to own nothing. Before the sun sets, I will be on the floor in my wedding dress. No longer a battered girlfriend; now, I am a battered wife.

Nine days later, April 29th, 1986 I give birth to my third child, LiSandra. Her nose and eyes are mirror reflections of mine. Soon, our family begins attending another church service regularly, and where Bruce leads, we follow. Walls and corners are smothering, so I sit near the end of the row with my children; close enough to see out of a small, pitched window, so that I can gaze at the sky.

The choir begins to sing "Amazing Grace." Pen in hand, I try to stay focused, taking notes, listening to a message about how Christians are all a part of the body of Christ.

After the sermon, everyone stands. "Come to the altar if you need prayer. Come and get set free; He who the Son has set free is free indeed," Pastor Butler makes the altar call. I cannot feel my feet, but I am moving towards the altar. Head down, shaking;

everything hurts. Clean and sober; I feel like I am fighting a constant war with an unseen enemy. For the sake of my children, I move forward, praying for the strength to stand and stay sober. I had tried before and failed. Today, I'm afraid of failing again, terrified of seeing the where-you-been look inside my children's eyes after every relapse. Afraid of the dreams that keep coming, even after months of sobriety — dreams of using again, dreams of falling again, drowning, deeper inside a widening trench. Often, I wake up in the middle of the night, chasing smoke through a bottomless, inescapable maze. God help me not to lose it all again.

Near the altar, I glance back at my children. Casita stands near her little brother and sister in the middle row of the church. I give her a smile and turn back towards the altar, hiding every sign of depression like a skillful illusionist. I never want my children to know the truth, but then even at their young age, I'm afraid they already do. Always careful to muzzle my cries, I force myself to keep it all in because *they can never know what happens behind closed doors.* Obscured faces look out from folding chairs that column on the right and left sides of the church. Others come to the front, praying, crowding the altar with shouts of "Glory Hallelujah!" and "Praise, Jesus."

The anxiety crowds out the fervent prayers of those around me. It's hard to pray when I am uncertain about tomorrow, and the next day, and the next. "God bless my children," I whisper, wanting better for them. I fall on my knees at the altar. "God, help me please," I whisper, remembering the time my addiction had become so bad, that I didn't think it could get any worse. Wanting desperately to heal and gain control of my life, I had checked myself into B.A.R.C. The Broward Addiction and Recovery Center had felt like a last resort. I was on the road to self-destruction, and everyone in my life knew it.

I do not remember the length of time I stayed at the facility, but I will never forget seeing the gentle eyes of Sister Brown; she is the pastor's mother. I didn't know she worked there, though I'd seen her at Refreshing Springs Church before. I had noticed her kind eyes watching me as I shuffled listlessly across the detox hall floor. Her expression conveyed the same message I once heard her speak about in church:

"You must take life one day at a time." The words echoed from her passing glance. When you are an addict, that's all you get; all you can bear is — one day at a time. There is nothing else. In the bondage of addiction and unrelenting anxiety, I believe tomorrow will never come. In a brief meeting with the center's therapist, I learn certain facts about addiction and "emotional blocking."

A therapist had explained the plunge of my dependency on alcohol and drugs is rooted in emotional blocking. "You must understand your addiction is a disease caused by unaddressed emotional trauma. You must heal the emotional pain, and then you can gain greater control over the physical pain and ultimately the addiction. You cannot continue to ignore your emotions. They are a part of you. Treatment will teach you ways of coping with your disease," the therapist told me. I heard her, but the threats in my secretive life still speak louder than her facts. I had not known where to start the process of healing.

How do I leave someone I love? How can I love someone who is beating me? How do I escape from a trench that continues to get deeper and wider? No one stopped the storms. What voice do I have to change it; to speak out against it?

Past trauma has wired me to be reactive. The present circumstances have bound me to silent apathy. Trapped on both sides; there are no exits, no way out. The inherent encore of history has circled back.

Eyes closed, I don't look at the faces of saints standing near. To avoid seeing any judgmental glances, I stare at the floor, thanking God for surviving these months, clean and sober. I had not thought the storms would last so long, yet by His mercy, here I stand.

"God, please help me. Every day is a struggle. It's hard to keep from fading in and out of time. I need you, God. I can't do this on my own." After I finish praying, I keep my eyes closed at the altar, standing still, waiting for something to happen. The problem is, I don't know what I am waiting for because I am unsure about everything—even God.

When Joyce was near, I had felt God in her gentle touches; I heard God in her songs. On the beach, I heard His voice in the wind. Now everything is wrong, and I wait for a miracle, a magical event that would change my life; some kind of sign from heaven, like in the Bible stories Joyce would always read to us. Seas parted, the dead were raised, blind eyes miraculously opened. Surely, there must be a miracle for me somewhere at this altar.

As I open my eyes and take the time to look around, there is a group of people surrounding me, touching my shoulder; still praying. I realize I was wrong. There is no judgment in their eyes, only compassion. I feel safe, accepted, and in time, I begin to experience the love of Christ in a new way. For the first time in a long time, I feel I have a place to belong; this is in fact, the miracle. If I am going to stay clean and sober, I need the people of God; I need the church. Healing will begin here—with the support of a community of Christian believers: The body of Christ.

The Idols of Pain

"This is slavery, not to speak one's thought." ~*Euripides*

Several months later in that same year, Leon is released from prison and comes to live with us for a few months. His mandatory sentence for the petty crime years ago had come with severe repercussions, including getting into more trouble and becoming more isolated, depressed, and angry. Leon and I make up for lost time, talking late into the morning hours while everyone is asleep. Injured during his incarceration, Leon describes prison life as he has experienced it. I listen. His hunched posture and downcast face seem to reveal the seasons of his repeated incarcerations. Like a guppy in a large pond of piranhas, he tells me about a broken system where, steel bars have taken the place of the chains of slavery, and prison guards, much like the desensitized traffic lights, just "doing their jobs" with no regard for the sanctity of human life. The rage of seeing him arrested all those years ago resurfaces as story after story reveals the hellish halls of the so-called justice system. As he continues to explain, his eyes look as though they are still locked away. I watch his mouth cave crookedly to one side of his face. While in prison, he got into a physical altercation that broke his jaw. Now, his jaw has healed that way; what a concept— a cruel travesty.

"It doesn't hurt anymore," he says after I ask him about it. "I did not steal a TV, Sandra. I did not take anything. I am telling you the truth. I can't believe Mama believed them. That hurts more than anything—she believed them cops. God help me, sis," he sighs heavily. The serrated lines across his jaw fall to one side. He drops his head in his hands. I have never doubted him. But, after all these years, I question the use of a corrections system that appears to destroy far more than it corrects.

"I believe you, Leon. I have always believed in you."

On August 19th, 1986, my 19th birthday arrives, and I help members set up the chairs for service at the Upper Room Church. The new journal entry in my Bible today is short yet meaningful: *I am so happy. Thank you, Jesus.* While the choir sings "I Got Joy," I clap my hands in praise. The burns on my fingers heal, and the black phlegm I used to cough up is almost gone. Grateful for the love and support of a community of believers, I celebrate sobriety.

Only God knows my heart, this feeling of joy and peace; only He could give this to me. I'm thankful. Once again, I can see my children's faces, hear their laughter and feel their sweet kisses. The blur of intoxication is gone, and I feel alive again.

After church, Linda comes over to visit. When we are together, time rewinds over us—opening a magical umbrella that allows us to become little girls again. We sit under it, laughing, talking, and singing all the Barry Manilow songs we fell in love with when we were children. Line by line, we know all the lyrics, every single word. His music makes everything feel new, like starting over.

"I wish Joyce were here right now," I tell her.

"Me too, Sandra." Linda sighs.

When Joyce is not sick, she stays busy working. And when she is not working, she seems to want to be alone. *The need for solitude runs in the family.* Later that night, Leon goes to bed. I sit in my room, holding LiSandra on my lap, Casita on the right, and BJ on my left. Singing to them before bedtime makes them happy, especially Casita. All dimples, she holds onto her brother and hums along with the melody. LiSandra looks up, smiles and coos while I hum the song from church tonight, "I Got Joy." Casita and little BJ lean on my lap, talking baby talk to their little sister. She giggles softly, looking up—always looking up. Casita holds her hand and smiles back at her. Their happiness means the world to me. My children are all I have; they are everything. But it seems, as long as life persists, so too will the storms. I could have never imagined it would be the last night I'd sing to my baby girl.

August 20th, 1986

Bruce comes out of the room, looking as if he is sleepwalking through a nightmare. It is early morning; the time when the sky is still and when you are not sure if you are sleep or awake.

"LiSandra is cold; she is not breathing!" His words stab me straight through the heart. In slow motion, I stand up, thinking I cannot be awake. Frozen solid to the floor, I am unable to process the overwhelming anxiety that paralyzes every part of me. Nothing makes sense. From shock and denial, everything shuts down inside me. There is no phone in the house; Bruce runs to the neighbor across the hall to call 911. My feet try to move toward my children's room. They cannot.

The paramedics arrive in what seems like seconds. They rush in past me, still frozen in disbelief of what is happening. The world slows to a dream's pace. With the next breath, I disconnect, convincing myself this must be a dream. *I am asleep. And when I awake, I will realize this was only a dream. Everything is okay. You are dreaming, Sandra. Just wait. In a few minutes, you will wake up, and all will be okay.*

The authorities take the family outside while they complete a preliminary investigation. I move mindlessly, detached, shattered into tiny floating pieces, like particles in outer space. Nothing registers until I watch the paramedics coming out the apartment door. I need to see my baby, but my body cannot move. I want to pick her up and tell her that I am here. Nothing makes sense; *I was just at church last night. Singing and clapping my hands, praising God for his many blessing, for life, for health, for sobriety.* Now, I watch the paramedics walk out of my apartment pushing a gurney, where a white sheet covers the small frame of a life, I once carried inside of me. *What is happening? Where are they taking my baby? God, what is going on now? Only You, God, can answer this for me. Where are you! Answer me!*

God is silent. Long after I receive the medical report, the questions still go unanswered.

The autopsy reveals the cause of death to be asphyxiation. Later I was told about SIDS, Sudden Infant Death Syndrome. The details show infant mortality affects six out of every 1,000 births in the first year of life and is higher among African American babies. I cannot accept the facts of the reports. All my life, I have believed every adversity was my fault. I cannot escape the scourge of self-blame: I should have done something! She was mine; why didn't I hear that she needed me. The depression from LiSandra's death is more than I could endure.

In denial, I lose touch with reality, refusing to believe LiSandra is gone. I relive the event, becoming afraid of the morning, dreading the dawn. In my mind, every morning, I see the gurney. A white sheet moves past me, but she is not there. Only a dream.

Despair.

Boyd Funeral Home takes care of the cost of LiSandra's burial service. The church fills with family and friends to mourn her passing. I cannot remember who came or who performed the eulogy. I only remember wanting to sing to her again. *"Because He lives, I can face tomorrow…"* I sing the song at her funeral. It is a song I learned from my sister Joyce a long time ago. I need her now more than ever, but in the grip of despair, I can't remember the faces around me or if she was there or not. The world looks hazy, like clouds sleeping on the ground. It is hard to see anything except for the delicate flowers, made of white cottony lace, adorning LiSandra's casket. At her gravesite, I wait on God. I have questions only He can answer. But God is still quiet today. The only sound is the clanking of the pulley lowering the snowy white casket into the ground. Black dresses and suits move across the dark green grass towards the cars parked on the reserved path of the Forest Lawn Cemetery.

"What is happening," I whisper in the wind, staring out over the graveyard, refusing to move away from my daughter's grave.

Linda takes my shoulder and pulls me into hers, "I'm so sorry Sandra." She pauses as if looking for more words to say. She wraps her arms around me and drops her head on my chest. I lay my head on Linda's shoulder and close my eyes. Strange, but I cannot cry right now; I need answers.

"Where are you, God?" I whisper, wanting to hear His voice, needing to find reason in the senselessness of it all. No fireflies, no tunnels, nothing can change what has happened. "Why God?" I ask, before vanishing into nowhere. I disconnect where no one can find me. I drift back in time.

Back to Tampa, where my mother's face lit up every time Joyce would take us to visit the family store, where my dad's Old Spice cologne would fill his barbershop and my heart with the scent of Christmastime. But this is not Tampa, and I am not a little girl anymore. This is where I am, my fate, my reality.

After the funeral, I hear the prayers of my church, family, and friends around me, but it will not be enough this time. I cannot stand this thorn, this pain. Unable to deal with the heartache of losing my daughter, I fall farther than I have ever been. I fall into a despair so bottomless that the days' pass and I am holding diapers and a baby bottle, walking aimlessly toward a voice that I swear is hers, calling me. But she was too young to speak; the delusions grow worse. Consumed by life, haunted by death, I disappear into the night.

I relapse.

The candle's flame chokes and flickers in the stale dead air. Not long ago, F.P.L. turned off the utilities. No payment, no electricity. I stare at the flame, going in and out of lucidity. Weeks pass after LiSandra's funeral, and someone is knocking on the front door. I stumble up to the peephole. It is Pastor and Sister Butler.

I don't open the door. They are saying something, but I am too wasted to focused long enough to hear the words coming from the other side. I stay quiet so they won't hear me, but I think they can smell the smoke and alcohol seeping through the doorframe. A master of disguise, a keeper of secrets, I sway like a ship without a sail near the eyehole. *When are they going to leave?* Their persistence tells me they know I am in here alone, and in an unredeemable state of relapse—slipping further away. My children are with family members, and I have convinced myself that my prediction would soon come true. *I will not see twenty years old.* It would be better if Casita and BJ forget about me now, while they are still young.

"We are praying for you Sister Sandra. We love you." I hear Sister Butler say. Her voice mixed with sadness and faith. I drop my head, and they soon leave. I stagger back to the round kitchen table, slightly upset. All the knocking blew my high. But I soon recapture it. Candlelight glows in front of me, and with each hit of cocaine, I lift away, past the shores of this earth with all its heartache. Through the haze of smoke, I see my brothers and sisters sitting on top of the stairs in Tampa. A fierce thunderstorm took out the power. Joyce lit a candle so we could see in the dark. But then again, more than the candlelight, it was the stories she told us, and the songs she sang that brightened the stairway during the power outages.

In despair, the world grows darker, and the downward spiral becomes an unrestrained jump—into freefalling. Two idols wait for me on the kitchen table. One sits in a small plastic bag and the other in a bottle of MD 20/20; they both promise to take all the pain away. I wait for answers that never come. When I am high enough, drunk enough, and numb enough, nothing else matters. I seek refuge from the gale-force winds I have no power to calm or control. I don't bother to pray anymore. Nothing makes sense. A hit from the crack pipe and all the unanswered questions fall into a deep sleep. Exhaling, I stare into the candlelight, watching the flame twist as the smoke blows pass it. My hands stop shaking. Every hurt and pain, I stuff it way down inside until I forget where I left it.

I take a long gulp of MD 20/20 between hits of cocaine. I had stolen the wine from the corner store near State Road 7. Slipped it right underneath my jacket pocket when the cashier turned his back to get cigarettes for a paying customer. The booze takes the edge off the cocaine, which I also stole. Just so you know, never turn your back on a crackhead. A dealer turned his back on his stash when an unmarked police car strolled near the back parking lot near 27th Avenue and Sunrise Boulevard; that's when I nabbed it. Kay took me by the high-traffic drug area some time ago. Addicts never forget the best areas to score dope. Like thieves, there is no honor among addicts and dealers. Selfish bloodsuckers, we take what we need and worry about the consequences later.

During the next drug run, I will pay the price for the crack I stole. I'm not sure which was more foolish: stealing from a crack dealer or returning to the same drug-infested neighborhood to score more dope; a crack-headed move only an addict could understand. The beating did not bother me so much. Through the years, my tolerance has increased. And besides, if I am going to get beat up anyway, I prefer to get beaten up by someone I do not know.

A flick of a lighter—I breathe in, taking another hit and soon, nothing else matters. The bruises, my car that I traded for crack, not even my next breath; nothing matters.

Life is but a dream, and just as soon as I wake up, I will be where I was before; the place before I had a memory, before my awareness of the world, before I ever took form in my mother's womb and took my first breath. Then, I will wake up safe and sound. There, I will be, nowhere.

Fiery trials and tribulations happen to each of us in various degrees; no one is exempt—we all have a story. Seasons of test and trial comes as a result of the human condition of sin; the thorns and thistles are a part of life. The voice of God speaks through the penned words in John 16:33,

"I have said these things to you, that in me you may have peace. In the world, you will have tribulation. But take heart; I have overcome the world." We often look for a reason why things happen, needing to make sense of it all. But that's where we fall. We can only survive when we forsake reason and embrace faith. With faith in God, we will overcome! If only we learn to run to the Cross of Christ; there we will find what nothing else can supply. We will find the *reason* why He came. Jesus offers us peace that surpasses all understanding.

Cracked Houses

"Perhaps the greatest social service that can be rendered by anybody to this country and to mankind is to bring up a family."
~*George Bernard*

Since the last relapse, Bruce has come after me more times than I can count. On the run, I find new places to hide from life and from him. His techniques don't work anymore. Whether he uses threats or his fist, he soon learns I will outrun it all. By now, I am good at it—a master of escape.

The pattern repeats week after week, month after month until the present reality mingles into new levels of insanity. Running is my weapon. Under the shroud of night, I disappear. Like my old Raggedy Ann doll, I smile with a painted face, but beneath the wide grin and fixed stare is a solid rage. And if I am going to die, I might as well be in on the plot to take my life. Flick, inhale, no future. In my skewed perception, nothing else exists in the world except for the tormenting pain and the shame that drives me to relive the past as if it is happening now.

I find myself wandering back to the same crack houses I once frequented; the door is always open. Crack houses are like cemeteries; the only difference is the dead still breathe. In the desperation of the insatiable cravings, the addiction drives me out from the crypt of the crack house, into the night where I do whatever it takes to escape the past. Ash and bone of lost souls wander within the tombs of childhood wounds and suppressed pain. Unkempt homes, abandoned buildings, and occasionally the apartment of a fellow crackhead all become my temporary shelters. In time, my addiction consumes everything. As with most addictions, crack cocaine demands all. Cars, homes, family, friends, your dreams, your life; all is sacrificed at its altar. In my addiction, I exchange the pain for a formless genie that moves, shifting into shapes of rapture and reprieve.

In the gutters and alleyways that lead to the crack houses, deals with the devil play out in the dark shadows of secret heartache. Under the dim streetlights, I find out that pain is a merciless pimp. Wild beasts trolling the street can smell a wounded heart from miles away; perhaps that's why runaways are easy prey. Pain demands worship. Its rules are scandalous, and it will cause its victims to forfeit tomorrow believing we only have today.

And in the throes of sorrow and addiction, tomorrow never comes.

I met Samantha on a crack binge during my last relapse. Those who know her call her Sam. I find her again and stay a few days at her house to hide and get high. No one will ever find me here. But I never get too comfortable. Like a nomad, even before my time in foster care, moving from place to place feels normal. No matter where I am, I anticipate the next run.

Samantha is a different type of addict. An overweight middle-aged woman—late fifties, early sixties maybe, it is hard to tell. To see her out on the street, you would never know she uses. Whenever I visit, there are usually people over getting high. Some pull at the lint on the carpet, while others stare nervously out of the window: the usual positions crack cocaine forces us to assume. Sam has the composure of a queen bee and everyone in the house, whether high or jonesin' for another hit, respects her. She ignores their paranoia, takes a hit off the pipe, and shuffles a stack of playing cards. It's hard to tell if she is high because her smooth demeanor never changes.

Tonight, I prepare to go out on a drug run. I place the crack pipe on the side table and sit up straighter when Sam asks me to go. A swallow of booze brings me down low, just enough to feel my feet touch the ground. After being such a monumental failure in life. I needed to get this right. Get the drugs, get back, and hear her say, "Good job." I want to know someone sees me as more than just a mess-up. She takes another hit and passes it to me. Her cards shuffle slowly near the small square table. She leans back into a wide white sofa and hands me some cash.

"Hurry back; be careful, the police are out heavy tonight."

"Yes, ma'am. I'll be right back."

You never know who's watching you. The crack hideouts near the Williams brothers' turf is a well-organized enterprise where drug dealers carry guns and dare anyone to come in disturbing the peaceful high of their customers. I circle the block looking for a sign; any indication that tells me the cops have not shut down operations for the night. I see a man standing near the edge of the dark, dusty path. He spots me before I see him. A quick inconspicuous nod tells me they are open for business. Rumor is the young brothers have an entrepreneurial drive that could parlay a $20,000 kilo of cocaine into a few hundred thousand in less than a month. The sale of heroin and marijuana adds to the revenue stream, making their illicit industry a one-stop shop. Whether the rumors are true or not—the larger the cash flow, the greater the consequences from rival drug dealers and undercover cops. We learn to watch our back when we play this decadent game. Whether a dealer or a junkie, there is an unchangeable truth; the end is the same. No one will come right out to tell you, but the rules of the game are simple: there are no rules. Sooner or later, we will lose.

With tunnel vision, I head straight to the back street, never once looking behind me. Impulse-driven, I don't care about the consequences. The vicious events of my life leave me reckless and numb to any repercussions that may come because of my actions. I have only one agenda: get the drugs, get back to Samantha's house, get wasted, and repeat as often as necessary. I park my car on a side street, making it past the first set of watchful eyes. A few steps away, my luck runs out. The business-minded brothers have a security guard who, ironically, believes I am an undercover cop and refuse to let me pass to buy the eight ball of cocaine I came for. I stood there for a moment with a 'you-got-to-be-kidding-me' look on my face. He cannot be serious. My stomach starts to reel.

Sam is waiting. The other crackheads at her house are waiting. I have their money and need to get back before she starts to think something went wrong. Going to another drug house to score is out of the question. After the first time I was hustled into buying synthetic dope from a crackhead posing as a dealer, I learn a hard lesson: only buy from dealers you know. But the sobering fact of the drug culture is that you never really know anyone. Remember, the code of honor—it does not exist.

The security guard has a good reason for his suspicions. The sheriff's office was casing the area near the Williams brothers' territory during that same time. For months, the suppliers, the dealers, and the buyers had been under police surveillance. But in the sick mind of an addict, nothing else matters. I need to get back to Sam. Just then, one of the Williams brothers steps out from the shadows of the trees that line the back trail.

"Let her pass. She's okay. I've seen her before." I held back a sigh of relief until I was well on my way, feeling his eyes on me as I walk through another dark path onto a dim lit porch. Getting to the actual hideout seems like a maze, which the dealers have changed with every new hint of suspicion. I cannot move fast enough to get back to the car. *I am not about to be busted.* Now, getting back with the dope means more to me than the next high. I remember wanting to get *this* right, wanting Sam to believe in me. But truth be told, my presence in her home, or any other crack house for that matter is only a means to an end. We are all on the take, each person in his or her own way. Cracked houses, broken lives; we become the very thing that we most despise. That night, I make it back to Samantha's house. After a few hours, I make another run. On and on it goes, set on reactive, I will keep running until I can outrun the hunters of my past. I will continue to chase the next high because my addiction gives me control over my demise. Chasing smoke offers a twisted sense of power, where I get to take part in what fate had started in my youth. It appears there is some truth to the old adage: "If you can't beat them, join them" — a pathetic excuse that allows you to go along to get along.

In the war on drugs, there are no allies. There is only greed. The word on the street is not make-believe; this is the real story. Greed runs a two-way cash market, where both the police and the dealers vie for the spoils. There are copious accounts of cops busting dealers, and taking the drugs and the money, not as evidence but personal profit. Once, I had gone to buy crack from a nickel-and-dime dealer Kay introduced me to just off of Broward Boulevard. Minutes before I had gotten there, the cops had raided the place. The door was busted wide open when I arrived. The residue of powder cocaine spilled over the table and floor. Every piece of furniture was broken or turned upside down. A few onlookers told me what happened just minutes before. The place was ransacked by raiders — undercover cops on the take. They claimed the spoils for the sake of their own idea of law and order. It seems if we try hard enough, we can justify just about anything.

A shirtless boy who looked to be about 16 had said, "They didn't take everyone to jail, but they drew their guns, told us to get down, and pocketed the dope and cash." As I drove away, I could still see the debris of broken pieces of furniture. In the rearview mirror, I remember the familiar scene of a cracked house I lived in long ago as a child. My doll somewhere stuffed in a garbage bag. Angry words like gunfire blasted through the air. My mother had had enough, and my dad was nowhere to be found. Today, driving away, chasing smoke, I'm reminded of a place called home.

In this gravity, time does not exist. I continue to make runs, get high, and take risks; it's all a part of the game. Crack cocaine weaves its black magic in my mind. Surely my young children have forgotten about me by now, and I pray their father moves on and leaves me the hell alone. My entire family has given up on me, so I believe — mostly because I have given up on myself. Drug addiction, like Rumpelstiltskin, offers to spin gold out of the tattered threads of my existence in exchange for my soul. But I lost my soul a long time ago. I remember the day she flew away, leaving me underneath the sick rhythmic thrusts of a monster. I have no soul to offer. I will trade what's left; whatever it takes.

The trade with addiction greedily accepts what I have. Women, men, or both join in where acts of decadence let you know just how deep the rabbit hole of sin can go. The men repulsed me; the women, I revered. I learned years ago that my body is not my own. Sex, from the beginning, had never belonged to me, but to a demon of lust, and now, to the idol of pain. Nothing really matters anyway.

Drug addiction is a prison more formidable than Alcatraz. I live within the barbed wire fence of its control. And now, when I am too tired from the lack of sleeping and eating, too broke to buy more dope, and too numb to care that I am wasting away, I stare up from the filthy floor of a crack house, remembering how I was once loved.

I think of Joyce. Her soft kisses and calming lullabies echoes across my deaden senses. Then, a group of crackheads yell and scream in the next room over from me in an abandoned building. I hear a tussle, someone points a gun; more fighting erupts, and all the while I sit staring into nowhere, looking at my reflection in the dusty window, humming the words to a song about a bluebird flying over a rainbow. Although I am numb to everything around me, I can still hear the words Joyce spoke long ago; words, like seeds planted in the soil of my childhood, "No matter what, you must trust God."

But too much has happened, and it's too late now. I feel abandoned, trapped inside a never-ending nightmare of a stormy existence. Tears fall, and I turn away from the window.

In time, I dry my eyes and keep moving, going back to the cracked houses, searching among the rubble for something that was lost a long time ago. Roadman's daughter, I stay true to the lineage of apathy and addiction. Watching the replay of history, I wait to see the little girl with braids in her hair, ten jackstones in her hand, bouncing a small red ball. But she doesn't come any more; not even in my imagination. I don't know how to rescue her, to save her, but I need to find her, if only to say, I'm sorry.

The Wrong Enemy

War on Drugs – 1987

By the end of 1986, I have found myself on the opposite side of America's war on drugs. The surge of crack cocaine has reached epidemic proportions as it spreads across the country.

The epidemic ravaged the lives of nearly 5.8 million people in 1985. President Nixon declared his "War on Drugs" in 1971; even so, the problem skyrocketed. Consequently, by the start of President Reagan's term, the drug hysteria was at an all-time high. His solution to the bleeding epidemic was to expand the war on drugs to unparalleled proportions: lock up offenders, and in some cases, throw away the key. The number of people in jail for illicit drug use was about to include one more crackhead.

Crack cocaine is public enemy number one, and the nation rages war on the elusive smokescreen of a "drug problem." I often wonder if this nation has ever considered the underlying issues surrounding the disease of drug addiction itself, and its self-destructive powers. Addiction has more to do with the individual, not the substance in and of itself. Blinded to the real enemy, politicians shoot in the dark at a mammoth problem and completely miss the mark. They declare war on the wrong enemy. It is often the inner pain that feeds the addiction.

Soon, Nancy Reagan, who I would like to believe was well-intentioned, starts her highly publicized campaign of "Just Say No" to drugs. I would've liked to have had a conversation with her, a woman to crackhead discussion about the zero-tolerance policies and her Band-Aid solutions to an epidemic that needed deep emotional surgery.

I would have liked to ask her if compassion played any part in the decision-making process that would affect so many lives. Moreover, I want to ask her if she could fathom the repercussions of having her voice and body stolen by wolves. Sold away in a flesh market where evil wears a joker's grin and yellow eyes. The rage waits for the day of vengeance, and until then, the victim's wilts, forced to linger between the reality of what has happened and the sweet void of insanity. Though I highly doubt the Secret Service permits crackheads in the White House, I would have liked to explain. On the other hand, if the policymakers have never experienced addiction, it is almost impossible to understand.

In my world, the word "no" does not exist. The threat of "Just Say No" or get locked up for a minimum of five to ten years, depending on the drug offense, is of little to no consequence. The disease of addiction has already imprisoned me, trumping the fears of my past. The empty values of this seen-and-not-heard culture make me a prime candidate for the government's idea of correction, while harsh drug policies all but reject the notion that educational programs just might make a positive impact on their war on drugs. But there is something more behind this drug war. Something crafty hides behind the smoke and devastation of crack cocaine.

In the same year, President Reagan enacts the Anti-Drug Abuse Act. The policy includes stricter penalties for dealers and drug users. The government spends over $1.7 billion to fight an enemy that methodically has found its way from the coca leaf fields of South America and pass border control to infiltrate the impoverished streets of America. One must wonder about the incredible ability of the shrewd coca leaf. Like many other destructive vices, it magically finds its way, debarking cargo ships and planes to infiltrate the nation's communities. Particularly the inner-city streets, where poor minorities struggle to survive. It creates the perfect conditions to decree a different kind of slave-trade.

The lethal flow of crack cocaine turns ghettos into death camps. And while crackheads like me— poor, black, and uneducated—pursue the next high, others are pursuing the truth behind the lies. Reporters and journalists begin to ask probing questions about the trail of cocaine in America. Journalist and investigative reporter Gary Webb, along with other community leaders, ponder the facts behind the influx of crack cocaine in the nation. There are floating suspicions of a dark alliance between the government and the pipeline of cocaine, which leads directly to the African American communities. Suspicions turn into allegations that try to find and expose the dirty politics behind the blood diamonds of crack cocaine.

Only a corrupted government could be involved in such a cold-blooded conspiracy. Is it all propaganda—half-truths, seeking to vilify government officials while side-stepping the more critical issues of poverty and the lack of educational opportunities, social programs, and employment in a post-Civil Rights America? Is there a drug epidemic or a systematic master plan to reinvent the idea of free labor and control once again?

In any case, the devastation of crack in America creates

another kind of holocaust, where a systematic extermination of the weak and the poorest communities implode. From the west coast to the east, corruption has no boundaries. Families, life's, souls, all stolen, imploding at the hands of organized greed. Whether imported by the government, the CIA, Colombia's cocaine cartels, or aliens from another planet—all of America would pay a high price. Addiction does not discriminate. The crack cocaine explosion in America causes an unprecedented chain of events no one could have predicted, and no one can stop.

The government has tough decisions to make. *What to do about the drug problem? How do we bring an end to the war on drugs? Education or incarceration?* The government makes the decision to build more prisons. In the heat of the war on drugs, plea bargains are few, no excuses are permitted, and little to no mercy is given to many drug offenders.

There is an insidious system governing this traffic-light society. It hangs high in the air, abusing its authority, disregarding human life, profiting off lost souls. The ideas of counseling and educational programs are all but overlooked. Perhaps because they would have proven unprofitable to the multibillion-dollar prison investors who need to keep their plantations filled—isn't that the reason why prisons are built? Arrest after arrest, the heart of the people bleeds while America takes its bow, as it reigns supreme as the country with the highest incarcerations of its own citizens. Over half of those incarcerated citizens are impoverished, uneducated, African Americans; the descendants of slaves. History replays its anthem of greed, oppression, and slavery.

Long before crack cocaine entered my life, riding on its Trojan horse to rescue me, I had met Becky and Jean. We used to work together at the Burger King on Oakland and Andrews Avenue after I left the beach franchise. Becky is a cute brunette with pale skin and beautiful blue eyes. Jean is a hippy redhead with the kind of friendly personality you often see from country folk. Jean's son, who is a carbon copy of his mother, had played with Casita while I cleaned the lobby tables and finished my shift. I have missed walking with Casita across the street to the Polar Cup shop for lemonade slushies, listening to the sweet tone of her voice. She'd smile so big, saying "thank you mama" with a piece of the lemon already in her mouth. I have missed the brain freezes we'd get when we took turns feeding each other spoonfuls of the lemon slush. But it's all gone now. Of all the things stolen from my life, my addiction stole the gift of time, seeing my children's smile, hearing their laughter, feeling the warmth of their touch. It's all gone.

Life is but a dream.

Set on reactive, I will stay on the run. Like the ocean's tide, the memories flow in and out. I remember the drunken nights my father came home after being gone for days. Alcohol addiction stole his heart, his smile, his kiss, and our melody on the moon. In the flow of addiction, I follow the footprints. After stealing from the register, I never go back to Burger King. The last time I had seen Jean, she was holding her son in her arms, telling me how worried she was about me. I was too far gone to respond to her nudging me to get help. That last time I saw Becky, we had been in a crack house together. She had a needle in her arm, asking a man if he was sure all the air bubbles were out before he shot her up again with heroin.

In the War on Drugs, politicians have it all wrong. There is an enemy, but it is not a drug, nor anything else outside the human heart. The chaos in this country has a sure source—a reason for all the cruelty, broken homes, greed, and lust. For countless centuries, it remains unseen, hidden stealthily away below the surface, like the roots of a sycamore tree; it goes deep.

Since my youth, I've heard the story of Adam, Eve, and a snake in a tree. It seems the same rebellion exists. 1 John 2:16 teaches that every malady of sin known to man comes from within; the lust of the eyes, the lust of the flesh, and the pride of life. I remember, as a child growing up in Tampa, at the old house built on top of a cemetery, Joyce rebuked an evil spirit called satan. In the Bible, God calls man's disobedience: sin. Stuck in a world that is upside-down, I feel the constriction of both, crushing around me. Still, I run to it; set on self-destruction.

Consequently, Gary Webb, the American investigative journalist and author of *'Dark Alliance,'* is blacklisted by the CIA for his reporting of the crack cocaine epidemic in America. Sadly, years later, he would be found dead in his home in Sacramento County. The report is a questionable "suicide" with two gunshot wounds to the head. The rumors were widespread about the branch of government where men, like coiled reptiles, strike against anyone who dares to try and prevent their covert operations. Century after century, from sea to shining sea, the accounts are all the same. History repeats, with stories of corruption and greed and snakes that speak from the high governmental branches of the trees.

In the grand scheme of things going on in this world today, it appears Solomon's words in scripture are true.
"There is nothing new under the sun."

Drug Sting

June 1987

Almost 20, and in my mind, time is almost up. On the run, I couldn't care less about the war on drugs. There's been a war going on inside me since God knows when. The hallucinations have gotten worse until schizophrenic-like symptoms bombard my inner world. I cannot remember when it happens, but I go home. I want to see my children before the voices make good on their threats. My clothes are two sizes smaller, and I avoid mirrors, light, and food. Bruce doesn't bother fighting with me. He sees how bad it is, and brings food to the bedside table, glances at my withered frame, and walks away. In my mind, I am beating fate at its own game—I am dying; I am winning. I remember feeling that Bruce somehow loves me despite his anger. Why else would he leave food on the bedside table for me to eat? Then I remember Edward, a rat named Ben, and the mixed signals, like the smells of perfume and cigarettes. The conflicting messages are not easy to forget.

I don't want my children to see me in the state I'm in, but my last wish is to tell them that I'm sorry for everything. I am nineteen years old, and I'm afraid that even God Himself cannot love a wretch like me. And with less than a year left on my self-imposed death sentence, I start the countdown in my head. Pastor and Sister Butler have come over to an apartment we have moved to off 27th Avenue—an apartment I hate more than all the others because of the thick backwoods that brought huge recluse spiders inside.

"How have you been, Sandra? We have been praying for you." They sit close together on the couch. The look on their faces is serious. They try to hide it, but I hear the hard sighs in between the words.

"Is there anything we can do to help you?" Sister Butler asks. Sitting across from them, I do not know where to start, what to say. I hear her talking to me, but I also hear voices coming from the faces on the wall behind her and Pastor Butler. Threatening faces that no one else seems to see. *Why can't they see them?* I fidget with agitation, feeling something crawling on me. And I just want to be left alone.

There are faces inside the walls, watching, waiting for me to say something wrong. I swallow hard, listening. *You better keep your mouth shut! Tell anyone, and you're dead! You are almost 20. Time is almost up! You will never be anything more than a worthless misfit, a drug head, a crack whore.* I shake, trying to turn away from the sound, but the faces surround me. *You had better run. Lock the door. Tell your mother, and I will kill you both. You are going to learn to like it.* The faces push out from the wall. I shift unsteadily away to the corner of the sofa. *God, I want to disappear. I am not well.* I stare out toward the space in between the kitchen and the hallway.

Sister and Pastor Butler patiently wait, but I do not have an answer. The question is too complicated. I have no clue of what I need, and I'm sure from the looks of it, I have lost touch with reality. But crazy or not, there are some things you never forget.

I remember the voices. Bruce stands nearby. His hand to his head—he looks tired. In the next few moments, I see him moving towards the kitchen. Bruce appears different. He looks at me with more pity than anger, but crazy doesn't equate to stupid—I know it is just a matter of time. The voices tell me to get out of the house. Pastor Butler takes my trembling hands and begins to pray. I do not remember the words of the prayer. I only remember a peaceful mist descending around us, filling the room. *Why haven't they given up on me yet?*

Slowly after, the voices, the faces, and the sounds fade out. I begin to feel peace for the first time in a long time. Looking up from my folded hands, I notice Sister Butler's eyes are soft with compassion and concern; there is no trace of judgment. She does not say too much tonight, but her eyes speak a message I will always remember. Her peaceful energy draws me. In the days following my breakdown, Pastor and Sister Butler and many other church members kept praying for me and believing for my deliverance even when I did not have the strength to care or believe for myself.

In the weeks and months that follow my recovery, we move yet again, and I try to fight the urges to use, especially after every violent episode. I want to believe Bruce can change, but his actions always speak so much louder than his words.

In the winter of 1986, my weight balloons to over 200 pounds. Where I can't smoke, I gorge myself, eating to replace the urges; trying to stay clean and sober. Time shifts, and I learn to play by life's rules without question or a crack pipe. The storms keep raging, but something is changing. I stayed home after the last fight with Bruce, wanting to stay close to my children, I did not resist his need to take whatever causes him to be angry out on me. The sand in the hourglass of my mind is running out. Chronic anxiety causes my heart to race, even while I am standing still. Trying to make up for lost time, I store up enough kisses and hugs from my children to take on my journey, wherever the last heartbeat sends me.

June 1987

I lay on the floor, between the wall and the bed. Bruce takes a hanger from the closet and threatens to beat me if I do not tell him the truth. He accuses me of stealing his stereo and selling it for crack. I remember lying there terrified yet enraged because of the false accusation. I think of my brother Leon, falsely accused, thrown into prison for something he did not do. I plead and beg for Bruce to believe me.

"I did not take a stereo. What would I do with a stereo?" I question. I am clean and sober. I am home every day, and I am pregnant. "I didn't do it," I beg. It all falls on deaf ears; he doesn't hear me.

I tuck myself into a tight ball before it begins. Being falsely accused almost hurts worse. When he finally walks away, his arrogance inflates, and after all these years, I remain perplexed at how he so easily transforms. One moment he is caring, laughing, making plans for a better future. The next, he beats me as if I am not the same person he was just tapping a tambourine with at church.

Memories of Tampa and the fights between my mother and father begin to emerge. I relive it all over again, as if it never ended, but transferred. Bruce knows I will never fight back. I do not resist because I am not sure how. I had learned years ago from Roberts's cruelty how to submit, take it lying down, and never tell a soul. I learn to be still and quiet until the darkness washes over me, and my body goes numb. He knows I don't want the children to hear the cries, so I silently scream inside until all I want to do is run away; particularly when his cruelty turns to rape. Still, I do nothing to change it.

June 29, 1987—I can feel the manic emotions firing through my veins as I drive my car on this fateful day. A day over a thousand eyes will sit and witness. Volcanic anger hides behind a polite smile as I make the first stop at Troy's Liquor Store. The desire to get drunk and high is gone, but the rage, self-pity, and bitterness drive me to even the odds the only way I know how. I go through the motions, buying a bottle of Peach Schnapps Liqueur. I see myself putting the bottle on the passenger seat. In the following moments, I tell myself that I cannot drink it. But rage grits its teeth, telling me to go; get high; get even! *Go and leave all the problems behind in a cloud of smoke. Hurry before it's too late.* I want to maintain my sobriety, but I have no defense against this injustice. I drive to chase what has felt familiar — an easy escape. The next stop is the drug house on 15th Street and 27th Avenue.

I don't remember the last time I came here but addicts never forget where to score *good* dope. However, the next series of events are unforgettable; not only for me but also for the thousands of eyes that would be watching TV tonight.

A man walks up to my car. He is wearing a baseball cap, blue jeans, and a red, striped polo shirt. I remember his clean-shaven face, but I do not recognize him, and this time, I don't care. I go through the motions, outside of myself. *I don't want to be here; I don't want to get high. I want to get even,* I think to myself. I want the power to fight back and take control of my life. Self-pity is a sly demon. It sits next to me, reminding me that I am a victim of my circumstances.

"I got them boulders. What you need?" the man wearing the baseball cap asks, leaning into the window. We make the exchange. But nothing feels the same anymore. Just then, I do what I am almost sure no clear-thinking alcoholic has ever done.

I offer him the liqueur I just bought. "Hey, I don't want to drink this. It's yours if you want it?"

The man is facing the street. I lean back and breathe, unsure of what I am doing here again. I think of my children, my unborn baby, my sobriety. I don't want to lose it all, but how else can I even the odds. The man looks at me, but instead of reaching for the bottle, he reaches for his baseball cap, tipping it before backing away. The next run of events happened too fast to remember the details. However, I did not have to worry about missing anything. Whatever I may have missed in the real-time shock of what is an undercover drug sting, is already recording for the evening news.

The police converged at all angles of the car with their guns drawn in my direction. Television cameras and news reporters move in, joining the circus sideshow. "Hands up! Don't move!" The drug dealer is an undercover cop, and the drug sting is captured live, making headlines in the *Sun Sentinel* newspaper. Cuffed by detectives, I hear the familiar refrain of the Miranda Rights.

"You have the right to remain silent."

Got it, I have been silent for years; no problem with that one, I think to myself as the metal cuffs click tighter around my wrist.

"Anything you say will be used against you in a court of law."

Cutting my eyes to the ground, anger building with each

breath. *What the hell!* I think to myself. *No law protected me from the beasts and the madness of this society. The time for words expired a long time ago.* I will remain silent.

"You have a right to consult an attorney before speaking to the police, and blah, blah, and more freakin blah." In my mind, everything he says means nothing.

By this time, I am not listening anymore. The words are empty, meaningless. I have no rights. Rights are for the rich, the white, the corrupt, and the well-pedigreed socialites of this greedy culture. These so-called "rights" are a standard procedure this cop must say to perform his job and uphold the contradicting laws of society; the same society that creates the very monsters it convicts. This cop is just another round-bellied traffic light. The badges and guns do not intimidate me, not from where I come from. I have seen horror and heartache face to face. *What can the law possibly do to me that life has not already done?* Jail is no threat to those who have been locked up for years in their own private prison; unable to break free.

My arrest in the citywide drug sting is more of a welcomed reprieve from the hell called home. The backseat of the police car is just another ride to the Neverland of my life's existence. And in my mind, I believe that in the eyes of these cops and the law, I am just another black, stupid, crackhead who has lost her way and ruined her own life. To these cops, this city, and this world, I am nothing but a lost girl, a useless menace to its *decent* society. I have always maintained the "right to remain silent." Nothing will change that now.

There are no available beds in the Broward County Jail—go figure. I sit on a bare mattress on the floor of the correctional facility. There are no windows to look out of and search for the moon; there is nothing but blank walls. Women of every race and age crowd inside the lockup, jabbering among themselves. I rub my fingers across a creased line on my wrist where the handcuffs have nipped the skin. Guards saunter about like zookeepers, easing up to the cells as if they are a different species from the rest of us. I remember the animals at the pet store my brother Michael and I had visited after school. It seems the staff at the pet store treats cats, dogs, and ferrets with more care, value, and dignity. The guards speak with short words and even shorter tempers, disconnected from any display of kindness or empathy. I don't know why I have expected anything different from the people who robotically work in a system that supposedly correct the destructive behaviors of mankind. *What a joke,* I say, staring out into the open space of the jail and then at the faces of my fellow inmates until the main lights go out. The ramblings quiet down, and between shadows of the light and the darkness, a regretful hush blankets the cells.

A young woman whisper,

"What are you in for?" A dim light glows from the corridor of the windowless room. It casts a soft shadow across her inquisitive face.

"A drug bust," I answer. Her eyes bulge, as she looks me over. Her short-cropped hair frames her attractive oval shaped face.

"You use drugs?"

"Not anymore. Well, I haven't used for a while now."

"You don't look like you belong here." She whispers with a raised brow. I wanted to tell her that I have no idea where I do or do not belong. Spurring noises catches my attention. I turn my head towards the hall of the jail, hearing clicking heels from the boots of a guard patrolling the cells. A memory flashes green. I see Dixie Court projects apartments and the seductive dance of cigarette smoke rising to the roof of a yellow Eldorado. The clicking heels of a Merchant Seaman move in harmony with the guards. More acid; I swallow, pretending to have it all together.

"What did you say? I ask, tilting my head, struggling to keep from zoning out again.

"I asked how many months you are." She says with a bright expression.

"Almost six." I keep my answers short, thinking of the moment my family sees the 6'oclock news. She tells me her name, but I don't remember it. It sounded like a nickname. I don't ask about her arrest. Life has taught me not to ask too many questions, and frankly, in sensory overload, I didn't want to know. Nonetheless, she tells me a part of the story of her arrest. She has no qualms about the charges, stating she will take whatever plea bargain they offer. An undercover detective posing as a John made her an offer she could not refuse. "I needed the money. What are you going to do? You have to survive the best way you can." she says shrugging her shoulders.

My stomach turns, thinking, *Typical of this society: to set you up, not to succeed, but to fail.* Blindside ambushes dressed up in sheep's clothing, you never see coming. Why not impose education as opposed to incarceration? How convenient to create the conditions that maintain the age-old system of greed and oppression. I soon let the thought pass, believing, that maybe, I'm just crazy.

I try not to stare, but she is beautiful. I shift my body on the lumpy mattress as she talks about parents who love and support her, regardless of her rebellious ways.

"Once I get myself settled, I want to finish school, get married, and have some kids. You know, live the good life." She lies back and gets quiet. In the crowded cell, another young girl, eighteen maybe nineteen years old, tells me about a nightmarish event that happened to her years ago, on an ordinary day. She said she was walking in her neighborhood when a neighbor, a few houses down, asked if she wouldn't mind coming inside to help him with his dog. She said he appeared to be a nice person. She went inside. After the door had closed, the man with his two dogs led her to a back room. Both were pit bulls. She said their fangs were all she could see when the man raped her. When he was done, he called them off and allowed her to leave. Just like that; as if nothing ever happened.

She said she never reported the crime, believing it was her fault for going inside his house in the first place.

"I don't trust anyone anymore." She whispered, staring down at the floor. She never told me what she was in for or how long. She didn't have to; the look in her eyes said it all. She is serving life. Almost immediately, we seem to connect. Listening to her terrifying story made my blood boil. I know the foulness of this pain. I live in the prison of its secret every day. Life: that's what we serve; that's what the pain demands. Victims basically assume the numbing position—never telling of the crimes, as if nothing ever happened.

You learn to 'deal with it.' To carry the weight of the ugly truth of what has happened to you, and like a solid iron anvil, you can never put it down. Seen but never heard, the young woman said she saw her rapist a few times after the crime, lurking around the neighborhood. I look away towards the ceiling of the jail cell, enraged, thinking, it never once crossed my mind to report the crimes against me. After so many years of silent shame, the pain and sense of worthlessness become normal. The reality is for every rape that goes unreported; the rapist is free to hunt and hurt again, while victims wilt in a silent bed of thorns. More acid boils inside of me as I think of every offense. Young, black, and uneducated, I knew without question, no one would come to my defense. No roadblocks or alerts go up for misfits like me. I wonder how many are silenced by the shame and society's decree to be seen, and not heard. She said after the rape, she was never the same again. That night, we talked until we ran out of words to say. Only rigid shadows move across the outer corridor.

I close my eyes thinking, is this the way life supposed to be? Is this normal? Like the thorns that grow on the stem of a rose, is this the natural order of things on this planet? Should I get tough, suck it up, and stop questioning everything? The questions follow me to sleep.

Before daybreak, a sharp pain in my side jolts me awake. Unsure of what the day would bring, I sit up on the mattress, pondering the events of my life. Bruce's anger and control have only intensified over the years, though I keep telling myself things would get better. Ironically, I feel safer since my arrest. Here within the confines of a jail cell, I am safely out of his reach. Free from my wild emotions that drive my life impulsively. Perhaps some divine intervention brought me here. Of all the places to find peace, I find it here at the Broward County Jailhouse.

It is not long before Bruce shows up and posts my bail. I wish he would somehow forget I am on the same planet. Once again, I return to his kingdom, believing I have no other choice. Conflicted, I cannot understand this twisted game of abuse and rescue. I stop trying and return to apathy — the easy state of do-nothingness.

Not long after, the day of my arraignment arrives, and I sit before a judge whose nose reaches towards the heavens as if he created it himself. Earlier, before the hearing, a public defender tells me he has been assigned to represent my case before the judge. I cannot afford to pay for an attorney, so as an indigent offender, the government has appointed Mark. I find it interesting that the same government that declares the charges against me appoints a white, blue-suited attorney to work for my best interest.

The Sixth Amendment right to an attorney comes with questionable conditions. Mark gives me the rundown of today's preceding. Alternating between a hand full of papers and his wristwatch, he looks down as he informs me about plea bargains and the charges the state has leveled against me.

"Crack cocaine carries a serious penalty," he says as he bustles through the documents. Incidentally, powdered cocaine carries a lesser charge than freebase. I sit and listen, thinking, *who comes up with this crap.* Not understanding the difference in the possession charges, nor a government who insists its citizens obey rules that it underhandedly violates, I stare obediently at him. I nod on cue, all the while, silently raging. *No crackhead or drug dealer I know owns the planes and ships that smuggle in the billion-dollar supplies of either powder or freebase cocaine in the country. There is a scheming supplier to the desperate demands of every addiction and every form of trafficking.* The rest is a matter of circumstance. Mark goes on to educate me about the court meaning of the terms: innocent, guilty, and no contest. He goes on to explain the implications of how I respond to the charges today. Keeping up with all the gobbledygook is too exhausting. My thoughts wander off as I watch both sides of the courtroom fill up with men and women chatting before court begins.

"Will the defendant please rise?" the bailiff says. I stand. "You have been charged with the possession of an illegal substance." The judge goes on, announcing every ordinance I have broken. His words, like sharp stones, hurl across the courtroom from his noble bench. "How do you wish to plead?"

The room begins to spin until I can see everything at once. Anxiety pushes through the nerves in my face and hands. I twitch. The closed-ended question allows no room for what my heart wants to explain. I try to swallow—I cannot. No matter how I answer, there is no freedom for me, not in this courtroom, not anywhere. The ghosts of the past and present take the witness stand; I alone can see them and hear their unrelenting accusations.

Your honor, she should have never been born. She is weak and worthless! She is a misfit and a menace to this decent society. Lock her black ass up and throw away the key! The voices jeer. And as with so many other times, I believe there must be something wrong with me. Something beyond the voices, addiction, violence, and emptiness. *Why was I born, and why have I survived so much in my life? What is it all about?*

Still, I listen and believe every indictment that reminds me of the past heartache I have caused my parents, the frequent abandonment of my children, and the indelible stains that cover me. I drop my head, wanting desperately to twirl the corner of my blouse around my finger. I do not move. I want to scream out at every offense that has come against my life. I stay silent. The question of "how do I plead," leaves no room for any such explanation. This public defender, this judge, and these people do not know me, or my history. They do not care to ask or find out why. *Why would anyone deliberately choose to destroy his or her own life? Why!*

The question of why is unprofitable. In this courtroom, there can be no excuses, no rhyme or reasons. Answers are black and white—no gray can exist. It is "crime and punishment" in this greedy government. No true advocate pleads my cause. I must deal with it all, face to face. And regardless of what happens today, nothing can right all the wrongs. I am a nineteen-year-old drug offender, sworn to secrecy by the ghosts of the past. And besides, nothing matters anyway because the voices remind me, I will not live to see my twentieth birthday. Time is almost up.

"How do you wish to plead?" The judge asks again. I clear my throat.

"Guilty your honor; I plead guilty."

I will receive no offers of an educational or counseling program from across this judges' noble bench. No positive reinforcement of an advocate or the connectivity of a mentor— someone who has conquered addiction and life and could help guide me out of the darkness of my mind. Instead, The Florida Department of Corrections orders me to complete two years' probation, mandatory drug testing, and community service. The gavel comes down. I walk out of the courtroom and into the world, engraved with a new label; prepared to assume a new position: convicted felon.

God never told us this life would be easy or even fair; however, he did tell us that before there is a problem, He already provides the solution. When the root of bitterness, revenge, and rage overtakes us, God provides a way of escape through the guidance of the Holy Spirit, cautioning us, in John 8:11, to go and sin no more. From the beginning of time, these lessons were intended to teach the law of cause and effect; every action is subject to this unvarying principle; for every action, there is a reaction. Therefore, Ephesians 4:31 instructs us to "Get rid of all bitterness, rage, and anger, brawling and slander, along with every form of malice." We become our thoughts, and if we are not mindful, a root of bitterness will grow alongside our attempts to live pleasing in God's sight, contaminating every effort with the poison of self-righteousness. We must get rid of it; confess and let go of every desire to even the odds. In my life, growing pass these thorns were hard lessons to learn.

Vengeance belongs to God; our calling is to love.

Great Grace

Summer, 1987

Her name means strong and free. Sharletta is a joyful gift God has given me in the year I have believed would be my last. Like a comic book hero from the Justice League, she came into my life on July 10th, 1987. Weeks before my 20th birthday, her tiny fingers lasso tightly around mine. She gazes at me as if she needs to give me a message from someone. She is a sweet little girl with deep brown eyes, wrapped in dark, beautiful skin—like the fertile soil of Africa where diamonds form. Somewhere between my release from jail and her birth, I begin to believe in miracles again.

And then, it will happen days after my 20th birthday comes and goes. My children surround me at the kitchen table. I coddle my newborn, and Casita, now five years old, jumps off the chair and stands in front of me. BJ follows. He is two.

"Mommy, I love you this much," Casita says, stretching her arms to the sides of her body. She holds the position, dimpled cheeks, smiling as though she sees someone else behind my tired eyes, someone that I do not know. She waits for me to stretch out my arms, pick her up, and dance around in a circle the way we used to. I am amazed she has not forgotten, and she makes me smile past the fatigue. BJ stands next to her, mimicking her movements. Their little arms reach out wide in front of me. They cannot have possibly known my fear has come full circle. The voices from my past tell me, time is up. I believe that at any moment something is coming to get me, to hunt me down and finish what it started in my childhood. The fear is very real, and I prepare for whatever will happen. I'm ready.

More isolated, and somewhat of a recluse, I wait. Days trudge slowly, and I secretly conclude my children will not miss a mother they have never known; I believed this for so long. I wait for the ax to fall. *Broken and uneducated, what could I possibly leave behind for my children to remember and build upon.* All I have are thorns and heartfelt words.

"I love you too," I say, looking at their arms stretched out wide, like a small army. Day by day, I try to deal with the problems of life and the decade of storms that continues to come without warning. Meanwhile, my children run to me, arms open wide, declaring a love that appears to keep no record of wrong. In time, their little arms and unconditional love begins to block the entrance of my irrational fears. Then, one day, something changes. I start to realize, that after all this time, I have believed a lie. *I am still here, still alive. Where did the threatening thoughts come from, and why did I think I would die before turning twenty? What caused it?* The unconditional love of my children helped to prove me wrong and made me want to fight the sickness in my mind. The process would take years. The impending doom of death and the chronic condition of life sit side-by-side staring back at me. Both are still the same mysterious forces. But I am changing. I begin to think about the future. A future I had thought would never come. It has been too impossible to believe I could live with the haunting anxiety, the unforgettable memories, and that I can survive it all. And though my mind continues to race against itself, little by little, I am becoming more aware: it is in my mind; not the present reality. *Just breathe*, I say to myself. *Breathe.*

The church fills for morning service. I sit towards the back row with my children next to me while their father sits on the deacon board since becoming ordained at Refreshing Springs. Pastor Bellamy will soon speak. I hold tight to my Bible, flipping through its pages, reflecting through the notes I wrote when I arrived at Simon House and St. Vincent's Home for Girls. It seemed a lifetime ago. I draw a heart next to all the Bible verses Joyce taught me. I miss her, but I know hearing of the craziness of the drug bust in the evening news only causes her more stress than she already has. A big part of me misses my family—the part that never grew up. I push away the thought and begin to write. Writing is an obsession. My pen is a lightning rod, pushing out currents of electrical energy faster than my motor skills can keep up. I learn that I must take notes to stay present or my mind will carry me away into a stupor. For this reason, and to this very day, I keep a pen and pad for note-taking.

Staying present is a constant struggle. When driving, I often get lost; a lot. Every day I must fight to be intentionally mindful and remain in the present to become more aware of what and who is around me. While I hide it well, being present will be a lifelong struggle. The memory bank in my brain forgets everything I do not write down. *Life is moment by moment, and the memories of the past are more real than what is happening now.* I can't explain this to others, especially those who already think they know it all. When someone is talking to me, I am not sure when I leave, how long I been away, or who I was speaking with. My mind wanders down trails of thoughts without my consent. The mental exhaustion makes me more absent-minded and even more standoffish.

For this reason, I like being alone. No one can judge me when I am alone. The solitude understands me—it always listens and allows me to come and go as I please. The social phobia makes me afraid that people will think I'm rude, disrespectful, or just crazy. If only they knew the impossible task of collecting thoughts that scatter like jackstones thrown across the floor, too far away to pick up. If only they knew, perhaps then, they would extend more grace, more patience, more compassion, and not take it personally.

Refreshing Springs Church becomes a refuge. Within the four walls of padded burgundy pews and stained-glass windows, I experience an unconditional love that encourages me to try and lift my head again. I hide the secret of my abuse, telling no one about the fear I have of the man I love and who is supposed to love me. I must honor him and do all I can to be a good wife and mother. I've failed so many times; he is diligent in reminding me of my disappointing actions and looks at me as he always has before. Still, I am my grandmother's girl, and believe it is my duty to honor and obey. After all, he is a hard worker and a good provider. He and his family have been there for my children throughout my battles with addiction. Aside from his controlling behavior and violent temper, he has admirable qualities that make me believe that one day he will change, and the dreadful fear I have of him will go away. For now, I wait.

Through the years, his abusive tendencies reveal an insidious pattern. It seems to have increased with each of my pregnancies. I resist the urge to ask if his father had abused his mother, and if he did mistreat her, how did it make him feel; I dare not ask the questions. Instead, I make excuses for his behavior until I convince myself that it is his right to be angry to the point of losing control. *Perhaps he feels out of control because society has taken so much control away from him, as it has for so many oppressed generations — like old rage demanding vengeance, but it shoots without aiming and takes the aggression out on those most vulnerable.* Or maybe he harbors personal frustration because of his relationship with his own father, which can lead to unpredictable rage. I understand the frustrations because I miss my dad too, but unlike Bruce, I am a runner, not a fighter.

Years ago, while I was living at the Women in Distress shelter, one of the group leaders spoke about the crime of domestic violence, asserting that "men who abuse women feel out of control, and it is a learned behavior from childhood, rooted in the emotional disorder of rejection and lack of confidence. The explosive behavior causes abusers to try to control the most vulnerable people in their life." People like me who will not fight back, who keeps secrets, and who blame themselves for the actions of others. I believe the group leader is right. If someone can learn to be abusive, they can unlearn it, by practicing the opposite: self-control, empathy, and kindness. But abusers must want to learn and practice new skills to gain a greater sense of restraint — it must happen intentionally, or it won't happen at all. Awareness is the key.

Months turn into years, and I reach the end of my probation. From October 1, 1987, to September 30, 1989, I complete my State mandated sentence. I pass every drug test and finally say goodbye to the stiff-necked probation officer who supervised my state probation — another traffic light, just doing his job. He has dutifully reminded me to wear the "Just Say No" button for the length of the probation. During the first year, I had wanted to take that button and toss it to a lonely catfish in the bottom of a riverbank. I had worn it only because it was an order. The button of correction has had no transformational purpose in my life whatsoever. I believe its only use is to humiliate, the same counterproductive goal as locking up humans behind bars with no commitment to correct and change destructive behaviors. *When people are caged and treated less than animals, how can the heart begin to change and evolve?* I often think about my brother's incarceration that left him with a profound sense of emptiness and a broken jaw. I rage at the United States of greed and waste and pray for change. God sees all.

After many years, I journaled the rage.

September — Journal:

Authority must come with responsibility. The authority to detain must also come with the responsibility to effect real change and transformation, not merely crime and punishment. So, America's penal system does more harm than good. The responsibility to educate and counsel offenders is paramount and must be a part of the process, from arrest to release. Understanding why people do what they do is essential to help the process of change begin. What pain and hurts are driving many of the destructive behaviors? It's time to get to the root of the problem! There should be no incarcerations without the motivation to impact positive changes in the lives of offenders. Something is very wrong in this society—something devious. And what of the recidivism rate in this nation, where individuals return to the vomit of what was forced down their throats? This society offers no place for human error and little expectation for redemption. How irresponsible of a nation to punish citizens for crimes, and rightly so for some, nevertheless, make little to no efforts to transform the heart and mind and heal the soul. Some would say it is not the responsibility of the nation to counsel but to cage humans. I disagree. This type of penal system is monstrous, irresponsible, and sadistic. It dehumanizes inmates, with no protection from further violence; some offenders will become more brutal and angrier. My brother, Leon, was violated and brutalized in every way; the details are too heartbreaking to write. How do you treat humans like animals and then release them back into a society where it is almost impossible to fit in and find their way back to feel again, love again, and live again? The prison system is devious and plays by its own set of rules. When greed is the dealer, the hand you're dealt is sure to lose; why has it continued this way? Rules where harsh societal conditions are created to ensure the bunks stay warm in the jail cells, while the fat-pocketed prison owners continue to invest in more prisons—modern-day slavery; different day, same greed feeding on the ignorance, poverty, and pain of humanity. It is no wonder why the moral fabric of this nation continues to decline. I feel blessed to have my arrest behind me. I will live with an arrest record for the rest of my life and the implications of a marred past that will haunt me, making it virtually impossible to get a job as a convicted felon. Still, others live behind bars for a lifetime, many for nonviolent crimes.

Many inmates die behind bars from neglect or at the hands of the very ones who are sworn to serve and protect them. Many of them were innocent, but because no one believed, the grave became their only reprieve—the travesty is beyond reason. How many people break the law because they were young, immature, wounded, mentally ill, or just made a mistake? How many was set-up by a corrupted system? How many did not break the law at all, yet the sham of justice twists its shape into the phrase: "Guilty until proven innocent." It seems in this country there is more faith placed in the training and taming of lions, tigers, and bears than humans. How many more before we evolve, before we understand what being human truly means? When will change come? The multiple accounts of corrupt cops raping, beating, and killing inmates are even more cause to change this inhumane, overcrowded system…now! I pray for change; right here and right now!

What is the objective of the penal system? I often wonder if its motive is more of greed and profit, rather than grace and improvement. The *system* seems to squander every chance to enact *change* but never failed to make inmates pay; even beyond what is reasonable. Eight years, 12 years, 20 years, to life; these sentences prove that there is no correction, no redemption, and no intention of rehabilitation which according to research, takes 3 years to rewire and transform the human brain. But then, when the agenda is profit, the transformation of a person's life yields no gain.

The cycle perpetuates itself at the cost of billions of dollars per year to maintain America's prison system with its cruel protocols; money that could be better used for state-ordered degree programs, education programs, mentorship, and counseling programs. Funding that would address the deep emotional wounds we hide or have no language to express. We must begin to heal this hurting nation; money that could educate citizens and build communities. When people know better, they will often do better, but are they truly taught to do better; are they educated beyond their thorns? On massive scales, the answer is no! Instead, greed rears its ugly head, and more prisons create the next invasion of the body snatchers. Like a gluttonous parasite, greed feeds on human ignorance and frailties. The irony is this: unless all human life is sacred, no life will be sacred — this is the certainty of humanity.

Across the nation, hearts continue to bleed under state-mandated prison sentences and plastic buttons that read "Just Say No to Drugs." What an insult; a mockery! All my life, I have seen people act like traffic lights — just doing their jobs, wearing human clothes, carrying guns and badges, black robes with stuck-up noses in positions of authority with blind control. What happened to compassion, connectivity, true correction, and accountability? Did it ever exist, or have I some mental illness?

Around and around we go on this revolving planet. With all the remarkable innovation in science and technology, humans seem to be devolving; into Neanderthals, stone-hearted cave dwellers; merely, sophisticated beasts.

The Anchoring

"You'll never get to a person's soul until you understand their hurts." ~ *Ravi Zacharias*

In church, two women walk by me, whispering something among themselves, staring me up and down before walking away. In my head, paranoia and suspicion are normal, no matter how distorted the thought. They don't even know me, but all the same, the enemy within, keeps me looking out at the world with distrust. Whatever they have said about me is probably true anyway. But today, I am too tired to care. I brush it off, listening to the music coming from the piano.

As the music plays, Pastor Bellamy walks out towards the wooden podium that stands in the middle of the pulpit. He holds a microphone, and the chords of music begin to rise. I stare out at him, grateful for all he and Sister Bellamy have done for me. During the passing years, they have become my family. Never once making me feel like a misfit or a mess-up. They seem to see something more; treating me like a daughter, they express a sincere love that anchors me deeper in my faith. As Pastor Bellamy begins to sing, I plunge beneath a healing flow, and it feels like God's grace—amazing grace. It is tangible. The powerful words of his song touch my heart, connecting to the deep sorrow I hide. I have never told him how the song reassures me and begins to help heal the brokenness. Verse by verse, the song marks the beginning of what will be the process of a lifetime of healing, anchoring me beyond my feelings, beyond the manic emotions. His eyes gaze above the crowd of faces, as he begins to sing:

> "Though the storms keep on raging in my life
> And sometimes it's hard to tell the night from day
> Still, the hope that lies within reassures
> As I keep my eyes upon the distant shore.
> I know he'll lead me safely to that blessed place he has prepared.
> But if the storms don't cease
> And if the wind keeps on blowing in my life
> My soul has been anchored in the Lord.
> I realize that sometimes we're gonna be tossed
> By the waves and the currents that seem so fierce

But in the Word of God, I've got an anchor
That keeps me steadfast and unmovable despite the tide.
So, if the storms don't cease
And if the wind keeps right on blowing in my life
My soul has been anchored in the Lord."

I try, but I can't hold back the tears. The melody, like a raft in the raging sea, holds me up. The words, like medicine pouring over me, healing the deep, unseen cuts of a broken heart. Somehow, it affirms and validates the years of not being seen or heard. Without me ever saying a word to anyone, his song speaks to me in the voice of the Holy Spirit saying, "I see you, I hear you. Now anchor yourself deeper; you must go deeper."

More than his songs, Pastor Bellamy demonstrates the love of a father, giving me a safe place to begin the process of healing and personal growth beyond my stolen childhood, beyond the thorns.

As time passes, Pastor Bellamy teaches me through his sermons and by his actions that my life has a purpose. I have an identity in Jesus Christ. Though the storms keep raging, I find a place to hide and a greater sense of peace. Refreshing Springs Church of God in Christ becomes a shelter from the constant calls of my addiction. The church becomes an intensive care unit where my pastor, First Lady, and church members shower me with love, kindness, and acceptance: the formula for all healing. Still, the battles were not over, and the storms kept raging. But something was different this time. Deep inside, I was changing.

Sunday School: Early morning
Mother Bellamy, the mother of the church, teaches me modesty; a lesson that is not so much about right or wrong, but of wisdom. I will never forget the day she walked up to speak to me.

Before the start of Sunday school, she takes me to the side, concealing a small safety pin in her hand. "I want you to know who you are," she says. Her eyes scan over me as if she sees someone else, someone worthy. "You are beautiful, baby. Let them see *only* your true beauty," she whispers the words as she fastens the top of my blouse. Her hands remind me of my grandmother: aged, wise, and loving. This is the first day I become aware of how I dress and that it not only affects how others see me but also how I should see myself.

I keep the pin, making sure my blouse is higher than my

cleavage. I want to be like her, to see the real beauty in everything and everyone. Her grace, faith, and inner strength are unwavering and undeniable. As a young woman, and as a child of God, I want to be like Mother Bellamy. Thinking back to this time, I realized these lessons can only be learned with a spirit of trust and humility. A transformation was taking place.

Fall, 1989-1990

"Repeat after me," I say, preparing to teach my children today's lesson. We sit on the couch passing handmade notecards back and forth. "This is a cat—C is for cat. This is a dog. D is for dog," I say the words and point to the pictures of animals and shapes I drew for my two youngest children to learn the alphabet. There are now five blossoming faces surrounding me. Last spring, Rick, Bruce's son, came to live with us. I love him as my own. He and BJ sit on the floor, stroking Jazzy, a stray cat I found months ago. He had been wandering the street, and I could not resist giving him a home. I have named him Jazzy because of the quick tempo, bebop way he moves and jumps around the house. He has become a part of our family. He wags his tale, contently listening to the lesson.

The same year, Angela, a little girl from the downstairs apartment, becomes my goddaughter. I care for her as my own, braiding her hair, teaching her the books of the Bible, and its awesome stories. She enjoys spending time at the house and never seems to want to go home. She blends in with my other children until their smiles all look alike. Her mother Brenda and I become friends, sharing secret heartaches and an occasional laugh while watching our children play together on the top floor of the apartment duplex. In time, Brenda allows Angela to stay with us. There are no words to describe the joy of having her always here. In my eyes, whether birthed from the womb or the heart, all children are gifts from God. Their laughter lets me know everything will be all right. Each child is uniquely different, but they all want the same things: to be seen, to be heard, to be loved.

Casita helps me with today's lessons. Colorful beads swing on the braids in her hair as she gathers the papers. She is a loving big sister who adores her siblings, and she is a great assistant, always ready to help with any task. Despite the irritation of chicken pox, she manages to be the first one to help with paper and pencils. First the Old Testament, then the New. Every week, I add another five books for them to read, memorize, and recite.

"I got it, Mommy," Casita says, passing me the materials for the next session of Bible lessons. Calamine lotion covers her from head to toe.

"Don't scratch baby, it will leave a mark," I tell her. She brings me the pink bottle to put more lotion on her arms and back. I buy books and magazines from Goodwill, building a treasure of lessons to teach my children at home. I crave knowledge, searching and circling words I am not familiar with in the dictionary. A timetable chart builds our math lessons, and then it is on to the subject of history. Home becomes the school, where I pass down the Bible stories, life lessons, and lullabies I learned as a child. When the day's lessons are over, we celebrate with a snack and a toast of cherry Kool-Aid. "Cheers!" We tap our plastic cups together.

"Mama, can we go outside to play now?" BJ asks.

"Yes, but stay upstairs where I can hear you. Don't let Jazzy out." The side door bursts open, and they are off to play in their own wonderland. In the quiet moments, I reflect on the past years. Staying clean and sober is a battle every day, a war against the enemy of me. I try to hide it from my children: put on a smile, never let them see. Through the years, abuse and addiction have kept me isolated, and other than an occasional phone call or a brief visit, time with my family is scarce. I miss them. My mother and siblings have scattered across the city, and just like old times, no one speaks of the thorns. My obscured past, my arrests, drug history, and volatile relationship are all separate parts of my life no one acknowledges, at least not to me. It is all too shameful, I suppose, or maybe it is easier to act as if nothing ever happened.

My mother remarried two years ago. She continues to work from sunrise to sunset, but she promises to take time off during the summer months to take the children on a trip to Busch Gardens. In the coming years, she will make good on her promise. They take trips to Lion Country Safari, and back to Busch Gardens Tampa again. Nearly every year, she whisks them away with her on vacation.

Time passes in a blink. Joyce is busy working and raising her family. She too remarries and seems to be feeling better after reoccurring bouts of debilitating fatigue. Remembering her tireless care of my siblings and me, I wish I could make every day as enchanted for her as she had made it for us when we were little. Linda and I keep in touch, and always seem to find a reason to act like silly girls, laugh until we cry, and never mention the past.

Grateful, I finally find my brother Leon after wondering

where he was for a long time. He has been arrested again and transported to a jail closer to the area. The reason behind his latest arrest is unknown, and I plan not to ask as I drive to the Pompano Jail. The short visiting schedule is never long enough. Before I leave, I promise to come back. As I stand to go, Leon asks, "Sis, how is Michael?" His lonely eyes peer behind a thick pane of smeared glass. He is in a wheelchair, and it looks as if he has been in another fight. I push back tears and try to give him a smile so he will remember to have hope. I want to hold him and tell him that everything will be all right. His voice scratches through the telephone receiver against the wall. *Jail corrects nothing,* I think to myself, looking at my brother locked away.

"Michael is fine. I don't get to see him much, but I think he is engaged to be married."

"Sis, can you tell him to come see me." Tears begin to drown the brown of his eyes. He looks at me as though I'm just a mirage in the desert of his incarceration.

"Yes, I will. I will tell him. And I love you very much. Don't worry; trust in God; He is with you." I say the words, but inside my heart breaks like a glass thrown against a wall made of solid iron; it shatters to see my brother locked up again, broken and frightened. On the way back home, I drive and let the tears fall where only God can see, whispering what only He can hear. *God, Please help my brother. He needs you. We need you. Please set him free.*

Such are the times when a "crime" leads you to prison's revolving door system—in and out you go; the same as you were before; same brokenness, same pain. Human lives are lost while prison investors gain. It's a travesty.

Before I left that day, I ask Leon, if he remembers where our father lived. He says our dad has not moved for many years, and that his house sits just off 27th Avenue. By the end of that week, I drive with my children to see my father. Turning off the back street of Sunrise and 27th Avenue, my heart races, the same way it did when I was a little girl in Tampa. It's amazing how time, like a Polaroid picture, can freeze us in place.

When I arrive, his wife Barbara greets us at the door. Gray hair peeks out from underneath her brown, short-cropped wig. My father married her years earlier. She seems delighted to meet my children and offers each of them a warm welcome as they sit on the sofa. "Your children are so polite," she comments before telling me that my dad is not home and that he has not been feeling well for quite some time.

Unmanaged high blood pressure has caused another stroke to the left side of his body, she tells me. "I tell him to stay home, but he is stubborn and won't listen. I'm afraid for him to drive, but he wants to come and go when he gets ready. You know your father, Roadman. Even when he is sick, he never stays in one place. His gambling has gotten worse, but at least he has cut back on drinking liquor," she says letting out a deep sigh. Barbara appears to be a kind woman who has the patience of a saint. Her fingers stiffen as she dabbles back and forth from the kitchen to the couch. She offers us something to eat, but I tell her we must go.

"Would you and Daddy like to come to church with us one Sunday?" I ask. "I would love to go baby, but ya' daddy, he won't be having anything to do with no church. He believes there's nothing but hypocrites in the church, rogue preachers, sluts singing in the choir and sissies playing the piano. I wanted to go to service a long time ago, but he picks a fight about it. I don't bother trying anymore." She looks at me, folding her hands on her lap with a calm dignity.

"Yes, ma'am. Well, maybe he will change his mind someday. I have been praying for him. I will pray for you too. Please tell him I came by."

Barbara gives us a wave as we get into the car. "Come back soon. Anytime you like. I'm always home," she says, standing outside her front door. "Yes, ma'am. Thank you. I will. Please tell him I'm sorry I missed him and that I love him."

"All right suga', I will."

"Good-bye."

My limited perception of my dad was frozen in time; back to when we shared tender moments, and my imagination provided a magical melody, created for just the two of us. Today, our dance is still the same; I wait on the moon for his heart to return; it would take a lifetime. Perhaps that is why God tells us that we must become like children. 1 Corinthians 13 speaks of a *childlike* love; a love that humbly waits though its heart continues to ache; a love that openly expresses truth and hope, believing all things are possible.

I Come

"The wound is the place where the Light enters you."
~ *Jalaluddin Rumi*

Some call it a rebirth, others say enlightenment; regardless of the name, one thing remains the same; the ego must break before we awake to who we really are; there is no other way.

While gathering for evening service at Refreshing Springs, Bruce's sister, Jamie, sees me coming into the church, and greets me on the steps.

"Hi, San, how are you doing?"

"I am good, Jamie. A little tired, but I'm okay," I say with my head slightly offside.

"When is the baby due?" she smiles, looking me over.

"The doctor says around the end of March if I carry him full term."

"Well let me know if you need anything."

"Thanks, I will." I walk towards the bathroom of the church and lean against the wall inside the stall. "Thank you, Jesus." My tears are of gratitude to Jamie and her family. I am indebted for all they have done for my children. She and her mother and her sister had helped take care of Casita and BJ during my many relapses. Overwhelmed with thankfulness, I have no other way to express my feelings; the tears are all I have to release the sea of emotion. When Jamie looks at me, I see no judgment in her eyes. It is as if she sees someone else. She invited me to be her Lamaze coach for the birth of her child. I swelled with honor. Happy she wanted me to be there.

On the way back inside for service, Sister Wiggins see me and gives me a big hug. She is a loving person: elegant, with the kind of personality that makes you want to be a better person, just because you know her. She has become like a godmother to me. More times than I can remember she has encouraged me beyond my many fears and doubts and taught me to let go and trust.

"Sandra, I miss you in the choir. You have a nice voice."

"Thank you, Sister Wiggins."

"I am here for you. I want you to know that whatever you are going through, remember, this too shall pass, and there is nothing too hard for God. I love you, and you can call me when you need me."

"Yes, ma'am, thank you, but I am fine," I smile as if all is wonderful with the world.

Inside the sanctuary, I sit near the back row, twirling my finger inside my blouse. Today has been a hard day. It started out that way since morning, but then again I don't know how to ask for the help I need. Keeping quiet is normal. I try to breathe. *Just breathe.* Something is missing, but only God knows the language of a lost soul. Pastor Bellamy makes the altar call, just as he always does at the end of every service. I waste no time; I know I need to go. At the altar, I fall to my knees. Prone to wandering away from my sanity. I come, desperate for something I have no language to explain.

A gentle hand rubs my back. "It's okay. Call on Jesus. He will answer," a church member says, handing me a tissue. "I cannot do this alone," I whisper, feeling the cravings, the fear, the anxiety—it will not go away. It is worst on stressful days, like today.

I have been clean and sober for over a year—still, something is missing in my life. Disillusioned, I feel my faith is not working. *Why am I still so afraid?* I try to keep busy, but again, the fear comes, sneaking up on me, like a phantom in the dark. *What am I missing? How do I know if I am doing this "church thing" right? How many times will God hear me cry? Could He grow tired of my constant pleas for help?* My battle with addiction is no secret; most of the congregation knows. But unless you have been an addict, it is impossible to understand. The ambush of anxiety and cravings comes like a thief in the night. And before you realize what has happened, it steals everything away again. The dreams of using, falling, dying, are real to the mind. My body reacts as though it is happening in real time, right now; it is paralyzing. The fatigue drains you from the lack of sleep. It is hard to sleep when you are running in your dreams and the storms inside keep raging. I wake up in cold sweats, thankful it had been just a dream, but too afraid to go back to sleep again.

At the altar, tears run over my knuckles into the folds of my palms. A part of me feels weak and ashamed for crying, especially in front of others. Long ago, I had sworn no one would ever see me cry. A voice, soft and gentle, begins to speak from inside of me. It interrupts the intense emotions. It tells me to surrender all, to empty myself and cast all my cares on the Lord. I have tried before, but they come back. *It is not that easy,* I think to myself. *I need a miracle.* I want God to speak and rebuke the forces that war against me. I want it all to stop: the desire to get high and escape, the sensual same-sex affections that I have tried to pray away, and the intense hatred I have for the men who have caused my deepest pain. I try to let go and claim the victory over my flesh, but it feels useless. Sometimes it works, but then, it all comes back again. The past revisits me, dragging me back to what feels like a mental purgatory where I am sentenced to roam in the trench of its despair. *God, just make it go away. Make it all stop!*

I recite the sinner's prayer more times than the beads on a rosary. Still, my emotions are tattered and my desires utterly sinful. I don't know what I am missing. *Lord, I come to you; where else can I go?* I have no other hope but the hope planted inside of me a long time ago. In Tampa, under a starry night sky, there were seeds of prayer, stories, and lullabies, but uncertainty comes and with it the confusion of not knowing if I am doing everything right or not. Just as I am, I come, calling out to an invisible God. The God of ancient scriptures that proclaim He sent His Son to shed his blood on a rugged cross for the sins of the world. I tell myself to believe. *I must believe. I need to know Him more. I need more of you God! I don't know how to do life.* I am on my knees, but the fear and doubts keep me feeling like a kite flailing against strong winds.

The voices and prayers of the saints around the altar become louder until the prayers turn into a symphony of worship.

On my knees, I whisper, "Lamb of God, please speak to my heart. Teach me what I do not know. Teach me how to trust you more. And until the storms are over, I will come again and again to kneel at this altar, to pour out myself like water until there is more of you and less of me. Lord Jesus, let me plunge deeper, beneath the fountain filled with the cleansing flow of the blood you shed on the cross at Calvary. Wash me, until I lose all my guilty stains. Father God, without one plea, I come."

When I remember this time, my heart fills with gratitude for the grace that brought me to my knees — repentance is a gift. Submission is a type of death where we kneel at the threshing floor; the place good and evil separates; the place where we yield our lives wholeheartedly in trust, allowing God to burn away everything in us that is not beneficial to the body of Christ. The threshing floor is the altar upon where we take up our cross to follow the Lord wherever He may lead. I didn't know it at the time, but I was learning how to live by faith with every earnest plea. "Create in me a pure heart, O God, and renew a steadfast spirit within me" ~ Psalm 51:10.

On the Outside

"A person can only be born in one place. However, may die several times elsewhere…" ~*Mahmoud Darwish*

1990

"I can't get a vein!" one nurse shouts. "There's no time, the baby is coming!" another nurse says near my feet. In the labor room at Plantation Medical Center, nurses barely have time to prep me for delivery. I feel little to no pain, only pressure, and I require no anesthesia as my baby begins to crown. In the evening hours of Thursday, March 29th, 1990, I give birth to my second son. Born seven pounds and fourteen ounces, he is healthy and active. My joy is indescribable. It surpasses the shame and emptiness of a decision I had made during an earlier pregnancy. I name him Cory Emmanuel. His name means *hollowed* and *God is with us*. He came into my life when I was desperately seeking change, needing to free myself from the past and allow God to fill the emptiness. Cory will be my last child by birth, and in my heart and mind, he is a miracle.

I didn't think I could have any more children after the abortion. In the throes of depression and addiction, I had felt a deep guilt only God could take away. I had been nearly two weeks pregnant by the time I found out. For a long time, I have justified ending that pregnancy because I had poisoned myself with crack and alcohol to the point that I believed the damage would be irreparable. Years after becoming clean and sober, the regret continues to haunt me.

Now, the painful thorns of the abortion begin to fade in the light of God's amazing grace. The moment I see my baby's face, holding my healthy newborn son, I feel God's mercy and forgiveness falling over me, covering me. I whisper, "Thank you, Jesus."

Today, God speaks. My heart hears Him clearly saying:

"See that I will make all things new."

The process of change begins, and I prepare to go back to school, a goal I have believed is too impossible for me. It's hard to focus on reading, writing, math, and science when the howl of wolves is still so deafening. But now, I am ready to fight for my education. The more I attend church and focus on the scriptures of faith, the more I believe I can accomplish almost anything. Believing in God helps me to believe in myself. I begin to study, while noticeably, Casita would walk around the house, quoting her favorite scripture from Philippians 4:13,

"Mommy, I can do all things through Christ that gives me strength," she says. She puts her Bible study lessons to good practice. Her snaggletooth smile helps reinforce my belief that God has it all under control, and that no matter what, I can make it through another day, manage the anxiety, and maintain my sobriety.

Bruce works hard and comes home late most evenings. I do not ask where he has been when he gets home after hours. I figure he is working overtime. He finds a way to make ends meet and takes care of the mounting bills. We rent a three-bedroom home in Parkway, and soon two new pets join the family, Sally, and Buffy. Sally is a spirited Calico cat we found as a stray. She often wanders off, but she knows her way home.

After losing my beloved cat Jazzy, I relinquish any illusion of control. I had tried to keep Jazzy inside the house. I wanted to protect him better than I had protected Midnight. He slipped out early one morning and died less than five feet from the front door. I heard him outside, crying for help, but it was too late. As I rush to the door, two stray dogs from the neighborhood had climbed the steps and mauled him to death. I cried for weeks during that time.

Now the family has a puppy. Buffy is a tiny little fellow. Bruce had given him to me as a gift on a Saturday afternoon. During a stop at Publix, he returned to the car, handing me the six-week-old puppy through the window. When we first drove up to the store, I had noticed an old man sitting on a bench near the supermarket with two puppies on his lap. Bruce must have noticed the expression on my face when I first laid eyes on the little, crème-colored dog. He said the old man sold him the puppy for $25.00. I couldn't stop thanking Bruce for getting him for me.

"I'm going to name you Buffy," I smile, snuggling with him. The children were equally surprised. On the outside, our family appears normal and happy. Casita and her sister and brothers lavish love on their new baby brother, I dive into my studies, and for a while, it feels like my life is going to be different, somehow better.

For the first time in my life, I begin to set goals. I lay the plans out in a spiral notebook. First, I will study to earn my high school diploma, and then I will apply to nursing school. Excited, I put stars next to each goal. Underneath the goals, I write a note to God, asking for guidance. Nursing school will help me do what I have always wanted: to care for people. As a child, I had watched the loving way in which my mother interacted with her customers at their Tampa store. I think about my sister Joyce. Her tender care during the early years has taught me the lessons of a love that makes the world go 'round. I want to share those lessons with others and somehow convey the joy and peace they gave to me. Nursing school will be a good start. It will make my parents proud, and prove that I have finally lived down the shame and mistakes of my past. Most importantly, it will set a good example for my children. As I prepare to get busy with my future, maneuvering around the barriers of the past, the inevitable happens. Again, I will stand face to face with a history that refuses to die.

The day starts out near perfect. Cory is in my arms; he is almost two months old. Casita, now eight, reaches out to hold her baby brother while I prepare hair supplies to braid the hair of one of my nieces who I am expecting to come over later in the day. I have just finished styling my daughters' hair and cutting then washing my sons' hair. My children gather in front of the television to watch the *Tom and Jerry* cartoon show.

"Mama, can you watch cartoons with me?" BJ asks.

"Oh, my goodness, baby, I love Tom and Jerry. I will be there in a moment, sweetheart. I just need to get ready before Sharon comes over. I have more braiding to do today, and I need to get lunch ready, but I will be there soon to watch TV with you."

These moments with my children are the last lucid memories I have of this day and time. A storm is brewing, headed straight for me. I take a direct hit. The memories come only in flashes, like lightning striking across the sky before touching the ground.

In broad daylight, it comes. I step outside on the front porch. I remember the sunlight, warm on my skin. Buffy follows close to me. I scan the yard for Sally. She is gone again. I turn to walk back inside the house, noticing Casita near the door. Bruce steps out.

I feel a whack against my head. I fall. Flashes of my daughter's eyes make me want to mute my screams. She stands in the hallway, staring with her arms down by her sides. She is horrified, but I cannot stop screaming. Bruce drags me by my hair, and I feel like I am plummeting down a dark black hole. Backpedaling against the air, my feet flail uselessly. Defenseless, my arms reach in every direction for help. No help will come. I look into my daughter's eyes, and I do not understand why I am the one feeling ashamed and guilty, but I am. *I am supposed to be a good example for my children, but I feel like a coward, a weakling, a nobody.* I try to catch my breath as the flashes of the present and past drown me. A culmination of every offense and every fear meet me here against the cold floor. Standing over me, demanding I assume the position. The last thing I remember is my daughter's face congealing between the sounds of my own screams as her father closed the bedroom door. Her eyes wide with dread, I never saw her blink.

It's 2:00 a.m. and the children are asleep. The house is quiet, and all goes back to normal as if nothing ever happened — as if, no crime was committed here. Buffy curls up on his dog cushion, waiting for me. Tomorrow, when my children awake, they too will be waiting, wondering, where is Mommy? Behind closed doors, they are oblivious to the fear and silent heartache. I felt powerless, unable to express the profound emptiness. Fight or flight, I react the same way I had since my stolen childhood. I waited for the crickets to lift their wings and play their symphony beneath the moonlight. That is my signal. That's when I run.

The relapse lasts less than a week. I want to be with my children — no matter the cost. Bruce greets me at the end of the binge with a 38-caliber handgun. If I were not already dead inside, I would believe he will kill me when he places it on the side of my forehead. His threats are all the same. Nothing has changed.

"If you leave me, I will kill you. I should kill you right now!" He spits. Pinned against the closet door, feeling the barrel against my head, I think to myself, *I already feel dead inside, so good luck with that.* An unusual calmness comes over me. The years of violence, fear, and anger crowd inside the bedroom; I see it all at once. I hear a gentle whisper, reminding me that somehow, I am still here, still alive, not by my own will, or the will of any man — but by some divine intervention. I believe with all my heart, whatever happens to me, will be the will of the all-seeing God.

He hits me with the handle of the gun. I fall to the floor, praying for God to help me, wondering if my children are at the door, listening the same way I had listened when my parents were at war. When Bruce backs away, I want to run, but I know I cannot run with my children. I have nothing to give them, and no way to support them on my own. Bruce has everything. He is cunning, charming, and he has connections; I do not stand a chance. I feel I have no real say in my children's lives, though they are mine and all I have in the world.

Every day after, I think about running. *Where would we go?*

And how can I live with myself if I take my children away from their father, knowing how it made me feel when my mother left my father? I fear my children will be angry with me if I take them away, and considering my history of drug abuse and mental health issues, Bruce would surely win any custody battle; if I ever survived long enough to make it to court. I feel there are no options. I had seen myself in my daughter's frightened eyes during the last violent attack. The way she stood cemented to the hallway floor, mouth gaped open. I had watched my mother and my sister go through the same cruel treatment. I could not treat anyone this way, not even an animal, yet here I relive the same cycle of violence, over and over again.

"God, where are you?" I whisper.

The depression and isolation that I lay at the altar of the church continue to hunt me down and find me. *Why?* I ask myself. My son has waited for me to watch the *Tom and Jerry* show with him, but I am afraid of the cat-and-mouse game he sees lived out in the house. My children have seen so much, too much. Seen and not heard, what goes on in this house, stays in this house — these are cruel unspoken rules, ones that I had honored for many years. I worry how it will affect my children. *Will my sons grow up to beat their wives? Will my daughters allow the same cruelty to come into their lives because of my inability to take a stand?* I feel helpless.

I need my family so desperately. I wonder if they would blame me; I wonder if they know what is happening behind closed doors. I believe that because of my past failures, they will think I caused it. Most often people expect the worst from addicts, even those who have overcome the strongholds of their addiction. Perhaps like Bruce, they too would believe I deserve this for whatever reason. I cannot tell my church family — especially now when Bruce holds a prestigious title in the church ministry. I turn my eyes upward, away from this place, this earth, and call on the only help I know.

"Lord, please help me," I look for a sign, a word, a miracle from God; anything that tells me He hears me, He sees me. But for now, the heavens are quiet.

Life goes back to "normal." At church, I blend in between the pews, hoping no one asks me about the bruises on my neck or the isolation that pushes people away after every polite hello. Loyal to the secrets and shame, I refuse to expose the abuse, choosing instead to keep quiet and assume the familiar position. My children play a few rows away from me, unaware of how the love I have for them helps me to manage these internal storms. If it weren't for that love, I would be long gone, on a plane, a train, or somewhere in a gutter still strung out on crack cocaine. But one day at a time, God's grace and mercy help me endure. He blessed me with these blossoms to assure me of this one thing: *He will make all things new.*

Waiting for service to begin, I sit alone reading a Scripture in the *New Testament,* Hebrews 11:1. It reads: "Now faith is the substance of things hoped for and the evidence of things not seen." I question my faith. *What does it mean to believe in what is not seen? Should I live my life based on what I can prove to be real, as my senses define reality? Do I deny my feelings for the sake of love? Pray tell, what is love?* Confused about the contradictions of this life, I ask God and wait for an answer. *What am I missing? Is this faith? What am I doing wrong?* Either I am crazy, or I was born on a planet I do not belong.

I call out to God until I finally learn the lesson of surrender. Until I let go of it all and begin to only "believe." No miracles, no signs come down from heaven. I decide to believe in His Word alone. I purpose in my heart to take it. I will not fight against the storms that continue to rage in my life. I try to deny my emotions. I want to fight and no longer worship the idol of self-pity that keeps me in a perpetual state of poor-me, why-me, pathetic victimhood. No matter what, I will stay close to my young children while I believe they still need me. At the risk of everything, I will believe in God and the joy that He promised to give me if I endure to the end.

In the uncertainty of the decision, I remember the words of my sister. Words spoken long ago, carefully planted — nurtured by time, watered by the storms and my tears. Like a seed breaking, dying below the earth, I feel the life of her words rising in me.

"Trust God, no matter what" Joyce had always said. I begin to trust God's will for my life, no matter what. Rise or fall, I will trust the Lord who created the heavens and the earth. Before the end of church service, I write the words from Philippians 1:21: "For me, to live is Christ and to die is gain." His grace is sufficient. I close my journal and my eyes, to just… breathe.

All or Nothing

We move again. Packing, unpacking and packing again before the last box is emptied. I don't bother to keep count of how many times. From my youth, I learned, just as the seasons change, so will my address. You simply adapt. I begin to search, finding out more about the Word of God. I lose myself between the pages of scripture in Bible study and the various notes from my schoolbooks. I prepare to take the General Educational Development (G.E.D.) test to earn my high school diploma.

Busyness can be a blessing and a curse. The blessing of it keeps me focused on the present tasks. The curse of it keeps me silently frozen, unable to confront the thorns of the past and take back my life. What we refuse to face never changes, and never heals. Between studies, I work several jobs. Braiding hair, cleaning houses, whatever my hands find to do. I take life one day at a time. Soon, the good times and the tough times look the same. But a battle was coming to test everything I know.

Pastor Bellamy gives me his blessing when I ask to start an exercise program in the back of the church. I was grateful to have a safe place to work out. The fitness classes start out with only a few members, but in a matter of months, the classes are packed. Soon Linda joins the fitness group; I felt so happy about that. The exercise classes help me begin the process of changing the negative energy, freeing me from the crippling anxiety, empowering me to want to dream again; I give it my all. After a few weeks, I joined the usher board, and then the choir; a new sense of purpose unfolds.

Tonight's Bible study fills both sides of the church. Pen, pad, and Bible in hand, I sit in the middle row, waiting to explore the various points of the text. My faith increases. Week after week, I sit to hear the word of God. I highlight Romans 10:17 in my Bible that says, "then faith *comes* by hearing, and hearing by the word of God."

I feel empowered. Moreover, I can ask questions. "There are no stupid questions," Elder Mark Johnson said to the audience. I begin to think critically about the answers. Slowly, my confidence grows. Since joining Refreshing Springs, I felt the words of John 15:12 come to life. The verse says, "Love one another as I have loved you." Though the storms keep raging in my life, my perception begins to shift. I have no power to change the severe tempest of my circumstances, but it starts to change me. In time, the word of God becomes a steady anchor. It begins to ease the anxiety as I learn to truly trust. "God is sovereign, and His will for our life is better than our own plans." I read in Jeremiah chapter 29. He is in control—not my past, not my sorrow, and not the erratic voices in my head that awake after every fight behind closed doors.

I focus, plunging deeper into the tasks of cooking, cleaning, cutting hair, braiding hair, checking homework, keeping up with field trips, and working on school projects with my children; these are the best times.

I find peace in my faith and in the words of the lullabies that I sing to my children. The melody is the same as when I was young. It offers the same calming tonic that had once soothed my soul.

> *"Love makes the world go 'round*
> *Love makes the world go 'round*
> *It's a time for beginning*
> *Love makes the world go 'round*
> *When we're together*
> *Love makes the world go 'round*
> *It's a time for beginnings*
> *Love makes the world go 'round."*

I sing, passing on the gift of the lullabies. In time, the word of God becomes louder in my ear, dulling the sharp-tongued ghosts of the past. As I bathe myself in the Word of God, it guides me, leading me around the landmines of automatic thoughts. The shameful stains of my past slowly begin to fade, and I purpose in my heart to be content and try not to complain when things are not going so well. Some days I manage to block out everything, but other days, it's not so easy. There are days I fall on my face, but then I get back up, dry my tears, and try again. Those days come to remind me, I am only human, and God's grace is enough.

Months pass and like leaves in a sudden gust of wind; my hands tremble. Powerful cravings hit me all at once. They come out of nowhere—no argument or fight spurred this call to get high. My stomach heaves in fits, waiting for the sensation of the first hit from a crack pipe, the first sip of alcohol, anything 80-proof will do. I find a quiet place, usually the bathroom. It's the only place I can be alone. But since growing in my faith in Christ, I know that I am never alone. Spiritual growth increases spiritual awareness, and now, I'm beginning to see beyond it all; this is a supernatural battle.

I sense a presence; a demon. It reminds me that I am a powerless victim, accusing me of allowing it all to happen. Praying, I bow my head. "God please help me. I can't do this by myself." I call on the name of Jesus, the One the saints' call the "Rock of Ages." The pangs of addiction are intense. My body revolts, wanting more than oxygen; it demands cocaine. I exhale, letting myself feel its torment and disapproval. I begin to rage war against myself.

The battleground is in my mind, and the spiritual battle is as real as the air I breathe. Anchored in my faith and armed with a deeper sense of purpose in Christ, the same battle that begins in my mind will end in my mind. I lean back on the bathroom commode, like the corner of a sparring ring, in a tug of war between my body that demands its own way, and the spirit that reminds me that the just must live by faith.

All at once, I remember there is a crack pipe, well hidden inside an old sock, stored inside a raggedy tennis shoe in the back of the closet. Addicts are masters of hiding things—mostly from ourselves. Home alone, I begin to dig through a pile of clothes I set aside to donate to The Salvation Army. Under the clutter, I find the dingy high-top Converse. I reach inside, pulling out a sock. Inside the sock are the spoils of my insanity: a crack pipe, a lighter, and the immense memories that drove me to escape its dreadful reality. The sides of the glass stem crusts with residue from the last binge.

Months without seeing it or touching it ignites a desire that moves wildly inside the pit of my stomach. As I hold it in my hands, I can feel the blood coursing through my veins with anticipation. A sick feeling moves inside until I can no longer sit up straight. My flesh demands me to light the fire that summons the genie. There is just enough residue in the stem to stop the tremors in my hands and make the memories fall asleep again.

"Three wishes!" it whispers to me. I sit up on the seat of the commode, listening to the familiar hiss. After all these years, the voices have not changed, but I have. I begin to understand the spiritual connection of my drug addiction. Rooted in pain and in the destructive emotions of bitterness, pride, and self-pity, it was not merely physical. Addiction is like a sweet-talking snake, a charming liar whose motives will always remain the same: to steal, kill, and destroy.

The inner battle with drug addiction feels like a twelve-round boxing match where I am both the contender and the opponent. Round by round, I am determined to fight; win or lose.

The pull of addiction is powerful. Like a dry leaf in hurricane force winds, drug addicts go where the habit blows; without question, we can't resist it in our own strength. Addiction cannot be fully explained or learned. Only an addict could understand the desperation, the crumbling, and the insatiable cravings; despite knowing that it could take our lives, still, we run to its call. Sweat trickles from my brow, as I begin to think about the subtle triggers that spur the call of the addiction. Fatigue, stress, and anxiety are all culprits of the human condition — unavoidable suffering. But for me, they are like menacing storms, causing me to want to escape to the illusion of a shelter made of nothing more than smoke and ashes. Fight or flight; this time, I choose to fight.

I will hold fast to my confession of faith and cling to the incredible story I have heard since childhood; the story of an innocent man, a crucifixion, and an old rugged cross. All my life, the love story of Christ has guided my heart. From sobriety to relapse, time and time again, I have sensed His great love lifting me, surrounding me, and restoring me. When nothing else could help get me through the diabolical cravings, His mercy has never ceased. With each surrender, I feel new strength. I am becoming free. Free from the guilt of the past, free from the shame that has lasted so long, and free from my sin and stains.

In Revelation 12:11, the Word of God proclaims, "And they overcame him by the blood of the Lamb, and by the word of their testimony, and they loved not their lives unto the death." Today, something had to die. Leaning against the sink, I breathe the words, "Christ redeems me." I tremble to think of His suffering, the price He paid to set me free from every stronghold. The tomb is empty; He lives; I need to believe this — with more than just my words. Face to face with this demon of addiction, I make a decision. Still craving, shaking in the bathroom, I make up my mind to believe in the promise of God, found in Jude 1:24: "God is able to protect us, to keep us from stumbling, and present us faultless before the presence of His glory with exceeding joy." I stand near the bathroom door, needing that strength, craving that joy.

All at once, I battle a lifetime of reactive impulses, feeling like it is the sixth round. I resist the urge to flick the lighter. Nothing feels *normal* right now; *normal* is to give in and let my flesh win. I fight. By round ten, I decide if I want to be free or remain a victim to the demonic genie of crack cocaine. I need to forsake a lifetime of misery, all or nothing. Self-pity and bitterness must be the first to die. Near the bathroom sink, I hold the crack pipe, remembering how I have allowed its lies to run roughshod over my life. Chasing smoke, it has told me my worth. It's all a lie! It insists that I assume the position of a powerless victim. It says, "it's your life, do what you want, what you feel. You have a right to get high, to get even."

"No more!" I speak aloud. "Satan, you are a liar." I am learning to fight, not in my strength, but in the supernatural belief that all of heaven is with me. I no longer feel the need to self-medicate because of the deep emotional pain. Bought with a price, by the blood of the Lamb, Christ, my King—He fights for me. I feel it. Deep inside, without a doubt, I know it.

"Listen carefully," The Holy Spirit speaks in a voice that surrounds me, wrapping me in what felt like a warm cocoon.

"You are not your own. Addiction can no longer afford you." The voice proclaims. A transformation is taking place beyond my ability to understand. Staring in the bathroom mirror, I splash cold water on my face, vowing that I will no longer allow my issues and anxiety to drive my emotions to the point of relapse. I hold fast to my sobriety. No matter what.

The Holy Spirit continues to speak to my heart, revealing the primary cause of my addiction is the deep emotional pain I suppressed. Year after year, a deep trench has collected offense after offense, with no recompense, no apologies. Unresolved grief becomes a thief when it is not confronted; I had allowed myself to wallow in its stench. The injustice of it all has fed the addictive behavior. The deep emotional wounds have demanded payment for every affliction and assault. Without justice, there is no peace. Self-pity creeps into the space where truth and justice never came; it makes the slow death of addiction tolerable, even acceptable to its victims. But it can never make amends for all the wrongs. No drug can ever change and correct the past and present pain of life. I need to accept that fact and understand the truth of why Christ came to earth in the first place.

From the fall of Adam and Eve to this very day, we have all lost our way; every one of us. The universal state of sin affects us all the same. But Jesus came to take our place, to give us hope, and guide the way out of the trenches. I feel Him, I hear Him. Tenderly, He speaks to my heart, "The only way out is through forgiveness." The words wash over me. I close my eyes, giving into the breathless flow of what feels like living and dying at the same time. *I must learn to let go and fully forgive.* I know it's the only way.

I must choose to let go of my right to hate and to even the odds. The process continues as I deny my flesh the right to its destructive craving. In Galatians 2:20, the Word of God declares, "I am crucified with Christ: nevertheless I live; yet not I, but Christ lives in me: and the life which I now live in the flesh I live by the faith of the Son of God, who loved me, and gave himself for me."

The final round comes, and I step out of the bathroom. The fight is over. I choose to forgive based on the belief that Christ, the Son of God, paid for every sin, every offense on the cross. Not just for me, but for every person who has ever hurt me. I must forgive all, every injustice, past, and present—all or nothing. At this moment, I declare my hope in God, allowing myself to feel everything and yet choose to be joyful in the midst of the storm. The bathroom transforms from a hideaway into a haven of praise. I breathe out, "Thank you, Jesus."

The struggle is just as real as before, but now, there is a greater sense of who I am and who is in me—guiding me, fighting my battles. To explain the paradox for others to gain a full understanding is impossible without an experience with the person of Jesus Christ. This truth is more of a revelation; an evolving of mind and spirit. His love overshadows every affliction, and I find new strength to endure the bouts of immense anxiety and erratic emotions. In my weakness, He is strong. In Christ alone, I became empowered to not only say no to drugs but also never need to answer the enticing call of the addiction; pride, hate, and unforgiveness is the devil's property; when we give it back, he can no longer trespass.

Through full surrender and forgiveness, I win the victory over cocaine and alcohol. "My grace is sufficient," He softly whispers to my heart as I walk to the backyard, open the trash can, and throw the crack pipe away with the rest of the garbage.

I never relapsed again, to this very day.

Addiction is indeed a slave master. The Latin term emphasizes that the very word means "enslaved by." As I look back to the years, I spent chasing smoke, I've come to know God as my deliverer. Deliverance from every bondage and stronghold begins with awareness. Until we are aware of the root of our addiction, we will be forever the slave to its hijacking mind games and deception. In Galatians 5:1, Apostle Paul admonishes believers to "stand fast; therefore, in the liberty wherewith Christ hath made us free and be not entangled again with the yoke of bondage." The root of every disease is the condition of sin, and the cure for sin is Jesus Christ. The price He paid on Calvary overrides death and disease; His blood makes us free. In Him, we stand strong knowing that "if the Son sets us free, we are truly free" ~ John 8:36.

A Lesson in Courage

"Although the life of a person is in a land full of thorns and weeds, there is always a space in which the good seed can grow. You have to trust God." ~*Pope Francis*

Winter, 1990

I stand in the living room, hesitating before I open a large manila envelope that just arrived in the mail. The sender is the Department of Education. It is the results of the G.E.D. test I took over a month ago. I swallow hard and open it. Overjoyed, I passed! I glide my fingers across the embossed seal on the diploma, remembering how I have dreamt of this day for so long. My first thoughts are of my parents and Joyce; I can't wait to show them. My mother comes to my graduation with a few family members.

My father cannot make it. I go to his house to show him my framed diploma, hoping that he would be proud of me. I wait. Ms. Barbara says she is happy for me.

"I'm sorry, baby. I'll tell him you came by," Ms. Barbara says, clearing teacups off the table.

"That's all right. Would you please tell him that I'm sorry I missed him again and that I love him?"

The following week, I apply for nursing school at Broward Community College. The cost and requirements for the prerequisite courses are more than I could afford. I decide to obtain my nursing assistant certification, work fulltime, and earn enough money to pay my way through college.

In the spring of 1991, I begin classes at the Coral Ridge School of Nursing on Oakland Park Boulevard, through the Broward Employment and Training Administration (B.E.T.A.) program. The nursing school is less than ten miles away from Fort Lauderdale beach and The Biltmore Hotel. Sometimes before school starts, I ride down to the strip; a strange nostalgia calls me back to A1A just to pass by The Biltmore. I turn off the road, barely moving, driving slow, remembering the shelter of the bathroom, and the way the morning sky would light a path across the water from the horizon to the shore. A sigh of sorrow and gratitude moves me on to school.

Ms. Mais, the director, is kind yet stern, with high expectations for each of her students. Rarely behind her desk, she moves meticulously through the rows, giving each student the time and attention needed to succeed through the rigorous training.

From the written and oral examinations to clinical competency, she devotes herself to us from the beginning to the end. There are no shortcuts, no late assignments, and no excuses in her class. Ms. Mais requires our absolute best: all or nothing. The need to succeed, to get this right, and to make Ms. Mais proud consumes me to the core. I give it my all, focusing my energy on every class assignment, and earn a 4.0-grade average.

The second floor of St. John's Rehabilitation Hospital will be my second home over the next several years. Caring for others gives me the greatest fulfillment. The patients become a part of my family. I work the third shift at St. John's, and study for final exams while my children are at school in the morning. After a while, my busy schedule catches up with me. One morning when I am waking up from a "quick nap," I notice my children lounging around the house in their pajamas. In a state of panic, I shout,

"Why aren't you guys ready for school?" I say, looking side to side, half dazed.

"You are going to be late! Hurry, get dressed!" I move like something is on fire, trying to find the car keys and put on my shoes. My children stare at me peculiarly and then back at each other.

"Mommy, it's Saturday. There is no school today," Casita says with a worried expression.

More times than I care to mention, my schedule gets the best of me. Still, another time I worked a double shift to cover for a coworker who couldn't make it to work. When I arrive home, Casita gives me a bowl of cereal. It is late, or early, I can't remember. However, I will never forget the moment she tried to take the bowl out of my hands. The conversation was brief.

"Baby, what are you doing?" I ask as she tugs on my cereal bowl.

"Mommy, give me the bowl."

"Why? I am eating."

"Ma, give me the bowl! You are not eating, you're sleeping." She tugs. I hold tighter, narrowing my eyes at her.

"I'm not sleeping. I'm looking right at you." I assert with a sideways stare. She lets go of the bowl, shaking her head at me. With one hand on her hip and the other under her chin, she says, "Mama, yes you were sleeping. Look at your chest!" Staring up at her from the recliner, I slowly look down. A trail of cereal cascades across my blouse. She is right. I had not realized I had fallen asleep. Fruit Loops and iced milk has spilled all over my chest. I laugh at myself; she laughs at me too. Without another word, I give up the bowl. Thinking we are right, we can be so wrong.

August 1992

Hurricane Andrew ravishes the southeast coast of Florida, causing billions of dollars of damage to infrastructures, homes, businesses, and hospitals. St. John Hospital makes room for the displaced patients from neighboring hospitals and nursing homes. The staff works around the clock to comfort and care for patients. A woman transported from a Miami hospital never makes it to our facility; she dies in route, still sitting in her wheelchair. It affects me deeply when I get the news. Most staff members work overtime, and on my days off, I volunteer to help out. Casita and Angela ask to come with me to help with the relief efforts. I remember feeling proud they cared enough to offer. After speaking to my supervisor about youth volunteers, Casita and Angela receive their volunteer badges from the receptionist, and we get to work.

Staff and volunteers hand out juice, food, blankets, and pillows to patients lining the halls of the hospital. We work into all hours of the morning, finding whatever our hands can do to help on each floor. In the aftermath of the Category 4 storm, I witness the remarkable spirit of people who care, not because of salary or a false modesty of just *doing the job*, but because of a sincere heart of compassion for their fellow human. Adversity seems to have a way of bringing out the best in us.

Weeks after the storm, I meet Anthony Moody, a young man who has been admitted earlier in the day; I am about to learn another lesson in courage. Anthony is on my list of new patients. On the evening shift, the fire alarm goes off accidentally, and I hurry in to comfort the patients and let them know that there is no fire and that everything was all right. Soon, I get to Anthony's room.

"Hello Mr. Moody, my name is Sandra," I smile, reaching my hand out to him, touching his hand. "I will be your nurse assistant. Do not be alarmed by the sound. There is no fire. Please let me know if you need anything. Are you comfortable?"

"Yes. Please, call me Anthony. It is nice to meet you. May I call you Sandy?"

"Yes. Sure. Most people do." Anthony has a cheerful disposition, and after talking for a while, I find out he is excited about his new electric wheelchair. From that very night, the young man captures my heart. In the passing days, I notice a determined spirit in him. Every work night, I look forward to speaking with and caring for him.

"Hi Anthony, I have the apple juice you wanted." I hold the

juice container and straw until his eyes tell me he is satisfied. "Anthony, I am going to turn you on your other side now, is that okay."

"Sure, Sandy. Thank you. I miss you when you are not here. How is your family?"

"Everyone is fine, thanks for asking." His huge smile warms the entire room as we talk about his family and the love of his life: his mother, Rose. We talk about his childhood and growing up in the seventies. He tells me of the time his muscles had become so weak that he could no longer walk. At the age of twenty-five, Anthony was diagnosed with muscular dystrophy. I listen intently, watching his head angle on top of the pillow as he shares his life's journey. I admire his courage.

On the nights he has trouble sleeping, he turns on his room light, and I come in to check on him. We talk until the indiscernible fears move on, allowing him to rest. "You have a soothing voice, Sandy. Thank you for taking so much time with me. I hope I am not keeping you from your other patients."

"No worries, Anthony. The floor is quiet tonight. Everyone is asleep, and the others have the front desk covered. It is my pleasure. Besides, it takes time getting used to new surroundings and new people; right?"

"I guess you are right," he says with a yawn. At almost 3 o'clock in the morning, I pull his blanket snugly underneath his chin as he begins to fall asleep. I prepare for the next shift. Serving others starts to transform me from the inside out. I feel useful and thankful to have the opportunity to give kindness and compassion to others who are hurting and afraid. I know what it feels like, and I want to make a difference.

Months go by, and during the time I have cared for Anthony, I never hear him complain about the debilitating pain and isolation he endures. As an insomniac, I can relate to the restless hours of wondering what tomorrow will bring.

Soon, Anthony becomes a part of the family, attending holidays, family dinners, birthday parties, and church functions. He falls in love with my family, and they fall in love with him, especially my mother. His kind heart and strong spirit teach me that after every storm, blessings will come if we have the courage to look for them. Anthony is my blessing, and every day, I learn a new life lesson that teaches me to see with different eyes; fearless eyes that see adversity, not as an opposition, but as an opportunity. It is a lesson in courage I will never forget.

Follow Your Dreams

There is a specific path we must take, following the intuition and instinct inside us that no one else may understand or perceive; still, we must listen to it, nurture it, and no matter what, run to it, until the dream becomes a reality.

"Are you ready, Ann?" My fellow classmate Ann Solomon and I prepare to march inside Coral Ridge Presbyterian Church.

"Yes, I am excited, "Ann says in her beautiful island accent. It is graduation day. We take pictures near the elegant water fountain outside the stunning cathedral established by Dr. D. James Kennedy, an eloquent pastor I have listened to on many occasions, so I feel honored to graduate here. I look for Charmaine, another classmate who has become a close friend, but I can't find her among the crowd gathering in the foyer. Ms. Mais waits for us at the front of the stage. One by one, white nursing uniforms march in to attend the graduation commencement.

It is a day of miracles, the day of my dreams. I have prayed for so long that this day would come, and now, it is here. My family members gather in the designated seating area, and before the ceremony begins, my mother calls out,

" Sydney!" she waves and calls from a seat near the left side of the church. I turn toward the sound of her voice, and when our eyes meet, there is no trace of the hard lines of heartache and disappointment. She looks proud. The look in her eyes makes me feel like a little girl again. Time rewinds, giving me a priceless gift, the one thing I've always wanted: her time. She sees and hears me beyond the thorns of distress from my years of recklessness. I smile.

"Hi, mama. Hi, Joyce."

"Sandy Patty! I knew you could do it." Joyce says with a lovely smile that lights up the room. My heart overflows. Turning back towards the stage, I whisper, "Thank you Jesus."

Ms. Mais begins the graduation ceremony, and with her regal presence, she starts to call the names of each graduate. Daphne and I look at each other at the same time. We have a lot in common. Both young mothers, both recovering addicts, both born-again believers, and now, we are both certified nursing assistants. "We did it!" she whispers to me. I smile back at her. Ms. Mais calls me up, and I walk across the stage to receive my certificate.

Weeks after graduation, Ms. Mais calls me into her office.

She has exciting news. It is regarding a poem I wrote while attending nursing classes. She put it in a newsletter for publishing. I can feel my heart beat in my chest as she tells me about the newsletter. The title of the poem is "Follow Your Dreams." She has more news.

"Sandra, I have spoken with the B.E.T.A. program coordinators about your progress. We have also followed up with your job performance at St. John's Rehabilitation Hospital. You have maintained an A average throughout the course, supported your peers, and proven yourself to be worthy of the honor of the B.E.T.A. Alumni of the Year. There will be a ceremony. Commissioner Clay Shaw will present you with the award, along with the Director of Nursing Services at St. John's. I will also attend the ceremony. Congratulations, well done."

I cannot find the words, wanting to say so much to show the deep appreciation I feel for all Ms. Mais has done for me since attending the Coral Ridge Nurses Assistant Training Program, but in the surprise of it all, my response was brief yet heartfelt. "Ms. Mais, I could not have succeeded without you. Thank you."

During the Alumni ceremony, Commissioner Clay Shaw and Ms. Francis from St. John's present me with the B.E.T.A. Alumni of the Year Award. I am nervous and feel unprepared to speak. Cameras flash and I try to keep from zoning out to someplace safer, somewhere quieter, a place where no one can judge me; that's what the voices come back to say. *Don't they know where I have been? I'm a misfit? I don't belong up here.* Although I am grateful, the stress of the honor is overwhelming. It is hard to explain the joy of being here, hearing the words that I've wanted to hear for so long, yet still feeling so unworthy.

When Ms. Mais had first told me about the award, I called my mother. She had said she would attend, and even bought me a dress for the occasion. Forty minutes have passed, and she still hasn't made it. Every time someone enters the dining hall, I turn, hoping it will be her.

Finely dressed waiters bring out dinner plates. I cannot eat. The smell of the food clashes with the acid already churning in my stomach. The social anxiety pushes me back in time, making me want to escape. As I stand at the podium, I look out in the audience at Ms. Mais. Her eyes glow like opals above a graceful smile. Seeing her happy expression calms my nerves. Nevertheless, with the sea of people watching me from behind white linen tables, elegant flowered centerpieces, and crystal glassware, I can't seem to remember the short speech or the poem I have prepared to read.

"Thank you, Ms. Mais, for all the love and support you give to your students. You have taught me more than a career. Because of your hard work and dedication, you have shown me a character of commitment and integrity. I want to thank Ms. Francis and Commissioner Clay Shaw. I wish my mother and father could be here today. Thank you, everyone, for this award. God bless you."

I know I had wanted to say these words, but I cannot remember what I said exactly. Anxiety causes me to straddle two worlds. After years of dissociating, my short-term memory suffers, floating away on its own, while the long-term memory refuses to let go. After the speech, I walk off to the side, where Commissioner Shaw and Ms. Francis are motioning for me to take a photo with them while holding my award. As I move towards them, the nervous spasms shift from my stomach to my chest. I nod, and with each flash from the cameras, I remember a surreal past where thorns jut out in every direction—from a felon, a junkie, and now, an alumni of the year. Breathing out, I smile. Hopeful but still afraid of the uncertain future. As I return to my seat next to Ms. Mais, my hands are still shaking. I breathe slowly and then sit back. It's over. I whisper, "Thank you, Jesus." It's over.

The Westside Gazette follows up on the story and after meetings with the journalist; I am on the pages of the Broward County's oldest and largest African American newspaper. The name of the article is "Cinderella All Over Again." I was grateful.

During that time, I wanted to visit Kay, check on her to see if she was doing better. I found out she moved. Her family lost the house. When I finally find her, she is still in a state of desperation. I ask her if there was anything I could do for her. She asked for cash, stating it was for food. I told her that I would buy her food, but I could not give her money; I know the genie well; the game is still the same. Kay gave me a grocery list, and after a trip to Winn Dixie, I wished her well. I never saw her again after that time. I pray for her to this day.

I drive to my father's house to share the news of the Westside Gazette, hoping he will be home. I am so happy that he is, and when Barbara walks into the bedroom to get him, my heart skips a beat. My children and I sit in the living room, watching him limp out.

"Hi, Daddy, we came by to see you before. I waited for you, but you were busy. I miss you. How are you?" I reach out to hug him. He looks weak and drops hard on the sofa when he sits. Barbara tells me that he has not been taking his pills as prescribed.

"I don't know why he is so stubborn," she says, looking at him the entire time. She drops her head and goes quiet.

"I'm all right, baby. Just a little tired," he says, leaning over to one side. He gives me a slight smile, and then clears his throat as though he has something to say. He doesn't. There are only quick hard breaths as if he forgets how to breathe each time he clears his throat. I don't tell him about what's going on in my life, even though it is good news; he seems to have enough on his plate. That part of our relationship has never changed.

"Daddy you must take your medication. Does it make you feel sick when you take it?" I ask.

"No, I just forget to take it sometimes." Barbara disagrees, mumbling under her breath. She laughs lightheartedly and gives the children snacks.

"Granddaddy, your pills will make you feel better," Casita says.

"Okay baby, I will. I'll try to remember."

"You don't have to remember, Bert. I give them to you every day, but you won't take them. There is nothing to remember. Just take them when I bring them to you," Barbara says standing in the kitchen. My father doesn't say anything. He holds the same look that I have always remembered. It is the look of a quiet wanderer, restless, preparing for the open road again. My heart is heavy after the visit. My dad's poor health has become more evident as he sat with us in the living room, and his apathetic silence reveals nothing has changed. I desire to connect with my father, beyond the past hurts and years of his absence, but he still seems so far away, though he is sitting right next to me. The ultimate gift from my father is not money or things, but the gift of his heart; that's all I have ever wanted.

I want to stay longer and help Barbara with his care, but he swears he feels all right and has plans to leave out before the end of the night. I begin to understand some of the reasons why everyone called my father Roadman; even in poor health, his mind is on the road. I wanted to ask him to come to church with me, but I remembered what Barbara said; he despises church. So, I didn't ask. Even after all these years, his wandering heart still seems to search for purpose and meaning. As we drive away, I ask God to save my father and to bring peace to his restlessness. I was seven years old when I first prayed that prayer, and I know God sees and hears and someday, I believe, He will answer.

Another Second Chance

"Struggle is a never-ending process. Freedom is never really won, you earn it and win it in every generation." ~*Coretta Scott King*

"Oh come all ye faithful, joyful and triumphant..." The children's choir from Refreshing Springs sings Christmas carols to the patients at St. John's Hospital. Pastor Bellamy and the church support the idea of reaching out to the patients with Christmas gifts and caroling. My heart is overwhelmed by the kindness and generosity of the congregation. The night before, the members of the church worked hard to prepare each gift. The children dress in angel and shepherd costumes, eager to hand out the presents wrapped in bows and tinsel. Patients who cannot speak audibly express an unspoken joy. Their arms reach out to offer a hug to the children. Other patients sit up straight in their beds, with wide, toothless grins, applauding the carolers.

"Thank you. Thank you!" a gray-haired woman says with her hands clasped underneath her chin. I am not sure who is happiest, the children or the patients.

February 1993

I receive a call from Ms. Mais. "Sandra, I want to let you know the school has decided to use your drawing in the classroom. The portrait of the heart you drew for the anatomy assignment."

Taken aback, I am not sure I heard her right. "The heart *I* drew, Ms. Mais?"

"Yes, Sandra, the replica is what I would like to use to show the classes." I am lost for words again. Recalling the anatomy assignment, I drop my head, holding the receiver to my ear.

The right and left atrium, the superior and inferior vena cava, the pulmonary arteries—it was one of the first assignments in the class, and one that I had enjoyed very much. I poured all my energy into the project, trying to depict how the human heart is more than just a blood-pumping muscle. Unlike any other organ in the human body, the heart is the life force, the center of the indiscernible soul. I hold the line, unsure how to respond. Trying to separate the part of myself that feels unworthy of such an honor, just as it did during graduation, the alumni ceremony, and the interview with *The Westside Gazette*.

"Thank you, Ms. Mais; I am happy to know that. Please let me know if I could ever be of service to you and the school. The nursing program has changed my life, and you have touched my heart in more ways than words can say. Thank you for everything."

"You are welcome, Sandra. Would you like to attend church with me this coming Sunday? I would like to talk to you about speaking at an upcoming graduation."

"Yes, ma'am. I would like to come."

In the coming weeks, Ms. Mais graciously invites me to speak at several of her graduate classes. Each time, I am always fearful of the paralyzing anxiety that causes my thoughts to scatter into nonsense. Nevertheless, Ms. Mais believes in me, overlooking my many quirks. Over the years, she demonstrates the genuine love of Christ in my life. She seems to see someone else when she looks at me. Someone I do not know. But I desperately want to.

Hidden behind my gratitude is the need to do more, work harder, and be better to make myself feel worthy of any love and kindness in my life. Impaled by a past where I feel unworthy of anything good, I strive to earn it. Year after year, no matter what I do, it is never good enough. I make myself work harder. I often drive back to the beach before going home from work. Looking out over the ocean, I remember an unforgettable past. As I watch the waves crash against the shore, I question who I am. I ask God, why. *Why is there a constant battle, a war raging inside of me?* Conflicted, I feel strong forces pulling me in opposite directions, like a divine hand pushing me forward, and an enslaving shame snatching me back, beneath the turbulent waves. *What is wrong with me?* I question everything.

The questions tangle up inside my head. *Who am I that there would be a fight in the first place? Why did I survive it all?* The questions are endless, and the answers come gradually, through the process of living. I would like to meet this girl who everyone sees but me. This person who dances and sings with the children of Refreshing Springs and wins awards to hang on the walls of a home where she still feels so small, and invisible—something is still missing. The heart connection of who I am—my true self. Driven by an impossible quest, I will keep working hard until I find it. Like a lost little girl playing jacks, trying to find true love and acceptance, I will keep struggling, throwing up my heart like a small red ball, hoping to pick up all the scattered pieces of myself, before it all falls down again.

The dining hall of St. John's Hospital fills with family, friends and staff members. Anthony cries and his tears wet the lapel of his white tuxedo.

"Why is he crying?" one of the staff members asks as I videotape the beautiful event.

"Because he is happy," I answer. With their wheelchairs side-by-side, Anthony and Shinetta pledge their love for one another. Shinetta is a lovely young woman who came to St. John's nearly a year ago. Balloons and ribbons decorate every corner of the room. The smell of Caribbean food and homemade pies fills the reception hall sending curious eyes inside the festivities. Anthony glows with utter bliss as we celebrate His wedding day. I feel so blessed to share in the joy of my dearest friend, and as I look around, happiness swells inside me from the love and the lessons I have learned here at St. Johns.

Panic attacks

Less than two weeks later, I am unsure of how to tell Anthony that I must leave St. John's Hospital. Secret frustrations at home imprison me to a fear I cannot seem to escape. Stressful triggers have begun to overwhelm my life again, catapulting me back and forth between the past and the present. Images flash in front of me — they are not real, but I flail at the air as though they are, and in every flash, there is an attack. Someone is hurting me, or an object is coming straight toward me. I flinch as if it is happening in real time. I clearly see their faces. Some faces are people I know would never hurt me. Still, they appear in the violent scenes — out of the blue, they lurch at me. *I know that I am not crazy.* I tell myself, *there is nothing there, no object, no attack, no danger; it is just in my mind.*

During my last week at St. Johns, I realized that I have a long way to go before I gain a real sense of wellness. Just when I think I have control, life reminds me that I don't. The other day, it got worse. On the way home from work, I can't get air. Out of the blue, it happens. Panic and anxiety overwhelm me while I'm driving. The car moves ahead, but something is not right. I pull over on the shoulder of Interstate 95. The dread is something I cannot control. I feel as if I am going to die at that very moment. The anxiety attack comes suddenly, without warning. Inside the car, I feel dizzy, like everything is spinning upward and away. My body detaches as if I am leaving it behind. I cry out for God to help me, thinking of my children. I pray to see them grow up. I breathe, slowly, calming myself. "God let me see my children grow up," I whisper. Most of the triggers that bring on the panic attacks are unknown to me, but slowly I will begin to learn.

The process of introspection will take years: I need to become a student of myself and my emotions. I am still learning to watch for the triggers that cause overwhelming anxiety. Years after my freedom from addiction, I am still trying to get well. Spiders, loud voices, and cigarettes are all triggers that evoke a particular memory, like a bad dream that is all too real. I must learn to cope, and deal with my body's survival-mode reactions. I try to fill up every hour of the day; the busier the better. Church activities replace much of the negative thoughts and compulsions buried too deep for me to reach and recognize at this point in my life. My church community offers me the support and patience I need to continue the process of healing. The journey is long, and reading is a part of my therapy. I repeat the scripture in Philippians 4:6-7 that says, "Don't be anxious about anything, but instead, pray about everything. Tell God what you need and thank Him for what He has already done." I recite the words, write the words, and learn to let go; breathe out; *This too shall pass.*

Months later, I get sad news about my father's wife. Barbara dies suddenly. She had been sitting in her room, resting in her favorite chair. It was there that she never woke up. My father cannot live alone, nor can he afford to pay his rent with his social security. He has never owned his home or anything else for that matter. He falls deeper into depression. I ache for him, and while going through his things, I fall back into time.

I remember hearing about land, owed and then stolen before my father's generation. African Americans continue to pay rent on property they are supposed to own; land handed down from their families; land; stolen by greed—the same tyranny that took human lives and their very identity. Such were the times. But history never seems to die, like a broken record it appears to repeat, waiting for someone to take a stand, repair the breach, and allow the music of love to play a new song of equality. My father's eyes tell me it is a song he has never heard. In this fallen world, such *are* the times.

I think back to my days in public school, listening to "America the Beautiful." The lyrics clash with the reality of this nation's brutal crimes. False freedom is no freedom at all.

"America! America!
God shed his grace on thee,
And crown thy good with brotherhood
From sea to shining sea."

The songs, the times, the nation, and this life all reminds me of the contradictions I've witnessed since childhood. The conflict between rich and poor, love and violence are all the same perplexing states, like the blend of perfume and cigarettes — smells that introduced me to a world of shame. Such is life on this stormy planet.

With no economic footing and little to no education, my father is left in the same state of survival. My heart breaks for him. The death of his wife and the need to transition suddenly take a visible toll on his already poor health. He has to leave so much behind. Though he never says, I can still see a whirling sadness in his eyes. I know that look all too well. It is the kind of look you have when you disconnect, waiting for the world to make sense. He does not want to leave his things, nor give up driving, but losing Barbara, his home, and his health, has left him no choice.

The year is 1993, but it might as well be 1974. I feel like I am 7 years old again. My father moves in with us. My world turns upside down, and then, incredibly, it rewinds. An enchanted ship has somehow returned to get me. Its sails catch the wind, reversing the course of time, giving me a second chance with my father. The voyage of a childhood that sailed away many years ago takes me aboard, granting me a gift. A gift I longed for all my life — the gift of my father's time. It is priceless. New phases begin to open. Stages of healing and maturing the parts of me that are still scarred and incomplete.

The clouds take shape, and the moon follows me home when my father is with me, just as it did when I was a child. Other times, my dad and I sit alone for hours talking and revisiting his daunting past. In time, I begin to have a better understanding of why he was so quiet and reserved over the years. He suffered from debilitating depression, assuming the position of a life with no compass to guide him from birth, where his mother died, to a society where he struggled to survive as a Black man. How do you manage life as a man, a father, and a human being when it's denied, and you feel like the whole world is against you? I think of how alcohol must have evened the odds for him as it did for me. When you are drunk, you do not need to know who you are. Intoxicated, all the questions, every injustice falls into a deep, deep sleep. As we talk, I never speak to my dad about my battle with addiction, the sexual abuse, domestic violence, or the Post-Traumatic Stress Disorder (PTSD) that often makes me feel like I am losing my mind. He has enough stress of his own to carry.

At the time, I was not aware I had the mental condition, and that it was one of the reasons for my impulsive reactions and chronic anxiety. The past and present trauma in my life keep me silent, hiding the fear and insecurity. Like breathing, it feels normal; the flinching, the scary images that come without thinking, and the denial of my own emotions; it all feels normal now. The years teach you to adapt and manage life the best way you know how. I understand my father's heart, even more today than before. I am his daughter, and more than his blood and his name, I carry the legacy of all that he is. When you get an understanding, empathy comes and fills up the empty spaces in your heart. Compassion drowns the disappointment of missing him all these years. And as 1 Peter 4:8 says, "love covers a multitude of sin." Life is not black and white, there are reasons why it unfolds in varying degrees of colors and contrasts; a reason why we were purposefully created like flowers in a garden; all different, yet all the same.

As we sit together, I think about the plight of the Black community, and the perpetual traumatic stress disorder brought on by a system of staunch bigotry and inequality. Like my father, I've learned to hide the conditions of a life impaled by piercing thorns. You take life as it comes and you keep it moving, while you wait for the world to change, or for Christ's return.

This is what the years have taught me. That is what my parents had to endure, and their parents before them. Perhaps, for this reason, no redress have come for the generations of families utterly broken by this *normal* dysfunction. *Why speak out when every hurt and offense is perceived as normal.*

In my flustered mind, I still struggle to think that *certain* human beings were denied the right to feel and express the emotions of anger, sadness, fear, and stress, and be seen and heard with equal empathy and care. But my mother's denial of her own emotions revealed this truth; more than her lips could say. I think of Mahalia's song, Emmett Till, and the awful expression on my mother's face that is still so haunting. My question remains the same as it was when I rode in the backseat of her car, watching the rainfall, like the tears of slaves from heaven. A thousand times, I ask *why*? Why are the hurts, oppression, and the pain of a black man in this country viewed differently, less valid and valued than that of Whites and other race groups in society? They are expected to just get over the mistreatment, the depression, the tyranny, and the unyielding discrimination as if nothing ever happened as if no crime has been committed.

The reparations given to the Jews, Japanese, and Native Americans for the human atrocities committed against them throughout history are public knowledge; however, with the Black community...the very ones that helped build America's massive wealth, there is unfinished business.

Like countless others, this is my father's reality, and now, it is mine. The upshot is seen across the country and felt around the world from the war on drugs to the vicious cruelty of law enforcement. It is real, tangible, and cannot be ignored any longer. It will not just go away; it must be confronted before it can be restored. After the Civil War and before President Lincoln's assassination, there was a visionary program, a crusade of sorts where land and resources could have changed the course of History and the lives of the African American community. Once President Andrew Johnson, the successor of Lincoln, got into power, the order was overturned and vetoed into oblivion in 1866; the land was returned to slave owners.

America the beautiful, where the majority embraces Christianity, yet around and around we go as if nothing ever happened; as if God cannot see; as if He hasn't given every follower of Christ the command to stand for the weak and speak against the greedy systems of this world. I question why people believe there is a God yet mistreat each other or remain silent at the mistreatment of their fellow human being. Did He not tell us in Micah 6:8 to "act justly and to love mercy and to walk in humility?"

The questions are disturbing because the answers are paralyzed — trapped between the lessons from the thorns of history.

Today, the signs are everywhere. It seems the violence, the profanity, and the word "~~nigger~~" are all the traits of a slave master, the same demonic system built on greed, selling human beings as property. Until now, quite insidiously, the slave has become its master's son. I think of my angry grandfather, Eddie, who had to sign his name with an X because, in this country, he was denied the right to an education. His history haunts me because it is a part of my present reality and that of my children. The deception continues to live and breathe with each new century. It lives in Bruce and all those like him, unaware of the transfer — fighting blind, against the wrong enemy. Hatred hides in plain sight, watching the generations assume the same twisted position of an oppressed past; a past where human rights are denied to the acceptable degree of being seen-and-not-heard, hence any signs of emotions — sadness, fear, anger, contempt, and disgust are unacceptable. The unrelenting hate penalizes you for having emotions, labeling you a convict, a "superpredator," and such, who "got the attention," not of a loving, healthy family structure, but of a lethal, evil, and monstrous social order that deemed human beings to be inhumane for no other reason than greed. The agenda of greed and personal gain has not changed since the nightmare of the Atlantic Slave trade, where African families sailed in chains to the Americas. History repeats, thereby creating the conditions and laws through which to reconstitute the same tyranny of hate and greed. Such are the times; you wait on the world to change.

A time where survival is all that matters, so you learn to just "get over it" or hide it until the inner rage causes the volcanic eruptions that are evident today. I look in my father's eyes, thinking of my children, wondering, *how much longer?*

The signatures on the Civil Rights Act of 1964 did nothing to change the heart of those who practice bigotry. Unaccountable for the human atrocities, the nation stays the course while the defenseless assume the position. Only God has the answers. But for now, heaven is quiet. Justice is silent, and the questions go quiet.

I glance at my father. He too is quiet. The answers must wait for another time, another day, and perhaps another place. A place, like heaven.

As the month's pass, I try to lavish him with the love of 10,000 lifetimes. I would do anything to make up for the sadness in his eyes. I try to show him that, to me, he is a great champion. But I am not sure if he can quite understand his worth; in my eyes, or his own.

Summer comes, and my car turns into a time machine. I drive with my father next to me, going just about everywhere together. I hurry to make up for the time we lost all those years ago. Pizza Hut, bowling, the movies, it does not matter the place. We are together, and my joy is indescribable. He sits with the usual solemn demeanor, watching me from the passenger seat.

"Daddy, are you okay?"

"Yes, baby, I'm all right," he says, slurring a little from the last stroke, but his eyes never stop smiling at me. I smile back; dancing on the moon.

On weekends at the bowling alley, my children boast of who is the best bowler, competing against each other as though they bet money on the game. It seems Bruce always bowls the highest score. On the sideline, I sit next to my father, cheering for the kids to get a strike. I am grateful for the fun times our family share. Nighttime, I listen out for my father's call. On the nights when he cannot sleep, I massage his back with the green rubbing alcohol he likes. It smells of menthol, and the joy it gives me to care for him surpasses every sorrow. Most nights we stay up watching old movies, just the two of us; those times are priceless to me. I cuddle up close to him; listening to his heartbeat. His Old Spice cologne still smells like Christmastime, and after all these years, the melody of our song is the same, as if no time has passed at all. While he is watching the movie, I breathe him in, closing my eyes; dancing on the moon.

On Sunday morning, we head out to church service and my father surprises me. "Baby wait for me, I'm coming with you," he says, limping out of his room with his hat in his hands.

I smile. It is the first time my father attends church with me. After Sunday school, I sit with him on the back pew for a few minutes before morning service starts.

"Daddy, can I get you some water or anything?"
His blue brim hat rests on his knee. "No baby. I'm okay." He stares out again as if he is miles away, but I am joyful because he is here. Soon, he begins to attend services regularly.

Sunday after Sunday, he sits and quietly observes. After a few weeks, a miracle happens. As the music plays, Pastor Bellamy makes an altar call: "Come to Jesus. He is faithful to forgive us for all our transgressions. Come and give your heart."

On my post, as I usher near the front entrance of the church, I see my father stand to his feet. One foot drags behind the other as he makes his way toward the altar. I hurry to his side. He smiles when he sees me. I smile back, remembering the silent whispers of a little girl. Pastor Bellamy asks those who have come to the altar to repeat the prayer after him. Together, my father and I say the sinner's prayer: "Lord I am a sinner, forgive me of all my sins, I believe you sent Jesus to die on the cross so that I can have everlasting life…" Once a man who said he did not believe; now my father is born-again. This is our miracle; an answer to a silent prayer that was prayed many years ago in the bathroom stall of Oriole Elementary school. God is faithful, even when we don't see a way, or understand His plan, we can trust that He is in control. My father's smile is different now: lighter, freer.

Since my dad has moved in, he and my mother have been talking again for the first time since I can remember. I watch them sitting together, having a cordial conversation. No arguing no fighting, there are only pleasantries surrounded by their grandchildren and family pets. As we sit in the living room, I take pictures so I will never forget the moment. My heart leaps. After all that has happened, there is peace between them. *God is faithful.*

One night, my mother comes over to take my father out to dinner. As he got his hat and coat, I tell him that I will wait up for him. As they drove away, I think of how different they both are. The war is over. They have finally decided to let it all go and forgive. "Thank you, Jesus," I whisper, staring out over the road.

My sister Linda moves back to Florida. She is expecting her first child. She comes to stay with me for a few months and asks if I would be her Lamaze coach. I am excited. With a pillow under one arm and a blanket under the other, we are ready. We attend Lamaze classes together at Holy Cross Hospital, and our bond grows closer than ever. It is a joyful time.

That same year, my brother Michael joins Refreshing Springs and soon marries. Pastor Bellamy performs the wedding, and during the reception, my parents smile and laugh as though they are teenagers again. In the passing months, I watch them become good friends and wonder why it takes a lifetime for us to realize we are only human; living in a fallen world; prone to make mistakes.

My father tries to hold on to his independence, often getting upset because he can no longer drive. He leaves the house, and when I get off work, I search his old neighborhood looking for him. When I find him, he is under a large shade tree with five other men, playing checkers. I wait for him until he is ready to come home.

One night, I could not find him. I searched his regular hangouts, asking the people who know him if they have seen him around today.

"No, we ain't seen Roadman," one of the old-timers says. I call 911 in a total panic. And then, I call my mother crying, worried my father was lost. She tells me not to worry.

"That's your daddy. He likes the road. He has been that way

since I met him. Always on the go. Don't worry; he'll be home."

She was right.

He comes home later that evening on the city bus. He is fine and says he had wanted to get out and go by his old house and neighborhood. I tell him I was worried and remind him to take his medication. He gives me the same coy grin and limps to his room. Grateful he is home, I breathe a sigh of relief. My father continues to long for the open road. The unsettled look in his eyes makes me wonder what he is still searching for. I pray he finds it.

Later that year, I begin working with my mother at Jade Ocean Cleaners on A1A near the beach. Larry Toroker owns the dry cleaners, running it with his wife, Ruth. Larry and Ruth make an attractive couple and are highly respected by many of the business owners surrounding the busy strip mall. They run the front desk while my mother works as the master seamstress. She wants me to be the silk presser and teaches me all she knows about the business. It really doesn't matter what she wants me to do at the cleaners. I only want to be near her, and somehow make her proud of me. Sometimes I still feel I could never be good enough, no matter what I do, regardless of my accomplishments in life. I will keep trying to be good enough, to feel worthy; to pick up all the jackstones that fell down, so many years ago.

Larry is a generous and kind man. He offers me extra time off whenever I need it for my children and father. He never deducts the time from my pay. And the opportunity to work with my mother is a pleasant experience because I get to see a side of her I have never seen before—not all work, she has a light and easy way about her that makes me feel like we would be good friends if we get to truly know each other.

"Sydney isn't Larry one of the most handsome men you have ever seen," my mother whispers to me as he walks toward the back to grab a customer's order. I smile, turning my head away. "Well he is!" she declares loudly. "God gave me eyes. I can look," she adds as Larry comes back towards the front. "Lillie, what are you up to now? Sandra, your mother is always getting into something. I have to keep my eyes on her. Don't believe anything she says about me." He grins on the way back to the front desk. We chuckle and get back to work. Their playful banter makes the job enjoyable.

On alternate weekends and some evenings, I work private duty as a nurse assistant for Mr. and Mrs. Polly. The couple and I become close friends, and they adore my children. They give three-year-old Cory the nickname, Tiger. Mr. Polly is a Vietnam vet who lost the ability to walk after the war. He is one of my most challenging patients. He has diabetes, and he often hides food he knows he is not supposed to have. His wife Fran fusses with him after she finds Toblerone Swiss Chocolate wrappers between his sheets; it is his favorite. Keeping his diabetes under control is a constant battle. I find myself in the crossfire, where the verbal altercations let me know the problem is about more than the chocolate wrappers or his diabetes.

One evening, Fran tells me why she becomes so angry. Broken capillaries run like spiky red lines across the surface of the pale skin on her face and neck as she talks about her husbands' affair. She says it happened many years ago, before the war, but the pain on her face tells me she has never gotten over it. Fran had been fighting breast cancer when he had the affair. Now as a cancer survivor, perhaps her disease is easier to fight than the feelings of betrayal. She has never found the ability to forgive him. She tells me she never will. Years later, it would not be diabetes, but an aneurysm that caused his death. I never see Fran again after that, but I think about her all the time. I think about how forgiveness can be hard, especially when the pain outlives the past; I understand this problem all too well.

My hectic schedule keeps me in a constant state of motion. The children are busy with school and church activities. Casita is now in 7th grade and attends Victory Christian Academy.

Tonight, she has a project due for class. On the floor, she and I work together with glue and cardboard to create a model of Noah's Ark. We add the animals two by two from magazine cut-outs, with a dove ascending through the small scissor-cut window in the upper-right corner of the Ark. Hours of cutting, gluing and pasting, and we finish before any flood comes.

"We did it! Thank you, Mama," Casita says half-asleep. Everyone has gone to bed. We hug and kiss goodnight. I stay up longer to make the ark just right for her, adding an invisible string to the dove's wings, so it looks as if it is in midflight, off to check for dry land—a place to call home. At 2 a.m. the project was complete.

Adrenaline, like a persistent force, moves me past the fatigue as I try to seize every moment of this second chance to create, color, and play again with my children. Their love means everything to me, and life feels brand new. God's mercy and grace give me a gift to recreate these precious moments that I had thought I could never get back. There is life after addiction. Despite the rubble of my past, God is making all things new, just like the lullabies said, "it's a time for beginnings, love makes the world go 'round."

The next day, Casita comes home from school wearing a big smile on her face, announcing, "Mommy, I got an A on my school project!" We give each other a high five.

"Good job, sweetheart!"

The Other Side of the Moon

We were all born here; among the thorns and thistles, but is this where we really belong? We strive for citizenship, riches, and fame, while all along, the sand in the hourglass of life continues to escape. The path toward paradise reminds us that hope placed in earthly things will only bring disappointment and grief; for all will pass away—this is a certainty. Faith in Christ promises life, today and forever.

Tonight, Pastor Bellamy preaches about heaven. "John 14:6 says Jesus is the way, the truth, and the life; no one comes to the Father except through Him."

Pen and notepad in hand, I take notes and ponder the belief of heaven and its streets paved with gold. *Could such a glorious place literally exist beyond this world of thorns and sadness?* I've heard many stories about heaven over the years. My grandmother spoke of seeing heaven before she died. When I was a little girl driving in the backseat of my mother's car, I heard Mahalia Jackson sing about joining a heavenly choir, and a sad story about Emmett Till who I hope made it through the gates. In the Book of Revelation, chapter 21, John, the apostle, wrote of seeing a new heaven and a new earth, the transformation of the saints of God, and a promise of eternal life. Still, I have many questions about all of this. There is so much I don't understand about the heavenly kingdom where no one ever grows old. I've heard the atheist logic that life is the random product of time plus matter plus chance. If this is true, what can people hope for, and why strive for life, liberty, and the pursuit of happiness if nothing beyond this imploding society exists? And what of dreams, visions, and the supernatural things that time, neither matter nor chance can explain away? Similar to the night, I saw the angel with six wings, it can't be described. I remember the vision clearly; it was more holy than it was supernatural.

I had finished my usual prayer in the privacy of the bathroom. Unexpectedly, it happens. It was not a dream. Before seeing the angel, I had been asking for wisdom and understanding. I had so many questions for God; questions of why He allows atrocities like the Holocaust, slavery, wars, genocide, and famine. Every night I asked—until the angel appeared out of nowhere.

Sitting up on the bed with the usual insomnia, I heard my name coming from a blinding light. He said my name twice; "Sandra, Sandra," I clearly heard His voice coming from the light, shining from every direction. Piercing and sharp, but the light did not hurt my eyes. Without question, I know His voice, His presence. I have felt it all my life. In the quiet whispers of Jesus, moving between the notes of my childhood lullabies, and in the eye of the fiercest storms, I heard Him.

"Behold!" He said to me as I turned to see the most breathtaking sight of an angel, too fearsome to look at for any length of time. I feel as if I would die from the sight of it. The angel never moves its mouth, yet it speaks clearly, "Fear not." But fear is the only thing I could feel. It has six wings, all stretched out, as it hovered near my bedside. I begged God to take it away. Weeks after the vision, I was still afraid it would show itself again, but the Seraphim did not appear a second time. God is such a mystery. No man can fully understand His ways, and among all the questions about heaven and hell, I have come to trust the mystery of the great love of Christ, His sacrifice, and His plan for my life. But sometimes, I still struggle with my faith. Life can be so uncertain, so unpredictable. And so, I move between faith and doubt, prone to wander and forget; prone to lose myself in the regretful past and the uncertain future. "One day at a time," Mother Brown told me, many years ago while I was in rehab; she was right. There are no easy answers in life. All we have is today, right now, this moment. But anxiety has a way of stealing the day, the moments.

After church, my father asks me questions about faith and the family of Jesus.

"Did Jesus have brothers and sisters from Mary and Joseph?" my dad asks leaning against the bedroom door entrance.

"I'm not sure, Daddy," I respond with delight that he has asked me a question about the Bible; he never has before. We talk about the church service tonight, lobbing questions back and forth.

The evening feels extra special, and our relationship grows stronger. Every moment with my father is magical. Ever since he joined the church, I have noticed changes in him. Now, I can see a light shining in his eyes. Instead of staring out into space, he seems more focused as if he is beginning to awake out of a deep sleep. And one night, when I come in his room to massage the green rubbing alcohol on his back—our nightly routine that soothes his itchy skin, I find him on his knees. He is praying. His hands folded beneath his bowed head. I hear his silent prayer and back slowly away, easing the door closed. Seeing my father in prayer is a marvelous sight. Again, the moment reminds me of the silent telegram I sent to God from the bathroom of my elementary school:

"God save my daddy."

"Thank you, Jesus," I whisper on the way back to my room. God never forgets; He answers prayer.

Less than a month later, my world is about to turn upside down. I see my father drinking juice. It runs down the sides of his mouth. Fear, like a sharp steel rod, strikes through my heart.

"Daddy, something is wrong, we have to get you to the hospital!"

He smiles and shakes his head, no.

"I don't need to go to the hospital, baby. I feel fine. I'm all right. You always worry. Don't worry so much," he says with garbled breaks between his words. He hates doctors; trusting them is a huge sore spot for him. He refuses to listen to my pleas for him to get a check-up. My father had been upset the day I had called 911 when he did not come home. Now, I notice his speech is somewhat off, his limp more distinct, and his shirt moist with juice. And he tells me not to worry and not to call for help.

"Daddy, please!" I beg. Still, he doesn't want to go.

I felt relieved and grateful when Bruce makes him get into the car and drives us to the hospital. When we arrive at West Side Regional Medical center, emergency room doctors immediately run blood tests and a CAT scan.

"Nothing appears abnormal," the doctor tells me.

"The CAT scan of your father's brain shows no new stroke activity, but we will admit him for additional testing and further evaluation." The doctor walks away, leaving me with more questions than he had time to answer.

"Everything will be all right, Daddy." I caress his hand while holding tight to my faith, believing God is going to fix whatever is wrong.

January 1994

I stay by my father's side until the days turn into weeks. The children and I stop by Hot and Now, the burger joint off State Road 411 most days so we can get a quick bite to eat and get back to the hospital. Family members gather every now and then to visit. Some people on my father's side I have never met before. Nearly every day, I take Alka-Seltzer to calm the stomach pains that cause me to double over on the floor of the bathroom; it seems my body reacts to the stress of what my mind refuses to believe—his health is deteriorating. My mother brings flowers, but her schedule at work keeps her from visiting as much as she would like. She often does both our jobs at the cleaners so I can spend more time with my father. Joyce and Linda visit, staying until late some nights.

We gather around his bedside and talk about old times. The glow on Joyce's face makes me believe she is feeling better. Through the years, I feel as if she has gradually pulled herself away, allowing us to practice the lessons of faith she planted from our youth. Despite the distance, my heart beats faster every time I see her. So many years ago, she gave us a gift; the amazing gift of a childlike faith wrapped up in stories, prayer, and songs that make me believe beyond what I can see. A faith that believes anything is possible; I believe my father will get better. Joyce stands near our father's hospital bed.

"I love you, Daddy," she says. Still wise beyond her years, Joyce speaks only of the good times.

February 14th

Linda and I pin up red hearts on the walls of my father's new hospital room. The doctor moves him from the stroke unit to a regular floor. Although my dad's health has not improved, I am hopeful.

"Happy Valentine's Day, Daddy," we say. He does not answer back. He gazes at the hearts decked across his wall and smiles. We take pictures and talk with him as if at any second, he will speak. He gives me the same coy smile as he always has since I was a little girl, skipping through his barbershop in Tampa. I miss the sound of his voice, but I am hopeful. I wait.

The nurse tells me about Aphasia, a condition that impairs the ability to speak. She tells me only time will tell whether he will regain the ability to talk again. I believe he will. My father has become incontinent—he can no longer control his bowels. I change his undergarments after I give him his nightly bed bath. His brown eyes say more than words could ever explain as I place the warm towel under his chin to soften his whiskers before his shave.

"There, all fresh and clean; you smell so nice." I splash Old Spice cologne under his chin after his shave and bath. He smells of Christmastime, and to care for him is a gift and an honor for me.

February 23rd- Jade Ocean Cleaners

"Sandra, you have a phone call. Sweetheart, I think it's about your dad." Larry's voice is solemn as he calls me to the front desk. My mother asks who is on the line. It is Gladys, my father's daughter from Miami. She is at the hospital.

"Sandra, you need to come. Dad stopped breathing just now.

He woke up, and he spoke. He asked for you."

When I arrive at the hospital, my father's room overcrowds with family and friends. Some people I still do not recognize.

"He asked for you, Sandra. We told him you were on the way. He is holding on," a voice in the crowded room explains. The nurse tells me the stark prognosis. She says the staff will do everything they can to keep my father comfortable. I thank her and block out the reality of his condition. I stay hopeful, waiting for a miracle; no matter what, I believe.

"Daddy, I am here," I whisper.
"Sandra," he says softly with a faint breath. *He sees me.*
"Hi," I say forcing a smile. *He hears me;* that's what my heart tells me. Hours pass, and his breathing stabilizes.
"He seems to be doing better," a family member says.
"We are going to head home. We will see you tomorrow."

Almost midnight, Bruce tells me I should go home too and come back tomorrow.

"I can't leave," I tell him. I pull down the side rail of my dad's bed so I can bring my chair closer, needing to be here. He has waited for me and now, I will wait with him through the night. And If I have to, I will wait another lifetime. I'm not prepared for what the wind whispered to me on the way to the hospital.

Bruce stays, understanding my need to be with my father. I feel grateful for him being there. The hours pass by with nurses coming in and out of the room. I lean against my father's shoulder, staring out at the blank TV screen, and then back at him. He gives a quiet sigh and presses his head closer to mine. The smell of his Old Spice lifts me away.

I close my eyes, and I am six years old again in Tampa. It was the last time my father picked me up off the floor and held me in his arms. Carefree, my little legs dangled in the air. His arms felt like the beams of a sturdy bridge that would carry me from my youth to adulthood, helping me find my place in this world. He never hit the lottery, but today, he is the richest man I know, because I was there when he gave his heart to Jesus and received the priceless gift of salvation and eternal life. Still, I am not ready to let him go; I'm no good at good-byes. I believed he and I would dance on top of the moon forever. That's what my heart told me.

February 24th

It is 4:25 a.m.; the sound of a death rattle interrupts the melody of our song. The heart-wrenching gurgles bring me back to reality. The sound is coming from my father's chest; he is dying. Bruce walks out of the room. Louder and louder, my father's breathing worsens. I want to defy the no-resuscitation order, but I knew the appointment of life and death is not mine, but God's. A part of me wants my father to fight, but his weary expression tells me he is tired; his eyes tell me the fight is over. He's preparing for the road again, but this time, he will not return to me. Not on this side of the moon. A tear rolls down from his soft brown eyes; it was the first time I have ever seen my father cry.

"Daddy I am here." I lean closer to him, holding his hand, listening beyond the rattle of pooling fluids. I ignore it, listening harder so I could hear the melody of our song one more time.

"I love you. I am here. I will not leave you. I will see you again someday." My father blinks his eyes while my heart is breaking into a million pieces, but I don't show it. I force a smile for him, just as he did for me all my life.

"Everything is okay, Daddy." I touch his face, soft and slow, hoping he will always remember our special dance and somehow take it with him. "God is with you always; He promises never to leave us nor forsake us," I whisper, kissing his forehead and hands, thanking him for being my dad; the best father he knew how to be.

At 4:30 am, the rattling stops. My father surrenders his breath to the giver of life. In those moments, I don't take my eyes off him, wanting him to know a part of me will go with him.

In the stillness, my heart beats alone, and I finally let the tears fall. "God give me strength," I whisper. A deep sorrow consumes me. *I can't hear it anymore. The melody is gone.*

Life is but a dream.

In this stormy life, our best just isn't enough. It enables us to see the human side of our place on earth. And it helps us seek the answers in the only place they can be found: in the Word of God. I share my father's legacy with honor and hope. I hope there is indeed a place called heaven. The one Mahalia sang about. I want it to be a loving place where all men are truly free. Where people are not judged by their skin color, class, or ethnicity. A world where love reigns without end and all things are new. Grief is a subject of life that I never properly learned, and so, I begin to wade between the past and the present; unable to move forward. This was one of the hardest lessons for me; I had a lot to learn about the transcendent and universal journey that happens to all life. In 1 Thessalonians 4:13-18, Apostle Paul tells us "not to grieve like those who have no hope." He goes on to write that belief in the death and resurrection of Jesus Christ means that God will also revive those who have died in Him. *I wish it were all that easy to understand.* But the reality is, I believed for a miracle that didn't come, and begin to question my faith. Wherever heaven is, I want to believe my father and I will see each other again there; somewhere on the other side of the moon.

Dead Girl Legs

God gave us a promise in the sign of the rainbow. Rainbows appear in the sky for the briefest of moments before, like a mist, their phenomenal radiance fades; it teaches us the wisdom of time, and the value of numbering our days.

I don't do well with goodbyes, mainly because I believed for a miracle that never came. After Sunday service, I walk toward the back to the church office.

"Pastor Bellamy, may I plant a garden?"

"Yes." He says without hesitation.

After Pastor Bellamy gave me permission to plant a flower garden at the church, I find an outlet to the inner sadness of losing my father. I have little to no idea of what I am doing; still, he gives me his blessing. I was grateful. After several trips to the Home Depot, my garden is almost complete. Thirsty flowers of every color border the outside walls of the church and around the palm trees in the parking area across the street. On the days when there is no rain, I water the flowers, waiting for new buds to bloom. After my father's funeral, I have found myself becoming angrier. Planting this garden helps me deal with the inner conflict. Going through the process of digging through dirt, pulling up rocks and weeds, and planting flowers help cool the burning acid in my stomach. Glib whispers about my sanity float around, but insults are nothing new for me. I shrug it off, learning to take compliments and insults as though they were the same; it's all fleeting anyway. My fragile state of mind has always been questionable, and even I marvel that I am not locked away somewhere in a straitjacket. Some days are better than others—such is life. Just a dream.

I stay for long hours at the church, planting, tilling the ground, trying to find peace. I think of my mother. She says she is worried about me because I wear my dad's old hat and jacket almost everywhere I go. I tell her I am fine, but inside, I'm downright mad. I wanted more time with my father, and now he is gone; it is too late, and I do not know how to mourn his death, particularly now that I am clean and sober. Crack cocaine and MD 20/20 had numbed the sting of LiSandra's death. Drugs and liquor are no longer options for me. I garden, digging deeper, trying to deal with manic emotions face to face and with my head on straight. Still, the anger eats away at me. I am angry at myself, at the world, and because I know God has the power to heal, I'm angry that He allowed my father to die. I blame myself; *I should have quit working so much and focused more on taking care of him.* I'm angry at the world for its racism, hatred, and greed that made my father believe he was less than human because of his nonwhite existence. Acid explodes inside, burning up until my throat hurts. Truth is, I wasn't ready to grow up; my dad had already missed so much of our life. And the reality was I could not go back in time. I rage as if I was a child again;

I don't recall any of this between the notes of the lullabies about an all-powerful God who makes all things new. What about the miracles? What happened to my dad's miracle? Life is so unfair! On and on, the musings went until I made myself sick, unable to let go.

Shoveling through the dirt of the garden, I question everything I think I know about life, but life keeps reminding me I don't know anything. Grief is a necessary process, but in my manic mind, life has cheated me again. I rage at the wind, remembering the stories of oppression, the apathy and depression that ensues, and the insanity of a world that deals you a hand that guarantees you will lose. *This society is a double-dealing thief.* Tears fall against the soil as I rage at everything around me. I dig deeper, stabbing at the hard ground with my hand shovel, trying to get past the pain. I shovel until blisters form between my thumb and index finger.

Snatching at the thistly weeds in the garden, I try to find the root, so it never grows back again. I try to refocus, to learn how to express anger appropriately, but I never learned to *"be angry, and sin not"* as the Bible instructs in Ephesians 4:26. Maybe, I am afraid of my anger because it mixes with emotions I do not completely understand because I have yet to learn how to develop a healthy relationship with them. There are many emotions that exist between the extremes of passivity and rage, but I'm still learning to find my way through the maze of my mind. Wiping the sweat from my face, I clench my teeth and dig deeper. Every now and then, I find myself shoveling mindlessly until I blink and watch the tears water the soil. I want to believe my father is in a better place, but I wasn't ready to say goodbye. *Are we ever truly ready? Why, after a childhood without my dad, would God give him back to me, and then take him away again?* Just when we were getting to know each other better, he is gone. I had waited for a miracle, but still, he died. *What is the point of it all?* I ask myself. *Why have faith?*

I plant more flowers, trying to fill up the emptiness inside. Some of the flowers wilt and die days after I plant them. The ground had not been ready, not soft enough to receive the seedlings. Day after day, I come back to the garden. I am driven beyond that which I can explain—determined to shovel, pull, and dig deeper, until the ground is soft enough to accept the new life I am trying to plant.

Saturday morning, I rise early to go to the garden. I see an empty space near the edge of the road in front of the church. I prepare the soil to plant more flowers there. Street litter, thick weeds, and rocks cover the surface of the ground. I clear the area and dig, pulling up more dirt clods, sharp rocks, and more debris. Morning fades and the heat from the afternoon sun scorches down until sweat trickles from my forehead. I keep working, hoping the flowers will like their new home.

On my knees, I water the flowers, and then, to the right, just down the street, I see police lights flashing near the end of the block. The commotion is less than one street away from the place of my arrest in the citywide drug sting. One after the other, the police come. I stand to my feet, brushing off the grass and dirt, and walk toward the end of the block. Police and Crime Scene Investigators begin rolling yellow tape around the fringes of the construction area on the corner of 15th and 27th Avenue. The open structure has gray cinder blocks scattered about the foundation of an unfinished renovation area. Whoever started the building process, didn't complete it for whatever reason.

"What happened?" I ask a man who is standing among the growing crowd of onlookers.

"Not sure, they say she was a young prostitute. She musta got with the wrong people." He says with his arms folded high up on his chest.

"Is she still in there now?" I ask, looking at the scene and then back at him.

"See right there, by that hole, down by the pile of cement blocks right there." My eyes follow his pointed finger through the opening of the topless building.

"Those are her legs?" I ask in disbelief of what my eyes clearly see. He breathes. "Damn shame," he says, still looking at her legs. I walk back to the church, unable to get her out of my mind. Her lifeless legs, ashen and stiff, covered with rotting skin. I cannot shake off the image. I wonder who she is, and though I didn't see her face, I wonder what happened to her and why. *How old was she? Where did she live? Whom does she belong to? Whose daughter, mother, or loved one lay dead among the rubble?* My heart hurts for whoever she was, for the dreams she may have had, and for the unfortunate events that ended her life on the corner of a dusty construction site. I walk slowly away, back to the church, and return to my gardening.

The sunlight fades, and I rake over the ground, smoothing out wood chips of mulch around each flower bed. After some time, Pastor Bellamy drives up and compliments the work. "You are doing a good job. The flowers look beautiful. Thank you, Sister Sandra."

Covered head to toe in perspiration, dirt, and grass stains; I look down at my pigeon-toed feet and smile. "You're welcome, Pastor Bellamy." I look up, partly embarrassed because I'm a grassy mess. The legs of the dead girl sit in the back of my mind.

"I have a fern plant in my office. Would you mind taking care of it for me?" he asks with his keys in his hand.

"No, sir, I don't mind. It would be a pleasure." Whatever my hands can find to do, I jump at the chance to be useful. He and I are alone in his office that sits on the right side of the church. The fern sits in the back corner of his desk. Pastor Bellamy spends a few minutes telling me how proud he is of my accomplishments and how much he likes my gardening. I remember feeling joyful at hearing that he was proud of me; words every daughter wishes to hear her father say. I sit with my arms slightly folded in the chair, brushing off blades of grass and speckles of dirt. Trying to relax, I unfold my arms, forcing my hands to sit still while torrents of anxiety flow pass my calm expression.

"I can take care of that for you now, Pastor," I say with the usual awkwardness. My hands begin to move clumsily by my sides. Any social interaction causes bouts of anxiety to rise; like breathing, it comes. *There is no spider; I am safe*, I tell myself, exhaling the images away. Pastor Bellamy hands me the potted fern and tells me to let him know if I need any plant food. As I stand at the back door to fill the planter with water, he asks me if everything was all right.

"Yes, sir. Everything is fine." I tell the lie out of habit, never sharing with him the truth of how I truly feel. Still, I think he can detect the desperate longings I try to hide. Like my father, Roadman, I muffle every emotion with apathy and continue to search for something that seems beyond my reach. Pastor Bellamy gives me a warm smile—like a father.

"Thank you again for taking care of the plant and for the good job you are doing around the church. We are here for you. The church is your family, and we love you."

"Thank you, Pastor, I love you too." I walk back to busy myself in the garden.

In the coming months, while I till the garden at the church, something is changing. I feel it. Something inside of me is starting to grow and die at the same time. Digging up the hard ground gives me a chance, not only to grieve but also to begin to heal the deep wounds buried inside — a pain that is too far to reach on my own. I dig deeper, feeling the Holy Spirit tilling the ground of my heart, surrounding me, teaching me the lessons of letting go, surrendering all. He reaches down below the depths of all that I am until I begin to understand the reasons why we must toil. A clean heart and noble character can only be cultivated and protected by the thorns; those difficult places and the hard times we face in life. When we embrace affliction, we become more like Christ — lowly and loving.

As it turns out, all those years I was coming to the altar of the church, kneeling, praying, crying; I was transforming. I was learning to die to the anger and misery. I just did not know it at the time, but my heart was changing. The transformation continues here in my garden. It offers an unexpected gift. Through gardening, I'm connecting with nature. Through connecting with nature, I'm undergoing a deep healing process; it is God's therapy. He has me exactly where he wants me to be. Among the seeds that break and die to have a chance to bloom to life, I learn to let go. And soon, the roots of faith and trust begin to spread wider, deeper, beneath my clumsy feet. Among the soil and nature's rhyme, God teaches me the lessons of the thorns. He alone is God, holding all power of life, death, and time. He is omniscient — all seeing, all-knowing. Not even a sparrow falls beyond His watchful care. Today, I believe He received my father's repented heart and restless spirit. I believe my father finally found what he spent a lifetime looking for: rest and riches beyond what could ever be earned or won. He found home. Knowing this is enough for me now.

After my father died, I thought I lost the melody of our heartbeat forever, and the enchanted childhood dance we shared on the moon was gone, but I was wrong. Nothing is ever truly lost.

As time passes, my tears dry, and Pastor Bellamy tells me to lift my eyes to heaven; that indiscernible place where all of our help comes from. He teaches us the scripture verse of Psalms 121 in our midweek Bible study. As I humble myself and listen, I find new strength. I learn to look up, be still, and trust in a God who works in mysterious ways. It is written in Romans 8:28, that He is working "all things for the good of those who love Him." I believe in His

Holy Word, even when I cannot fully understand it all.

In time, I could hear the melody again; my father's and mine. It is there, in the quiet night sky, in the smell of Christmastime, and in this garden where I learn the poetry of how life is never complete until it surrenders, dying to its present form. Like a caterpillar, surrendering its earth-bound existence to become a butterfly; a completely new creation; so, we too shall be changed. 1 Corinthians 15:52-54, says, "The trumpet of the Lord shall sound, and in the twinkling of an eye, we will be changed from mortal to immortality. Death will be swallowed up in victory." This is the hope we have in Him; the great mystery of life beyond the veil of this human existence.

I garden, and among the flowers that bloom, I can hear God speak to me, reminding me that soon He would make all things new again. I feel His grace, and as my attitude begins to change, grief turns into gratitude. I begin to recognize the gift of a second chance God gave me to spend time with my dad before his death. A second chance to live beyond the prison of disgrace, depression, and addiction. There is a joy now, springing up among the colorful blossoms around me and the thorns that impale me. There is purpose in both the blossoms and the thorns. They are symbols of His amazing grace and the deep change He is completing within me. As I meditate and mature in His Word, it speaks of the realization of His divine intervention.

The fact of the matter is, if it had not been for the grace of God, the dead girl in the abandoned building could have easily been me. There is no question in my mind of how I survived the daunting years. God's grace and mercy brought me through. I believe that His angels have watched over me all my life. I think back to many years ago in Tampa with my father. God gave us the melody of our heartbeat from the very beginning. Before He called my father home, God reunited our hearts, giving us the second chance of new memories to share, new melodies to dance to, and the gift of salvation, a promise before the final breath to one day make all things new. No sadness can steal this truth away. In this moment, I am here, alive, and becoming free.

Now, in my garden, I worship, tilling the ground, humming a joyful tune; a new song to my Savior, Jehovah-Rapha, which means; the Lord who heals; who makes the bitter things sweet.

"I love you, daddy," I whisper, gazing beyond the clouds. "See you in heaven." I smile, breathing in His peace, noticing new buds sprouting out from beneath the stems of the beautiful flowers around me. They reassure me of His promise: He *is* making all things new. Jesus, the Hope of glory; the wonderful Counselor; the composer of the melodies, and the maker of the moon.

Sometime later, while clearing my father's things in his room, I found a picture and a small book under his pillow. The picture was of him and me, sitting together in the church, and the small book was his personal bible.

In the back of the bible, on the last page, was his scribbled signature and the date he accepted Christ as his Lord and Savior. To this very day, that picture and that book brings me great joy and reminds me that God's timing is perfect. From birth to death and beyond, He orders our steps; we only need to surrender completely to His divine order.

Blossoms on a Thorn Bush

Home from school, my children start their homework, and Casita, now in 7th grade, shows me a dance she has learned at Victory Christian Academy. When she and Letta were younger, I had put them both in ballet classes at the city's community center. Now the early years of ballet classes shift, changing into what Casita calls "praise dance."

"Sit right here, Mama. I want to show you my dance routine," she tells me before turning on the music. I sit on the sofa with my younger children folding themselves snugly around me. The music starts and Casita raise her arms gracefully into the air to the song "I Surrender All" by CeCe Winans. In quiet awe, I sit back watching her twirl and move, thinking how fast she is growing up, remembering how her little arms use to stretch out to the side as she spoke the words, "Mommy, I love you this much."

She watches me watching her, making sure I don't miss a thing. I smile and nod to the beat, while all at once, my mind straddles two worlds, and I see them both in full color like they are happening in real time. I hear laughter, and circling Casita, I see the translucent figures of my sister with her living dolls dancing the waltz. I breathe, as the past and the present unites me to the rhythm of a lullaby, showing me that Joyce was right—beyond the shadows of sorrow, God makes all things new, and love makes the world go 'round.

"Baby, that was beautiful. How long did it take you to remember that routine?"

"We learned it at school," she says and later asks me to dance with her. Soon Casita and I will perform the dance together at Refreshing Springs. It will be the beginning of a new praise dance group called Expressions of Worship. Eventually, the children of the church will rehearse and perform their praise dances for the holidays. Cheerleading, stomping, and theatrical performances become yearly events. The task of program coordinator becomes an unexpected blessing. I begin choreographing dances, writing songs and cheers. Soon I discover hidden gifts nestling among the thorns.

The movement of dance begin to transform the fear. My mind has always been the keeper of secrets where disturbing images creep in front of me, pictures no one else can see moving, lurching, attacking, and then stealthily vanishing out of sight; I'm used to it now, and honestly, somewhat immune. Teaching praise dance begins to help realign my thought patterns—giving me more control of the frightening scenes. Worship music, combined with dance movements, gradually strengthens and empowers me to do what 2 Corinthians 10:5, instructs: "take every thought captive to the obedience of Christ."

My imagination has become so intense, that I can hear a song one time and choreograph an entire dance, seeing it inside my head from beginning to end. In time, I learn to regulate the triggers, and when the flashbacks come, I make them apart of the dance. When the angry faces growl, reaching toward me—I close my eyes and find the memory of the dance my sister taught us, twirling us around the living room in Dixie Court until we were dizzy with laughter. Now, all I need is the music, and I guide the movements until the mental invaders become my willing dance partners, bowing to my eight-count.

I lead the dance, and little by little, the movement begins to transform the inner struggle and the Tourette-like tremors I have tried to keep from public view. Unwittingly, my daughter has brought dance back into my life. The dance tells a story, and after months of rehearsals, the children become the storytellers. With every movement, the words come alive.

Tonight, at Refreshing Springs, as Casita and I prepare to perform the dance, "I Surrender All," I remind myself to let go of the resentment in my marriage and secretive past, and worship with my whole heart. Praise and worship are the keys that unlock the doors to set the captives free. I lose myself behind the veil of an unseen realm. There, all regret falls away. This lesson is a "one day at a time" process because tomorrow is still too uncertain when you are in a relationship with someone who sees you as a person you no longer want to be; a person who is waking up from sleep after being stuck for so long in Neverland.

As I dance with my daughter, I remember the faceless girl down the street; I couldn't forget her; thinking of her dead legs. *What was her name? I remember wishing that I knew her name if only to whisper it in prayer.* When the music ends, my daughter and I curtsy. And as we bow to the audience, I glance at my legs and feet, grateful for God's grace and mercy that saved my life from the deathtrap of addiction. More times than I can remember, God has rescued me from the valley of the shadow of death.

Staring out over the crowd my mind replays it all again: the girl in the building, and how her story ended. I pray for her, hoping there were angels there to comfort her the day she died; *Wishing they carried her away to a peaceful place where all things are new, and she can begin again.* I pray she made it to heaven.

For many years, teaching praise dance blesses my life. But when the music stops, and the world is still, the voices come again. And from time to time, the images visit me as if it just happened yesterday. Leaving the past behind is not easy when it refuses to let you go. But for me, His grace is enough. *"All to thee my blessed Savior, I surrender all."*

1994-Fort Lauderdale, Florida

"Do it again, Mommy!" My children roar with laughter as we jump the high tracks on Sistrunk Boulevard near Betty's Soul Food Restaurant. Our destination is not very far. We head east to catch an afternoon matinee at the movie theater. I take this route when we go to the movies or the beach because the children love going over the steep tracks.

"Mama, do that thing with your hands again, and go faster!" BJ says as I make the first U-turn.

"Yeah, Mama, go faster," Cory shouts. I pretend to shift gears on the automatic Cordova while making vroom-vroom sounds like I am the world's fastest race car champion, Speed Racer. My children bring it all out in me; a jovial sense of freedom, so carefree that I'd swear God is blessing me with another second chance to be a silly kid. Squinted eyes, I make the sound effects, until my children burst with shouts of glee. "Go! Go! Go!" they chant loudly.

I bring my sunglasses to the bridge of my nose, looking to the sides of the road to make sure no cars are coming from either direction. The pedal to the metal sends the car airborne, flying across the tracks. All four tires off the road. We lift off, unable to contain our laughter. The car lands solid, and our seats rebound like a trampoline. Ecstatic, Cory looks at me, his eyes full and bright with boyish charm. A huge smile springs across his face as he cheers with both hands up.

"Mama, do it again! Do it again!" I can't resist. I reach for the volume, turning it up. Simon and Garfunkel play on the radio, and there's magic in the air. The wonderful thing about children is their hearts—it is teachable and compassionate. No matter what, they will often love what we love, and do what we do. Where I once felt a misfit, an outcast, my children embrace my quirks, my songs, and my sense of adventure. With every moment, they make life feel brand new. We sing aloud with the music booming from the cassette player. Line by line, with Paul Simon and his band of South Africans, we sing out,

> *"If you'll be my bodyguard*
> *I can be your long-lost pal*
> *I can call you Betty*
> *And Betty when you call me*
> *You can call… me… Al*
> *Call me Al."*

After about the eighth or ninth time jumping the tracks, we finally make it to the movie.

Most of my life, I have never really had a sense of humor, but my children are changing me in more ways than I realize. For so many years, I have disregarded myself: my emotions, my rights, my value. My children are becoming my life's most excellent teachers. They seem to start with the most important lesson of all: self-regard. They are growing so fast. And as their colorful personalities begin to emerge, I find the parts of me that never grew up. The simple emotional needs of every human being like creative expression, confidence, structure, acceptance, self-awareness, and boundaries. I begin to try and learn it all again. Arrested in my own development, I have lacked much as a parent and as a whole person.

Through the journey of parenting my children, I discover a beautiful lost world. In every interaction with them, whether one of conflict or pleasure, a light shines inside the deep trench of my repressed emotions.

I remember a time, one Saturday afternoon. I was not well. Casita wanted to move her bed to the left side of her room, the headboard facing left. I totally freaked out.

"No! Absolutely not! You cannot turn your headboard in this direction." I moan, frantically turning it back—facing the right. There was a sense of desperation I could not understand at the time.

"Mom, I just want a change in my room, like when you change the living room furniture around," she protests respectfully. The discussion is over; her bed must face the right side of the room! Casita stands by her closet with a puzzled look on her face. I have no way of telling her that I am afraid. I cannot put the fear into words; even I cannot understand my crazy reaction to such a minor request. After all, it is *her* room. The problem is not the positioning of the bed, but my inability to halt the transfer of a fearful memory. A part of my mind was still straddling the past and the pain of losing my baby. I had to learn—*this* is not *that*; her bed is not a coffin.

During the funeral of my daughter LiSandra, her small white coffin was facing the left. At the time of her death, I resorted to getting drunk and high to help me suppress and forget the incident ever happened. I have never dealt with the pain of losing her. Somehow my mind transferred the fear to the here-and-now. When deep trauma wounds you, the past is never over; history never dies; it repeats. The irrational response has taught me that I have a long way to go before I can come to grips with how much the past directly affects the future.

It will be years before I begin to understand the magnitude of my repressed emotions and its effects on my life. I need to learn to separate the two dimensions of time, which I have straddled for as long as I can remember. The past and the present always collide, sending me into a state of inertia—like being paralyzed, where real change can seem impossible. In times like these, the words of Mother Brown still echoes from the halls of the BARC Rehab center, reminding me to take life "one day at a time."

Time sails by and my children share a special gift with me. Day by day, like undercover agents, they sneak the broken parts of me inside their own childhood, bypassing the forbidden gate of time. I continue to heal inside their carefree world. Love is a powerful healer. I channel the anxiety into what seems to be endless energy. The love I have for my children continues to inspire me to look beyond the present circumstance. Children are magical, and in our world, there is no such thing as too much playing, singing, or goofing off. I relish in it all. Cory and BJ put on recurring comedy shows, where they come into my room, one in front of the other. Cory talks, while BJ stands behind his back, moving his hands like a puppet to each of the words. Their impromptu skits are hilarious. Tears roll from my eyes from laughing so hard, and my stomach hurts because they will not stop acting silly.

Day after day, hour after hour, we play until they get tired. We sing until our voices are gone. We hit the road, driving anywhere and everywhere with the radio turned up until the sound vibrates against the windows. The van rumbles with music and the magic of true love—my children. For me, music makes the moments special. Joyce made it that way when I was young. And now, just as soon as we finish singing one song, we begin with another. Neil Diamond sings a love song; a song about what matters most; the one song that steals my heart away;

> *"Money talks*
> *But it can't sing and dance*
> *And it can't walk.*
> *As long as I can have you*
> *Here with me, I'd much rather be*
> *Forever in blue jeans baby."*

We sing even louder, playing the cassette until the ribbon breaks. But Angela, who is growing up to be diplomatically tenacious, is determined to fix it. After a few moments, she does, and the singing begins again. I don't know how she did it, but she has always had that fix-it-spirit about her. We make it to the park and there we swing, and sing, and play until there is nothing left to do but eat again. Before sundown, we are off to another adventure. Life is but a dream—a magical, wonderful dream.

My children are my paradise, my beautiful blossoms, my rite of passage from a childhood plagued by sadness to indescribable joy.

I balance the roles of playmate and mother, unaware of the therapeutic impact of the parent-child relationship. Without ever knowing it, my children become my counselors. They surround me, like blossoms on a thorn bush, covering me with an assortment of colorful hues in layers of love and acceptance. In time, I could no longer trace the thorns; the places inside that was so broken and torn from a lifetime of despair. My children are like comic book heroes that have somehow come to life. Flesh and blood defenders of the Justice League that came to save the day—my superheroes

Soon, we move into our first house. After months of praying and working with realtors, we sign the papers. It is ours. The years bring more lessons as I teach my children to drive and brake gently. More gatherings with family and friends, and more of everything that makes life look normal. Bruce seems cordial and supportive, but the distractions of laughter, flowers, decorative birthday parties, and the romantic hours are not enough to make me forget who I am in his eyes. I know my place; I stay in it. As Buffy and I sit on the front door steps watching him play basketball with the children, I want to believe he has changed, and that he will not hit me again. For years, I have learned how to keep the peace, be submissive, obey, and assume the position. I know the line. For now, I will not cross it, even if I smell the scent of another woman on him. Some things haven't changed at all.

Sebastian, the crab, sings "Under the Sea" for the hundredth time. After the movie, I knew Letta was going to ask the same question, in three…two…one,

"Mommy, can we watch the movie again?" Letta asks with soft ringlets from her curly hair flowing across my lap; it never fails—it is her favorite movie.

"Sure, sweetheart" my reply is always the same. The children snuggle under their blankets as the VHS tape of the Little Mermaid rewinds. Even when the tape is not playing, they are still singing the Disney song. I'm not sure how to feel when they all ask me to make crabs for dinner. Yet again, we jump in the car in search of blue crabs. When we return, the theatrics begin. On the kitchen counter, a few crabs escaped out of the bag. I laughed, watching the children square off with the angry crabs running sideways with their claws snapping at the air. BJ grabs a spatula and sword fights with the last crab before we finally get it in the pot. With all my heart, I wanted those happy times to last forever. But it would not last, and the clock was ticking louder. The boomerang was on its way back.

Summer 1996

Linda brings her baby daughter Dionna over to spend the weekend with us. Before her feet can touch the ground, my children rush to pick her up. They take turns cuddling and utterly spoiling her with attention. Seen and heard, they all lavish love on one another. I determined that in my home, with all children, the need for attention, care, and emotional expression was not only a right but an absolute must! Letta has a particular fondness for her cousin, and often wants Dionna all to herself. Linda and I watch Dionna as she runs and plays through the house with my children, remembering the miracles of the past, grateful for how we survived it all. Today we share the joy of new miracles in our life; including her daughter, Dionna.

In early June, Dionna had been born blue as the northern night sky. At the beginning of Linda's labor, we had felt confident that the Lamaze classes we attended had prepared us for a smooth labor and delivery. But there is no way to prepare for the unexpected. Joyce met us at Holy Cross Hospital, and we get ready to welcome Linda's new bundle of joy into the world.

"Push when you feel the next contraction," The nurse had said, unable to hear the baby's heartbeat. "Don't push! We need you to turn." The nurse said urgently.

"Breathe with me," I told Linda. But the hysteria was too much. Wire probes were attached to her baby's head during the delivery. The medical team desperately tried to find her heartbeat.

"Don't push!" the nurse asserted again. When Dionna was finally born, she was motionless, and her skin was blue, nearly purple, like a breathless flower. Straightaway, the medical staff had taken her to the side of the room to try and revive her. Linda hyperventilated; her eyes following in the direction of where the nurses placed her quiet little girl.

"Look at me, Linda. Everything is all right. She will be okay. She is beautiful." As I tried to comfort her, Joyce went into the bathroom to pray.

"Linda, I need you to breathe with me." I pulled myself closer.

"What's wrong, Sandra? What is wrong with my baby?" Linda's tears poured down the sides of her face while Joyce's prayers echoed from the bathroom.

"Linda, she is beautiful. Everything is all right. You must trust God." I heard His voice; it was crystal clear, telling me everything would be just fine. And so, it was; her heart begins to beat. After a short stay in the NICU, Dionna was discharged.

Now, watching her run and play reminds me of a God who works in mysterious ways, and that miracles still happen. Linda leans into me, smiling, grateful. We embrace, and as I stare away, listening to the children play, I hear the Lord's voice in my heart; "See that I will make all things new."

Some miracles come in an instant, while others happen over a lifetime, through a process of highs, lows, and grueling effort. The master teacher of experience has taught me well, and therefore, I have no choice but to believe in the God of miracles; great is His faithfulness. In my life, I've learned that the unexplainable signs and wonders are not the only events that define a miracle. The fact is when we survive unimaginable pain and sorrow, and still choose to be grateful, joyful, and thankful, no matter what; to keep moving forward in the face of every storm and uncertainty—this is a miracle. Perhaps, it is the greatest miracle of all.

Three-Strand Cord

Memorial Day – 4:30 a.m.

The family awakes to prepare for a picnic on the beach. In the coming years, I make the outing our family tradition. Half asleep, the children pile up in the backseat with the picnic basket, their kite, beach balls, and blankets. Buffy is wide-awake, moving back and forth from my chest to the car window—always ready to ride. I clutch my father's hat, carrying it with me in remembrance. Sometimes, I just need to feel a part of him against my skin. We hurry to make it before the sun comes up. The air chills with the morning breeze, and we spread out our blankets on the sand. The early morning menu is always the same: Dunkin Donuts, coffee, and hot chocolate.

"Boston Crème, please," the boys say. The girls are happy with glazed and double chocolate. I look out over the horizon, a gleam of light peers from out of the sea. The sun is slowly waking up, and the waves bring back memories of days gone by. The children run, kicking up sand behind their heels. Bruce and I keep a close watch on them by the ocean's shore. Pulsing waves crash against the shoreline pushing brown and green colored seaweed upon the sand. Buffy curls up against my legs while the sun sprinkles golden rays of orange, red, and blue on the water; I breathe it in. Coffee in hand, I sip, thinking of my grandmother, Rachel. The smell of her coffee in the morning made me love it before I ever tasted it. Being with her on the farm, all those summers ago, had been the closest thing to heaven for me. My heart misses her today, yet, I sense that she is close to me. Strange, but I can feel her presence.

Buffy seems a little restless. He snuggles up under my chin, trying to make himself comfortable.

"Guys stop throwing sand. You might get it in someone's eyes," I tell my sons.

"Yes, ma'am, Mama." They reply, already covered from head to toe. Looking out from my blanket with Buffy, I smile, thinking of how fast they are growing up, remembering the funny faces they make taking their weekly spoonful of cod liver and castor oil to keep the flu away. The numerous spats they had over somebody coming into someone else's room without permission, and the complaints of "Mom, so-and-so is bothering me." Being a mother is the best and the most challenging part of life; a marvelous journey.

Our family has had its share of sibling rivalry. Most of the conflict is resolved by offering my children two choices, "Say you are sorry, kiss and hug, or everyone is in trouble!" I'd warn. Most of the time, it works. Before long, they hug each other, start laughing, and soon forget what they had been upset about in the first place. I've seen enough strife for a lifetime. Avoiding it at all cost is a daily pursuit. Nothing means more to me than to see them loving each other unconditionally.

Watching them play warms my heart past the chilling memories that meet me here at the ocean's edge. For some reason, I have always needed to be here. Something pulls me to the sea, something unexplainable. Someday, I hope to share the significance of this place with my children. One day, I want to explain the reason I bring them here. Not only for tradition or the beauty of the vast ocean, but there are lessons I need them to know that only the thorns can teach.

Off in the distance, a homeless man sits aloof near the road. I walk over and offer to share what we have to eat and a few dollars. My son BJ smiles at me. I nod, wanting them to know that we have a serious responsibility. *I want to do more. God show me how* I think to myself walking back to the blanket. *We must be our brother's keeper. We must try harder to love and care for one another.*

When they are older, I pray to have the courage, the wisdom to explain; to find the words to tell them about what happened here. On this beach, in this very spot, I think of how God's grace and mercy found me. I watch the sun come up, remembering the unforgettable flashes between life and death. I exhale, thinking of what I survived. I turn toward the road. Right across the street are the memories of a lost little girl, the ache of hunger, and a cold bathroom floor at The Biltmore Hotel.

The tide brings in memories of wolves dressed up in human flesh, and a rat named Ben running across Edward's TV screen. Time won't let me forget. But God is transforming the baffling emotions and renewing my mind. Where I once was drowning, I am becoming free. Sold in the shadows, yet now all I have is sympathy for the ones who caused the unimaginable pain. This is the power of Christ in the life of those who believe — the ability to forgive; I know that now, more than ever before. My life is not my own, and I pray that one day I can help my children understand who Jesus truly is — more than a story or a legend, He is life, He is love, He is all the world to me. *How do I teach my children the lessons of the thorns? How do I show them how to trust in the mystery of a God who does not save us from tribulation and the storms, but delivers us through it all?* One day I hope my children will understand that if it had not been for the grace of God, I would have perished many years ago, beneath these waves, right here on this beach, before they were ever born. *God help me to explain the unexplainable. Help me to teach my children the reality of what it means to follow Christ Jesus with all their hearts, mind, and strength.*

"Mommy…Ma, come fly the kite with me," Cory says. I inhale, staring up at him. My mind shifts back, and I feel the warm sun on my face. The spray from the sea caresses my skin. I sit up to listen.

"Yes, baby, let's see how far we can make it go." Seagulls fly above us, and the kite lifts off, flapping and whistling through the air.

"Mom, we are almost out of string," Cory holds onto the small black reel, glancing from his hands to the kite, and then back at me.

"Hold it tight, baby." The kite soars, pitching against the wind.

"Mama, what if the string breaks?" Cory asks. "I don't think it will break, my love. See the thread. There are three strands tied together. Don't worry; it won't break. If you hold it tight and don't let go, I think it will be okay." The kite zigzags high up in the air. Cory stares up, carefully watching. My thoughts trail away, through the clouds and sky, thinking of the songs, stories, and lullabies from my youth. They had been like the three-strand cord of the kite string that has kept me from giving up and losing my mind completely. The lessons they have taught me secured my faith. From the very beginning, the prayers gave me a point of reference. The stories made me believe. He continues to prove that He is holding on to me; even when I cannot trace Him. And because I know He won't let go, I'm not that easy to break.

Winter, 1997

My mother takes the children to Lion Country Safari. Every year, she plans to take them with her on vacation. I am happy she is finally taking more time off from work. Life is changing every day. But of all the things that are changing, some things stay the same. My marriage remains an institution of compromise and fear. I never question Bruce's whereabouts when he is out, or the phone calls that come in the middle of the night. I assume the position, conditioned not to question his actions. I continue to keep busy at the church, with my children and other responsibilities. They are the focus of my attention. And if I never look inside myself, or try to rise beyond the trench of my fear, I can carry on with the pretense.

The more time I spend with my children and at work, the easier it is for me to cope with life. The school plays are always fun. I will not miss one event. Letta and I dress up like Christmas bells during one of the holiday programs at her elementary school. Watching my baby girl onstage takes my breath away. Her smile and curly locks of hair: I don't want to miss a thing. It is a delightful time watching her grow, and now that she is older, we spend evenings creating science projects for her class assignments. Tonight, we gather supplies to build a massive rotating eye for her school's science fair. I watch excitement fill her gaze as we complete the last details of her project. I tell her how proud I am of her for finishing the challenging assignment, and how working with her makes it even more special.

Cory starts to play guitar, but after I take him to his first lesson, he hurts his arm jumping off the bed. I have warned them at least a thousand times.

"Guys stop jumping on the bed! You can get hurt. How many times do I have to tell you?" Of course, they keep jumping. Boys! Go figure.

Cory needed twelve stitches in his elbow after he leaped off the bed and hit the glass on the frame of the new Michael Jordon poster I had bought for their room. My nerves unravel, rushing him to the ER. Even so, with all the challenges of parenting, they bring me special joy and contentment. I never thought I would ever be worthy of such happiness, but with each new day, they show me the love of a lifetime.

Near bedtime, I go into their rooms, and though they're older, they still wait up to hear their lullabies…

"What song would you like me to sing tonight?"

"Mama can you sing that song, 'God is watching us, From a Distance?'" Casita says. Letta agrees. I sing, and afterward, go into my son's room. They are waiting up.

"Mom, please sing "Somewhere over the Rainbow?"

After the lullabies, we kiss goodnight; these are the best of times.

But as the years are passing, I notice something's subtly

happening. At night, BJ becomes afraid, and so does Letta. The fear seems to come out of nowhere, but that's impossible. Like the footprints on the stairs, fear comes back through open doors; passageways of time where generations had been before and failed to set things right—the boomerang was circling back. We pray together and repeat the scripture from 2 Timothy 1:7, "For God hath not given us the spirit of fear; but of power, and of love, and of a sound mind." I buy BJ a stuffed lion, and we decide to name it Courage. I sit longer, talking to Letta, praying away the night terrors. I try to take their mind off what seems to be irrational fears. But there is nothing irrational about compromise—it sends the same boomerang back again.

The demons we fail to confront and defeat in our own lives, will often return to plague the young hearts and minds of the next generation. After fasting and praying for my children, their fear subsides; however, until we destroy the *root* of sin, the spirit of fear will always have a way back in—everything begins at the source.

During the summer of the next school year, BJ begins piano lessons and soon starts writing his own music. I love to hear him play and soon decide to turn the back room into a music studio, painting it blue; his favorite color. My stepson, Derick has grown almost taller than me, and just as it was from day one, I love him as my own. Angela and Casita will be turning 16 in a couple of months. I am not sure where yet, but we are planning a sweet sixteen party for them both. I make a list, and then another list so I don't forget where I put the last list. Short-term memory continues to be an issue and will be for years. I have learned enough to know that I cannot always trust myself to remember. I need back-up. I plan the girl's party early. The cake, candles, food, guests—which often include the neighborhood children and their friends too. The more, the merrier.

Today, my children and I return home from the grocery store, and Cory gives me "the eye."

"It's on, Mama!" Feeling sure of himself, he carries a large pack of tissue.

"I'm gonna get you today! Prepare for war." We put the groceries away, but the twelve-pack rolls of Cottonelle toilet paper get opened and used for a unique game we play. On the other side of the house, my sons clown me, bragging about winning the last match.

"Bring it!" I tell them, gathering rolls of toilet paper like ammo. We get ready for my idea of war. I roll my neck, stretching my arms up, ready to rumble. Determined to win this time I yell,

"Let's do this!" Toilet Paper War is a game I had started with my children years ago. The rules of the game are simple. We each take several rolls of toilet paper and throw it at each other.

Each direct hit earns a point, but most importantly, the winner gets bragging rights that last until the next trip to the grocery store. I'm not sure who loves the game more, my children or me. It is a fun game and kind of silly, but I use it to teach a valuable lesson. My competitive sons take no prisoners. They play to win. We get into position, bunkering down behind the furniture and out of the line of fire. Rolls of toilet paper hurl toward me like missiles. They ricochet off the wall and land near my makeshift dugout behind the sofa. When I think I have a remote chance of outmaneuvering my energetic sons, I throw my roll up like a live grenade. BJ catches it. Cory fires back, using my artillery against me. Buffy barks as if he is making SOS calls in my defense. It doesn't work. I take a direct hit, falling to the ground as if mortally wounded. My sons shout in victory.

"Got you, mama! We win again!" Cory says. The sweet taste of victory is written all over BJ's face.

"I'm gonna get you guys next time," I declare, before walking into the kitchen to prepare lasagna for tonight's dinner. By the end of the game, streams of toilet paper teepees across the furniture and carpet. My sons clean up the battlefield, rerolling the loose ends of tissue before putting it in the closet. I cherish the fun time, but there's a lesson I want to teach them here—a different kind of war. A war where no one bleeds, there's no broken hearts and no scars. Silly as it may seem, but I want to shield my children as long as possible from the grim reality of life, at least the part of it that I have seen, including divorce. Compromise keeps me in my place, daring not to disturb my children's fairy tale. And because it happened during the year of his birth, Cory is too young to remember the Operation Desert Storm Gulf War going on in the world or the domestic war going on in his home. I want to protect them as long as possible.

From the days of watching my *Underdog* cartoons, it seems nothing has changed. Like Simon Bar Sinister, power-crazed louts are always taking more than what they need, exploiting the weak, and manipulating the simpleminded. War and chaos always follow greed, it seems. And like the corrupt leaders in history, they are all but one bomb blast away from total ruin. In Mark 8:36, the scripture asks, "what do you benefit if you gain the whole world but lose your own soul?" And what is the future for our children, and their children?

Playing Toilet Paper War with my children allows me to create an idea of combat where there could be no casualties. No matter how hard you throw it, the soft tissue bounces off, leaving no harm done. Call me crazy, but the reality of war has been all too real for me. All my life, I have either run away from conflict or neglectfully ignored it. I have never learned the rules of engagement in the seen-and-not-heard culture in which I grew up. Always the timid introvert, I have a hard time saying the word "no," let alone actually engaging in a battle where I stand up for my rights and the rights of others. I am still too afraid to confront the fear that sleeps next to me. In the secret places of my life, every time I try to rise above the trench in my mind, fear drags me back, demanding that I assume the same weak position. In doing so, I keep the peace.

George Orwell once wrote, "If you want to keep a secret, you must also hide it from yourself." In good times, I foolishly told myself that the terrible times never happened; after spending a lifetime acting as if nothing ever happened, it becomes habitual. I wanted to believe that Bruce has changed and that he will never hurt me again. I thought the love I have felt for him would be enough. Victims of abuse and violence are grand illusionists. The show we put on is indeed Oscar worthy.

For the sake of love, we believe in lies. Silently, we move through time, feeling the ache of all we've compromised. But as my children grow older, wisdom pulls my attention, making me more aware of a lesson I've tried to run from for most of my life. The real lessons of war are not the war of my parents or grandparents, nor is it anything made of flesh and blood. In Tampa, on top of the stairs in an old house, my sister would pray, warring with her words, against an indiscernible enemy.

The truth is there are times in life we must learn to fight. The first rule of engagement is to recognize the real enemy. It is an unseen force, but just as real and destructive. President John F.

Kennedy once said, "The only way to secure peace is to prepare for war." The dreams I once had of becoming a police officer and joining the military are long gone, and at this point in my life, I question if I might've done well in the field. It would be years before I understood the words of 2 Corinthians 10:4 that tells us, the weapons of our warfare are not the weapons of the world. Instead, they have divine power to demolish strongholds. The strongholds of human reasoning and false arguments. I have learned many lessons in my life, and above all else, I only want peace. But peace has a price; which makes war, necessary.

No Weapon

"You can be the most grateful person in the world, but if you have not arrived at the place God wants you to be, to do the thing God has destined you and only you to do, that longing will never go away." ~T.D. Jakes

Pembroke Pines, Florida

The Expressions of Worship dancers gather in a circle for prayer. "Lord, bless us to dance for your honor. We praise your Holy name. We belong to you; use us to bring you glory. Thank you for allowing us to be here. We worship you alone. In Jesus name, we pray. Amen." After I led the prayer, the praise dancers line up one by one. After the final wardrobe and hair check, they are ready and excited to perform for the outdoor AIDS charity event where the Grammy award-winning singer Donnie McClurkin will appear and speak. The dancers pace the courtyard, waiting for the call to come onto the platform. "Don't be nervous. You are ready for this." I say, trying to encourage them beyond the excitement that mixes with anxiety.

Just weeks earlier, the dancers had won their first award at the Jesus Christ Supernatural Church. They had danced to the Fred Hammond song "No Weapon," a song about God's divine protection against every snare. The dance had been more theatrical than liturgical. Dancers dressed in costumes of angels and demons to characterize the spiritual warfare that goes on every day; often beyond our awareness. As a choreographer, I wanted to unveil the unseen battle. A battle not of flesh and blood but between good and evil, where principalities rage war against all that is right and good.

The real enemies are not the people we yell at in traffic, disagree with at work, or fight inside our homes. In the Book of Ephesians, chapter six speaks of this enemy. It is satan, the father of lies, the enemy of our souls. He is the author of pride, greed, and lust. But as children of God, we can stand on God's promises and trust that no weapon formed against us will prosper. The Lord is our defender and protector. The words of the song came to life in the dramatic dance. When the praise dancers took home the first-place award, I could not wait to hand it to Pastor Bellamy. Later I had received a call from Pastor Lomax of the Fountains ministry in Pembroke Pines. He invited us to dance for the charity event. I was amazed and honored to have the opportunity to serve.

Now at the AIDS charity event, the music ends, and the dancers bow before the crowd. Never once during the event, did I connect with the significance of how time ushers us into a higher purpose, to do what God has destined us to do — to let go. Flooded with gladness, I stand on the grass near the amphitheater. The dancers performed with such grace and beauty. Watching from a distance, I see Donnie McClurkin greeting the dancers on stage. The look on the children's faces spills over with joy. I smile and look across the field of green grass, praising God for all He has done. I am thankful to be alive, to witness this beautiful day. The road has been so long, yet here I stand, under the shadow of the wings of the mysterious God who makes all things new. The taste of addiction has long gone, and the howl of wolves moves only through the dark recesses of my memory. "Thank you, Jesus," I whisper as I wrap my arms around myself.

The Lord has given me the gift of these beautiful children. Their love and laughter are the blossoms that cover me, keeping me in the present moment, and helping me to continue moving forward. Glancing toward the stage, I remind myself not to take anything for granted. I think to myself, *it's all so glorious; the smell of the green grass, the feel of the evening breeze gently touching my skin, and the vision of the children dancing before the crowd.* Today, my beating heart tells me that my life has a purpose and that there is more to come, beyond the thorns.

On the way home, some of the dancers wear a speechless glow on their faces; others are still giggly, enchanted by the opportunity to meet the gospel star. Sixteen chattering dancers all pile inside my old green Windstar van. "Who wants ice cream?" I shout. The van erupts with the happy shouts of praise dancers.

Through the years, I thought I was teaching them, but in fact, they continue to teach me, showing me the true beauty of life. They show me a different reality than the one my past has groomed me to believe. It boldly contradicts the skewed views of my self-perception. The voices that once dominated my thoughts with accusations of worthlessness go silent when I am with them. I'm finding peace, acceptance, and confidence unlike any I have ever known. Looking back in the rearview mirror, I tilt my head, smiling as they start singing at the top of their lungs,

"No weapon formed against me shall prosper...it won't work."

Breathing out, I drive slowly, listening to the children sing, never wanting the time with them to end.

Children are the most precious gifts. I don't think they will ever fully know how they have blessed my life. Driving down Sunrise Boulevard, I glance down the street, where just a few blocks away I would walk for days, aimlessly chasing smoke, strung out on crack cocaine. The chains of addiction are gone, but a longing deep within remained. For so many years, something had been missing in my life, something intangible; something I couldn't deny or explain during this time, but my answer was coming. Life teaches us patience; it is indeed a wise virtue—a benefit to all who practices temperance: the byproduct of waiting. In a society breed for instant gratification, we must increase our ability to pause, embracing calm patience, trusting that God sees us, hears us, and is faithful to see us through to the end. Isaiah 40:31 teaches, "But they who wait for the Lord shall renew their strength; they shall mount up with wings like eagles; they shall run and not be weary; they shall walk and not faint." In the treasured words of my sister, Joyce, "Steady as you go."

Dying to live

Plantation, Florida – 1997

The years have flown like dust in the wind. You blink and the moment is gone. My restless mind has always pondered about life and time. Time is such a peculiar concept; how it moves in circles; the way it comes back almost purposefully just to check and see what humanity has learned. Then it goes away and returns again, evaluating how we have used its knowledge, since the last time. The ancient wisdom of time seems to implore us to understand its lessons, begging us to get it right finally. Only then, can it offer us the gift of transcendence.

At church, the pain of loss overwhelms the entire congregation. Some of our loved ones and friends have gone on to be with the Lord, including the young sons of the first family. And though their sorrow is inconceivable, Pastor and Sister Bellamy and the Refreshing Springs Church family still sing of God's faithfulness. We clap our hands as the choir begins to sing "He'll Welcome Me,"

> *"I'm living this life just to live again*
> *And with the Lord I know that I shall reign*
> *I shall not stray, with Him I'll stay*
> *He'll welcome His children home one day*
> *Like a thief in the night He shall return for me*
> *That's the day that He'll come and fly away*
> *You'll see, Jesus will welcome me home."*

As believers of the Gospel of Jesus Christ, it is not always easy to understand why God allows the storms. *Why do some receive healing, while others die; too soon? Why does evil seem to prevail while love and goodness wax cold?* Christ tells us in Matthew 16:24 to "take up our cross and follow Him." We do not get to choose the calling or the cost. By faith, we trust His sovereign hand, believing His grace is sufficient.

Still, in this fallen world, we are prone to wander, easy to forget what matters most and fall into depression and apathy. For most of my life, I have lived with an intense degree of uncertainty; marked by an unseen force that guides me toward what I have yet to see. So, it's no wonder why I often feel time watching, slowing me down when it needs me to focus, and speeding me up to save me from myself and the reality of the thorns.

Time prepares to offer me an obscure gift. A token of which to spur me in the direction of my destiny, towards the transcendent knowledge of God's love and power that is made perfect—only in our weakness.

Determined to keep up my busy schedule, I move, full speed ahead; work, dance practices, and clearing the weeds from the flower garden at the church. But, in the past several months, I have not been feeling well, often becoming tired and achy. It is getting harder to keep up with it all. Remembering how hard my mother has worked for most of her life, I refuse to stop. Staying busy forces me to forget, but the stress of all I've repressed is about to turn the tide on my busy life. As I am leaving the parking lot of the Vitamin Shoppe on Oakland Park and Interstate 7, an unfamiliar pain sits on my chest. The unexplainable pressure sent shockwaves through my heart as if some lightning storm is happening inside me. I cannot ignore it—there is something terribly wrong. I drive myself to the emergency room.

Westside Medical Center-Fort Lauderdale, Florida

At the hospital, doctors perform a series of test. The nurse injects blue solution into my vein while I walk on a treadmill, feeling like the bionic woman with all the wires connected to my skin. After the stress test, the nurse sticks more wire pads on my chest, arms, and legs. "This will not hurt," she explained. "We need to do an EKG, to see why your heart is beating irregularly."

The electrocardiogram did not take long. I receive the first diagnosis. The doctor informs me of the dangers of stress. "It is a silent killer," The doctor cautions. "You must slow down, take some time off, and stop running yourself at this current pace." The doctor has no idea what he is asking me to do. I need to stay busy, and the mere thought of slowing down is out of the question, but for now, I have no choice. The medical staff tells me I must stay for a few more days in the hospital.

The doctor admits me to Westside Regional Medical Center for further evaluation; I will miss the program at church tonight. The children have been practicing for months. I call Sister Wiggins, who I now lovingly refer to as Mama. Over the phone, I hear traces of worry between her words of comfort. "We will be praying for you, baby. Do you need anything?"

"No thank you, Mama. I'm fine. Tell the children that they will do well tonight. They know all their lines. They have rehearsed their dance and songs. They will do fine without me." Hemmed in between blaring white sheets, I fluff my pillow, imagining I am with the children.

After the program, Sister Wiggins calls me. "Sandra, they did a great job. Pastor Bellamy was proud." After the phone call, I turned towards the window of my hospital room, smiling past the strange alien pain in my back and stomach. Thankful everyone had a good time; I breathe out and fall asleep. After a few days, I am released to go home.

Gardening has become a bit much, but I push past the growing fatigue to pull out the wild weeds growing up among the blossoms. Since my release from the hospital, I try to take it easy and follow the doctor's orders. Still, something is not quite right.

Christmas comes, and I stay home while Bruce takes the children to celebrate with his family. I will never forget how lonely I feel this day. It is the loneliest Christmas I can remember. I think of my father, and how my mother loves Christmas. I miss my siblings and my children but being alone was probably for the best.

In the past weeks, I become more withdrawn. As I lay in bed, I realize just how much I have become dependent on an activity-filled life to feel useful, to cope. The trench of isolation widens, and with it, the familiar spirit of depression from all the uncertainty about my health visits me. In the melancholy mood, I flow back in time to when I was younger, listening to Kansas, a 70s rock band, singing "Just in the Wind." That's what today feels like for me; everything is unsure; I'm just in the wind. I remember thinking how much the song reminded me of the scripture in Ecclesiastes 1:14. Solomon, the richest man in the world, must have felt this way when he wrote; "I have seen all the things that are done under the sun; all of them are meaningless, a chasing after the wind." The uncertainty seems to never end in this stormy life. Even so, the anchor of my faith holds firm to the rock of my salvation.

After a few months, I begin to face another strange health crisis. Underneath my breastbone, on the left side, an abscess appears. *What is happening now?* I ask myself. Painful and sore, it feels like a bleeding ulcer — as if the culmination of all the years of repressed ire and secrets had boiled to the surface. Swallowing becomes increasingly difficult, as though I have a sore throat that has traveled, spreading from my neck and out across my entire chest. It is hard to eat, and my clothes begin to sag. I go back to the doctor, and I remember feeling grateful for health insurance. Bruce has always made sure we had every kind of coverage, just in case. He always says it is better to have it and not need it than to need it and not have it; he is wise in that aspect of things.

After examining the raw ulcer, the doctor continued to believe the condition was stress-related. He prescribes a topical solution and orders me to rest. Still, the condition worsens.

Weeks later, strange rashes, like lesions, begin to appear on my hands and arms. Soon, it spreads to my face and abdomen. At first, I am not alarmed. I figure it is something in the dirt from all my gardening or the stress of my hectic life. I was wrong about both. After a skin biopsy, I receive the second diagnosis: a skin cancer called Kaposi sarcoma. A viral infection causes the skin disease. The dermatologist advises me to have a complete blood check to determine the underlying cause of the aggressive tumors — every issue has a root cause. I had been sure the hospital ran a full series of blood tests. Nevertheless, two weeks later, I receive the third and final diagnosis.

Dr. Mestre's office, Plantation, Florida
My mother's voice echoes across my memory as I stare at my feet dangling off the edge of the examination table. "*Sydney, tie your shoelaces before you fall.*" While I wait for the doctor to come in, I breathe out, drifting back in time to Tampa's red brick streets. I was five years old, skipping, twirling, and dancing with clumsy feet, carefree inside my parent's store. In my childhood daydreams, I had battled monsters with a golden scepter that sparkled with magical powers that would make the world a better place for all people. But today, I have nothing in my hands. There is no magic wand that I can wave that would change this fate. At thirty years of age, I prepare to face another monster that is as real as all the others in my life have been.

The doctor comes in, and I lift my head and sit up straighter, readjusting the wide-brimmed hat that shades the lesions.

"Hi Sandra, my name is Dr. Mestre." He reaches out to shake my hand and holds it longer than most handshakes I can remember. "How are you feeling today?" he asks.

"I'm good, sir." I smile, but, I can no longer hide behind the polite lie. The dark flaky patches of skin covering my body beg to differ; I am far from being *fine*. The truth is I have not been fine for a long time, and all that I have suppressed through the years, hiding from public view, must now make room for another piercing thorn.

Dr. Mestre holds a folder in his hand with my name on it. He places it on the counter. With gentle brown eyes, he looks directly at me. I wait for him to turn away from the sight of my unpleasant appearance. He never does. I sense compassion in his tone. "We have the results of your tests." Straightforward with his words, he begins to inform me of the clinical implication of a high viral load and a low CD4 count. I've worked in the medical field, but my experience does not stop time from standing still long enough for me to pay close attention. I will soon learn a broader lesson in immunology. According to the Center for Disease Control, the normal range for the T-helper or CD4 cells is 500-1500. These cells act as an army to defend the body against infections. The lab test has shown my CD4 count is two and my viral load is extremely high. My body is under attack and has been for quite some time now. Dr. Mestre explains why.

"Your blood test is positive for the HIV virus. The disease is advanced. You have AIDS." In the final stages of the infection, I look out from under the wide-brimmed hat, motionless. I have little to no immunity, which explains the swollen lymph nodes, chronic fatigue, and the opportunistic skin infection, Kaposi sarcoma. My body has been under attack. Apathy has kept me passive, unable to fight for my life, my voice, and my rights for so long. And now, hiding beneath the surface of all the thorns—the repressed emotions, was a ferocious virus.

The diagnosis of AIDS is like a lightning bolt striking the same burnt land that has been hit year after year, blow after blow, thorn after thorn. The anguish of my life's journey has built up an immunity to the shock and dread of learning I have the fatal illness. Surviving the inconceivable events of a stolen childhood, ravenous wolves, and domestic violence feels like a bolt of lightning setting fire to the same patch of burnt land. And the peculiar thing about lightning is that it will often strike the same area again and again, but it cannot set fire to land that has already been scorched and charred. In other words, the threat of death had lost its sting. After surviving so much in my past, I know God is with me now. His grace is enough; no matter what.

Calmly, I swallow, I breathe and listen as Dr. Mestre continue to speak.

But what did I really know and understand about the

frightening disease that had already claimed the lives of so many people? What does any of us truly know about anything until we have experienced it for ourselves? Millions have been infected with the deadly virus, from Rock Hudson, Arthur Ashe, to the famed pianist Liberace, who I loved listening to as a child. At St. John's, I worked with many patients, from AIDS to Alzheimer's, I saw only the person, never the problem. Providing care and comfort was all that mattered. I remember caring for a patient dying of AIDS. As he took his last breath, I sat by his bedside, whispering a prayer, hoping it made him feel less afraid as he slipped away.

The disease does not discriminate, regardless of race and sexuality. Rich or poor, the universal threat of HIV/AIDS is as real as it has been since the first known cases in the early 1980s. Likewise, the stigma attached to the disease is similar to the same socially unacceptable mark of the dark skin I was born in and the disgrace of sexual abuse and trafficking; unless it is experienced, it cannot be fully understood. After a life of adversity, I prepare for yet another fight, but this time, it would be different; very different. The definition of resistance is the ability not to be affected by something, especially adversely. Fear had controlled me for most of my life, but now, gradually the deadly disease begins to build another layer of resistance in me. In time, it would begin to reveal itself not as a foe, but an unassuming ally.

As Dr. Mestre begins a baseline evaluation, I forego any need to explain or defend myself as to how I became infected with the virus. In my world of thorns, if there is one thing I do well, it is taking full responsibility. The many years as an addict left little to question. Forget any variables that may exist. Moreover, at this point, blame is useless. Dr. Mestre informs me of the next steps, including notifying family members for testing and emotional support. "1 in 5 people don't know they are infected. Getting tested saves lives." I listen, taking in his words of comfort and thoughtful advice, holding onto his gentle tone.

Sitting calm and still on the examination table, I continue to listen to the facts as Dr. Mestre informs me of the options for therapy. Medications also known as Antiretroviral Therapy (ART). A combination of three drugs: Combivir, Viracept, and Reyataz will be the first prescribed. The powerful drug combination is a part of a class of Nucleoside, Nucleotide Reverse, and Transcriptase Inhibitors (NRTIs). *God seems to work in three's,* I think to myself. These drugs prevent the virus from replicating or making copies of itself within the cells. The side effects can be toxic, but there are no other options for me. As it stands today, I will need to take the highly active antiretroviral (HAART) medication daily, for the rest of my life.

Dr. Mestre writes the prescriptions and places them in my hands. "No skips," he says earnestly. "Take the medication every day at the same time; that's the only way to manage the virus." He tells me new medicines are coming, and how important it is to stay adherent to the regimen. His hand touches evenly over mine, covering the unsightly blemishes. "We are going to fight this together." He reassures me with a trusting nod. The look in his eyes tells me I am not alone in this battle; it made all the difference in the world.

"I will see you in three months. In the meantime, call me if you need anything." I remember the ride home that day. A part of me felt almost numb, but at the same time, I think about all the daunting years and the grace of God that keeps me, day after day.

When I arrive home, I walk into the room and shut the door to speak to Bruce. The discussion about the diagnoses and him getting tested was brief. I'm not sure why, but I had expected the indifferent response. I wanted to talk about the therapy and possible counseling my doctor spoke about, but there is no exchange, no room for such an intimate conversation. Much like the past traumatic incidents, the news of the disease is as if it didn't happen and did not matter.

As time went by, Bruce rarely speaks to me about the diagnoses. Months pass, and I go to my medical appointments alone. We go on as if it is just one more thing to hide. In a sober moment, I remember back to the time I spent in foster care, listening to the words of Gladys Knight like a looming prophecy—the anthem of co-dependency:

"We go on together living a lie
because neither one of us
wants to be the first to say goodbye."

My disease becomes like the rest of me, a temple of secret thorns sprawling along the high walls of a deep impassive trench. Yet again, blame is useless; it changes nothing. After the diagnoses, I withdraw even further away inside myself and my faith. People talk. I hear it, and I don't hear it. The stress triggers the memories of cocaine and alcohol, but never the call of them; when God healed the emotional pain that was stuck inside me, addiction had nothing left to call to—I was free! Much has changed. I do not need to self-medicate from the mental and physical distress of the diagnoses—which is very real and often requires support. I square my shoulders and keep moving forward.

In the mid to late 1990s, the public perception of AIDS continues as it did almost two decades ago when the epidemic first appeared. And though antiretroviral drugs save countless lives by stopping the reproduction and spread of the virus, its fatal reputation lingers in the minds of the misinformed. I don't tell my family about the diagnoses. The last thing I want is for them to feel afraid, or worse, feel sorry for me. I have been victimized all my life, and now, I refuse to be a victim of ignorance. With all the campaigns launching globally to raise public awareness and understanding of HIV treatment, transmission, and risks, many people still view AIDS as a curse and a death sentence. Type-casted as a killer, the stigma of an AIDS diagnosis is difficult enough without the discriminating delusions surrounding the disease.

The worst thing about hiding is that I hide from the only person who can change the course of my life. When we are not free to be ourselves, to express our heart, and to speak out against injustices, we hide from our true selves, hindering our liberty. We cannot receive the emotional support needed to overcome the social stigma and the inner voices that tell us how polluted we are, and how irreparably damaged our lives has become. Voices I have heard my whole life. *Reject, misfit, outcast,* they say of me. Now to the list of ridicules, adds the label of *modern-day leprosy.* But it doesn't matter. I am determined to press on, and move forward, no matter what.

Life has always seemed to be like a sparring partner—blow after blow, I take it; get up, and move forward. I absorb the emotional impact of the disease while managing the drug therapy, full-time work, caring for my children, and church activities. But I can't escape the stares. At work, choir practice, and while teaching Sunday school, I feel the curious eyes peering pass the thick layers of makeup I put on every day to try to hide the dark blemishes on my face and arms. I guard my trench of secrets well, hiding behind my busy schedule, and a smile that tells the world, "I don't need help. I'm just fine."

The worst lie is the one you tell yourself. At home, as soon as I close the door, and stand alone, looking at my reflection, I must face the truth. Not the reality of what I see, but the truth of what I don't see. Something is missing in the eyes of the person staring back in the mirror. It has been missing for a long, long time. There is a part of me that dares to think I could find her again. I remember the moment she left me on 24th Street. Before the wolves, violence, and addictions, she made me dream of doing impossible things.

Once upon a time, I believed in her, but now, I cannot trace her in the weary eyes of the person staring back at me. Without a doubt, I know God loves me; still, I am afraid. Not of AIDS or anything else that threatens my life. Now, my only fear is that I will never find the little girl with the braids and barrettes in her hair, who twirled around without a care in the world. She made me feel, alive. Strange, but since the diagnoses, I miss her more than ever.

That night, while I'm in the bathroom, I decide to throw the makeup in the trash. With all the money it cost, it does a poor job of hiding the flaws, and I am getting tired of hiding, tired of the secrets, just plain tired. A societal misfit, I have seen the disapproving eyes of others all my life. *Let them see! Let them talk!* The way I look at it, God is going to either heal me or take me home to be with Him. Either way, I win. I no longer need all the answers.

Tired of the endless striving, my place is to trust in Him, surrender to His will and His plan for my life. In Romans Chapter 8, the first verse says; "There is therefore now no condemnation to them which are in Christ Jesus, who walk not after the flesh, but after the Spirit." I hold tight to the truth of the law of the Spirit of life in Christ.

As I look at my sickly reflection in the mirror, I sense death waiting, stalking me as it has done most of my life. Fed up with its bullying, I speak to it, staring back at me, with my own eyes. It taunts me and tells me I am nothing. I stop listening and start talking back—confronting the voices.

"I know you!" I rage with tears streaming from my eyes, allowing myself to express the one emotion I had been denied: anger.

"Your fear has ruled my entire life! Go ahead; I am not afraid of you anymore. You can kill me, but with my last breath, I will give God the Glory." I watch the tears roll over the dark flakes of skin. Staring at my reflection, I run my hands across my face, drying my eyes, ready to fight the only way I know how: in the spirit.

I rage war with the Word of God as my weapon. I proclaim the words of 1 John 4:4, that declares:

"I am of God! I overcome it all because greater is He that is in me than he that is in the world." I breathe, feeling free!

"Shoot your best shot, devil!" I shout aloud, refusing to cry again. "Go on! Do what you gonna do! But I declare my last words will be praises to my God!" I begin to worship, lifting my hands, praising God louder in the bathroom until it becomes a sanctuary of praise and worship until nothing else mattered.

I remember that very moment, in the bathroom; I felt the fear of a lifetime losing its grip on me. What we think and believe shapes our reality. In Philippians 4, Apostle Paul writes about a secret—the mystery of being content in every situation, no matter what.

Faith believes that through Christ we can do all things. Being in this state, embracing this mindset, attracts and creates to us more of what we were designed to be; the very essence of love. My journey was far from over, but that's okay because every morning His mercies are new, so I dedicate my life to Him again and again. And if I fall, so be it. He lifts me up. He will make me stronger. I felt grateful for all I had and for all I've survived. I am here! The words my sister planted in the soil of my childhood holds firm, sprouting up inside my heart: *no matter what*, I have made my choice. I will trust the God who created the heavens and the earth. The God of Abraham, Isaac, and Jacob. The God who promised to make all things new. All to Jesus, in life, in death, and in the uncertainty of everything; I surrender all.

I Wish...

"Understand that the right to choose your own path is a sacred privilege. Use it. Dwell in possibility." ~*Oprah Winfrey*

Gradually, my faith grows stronger as I continue to hear God's word and apply it to my life. But when there is compromise, the more things change, the more they will tend to stay the same. My marriage remains a farce; an institution where history continues to repeat as if nothing ever happened. Remembering how my parents lived different lives in the same home, I resolve to focus on my children and writing. In the passing days, journaling becomes my escape, and soon, I turn my thoughts into songs which years later, I would publish. Near the end of 1997, I write "Let the Monsters Come." It is my fight song.

Writing music is like a honing tool that sharpens my will. And as death waits for me, I remind the devil that Jesus has victory over the grave and to live is Christ, and to die is gain; a win-win either way. I begin to speak the word of God out loud over my life. Psalms 27:1 says "The LORD *is* my light and my salvation; whom shall I fear? The LORD *is* the strength of my life; of whom shall I be afraid?"

January 1998

Family and friends come together to celebrate Casita's and Angela's sweet sixteen party. Planning the celebration is bittersweet. The older they become, the less they appear to need me. Now, at sixteen, they have plans and dreams of their own. Casita wants to go into the medical field, and Angela desires to join the military. After all these years, Casita still has a caring spirit, and true to her favorite scripture, she really believes anything is possible. Angela's independent nature blossomed early, and it's no wonder she wants to serve her country. I remember her preteen mutiny against the ribbons and curls I used to put in her hair. Angela had served notice to me that she has been growing up faster than I cared to admit. I pray whatever their dreams for the future that God's favor will go with them, and they remember the many lessons from their youth. I pray that they embrace the good, learn from the bad, and live in the truth of the One who promises to make all things new.

As I prepare the tables for the food and birthday cake, I wonder where the time had gone; it passes so quickly. They both sit at the head of the table, wearing their sweet sixteen tiaras. The wind blows and the paper cups I placed on top of the white plastic tablecloth tip over; the spill pulls me back in time.

I think of when Casita and Angela were about nine or ten years old. I had called them at the kitchen table for another lesson. The kitchen table had become the place of many life lessons, but this day would be different.

"Come to the table. Bring paper and pencil. Something is going to happen to you very soon. And I don't want you to be afraid. It is natural, and it will be one of the signs that you're becoming a young woman." I tell them

As they sat at the table that day, I made a simple sketch of the anatomy of the female reproductive system. "I want you to know what to expect before your menstrual cycle begins. They listened and copied the drawing. They asked questions, and before the lesson was over, the puzzled look on their faces turned to confidence. Teaching these lessons were vital to me, wanting my daughters to know themselves and understand the things I did not, including their bodies and how it works. Most of my life, my body never felt like it belonged to me. It's no wonder why I was such a poor steward of it in the past. Confidence in the life of a young girl is crucial.

Knowledge is power. Teaching empowers, and the lesson that day ended with the importance of taking charge of their life; never relinquishing it to impulse or fate. Soon, it would be Letta's turn to learn. Problem is, inside I feel like a fraud, teaching empowerment while being stuck in a marriage that is as toxic as when it first began. Breathing out, I try to quiet my mind.

Bursts of laughter erupt beneath the carport as more friends and family gather for the birthday celebration. I remember the constant chorus of questions from family and friends.

"Hi, San, what's up? How are you doing? How's work going?" they ask.

"I'm fine. Thanks. How are you guys?" I keep moving. Politely inching away; still replaying the memories of motherhood and life lessons. Always lessons. Between the scattered episodes of addiction and depression, my children have been the best part of me. Without ever knowing it, they have played a central role in my recovery. I think back to the fierce storm of 1992 when Casita and Angela wanted to come and volunteer at St. John's Hospital. Several years after that, they asked to go with me to The Heart Walk charity on Fort Lauderdale Beach. I remember feeling so happy that they wanted to come, especially when they could have been hanging out with their friends. The Heart Walk was during the year I earned my group fitness certification with Candy Colby's Body Factory.

As a chubby kid, I use to watch Candy Colby on TV exercising with leg warmers and big gorgeous hair; I laugh to myself, remembering who I was then. Joining her team had been a surreal experience. After the event, I got the chance to introduce Casita and Angela to one of the pioneers of fitness, Cassandra "Candy" Colby. During that time; after my battle with drug addiction ended, the struggle with my weight began. Chronic anxiety kept me craving, never full, never satisfied. Eating became how I avoided dealing with life.

Sometimes, unknowingly, we can trade one addiction for another. My weight ballooned to over 260 pounds. Joining Candy Colby's Body Factory helped me to get control of my emotional eating and get moving with purpose and greater resolve. After all this time, the gift of exercise Joyce gave to me still blesses my life with a natural high and impulse control. Without fully understanding it, I was undergoing a medication-free therapy; holistic with the only side effects being sweat and sore muscles from working out; I was blessed beyond what I could realize.

At the end of the Heart Walk, the girls and I stood together, posing for another picture. My emotions were a mix of regret and delight, but I was adamant about making positive changes. "Say cheese!" a fellow fitness member told me. I remember the sun shining warmly around me near the very place where I first rode in the back seat of a police car, over 17 years ago.

"Mama? Ma! Mommy!" Casita's voice tugs me back to the birthday party.

"Say cheese, Ma." I turn my head, noticing everyone standing around.

"Come on, Mommy. Take a picture with me."

"No baby, Mama don't want to take any pictures."

Casita pauses before giving me a look that says she will not take no for an answer. I keep busy cleaning. On the grass, I watch the children run, playing with their cousins. Letta gives me a wave before she bounces off like Tigger from Winnie the Pooh; she is growing so fast. I rest my head in my hands for a moment, breathing out the growing anxiety; still working on social interactions. Seeing Letta's smile helps with that; my children have a way of making everything enjoyable, but now, that they are getting older, I don't want to pretend anymore. *How many times can we forgive as Christ commands, while we continue to live with the same set of circumstances?* I think of my grandmother, my mother, and sisters. After a lifetime of secrets and self-preservation, humility takes a backseat to bottled-up anger. The cat-and-mouse game is still the same. Regret and resentment find me again, reminding me that some things will never change. Even when all seems calm, I live under threat, and I will never be safe as long as I stay and continue to play by his rules.

Standing in the front yard, I think to myself; I have been smiling for years in this marriage while wanting to scream. But for the sake of my children and the "idea" of family, I remain silent to domestic violence and the constant intimidation. And when the phone calls come in late at night, my heart begins to make dark wishes; wishes for vengeance; wishes for harm because of the repeated torment. Tired of it all; I want out!

How can God complete His work in my life and create a clean heart inside when so much anger hides there? How can I leave; how do I start over? The struggle to stay in this marriage is real; *damned if I go, and damned if I stay*; apathy becomes the only way to survive a relationship of compromise—what we do not confront, will not change. I want to take ownership of my life, unsure where to begin; who to tell; who to trust. One-step forward, two steps back; that's what it feels like; playing this game of pretend keeps me stuck, and sometimes, it feels useless. But I know, I have a decision to make.

For now, while I busy myself cleaning the tables, planning parties, and being a good mother and wife, I meditate on scripture I learned in Bible study; Romans 8:37 says "it is written that we are more than conquerors, through Christ who loves us and gives us victory in all these difficulties." And so, I press through it, even when I am fed up, and just want the roller-coaster ride to stop. I continue to walk by faith, believing that I am victorious, and I'm free. I stand on the word of God in Romans 4:17 that says to call things into existence, as though it was already true—already done; now!

I breathe out, believing my change will come.

The warmth of the sunset reminds me that it is a good time to bring out the Neapolitan ice cream. The birthday candles light up, and a chorus of singing begins: "*Happy birthday to you. Happy Birthday to you…*"

"Blow out the candles and make a wish," we tell the girls.

Soon the festivities turn into a food fight. Someone throws

cake. Another person makes a water balloon and throws it. The next thing I know, there's an all-out frenzy of cake icing and water balloons flying towards a crowd of guests moving too slow to get out of the way.

As the daylight dwindles, Casita calls me again. "Mama, come take a picture with me."

"Baby, I am trying to clean up. I'm not dressed for a picture." I try to think of another excuse as she reaches for my bag.

"Please, Mommy."

I drop the trash bag without another word. Casita pulls me tightly to her side. "Smile, Mama."

I smile, while the camera captures the blemishes in time.

"Mama, …you still look pretty," Casita kisses me.

Near the close of the sweet-sixteen party, I step away. Buffy follows my every move as I seek solace in the relaxing task of cleaning. I lower the front of the large-brimmed hat. In a quiet corner with my head down, I make wishes of my own. I wish to find my way out of the trench of thorns that keeps me impaled to a daunting past that will not allow me to break free completely. I wish to completely forgive and find the meaning of a marriage where I'm faithfully reminded of how inferior and stained I am. I wish to find the voice of a little girl who was lost so long ago. In the quiet moments, I still long for her, feeling a deep sense of emptiness. I look toward the sky wondering, hoping she returns to me. I pray to find her someday.

As a child, I heard the poem, "Starlight, star bright… I wish I may; I wish I might…"

Choosing your own path is your responsibility. James 2:26 says, "For as the body without the spirit is dead, so faith without works is dead also." All the hope, faith, and wishes I've made through the years were sincere, yet it was not enough. 3 John 1:2 says, "Beloved, I pray that you may prosper in all things and be healthy, even as your soul prospers." The more I begin to understand this; the more my heart continues to change; assuming the position is no longer acceptable for me—I'm not who I was, but I was far from who I was going to be; who I was called to be: a prospering *soul*. In life, there comes a time when we must take action to be free, joyful, healthy, and prosperous. It is our God-given right!

Through the years, I have learned of the power of words. Proverbs 18:21 says that "death and life are in the words we speak." Like a force of nature that blows everything out of place, the right words spoken at the right time can create the perfect conditions that will stir us, motivate us, and usher us out of the firm belief that we are not powerful beings. Indeed, we are powerful beyond our understanding.

2000

Steadily, the questioning stares from family and friends become less noticeable. In the coming months, my life takes on a new transformation. As the blemishes begin to fade slowly, so does the lingering fear. During this time, Dr. Mestre introduces me to Dr. Grenitz. He becomes my gynecologist and together, we partner in my health. With each visit I feel more confident, taking a vested interest in every aspect of my life, health, and wellness. I am learning more about my condition and practicing healthier eating habits. My doctors invite me into their lives by sharing delightful stories of vacations and family weddings. I am blessed with a medical team that makes me feel like I am more a family member than just another patient and case folder; it feels incredible. They empower me to fight for my life — every part of it. And while my physical health strengthens because of powerful medicines, my mental health begins to absorb the ensuing gift of emotional wellness

Today, I arrive for my annual follow-up. The lesions are gone, and the opportunistic infections have cleared up. The doctors' visits have tapered from every three months to every six months, and now, once a year. Dr. Mestre greets me with a grand smile.

" You are doing well, kiddo. Your CD4 is high, and your viral load is still undetectable. You're doing great. How do you feel?" He asks, still smiling at me.

"I feel well, um I..." I clear my throat. "Dr. Mestre, I just want to say thank you. You helped to save my life. And I just needed to tell you that, I..." Overcome with emotion; I drop my head.

"You did it! Your lab results have been fantastic. You are still exercising and eating healthy. I am proud of you, and you should be proud of yourself.

"It's not me, Dr. Mestre, but my faith in God," I respectfully affirm.

"Yes, but God doesn't force us to do anything, you are doing the work you have to do to stay healthy and get your life back. I'm proud of you."

As Dr. Mestre speaks, I'm reminded again of the verse in the Book of James that says, "Faith without works is dead and useless." He is right.

He asks me about the fitness classes I teach, my goals, and my dreams. It touches my heart the way he listens so attentively and remembers our last conversation. His questions tell me that I am not the disease; I merely have acquired it and must continue to take care of myself to stay healthy.

I keep a book in my hand, and often share it with him — reading is one of my greatest pastimes; it keeps my mind in one place. Sitting on the exam table, I tell Dr. Mestre about the dietary changes I've made. "Since I started Dr. Lams and Dr. Cristiano's Eat Right for Your Blood Type programs, I have the energy to teach multiple fitness classes every week, and I feel a sense of wellness I have never had, even before my diagnoses," I explain. We talk about our personal battles with weight gain, and the topic gives me the opportunity to share the details about the book I ordered from the Trinity Broadcasting Network with Paul and Jan Crouch.

The title is *Blood Types, Body Types and You*, written by Dr. Joseph Christiano. With this information, along with Dr. Lam's research on nutrition, I commit to following the list of healthy foods for my O-positive blood type. The knowledge has completely changed the way I view health and nutrition." No wheat, no shellfish, no dairy, no pork, no sodas, and on and on I explain the mind-body connection I continue to learn.

"I simply eat the food that is right for my blood type while avoiding the foods that are not," I say, showing him the book in my bag. Dr. Mestre nods and listens. I nod, smiling back at him.

"Have you ever thought about writing a book of your own?" he asks.

"No sir, I haven't."

"You should. You have come a long way. You have survived a lot of adversity. You have come from a CD4 of 2. You are healthy and doing excellent. Hearing your story, seeing how far you have come, you should tell your story. It is inspirational. Sandra, you are a special lady." He stands and closes my file. A look of expectation flows toward me from his gentle glance. I stare down at my hands, unsure of what to say. So, I just breathe.

When I leave the office, I think about Dr. Mestre's life-affirming words. *He truly believes in me. But how could I write about the secrets that have haunted me for so long?* I question the ongoing conflict of my perception; sometimes, I don't trust it. At home I live in a marital purgatory, paying an endless price for a past that is gone but never over. I drive slowly, wondering *how it is that Dr. Mestre and others see me so different*ly? They speak to me as if I am worthy of real intimacy, love, and respect; as if I am someone else — someone not irreparably broken. Even so, sharing my secrets with my infectious disease doctor is easier than telling it to the world.

Besides, I never thought about writing my story because I never thought I had anything of value to say. *Who would want to hear about such despair and heartache?* Moreover, I am not ready to give my secrets away. They are the only things in my life that no one can steal, no one can snatch away from me. My secrets are my own — buried possessions too unbearable to dig up and share with anyone else.

In the passing years, Dr. Mestre continues to remind me that he would be waiting to read my story. But I'm not sure I dare to relive and write about my life. The shameless cruelty is more than I care to share and relive again. *How can I unveil a past that continues to grieve the hidden parts of me? How can I write about what I have been trying for years to forget?* Such an endeavor would require me to forsake every lingering nuance of shame and self-preservation; ultimately, giving myself away. I am not sure I have that kind of courage. It hurts to be vulnerable, to let people in. Just the thought of it was too much. Telling my story would be a journey I could never achieve in my own strength. I breathe, thinking,

Thy Kingdom come, Thy will be done. On earth as it is in heaven…

The Last Threat

"When we are no longer able to change a situation... we are challenged to change ourselves." —Victor Frankl

There comes a time in life when we must face our worst enemy. Often, the one person responsible for oppressing us, mistreating us, and keeping us down, is the person in the mirror— that judgmental person; staring back in the reflective glass. An elusive self-perception keeps me paralyzed, unable to decide for my life. I have trembled at the shadows of a dead past for years, rehashing the multitude of mistakes I made in my youth and as an addict when God's word counsels me to stop looking back and start pressing towards His call, His plan, and His purpose. I have held myself captive to the erroneous belief that I must satisfy the expectations of people in my life, earning their acceptance while neglecting the spirit of true love and peace Jesus died to give me.

After battling addiction and disease, I prepare for another fight; it will be the fight of my life. The battlefield is the same: my mind. The battle is against co-dependency. I refuse to continue to repeat the abusive patterns of my history. After years of assuming the position of powerlessness, I am changing. My sense of self-worth is transforming, like the metamorphosis of a chrysalis. I once thought I could never be worthy, confident, or strong enough to rise above the deep trenches of my past. But God is not finished with me yet.

God speaks to us through the wind, in songs and hymns, and through those who speak His language—the language of love. Tonight, at church, He speaks to me through the wise counsel of a virtuous woman name Sister Georgette Graham.

"If you have a minute, I need to talk to you after rehearsal," Sister Graham tells me in a tone that makes me feel a tad defensive. She sits on the third row, watching her daughter Kayla and the other children learn the new dance routine. Georgette works as a schoolteacher and helps me with church practices with the children. She manages to attend the rehearsals, despite the tough battle with Lupus. She has always given me tremendous support with the children, but tonight, the prophetic words she speaks will begin to shift my life into an entirely new direction.

I stand to the side, repeating the same four words, "Let's do it again." The music plays, and the dancers start from the top;

practice goes on for hours. I walk back to catch the full vision of the choreography and the flow of the dancers. I sense Sister Graham's eyes, watching me more tonight than usual.

"Again; from the top," I say, noticing Letta's face.

Letta has become a strong praise dancer, but I worry. She looks tired in rehearsal today. She has bad dreams at night, and at times, I see a reflection of myself in her beautiful brown eyes. I pray over her, reciting the same scripture "For God has not given us the spirit of fear; but of power, and of love, and of a sound mind." I try to be bold as I say the words, but the truth is I have taught her how to be afraid. Children will often flow in the same energy as their parents—repeating the patterns. My mind has been far from sound. My life contradicts with my belief. *How can I tell my daughter not to be afraid when the same spirit of fear has dominated me for most of my life?* For years, I showed her a double standard, smiling while allowing myself to live in abuse and fear. Claiming victory in Jesus and crying behind closed doors.

I thought I was living in faith, being a loyal wife and mother, waiting for something to change. But faith and apathy can look the same when you are waiting, trying to find your way through the torment and the mental maze of a marriage where nothing is definite. But now, I am allowing myself to grow up and learn the differences between love and control, faith and apathy. Significant differences exist between the two sets of beliefs. Faith moves you to action, while apathy lulls you into the deep sleep of compromise.

Watching Letta dance, I think back to a time, not long ago, when she came to work with me at the dry cleaners. She works hard and earns money to save in her piggy bank. I rarely say no whenever my children want to come to work with me, enjoying their company, remembering how much I loved visiting my mother while she worked at the store.

Friday comes, and Letta smiles as she gets her pay and runs to the store a few doors down from the cleaners. "I'll be right back, Mommy!" she shouts skipping away.

"Stay together, and hurry back," I tell her as she leaves with Larry's older daughter, Dawn.

When she returns, her face is full of joy.

"Mommy!" She says. I know that look.

"I got something for you." Her hands behind her back, she rocks cheerfully from side to side.

"What are you up to now sweetheart?" I ask, aware of the answer. She eagerly waits, letting a magical childlike tension build before she reveals the gift her eyes have already given away. She extends her hands up towards me, holding a bouquet of flowers and a small teddy bear that wears a stitched smile as wide as hers.

"Surprise!" She beams with the curly strands of her hair bouncing near her big bright eyes. I stop my press machine.

"Thank you, baby, but I gave you money to buy something you wanted for yourself. You worked hard all week, and you are always buying things for me. You are my gift. I want you to get something that you want for a change. I love my flowers and teddy bear, but I would like you to think about yourself as well," I try to explain.

She looks at me, blinking through the steam rising from the pressing machines, "I'm fine. I wanted to get something for you. I love you, Mama." She wraps her arms around my waist.

She seems to lose herself in the practice of pleasing others, as I did. We are both middle children, compromisers, always wanting to keep the peace, and I worry about all she has seen over the years. Or maybe, it's paranoia; my flawed perception, thinking *this* is *that*, again. Whatever the case may be, I want her to be a fighter and never allow anyone to mistreat her. But, how can she? I am her first teacher, the one example of what a woman should be. *How can I teach her courage and self-worth? How do I show her boundaries, when every line in my life has been crossed, violated, and I never said a word against it? How do I teach her not to allow herself to be a target of the misguided anger of others?* I didn't have all the answers.

In a circle, the dancers hold hands. We end practice with prayer. "Good rehearsal. See you next week. Remember to learn the new music and practice the dance routine at home," I remind them, and prepare to clean the church.

Sister Graham glares at me,

"Sister Sandra, I need to tell you something." She grimaces, and I tell myself whatever she has to say, will be some form of criticism. My mind has a habit of drawing all kinds of conclusions before I get all the facts: a character trait I strongly dislike about myself. After a lifetime in fight-or-flight mode, my guard is always up. I remind myself to stop thinking and just listen.

"Yes, ma'am, I'm here," I answer.

"Sister Sandra, I need to tell you that I have been watching you wear yourself down." She begins to name all the programs, rehearsals, and church duties that I have taken on. She mentions my hospitalizations and feels I need to take time off to care for myself and completely recuperate.

I hear her, but she doesn't know. For many years, busyness has been my weapon of choice. To slow down is to disarm me, leaving me vulnerable to blindsided emotional attacks—in moments of high stress, the disturbing images still come. I constantly overextend myself to please others and to make sure I complete all tasks well. In my mind, there is still a damning voice that insists that I earn the love and approval I desperately wanted. To fall short in any area would be unacceptable; breaking free from childhood trauma is an ongoing process.

Sister Graham was just getting started. She proceeds to share a piece of information of which she cannot possibly know the details. It is something that happened many years ago when I was a little girl. "Sandra, I need you to go find where you lost the ability to say no." Her words are almost angry. She gives it to me straight. "You have lost yourself. You have lost your ability to say "no" and really love and care for yourself. You must go and find it!" Her eyes are stern, unblinking.

As she walks away, I stand there, trying to calculate the number of times I have said the word no. *No, I do not have time; no, I do not like staying up late when I need to get up early, no, I cannot fit one more thing on my plate, no, you cannot treat me that way, and no, I won't shut up because you don't want to be held accountable for your actions.* On the drive home, a light comes on inside me, shining inside a dark tunnel I dare not enter again. Sister Graham is right. I lost myself many years ago—Robert, like many others, took my voice, my right to say "no." I never made the connection. Sister Graham's message tells me, *I will never find her in this fearful trench of secrets. And I will never understand where to search if I continue to try to please everyone else in my life, at the expense of forsaking the lost parts of who I am—who I was before the monsters came and the nightmares began.*

In December, that same year;

A baby girl comes into our life. She is a miraculous little princess. I call her Precious. Her name is Jontavia. She is Bruce's niece, and though the adoption is supposed to be temporary until her parents got back on their feet, the family loves her as our own. I spend much of the time singing to her to calm her chronic colic. The first day she comes home, she is sick with an awful cold. Her stuffy nose and constant chest congestion persist even after the visits to the pediatrician. After nearly six weeks of warm baths, vapor rub, and amoxicillin, she gets better and began sleeping through the night. After school, the children gather on the bed in my room. Arms and legs stretch out everywhere. They will not move until they hear the sound of their father's car pull up. Meanwhile, Precious goes from one end of the bed to the other.

"It's my turn to hold her," Letta says.

"No, it's my turn," Cory harps back. They go back and forth, fussing over Jontavia.

"She is not going anywhere guys, she is a part of the family." I smile and rest against the pillow, pinned to the bed by Derick's feet across my legs and BJ's head on my shoulder. Pins and needles start in my toes and travel towards my back, but I won't move; this is my heaven.

My room is the hangout, and every day I fall deeper in love with my children. Cory and BJ make me laugh until I cry as they continue performing skits with the silliest expressions on their faces; their goofiness hasn't changed a bit. They remind me of Michael, my brother. In a constant state of comic relief, they would stand in the doorway, one in front of the other, performing their nightly comedy routines. I am not sure where they come up with this stuff, but it is like medicine. I have never told them that, but somehow, I think they know. They make me laugh until my sides hurt; it's a good hurt. It loosens the fetters of isolation that still holds me in this house. The children and I have grown up together, and now we begin again with little Precious. As she grows, I try to get her to call me auntie. But she echoes my children and starts to call me mommy. After a while, I just gave up and let her call me whatever made her happy. I find a special song just for her. It makes her smile, so I sing it to her every day:

> *"You are my sunshine, my only sunshine*
> *You make me happy when skies are gray*
> *You'll never know girl how much I love you…"*

History Repeats.

In late Autumn, I stand pressed against my bedroom window, shrinking from Bruce's angry hands, thinking I have had just about enough. Bruce shifts back into abuse mode, and I will be damned if I continue to live in this fear. My mind tells me to fight, but my body assumes the same reactive position before I realize, there is a pattern here that also involves the children; be it jealousy or some twisted rivalry, His violent reaction is the same as he slyly regains the *attention* to thwart my bond with the children. The picture emerges; I make the connections; abusers must control absolutely everything.

But now, I speak out, telling him, what I have wanted to say for years; I want a divorce. Bruce warns, "If you end my marriage, I will end your life." Again, the threat comes. Earlier today, I attempted to have a *cordial* conversation with him about everything. I had thought after all these years he would change. But I was wrong. His abusive nature has never died. It has waited in the shadows, returning each time I begin to feel alive, and want to break free. Abuse will always remind you of whom you were, which requires you to assume the same powerless position: seen and not heard. The same position that does not allow anyone else to love you for fear you may learn to love yourself. He never admits to the abuse nor assumes responsibility for his actions. And what is not acknowledged, will not change.

What was I thinking? I try, asking to speak with him, wanting to express my love and sincere appreciation for all the *good* he has done through the years, despite his violent temper? He had been a hard worker, providing for the family as best as he could. I remember the years during my addiction when he'd search the crack-infested neighborhoods to find me. And, there were good times: A cruise, breakfast in bed, holiday vacations. You can try to name it all, but it would be too impossible.

I have always given him the benefit of the doubt, and the truth is there is never all bad or all good in any of us; we all sin. In the biblical scripture of Romans 3:23, this fact is clear: We all fall short of the glory of God. Yet, infidelity, abuse, and manipulation corrupt every *good* deed, revealing a root of intimidation, control, and ultimate rule — not love or respect. Love and reward are very different. One is unconditional; the other expects obedience; it demands you to assume the position of a slave. And like the familiar smells of perfume and cigarettes, I've grown used to them both; as though they were the same. But the thorns have taught me well; they most definitely are not!

I try to reason with him, but he cannot hear me — that hasn't changed at all. Reason requires listening, and throughout the years, his opinion was the only one that mattered. I have played the fool, allowing it for so many years, until I believed it to be normal to live in fear of a man who was supposed to love me. *But I am tired of being afraid.* Sick and tired of assuming the same powerless position day after day, year after year. And though I remained calm, I wanted to shout;

To hit someone is a crime. To make someone feel afraid is equally a crime. To scream, bully, block the doorway, intimidate, and threaten someone are all offenses against the laws of God and humanity. He looks at me as if I am the same young girl he could hit and control, and the same teenage crack head that lost her soul. But he is very wrong. The years may not have changed him, but they have changed me.

I rage inside, thinking of how my submissiveness rewarded him with some sick rush of power. My failure to expose him enabled the grand illusion of one big happy family to continue all these years. I have learned that we teach others how to treat us, by what we allow or forbid. I have allowed it for so many years, that now I am expected to assume the same position without defiance. But the devil is a liar. I come to the harsh realization that until he confronts his hunger for control and his volatile nature, he will never change. Moreover, I can never be free until I demand my freedom, unapologetically.

Bruce knows I will not leave because of the children; this was clear years ago. Abusers use their children as pawns to gain an advantage and maintain control. As I become more aware, more empowered, I realize there is no easy way out of this quicksand. And just as it was with my parents and my sister, I knew divorce could devastate my children.

Before the last threat, the discussion started peacefully. As we walked across a small bridge in the area, I took a deep breath to explained,

"We met when I was only a child…," I tell him, wanting to be completely honest, trying to find words to express what is in my heart. "I was only twelve and a runaway when we met. We both were very young. I love you, but I would not have chosen you to marry. I was too young and broken to make any decision about my life. We both were too young. And now, I need to be on my own, to find what I am looking for — something I've lost."

I tried to explain, but so many words got in the way. Simply put, I no longer want to be married to him because I no longer want to feel afraid, but I didn't say that, for fear of how he would react. I could never truly express how I felt, but the truth is, I am tired of feeling like I owe a debt that I can never repay. All people have a right to feel safe and loved. And with him, I never did. Never safe, never loved, never so much as an orgasm in the *act* of his satisfaction.

As I try to explain, he waits. I think he has heard me out, and perhaps understood what my heart was trying to say. Maybe he has changed, and now, will finally allow me to express myself. But again, I am wrong. The passive-aggressive game he plays goes into overtime. He waits until he is ready, which is usually behind closed doors; that's when all hell breaks loose.

Once again, I find myself cringing against the bedroom window as Bruce towers over me. *If I am going to die, it had better happen quickly, because now, I am done with this foolishness and this endless cycle of cruelty*. I'm done with this fear; done with feeling helpless. Since childhood, I've been looking out of bedroom windows — crying, waiting, hoping. No more! Breathing out, I fast-forward; propelling through time — waking up; preparing to take back my voice; my dignity; my power of choice.

I run out of the bedroom, towards the phone on the kitchen table. Grabbing the telephone receiver, I dial 911. Up until this point, I could not have imagined reporting the crime. The risk of losing it all was too high, too much to lose. Now, I couldn't care less. I am sick of it! Every atom in my being makes a quantum leap to break free.

Bruce runs to the other side of the table and snatches the phone line out of the wall. At that very moment, for the first time, he looks at me differently, as if he sees someone else — someone who would no longer pretend like nothing ever happened; someone who could no longer assume the position; someone who is, awakening. Casita steps towards the table, speechless, frozen to the floor with her mouth partly open. The fretful look in her eyes makes me step back and calm down, but I know I could no longer continue to make excuses for his mistreatment.

How many times must children witness these crimes before they begin to believe it is normal? Enraged, I could spit fire. Mostly because my daughter has seen this violence before she could even speak. Tonight, I look in her eyes, and I remember my baby, watching; she is now a young woman, and she is still watching. Now, Bruce looks at me as if I'm the one hurting him — denying him the power he needed to feel alive; and there lies his disease — the need to control; to hurt another for the sake of his own misery.

I prepare for divorce, but it would mean leaving my children because it is impossible to co-parent with an abuser. He would surely find me, just as he did so many times. Leaving my marriage would mean breaking a vow of for better or worse, but vows mean nothing in abusive relationships.

Leaving would also mean breaking my children's heart and risking the retaliation of a man who would surely make them take sides. Controlling spouses often resort to threats and lies that damage the relationship between the exiting spouse and the children, hurting both parent and child—all consequences abusers care nothing about. I pray for God's guidance as the last threat lingers among the others; threats of death alongside the promise that he would make sure that my children "would hate me for leaving him." I'm done with this twisted game! God is not deaf, nor is He blind. He has been faithful and true, all through the years. He promises to defend the defenseless. And like the words in my sister's lullaby, someday, He will make all things new.

Needing more time with my children, I wait. Big mistake! Staying with an abuser for any amount of time is not wise,

I never speak to my children about their father's abuse. I have tried to honor him and wanted them to do the same, as I honored my father, despite his ways. But children are not stupid. They hear and see what their hearts are too afraid to say, just as I had listened to my parent's nerve-wracking fights. The fear of losing my children again keeps me close.

In the coming months at church, Bruce switches his attitude; a ploy he had used before—back when he swore, he had changed; typical. Using his well-guarded public image to hide behind. He laughs and smiles before the congregation as if he is above reproach. While at home, he backs off, changing the method to his madness. Some days it's hard to decode his actions. Months of peace followed with flowers and praise. I know this game. I question within myself the identity of the God of whom he speaks on the nights he preaches behind the pulpit. As the congregation of animated parishioner says amen, I wonder if he believes in his own hypocrisy. Either something is very wrong with this scene, or the years I spent as a crack head has numbed me to any sense of reality. I sit silently, watching, waiting.

Since the last threat, the spell of co-dependency begins to break. And for the first time since we met, I take back my right to say the word "no." Freedom comes first, by the words we say.

No, you cannot touch me! No, you cannot say whatever you want to say because I am done listening. No, you can no longer tell me lies, and I believe it. No, you can no longer control my body and mind. I snatch it all back, waiting for the right time to get out for good. It was liberating. For the first time in my life, since I could remember from childhood, my body was mine: only mine! The rebirth of self-confidence was beginning deep inside.

I became open to an emotional affair, because I no longer

wanted to care, to hurt, and fear him. In all-out rebellion, I seethe beneath the surface. We live separate lives in the same house. And just thinking about the way he has treated me turns my stomach inside out, and I ask myself why I allowed it for so many years, just as my mother did before me. I remember my sister, Joyce, a highway, and the thought of broken glass scattered in every direction. No matter what I choose to do, I will bleed. I know firsthand of the effects divorce has on the family. I hurt for the hearts of my children, the same way I ache for the little girl that once lived inside of me.

As time pass, I refocus my energies on school projects, piano lessons with BJ, church programs, a business school at the local library, and motorcycle training, a hobby I have wanted to pursue for many years. One of the first lessons I learned from my instructor at the Motorcycle Training Institute was not to look down. I had to learn to defy the natural impulse to drop my head, doubting myself. "Eyes open, head up. If you look down, you go down. Look ahead, to where you want to go. Don't look down!" The instructor would say over and over again. I sit on my bike, listening pass the revving engines of motorcycles around me. Across time, I hear the sound of my sister's voice as we danced the waltz. *Chin up, Sandy Patty. Don't look down.* I blink and refocus. Eyes straight ahead, I begin to shift forward — from neutral, into third gear.

Some days are harder than others, but channeling my energy serves a dual purpose. It allows me to move forward with my life, and it helps me to forgive the crimes of the past. I know I must let it all go; once and for all. I have tried before, and twice before that. It is not an easy thing to do. I must take ownership of the things that I allowed in my adulthood, no matter how my childhood may have influenced the self-destructive reactions. Right now, the choices are mine alone, as are the consequences. I have tough decisions to make, and sometimes forgiveness is the hardest thing to do.

I want to forgive, but how do you let go of something that will not let go of you? How do you forget the years of torment where you bought into your own abuse, believing you deserved to be hit and mistreated? This to me is mental illness. Like racism, intimate partner abuse is a mental sickness. To abuse someone and to allow abuse is one of the worst forms of mental illness. Ignorance is bliss, and when it comes to domestic violence and every other dreadful life experience, it is also a mental disease. If we believe we are all made in God's image, how can we carry out such cruelty? I want to forgive and let go, and start my life over, but I know if I allow myself to stay in a toxic marriage, forgiveness today will inevitably turn into resentment tomorrow.

My marriage only grew worse, and I became more embittered, thinking about my grandmother, my mother, and both my sisters, Joyce and Linda — all were victims of violence from men who were supposed to love and care for them. Co-dependency and self-hatred walk hand-in-hand to plague the next generation with its fear and "normal" dysfunction. And like a loveless love song or a fairy tale with no happy ending, domestic violence threatens the very core of every community. I must learn how to catch this boomerang before it reaches my children. In my heart, I whisper, *God will guide me. I put my trust in Him.*

Breaking the toxic bond of co-dependency begins with taking responsibility; We must forgive ourselves before we can genuinely forgive anyone else. The secrets I swore I would take to the grave, kept me impaled to a shame that does not belong to me; we must share our stories. Abusers and victims of abuse can heal only when the co-dependent nature of the crime is exposed, confronted, and resolved. And though the crime of domestic violence is complex, I removed myself from the belief that Bruce, in any form, hates me. His inability to perceive the real enemy cause him to feel out of control to the point of hating himself.

Ephesians 5 explains that, "husbands should love their wives as their own bodies. He who loves his wife loves himself. Indeed, no one ever hated his own body, but he nourishes and cherishes it, just as Christ does the church." Abusive spouses despise their own flesh; unable to understand the projection of their own inner hatred. Men desperate for control, yet out of control; hungry for power and rule, they grasp the wind, reaching for the illusion of domination. History echoes the evil of controlling men who incidentally cannot control their own heartbeats. All is vanity until we fall on our knees at the nail-pierced feet of the One who died for every sin. Only then can we see our own wretchedness and return to the God of love who created all life, deeming it sacred and worthy.

I was determined to write new vows for my life. Vows to love, honor, and cherish the gift of life God has given me. A pledge to never give away my power of choice again, and to listen to the sound of my voice. The lesson begins today, using our God-given right to be joyful regardless of uncertainty; we must believe our change will come, and in our ability to make that change happen.

When we proclaim faith in Jesus Christ, yet deny the power of God to change our life, we are brain-dead or simply an undercover atheist. We must believe our change will come. I believe; no matter what!

The Ache of Compromise

"From the beginning of our history, the country has been afflicted with compromise. It is by compromise that human rights have been abandoned." ~ *Charles Sumner*

Winter turns to spring, and tonight, my children scattered throughout the church. They are growing up faster than I can keep up. Cory will begin driving lessons next summer; his feet can almost reach the floorboard of my car; I gather my thoughts and stand to go.

Outside the burgundy doors of the church, Pastor Hall, an associate pastor, and a talented pianist stops me as I prepared to head home from the weeklong revival.

"Sandra, you should teach. You have a gift for it." He says to me; out of the blue. I have never really thought about it, I just do it. Immediately, I thought of my sister. Joyce spent her life teaching us just about everything. Her energy and diligence to care for us is the gift Pastor Hall sees in me. Joyce led by example, showing love in the way she cooked, cleaned, and taught us the amazing stories of the Bible; even her discipline was loving because it taught us right from wrong. She was indeed the angel in the garden, planting seeds that would never leave our lives. The good manners, love and respect, and faith in God blossoms through every storm and adversity.

And now, my world is teaching children to sing, drive, dance, and learn of a God who gives us second chances to make life right again.

"Thank you, Pastor Hall. I appreciate that." I remember feeling grateful for his thoughtful words, but I also know, with all I have taught my children, compromise is a lesson I wish I could change for their sakes. For too long, I've remained silent.

Earlier, during the revival at church, Casita sat near the right side, a few pews away from the drums and organ. I glanced at her, and then, turned away. My heart ached because I know the hypocrisy of all they have seen between home and church. Growing up, I resented the mixed messages of church compared to the realities of the world; something did not add up. Faith loses its power and authority when the messages at church and home do not agree. I fear the church will stand in critical judgment in the eyes of my children as it once did in mine, and they will assume the same position of going along to get along. I pray they see past the aches of my compromise and learn to seek the true face of Christ and His plan for their lives. The contradicting views of church, marriage, and honesty are baffling, like trying to walk on a tightrope that splits off into two different directions. No matter the next step, you will fall.

Casita is turning 18. She glows with grace and beauty. The little girl I carried in foster care, sewed two pink gowns for at St. Vincent, braided her hair, and sung lullabies to, is all grown up. She has asked me if she can have her birthday party at her favorite restaurant: Olive Garden. It was the same place she had wanted her 17th birthday party. The most astonishing thing to me is that she is still the same fun-loving girl who loves to sing and dance. Now it was time to commemorate her coming of age, making plans for her party, and spend hours braiding her thick dark hair. Seeing her smile, hearing her laughter, surrounded by her closest girlfriends, are wonderful gifts. I breathe, thinking, *we have come so far by the grace of God. Thank you, Jesus.*

January 24, 2000

Both sides of the family join in the celebration. During the party, I give my usual smile to take pictures, but inside I grow more restless of the facade. A few months later, the children gather in the living room waiting for their big sister to come out of the bathroom. She steps out a vision of loveliness, wearing a long, princess prom gown with golden sparkles glittering off her shoulders. Her Auntie Linda waits to drive her to the prom. Tearing up, I want to remember the way she looks, the special way she glows tonight, and the fragrant corsage laced around her wrist.

"Mom, how many more pictures are you going to take?" Casita asks with her head leaning off to the side.

"Just one more picture, sweetheart."

"Ma, you said one more, ten minutes ago," she laughs.

"Hold that smile!" I say, wanting to freeze time. The feeling was different for me; more of every incredible feeling I could think. Looking back from where I was many years ago, seeing my daughter dressed for her high school prom was magical.

Linda drives away with Casita and her prom date Kevin in the back seat. This feeling is a new *normal*, and no words can express how happy that moment made me; beyond grateful; only God could know.

Another year of teacher's conferences and school projects come to a halt as the school year hurries towards summer vacation.

It has been a busy year of helping my teens and preteens learn to listen more attentively to their teachers while managing their active church and social life, which to them, seems to be more important than life itself. I laugh, thinking about the parent-teacher meetings.

"Your son is a good student, but he must stop interrupting my class," one teacher told me of my son BJ. He gets his title of class clown honestly. I had received a trophy for Class Clown at Oriole Elementary; I was extremely proud of myself. I may not have understood math too well, but I knew how to goof off and make the entire class laugh. I am not sure, but I think, often, the funniest people are the ones who are hurting the most.

Then there was the time when Letta's elementary school teacher who had called me in for a conference about her constant talking in the class. No news flash there, I had been completely aware of her gift of speaking without ever needing to take a breath. In the hours, it takes to braid her hair, I never get tired or bored because she is always good company and the conversation is lively.

Now that Letta is older, something was changing. She has become somewhat guarded, but, aren't all teens a bit secretive? All children reveal one or more characteristics of their parents. Like my mom, work speaks my value, and like my dad, the road calls to me. Through the years, my children have seen and heard more than I want to believe, and as I've met with my children's teachers, I know that their actions have not always been their own, but a combination of their environment, childhood experiences, and the ailment of a home ruled by secret fears and control. Growing pains exist in every family, but when a bloodline of fear and intimidation runs beneath the roots of the family tree, it is not merely hormonal, but the vicious repeat of history.

Through the years, my children have had their share of rebellion, even running away, and after much prayer and fasting, coming back home. Was this normal adolescent behavior, or is there a widening trench? Proverbs 28:13 teaches that "whoever conceals his wrongdoings will not prosper, but he who confesses and forsakes them will obtain mercy." I sensed the transfer; the boomerang effect of Exodus 20:5, warning families of a visitation of iniquity passed from "fathers upon the children unto the third and fourth generation." The same sin will continue to plague the next generation unless it is broken by the act of repentance.

The Warrior

Spring, 2000

The passion and dream of joining the military, serving on the police force, and defending the rights of others remain alive in me. And though I filled out an application for the academy, one look at my arrest record and I walked out wondering why I even tried. Today, I was about to get a reminder of why I survived such a long battle; why God preserved my life through the fiercest storms. Psalms 37:23, reminds us to embrace every moment; every step; for it has been assigned by the one who calls us from the battle to victory.

Casita prepares for yet another milestone: high school graduation. "Ma," Casita knocks from outside my bedroom door.

"I'll be right there dear." When I open the door, she is standing in front of me holding a large square package, the size of a wall poster.

"Mama, I got something for you." She smiles.

In an instant, time rewinds to when she was four. "Mommy, I made something for you." She holds a portrait of flowers and hearts. "I love you this much," she'd say with arms stretched out to her sides. The little girl is all grown up, but the dimpled smile is still the same. I stand at the door, in awe of the amazing grace that has brought us so far.

"Hey, Mama, open it. I've been saving for a while to buy this." She says as we walk over to my bed.

"Thank you, sweetheart" I sit, opening her gift. Casita stands in front of me. Underneath the wrapping paper is an 11x14 canvas, encased inside a golden frame. In the center of the painting is a poem written by Larry S. Clark.

"I hope you like it," she says, staring at me as if she needs me to see something more than my reflection in the framed glass. "Read it, Mama. Read it out loud," she asserts, sitting next to me. I cannot help but smile, but when I begin to read and understand the message of the poem, it turns on a light—a bright light that shines deep inside an empty tunnel. The title of the poem is "The Warrior:"

> This morning my thoughts traveled along
> To a place in my life where days have long since gone
> Beholding an image of what I use to be
> As visions were stirred, and God spoke to me.

He showed me a warrior, a soldier in place
Positioned by Heaven, yet I saw not the face.
I watched as the warrior fought enemies
They came from the darkness with destruction for me.

I saw as the warrior would dry away tears
As all of Heaven's angels hovered so near.
I saw many wounds on the warrior's face
Yet weapons of warfare were firmly in place.

I felt my heart weeping, my eyes held so much
As God let me feel the warrior's prayer touched.
I thought "how familiar" the words that were prayed
The prayers were like lightning that never would fade

I said to God "Please, the warrior's name."
He gave no reply, He chooses to refrain.
I asked "Lord, who is broken
that they need so much prayer?"
He showed me an image of myself standing there.

Bound by confusion, lost and alone,
I felt prayers of the Warrior carry me home.
I asked, "Please show me Lord, this warrior so true."
I watched and I wept
For mother, the warrior was you.

My daughter's gift strikes like lightning, burning through each accusation that still echoes in the corners of my mind. As I read the last line of the poem, I think, *a warrior; is that how she sees me?* After a lifetime of relentless voices degrading me, shaming me, making me feel weak for not fighting back, she calls me a warrior. My daughter sees me, not as a failure or disappointment, but as a warrior, a soldier in the fiercest military; the Army of the Lord.

The gift encourages me, making me question my identity. By now, I should know who I am in this world, but when you've wandered through your life in a trench with thorns on every side, confidence is a foreign language that I'm still learning to speak.

"Thank you, Casita." I am deeply touched. She stood up and looked at me.

"I love you, Mama," she says. It was like she was trying to break a spell cast long ago. We embrace, and she walks out of the room.

Long after Casita gets married and leaves home, the poem will hang on the wall near my bed. For the next three years, it will serve as a reminder to break the curse of apathy and stay on the battlefield of faith.

The words of Casita's favorite lullaby move across my memory: "*God is watching us, from a distance.*" He will soon speak to me again, and faithfully guide my stumbling feet towards freedom. The freedom of choice is a powerful position. Even God Himself allows us this. In Joshua 24:15, it is written, "And if it seems evil for you to serve the Lord, choose you this day whom you will serve; whether the gods which your fathers served that were on the other side of the flood, or the gods of the Amorites, in whose land you dwell..."

Still awakening, I realize the apathy and fear that has kept me enslaved to a trench that has me unable to move beyond the secrets of my past; secrets of abuse, HIV, rape and trafficking. More than anything, I want to climb out. I want to be free from every voice that silences me. The spirit of fear tells me the same old story; it is better to stay in your place, assume the position, seen and not heard, numb, powerless, afraid — nothing new; all the same lies. Still, I stay in this house, needing to be close to my children while wanting to get out.

Since childhood, there had always seemed to be a tug of war between fear and faith. Some days up, other days I cannot tell. Doubt keep me always wondering, *am I doing this right?* But God's Word reminds me that the battle is not mine; He fights for me. When I look back over my life, I see, again and again, how He has delivered me from the shadows of death. Surely now, He will deliver me. I pray, asking God to show me the way out, questioning my marriage. *Can divorce ever be of God? What of the men who treat their wives treacherously? Who defends us? What are our rights? What are the consequences for the next generation? God show me the way.*

The coming years will reveal how much my children already know, and how that understanding influences their lives. They follow, almost instinctively, in our shoes, absorbing everything; the good, the bad, and the unspeakable. This was transgenerational grief and trauma; *The root must be confronted and destroyed before the family can completely heal. The process was beginning.*

"Where Are You?"

> *"Not until we are so lost do we begin to understand ourselves." ~Henry David Thoreau*

"Where are you?" Angela asks. But I don't know how to answer. The stress of last month's event triggers severe anxiety. Overwhelmed, I float in and out, trying to disconnect from the roller coaster. Letta, my daughter, is all I can think about. The unpredictable turns and plummeting drops of life are like shockwaves after an earthquake.

"You're not listening," Angela says as we stand near the hall of the church. I stand on my post ushering, and after she informs me she is soon going into the Air Force, I remember telling her how proud I am of her, and then my thoughts trail away to the strain of the previous week. The scene replays as if it never ended.

On the way to work, I suddenly feel sick, making a U-turn, I break the speed limit to get to Letta's high school. The foreboding sense of urgency hurls me back to the past. Call it paranoia or mothers' intuition; I must get to her school; something was wrong. I couldn't shake the overwhelming feeling that my daughter is in trouble. When I made it to the lobby of North Lauderdale High, the guidance counselor told me she was not in class and was marked absent. I doubled over as she confirmed my fear. I ran upstairs to speak to the campus police.

"My daughter is missing! She is not in school. I feel something is wrong. Please help me!" The campus police looked at me as if I have a third eye. They react as if my distress is something they hear happening all the time. I break down, and the stress of it overwhelms me to the point of near collapse.

"Calm down Miss, teenagers skip school all the time," the cop replies with a casual smug.

"You don't understand. I know my daughter; she can't just skip school. She takes the school bus. Where will she go? I feel it in my gut. I know something is wrong!" They told me there was nothing they could do until she was missing for more than twenty-four hours. I fell apart.

"Sorry Miss, after the age of sixteen, your daughter is no longer under the truancy law. If she is a runaway, you cannot make her go to school or come home."

"What! What are you talking about? Did you hear anything

I just said? She is not a runaway! Something is wrong; this is not a case of a runaway teenager. She got on the school bus this morning. I know she came to school, but she is not in class. We are wasting time!" A group of students heard me down the hall and stopped to tell me they saw my daughter walking out by the bus area.

"I know her. She walked near the apartments north of the school," one male student remembered.

"Was she alone?" I ask.

"No, she was with someone, a man. That's all I know."

"Can you please give me a description of him?" I pleaded.

"Brown-skinned, five-nine, medium built, black guy," he said clearly. I ran out of the school and drove in the direction the student said he last saw my daughter. I could feel her near; in my bones, she was close. Tunnel vision, I prayed, ignoring the floating specks of light; my blood pressure was rising. It was hard to breathe because I knew history was beginning to repeat itself. I rode out the panic attack with one focus: find my daughter!

"Breathe, Sandra," I spoke aloud, barely able to swallow after I said the words. "God please help me!" I readied myself for the unexpected.

Three blocks away from the school campus, I pulled into an apartment complex. Rows of gray townhouses eerily remind me of Robert's Merchant ship. Dwarf shrubs sat vertically between small lot lines, separating each townhouse door. I got out of my car, scanning the property.

"Holy Spirit, please help me," I whispered. I heard the voice of the Lord telling me to look straight ahead. "That's the door," I said; I know she is here. I knocked. There was no answer, but I wasn't going anywhere without my daughter. I called the campus police.

"I need help now. Please come! I know my daughter is here." The campus police were on the way. I kept my eyes on the doorknob, but I heard the Lord telling me to be still. When the police arrived, they asked me how I knew my daughter was in that apartment.

"I just know she is, please hurry." They both look at me as if I was a lunatic and gave me the same traffic-light stare as they did on the second floor of the school.

"Sorry, ma'am. We can't just go in because you think your daughter is in there. I told you, your daughter has the right to be in there if she wants to. She is over sixteen."

"She is a child; I don't care what you say. Teenagers are still children, and she could be in danger." I take my cell phone and call 911. I interrupted the operator on the other end before she can complete her words.

"911, what's your emergency, do you need fire or—"

"I need help. I have the campus police here from North Lauderdale High; they are refusing to get my daughter from an apartment where I believe she is in danger. Please come, please help me!" I screamed with all my might, trying to reach through chasms of time, to find the voice of a child that was never heard. I was desperate, crying for my daughter; crying for myself because somewhere inside of me there is an empty space. It was abandoned nearly thirty years ago because no one ever came. Every atom within me roared, *I am not going anywhere without my daughter!*

A few minutes later, two North Lauderdale city police officers arrive. "Please, stay back ma'am; we will go investigate your suspicion." The campus police wait skeptically to the side. I paced by the patrol car, burning anger building inside me because of the police officers' desensitized attitudes. Moments later, my daughter comes out with her book-bag, and a man comes out in handcuffs.

There is no way I could have known she was in there; God led the way—of this I have no doubt. I also had no idea who this person was or if he had a criminal background. Later, one of the lead detectives will tell me he was a repeat offender, already on probation for soliciting a minor.

I can breathe again. "Letta are you okay?" I asked, trying to stay calm. She looked away, blankly; I know that look all too well. She was safe, that's what mattered most, but I also wanted her checked at the nearest women's crisis center. The police agreed, and state it would be necessary for the criminal case.

At the crisis center, I held her hand, ready to listen when she felt ready to talk. I needed to show her unconditional love and support. There will be time to talk later. I wrapped her in my arms.

After a full physical examination, the center made its determination: no sexual assault occurred—she had been untouched, unharmed. It feels as though a thousand-pound weight has fallen off. We had gotten her out in time. After leaving the center, we spend time talking with the detective about the criminal case. He informed me there will be a court hearing and that he will keep me informed of the date.

"I'm going to handle this case myself," he said. "This guy has a habit of soliciting minors. His rap sheet is long. It is a good thing you followed your gut. We got your daughter out in time. He is not supposed to be within 500 feet of a school. He has violated his probation, and I want him off the streets for good."

Weeks later, I stood in a courtroom. My daughter and I are on one end, and the offender's mother and pregnant girlfriend are on the other. His mother cries, while his girlfriend walks over to me. "Please don't press charges; I don't know what I am going to do. Our baby is due in less than a month. I am so sorry for what has happened," she weeps.

"The case is not in my hands," I tried to explain. "I am sorry. I cannot control the judge's ruling in any direction. It is not in my hands. I will pray for you and your family. I too am truly sorry any of this happened."

The bailiff calls the court to order. The judge's ruling is harsh. After his mother and girlfriend hear the sixteen-year sentence, their sobs fill the courtroom. I tilt my head down and away, questioning the system more than the offender. He is a repeat offender. There had been no correction the first few times he was in jail for doing the same crime. What is the point of incarceration if it corrects nothing? *What will change now? Will he get out and attempt to do the same thing again, because of a penal system that fails to offer the correction needed to change his life? Or is this man an unredeemable beast?* My heart breaks for both sides of the family. *I don't have the answers.*

The sound of the judge's gavel comes down hard, and the guards take the defendant away.

The words in Jeremiah 17:9, describes how "the heart is deceitful above all things, and desperately wicked: who can know it?" No law can change its wickedness. God alone changes and transforms lives. He alone renews the heart and mind. In the book of Romans 12:2, the answer is clear,

"Be not conformed to this world: but be transformed by the renewing of your mind, that you may prove what is that good, and acceptable, and perfect, will of God." *I wonder what would have happened if, in prison, the word is taught in truth and love, instead of a penal system of crime and punishment which further dehumanizes offenders, adding insult to injury.* The very system is a travesty of justice.

"God, please help us," I whisper in the hall of the courtroom. *How do we get this right? When will we get it right? When will we see that without the law of Christ to guard and guide our lives, without his grace and mercy, we are lost?*

After the incident, life goes back to its apathetic norm. Again, as if nothing ever happened. My daughter attends a private school, and we try to move past the episode. As the days go by, I listen to my daughter, and I hear myself; her fears were my fears. The careless attitude that had caused her to put herself in a dangerous situation is a learned behavior. A lesson taught by my secret apathy. I can do nothing but offer her love and understanding while trying to show her that her worth is more valuable than all the stars in the universe. Perhaps my daughter would have believed me if my actions had not been speaking so much louder than my words.

My apathy and lack of self-worth had taught her to keep secrets, and now, I'm afraid of the secrets she may not tell me, the same way I have not told my mother. I hid my secrets from my children, believing if I said anything, it would hurt them, but the truth is ignorance is a painful thorn because what we don't know will hurt us. I must find a way to climb out of this trench and catch the fateful boomerang that has circled back again. For the sake of my children, I must find a way.

In Hosea 4:6, the word teaches "…people perish from a lack of knowledge." Ignorance is a slow-acting poison that moves through the generations where no one stops to think and ask, why. The issues I fail to talk about affects my children; this is one of the many evils of domestic violence. The victim routinely assumes the shame and guilt. The lesson we must learn is to stop pretending like nothing ever happened. Until the inner world changes, the outer world will remain imprisoned to the patterns of making circles around the painful thorns of our circumstance. Thorns are only thorns; they can keep us in our place or spur us to change; it's up to us to choose what we will do.

The Real Enemy

"Rough, boisterous, stormy and altogether warlike, I am
born to fight against innumerable monsters and devils."
~Martin Luther

When I was in DCF custody and foster care, the "no fighting"
rule was confusing because all my life it felt as if I was in a fight
with both hands tied behind my back, never throwing a punch. In
this world, every day we must face adversity in one form or
another. I have learned that the fiercest battle is within. A war with
our sinful flesh and the pride that so easily besets the heart. But
there is another war, a battle we *must* fight with our hands tied, and
without ever throwing a punch. In 2 Corinthians 10:3-5, the Apostle
Paul teaches that although "we live in the world, we do not wage
war as the world does. The weapons we fight with are not the
weapons of the world. On the contrary, they have divine power to
demolish strongholds. Prone to wander, I remind myself of these
words again.

We demolish arguments and every pretension that sets itself
up against the knowledge of God, and we take captive every
thought to make it obedient to Christ." One of the greatest lessons
we must all learn is that the battle is already won.

Alone in my room, I get down on my knees, praying,
desperately needing strength to rise above it all. I run my hand
across my forehead, closing my eyes, feeling like a leaf on a vast
ocean, drifting along with the motion of the waves. The signs of the
same patterns of behaviors are starting all over again; I observe it
in my children, and the way I see it, I have two choices: stay down
inside this generational trench of violence and apathy or find a way
to climb above it for myself, my children, and for future
generations. In the solitude, I rummage through old books and a
box full of pictures that never found their way inside the family
photo album. I come across a paperback workbook I received some
time ago. I think back to the Thursday night when the associate
pastor, Elder Mark Johnson, passed around the workbooks written
by authors Jerry & Carol Robeson. Pen in hand, I was ready for the
new course study. The workbook title is *Strongman's His Name,
What's His Game?*

"Tonight, we are going to talk about spiritual warfare," he said. "We do not fight against flesh and blood people, but against the rulers, against the powers of evil, against the forces of darkness, and against spiritual wickedness in the high places." Late-comers join the study, and I wait for the right time to ask a burning question. "Therefore, put on the full armor of God, so you will be able to resist the devil. Strongman is his name, and tonight we are going to the enemy's camp to take back everything he has stolen. Satan has a game plan, a cunning strategy to steal, kill, and destroy our destiny. We are going to explore his weaponry, learn his tactics, and destroy the strongholds he tries to place on our life," he declares with a military fervor. "You can only defeat the enemy of your soul through the Word of God and blood of the risen Savior, Jesus Christ. Without God, you can do nothing, and you would surely fail," he says pacing the carpet in front of the pews.

"Prayer is a powerful weapon. You must use the principles of prayer to fight this spiritual warfare. We need to learn the authority you have in Jesus Christ." Elder Johnson continues the study. And I can't help but wonder why when I pray that sometimes things seem to get worse. Life feels like a roller-coaster ride, and I do not like roller-coasters. *Why does God allow so much evil, what does it all mean?*

"It's Q&A time, does anyone have any questions?" He asks. I raise my hand, honestly believing no one could have the answers to my questions. Still, I ask, "Why does God allow so much suffering? From the Holocaust to slavery, are we all just going through the motions from birth to death? Greed, poverty, and diseases are rampant. Ever since Adam and Eve sinned, society continues to decline. We are all born in sin. As a people, there is progress, but the world remains in turmoil. I believe God is all-powerful, but why do these things continue as if we are just going through the motions here on earth?"

"No," he answers, taking a step toward me. "We are not just going through the motions. God has a divine purpose and plan for every one of us. We must trust His plan and will for our life. The scripture declares that "God will never leave nor forsake us." When sin entered the world through disobedience, it brought the curse. Jesus came to be the propitiation for sin, and he broke the power of sin, death, hell, and the grave. However, God doesn't take away our free will. Scripture says, "choose you this day who you shall serve." The choice is ours, but we do not have to yield to sin. We have power over sin through the love of Christ. satan desires to make us doubt the love of God through trials and hard times. But satan is a liar, and we can only defeat him when we know and understand the Word of God. It is our weapon."

The unseen war Elder Johnson spoke about that night is a battle I have seen all my life. As a child with dreams of being a soldier, serving my country, and joining the police force, I could not have imagined the galactic war raging around me. If my life is going to change, once and for all, I must take responsibility for the ripple effects of my passivity. No one else can do that for me. Anxiety was the tool the enemy had used to keep me subservient, manipulated, and easily controlled. I want a divorce, but I am not sure if that is the answer. Solutions do not come easy when you love someone and wait for something to change, but it never does.

Apathy is a trap that sets the bait for co-dependency. It causes you to waste away, waiting for someone or something else to change what only you can. I can no longer cast blame on Bruce for a life I allow. My silence is consent. I should have spoken out, but when mistreatment feels normal, what is there really to speak out against? The greatest ploy of an enemy is to make you believe he doesn't exist.

Once again, my focus begins to shift. The more I learn, the more the power of knowledge holds me responsible for my own life and transformation. Blaming others doesn't work. My life is my choice, not the consequence of my past, my parents, stepfather, the wolves, the culture, addiction, or an abusive spouse. In the book of 1 John 4:4, the word declares, "...Greater is He living in me, than he that is in the world." He will go before me to fight every battle. In an upside-down world, full of noise, doubt, compromise, and uncertainty, I must remind myself, every day, that I am not alone—God is with me. And if God is for us, no weapon, no devil, and no power can stand against us. My trust is in Him alone!

There is an evil in this world; a cruel energy, not a color of skin. Not a man, woman, or even beast, but a ruthless cruelty of an evil origin; void of mercy, human kindness, and love. The same cruelty of the holocaust, slavery, war, and genocide is the very same evil that shifts and hides inside hearts filled with ego and pride.

1 John 3:8, declares "The one who practices sin is of the devil; for the devil has sinned from the beginning. The Son of God appeared for this purpose, to destroy the works of the devil." True humility is the wisdom that defends us from ourselves; the blood of Christ defends us from all else.

New York

"The secret of health for both mind and body is not to mourn for the past, nor to worry about the future, but to live the present moment wisely and earnestly." ~*The Buddha*

September 2003

The bars of the mental prison begin to open wider, and the sense of freedom feels scary and intoxicating at the same time. Change is coming. My girlfriends Kim and Olga, and I begin spending more time together after church. After meeting at Refreshing Springs almost a year ago, we have become good friends. Last year, the Church gathered to remember Sister Graham; it was a challenging time. Her passing came unexpectedly. I cried on her mother's lap the morning she went to heaven. That was the day I made a promise to her. I would always honor her memory and the caring words she spoke to me that day after practice. "Go find your voice, your 'no.'" She told me. I can still hear her encouraging message speaking to my heart.

I tell myself that I *will* accomplish my goals. My friendships with Olga and Kim are essential parts of the process of learning to move from isolation to trust. They have become irreplaceable in my life, embracing my corny ways and nerdy study habits; I trust them and feel a level of comfort around them that helps me cope with the changing tides. Friendship is a gift.

Later the same year, Kim and I take a road trip to visit her family in Pennsylvania. I'm happy to drive her, insisting that she shouldn't take the Greyhound bus when I can drive her wherever she wanted to go. Roadman's daughter, I'll make any excuse to be out on the open road. Besides, Kim cannot drive, and I feel the bus ride would be tiresome for her 8-year-old son Nathaniel, who has autism. Although my teenagers didn't want to make the drive up, but 4-year-old Precious had wanted to stay by my side. She joins me on the long excursion.

"Look, Mommy, over there!" She repeats every time she sees a pasture of cows or horses. The rhythm of the road carries me away. I sing the songs on the radio, while Kim mumbles in her sleep, and Precious shifts from entertaining me to bossing Nathaniel around. "Hold it, hold it!" she shouts every time Nathaniel says he has to use the bathroom. She says it often. It seems we stop every other hour. When I think everyone is asleep, Precious asks me,

"Mama are you, all right?"

"Yes, baby. I thought you were asleep with everyone else."

"No, I'm not sleep, Mama. I want to stay up with you," she says. "Okay. How about a song?"

"Yes." She smiles.

"You are my sunshine, my only sunshine; you make me happy when skies are gray. You'll never know dear; how much I love you. Please don't take my sunshine away."

We sing until she falls asleep. Like magic, it works every time.

Visiting with Kim's family is an enjoyable experience. Her aunt makes me feel like family. From the very moment we meet, I feel accepted, celebrated, and loved. We attend church together on Sunday, and before night falls, the children and I are skating up and down the long Pennsylvania Street. It is like being with family members I never knew I had.

"Thanks for making lasagna tonight, Sandra. It's delicious. Can you stay longer? Do you have to leave by the weekend?" Kimberly's aunt asks me as I finished serving dinner.

"I need to get back to work soon, but I will miss you; you are so kind."

Later that night, Kim and I go for a long walk down the back-winding roads of her aunt's home. We talk about life and laugh about how I ran the red light when I first drove into the city. I hadn't seen the traffic signal positioned on the side of the road. New state, new road signs, and signals; every day the world presents new lessons.

The sky grows darker and the night air carries the scent of fresh green grass in every direction. The cricket's song is louder here; I listen and allow their gentle energy to lead the way. We slow our carefree stride, and I begin to see flickers of light moving in the grass, up ahead, to the sides, and all around us they float, glitter, and dance.

"Kimmy, do you see that? They are everywhere!" I asked, moving closer to the open field.

"Oh, those are lightning bugs. I have seen them since I was little. If you look close, they almost look like sparkling jewels. See right here, below the wings," Kim says, holding one in the palm of her hand. "You never saw a firefly before?" she asks.

I breathe, beaming with ecstasy, staring out, turning around in a circle like a child. *They are all around me.* I'm in awe of the little magical messengers only a great God could create. I raise my hand to my face, remembering how they had guided the way through the dark tunnels of my mind. Filled with emotions I cannot express, I smile, more to myself than at Kim. "Yes, I have seen them before, but not quite like this. They are so beautiful."

After the visit to Pennsylvania, I drive to New York. I couldn't come this far without going to the place Midnight, and I had stayed up for hours dreaming of; listening to Frank Sinatra sing about the magic of New York. In a word, I feel blessed. The excitement is beyond imagination.

"Are we there yet?" Nathaniel and Precious ask at least 20 times before we get out of the Holland Tunnel, and I can't blame them; The tunnel goes on for what seems like a hundred miles. But I love every moment of it. Nostalgia falls in between the honking horns echoing off the tunnel walls, and Billy Joel singing on the radio. The New York state of mind he sings about fills me with a sense of belonging. Right here, right now, I belong. Enraptured, I sing to the top of my lungs,

> "I know what I'm needin', and I don't want to waste more time
> I'm in a New York state of mind."

In the heart of New York, we visit Ground Zero to offer homage to the heroes and victims of 9/11. "Get hands; let's pray," I tell the children. I had known they would be too young to understand, but they are old enough to follow our lead as we whisper a prayer of healing for the tragedy that took place here. Kimberly prays, and soon the bustling noises of traffic and people passing by trail away down the iconic roads of the city that never sleeps.

I pray, remembering where I was the moment the planes hit the towers. Working at my part-time job at Blue Green Resort in Fort Lauderdale, I had dropped the phone, listening to the muzzled screams of a woman watching television on the other end.

"A plane just hit the Twin Tower!" she screamed, and then the phone went dead. At that moment I alerted my supervisor, and the instant he turned on the office television, the world had changed. My colleagues and I watched in horror just as the second plane hit. With one hand over my heart and the other covering my mouth, a thousand questions ran through my mind all at once.

I question the evil that seeks to kill, steal, and destroy for no other reason than the fleeting illusion of power and control. I have seen the same evil prevailing in the world—all my life, I have witnessed its tyranny. The battles of the Underdogs vs. the evil villains, like Simon Bar Sinister; hell-bent on ruling mankind, there seems to be no end to this thing called evil. Whether the terrorists are foreign or domestic, evil needs no visa or passport; it only requires a place to hide. It creeps, hiding inside empty hearts that beat with the practice of sin and self-righteousness, believing in nothing beyond its vanity. It hides behind sheep-like grins and ill intentions that you never see coming until the door closes behind you. It stews in men and women who refuse to deny their racism, pride, and hate. Life is a boomerang—what we throw out, comes back again into the hands of the next generation. Time waits for us to get it right.

I look out over Ground Zero, bowing my head; I pray for change. I imagine on this land, where the sky went black under the dark ashes of terrorism, that perhaps people can begin to learn a new language. The universal language of a love that would awaken us and enrich us with the truth of who we are: we are human. We are all created beings, designed by the Hand of an amazing God who, like Mr. Jim the Artist, paints with many colors, and requires but one law; the law of love; the love of God, and the love of our humanity. We must learn to live beyond our "feelings," and choose to *be* love. Feelings are mutable states of mind that drive our actions toward what we decide to do or be. For we are not human feelings, we are human beings; therefore, we do not have to feel a particular way to be what we or do whatever we choose.

Everything must come back to love, or there will be more terrorism committed by forces that have no regard for life, whatsoever: neither black, red, yellow, or white. *Every human life must be revered as sacred or no life will be sacred.* This is an inescapable truth; an unchangeable law.

"How long do you think it will take to rebuild the towers?" Kimberly asks, looking out over the renovation efforts that have already begun.

"I'm not sure. I hear it will be different from before; more of a memorial." I glance out over the skyline, praying that the terrible experience could make us better as a people, and somehow cause us to evolve in our thinking and knowledge about our existence on this planet. How quickly we forget the rubble and ash of 9/11, and how it united the nation beyond our practices of greed and bigotry.

The media scenes had been unforgettable. Among the falling embers, we witnessed people risking life and limb to save their fellow human being. Many perished in the effort. Grayish soot rained over faces and skin until no one could tell the difference between black and white, rich and poor. Everyone looked the same, struggled the same, and mourned the same. No one asked about religion or sexuality. No one cared about who belonged to the Democratic or Republican parties. In those moments, money and material possessions were of no consequence. The absurd lines on the color bar of ethnic categories ceased to exist.

The madness of the terrorist attack distracted us from the senseless divisions of race and hate. All the trivial views took a backseat underneath the dark hue of toxic clouds. I pray aloud, hoping that we can see beyond the smokescreens that the *real enemy* uses to continue to divide us and destroy everything that is good and right. I wonder how much longer it will take before we realize, underneath the fragile covering of skin and bone and shifting cultures, we are all the same, all human—all the color of tears and the sound of laugher.

Kimberly, the children, and I get in the car and head out again. The drive through the littered streets of Manhattan brings back memories of when I was a little girl watching Frank Sinatra and the Rat Pack with Midnight. Surrounded by buildings, roads, and sculptures I have only seen on the TV screen feels like an incredible dream where you can almost feel the heartbeat of everyone around you. We park, and I see a New York City police officer standing alone near his patrol car. I walk up to him and ask if he would take a picture with me. Silly I guess, but I cannot help myself. He smiles back at me and says, "Yes." I felt honored. Kim takes the picture, and after a brief chat, the officer and I bid each other farewell.

"Welcome to New York," he says.

"Thank you, Officer." I smile and make my way across the sidewalk; gliding on sunshine. Soon, Jontavia runs up to a huge bronze bull on Broadway near Wall Street. I snap pictures of her standing next to the enormous sculpture. She poses with a smile that tells me she is in her wonderland and all is right in the world. She skips and jumps around in circles with Nathaniel. The glimmer in her eye makes my heart soar.

"Sure, baby. Let's go find a boat!"

"Yeah!" she shouts, running towards me waving goodbye to the big charging bull sculpture. Nathaniel is not too far behind her.

"Where are we going to find a boat?" Kimberly asks.

"I figure we can catch the ferry to Ellis Island and the Statue of Liberty. I think the children will love it. We've come this far. Let's keep going!" I tell her. She agrees.

The streets of New York move faster than I can take it all in. The brilliant Manhattan skyline wraps around me with an intoxicating sense of freedom, like the arms of a gentle lover; you never want to let go. The blaring sounds of yellow taxicabs driving behind me turn into a sweet symphony of chords and strings that play the love song of liberty.

On the drive home, I tuck away the memories for safekeeping. The entire trip has been an experience I will cherish for the rest of my life. Meeting Kim's family, visions of Precious and Nathaniel playing near the stern of the ferryboat, thrilled by the foamy waves and the bubbles that jetted out from the rear of the boat. Listening to the children chatter on and on until they fell asleep; all reminds me of why God said, we must become as children. Childhood is such a wonderful time. I want to preserve it for them for as long as possible. Ellis Island and standing underneath the torch of the Statue of Liberty: it was all a gift to me. A wonderful gift from an unseen lover who continues to call me away from myself to new experiences, new knowledge, and new opportunities. He calls me into fields of green, adorned with dazzling fireflies like winged jewels. I feel Him calling me to all I have lost. Beyond Neverland, into a place where He will make all things new.

As I make the long drive back home, He whispers to my heart, "He, who the Son sets free, is free indeed." Softly, He impresses in my heart, *come away with me*. I hear Him, calling me to an unknown place. I feel ready for anything.

Social Responsibility: We Are One

"The simplest acts of kindness are by far more powerful than a thousand heads bowing in prayer. "*Mahatma Gandhi*

After the road trip, my children and I make up for lost time. Balancing time between them without someone feeling slighted is challenging, to say the least, especially when we go motorcycle riding late into the night.

"It's my turn, Mama; you took her the last time," Cory complains.

"Hop on the back. Let's go." My children and I ride on my Harley until one gripe about the other having more time. We ride until everyone is happy. Though they all like to ride, Cory seems more interested in learning about motorcycles and how they work.

Some nights I ride out alone—the restless nights when the children are asleep, and my mind refuses to stop racing, thinking about everything that has happened in my life. Incapable of sharing my story or telling the secrets that pursue me, I ride. I think about Dr. Mestre's urging me to write a book and tell my story. How can I talk about the heartache, and who, besides God himself, could possibly understand it?

I ride, letting go. It was during one of those nights that I rode to see my sister, Linda and the friend of my secret garden, Pamela. They both lived in the same apartment complex near 56 Street. They took turns riding on the back of my Harley. I rode them up the long stretch of State Road 7, revving the throttle with the intoxicating sense of freedom—something is changing. I feel it deep inside. During that time, both Linda and Pam were pregnant with sons. And though I could not give birth to any more children, I too felt pregnant; the offspring of freedom was growing inside of me, moving, shifting, preparing me to live beyond the confines of my past; beyond the thorns.

Summertime on 14th Street

On the weekends, there is no such thing as a clock, or time, or curfew. Such restraints do not exist in our world. Well, at least not on the nights my children and some of the neighborhood children are together. We prepare to *roll-out*. There are but three rules: be safe, stay together, and have fun.

"Okay guys, I need your parents' permission before we ride out tonight. We are not getting back till late again."

"Mom, their parents don't care about the time we get back. They already said if they are with you, they can stay the entire weekend," BJ says.

"That's right, Ms. Sandy, my mom's going to say the same thing she always says when I ask to go with you. 'Bye!'" Roberto says impatiently.

"I still need to get your parents' permission. They should know where you are every minute. Let's go." We stop at Roberto's house first. After the last house, the kids look at me and say, "See, we told you so."

"Yes, you guys did, but better safe than sorry. Let's go have fun!"

The ground rumbles as our gang of bicycles and rollerblades rush the pavement. The zing of tire spokes and the steady strokes of our wheels on the asphalt fill the warm night air. We stay together, riding for hours, miles up the street, from Sunset Strip to University Drive. My energy is endless, and with it, I want to teach the children lessons while having fun at the same time; the lessons are of teamwork and compassion. We ride as a team—no one left behind. On the back road of the highway, I scan the street for anyone who appears to be homeless. Anyone sleeping on a bus bench, or the sidewalk. I seek the chance to help as much as I can. I hide money in the folds of my socks for such occasions.

BJ spots a man on the bus bench next to the IHOP restaurant. "Ma, look at that guy over there. Can we help him?" I hand my son money.

"Listen, don't startle him, he might be sleep. Remember to be kind and respectful when you speak to him."

"Yes, ma'am." He and Roberto go together. I watch from a few feet away pressing the rubber break on my rollerblade against the pavement. Brea, my goddaughter who had wanted to ride with us tonight, hangs close to my side with the rest of the crew.

My mind travels back to the cold nights of 1981 when I was thirteen, pregnant, homeless, and hungry. I don't know where I would be without the compassionate people who helped me, clothed me, fed me, and loved me through life's storms. People whose actions said *I see you and I care.* People who were *God with skin on.* I want to teach the same lessons to the children; lesson that calls attention to the fact that we are our brother's keeper, and all life is sacred. Everything we do for others matter. It is our social responsibility to see and to care. What we make happen for someone else, we make happen for ourselves; we are all connected. For we are spirit beings; we are one.

Kindness and compassion are the defining factors that separate the cold nature of wild beast from humanity. The human condition of sin graphs us all into the same spiritual poverty. I thank God for Jesus Christ, for His sacrifice, for saving me. After all I have been through and all I have seen, I know this much is true. The scripture speaks of Love being "the principal thing."

The night air blows warm. My son rushes up to me.

"Mama! He said thank you; he told us he was from out of town and has no place to go." BJ's concerned expression touches my heart; I see it in his eyes—he cares deeply. That means everything to me as a mother.

"Well, we will pray for him, and thank God for whatever we can do to help. All we have God has given us. We must try to bless others who are in need. Roundup guys, let's go." The nights we ride out are among the happiest times of my life. We are together, and right here is where I want to be. I pray the children will remember the lessons: to see and to care for others.

Winter comes.

Late in the year, the sadness comes again. The night air is cold and still. I slump on the porch with a white box on my lap. Precious is trying to talk to me, but all I can hear is digging and the voices it triggers. All I can feel is heartache. My sons and Bruce dig a hole in my flower garden in the front yard of our home. My beloved Buffy has died. The stress surrounding the accident that took his life sends me into a familiar depression. After fifteen years of his unconditional love, I was not ready to say goodbye. Hard tears fall on top of the white box holding an animal that showed a tenderness and kindness many humans fail to show.

"Mommy, what's wrong?" Precious asks, crying because she sees me crying. Grief-stricken, I cannot answer. In the next few seconds, everything stands still around me. All at once, the digging stops, my weeping stops, and the only sound that remains is the voice of a little girl singing with her hands lifting my head. She cries and sings aloud, "Mommy, you are my sunshine, my only sunshine; you make me happy when skies are gray..." She holds onto my face with both hands.

"Mommy, please sing with me." she pleads. My heart breaks, and I have no voice left from crying with my sons all the way home from the veterinarian.

I wrap my arms around her to comfort her. The memories of the day's events still breaking, rolling over me like billowing waves, reminding me of the uncertainty of life. My sons stood by my side as I held Buffy for the last time after we rushed him to the animal hospital.

The vet had told us there was no hope. He had to be euthanized after he was hit by a car near the side of the neighbor's yard. The car did not see him on the grass. I fell apart when the vet told me the damage, at his age, was irreparable. My sons stroked his fur. In the cold room, we stood close, crying, unable to let go.

"I love you. Thank you for coming into my life." I whispered, holding onto him. I failed to be strong enough to comfort my sons. They tried to comfort me. No comfort came that night for anyone. When the vet came in to take him, I had told her I needed more time. She left out again; twice more after that. I have never been good at saying goodbye. It rained all the way home. Precious was too young to understand what happened that day; she was only four years old. But somewhere in her heart, she believes our happy song could somehow make everything okay again. Teary-eyed she kept on singing, trying to find our melody;

"Mommy, sing with me. *Please don't take... my sunshine ...away.*"

Some say time heals all wounds, but I disagree. There are some wounds and hurts that time must carry us through until we finally understand the lessons it wants to teach. The existence of all creation are great mysteries of God in which we can only find peace when we begin to see both life and death, not merely as a gift or a burden, but as awesome responsibilities, we must face courageously—without fear or apathy. Nothing belongs to us; absolutely nothing. All belong to God. Letting go of the need to want things to be different allows us to live in the present, reject the ego, and fully trust. Proverbs 3:5-6 tells us how to overcome every heartache and circumstance by trusting in the Lord with all our heart, leaning not on our own understanding, and in all our ways we are to submit to His will, and He will direct us all the way home.

Above the Trench; Pikes Peak

"The only way to get out of a deep trench is to begin to climb, one step at a time." ~*S.M. Anderson*

Colorado Springs, Colorado – 2004

I receive a call from Angela. Her second daughter, Aleesha is born, and Angela makes plans for me to fly out to Colorado where she now lives and works at the Peterson Air Force Base. Weeks before my flight, my Harley stalls in the middle of Interstate 95. First the ignition switch, now the carburetor. By the grace of God, it starts before the flow of traffic rushes into me. I have had narrow escapes before, and now, I am more convinced that the angels, who have been watching over me all my life, are watching now. It is Saturday. I visit Shirley and John, the leaders of the Harley Riders motorcycle club. We reminisce about the rides to Fuddruckers on Federal Highway and the biker convention at Oswald Park—I will miss it. Shirley looks disappointed when I told her about my plans.

"I'm sorry, I need to leave. I don't know what's going to happen," I tell her. "But something has got to change. I've got to find a way to get out."

"I understand, Sandy. You gotta do what you gotta do. God won't lead you wrong." After that night, I never see Shirley again. I know once I get out, there will be no looking back; everything will change. That is the price I will pay for freedom. Change will always require something from us. Quite often, a part of us will need to die so that a new nature can come to life within us.

I cannot explain the strong pulling I feel deep inside me. God is calling me away, somewhere I do not know. All my life, I have heard His voice and felt the shadow of His wings, even in the darkest times. Even in my lowest depravity, I felt His love. I feel Him now.

In the same year, I leave Refreshing Springs, and my life begins to transition. While the fears of my past demand I assume the same passive position, a spirit of liberation was rising inside of me. Year after year, I have been finding the broken pieces of myself. God begins to reveal the vulnerable places in my heart that I cannot trust; areas where I am prone to wander, run, and leave it all behind. God sees what man cannot see. He knows of the emotional strongholds that continue to unfold inside my heart, revealing its wicked tendencies. Only human, I know that faith is a daily practice.

Wild thoughts and unstable emotions sneak inside the secret places of my heart, running roughshod, stuck between the thorns of the past and the hope for a better future. I have pretended for so long, protected secrets for so many years, that often I feel like I do not have an identity of my own. Like a chameleon, I became what others needed me to be, neglecting my own personality, my voice, and my right to be free. And in the quiet times of my life, I still feel like a vulnerable little girl, waiting for her Father to come rescue her.

Saturday night church service, Fort Lauderdale

In my white usher uniform, I stand at the door greeting guests gathering for a program at the church we are visiting. It is great to see Pastor Bellamy again. He and a few of the members question why I'm ushering, especially during such a prestigious event.

"Shouldn't you be in the pulpit wearing a first lady hat?" someone comments. I don't feel the need to explain. I stay on my post. Head high, I square my shoulders. Ushering is what I want to do. But most of all, I will not play the 'religious' game. I fear God and refuse to accept a 'title' I know He does not want me to take.

He knows about the secret society I built up inside where a roundtable of rebellious emotions demands justice against the years of affairs and abuse. He sees the anger and pride pounding its fist on the door of my heart. God watches the goose-and-gander games I play, going through the motions as if we believe what we say, trying to *look* the part of good church folk. We only fool ourselves. Bitterness and secret heartache can become like toxic waste inside of us until we *choose* to get free. God knows about the emotional affair and the late-night phone texts that dare me to do to him what he has done to me. Infidelity and abuse seem to be thick as thieves — walking hand in hand. Where I haven't been able to fight back with my fists, I have felt justified to do so with my heart. Marriage can be one big illusion, like a dream that felt real until you awake and realize the joy you thought you had is gone — or worse, it was never there.

"Lord, help me." I pray. I don't want to hurt my family, my children, but I'm done with this twisted game. I'm too tired to pretend anymore.

June 2004

I board the American Airlines flight to Colorado Springs,

Colorado. After speaking to Angela, she has agreed this is a good time to fly out. I cannot wait to see the children and spend time with her family. The anticipation mixes with motion sickness as the plane taxies down the runway. I roll a narrow bottle of Dramamine between my fingers, waiting for the tablets to take effect.

The plane goes airborne, and I fall back in time to the day Angela's mother, and I drove her to the airport to see her off to serve her country. Brenda and I stood motionless until the plane disappeared behind the clouds. The years of parenting had come with its share of ups and downs, stages of failure, success, and uncertainty. That day, Brenda asked me, "Sandra, what's on your mind; are you feeling alright?" For the first time in a long time, I felt like I did not have to pretend or lie.

"I will be okay. God's got me. No matter what, I will be fine,"

Upon my arrival, the cold Colorado air meets me with Rod patiently waiting to pick me up from the airport terminal. As we drive onto the highway, I am not sure if it is the thin air or the magnificent overlay of mountains that takes my breath away. By the time we arrive at the apartment, huge chunks of ice are falling from the sky. Rod and I sit in the car and wait until it lets up. It hails for nearly an hour.

Angela is at work, but I get to see the children as soon as I make it through the front door. Brenda had arrived before Aleesha was born, and after climbing the outside staircase to the apartment, I finally get to see them face-to-face. I am a Nana, and hearing the word come from little Ashley's lips is like hearing the voice of God reminding me that He makes all things new.

"Hello, Angel Eyes," I whisper holding little Aleesha, unable to describe the joy flooding inside me. It's close to what I believe heaven would be like. I hold onto her, never wanting to let go.

The following morning, Angela and I attend Aleesha's doctor's appointments. There are some challenges with her health, but Aleesha is strong like her mother. She steadily improves.

"Brenda, I miss you. How have you been?" I ask while we all sit in the living room together.

"Fine, fine, girl you know me!" she says with a lighthearted laugh. She and I relive old times, and I begin to think, *this is what normal must feel like.* It is the feeling of complete acceptance. The approval of knowing you are loved just the way you are, with no motives, pretense, or hidden agendas. I breathe in and out, allowing myself to feel it. I stand behind a chair near the window, braiding

Brenda's hair, laughing and talking the night away. Her voice feels like a warm cup of tea that I want to drink slowly; because of how tranquil it makes me feel. She has never changed. Whether you are a prince or a beggar, she has the uncanny ability to pick up your spirit with her cozy personality.

On Thursday morning, Angela drives me to the Peterson Air Force base and introduces me to her team. A group of uniformed officers surrounds me near Angela's work area. "It's a pleasure to meet you," I say.

"Angela told us you were coming. We hope you enjoy your stay," an officer tells me.

"Thank you, sir. I am glad I could come."

"Welcome to Colorado." Another airman says.

"Thank you, sir."

My eyes veer just over his shoulder, through a broad, oblong window. In the distance, I watch translucent clouds open, allowing sun rays to pour through them. I look at the rosy light cascading over the top of the spiky mountaintops.

"Come on; I want to show you my workspace," Angela says. After the tour of the control tower, she takes me to her work area. Dozens of family photos encircle her computer and up the sidewalls of her cubicle. The carousel of memories made the Air Force base feel like a home away from home. Staring at all the pictures, I smile at a memory of her praise dancing. She spins gracefully across my mind; always putting her all into the dance. I remember a wonderful gift she gave me. It was just before her 18th birthday; she wrote me a poem, presenting it to me after dance practice: "The Peacemaker" she titled it.

Angela has always been a freethinker, unaffected by the opinions of others. She looks at me as if I belong to her, and she to me. Over the years, I have come to admire her teachable spirit, the lively humor of her heart, and her resilient confidence—everything I was not at her age.

"Thank you for showing me around, sweetheart. I am so proud of you," I say, wanting to tell her so much more, but unable to find the words. Her crisp uniform reminds me of the dream of a little girl who wanted to join the military and work in law enforcement. I stare at her and smile. She is not aware of it, but vicariously; she gives me the blessing of that childhood dream. A dream that lives on inside the lovely woman she has become. I flood with delight, overwhelmed by God's grace that I am even standing here, still alive today.

"Are you ready to get something to eat?" Angela asks me.

"Sure baby, whenever you are ready." When we left the Air Force base, I stare out over the Colorado horizon, in awe of the majestic mountains. It is a different world here. A world I use to imagine I was a part of when I was seven years old, listening to John Denver sing "Rocky Mountain High." In two months, I will be thirty-seven years old, and I'm still in love with his music and the message of "coming home to a place you never been before." That place is here; right now. It feels up my senses—every part of me; all around me; feels like home. A place I have never been, but amazingly, like Deja Vu, it feels like I have.

Angela drives, and I stare out of the window, listening to a call in the wind. Beyond the hazy Colorado sky, I could swear I heard a far way voice, calling to me—high in the cleft of rocks. Just over the range of mountains. Not an audible sound, but an inner whisper that pulls me toward something I cannot explain. It is something too impossible to understand, and too inescapable to ignore. *"I'm here, waiting for you,"* the voice says. *Come away.*

The flight must have given me jet lag. On Friday night, I prepare one of Angela's favorite meals, lasagna, and garlic bread. Rod has a few helpings.

"Are you okay?" Angela asks me. Lost in thought, I push a piece of the lasagna around my plate, thinking of how fast time has flown. I miss those times with my children, but I feel an inner force pulling me beyond the comfort zone of all I know. "Yes, baby. I am fine. I was just thinking about some things.

After washing the dishes and the Prego sauce stains off the stove, I sit to hold Aleesha while Ashley snuggles up close to my side. Before bedtime, I sing them a soft lullaby, a song about a Redeemer who makes all things new. Soon, Angela steps out of the room and puts the children to bed.

"Good night sweetheart. I love you." I tell her.

"You too. Get some rest, you look tired." Angela says; she is right; I am tired. A lot is going on in a short amount of time. Traveling, cooking, long hours of hair braiding; it is all catching up to me, mainly because I am not sleeping well at night on the narrow sofa. But there is more than just the physical fatigue that causes me unrest.

My life has reached an impasse. Emotionally and mentally exhausted, sometimes I think the harder I try the more exhausted I feel; like a little girl trying to pick up jackstones, only to drop them all again.

A part of me feels like I am preparing to die, while another part of me feels like I am just starting to live. Whatever it is, I'm determined to climb out of the trench that has held me for so long. Above my apathy, and the struggle to be good enough, to be worthy of true love; I am ready for change. But I have been ready before, and still, I did nothing but wait for something else to change. I cannot wait any longer. *How much patience is too much patience before we act?*

The house goes quiet; I step out on the patio and stare out towards the mountain range. It shrouds with a consuming darkness. A moth, charmed by the outside porch light, moves its wings in slow motion—as if it is hypnotized. I stare at it, feeling the chilly Colorado night air, thinking; how *fear had hypnotized me for most of my life.* I look out at the sky, feeling the same powerful yearning. In the depth of my core, an aching loneliness keeps me searching. I think of my father and the lost look in his eyes that seemed to last a lifetime. As I stand outside in the corner, near the edge of the fenced-in patio, I hear the echoing again. A small voice floats on the wind, far away in the distance. I close my eyes to try to capture the sound more clearly, but I can't. Like the stars, it is too far away. I could swear it is coming from the mountain range. I notice the leaves rustling in the trees in front of the apartment and soon talked myself into getting some rest.

That night, I turn in, pulling the covers over my shoulders. At 3:00 a.m., I hear the small voice calling out to me. It pushes me awake, becoming louder than before. I sit up on the couch trying to get a hold of myself.

The voice is delicate and sweet. It calls to me from within and without at the same time. *"Come up to the mountain. I'm waiting for you,"* the voice whirls around me, like a child on a playground, whispering a secret no one else can hear. I listen, holding onto her voice as if my life depends upon it.

I take my cell phone and look through my list of contacts for my doctor's number, thinking of how to ask the question I need to ask him. It is 5:30 a.m. when I make the call, leaving a message on his 24-hour voice mail service. The call is to my physician, Dr. Alberto Mestre. I wait for his reply, but in my restlessness, I decided that it's time; now or never; I must begin to conquer a history of fear, co-dependence, and apathy. I tell myself what I must do. *The only way to get out of a deep trench is to begin to climb out!*

Less than an hour later, Dr. Mestre returns my call. "Hi,

Sandra, I got your message. I'm proud of you, kiddo. Your labs look great, and I don't see any reason why you can't climb a mountain. Pursue your dreams, climb your mountains! Live your life! You are doing just fine."

"Thank you, Dr. Mestre, sometimes I still feel so unsure. Getting your opinion means a lot to me."

"You got it, and hey..." He pauses.

"Yes Dr. Mestre?"

"I will be waiting for that book. You have come a long way. Talk to you soon."

We hang up, and I prepare to head out at 7 a.m., determined to climb Pikes Peak—the highest summit in the county of El Paso. Listening to Dr. Mestre' words reaffirm me. Hearing the small childlike voice gives me no other choice. I must go. Before the dawn breaks, I ready myself with a backpack, a bag of nuts, and enough water for one day's hike. I knock on Angela's bedroom door.

"Come in." She says, already awake.

"Sweetheart, I will be back sometime tonight."

Before I can explain any further, Angela stands up and slows my roll.

"Wait. What? Where are you going?" she asks curtly.

"I'm going to hike Pikes Peak. I don't want you to worry; I should be back before nightfall." I assure her, noticing she has dropped the clothes she was holding a second ago.

Angela is not one to mince words, but she already knows; my decision is not up for debate. She stares at me for a moment, shifting a concerned gaze from my eyes to my clothes. Before I can turn and head out the door, she stops me.

"Okay, but you can't go like that!" She moves toward the closet." You're going to freeze if you go dressed like that." She digs through clothes trying to maintain her military composure, but the curve of her mouth tells me she is more than a little worried. But remembering the words from the book at the bus stop, on the beach as a pregnant teen, I take no thought about clothes or the mountain air. I have no worries, no cares; except one: *I must climb.*

"Here, put these on, and this, and this too. The air is thinner and colder on the mountain," she says, watching as I layer on a pair of her long johns, a long sleeve shirt, a hat, boots, and her heavy military jacket.

"That's better." she breathes.

I can hardly move with all the clothing, but I grin at her, thinking of how the roles have reversed.

"Thank you, baby, I will call you to let you know how far I've made it," I say, trying to relieve her obvious doubts. It doesn't work. She orders her husband, Rod, to get up, get dressed and go with me.

"I don't want her going by herself," she tells him. Barely awake, he stands there with his mouth open. His wide eyes and the deep wrinkles running across his brow tells me he had no intentions of leaving the house today, let alone hiking a mountain.

"Baby, it's okay. I will be all right by myself," I say trying to make it out the door before the day breaks. But Angela does not make it negotiable. She pulls rank, giving Rod a look that is as serious as the threat of court-martial.

Rod gets ready, and we head out the door. "I must hurry if I am going to make it up the mountain and back before nightfall," I think out loud. Rod remains silent, and we get a move on; the sun is rising quickly. I have lost nearly 45 minutes of my projected start time, making sure Angela was satisfied. On the way to Pikes National Forest, I think of where the time has gone. Thinking about the wasted years as an addict, I take a deep breath, move forward, and try to let go of the regrets that still lingers around the corners of my mind.

As Rod and I step onto the base of the trailhead, we read a serious warning for all who desire to hike Pikes Peak. "Stay on the trail," the sign cautions. A man holding a broom beneath a small wooden canopy walks up to me. I remember his smile as he reached out to me; seemingly from out of the blue. Few words were spoken as he placed a small pendant in the palm of my hand. "Thank you, Sir," I said looking at his unexpected gift—a gold angel pendant. We shared a tender embrace, and soon, he was gone. For a moment, I looked up towards the sky, exhaled, and pressed onward.

Step by step, I take it all in; the beauty of this wildlife paradise enraptures me. The sound of the mountain bluebirds singing, tall, majestic trees with branches stretched out like arms welcomes me to come, and continue going further, higher. Massive rocks border the trail near the switchbacks, and the smell of perennial flowers swaying near the Ponderosa pines invites us to go all the way. Miles pass beneath our feet, but for me, it feels like floating. We take pictures on the trail, and I greet the other hikers coming and going in either direction. "Good morning," I smile, pushing ahead. *My sons have always told me that I am overly friendly,* I laugh inside thinking, they must be right. After we hike nearly six miles up the mountain, Rod bends over, visibly winded. "Are you okay, Rod?" I ask, turning around to check on him.

"Who do we think we're kidding?" he says. "I can hardly breathe." He puts his hands on his knees and drops his head.

"I'm sorry Rod. You can turn back if you need to, but I have to go on. I can't turn back." After a few moments, he pulls himself together and moves forward. I'm not sure if it is the fear of something happening to me or the fear of facing Angela that makes him continue the hike.

"So why don't you make yourself a promise to quit smoking cigarettes after we make it to the summit," I suggest.

"Yea, that's a good idea, I've wanted to quit."

"You can do it, Rod."

"That sounds like a plan," he says, forcing a half-smile. We push on ahead.

For years, I have dreamed of seeing a mountain, and now, to climb one is surreal. Each step is a magical journey — as if it has been ordered beyond what my mind can imagine. As I hike Pikes Peak, my sister's song plays in my memory. A song about climbing every mountain until your heart finds what it has been looking for. I feel like a child again, living a dream, a beautiful dream where I am standing on a rock that is bigger, higher than any fear. *If I can reach the summit, I can do anything*, I tell myself. 6,500 feet, the air gets thinner and colder as we pass foliage the size of elephant ears.

"Look, Rod, over there!" Enormous antlers crown the head of a stag feeding in the dense glade. I hurry and take a picture before he gallops away. Thick fog spreads across the clearing where a humble log cabin sits upon a wooden porch. Lively green-colored paint frames the outer door and window. Gold letters spell out the words: BARR CAMP.

"Come on, let's go in," I tell Rod as we scamper over a narrow footbridge. When we go inside, the cabin feels warm and cozy, a hikers' sanctuary, and to my surprise, someone has made spaghetti on the black coal potbelly stove sitting in the middle of the room. It looks exactly like my grandmother's stove and the welcoming feel of the air reminds me of her home in Havana.

I did not expect this place. In the urgency to climb, I did no research to prepare for the hike, the mountain, its terrain, its critters, and its climate. I only knew I had to climb and make it to the summit. Later I will find out that many years ago, a church had established and operated the camp; perhaps for weary, unprepared hikers.

The Barr Camp is a blessing in disguise, especially for the

news we were about to hear. The caretakers inform us of pending danger. The report of a storm radios in from mountain rangers at the peak.

"It is a thunderstorm at the summit; no one can climb for the rest of the day." The caretakers alert us we cannot go forward, but I refuse to go back. I think of Angela; she will worry. I try to call her, but my cell phone has no signal. One of the caretakers' kindly hands me a phone. I step to the back of the cabin, take a deep breath, and make the call.

"Hi Angela, I'm calling from the camp's phone, my phone has no signal. There is a storm on the top of the mountain, and we cannot climb until morning. We are going to stay at the Barr Camp tonight. Don't worry, we are safe. The people here are very nice. The caretakers even made spaghetti." I explain, trying to sound upbeat so she would not worry. "Everything is okay. We will head out at daybreak tomorrow."

I pause, wondering if she heard me through the static on the line.

"Are you sure you're, alright?" she asks. I can hear the concern in her voice.

"Yes, baby, we will head out in the morning, the storm should be over by then. Don't worry. I will see you when we hike back down the mountain."

"No, don't hike down! I will drive up to get you tomorrow. I will be there by the time you reach the summit. Stay put!"

"Okay sweetheart. I love you," I say with a cheery voice, hiding my fatigue. I know she will worry tonight, but there is no turning back for me, not anymore. There are some mountains that faith can move, but there are others we must climb; something is calling me; I cannot turn back.

Exhaustion sweeps over me in waves. I push and pull against it, but with little to no sleep last night, my eyes burn and the nerves in my arms and legs quake. My body wants to rest, but my mind steadily runs. We have no money to pay for the food or the stay at the BARR camp, but I trust in God; no matter what. The uncertainty, the thin air, the lack of planning; it is all okay. I know God is here with us.

Inside the BARR camp, we settle in with the other hikers. "Put your finger in here," a male caretaker tells us, measuring our blood oxygen level. I think how the caretaker looks more like a Hawaiian surfer. I feel awkward as I placed my finger inside the small white Oximeter. The nail bed in my forefinger is cracked and dark. After years of twirling and squeezing my finger to numb the inner pain, the entire nail has died.

"How am I doing?"

"Well Miss, at this altitude, I'd say you are doing great for a Floridian." He shows me the numbers on the monitor. "Listen, don't worry about the storm. It happens all the time up here. Have some spaghetti." He tells Rod and me.

"Here are your bunks where you can sleep tonight." He shows us a dorm-like room with bunk beds and a few cots. "Everyone camps together here in this room. That flashlight hanging on the wall is for nighttime. Your kidneys tend to work overtime at this altitude, so when you need to use the bathroom, take the flashlight with you so you can find your way in the dark. The restrooms are outside, to the left. And don't worry—the mountain lions will see you before you see them." He laughs, but I am still working on my sense of humor. I wait for him to say, "Just kidding," but he never did.

"Thank you, sir," I tell him. Rod slumps by the fire, near the potbelly stove. The worn-out look on his face tells me he is not in the mood to laugh or talk. He manages a lighthearted conversation. After we eat, we settle in with the rest of the hikers in the bunkroom. The Barr Camp is full tonight. And as everyone falls asleep, heavy with spaghetti, I lay awake wondering why I feel so tired but can't find rest. So much is happening around me, inside me.

The night awakes, and my senses are in overdrive. I imagine a mountain lion is prowling, a bushy-tailed coyote scavenging, a slithering snake flicking its tongue just beyond the crest of rocks outside the camp. Everything in me feels alive to every sight, sound, and smell. I try to close my eyes, breathing in the moonlight that beams in through the cracks of the cabin, but sleep won't come. The nerve endings in my fingers and toes tingle and twitch. I must be exhausted because I feel like I am drifting on the outside of my body, a heartbeat away from leaving the world behind.

On the top bunk, I whisper to myself, "Go to sleep, you need to rest to finish the climb in the morning." But my brain won't listen. It keeps on going, racing with thoughts. Hours pass, and I ease down from the top bunk to go outside to the bathroom. Rod must have been sleeping with one eye open. He sits up on his bunk like a security guard.

"Where are you going?" he asks.

"To the restroom," I whisper, not wanting to disturb the

restful snorts and wheezes of the other hikers.

"What time is it?" he yawns. "I'm not sure. It feels like it is around two or three in the morning. I'm going to the bathroom. Be right back." I tell him, lifting the wide-faced flashlight off the nail.

"Wait, I don't want you to go out there alone." Rod hurries to the side door. The chilly air reminds me to thank Angela for making me dress warmly when I see her tomorrow.

Rod eases the door closed, and we step outside into a darkness I have never seen before; I cannot see my hand in front of my face.

"Hold the flashlight down so you can see where you are stepping. Careful, don't fall, watch the rocks," Rod says, his voice shivers in the frosty air. I hear him but cannot see him. He holds onto my elbow.

"I can't see the direction I am going. Where are the bathrooms again?" I say, standing still to shine the flashlight out in front of me. Two round eyes peer out into the darkness. *Perhaps it is only an owl gawking out into the night.* I swallow and refocus my steps.

On the way back to the Barr Camp, I almost trip over rocks because I am holding the flashlight up to see the direction I want to go, instead of down at the ground. In such thick darkness, it is hard to do both. A few steps away from the cabin door, a whisper floats through the wind. *"Stand still and look up."* I hear it, keeping the flashlight down at my feet as I lift my eyes toward the sky.

In a blink, I want to disappear as I stand beneath what appears to be billions of stars—like jackstones clustered together, too magnificent for my mind to grasp. Unlike the Florida night sky, where light pollution often hides the stars, nothing hinders their splendor here on this mountain. They shine above me as if they have been waiting to show me their brilliance and teach me to be still long enough to connect to what I was already a part of; the amazing universe. A wondrous creation, so mysterious, so beautiful, the moment takes my breath away, and I want to stay here forever. Looking up, I feel so small, like nothing really matters. Or ever did. The doubts and fears are all so trivial underneath this starry night sky that whispers to me, *let go.* I breathe out against the chill of the morning breeze, "God you are so awesome!" In this very moment, I feel like I could fly away beyond the stars.

I breathe in, ready to try—ready to let go and learn the true meaning of what it means to walk by faith and not by sight. After a lifetime of working to be good enough, trying to pick up the scattered pieces of my life, I see the stars as I have never seen them before. A sky filled with scattered jackstones only His hand is high enough, big enough, and wide enough to pick up. I thank God for the storm at the top of the mountain. If I had hiked on yesterday, I would've missed this moment; I would've missed the stars.

On top of the bunk, I sit, thinking, *there is so much more to this life than I can ever understand. The mysteries of an eternal, living God is beyond what my simple mind can conceive.* I close my eyes and let go.

Just a few hours later, soft shimmers of sunlight drizzle into the cabin. The dawn breaks and I splash cool water on my face and throw my backpack over my shoulders.

"Did you get any rest?" Rod asks.

"A little. What about you? How are you doing?"

"I'm ready to go home." He lets out a homesick grunt, stretching his arms to the side. On the way to the door, I thank the caretakers for their kindness. The morning air is cold and crisp. *I must fight this fatigue,* I think to myself, stopping to tie my boot lace tighter. A dizzy spell hits me as I stand up. The floaters come, like tiny specks of light, but after a few seconds, they are gone. Rod gives me a worried look. I smile at him, ready for whatever the day holds.

You don't notice how warm it is inside until the mountain air hits through your clothes. I get my bearings, and we head up the trail.

"Don't get lost. Stay on the trail! Don't wander off the trail!" The caretakers' voice echoes behind us.

The beauty of nature stirs me fully awake, and we resume the hike with a new friend.

"Hi, my name is Mitchel," he says, wearing a hat that slightly reminded me of the actor, Paul Hogan, from the movie *Crocodile Dundee*. We hike the trail together until the reality of the altitude and unstable terrain slow my pace. We stop for a couple of minutes. On the short break, Mitchel offers us peanuts. We reached 10,000 feet exhausted: my breaths are labored, and my head swims from the increasing fatigue. At virtually 12,000 feet, we pass an area called the Bottomless Pit Trail. Rod and Mitchel crack open more peanut shells to refuel as I sit against a rock boulder overlooking a narrow brook. "Smile guys." I take their picture, ignoring the ache in my feet, which have swollen during the night. No matter, I move ahead with one thought: make it to the top; no matter what.

Lush trees and hanging vines decorate the area around a slow-moving stream, adorning it with breathless serenity.

Something's telling me I am a part of it all. Amazed by God and the wonder of this place, I'm overwhelmed to know that life and death are both the same finite conditions moving within the omniscient control of an infinite God. I am here, right now. Alive, somehow through it all. No one can steal this moment, this memory, and this peace. As I continue to climb, I begin to hear more clearly. The demons that have haunted me, chasing me inside the deep trench of shame, and self-doubt, start to fall back; they cannot breathe at this altitude. They cannot follow where God is leading me. There are no voices; only peace.

I hear the wind, and I feel God reassuring me that "no weapon formed against me will prosper." I hear His voice, encouraging me that goodness and mercy will follow close to comfort and guide me, even when the storms don't cease.

Rod, Mitchel and I trudge on. I notice the burnt shaft of a tree, splintered down the middle. The charred bark looks as if lightning struck it; possibly from the storm last night. At 13,000 feet, the air feels torturously thin and dry; it is another world. The hike takes us into the alpine zone, where only willow bushes and wild grass can survive the thin air of this high altitude. I have had no idea of the danger of the atmospheric pressure at this level until I begin to feel it for myself. But there is no anxiety. I climb to die, or I climb to live — determined not to be afraid of either. Not anymore. I pull myself up over rocks, beyond my comfort zone. I command myself to keep moving forward. Hikers straggle around us, some ascending, others descending the mountain. Hours pass with one, maybe two hikers still moving on. If there are more, I can't really tell at this point. My head hangs low from the pressure. I must stop to breathe, and with the next breath, I press on. A small pale spider moves past my feet, crawling between the rocks; it is real; I do not flinch. Mitchel hikes on ahead and soon, out of view.

Breathing in the frigid air causes my chest to hurt from the inside out. I shake my head, trying to control the dizziness. My throat is parched, but I cannot drink for the need to go to a bathroom, which is nowhere around. I see a yellow-bellied marmot watching from just above a cleft rock ledge. The animal looks playful one moment, and cautious the next. It scurries inside a nearby burrow.

Little to no words passes between Rod and me. In huffs of silence, we climb over huge rocks where we now need our hands and feet to get beyond the next crest of boulders. I can no longer tell if we are on or off the trail. The steep moss-covered sand stones offer no sign of the previous path. I trust God and stay the course, discerning that He has been directing me the whole time, ordering every step. Gradually, I lift my head and turn around in a circle, beholding the beauty of snowcaps inside the pockets of the mountain. As far as the eyes can see, there is nothing but chasms of peaks and valleys of mountains crowned with silvery clouds. The sight is glorious!

We press through a maze of rocks bordering a narrow incline. I feel revived after seeing signs of the journey's end. The last mile before the summit and the hike takes us pass the 13,300-elevation point. The wind circles around me and I hear a small voice inside: *"You are almost there."* Rod reaches another posted sign. I lag behind, but after a few more steps the sign comes into view. "16 Golden Stairs." Reading the words felt unreal, like hearing a countdown in a fight with an unbeatable foe, yet here I am, grateful, still standing.

The bends and twists of the switchbacks challenge me beyond the brink of my strength and cause me to sit for longer periods.

"Go on ahead. I will be okay. See you at the summit," I say to Rod, feeling like I am breathing through a straw. I need this time to be alone, with God. I've known this breathlessness all my life. And now, it feels welcoming, normal. I embrace the moment, believing with everything in me that He has brought me to this mountain. I ascend slowly, asking God to show me what He wants me to see, and teach me what He needs me to know. *What is the meaning of it all? The mystery of life and death, with all its joys and sorrows, and more importantly, where is my place? What is my purpose? Where do I belong?* In the distance, I see a tall platinum binocular telescope mounted on the flat plateau of the summit. Some people are waving; others clap and cheer as hikers make the final ascent. Almost there, I push harder, leaving the unanswerable questions in the clouds surrounding me.

The wind loops around my feet and then moves up in a skipping motion. After all these years, the wind feels the same since the days I sat on the stairs in Tampa, listening to the stories of God. I feel His Holy Spirit surrounding me, and with it, a gift. A childlike voice, small and sweet; tugs inside as my feet touches the summit. *I knew you were coming. I've been waiting for you,* the voice giggles from a place untouched by the cares of life and unhindered by time. On the summit, I lift my eyes, and she is there, around me, inside of me; everywhere. I see her; she is beautiful! I fall to my knees—

breathing in the very essence of who I am, the person I was created to be before the storms came and caused me to forget my God-given identity.

"Praise God! I climbed! I made it!" I breathe aloud. Overwhelmed by the experience of finishing the hike, I let the tears fall. They are tears of unspeakable joy mixed with relief. In that extraordinary moment, I feel more alive than I can ever remember feeling before. I can feel God's grace returning everything that was stolen; lost in time long ago. *I reached the top. Thank you, God!* I close my eyes, and she is there — the little child; smiling, strong, beautiful, flawless, and unashamed. And then, I hear Him. He reminds me that before I was formed in my mother's womb, He knew me, and loved me. I can feel her moving, floating above ground as if she is being carried. She wears a long purple dress made of the finest silk. I remember; purple was one of her favorite colors. Like a kite, it catches the wind and sparkles against the sunlight. Her voice sounds the same: seven years old and filled with impossible dreams of changing the world. She reaches out to me with empty hands, yet they hold the valuable lessons from the thorns.

Let go. We don't have to try anymore. I hear her voice inside of me, like currents of energy vibrating, flowing through every fiber of my being. "No more striving, no more trying to be good enough," I whisper, feeling her close to my chest. *No ball, no jacks, no more guilt or shame, we can empty our hands and just let go of the past. Let go of the unanswerable questions. God alone knows the answers. He paid our ransom. He took the thorns and transformed them into a glorious crown. A crown He wore to Calvary! The crown of thorns was the exchange for every sin and all the pain; He died to make us free!*

I see her smile the same way she did that day in our father's barbershop. She begins to dance around, twirling like a carefree ballerina. She turns, moving closer to the edge of the mountain, unafraid of falling; I hear her voice inside, tenderly speaking to my heart. *Nothing can separate us from His love. Remember the stars*, she whispers and twirls, dancing above the mountain. She laughs and speaks to me as if she knows the unknown; as if all this time, she has been home, sheltered in the arms of our God. I begin to understand better, that from the ocean's edge to the top of this mountain, He was there all the time; in both the thunder and the silence.

Tears fall as I listen to the voice of my soul telling me of a love that is higher, deeper, and wider than I could ever hope, imagine, or think. She tells me of my price: it is immeasurable, far beyond all the stars in the sky. I feel a rebirthing, and for the first time in my life I could truly speak the words, "He restores my soul." He sees, He hears, and He answers! *I feel a profound sense of freedom, rising inside me. Enraptured – It feels amazing!*

As I stand to my feet, I knew I would never be the same. Redeemed and armed with a renewed sense of purpose, I'm ready to move forward, out of the trench of secrets, sadness, and self-doubt. I know now that I had been enlisted in His Army – the Army of the Lord, where every battle belongs to Him, and the course through basic training has led me here. "Great is thy faithfulness," I whisper, looking out over the mountain range, vast and beautiful. I speak the Word of God over my life and the life of my children and the generations to come.

The journey to catch the boomerang and choose the life God planned for me begins here and now. And though I know it won't be easy – the storms will come and go, I will continue to trust in the One who holds my future. His love is my strength and my song. His Word proclaims His faithfulness and His promise to "remember His people unto a thousand generations to those who keep His commandments."

Just then, Angela steps behind me with a big smile, and a sigh of relief. Her mother, Brenda, has made the drive up Pikes Peak Highway with her. Brenda makes snowballs. Angela and I embrace. She holds me close, exhaling before letting go.

"I was worried. How are you?" she asks, looking at me with an expression that lets me know that nothing will change the love we share.

"I'm good baby. Thanks for driving up." Brenda dashes from behind the Pikes National Park sign, throwing snowballs at us. She misses. I guess it's hard to laugh and aim at the same time; another good lesson to learn.

"Hey, Sandra," she wheezes, holding a hand full of snow.

"Hi, Brenda thanks for coming up. Where's Rod?" I ask, staring out towards the visitor's area near the center of the summit.

"He is in there," Angela replies. I imagine he is thawing out, somewhere near a warm fire, vowing to leave me at the airport the next time I come back to town. When I walk inside the Summit House, Rod is sitting with Mitchel and other hikers who made the journey up Pikes Peak. I feel a special connection with them; we hiked together. We refused to give up.

"You would've made it the first day if I hadn't slowed you down," Rod says with a smile. I smile back at him.

"I'm happy you came. Thank you, Rod. I couldn't have made it without you." Mitchel sits next to Rod and takes out his phone.

"It was nice meeting you both. Give me your address, and I will send you the pictures I took," Mitchel says. We trade addresses and say our good-byes. Angela heads to the car, to prepare to make the long drive down the mountain.

"I will be right there dear," I tell her, needing one last moment to reflect and look out above the clouds surrounding the crest of Pikes Peak.

There are times when life can seem like an impossible dream. On top of this vast mountain, with its peaks and valleys, I hear echoes of the songs, prayers, and stories from my youth. They are the three-strand cord that has fastened my life with faith in Christ and kept me anchored through every trial and storm. *"Climb every mountain, ford every stream, follow every rainbow, till you find your dream."*

More than thirty years have passed since my sister sang this song to my siblings and me. Standing on the summit of Pikes Peak, I felt her fervent faith, echoing across time. My heart is grateful for the seeds of faith and love that were planted in my life so long ago. I owe my life, my all, to God. Because of His great love, I was not consumed in the trenches of my past. I could have died in my sin, but He saved me. His grace has kept and preserved my life. The search for my soul and the right to reclaim her voice had brought me to an elevation beyond what I could have dreamed. I stood on the mountain, lifting my hands, unashamed, praising the name that is above all names: the name of Jesus, Yeshua HaMashiach, the King of Israel, the King of Glory.

All my life, I have heard my mother say the words, "Thank you, Jesus." After all these years, the three words remain the unceasing hymn of my heart. I realize the toughest part of my grandmother, Rachel, my mother, Lillie, and my sister, Joyce was not found in their own strength, nor in the ability to work hard or do the right things, but in the steadfast faith in God and His great love for humanity. No matter the circumstance, they continued to believe in a God who permits the storms to come, a God who, while we were yet sinners, sent His Only Son to die for the sins of the world. I am grateful! Faith and heartfelt repentance are gifts from God—the calling to a higher state of being in our human existence. The love of Christ shields us through the storms and offers us the promise of hope that we will overcome if we have faith; no matter what. After a lifetime, waiting to hear a love song; a song of true love, I hear it now.

The greatest lesson from the thorns is that God's grace is sufficient. No matter what we may face, the Cross of Calvary is enough. When life does not make sense, His love is enough. Christ the hope of Glory, who made himself a curse for us, has come to set us free from the trenches of sin with its shame, fear, hate, and bigotry. He calls us to a new identity in which we will produce the fruits of love, joy, peace, patience, goodness, gentleness, and self-control; as written in Galatians 5:22. For then, life shall be "on earth as it is in heaven." A life where we love each other, as God loves us.

I remember looking at the sky that day, thinking about the changes I had to make, choices to confront the past, heal the buried wounds, and embrace the unknown future; feeling it all. I hold fast to the belief that because God lives in me, I can face tomorrow, courageous and unafraid. His voice moves in the wind, and I can hear Him speaking freedom to every captive heart. He sees, He hears, and He loves each and every one of us. God's words proclaim that we are no longer slaves to sin; we are daughters and sons. Christ wore the crown of thorns for all humanity. Therefore, we are free to choose, to love, to forgive, and to live virtuously by the act of our human will; surrendered to the power of the Holy Spirit. 1 John 4:10 speaks of this eternal truth: "For *this* is love—real love, not that we loved God, but that He loved us and sent His son as the atoning sacrifice for our sins." Jesus Christ is God's love song to the world. After all these years, I can still hear the melody. He sings it over me now!

While mountain badgers played in the distance, I listened, breathing in the sweetest melody that will forever play inside my heart. From the mountain of Pikes Peak, I glorify His name, to the four corners of the earth resounding across the plains; is the song from my youth, my sister's lullaby, about a love that makes the world go 'round, and a God who makes all things new.

"... *It's a time for beginnings; Love makes the world go 'round.*"

Rod, Mitchell, and me. (Top left) a stranger I met at the base of the mountain. He gave me an Angel pendant. Pikes Peak, June 2004

Pikes Peak Summit after two days. Colorado, 2004
"Great is Thy Faithfulness"

Epilogue

Becoming Teachable, Breaking Free

Beloved, do not be surprised at the fiery ordeal which is taking
place to test you [that is, to test the quality of your faith], as
though something strange or unusual were happening to you. But
insofar as you are sharing Christ's sufferings, keep on rejoicing, so
that when His glory [filled with His radiance and splendor] is
revealed, you may rejoice with great joy.
~*Peter 4: 12-13*

Breaking the Silence

In July 2004, I took back my life, no longer allowing my past
to define my future. I filed for divorce through Broward County's
Legal Aid, and broke the silence of domestic violence, vowing
never to allow myself to live in fear again. The threats continued
after I got out of the toxic relationship. I had to live in my car from
time to time and soon traveled out of town to feel safe from his
growing threats. The fear and oppression do not end when you get
out; often, it will increase. But I want you to trust God, get out, get
safe, no matter what! Ironically, living in my car made me feel freer
than I did in my home. I was free from the control of co-
dependency, free from the madness, free to start my life again, on
my terms; unapologetically.

There is never an excuse for domestic violence. It is a
criminal act! And unfortunately, because of the stigma and shame,
the violence continues; unreported — to the degree that, for many, it
seems *normal*. When we allow mistreatment, it only continues. It
will not improve if you do not act! I had to learn to stop making
excuses and take action. Nothing will change, for the abused or the
abuser until you decide to change it. Change begins with a
psychological uprooting of the self-loathing that leads to feelings of
worthlessness. When you value yourself and understand your
worth, no one can devalue you. Until we reach that point, we will
continue the vicious cycle, often passing the abusive patterns to our
children and our children's children. It's time we catch the
boomerang, for once and for all. Know who you are in Christ. Know
your worth. Love yourself; free! You are priceless! You are
beautiful!

End the violence! No excuses! **Hands off**! Period!

The damage caused by domestic violence goes deeper than most people can understand, destroying families and communities—around the world.

No apology or restraining order can erase the fear that remains after the violent attacks and passive-aggressive behavior of intimate partner violence. Trusting in the word of God is vital to restoring mental and emotional health. In Isaiah 54:17, God's words proclaim, "no weapon formed against us will prosper." During that time, the judge presiding over the process of restraining orders was inept, and clearly unfamiliar with the dynamics of abuse and the shame that forces victims into the brutalized swamp of silence. In all fairness, a judge is just a man, doing his job. Like the high hanging traffic lights, keeping law and order on streets—completely unaware of what's going on inside the cars passing by underneath. Court judges often have no idea what goes on behind closed doors. But God sees all. He will fight for the defenseless and stand against the proud. He will provide every *report* necessary to accomplish His will and plan for our life. God's judgments are true—the only truth!

We must begin the process to heal ourselves, and to not fall into the trap of co-dependency, shame, and self-abandonment where we wait; hoping that someone else will heal us and rescue us from ourselves and circumstance. Vengeance is God's, not ours.

Finally, and most importantly, we must forgive wholeheartedly and trust the Lord to fight our battles. When we return kindness for evil, we show forth the universal law of love; thus, proving we are indeed the children of God and followers of our Savior, Jesus Christ.

Incidentally, for the first time in my life, since living on my own, I was no longer afraid of the dark. "Strange thing," a counselor told me after I explained how I can now sleep in pitch-black darkness, alone and unafraid. "It was never the darkness that frightened you. It was people," she said. I never knew about the social anxiety and the other mental disorders that grew like thorns on the stem of a rose. I refused medication for my mental dis-ease. God's word is my cure and has been for many years. The more I understood, the less afraid I became. It seems we only fear that which we do not understand. For this reason, Proverbs 4:7 says, "Wisdom *is* the principal thing; *therefore,* get wisdom, and with all thy getting get understanding."

As a victim of domestic violence, I often felt like I was going crazy. The emotional and spiritual contradictions are confusing. You can love someone desperately, endure the torment of their violent and controlling attitude, and yet find it impossible to leave. According to the United States Department of Justice, "approximately 1.3 million women and 835,000 men are physically assaulted by an intimate partner annually in the United States." This number continues to rise. Rape, stalking, physical violence, and mental abuse are all forms of immoral behavior that often goes grossly unreported. Many of the crimes against my life went unreported because of the shame, stigma, and powerlessness that surrounds the dehumanizing acts.

Many never break free to tell their story. Many have died hiding the crime behind closed doors as if nothing ever happened. Please love yourself enough to say something to someone you trust. You are created in the image of God. He sent His Son, Jesus Christ, to set us free from every bondage and stronghold. It is our responsibility to love others as we love ourselves, but if you do not love yourself, you can't truly love anyone else. It's time to heal. It's time to love and nurture the precious gift of life God has given you. If you or someone you know is trapped in an abusive relationship, don't wait another day. You are courageous, and leaving an abusive relationship will help both the abuser and the victim begin the process of healing and restoration. Get out and get help! Now! 1-800-799-SAFE (7233) and call 911.

"Our task must be to free ourselves... by widening our circle of compassion to embrace all living creatures and the whole of nature and its beauty." ~ *Albert Einstein*

Forgiveness, the Only Road to True Freedom
Each of us must take responsibility for our own actions! Blaming others is a waste of time because it seeks to remove the accountability we have for our life. We must take full responsibility for our healing journey. To move forward, we must let go of the past, forgive all who have wounded us, and forgive ourselves. We cannot achieve wholeness if we cannot forgive, nor can we be forgiven. Christ commands that we forgive and love one another (Ephesians 4:32). This does not mean that we allow ourselves to live in fear or abuse. However, it does mandate that we can set ourselves free by forgiving and living in the light of God's glory and grace. In forgiving and praying for Bruce and all my abusers, I

found joy and peace I cannot explain. The joy is indescribable, and the peace surpasses all understanding. In the 8th chapter of Nehemiah, are the words that would become the anthem for my life; "The Joy of the Lord is my strength." Forgiveness sets us free to experience that joy!

Forgiveness is a choice, and it is the first step to obtaining wholeness and complete healing. I have spent countless hours praying for all those who have hurt me, wishing them peace, prosperity, and joy — hoping they come to the saving knowledge of Christ and His plan for their life. There is no room in my heart for hate. Unforgiveness and hate is a self-served poison — refuse to drink it. Love your enemies — this is the power of Christ. When we refuse to forgive, we sentence ourselves to a lifetime of bitterness, addiction, and mental and emotional disorders. Like arsenic, resentment is a slow acting poison that builds up over time. The longer we refuse to release it, the more difficult it becomes to let go. In time, it will consume us, and destroy our God-given destiny. Proverbs 20:24 says that "a man's goings *are* of the LORD; how can a man then understand his own way?" Without God, we are lost and capable of the most horrendous acts against each other. We are all slaves to sin. Therefore, we must trust God's purpose, and seek to understand that whatever the enemy meant for evil, God plans it for our good. The Word says that "all things will work together for the good of those who love the Lord" - Romans 8:28. When we forgive each other, our trust in God becomes evident. Freedom waits on the other end of forgiveness. It is the only way to become, completely free!

" If you are teachable, it's fixable." ~Dr. Paul Hegstrom

The key to therapy is awareness; however, awareness gets our attention, only when we are ready and teachable. Healing never happens in anger, judgment, and isolation. Once we become aware of the root, the cure presents itself, and the healing will begin. Confidence is a daily practice, and healing is a continuous process. A healthy community of believers is necessary to survive the trauma and regain purity of thought and wholeness. Most of all, we need to learn how to become teachable. For me, becoming teachable happened when I learn how to trust again. I began to discover more profound truths for my life through watching, *The New You* by Dr. Paul Hegstrom. God led me to the Cognitive Behavioral therapist who spoke truth and life into my brokenness — ultimately helping me "make sense of the craziness." I believe it is this "craziness" that creates our addicted society. I never met Dr. Hegstrom face-to-face, but after a month of viewing his tapes, increasing awareness, and being teachable, my life was never the same.

Dr. Paul Hegstrom of Life Skills International explained in simple terms that "if you are teachable, it's fixable." As I ordered and watched the tapes from his teaching of *Confronting Your Anger,* I began to understand the body-brain connection, and how God could help me confront the rage that I denied I ever had and rewire my brain (mindset). Dr. Hegstrom said, "When we have been wounded in childhood, our emotions freeze us in the age of the wound, often locking us up for a lifetime. There, we become stuck." How do we reach maturity when our emotional development is frozen?

Dr. Hegstrom shared his personal journey of how he was once a violent abuser. His wife, Judy, suffered for many years because of his uncontrolled anger. He was unaware of how the wounds of his childhood negatively affected every aspect of his life. Like Dr. Hegstrom, many people have no idea how the childhood wounds of rejection, abuse, and neglect create thorns of anger, depression, and anxiety to grow deep inside of us. Professional help is necessary to confront the emotional pain. When awareness increases, we see ourselves in ways we had never seen before. After years on my own, my emotions were like land mines; I needed the only One who knows how deep the pain and sorrow goes. His name is Jesus: The Wonderful Counselor. Dr. Paul Hegstrom emphasizes the importance of faith in Christ for restoring lives. There is help for abusers and victims of abuse when we seek to better understand why we do what we do. Only then can we gain wholeness and healing through the process of regeneration?

I needed to get real with myself. For decades I had ignored the pain until mistreatment, bondage, self-hatred, and guilt became my normal. Learning to renew my mind and rewire my reactive brain is a process that takes time, often a lifetime, but the pursuit is worth every effort. I am being made new, freed from the tangled knots of co-dependency. Dr. Hegstrom teaching on *Your Brain and the Spoken Word* helped me understand I no longer needed someone else to make me feel worthy or valued. The Christ-centered teachings helped to answer many of the questions I needed answered. First and foremost was the question of my true identity: who was I before the sexual abuse, before the rejection, and before I was raped and sold for an undisclosed price to Edward. Today, my identity is salvation in Jesus Christ. In Him, my life, my hope, my all is found.

Acts 17:28 — "In Him I live, move, and have my being."
Becoming Teachable
The Process of Healing

The process of regeneration often takes a lifetime, but it can happen; one step at a time, when we refuse to stay bound by fear and shame. When we seek and find the voice hidden way down deep inside the unspeakable pain of our lives, we can break the destructive generational cycles, and find the joy, peace, and acceptance that Jesus died to give us. Though today, I still find myself, from time to time, twirling the edges of my blouse, and even flinching defensively at the air, His grace is sufficient. God's voice becomes louder as we stay in the word of life. Daily, I learn to take every thought captive to the obedience of Christ (2 Corinthians 10:5). That's why He came. That's why He died: to give us peace that surpasses all understanding. Through Jesus Christ the Lord, we can do all things; even climb the mountains that refuse to move. I was forty-four years old when I told my mother the reason I ran away from home so many years ago. It was difficult, scary, and the main reason I stopped writing this book back in 2007. In order to continue my journey toward healing, I had to renounce my loyalty to the shame and painful secrets of the past. Complete surrender to Christ results in the deep excavation and reconstitution of the body, mind, and soul. The result is complete wholeness and new life.

Interviews with my mother and siblings were a major part of completing this book. In separate talks with my family, I was able to piece together the unspeakable events from childhood. After each interview, my heart would bleed again. Not just for my pain, but for the pain of my entire family and for all those trapped in the systematic cycle of abuse and apathy—both are destructive. In Christ, we continue our individual journey towards healing and wholeness. *"His grace has kept us safe this far, and His grace will lead us on."*

Healing from secret shame is a slow process; nevertheless, victims of violence can regain their freedom from the bondage of fear by speaking out against it. Find your voice and speak out. Reliving the past is painful, and writing this book was a huge part of the healing process. The journey was cathartic because I could clearly look back and see the amazing love of a God who rescues us from every treacherous snare. His amazing love ransomed my broken life, and to all who believes in Him, He wants you to experience peace and love that is better than anything this world can offer.

Incidentally, in 2015, my mother noticed my dead fingernail. The years of twirling, numbing every pain, left me with the reminder. God used my mother to bring the dead nail bed back to life; even after a doctor told me the damage was irreparable. My mom used an ointment I had never heard about, and in time, the nail healed, completely. God works in mysterious ways.

Learning to Trust

The process of baring our souls, exposing secrets, and learning to trust again is not easy. But it's the only way to regain control of our lives and stop the cycle of abuse that stretches its tentacles towards the next generation. I have watched the skeletons of the past, creep out from the shadows of my apathy, and take on the skin of the next generation. Before the trench of abuse and addiction widens, I am committed to breaking the silence.

Through trials and tribulations, the pain may never go away completely; but God's grace is sufficient, and healing only happens when we confront our wounds and pursue wholeness in a safe environment of truth and love. Multiple disorders can develop because of long-term abuse. Often, the stigma, repressed anger, self-pity, and bitterness keeps us stuck, unable to seek the help we so desperately need to mature beyond the emotional injuries and reach our fullest potential. My personal journey towards healing and wholeness began with learning truth; the truth that I was not dirty and damaged. The truth that rape and abuse is never the victim's fault. And the truth of who I am in Christ; a new creation: no longer a victim. In 2 Corinthians 5:17, the scripture says "Therefore, if any man *be* in Christ, *he is* a new creature. Old things are passed away; behold all things are made new." I had to fully believe what God was saying and allow His truth to drown out the lies that were spoken over my life since childhood. Learning to trust again was perhaps the most difficult. The voices are always telling you to keep quiet, you are crazy, and no one cares anyway. The truth is you are loved, priceless, fearfully and wonderfully made.

"We need more light about each other. Light creates understanding, understanding creates love, love creates patience, and patience creates unity." ~*The honorable, Malcolm X*

Reformation and Reparation: God is The God of Justice!

As I reflect on my journey, I question a prison system that is more like modern-day slavery which perpetuates the social conditions that degrade the human spirit. The times I spent in jail could have lasted just as long as my deep pain, if God had not intervened. Juvenile detention centers and prisons are filled with hurting people who have found themselves on the wrong side of a system that is just as broken and ineffective to change the heart and restore the soul. The penal system and many social service programs fail to promote real change when the focus is on greed, punishment, or Band-Aid solutions that only skim the surface of a deeper problem. Getting to the root cause of destructive behaviors is the only way to achieve restoration and true healing. The root causes of many societal woes occur in childhood neglect, trauma, and abuse. More than once, I have broken the law. The fear of prison did not change my heart. Only the love of God restrains the conscience, renewing a right spirit where there was once only brokenness.

His law is love, and when we truly love, we cannot commit a crime against our neighbor, our community, or our country. The love of God seeks to heal what the law of man tries to punish. The contradictions of laws, freedoms, and punishments are a sickening setup designed to incriminate what it subtly creates. This present system is not the vision of our Founding Fathers and those who fought for true freedom and equality of all human beings.

My father represented many people, brainwashed, like Underdog, going inside phony phone booths set up by a corrupt system, seeking the power of truth; in search of the promise of life and liberty. In time, the pieces to the puzzle began to fit, revealing further thievery by a system that denied human beings education and human rights but allowed bars and saloons on every street, drugs, strip clubs, and pornography. Inner cities implode because many people are living in survival mode—shooting without aiming because desperation leads to further depravity. See now, how it all adds insult to injury, replacing illegal gambling with a taxable lottery; another distraction away from the fact that there is land owed that's supposed to be the economic footing in this country. Instead, many spend what little they have on the hope of hitting it big or winning just enough to dig themselves out of poverty. Tyranny transforms, mimicking social reform, but there is a bigger picture to the pursuit of life, liberty, and happiness. It's time to address the matter, once and for all; no more waiting for change!

This is a clarion call for change, for justice, and for the long-awaited economic reparations owed to the descendants of slaves; the Black American community: repair, rehabilitation, education, and land. "You may choose to look the other way, but you can never say again that you did not know." ~*William Wilberforce.*

As the leader of the movement to stop the slave trade, Wilberforce believed in the power of God to do the impossible. After a lengthy campaign against the powers and principalities of greed, Wilberforce achieved the impossible. In 1807, the Slave Trade Act was passed, and in 1833, the Slavery Abolition Act ended slavery in most of Britain. God is a God of justice for all people! Today, after nearly 400 years, the plight for human rights calls into attention the epistemic injustice of a people so conditioned by the psychological warfare of slavery that the identity of the true self and soul remains lost—no other race has undergone such an identity crisis, self-destruction, and internalized hate and racism. The iniquitous ruin must be healed.

Amidst the great strides in this country in the areas of social justice, the *illusion* of fairness and equality is not enough. Restorative justice must occur to repair the damage—wounds so deeply entrenched that it causes a nation of people to refer to themselves by the same name, the same deplorable word slave masters used to refer to human beings — the same word used during many lynchings. The word is, nigger. This inhumane word was intolerable during slavery, the Jim Crow era, and today it remains unacceptable; no matter who's saying it! It is the language of transgenerational trauma and PTSD. It is time to do the impossible; time for repair, time to heal! God is a God of Justice; therefore, it's time for reparations! It's time to change the world rather than waiting on the world to change! We are one!

> "We learn to be racist; therefore, we can learn not to be racist.
> Racism is not genetic. It has everything to do with power."
> ~*Jane Elliott*

The Poison of Pornography; The Freedom of Purity
The concept of our freedoms is not freedom at all; hence, not a real choice. If we were all born in sin and shaped in iniquity (Psalms 51:5), then freedom only comes when we can choose not to be in bondage to our sinful nature. True freedom can only exist when we are no longer ruled by our corrupt flesh. Galatians 5:13 teaches us how to use our democracy: "You, my brothers and sisters, were called to be free. But do not use your freedom to indulge the flesh; rather, serve one another humbly in love." Sin offers a counterfeit freedom; a trap and a blatant contradiction. A prime example of these contradictions is the evil empire of pornography. Pornography violates human dignity. The entrapment of pornography, and similar freedoms of expression,

often leads to insatiable and deviant appetites. Pornography is a "lawful" enterprise with ruthless ramifications. I was a child when my stepfather threw a *Hustler* magazine on the bed. He did what many others do when they are bitten by the venom of pornography. He acted out the disgusting images—unlawfully. Generations of children have assumed the position of the evil empire of pornography with no protection from the monsters this "freedom" has created—and continues to produce. As the pornography industry increases its multibillion-dollar revenue, so have crimes against women and children increased.

I would question the influence of viewing images of sexually explicit acts, bestiality (sex with animals), and violence against women and children. Can what we view affect our sexual appetites? Can what we eat affect our health? The exploitation is blatant, removing the value of the human soul and the safeguards of the human conscience. And where there is no conscience, anything goes. Humans become beasts; dehumanized, desensitized, and lawless.

The despicable production of child pornography continues to rise. No longer does it hide behind closed doors, pornography boldly creeps into homes where there are unsupervised cell phones, computer screens, and other forms of technology; which are all highly addictive. Even the messages in the music twist the beauty and sanctity of sex into a boorish act where true love and commitment does not exist; this is demonic. The hidden evil forces distort sexuality and the hearts and minds of adults and children until the very essence of human sacredness is lost. Wise parents will keep these devices under watchful surveillance. If we fail to do so, the cost for the next generation will be incalculable.

These *nefarious* freedoms destroy the family, the community, and ultimately, all of society. I often think, between the gross profanity in today's culture and the pervasive flashes of pornography, childhood is becoming an extinct stage of human development. German Pastor and Theologian, Dietrich Bonhoeffer once said, "The ultimate test of a moral society is the kind of world that it leaves to its children." Understanding this, we must stand firm in the face of these "evil freedoms," to resist them, and rescue childhood for generations to come.

Where is the line between decency and depravity; holy and unholy; right and wrong? Show me a nation where there are no ethical boundaries, and there, you will witness the end of civilization. Understanding this, what then are these freedoms ultimately creating? Sex crimes are at an all-time high. Pornography is the demon that opens the gateway that spawns' deviant acts against the human conscience. And I personally believe that sex trafficking leads this demonic regime.

According to the latest research and the Rescue Freedom organization (2016), "Sex trafficking is integral with pornography. Pornography fuels sex trafficking: they are one and the same. It is reported that almost 49% of those trapped in prostitution were made to participate in pornography." Pornography is also a form of visual sex trafficking that encourages and supports the immoral industry. We must seek purity of heart and mind, according to how God created it. Proverbs chapter 23, verse 7 "As a man thinks in his heart, so is he."

Sex trafficking is a billion-dollar industry, where women and children, both girls and boys of all ages are sold to the highest bidder at the rate of over $27,000,000 worldwide and growing. Sex trafficking is a crime that is as old as slavery. "There is nothing new under the sun" (Ecclesiastes 1:9). It hides in the dark shadows of the worst of humanity. Pornography further propagates the voracious appetite of the monstrous trade. The National Human Trafficking Hotline is 1-888-373-7888.

In a quote from apologist Ravi Zacharias, "...the fanciful thoughts of the man or woman in front of you there, in order to provoke just the baser instincts and ultimately leave you unsatisfied and insatiable. Because what they are pandering to you is not a person. What they are enslaving you to is a feeling that no one person can ultimately satisfy!" The images of pornography ravaged my childhood and distorted my sense of sexuality. Unwanted memories continue to flash across my mind to this day, but I have learned to replace them with continual prayer and study in the word of God, believing the blood of Christ covers me.

Every day is a choice to live above the desires of the sinful flesh and seek His righteousness for my life. Regaining purity is a lifelong pursuit, an important part of healing, and essential to achieving sanctification in Christ. Many years have passed, and through faith, I continue to live my life in sexual purity, taking every lustful thought captive, to live as God instructs in 1 Peter 1:16, "...be ye Holy, for I am Holy." No longer will I *assume the position* of sin, unresolved grief and trauma. I choose His original plan of sexuality — one man and one woman multiplied to keep civilization alive; God's design produces life; all else selfishly leads us to extinction. No matter the reason; be it the pain of abuse, "born that way," or the freedom to choose, God tells us to be born again — into sexual purity! For the sake of

Christ, I will carry my cross!

True love is acting in obedience to the teaching of Christ by the Spirit of God: The creator of all things. John 13: 34-35 says "A new commandment I give you: Love one another. As I have loved you, so also you must love one another. By this, all men will know that you are My disciples if you love one another."

Mentor Nation — Knowledge is Power

"Tell me and I forget, teach me and I may remember,
  involve me and I will learn." *~Benjamin Franklin*

Mentorship helps change, heal, and transform lives. When we change ourselves, we change the world: Our world! Personal transformation is not achieved alone: we need mentors. Mentors are gallant guides of wisdom and understanding. They help to show us our blind spots and offer the encouragement we need to reach our fullest potential. Unlike the traffic-light personalities I have witnessed working in human services — functioning without feeling; mentors are lighthouses; selfless individuals who shine, helping others to find their way back to shore, out of the storm, and safely home. Mentors give us a new vision of how we see ourselves.

And in the springtime of 2008, God sent such a person in my life. It was on a Saturday morning as I prepared to teach my 8:30 a.m. Step Circuit class at LA Fitness in Palm Beach Gardens. A young woman walked toward me from the back of the class. She reached out her hand, introduced herself, and my life has never been the same. Her name is Wienna Jane Hamilton. Many years later, she, along with her husband Earl, continues to reach out to countless individuals with the support and wisdom of Godly mentorship.

Wienna's mentorship edified me, sharpening my mind, helping me to become more effective to carry out the good works God has called me to accomplish. While on a road trip, her thoughtful words blessed my life. It was a time I will never forget.

"Sandy, I want you to understand your value. God made you awesome." Wienna was trying to teach me what I had not fully learned as a child or young adult — a practical lesson in self-efficacy. "Sandy, I want you to know the truth of who you are in Christ Jesus. You are His child, made in His image. You are filled with the fullness of God because He bought you with a high price. You are justified by faith." She said, pausing for a moment as if to let her words soak in before she begins again. "Sandy, it is as if you have never sinned. We are to have a clear conscience because God removes our sins as far as the east is from the west. Your sins are not covered but removed forever."

She spoke of the scripture in 1 Peter 2:9, "You are a chosen generation, a royal priesthood, a holy nation, a peculiar people that you should show forth the praises of him who hath called you out of darkness into his marvelous light."

In time, I begin to understand the plan of why God *chose* Wienna to be my mentor. She came to help me complete the process of healing and transformation. Life is a process; a continual journey toward sanctification in Christ.

"You are not defined by your past circumstance, but by who God says you are. We overcome by the blood of the Lamb and the word of our testimony." Wienna soon shared her personal testimony with me. I begin to understand her passion for God's people and the fervent energy behind her advocacy. "We need to create a counterculture," she would say. I believe it's time. A counterculture will renew our minds and turn the tide on our rebellious nation, ultimately turning our hearts back to God.

Wienna is the founder of Creating Leaders International. She has a mission of helping girls and women transition through life circumstances and transforms by the power of the Word of God. Wienna's passionate advocacy for the hurting and the lost is a testament to her own journey of healing. I am grateful for her mentorship. She is a lighthouse to many.

"You, yourself, as much as anybody in the entire universe, deserves love and affection." ~ *The Buddha*

Integrating Education and the Model of Christ

Education changes lives. A powerful scripture in the word of God underscores this fact, "My people perish from the lack of knowledge…" (Hosea 4:6). Education changes us as the Holy Spirit guides us. That is how transformation happened in my life. All people are capable of deep change and transformative learning. From William Wilberforce, who was transformed by the saving knowledge of God, to Helen Keller, whose life was forever changed by the fervent passion of her teacher, Anne Sullivan, transformation can happen, but it must first happen in our hearts. We must care enough to make the mind, body, spirit connection. We must help people grow up; do not throw people away; as if they are replaceable. They are not! This is my professional philosophy. No one is beyond the reach of God's grace and the power to truly change destructive mindsets and behaviors. Romans 12:2 declares, "And be not conformed to this world: but be ye transformed by the renewing of your mind, that you may prove what *is* that good, and acceptable, and perfect, will of God."

"Everything is as it should be." *~Casburn A. Spencer*

When we surrender and trust God with our life, "everything is as it should be." In 2006, with the love and support of Mr. C. A. Spencer, I continued my journey toward wholeness and education. More profound healing began in me, as the emotions that were frozen in time by the pain of pornography and the crime of sexual abuse was forced awake. I had to face my past, relive what I had tried a lifetime to forget, and confront everything that I subconsciously suppressed. The tender sting that came at this point in my life was the antiseptic on a raw wound that needed to heal. In time, I begin to understand that the same venom that froze me as a child, became the antivenom to unfreeze me so that I could start the process of excavation—digging up the past to heal my future. Recovering in the aftermath of trauma is hard, but I promise, the process is rewarding; we have a god given right to be free from it all.

In 2009, I earned my Associates degree in Health Care Administration, and in 2011, my bachelor's degree in Human Services Management. I pressed onward, and on August 14th, 2013, I obtained my graduate degree and later walked across the stage with Palm Beach Atlantic University graduating class to receive my master's degree in Leadership. I could not have obtained these achievements without this brilliant man who believed in me. I will be forever grateful to C. A. Spencer for his patience, dedication, and gentle acceptance. Today, I move forward with doctoral studies at Liberty University in Virginia. No achievement happens without the love and support of others. I am thankful for all the men and women who are dedicated to doing more than just their job; they are passionate about changing lives. My journey continues with education and advocacy, and my heart is filled with gratitude for the Body of Christ; the lighthouses.

The Hope and Help Center

In 2013, I had the pleasure of meeting Dean Hutchins, a case manager at the Hope and Help Center. Like so many others, Dean is a lighthouse. He helped to inspire me beyond the stigma of

HIV/AIDS and encouraged me through one of the most challenging seasons of my life. Later he invited me to join the awesome team of advocates and care managers to fight the stigma and take action against HIV/AIDS. The compassionate men and women of the Hope and Help Center of Central Florida became my second family, united in the fight. According to the Center for Disease Control, more than 37 million people are living with HIV worldwide; many are unaware. 2.6 million are under the age of fifteen. More than 230 people contract the virus every hour. HIV/AIDS has no face, no race, and no age, no culture, and no background. Like the color of tears, it speaks to our humanity, crossing every cultural divide, calling us to come alive and unite as one people.

"People are our Practice." ~*Jerry Ellis*

The Law of Love in Daily Practice

My work in human services, health and wellness, and as a counselor is most rewarding. Today, God continues to speak through those who follow His ways. God has led me to great leaders on my journey. I call them my spiritual fathers. They are powerful lighthouses, shining for the glory of God; teaching us the way home. Bishop Larry E. Bellamy gave me a safe place to heal and taught me that "if the storms don't cease, my soul is anchored in the Lord." And so, it remains. Ravi Zacharias of RZIM Ministries teaches me how to defend my faith in Christ without compromise. Dr. Paul Hegstrom of Life Skills International teaches that "if we become teachable, we are fixable." His teachings helped me make sense of the nonsense. Bishop Thomas Dexter Jakes of the Potters House counsels, encourages, and strengthens my faith through practical applications of God's Word, and storytelling abilities that surpass imagination.

These teachings are powerful and life-changing. I am grateful for the Godly men the Lord has placed on my journey. Psalm 119:105 says, "His word is a lamp unto my feet and a light unto my path." We are stronger when we focus on God's word of truth, every day, every hour, and every moment. Daily, I bathe my heart and mind in the wisdom of God's Word. In His Word, we are born again and made clean. In His Word, perfect peace is found. The peace of God guards my mind, countering the voices and images that flare in stressful times. Faith comes by hearing, strength comes from doing. God has called us to be "doers of the Word" (James 1:22). Of all the voices in my life, His is the voice of truth. I pray to endure to the end, to hear Him say, "Well done." And just as the love of Christ restored my shattered life, His law of love can restore broken hearts, heal our nation, and change the world.

Christ: The Only Hope for America and the World

It is written, in 2 Chronicles 7:14; "If I shut up the heavens so that there is no rain, or if I command the locust to devour the land, or if I send pestilence among My people, and if My people who are called by My name, would humble themselves, pray and seek My face and turn from their wicked ways, then I will hear from heaven, and will forgive their sin, and will heal their land." This promise is true for our world today.

A Plea for Fathers

Fathers must return to the children! Your presence, time, love, and touch are imperative for raising a generation of healthy, compassionate, and well-balanced families. The history of stolen men from society has left a gaping hole in the hearts of countless families. The consequences are widespread and devastating. Jonathan Perz (2001), wrote: "There is no role in our modern society that suffers greater neglect as far as God is concerned than that of the father. Not only has God given men the incredible privilege of imitating Him as Father, He has placed upon the shoulders of fathers an incredible responsibility. By God's standards, anyone who is a father should first be a husband (1 Cor. 7:1-5). Otherwise, souls are guilty of the sin of fornication (1 Cor. 6:9-10; Gal. 5:19-21). Therefore, being a responsible father first necessitates being a good husband. One must love, honor, nourish and cherish his wife in every aspect of her life (Eph. 5:25-30; Col. 3:19; 1 Pet. 3:7). Only then will one be prepared to be a good father."

The cry of my heart is for every child to know the love of a father. Family order is the mandate of God that provides the framework for every society. The foundation of every family will flourish when parents practice the fundamental values of love, compassion, respect, and unconditional acceptance. Without these essential values, the nation will continue to implode — one home, and one community at a time; through the depreciation and devastation of divorce. The result of a valueless society will ultimately crumble because of disorder and the chaos that ensues. Children are the most vulnerable; therefore, there must be an awakening to restore the family and end the cycle of grief, dysfunction, and transgenerational trauma. Fathers take your rightful place in the family with love and servant leadership. We need you!

Photo Album

Love awakens us from within, causing us to see with different eyes. The Apostle Paul wrote, "I pray that the eyes of your heart may be enlightened so that you will know what the hope of His calling is, and what are the riches of the glory of His inheritance in the saints" Ephesians 1:18. When we humble ourselves to learn to embrace and cherish His calling for our lives, we can truly understand how to love and cherish our families, communities, and the world over.

June 1994, Pizza Hut. My dad, Bertram and me.
The emotional, physical and spiritual well-being of the family are greatly influenced by fathers. The heart of fathers must return to their children. Society depends on it.

Photo Album

Easter Sunday, 1976/ Mizell Studios with my mom, Lillie, and my siblings: Linda, Leon, Michael, and me.

(Left to right in both pictures) Linda, Leon, Lillie, Michael, and me; nearly 40 years later. Psalms 36:5- "Your love, O LORD, reaches to the heavens, your faithfulness stretches to the sky."

"Looking unto Jesus the author and finisher of our faith..." ~Hebrews 12:2
My siblings: Joyce, Leon, Michael, Linda, and me

Family: the place on earth where love and acceptance should resemble heaven on earth!

Right to left) Joyce-our lullaby singer, Leon, Linda, Michael, and me. Miramar, Florida, 2006. The Lord is faithful.
Psalms 91:
"He that dwelleth in the secret place of the most High shall abide under the shadow of the Almighty..."

Photo Album
Childhood: The foundation of life and love

BJ turning 7 years old; 1992,
surrounded by his brothers and sisters.

Casita and Angela(Below) Candy Colby's
Heart Walk, Fort Lauderdale Beach; 1993

(Above) Letta, Casita, Jontavia,
and me. Christmas, 2003

Photo Album

Philippians 4:13 – "I can do all this through Christ who gives me strength." As a little girl, Casita would repeat this verse. Today, her strength and fortitude is the inheritance of the Great God who keeps His promises. (Right) Ava, Joseph, and Casita (Left) Dionna with Ava

Grandma and her, Ava Girl

Photo Album

Baby Letta and me, 1987

My beautiful baby girl, Sharletta,
in the garden at church. 1993

(Left to Right) Letta, me, and Casita, 2015

Precious and me, 2005, Road trip to
Pennsylvania and New York.

1994; My parents, Bertram and Lillie. Sometimes it takes a lifetime to learn to let go, forgive, and simply… love.

"Come now, let us settle the matter," says the LORD. "Though your sins are like scarlet, they shall be as white as snow; though they are red as crimson, they shall be like wool.
~Isaiah 1:18

Photo Album

Mi Casita, Mi Corazon
My Home, My Heart. Through
the years, God has kept us,
protected us, and shown His
wondrous mercy and love.

"Come, thou Fount of every
blessing, tune my heart to sing
thy grace; streams of mercy,
never ceasing, call for songs of
loudest praise…"

Photo Album

Beautiful blossoms; Angela and Casita (above). Angela, Sharletta, and Casita, 1995. (Below) High School graduation for Casita and Angela, Class of 2000

Photo Album

(Above) Angela and me, 2009
(Middle) Expressions of Worship Praise Dancers, 1996
(Below) Angela comes for me and Rod at the summit of Pikes Peak

Through the years, love grows as the seeds we plant take root and bloom.

Ms. Francis, Congressman E. Clay Shaw, and me
at the BETA Alumni of the Year Ceremony; 1992

Cory Easter Sunday, 1993

Cory and me, 2007.
There is a love song in my heart, it beats a rhythm from the sea. A melody of you and I, flying kites, so high above the sky.
Tis my love, my son, for thee.

Casita, Cory, Buffy, Trooper, and me, 1990

For my children, I will continue to climb, to learn, to break every generational stronghold. For my God has given me the authority to command their freedom! Psalm 103:1-22 says, "Bless the Lord, O my soul, and all that is within me, bless his holy name! Bless the Lord, O my soul, and forget not all his benefits, who forgives all your iniquity, who heals all your diseases, who redeems your life from the pit, who crowns you with steadfast love and mercy, who satisfies you with good so that your youth is renewed like the eagles."

Matthew 16:19, declares,

"I will give you the keys to the kingdom of heaven, and

whatever you bind on earth shall be bound in heaven, and whatever you loose on earth shall be loosed in heaven." This is my trust: "Know therefore that the LORD your God is **God**; he is the **faithful** God, keeping his covenant of love to **a thousand generations** of those who love him and keep his commandments.

(Above left) BJ and me, 1992, (Middle) Port Charlotte, Florida (Right) 2014

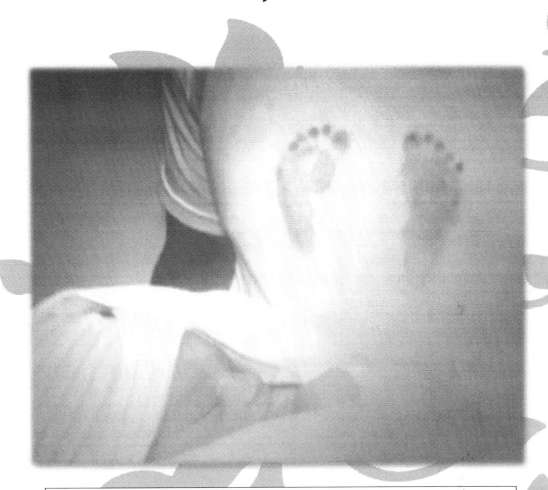

All the earth is created in the home by those who have the awesome responsibility to demonstrate love, respect, appropriate discipline, and unconditional loving acceptance. For all that little eyes see, and little ears hear, there are little feet that will surely follow; step by step.

"Train up a child in the way he should go,
And when he is old he will not depart from it." Proverbs 22:6

Photo Album

"In my eyes, whether birthed from the womb or the heart, all children are gifts from God. Each child is uniquely different, but they all want the same things: to be seen, to be heard, to be loved." (p. 308)
(Left to right)
Ava, Derick, Christina, Cory, CJ, and Jasia.

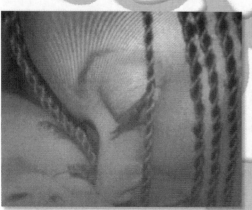

Photo Album

My son, BJ and Ashley Family. 2 Corinthians 5:17: "Therefore, if anyone is in Christ, he is a new creation, the old has gone, the new has come."

Pamela and me, 2011, College Graduation/ Friend of my secret garden

Olga, me, and Kimberly preparing for the Night of Joy at Disney, 1993

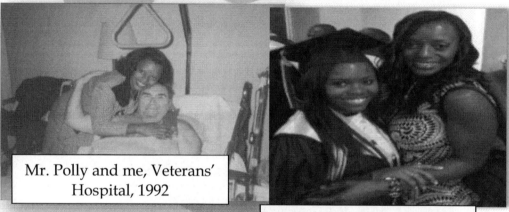

Mr. Polly and me, Veterans' Hospital, 1992

(Right) Dionna and Auntie; 2007

Anthony Moody and me, St. John's hospital, 2013

Isaiah 65:24- "Before they call I will answer; while they are still speaking I will hear."

Love can restore the world, because it first restores the person.
Palm Beach Atlantic University, 2013

For my children, grandchildren, godchildren, and all people, I will testify that the love of Christ is the answer for the world. He is the Way, the Truth, and the Life.

(Above)My Super Woman, Sharletta, and the blossoms born from my blossoms

Hearing the word, "Nana" for the first time, was like God saying, "I love you, and I will never let you go." Indescribable joy.

"If the Son sets you free, you will be free indeed."
— John 8:36

Psalms 1:1 says, "Blessed is the man who does not walk in the counsel of the wicked or stand in the way of sinners or sit in the seat of mockers. But his delight is in **the law of the LORD**, and on his law, he meditates day and night. He is like a tree planted by streams of water, which yields its fruit in the season and whose leaf does not wither. Whatever he does will prosper."

"My mother, my gift, my love."
Mother's Day at
Calvary Chapel, Fort Lauderdale.
"Thank you, Jesus."

Experience: that most brutal of teachers. But you learn, my God do you learn. ~C.S. Lewis.

Acknowledgments

This list is not exhaustive, as there are so many individuals to whom I owe a debt of gratitude.

My physician and friend, *Dr. Alberto Mestre* and his staff. You believed in me and inspired me to write this book. I cannot thank you and your team enough for your compassion, care, and commitment to saving lives. In my eyes, you are so much more than a caring physician; you are a true humanitarian.

Joyce, thank you for all the things you taught me. I could not have completed this book without your untiring involvement to help me put all the broken pieces together.

Cassy, for supporting my dreams and education. I could not have made it through hours of study and final exams without you. You have been my most excellent teacher, therapist, friend, and love. I am forever grateful. Thank you for reminding me of the stars.

My mother, *Lillie Robinson*, thank you for your love and support in compiling years of information into late night hours of conversation. I am blessed to have you in my life. The day I handed you the "Stole of Gratitude" was a dream come true. I could not have written this book without you, traveling back in time with me, digging through the rumble of a painful history. Thank you for all your love and support. I love you.

For my father, *Bertram Roosevelt Anderson,* my heart's melody.

Leon, Michael, Linda, God is faithful! Thank you for sharing the journey with me. I love you more each day. Thank you for your contribution of interviews, reliving the past, and your steadfast encouragement.

To all my beautiful blossoms: Casita, Bobby, (LiSandra), Angela, Derick, Sharletta, Cory, Jontavia, Jasia and for all my god-grandchildren, and grandchildren. For your love, your laughter, and the unique way each of you shares your life with me. My prayer for each of you is to come to know and follow Christ as your personal Lord and Savior. Seek Him, and you will find Him. Learn the lessons that can only be taught by God. He desires to create a clean heart and to renew a right spirit within us. Remember, Mark 13:31 — Heaven and earth shall pass away, but God's word shall never pass away.

Pamela and family, I will always treasure our friendship.

Cleveland Mack, thank you for being there on my road to Neverland and being a true friend.

The *Women in Distress* organization, for your tireless

devotion to women and families.

Refreshing Springs C.O.G.I.C., thank you for giving me a place to grow up, heal, and learn the Great Gospel of Jesus Christ.

My *Godmother Andrea;* for never letting me quit and for reminding me that "God is in control!"

Kimberly Nance, Olga Anderson, for your unwavering love and friendship that carried me through the darkest days; I thank you.

Cohort 26 and my professors at *Palm Beach Atlantic University*, the greatest people are the ones who see your thorns and remind you that they have a purpose. Thank you for helping me see with new eyes.

Eddie Osorio, for giving me a very special day: High school prom. My godson, I will always adore you.

Mr. and Mrs. Earl and Wienna Hamilton, for your love and support. You are true ambassadors for Christ and loving representatives of his loving kindness and grace. Your friendship and mentorship are blessings in my life.

Dr. Susan Gipson, Rose Etienne-Gibson, and my Palm Beach Lakes High family, for your encouragement, patience, and steadfast support of my education. I am forever grateful.

Pastor Neal Waugh of Community Marketplace, for your outstanding commitment to community improvement, Christian unity, and social reform.

Mr. and Mrs. Jerry and Ingrid Ellis, for showing kindness and compassion to a stranger, and making your heart her home. "People are our practice." Thank you for being a beautiful example of what it means to practice love, kindness, and charity.

The Hope and Help Center of Central Florida and the *Pine Hills Walgreens family* thank you for your kindness, support, tireless work, and undying commitment to the mission of saving lives and impacting the community.

FoundCare Health Center, an organization of compassion, for your support and acceptance, I am grateful.

Jessica Pazou, of Benin West Africa Lauretta Beauty Shop, for your special encouragement and prayers during this process.

To the reviewers and supporters of this project, *Steve White, Kizzy Watkins, Autumn Condio-Hollis, Robert Reyes, Rose Etienne-Gibson, Linda Anderson-Davis, Meredith Noseworthy.*

Project Investor, *Cory Emmanuel*, for your love and support. Photographers, *Adriana Harris, Huong Webb,* and *Kurt Adamie.,*

For my grandmother, Rachel; "The prayers of the righteous avails much and has great power and produces wonderful results." ~James 5:16

The Sword of the Spirit is the Word of God

"Wisdom is the principal thing; therefore, get wisdom: and with all thy getting get understanding." — Proverbs 4:7

"Be strong and courageous. Do not be afraid or terrified because of them, for the LORD your God goes with you; he will never leave you nor forsake you." — Deuteronomy 31:6

"God is spirit, and his worshipers must worship in the Spirit and in truth." — John 4:24

"But they overcame him by the blood of the Lamb and by the word of their testimony, and they did not love their lives so much that they were afraid to die."

— Revelation 12:11

"For God, who commanded the light to shine out of darkness, hath shined in our hearts, to give the light of the knowledge of the glory of God in the face of Jesus Christ. But we have this treasure in earthen vessels that the Excellency of the power may be of God, and not of us.

We are troubled on every side, yet not distressed; we are perplexed, but not in despair; Persecuted, but not forsaken; cast down, but not destroyed; Always bearing about in the body the dying of the Lord Jesus that the life also of Jesus might be made manifest in our body.

For we who live are always delivered unto death for Jesus' sake, that the life also of Jesus might be made manifest in our mortal flesh." — Corinthians 4: 6-11

"The Lord will rescue me from every evil deed and bring me safely into his heavenly kingdom. To him be the glory forever and ever. Amen." — 2 Timothy 4:18

"Give all your worries and cares to God, for he cares about you." — 1 Peter 5:7

(Above photo) Sandra and Dr. Nicholas Palmieri at Palm Beach Atlantic University Masters Ceremony 2013, West Palm Beach, Florida.

Made in the USA
Las Vegas, NV
14 June 2021